California Real Estate LAW

EIGHTH EDITION

WALT HUBER
GLENDALE COLLEGE
CA Lic. #00363967

KIM TYLER, JD
SHASTA COLLEGE

JIM CUNNINGHAM
REVIEW EDITOR
CUYAMACA COLLEGE

DERRY KNIGHT
REVIEW EDITOR
AMERICAN RIVER COLLEGE

COPYRIGHT© 1989, 1991, 1997, 1999, 2001, 2003, 2004, 2007, 2010, 2013 - 8th Edition

EDUCATIONAL TEXTBOOK COMPANY, INC.
P. O. Box 3597
Covina, California 91722
(626) 339-7733
FAX (626) 332-4744

www.etctextbooks.com

Call Glendale College Bookstore (For placing single orders - see form on page 610)
1-818-240-1000 ext. 3024

Library of Congress Cataloging-in-Publication Data
California Real Estate Law/ Walt Huber and Kim Tyler, J.D.

Summary: Covers all material in California Real Estate Law classes with special emphasis on California real estate laws. Very clear and simple language, easy-to-read format with photographs, charts and graphs. Includes glossary and index; suitable for the consumer, students and teachers seeking information about personal real estate transactions.

1. Real estate business-Law and legislation-California 2. Real estate property-California Real estate 3. Real property-California

346.79404 [347.9406437]

ISBN: (10-digit) 1-6268-4-000-8
        (13-digit) 978-1-6268-4000-3

Preface

This Eighth Edition of *CALIFORNIA REAL ESTATE LAW* is an essential textbook for potential real estate salespersons and brokers, a valuable reference book for practicing real estate professionals, and an excellent resource for buyers, sellers (or anyone else) with an interest in the ownership and transfer of real property.

As is appropriate, we've updated the most relevant California Association of Real Estate (CAR®) forms and made revisions to many real estate laws. But because the industry is as fast moving as it is, we found it important to include a new section on mobile technology. Downloadable CAR® zipForms® have changed the way professionals do business. What used to take days can now take minutes.

On the topic of the fast-moving industry, the **Department of Real Estate (DRE)** has recently changed its name to the **Bureau of Real Estate (BRE)** now under the Department of Consumer Affairs (DCA), and Wayne Bell has been appointed as the new Commissioner of Real Estate.

This new edition also includes the full text of the **Statewide Buyer and Seller Advisory (SBSA)**, which is an excellent resource when it comes to protecting brokers against potential liability for matters in which they are not expected to have expertise. That alone makes keeping this book on your bookshelf worthwhile (see Chapter 6).

We'd like to thank the many people who helped make this book possible: Colleen Taber, executive editor; Rick Lee, prepress editor and layout; Troy Monroe Stacey, graphics; Philip Dockter, art director; and Melinda Winters, cover design. Additions and revisions were made with the help Jim Cunningham, Cuyamaca College.

Special recognition must also be given to our legal review editors: Donna Grogan, CPM, El Camino College; Carol A. Jensen, City College of San Francisco; Lance Shoemaker, JD, M.C.P., M.A., West Valley College; Gary Goldberg, Santa Barbara City College; Ed Culbertson, JD, Mira Costa College; Shadrick Jefferies, JD, San Diego Mesa College; Robert Von Esch, Jr., Esq., Fullerton College; Aaron D. Grossman, Shasta College; Derry Knight, American River College; Robert E. Brode, Esq., College of the Canyons; and William A. McGrath, JD, Sacramento City College. Thanks to this great bunch of Law professors at East Los Angeles College for their support: D.E. Rodriguez, V.J. Cleva, O.V. Anderson, and R.C. Lipscomb.

This Eighth Edition also benefited from the wisdom of: Nick Zoumbos, San Bernardino Community College; Ken Merrill, Cerritos College; Dr. Chris Hamilton, Golden West College; Robert Palazzo, Moorpark College; Frances K. Jackson, San Diego City College; Mark P. Cazem, Santa Rosa Junior College; Dr. Ronald A. Goularte, DeAnza College; Victoria Armstrong, San Joaquin Delta College; Lance McHarg, Vice President, Real Estate Trainers; Lorraine Santirosa, SanDiegoMilitaryRelocationExpert.com, Keller Williams Realty, SD Metro; and Regina P. Brown, President/Broker, Realty Pro Academy.

TABLE OF CONTENTS

TABLE OF CONTENTS

TABLE OF CONTENTS

Around California...

New Disclosure Requirement

As of July 1, 2013, Purchase Agreements for residential property must contain a statutory notice directing buyers to the general location of pipelines under the National Pipeline Mapping System. (The newest CAR® Purchase Agreement should contain this notice.)

New Licensing Laws

The exemption of the two-year experience under a broker for licensees with a four-year college degree has been modified so that the broker-applicant's course of study must include a major or minor in real estate.

Helping Distressed Homeowners

As of January 1, 2013, for short sales, a first trust deed lender for an owner-occupied property with one-to-four residential units cannot proceed with a notice of default, notice of sale, or trustee's sale if a short sale has been approved in writing by all the parties (e.g., first lien, junior lien, and mortgage insurer, and the servicer has proof of financing or fund to close escrow. For loan modification, the first trust deed lender generally cannot proceed with a foreclosure as long as the borrower has submitted a complete application for an owner-occupied property with one-to-four residential units.

DRE Citations and Fines

The DR can issue a citation and $2,500 fine if, upon investigation, it has cause to believe that a licensee has violate the DRE rules, or an unlicensed person has engaged in licensed activities. **Cal Business and Professions Code 10080.9**

Protecting an Employee's Social Media

An employer is prohibited from requiring or requesting an employee or employment applicant to access personal social media in the employer's presence, to disclose a username or password for personal social media or to divulge any personal social media. An employer is also prohibited from discharging or disciplining, threatening to discharge or discipline or retaliating against an employee or applicant for failing to comply with a request that violates these rules. For purposes of this law, social media is generally defined as an electronic service or account, including websites, blogs, emails, text messages, photos, videos and online services. **Cal Labor Code 980**

CHAPTER 1
An Introduction to Law

CHAPTER OVERVIEW

This chapter is a broad survey of the legal system in the United States, with a particular focus on California's system. It begins with a discussion of the nature and purposes of the law, and explains some fundamental legal categories and concepts. It goes on to discuss the sources of law: constitutions, legislatures, courts, and administrative agencies. It also examines the judicial system in detail, and describes a typical civil lawsuit from its outset through enforcement of the judgment.

You should come away from this chapter with a better understanding of how laws are made and how legal rights are enforced. This information serves as a backdrop for the rest of the book.

I. Law and the Real Estate Profession

The law has a tremendous impact on a real estate agent's work. Hundreds of federal, state, and local laws control the use and transfer of real property. They affect property values and shape transactions. The real estate profession itself is also strictly regulated.

Laws also prescribe the agent's qualifications and his or her duties to clients, customers, and employees.

The impact of law is growing, too. In some areas (environmental law, for example) regulations have multiplied dramatically in recent years. In other areas, legal standards of conduct are being raised; a landlord or a broker might now be held liable for conduct that would not have been the basis for a lawsuit 15 years ago.

Avoiding legal jeopardy is one of the most compelling reasons to learn about the law. It's a rare real estate agent that isn't at least threatened with a lawsuit from time to time. Even if you would never think of doing anything dishonest, you could end up paying for the consequences of an innocent mistake. A firm grasp of your duties toward the buyer and seller minimizes the risk that you will be sued.

As a well-informed agent, you can reduce the possibility of litigation between yourself, the buyer, and the seller. By recognizing issues that could give rise to a lawsuit, you can help the parties clarify their agreement and avoid misunderstandings.

CHAPTER OUTLINE

Learning about the law is not just a matter of memorizing rules, however. It's important to understand where the rules come from and what backs them up. "The seller's agent must conduct a diligent visual inspection of the property." Who says so? What happens if that rule is ignored? How is it enforced? Can the rule be challenged or changed? Knowing how the legal system works gives the rules substance. In learning how laws are developed, you'll see that it is sometimes possible to influence the process to advance your clients' interests and/or your own.

Of course, learning about the law won't enable you to give clients legal advice or to act without legal advice yourself. However, it will give you a clearer sense of when legal advice is needed, and when it is needed, you'll be better equipped to assist a client's or your own lawyer in analyzing the situation and preparing the case.

II. The Nature and Functions of Law

The purpose of law is to govern the conduct of individual members of a group.

The **LAW** *is a system of rights and duties established and enforced by a government.* It takes the form of general rules that citizens and everyone else in the government's domain must obey.

> **Example:** The law sets out rights and duties connected with land ownership. As a landowner, A has a legal right to the exclusive possession of his property. This creates a corresponding legal duty for others to avoid entering the property without permission. If someone violates this rule, the landowner, through the legal system, may enforce his rights by ejecting the trespasser.
>
> On the other hand, A has a legal duty to maintain the property so that a person entering it at his request will be reasonably safe. If A fails to live up to this duty and someone is injured as a result, the person will enforce A's duty through the legal system by requiring him to pay compensation to the injured person.

Most basically, law establishes order.

Without law, might makes right; the strong and ruthless may use violence and the threat of violence to dominate anyone who is weaker. The law lays down rules of conduct based on other considerations besides brute force. A court or other tribunal serves as a forum for resolving disputes without violence. Thus, law makes it possible for people to live together more or less peacefully.

An important function of the law in any complex society is the **enforcement of promises**. Commerce depends on promises: a builder who agrees to construct a house must be able to rely on the owner's promise to pay for the house. Otherwise, the builder would have to demand payment in advance; in that case, the owner would have to rely on the builder's promise to go through with the work. By enforcing certain promises called contracts, the law makes it possible to plan ahead and to deal with strangers.

The contract is the basis of all business transactions.

In the United States today, the law reflects widely accepted ideas of fairness and equality. We have laws intended to protect people not merely from physical force, but from many forms of

---

Functions of Law

The law serves a number of related functions, including:

- Establishing order
- Resolving disputes
- Enforcing promises
- Preventing exploitation
- Promoting equality

---

exploitation. For example, a real estate agent is not allowed to take unfair advantage of a buyer by misrepresenting or concealing facts about a property. We also have laws that promote equal treatment: a real estate agent may not refuse to show a couple a house because of their ethnic background, race, or religion.

A. MORALITY AND EFFICIENCY

Laws preventing exploitation and promoting equality are examples of "sociological jurisprudence," where law is used as a tool for reforming society. Unfortunately, law has also been used as a tool for oppression. For example, in the 1850s and 1860s, many white Californians felt their jobs were threatened by an influx of Chinese immigrants who were willing to work for low wages. The state and city governments responded to this situation by issuing tax and licensing laws designed to create social and economic hardships for the Chinese.

It's clear that a society's laws are closely connected to its ideas of justice and morality. Although the law reflects and often changes with public morality, they are by no means the same thing. There are many moral issues that the law does not address, leaving them up to the individual's conscience, to families, to churches and other organizations, and to public opinion.

Morality is not the only force that shapes the law. Efficiency, more than justice, is the goal of many rules. When there are two ways of doing something, both may be equally effective, yet a law (a building code) may arbitrarily choose one method and require everyone to use it because uniform procedures help society run smoothly.

What is moral or ethical may not be legal. What is legal may not be moral or ethical.

III. Historical Background

A. ENGLISH FOUNDATION

When English settlers colonized the New World, they brought English common law with them. After gaining its independence, the United States retained many aspects of English law and legal institutions. These are still the foundation of the U.S. legal system.

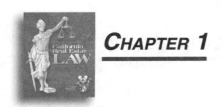

For example, judges in the U.S. have played almost as great a role in establishing rules of law as our legislatures have (see the discussion of sources of law below). This is based on the English model and it contrasts with the European tradition. In France, Germany, Spain, and Italy, lawmaking has been more strictly reserved to the legislatures, and judicial decisions have not carried nearly as much weight.

Many of our basic legal concepts and rules were inherited directly from English **COMMON LAW**, *which is the body of law derived from judicial decisions rather than from statutes or constitutions.* Common law is codified in California. California Civil Code 22.2 provides that the "common law of England, so far as it is not repugnant to or inconsistent with the Constitution of the United States, or the Constitution or laws of this State, is the rule of decision in all the courts of this State."

B. SPANISH INFLUENCE IN CALIFORNIA

The Spanish first arrived in California in 1542, and began to occupy it in 1769. California became Mexican territory in 1822, but was ceded to the U.S. in 1848 by the Treaty of Guadalupe Hidalgo. It became a state in 1850.

Under the **TREATY OF GUADALUPE HIDALGO**, *all public lands belonging to the Mexican government in California became public lands belonging to the U.S. government.* However, the treaty provided that the U.S. would respect all private property rights established by the Mexican government.

A Board of Commissioners was appointed in 1851 to review Mexican land grants. Anyone claiming title to land in California based on a grant from the Spanish or Mexican government was required to present a claim to the commissioners for settlement. If they confirmed that the grant was valid, the claimant was issued a patent (an original deed) by the U.S. government. If the commissioners rejected the claim, the land became public.

Of course, California had been governed by Spanish and Mexican law while it was under Spanish and Mexican rule. U.S. law (with its English roots) displaced the Spanish and Mexican system.

The Spanish left their mark in a few areas of law. For example, California's community property laws (see Chapter 4) originated in Spanish law. These rules are also used in a number of other western states, but they aren't used in eastern states, where the Spanish colonial role was very limited.

Community property states include Arizona, California, Idaho, Louisiana, Nevada, New Mexico, Texas, Washington, and to a certain extent, Wisconsin.

IV. Legal Categories and Concepts

A. SUBSTANTIVE LAW AND PROCEDURAL LAW

In a complicated society like ours, the law covers a vast area. Mapping out some fundamental categories and concepts will make it easier to explore.

One of the most basic divisions in the law is the distinction between substantive law and procedural law. **SUBSTANTIVE LAW** *establishes and defines rights and duties.* **PROCEDURAL LAW** *sets out the methods of enforcing substantive rights.*

Example: The rule that an easement appurtenant runs with the land is substantive law. It gives a land purchaser the right to use a previously established easement.

If the purchaser is prevented from using the easement and wants to assert his/her right to do so, he/she can start a lawsuit. There are rules prescribing how to go about it: file a complaint with the court, send a summons and complaint to the other party within a certain number of days, and so forth. These rules that set out the procedure for enforcing the easement rights are procedural laws.

B. CRIMINAL LAW AND CIVIL LAW

Another fundamental distinction is the one between **criminal law** and **civil law**.

A person who fails to live up to a legal duty, or fails to respect another's legal right, may cause harm to a person or to property. The failure may be accidental or deliberate. The injury may be slight or serious; physical, emotional, or financial.

Someone who has been injured as the result of another's act generally has the right to sue that person for compensation. The government offers a forum (the court) for resolving the dispute. *When one individual sues another, it is called a CIVIL SUIT, a CIVIL ACTION, or CIVIL LITIGATION.*

A law is worthless without a means of enforcement.

Certain harmful or potentially harmful acts are classified as CRIMES. In general, crimes are those acts that are particularly dangerous to society.

Example: Accidentally rear-ending another car causes harm, but it isn't a crime. Drunk driving is a crime (even if the driver has not caused an accident) because it has the potential to cause a great deal of harm.

Because crimes are so disruptive, the government takes a greater interest in them than it does in other harmful acts. Instead of simply offering the injured person an opportunity to sue, the government itself (represented by the public prosecutor) prosecutes the person accused of a crime. The government may start a criminal action without the victim's cooperation, or even if there was no victim. A civil suit, on the other hand, will only take place if the injured person decides to start one.

Civil cases and criminal cases have different purposes, so they offer different remedies. Most often, the goal of a civil suit is simply to compensate the injured person for the harm that was done. *The remedy granted is usually a monetary award (called DAMAGES)* paid by the person who caused the harm to the injured person. The damage award is usually limited to the financial losses that the injured person incurred. These might include lost profits or wages, money spent on repairs, or medical bills.

> **Plaintiff:** the person who files (starts) the civil lawsuit
>
> **Defendant:** the person who defends against the civil lawsuit
>
> **Litigant:** both plaintiff and defendant are called litigants

A criminal action has broader goals: to punish the wrongdoer and prevent him or her from committing more crimes, and to deter others from committing similar crimes. The penalties are not based on paying for the damage done. A person convicted of a crime might have to pay a heavy fine to the government, even if the criminal act (such as drunk driving) did not result in any actual damage. He or she might also have to serve a jail sentence.

CHAPTER 1

The same harmful act might lead to both a criminal action and a civil action.

> **Civil Suit**: a lawsuit to compensate an injured person for the harm done (usually through monetary awards)
>
> **Criminal Action**: prosecution by the government (usually the state) for committing a crime. Conviction may result in fines and/or punishment by incarceration (jail time)

Example: A drunk driver causes an accident, injuring several people. The government brings a criminal action against the driver, resulting in a fine and a jail sentence. The criminal action does not compensate the victims. They will have to sue in civil court to force the driver to pay for their medical expenses, lost wages, and car repairs.

Real estate lawsuits are almost always civil, not criminal. The main exceptions to that rule are cases involving fraud. For example, the victim of a fraud can bring a civil suit for compensation. If the fraud was serious enough, the government will also impose criminal penalties. (See Chapter 6 for a discussion of fraud.)

Since most real estate disputes do not involve crimes, the focus of this chapter (and of the book as a whole) will be on civil law.

C. BASIC CIVIL LAW CONCEPTS

As our laws have grown more and more complex, it has become necessary for most lawyers to specialize in a particular area of law. Their specialties correspond to all the different areas in which disputes arise: real estate law, corporate law, family law, personal injury law, and so on. There are three fundamental categories underlying all of these specialties:

1. contracts,
2. torts, and
3. property.

Each category represents a group of basic legal concepts, relationships, and principles.

1. Contracts

A **CONTRACT** *is a legally binding promise.* When two people enter into a contract, they voluntarily take on legal (binding) duties toward one another.

Example: If A contracts to sell B his bike in exchange for $100, A has a legal duty to give B the bike, and B has a legal duty to pay A $100. Without the contract, A had no duty to give B the bike, and B had no duty to pay A $100. By entering into the contract, they voluntarily assumed these binding duties.

A whole body of law governs legal relationships based on contracts.

These rules apply to real estate contracts, employment contracts, and sales contracts. They apply whether the contract concerns tomatoes, a condominium, or commercial shipping.

Various laws make special exceptions for certain kinds of contracts, but there are modifications of the basic rules that govern all contract relationships. These basic rules, as they apply to real property contracts, are discussed in detail in Chapter 7.

Contract law involves a duty by each party to the contract and owed to the other party in the contract. Breaking this duty may get you sued for breach of contract.

2. Torts

Other legal duties are not voluntarily assumed. Instead, they are imposed by law. *The law requires everyone to take reasonable care to avoid injuring another person or damaging someone else's property. A failure to behave as a reasonable person is a breach of this duty of care. It is called a **TORT**.* Torts are sometimes referred to as "civil wrongs" to distinguish them from criminal wrongs or crimes.

Example: Running desperately through the depot to catch a train, "A" accidentally knocks "B" down. "B's" arm is broken in the fall. A has breached the legal duty to use reasonable care in passing through a public place. In other words, "A" has committed a tort against "B."

TORT LAW concerns a group of laws involving civil duties and standards of reasonable conduct owed to persons generally, and not imposed by contract, including laws relating to negligence, trespass, and fraud. There are rules for intentional and unintentional acts, public places and private homes, family members, business associates and total strangers. Torts connected with real estate are discussed in Chapters 6 and 15.

3. Property

PROPERTY LAW concerns ownership of real or personal property. It includes rules about acquiring ownership and losing ownership, and about the rights and duties that ownership carries with it.

Example: A gives B a deed granting B title to Blackacre, a piece of property in San Francisco. The deed confers the ownership of Blackacre onto B. The law grants B, as the owner, the right to use, encumber, will, sell, or ignore Blackacre. The law (in the form of a zoning ordinance) also places some restrictions on B's

> **Contract:** a legally binding promise
>
> **Tort:** breach of a duty imposed by law
>
> **Property Law:** laws concerning ownership of real or personal property

use of the property: B may build a house on Blackacre, but not a shopping mall. The law also imposes a duty on B to pay taxes on the property. These rights and duties are the automatic consequences of ownership.

Nearly every specialized area of law involves contract, tort, and property issues to some degree. A lawyer specializing in maritime law might have to deal with the legal problems surrounding a contract to ship goods to Japan, an accident at sea in which crew members were injured, or transferring ownership of a vessel.

CHAPTER 1

Contract, tort, and property issues can also be presented in a single lawsuit.

> **Example:** A and B are neighbors. A has an easement over B's property for a driveway leading to his own property. A and B disagree about where the boundary between their lots is located.
>
> A leased his house to C. A believes the lease expired at the end of the summer, but C won't give up possession, claiming the lease was supposed to last until the end of the year.
>
> One day C slips in the driveway and breaks her collarbone. It's not clear whether she was on A's property or B's when she slipped, because of the boundary dispute.
>
> In order to determine whether either A or B must compensate C for her injury, the lawyers will have to sort out contract issues (Had the lease expired? What evidence can be introduced to prove the contents of the agreement between A and C?), property issues (Who owned that part of the driveway? Did A have a responsibility to maintain the easement? Did C have a right to use the easement, or was she trespassing?), and tort issues (Did C slip because someone failed to make the driveway reasonably safe? Or was it because of her own carelessness?).

V. Sources of Law

Who makes the laws? The simple answer is that our government does. In the United States "the government" has several facets, and each of them plays a role in lawmaking.

Governmental power is divided between the federal government and the 50 independent state governments, and in each state there are regional and local governmental bodies.

To complicate matters even more, there are different sources of law within the federal government and each of the state governments.

A single legal problem can involve both state and federal laws, or be the subject of constitutional provisions, statutes, court decisions, and administrative regulations.

A. CONSTITUTIONS

A **CONSTITUTION** *is a grant of power to a government.* It sets out the government's basic structure and defines the limits of the government's power.

A constitution is, in effect, the fundamental law that all other laws must comply with. In issuing a new law, a government sometimes exceeds its constitutional power. The new law is then **UNCONSTITUTIONAL**: *it is an illegal law and cannot legally be enforced.* Even a constitutional law can be applied by a government official in a way that oversteps the limits of the government's power. In that case, the law still stands, but the official's action is unconstitutional and illegal.

Checks and balances—the court decides the question of constitutional or unconstitutional.

Constitutions are intended to be long-lasting documents that provide government stability. They can be changed (**amended**), but the procedure for amending a constitution is more difficult than the procedure for changing an ordinary law.

Sources of Law

1. Constitutions
2. Legislatures
3. Courts
4. Administrative Agencies

In the United States, there is a federal Constitution that applies to the whole country, and each of the states has its own constitution as well.

1. Federal Constitution

The United States Constitution was drawn up at the Constitutional Convention in 1787, approved by the states, and adopted in 1789. The Constitution declares itself to be the "supreme law of the land" (Article Vl, Section 2).

a. Power of the Federal and State Governments

The U.S. Constitution defines the relationship between the federal government and the state governments. Only the federal government may make laws concerning certain matters, which include interstate commerce, wars and the military, immigration, bankruptcy, copyrights, and patents, and the currency (Article 1, Section 8).

There are many other areas in which both the federal government and the state governments can and do make laws. Discrimination and environmental protection are examples.

There are also matters that are left up to the state governments. These include the ownership and transfer of real property. As a result, most of the laws affecting a piece of land are created by the state in which the land is located.

If there is a direct conflict between a federal law and a state law (so that a person could not comply with both the federal and state law), or if the federal law expressly provides that it preempts state law, federal law prevails. In other situations, the state law may cover the same subject matter as the federal law in a way that complements, rather than conflicts with, the federal law.

Federal law prevails over a conflict or less stringent state law.

b. Protection of Individual Rights

*The first ten amendments to the U.S. Constitution are known as the **BILL OF RIGHTS**.* They were adopted in 1791. The Thirteenth, Fourteenth, and Fifteenth Amendments were added soon after the Civil War. Together, these amendments protect the rights of individuals by limiting government power. The protections range from freedom of religion to the right to a jury trial.

Some of these amendments have a particular impact on property and the real estate profession. These include the following guarantees:

1. due process,
2. equal protection,

11

3. just compensation,
4. no unreasonable searches or seizures, and
5. protection against certain government, or state, actions.

Due Process. According to the Fifth and Fourteenth Amendments, no one shall be deprived of life, liberty, or property without due process of law. This is known as the due process requirement. Due process requires a fair hearing by an impartial judge.

Example: A real estate agent is accused of grossly misrepresenting the condition of a home. The Real Estate Commissioner has the power to revoke an agent's license for this misconduct. A real estate license is considered "property" for the purposes of the due process requirement. As a result, the Commissioner cannot deprive the agent of his/her license without first holding a hearing that gives the agent an opportunity to tell his/her side of the story.

Due Process: requires that no person be deprived of life, liberty, or property without a fair and adequate process.

Equal Protection: the government may not adopt laws that unfairly discriminate between different groups of people.

Just Compensation: if the government takes private property, it must compensate the owner.

Unreasonable Search and Seizure: the government may not search you or your property without probable cause.

State Action: the government may not take action to interfere with certain rights.

Equal Protection. The Fourteenth Amendment also provides that the government may not deny an individual "equal protection of the laws." The equal protection requirement prohibits governments from adopting laws that unfairly discriminate between certain groups of people.

Many laws involve some sort of discrimination. For example, a law that says a person must have a real estate license to negotiate the sale of land can be said to discriminate against people who don't have licenses. But that discrimination is not considered unfair, since people with licenses are usually better qualified to negotiate land sales than people without licenses. Discrimination on the basis of race, ethnic background, or gender is considered unfair, however. That kind of discrimination generally violates the equal protection requirement.

Just Compensation. Another provision of the Fifth Amendment prevents the government from taking private property for public use "without just compensation." The government has the power to take your land for use as a public garden or parking lot, but the Constitution requires the government to pay you for the fair value of the property it takes. (See the discussion of eminent domain and condemnation in Chapter 10.)

Unreasonable Searches and Seizures. The Fourth Amendment prevents the government from making "unreasonable searches and seizures" of an individual's person or property. A search warrant issued by a judge is required, and a warrant may only be issued if there is "probable cause" for a search.

The Fourth Amendment is applied in criminal cases. In that context, probable cause means that the government must have reasonable grounds for believing that a search will uncover objects used in the commission of crime.

The Fourth Amendment also applies to "administrative searches," such as a routine inspection by the fire department or health department. A search warrant is required for inspection of a residence or business, unless there is an emergency or the owner or occupant consents to the inspection.

It is not necessary to show that there is probable cause to believe the administrative search will uncover a code violation in a particular building. A legitimate government interest in conducting inspections in that neighborhood is sufficient basis for the issuance of a search warrant. (*Camara v. Municipal Court*, 387 U.S. 523 [1967], and *See v. City of Seattle*, 387 U.S. 541[1967].)

State Action. It's important to understand that the federal Constitution's protection of individual rights is primarily protection against abuses by the government. It generally does not protect a person in relation to private individuals or entities. For the Constitution's protections to apply, there must be state action, which is action by a government or a government official.

> **Example:** The First Amendment protects freedom of speech. A city cannot pass a law or take action to prevent groups of protesters from gathering on city sidewalks or in city parks for political rallies. That interference with their freedom of speech would violate the First Amendment.

On the other hand, as far as the federal Constitution is concerned, the owner of a shopping center may prevent the same groups from gathering in the center's mall or parking lot. Because the shopping center is private property, this policy does not involve state action, so it is not considered a violation of the First Amendment. (*Hudgens v. NLRB*, 424 U.S. 507 [1967].)

A city or state may pass a law requiring shopping center owners to allow peaceful protests on their property. Such a law would make a shopping center owner's interference with an orderly protest illegal, even though that interference would not be a violation of the federal Constitution. (*PruneYard Shopping Center v. Robins*, 447 U.S. 74 [1980].)

2. California State Constitution

The current California State Constitution was adopted in 1879, and has undergone numerous amendments over the years. It begins with a Declaration of Rights. Among many other guarantees, Article 1, Section 1 provides: "All people are by nature free and independent and have inalienable rights. Among these are enjoying and defending life and liberty, acquiring, possessing, and protecting property, and pursuing and obtaining safety, happiness, and privacy."

The right of privacy guaranteed in the California Constitution is not specifically mentioned in the United States Constitution.

After its Declaration of Rights, the California Constitution outlines the structure of the state government, and treats a variety of subjects (such as education, taxation, and labor relations) in detail. Articles X and XA are devoted to water law and water resources development; Article XXXIV is called the Public Housing Project Law. Other sections of particular interest to property owners and real estate agents include Article XIV, Section 3, which provides for mechanics' liens; and Article XX, Section 1.5, which protects

CHAPTER 1

homesteads from forced sale. (See Chapter 3 for more information about mechanics' liens and homesteads.)

Many of the state constitutional rights overlap with those protected by the U.S. Constitution, such as freedom of speech and due process of law. In some of these cases, the California Constitution may offer greater protection than the U.S. Constitution. For example, the state Constitution's freedom of speech provision has been interpreted to apply to shopping center owners as well as to governments, even though the federal Constitution's does not.

www.leginfo.ca.gov/const.html
California State Constitution

B. LEGISLATURES: STATUTORY LAW

Legislatures are the dominant source of new laws in the United States. Representatives elected to the U.S. Congress, the 50 state legislatures, and county and city councils across the country make thousands of new laws every year. *The laws adopted by Congress and the state legislatures are called ACTS or STATUTES. The laws adopted by county and city councils are generally called ORDINANCES.*

1. The Legislative Process

The members of a legislative body write and adopt laws through a process of argument and compromise. Each legislative body has its own procedures. For example, here is a brief outline of the procedures used in Congress.

Congress is divided into two houses, the Senate and the House of Representatives. A *proposed law (called a BILL)* is introduced in each house, often at the suggestion of a government agency (the Department of Housing and Urban Development) or a lobbying group (the National Association of Realtors®).

In each house, a legislative committee (e.g., the Banking Committee) analyzes and revises the bill. A Senate committee and a House committee often make different changes in a bill so that different versions develop.

Next, the whole Senate and the whole House each consider and vote on that version of the bill. If a majority in either house votes against the bill, it dies. If a majority in each house votes in favor of the bill, the two versions must be reconciled. A conference committee of both house members works out a compromise version. If a majority in each house votes for this compromise version, the bill is passed.

The final stage of the legislative process involves the president. The president can approve the bill by signing it, or can take no action on it. Either way, the bill becomes law. However, if the president **vetoes** the bill, it will not become law unless Congress votes to **override** the veto. To override a presidential veto, a two-thirds majority in each house must vote in favor of the bill. If the bill can't muster this strong support in Congress, it dies. If the veto is overridden, however, the bill becomes law in spite of the president's disapproval.

The California legislature follows a similar procedure. It is also divided into two houses, the state senate and the assembly. The governor may veto legislation.

Most legislation becomes effective on January 1 of the next year. If it is critical that a law be effective immediately, it is called "emergency" legislation and is effective when signed by the governor.

A citizen can influence the legislative process. First, of course, you can vote for representatives who seem likely to promote your interests. You can also join or organize a lobbying group that will propose new legislation or revisions to the representatives. When the legislature is considering a bill that you support or oppose, you can urge your representatives to vote for or against it.

2. Codification

Once a new statute or ordinance has been formally adopted, it is published. It is the legislature's pronouncement of what the law on a given issue will be, from the effective date forward.

Some statutory laws are simple and clear; many are long and complicated. Some address a very narrow issue; others cover a large area. *At times, a legislature will gather up all the laws on a particular subject, reconcile them and clarify them, then set them out systematically in a comprehensive compendium (or collection) called a* **CODE**. *This process is called* **CODIFICATION**.

www.leginfo.ca.gov/calaw.html
California State Codes

In some states there are only a few codes, but the California legislature has codified most state law. Laws affecting property and the real estate profession are mainly found in the Civil Code and the Business and Professions Code (see **Figure 1-1**).

Figure 1-1   **California State Codes**

Business and Professions Code	Insurance Code
Civil Code	Labor Code
Code of Civil Procedure	Military and Veterans Code
Commercial Code	Penal Code
Corporations Code	Probate Code
Education Code	Public Contract Code
Elections Code	Public Resources Code
Evidence Code	Public Utilities Code
Family Code	Revenue and Taxation Code
Financial Code	Streets and Highways Code
Fish and Game Code	Unemployment Insurance Code
Food and Agriculture Code	Vehicle Code
Government Code	Water Code
Harbors and Navigation Code	Welfare and Institutions Code
Health and Safety Code	

C. COURTS: CASE LAW

Although legislatures are the main source of new law, the courts are also an important source. Courts do not issue general rules in the same way that legislatures do. A legislature can make laws on any subject it chooses (as long as it doesn't violate the federal or state constitution). A trial judge only addresses a point of law if it is at issue in a lawsuit. *The law is interpreted and applied in published written opinions of the Court of Appeal and the Supreme Court in court cases that are referred to as CASE LAW.*

Historically, the courts were the primary source of law in the English common law system (in contrast to other European countries, where statutory law was dominant). The term "common law" therefore refers to judge-made case law, which we inherited from England, as opposed to statutory law or constitutional law.

1. Dispute Resolution and Lawmaking

A judge's primary task is to apply the law and to determine where justice lies and the facts between the parties. One person accuses another of breaching a contract; the other denies it. They can't work out their disagreement, so there is a lawsuit.

In the course of resolving a dispute, a judge will often have to apply the law. Applying the law to the facts is not a mechanical process. Nearly every case presents a new combination of circumstances, and many raise issues that have not been settled by existing law.

Example: It is an established rule that a seller's real estate agent must conduct a visual inspection of the seller's house. If the agent discovers any defects, they must be disclosed to the buyer. The agent does not have to inspect areas that are not reasonably accessible to visual inspection.

A's house has a small attic, really not much more than a crawlspace. It can only be reached through a trap door in the ceiling. A's broker, B, inspects the house, but she does not look at the attic. After C buys the house, extensive dry rot is discovered in the attic. C sues B because she did not discover this problem and disclose it to him.

The judge must decide whether B's duty to inspect the house included looking at the attic. Was the attic reasonably accessible to visual inspection? The established rules do not address this particular question.

The way the judge answers this question will, of course, directly affect the parties involved in the lawsuit. If the judge says the attic was reasonably accessible, then B had a duty to inspect it. She will owe C compensation for failing to discover and disclose the dry rot problem.

Under certain circumstances, if the judge's conclusion is upheld by the Court of Appeal in a published opinion, it may affect not only the people involved in this particular lawsuit (B and C), but everyone who is in a similar situation. It may be that every broker confronted with an attic trap door will have to climb up a ladder and inspect the attic, or risk liability.

2. Stare Decisis and Precedent

An Appellate or Supreme Court's published decision in a specific case becomes a rule of law or precedent. The precedent will be applied to all future cases because of the doctrine

CASE LAW CITATIONS

Judicial opinions are published in books called case reports or reporters. Case citations—references to particular cases in the reporters—are given in a standardized form.

EXAMPLE: *Riddle v. Harmony*, 102 Cal.App. 3d 524 (App.1 Dist. 1980)

The citation includes the name of the case, followed by the volume (102) of the case reporter California Appellate Reports Third Series (Cal. App. 3d) where the opinion can be found. Then it states the page number (524) the opinion begins on. The citation ends with a reference to the specific District of the Court of Appeal, if a District Court of Appeal decision, or "Cal." if a Supreme Court decision.

There are separate case reporters for most state appellate courts in the country, as well as federal case reporters. In addition, there are regional reporters that compile important cases from state courts in a given region (the *Pacific Reporter* with 15 states and the *Northeastern Reporter* with 5 states, for example). Each reporter's title has its own abbreviation for purposes of citation (such as 532 P.2d 1226). The case reporter abbreviations that a Californian is most likely to encounter are:

State Court Decisions

Decisions of the California Supreme Court:

California Reports: Cal. (beginning to 1934); then Cal. 2d (1934-1969); then Cal. 3d (1969-1991); then Cal. 4th (1991-).

Decisions of the California Court of Appeal:

California Appellate Reports: Cal. App. (beginning to 1934); then Cal. App. 2d (1934-1969); then Cal. App. 3d (1969-1991); then Cal. App. 4th (1991-).

Decisions of both the California Supreme Court and Court of Appeal:

California Reporter (began in 1960): Cal. Rptr. (beginning to 1991); then Cal. Rptr. 2d (1991 - 2003); then Cal. Rptr. 3d (2003-).

Example: *Reed v. King*, 145 Cal. App. 3d 261, 193 Cal. Rptr. 130 (1983)

Decisions from state courts in California and 14 other western states:

Pacific Reporter (dropped California Court of Appeal decisions in 1960) P., P.2d, P.3d in 1930-).

Federal Court Decisions

Decisions of the U.S. Supreme Court:
United States Reports   **U.S.**
Supreme Court Reporter   **S. Ct.**
Decisions of the U.S. Courts of Appeal (including the Ninth Circuit):
Federal Reporter   **F., F.2d, F.3d**
Decisions of the U.S. District Courts:
Federal Supplement   **F. Supp., F. Supp.2d**

A citation to a case from a federal court of appeals includes the circuit number in parentheses, along with the year the case was decided. A Ninth Circuit decision would be cited like this:

***Trident Center v. Connecticut General Life Ins. Co.*, 847 F.2d 564 (9th Cir. 1988)**

A citation to a case from a federal district court includes the name of the district in the parentheses. A decision from the Eastern District of California would be cited like this:

***Furey v. City of Sacramento*, 592 F. Supp. 463 (E.D. Cal. 1984)**

Stare decisis: doctrine requiring lower courts to follow published Appellate or Supreme Court's earlier decisions.

Precedent: a previously decided case concerning the same issues as a later case.

Jurisdiction: an area under the authority of a particular court.

of *STARE DECISIS, which holds that once a higher court has decided a particular point of law, lower courts faced with the same issue must decide it the same way.* ("Stare decisis" is a Latin phrase that means, roughly, "to abide by things decided.") If the court of appeal in the previous example ruled in a published opinion that the attic was reasonably accessible to visual inspection, the doctrine would require another court in a later case involving a similar attic to rule that it also was reasonably accessible. *The Appellate or Supreme Court's published decision is called PRECEDENT,* and it is **binding** on lower court judges.

Stare decisis is important because it leads to predictability and stability of court law.

Stare decisis is not a law, but a policy that judges have followed for centuries (we inherited it from English common law). It tries to ensure that two people who do the same thing will be treated the same way by the law. This fits with our sense of fairness; it also makes the law more predictable. If a binding precedent holds that an attic with a trap door is reasonably accessible, real estate agents are given warning that they had better go to the trouble of climbing up into such an attic.

Not every court decision is a binding precedent for all other judges, however. It depends, for the most part, on three factors:

1. jurisdiction,
2. position in the court hierarchy, and
3. a written opinion.

For a judge to be bound by the Appellate or Supreme Court's published decision, the other court must be in the same jurisdiction. A *JURISDICTION is the area under the authority of a particular court.* To take a simple example, the jurisdiction of the California Supreme Court is the state of California. A decision of the California Supreme Court is not binding on a Nevada state court.

Within each jurisdiction, courts are arranged in a hierarchy, with numerous courts on the lowest level and a smaller number of courts on each higher level. There may be just one judge or several judges on a given court, depending on its function and the population of the area it serves. A judge is required to follow the precedents decided by a higher court in the same jurisdiction (see **Figure 1-2**).

Intermediate Court A hears a case involving an attic with a trap door and rules that such an attic is reasonably accessible. All the judges on Lower Courts A1, A2, and A3 are ordinarily required to follow that precedent if a similar case is brought before them.

An appellate court is free to override its own precedents.

Example: Two years later, Intermediate Court A hears another attic trap door case. The judges on Intermediate Court A would ordinarily follow their own court's precedent, but this time they reconsider the earlier decision and decide to overrule it. They hold that a broker is not required to inspect an attic if it can only be reached by climbing up a ladder and through a trap door.

Figure 1-2

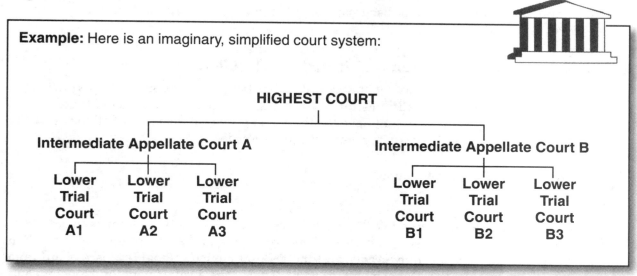

Example: Here is an imaginary, simplified court system:

If the earlier case had been decided by the Highest Court and not Intermediate Court A, the precedent could not be overruled by Intermediate Court A.

Judges can't overrule precedents decided by a higher court.

No decision can be a binding precedent unless a written **opinion** is published. All Supreme Court opinions are published along with many Court of Appeal opinions and, on rare occasions, a Superior Court appellate opinion. *In addition to stating the court's decision, an OPINION describes the facts of the case and the court's reasoning*: why it concluded that the attic was not reasonably accessible, and why it did not hold the broker liable. Courts prepare written opinions for every case decided on the merits, but publish opinions only for their most important cases.

By reading the higher court's opinion, a lower court judge can determine how similar the facts of that earlier case were to the case he or she is deciding, and whether the same reasoning applies. When the facts are significantly different, the current case is **distinguished** from the earlier case. If the current case can be distinguished, the lower court judge can reach a different result than was reached in the earlier case.

Even though judges are not bound by lower court decisions or decisions from other jurisdictions, they often take those decisions into consideration. A well-reasoned opinion from another jurisdiction may be persuasive.

Example: A judge in California is deciding a case involving a very unusual type of easement. Although no other court in California has ever dealt with such an easement, courts in other states have. The California judge reads opinions from courts in New York, Florida, and Alabama. The Florida court decided the easement was valid, but the New York and Alabama courts decided it was invalid. The Florida court's reasoning makes much more sense to the California judge than the other courts' reasoning. He rules that the easement in his case is valid, and writes an opinion that is based on interpretation of California law that is analogous to the Florida court's reasoning.

CHAPTER 1

The relationship of different courts and the process of deciding cases are more complicated than this initial discussion might suggest. They will be examined in greater detail later in this chapter.

D. ADMINISTRATIVE AGENCIES: REGULATIONS

Over the past few decades, another source of law has become increasingly important in the U.S.: federal, state, and local administrative agencies. Executives (the president, governors, and mayors) and legislatures do not have the time or expertise to take care of all the details of a complex area of law, so they create administrative agencies.

www.lib.lsu.edu/gov/fedgov.html
Federal Agencies

There are agencies concerned with nearly every aspect of society. Federal agencies range from the Department of Housing and Urban Development and the Environmental Protection Agency to the Internal Revenue Service and the Federal Housing Finance Board. California state agencies include the Department of Real Estate, the Department of Housing and Community Development, and the Coastal Commission. Every county and city has a zoning authority, a building department, a planning commission, etc.

1. Rule Making

An *ADMINISTRATIVE AGENCY is usually given broad powers within its area of authority. This includes the power to issue regulations that have the force of law.* For example, the California legislature, in Business and Profession Code § 10071, granted to the Real Estate Commissioner the "full power to regulate and control the issuance and revocation" of real estate licenses and "to perform all other acts and duties" set forth in the Real Estate Law. Using this authority, the Real Estate Commissioner has issued regulations prohibiting the discriminatory sales practices called blockbusting and steering (see Chapter 14). An agent who violates these regulations may have his or her license revoked. The Department of Real Estate also has the power to fine agents for violations.

Before issuing a new regulation, an agency generally requires publishing a notice of its proposed action at least 45 days in advance. This gives interested parties (such as real estate agents or homeowners) the opportunity to express their ideas and concerns. In some cases, the agency holds a public hearing on the proposed new rule, and in others, the agency will ask for written comments. If you file a request for notice with an agency, they'll mail you a notice of proposed rule changes.

A new regulation must, of course, be constitutional. It also must not conflict with a statute or exceed the authority granted to the agency by the legislative body or executive creating it.

2. Adjudication and Enforcement

Detailed regulations give rise to many disagreements: licenses, permits, and benefits are denied or revoked, rules are violated. These disputes would overwhelm the court system, so most of them are decided by the agencies themselves.

Many of these disputes are handled through an informal process of negotiation. When a significant liberty or property interest (such as a real estate license) is at stake, the agency usually must hold a formal administrative hearing to comply with the Constitution's due process requirement. Administrative law judges hear these cases and propose decisions to the Real Estate Commissioner.

An administrative law judge is an expert in the agency's area of authority. He or she is supposed to consider disputes impartially, rather than taking the agency's point of view.

If you're unhappy with the Commissioner's decision, there may be a board of appeals within the agency that will review your case. If you're dissatisfied with the board of appeals' decision, you can appeal again, this time to the court system.

On license application matters, a court is not very likely to overturn the agency's decision so long as the record contains some evidence to support the decision and the agency has not exceeded its grant of power or failed to follow required procedures. In discipline against existing licensees, however, a court can exercise its independent judgment on the evidence, in some cases overruling the administrative agency despite no agency violation of procedures.

The appeal to a court helps prevent an abuse of discretion, fraud, or injustice or lack of due process by a government agency.

E. INTERACTION OF LAWS

Constitutional provisions, statutes, case law, and administrative regulations are not isolated from one another. They are often complementary, and a judge may apply all of them in resolving a lawsuit. There is also interaction between them: a statute or a regulation can be held unconstitutional; new case law can be developed to interpret a statute; a new statute can replace old case law.

1. Judicial Review

The concept of unconstitutionality was introduced earlier in this chapter. If a law exceeds the limits of government power granted by the U.S. Constitution or the state constitution, it is unconstitutional.

Judges determine whether statutes, ordinances, or regulations are unconstitutional. The Constitution did not expressly assign that role to them, but in an early case, the U.S. Supreme Court declared that the judiciary had that power (see *Marbury v. Madison*, 5 U.S. [1 Cranch] 137 [1803]). **Judicial review** of legislation and regulations is established and accepted today.

Judges do not routinely review all of the statutes adopted by a legislature or all of an administrative agency's regulations. Someone who believes he or she has been harmed by an unconstitutional statute or regulation must file a lawsuit challenging the law's constitutionality before a court will review it. When a court decides that a law is unconstitutional, it cannot be enforced. The law is struck down. At that point, the legislature or administrative agency may try to revise the statute or regulation to bring it within constitutional limits.

A judge often must put aside a lifetime of personal opinions, beliefs, and convictions in order to determine a case guided by precedent and legislation.

INTERACTION OF LAWS

A judge deciding a lawsuit may consider all of these questions:

Has there been any violation of the state or federal constitution?

Are there applicable statutes?

Are there applicable agency regulations?

Are the statutes or regulations constitutional?

Have similar cases been decided? → **Are the prior cases binding precedent?**

---

2. Statutory Construction

The most common kind of interaction between different types of law occurs when a judge applies a statute in a lawsuit. This is a straightforward task when the facts of the case clearly fall inside or outside of the statute's rule. However, it often isn't clear whether the statute covers a particular situation or not, so the judge must decide. The meaning of the legislation is obtained by statutory construction. Judges have to interpret administrative regulations in the same way.

*In interpreting a statute or regulation through **STATUTORY CONSTRUCTION**, the judge's goal is to carry out the intention of the legislature or the administrative agency.* To return to the attic example, a statute may say "reasonably accessible to visual inspection," but the judge must decide whether the legislature intended that phrase to cover climbing through a trap door into an attic.

When judges interpret a statute or a regulation, case law is grafted onto the statutory or regulatory law. A whole series of cases may develop the meaning of a single statutory phrase such as "reasonably accessible to visual inspection": one case says you have to climb through a trap door into an attic, another says you don't have to go up on the roof, another says you have to crawl through a hedge to look under the back porch.

The legislature may disagree with some of the case law that develops through this process of interpretation. It can then rewrite the statute to make it clear that you don't have to climb through trap doors or hedges, or to make it clear that you do have to go up on the roof. The revised statute will supersede any case law that conflicts with it. An administrative agency can also revise its regulations.

The process of judicial interpretation will begin all over again with the revised statute or regulation. There's no such thing as a perfectly clear rule that covers all possible cases and requires no interpretation. This interaction between statutes, regulations, and court decisions is a necessary part of the law.

VI. The Judicial System

As you've seen, judges resolve disputes by interpreting and applying existing laws. This section of the chapter focuses on the structure of the judicial system. It explains the different functions of trial and appellate courts, and outlines the state and federal court systems. It also describes some rules that limit access to the courts.

Both the federal and state systems are overcrowded; there are too many cases and not enough judges to hear them, which often causes long delays. A number of the procedures and limitations described here were developed to help with this problem. They are intended to reserve the courts' resources for the cases where adjudication is most necessary and most likely to be effective.

A. TRIAL COURTS AND APPELLATE COURTS

The fundamental court proceeding in a lawsuit is the **TRIAL**. The general outlines of a trial are no doubt familiar to you: lawyers present arguments and evidence, witnesses testify and are cross-examined, and a jury or a judge decides the case. *Trials take place in a jurisdiction's lower courts, so those are often referred to as* **TRIAL COURTS**.

If you're dissatisfied with the outcome of a trial, you have the opportunity to appeal at least once, provided that you satisfy the grounds for an appeal. Grounds for an appeal include judicial error, lack of substantial evidence to support the decision, and a clear abuse of discretion in making the decision. On **APPEAL**, *you are asking a higher court in the same jurisdiction to review the trial court's decision. A court that has the power to review the decisions of lower courts is called an* **APPELLATE COURT** *and is said to have* **APPELLATE JURISDICTION**. (Trial courts are said to have **ORIGINAL JURISDICTION**, *because they hear cases for the first time.*)

The role of the court of appeal is to review the trial court's record (court files and transcripts) to decide if any legal errors were made.

Many people expect an appeal to be just like another trial, but it is a very different proceeding. To try every appealed case all over again would be extremely expensive, both for the parties and for the court system. As the evidence is not presented again, the witnesses do not testify again, and there is no jury.

Appealing a court decision does not mean there will be a new trial.

The role of the court of appeal is to review the trial court's **TRIAL RECORD** *(court files and transcripts)* to decide if any legal errors were made. It also includes any exhibits that were introduced at the trial. An **EXHIBIT** *is documentary or physical evidence: a listing agreement, a deed, fingerprints, or an old tire.* In reviewing the record, the appellate court is looking for errors committed by the trial judge. Most appellate courts will only change a trial court's decision if:

1. the judge or jury committed a legal error,
2. the error concerned a question of law, and
3. the error was prejudicial.

1. Questions of Fact and Questions of Law

All the issues in a trial can be classified as either questions of fact or questions of law. A **QUESTION OF FACT** *is any question about what actually took place:* Did A tell B she could lease the apartment for nine months or for a year? A **QUESTION OF LAW**, *on the other hand, is any question about the application of law on a particular point.* For example, is a lease for a year and a half valid if it isn't in writing?

*Questions of fact are decided by the **TRIER OF FACT**.* In a jury trial, the trier of fact is the jury; in a nonjury trial, the trier of fact is the judge. Questions of law, however, are always decided by the judge, whether or not there is a jury.

A case that is decided by a judge instead of a jury is known as a "bench trial."

An appellate court generally accepts the trier of fact's conclusions on questions of fact. The trier of fact had a better opportunity to assess the credibility of witnesses than the appellate court. The trier of fact heard the testimony firsthand and could observe the witnesses as they were testifying, whereas the appellate judges only read a transcript of the testimony.

If the trier of fact concluded that the plaintiff fell on the sidewalk instead of the porch, the appellate court will presume that conclusion is correct. An exception is made only if the trier of fact's findings are completely unsupported by the evidence.

In many jurisdictions, appellate courts follow this rule whether the trier of fact was a jury or the trial judge. In California, state appellate courts also follow this rule. The trial court's resolution of a disputed fact issue must be affirmed so long as the finding is supported by "substantial" evidence.

Any appellate court's main focus is on the questions of law, reviewing the record to see if the trial judge decided any of those incorrectly. The trial judge may have made a mistake about an established point of law or may have ruled on an issue that had never been decided before, and the appellate court might disagree with the ruling. In either case, the trial court is said to have "committed a legal error."

a. Prejudicial Error and Harmless Error

If the appellate court finds that the trial judge committed an error, it considers whether the error was prejudicial or harmless. A ***PREJUDICIAL ERROR*** *is one that adversely affected a substantial right of one of the litigants.* This is generally interpreted to mean an error that may have made a difference in the outcome of the trial. *If the trier of fact would almost certainly have reached the same final decision if the error had not been made, the error is considered **HARMLESS**.*

b. The Appellate Decision

The appellate court can agree with the decision of the trial court, agree in part and disagree in part, disagree and reverse the trial court's decision, or disagree and reverse with directions to the trial court.

When a trial court's decision is reversed, the appellate court may also reverse with directions expressly requiring specific further proceedings in the trial court. If the case is remanded, the appellate court may order the original trial judge to conduct additional proceedings, or it may order a new trial.

c. Supreme Court Review by Petition

A litigant dissatisfied with the result of an appeal may petition to an even higher court. While a first appeal is generally an **appeal by right**, a petition for review is often **discretionary**. (The litigant petitions the high court to hear the case, but the high court may refuse. In fact, because the courts are so crowded, the great majority of discretionary appeals are turned down.) Supreme Court review is granted in civil cases when necessary to secure **uniformity of decision** among the appellate courts or to **settle important questions of law**.

B. STATE COURTS AND FEDERAL COURTS

Just as there is a federal legislature (Congress) and 50 state legislatures, there is a federal court system and 50 state court systems. The federal court system isn't centralized in Washington, D.C.; there are federal courts in every state, along with the state courts. The jurisdictions of federal courts and state courts usually overlap.

Taking a closer look at the concept of jurisdiction will make it easier to understand the two systems and their relationship to one another. You have already seen how a court's jurisdiction can be limited to a particular geographical area: the California state courts generally don't have any authority over what takes place in Nevada. But jurisdiction can be limited in other ways as well.

A court's jurisdiction may be limited to a certain type of lawsuit, such as tax cases or patent cases. *The types of cases that a court has authority to hear are called its SUBJECT MATTER JURISDICTION. A court that is not limited to a specific subject is called a COURT OF GENERAL JURISDICTION.*

There may also be monetary limits on a court's jurisdiction. For example, some courts can only hear a case if *the amount of money at stake in the dispute (called the AMOUNT IN CONTROVERSY)* is more than $75,000. Other courts can only hear a case if the amount in controversy is $5,000 or less.

Limitations like these define the jurisdiction of the various state and federal courts. We'll look at the California state courts, then at the federal system, and then at the relationship between the two.

www.courtinfo.ca.gov
California Court System

> **Download Superior Case Summaries Online**
> Some county's make superior court case summaries available for download on the Internet.

1. California State Court System

The two types of California state courts are the trial courts and the appellate courts. The two types of appellate courts are the courts of appeal and the California Supreme Court.

All judges in the California state court system are elected, rather than appointed. However, the governor can appoint a judge to fill a vacancy if one occurs. Superior court judges serve six-year terms, and Court of Appeal and Supreme Court judges serve twelve-year terms.

a. Trial Courts (Superior Courts)

A judge or a jury in the trial court (Superior Court) hears testimony and evidence and decides a case by applying the law to the facts of the case.

Superior Courts are general jurisdiction courts, which, as explained earlier, means they have the ability to hear and decide a wide range of cases. Superior Courts try all criminal cases. They also try civil cases where **damages** are sought, which are divided into two

California's Court Structure

Supreme Court

California Court of Appeal (6 Districts)

First District
San Francisco

Second District
Los Angeles and
Ventura

Third District
Sacramento

Fourth District
San Diego,
Santa Ana, and
San Bernardino

Fifth District
Fresno

Sixth District
San Jose

Superior Courts
At least 1 in each of the 58 counties

categories: those which seek more than $25,000 (unlimited), and those that seek less than $25,000 (limited). The Superior Court is also the trial court for civil cases where the plaintiff is seeking a remedy other than a damages award, such as **specific performance**.

There is at least one Superior Court in each of the 58 counties, and the number of judges on the court depends on the county's population.

Small Claims Division. Each Superior Court has a small claims division for resolving minor civil disputes quickly and inexpensively. Small claims court is a **limited jurisdiction court**. The amount in controversy must be $10,000 or less for natural persons, or $5,000 for others (corporations or other entities). No one can file more than two claims for over $2,500 in one year in small claims courts in California. An unlawful detainer action (eviction) cannot be heard in small claims court.

To save time and expense, the small claims process is simplified in several respects.

The Superior Courts handle:

1. all criminal cases (felonies, misdemeanors, and traffic tickets);
2. all civil cases (family law, probate, juvenile, and other civil cases);
3. appeals of small claims cases and other civil cases worth $25,000 or less, and
4. appeals of misdemeanor cases.

There is no jury. Neither the plaintiff nor the defendant can be represented by a lawyer in the courtroom. (They are allowed to consult lawyers about the case, however.) The plaintiff gives up the right to an appeal, but the defendant still has the right to an appeal, since he or she was not the one who chose small claims court.

The appeal is a completely new trial held in the appellate department (unlimited jurisdiction branch) of the Superior Court. This trial is different in that the parties can be represented by attorneys. Once the new trial results in a judgment, the judgment is final and there is no further appeal.

b. California Court of Appeal

The **COURT OF APPEAL'S** *primary function is to determine whether there has been an error at the Superior Court level, and if so, to remedy it.*

In California, over 15,000 Notices of Appeal are filed yearly. They include approximately 6,300 criminal cases, 6,100 civil cases, and 2,600 juvenile cases.

The state is divided into six appellate districts, each having jurisdiction over several counties. The First Appellate District includes San Francisco; the Second District includes Los Angeles and Santa Barbara; Sacramento is in the Third District; San Diego, San Bernardino, and Orange County are in the Fourth District; the Fifth District includes Fresno, and the Sixth District includes San Jose.

Each appeal is heard by three justices of the Court of Appeal, who will render the court's decision.

The number of judges in each district depends on the population: The larger appellate districts contain more than one division. For example, the Second Appellate District has seven divisions.

A state Court of Appeal's opinion is published only if it involves an important new issue, or changes an established rule.

Approximately eight percent of Court of Appeal majority opinions are published yearly.

The published decisions of any of the Courts of Appeal are binding precedents for all the trial courts in the state (Superior Courts). This is true even when the trial court is not in the same Appellate District as the Court of Appeal that established the precedent.

Example: A San Diego County Superior Court judge is hearing a case involving breach of contract. In resolving the questions of law that the case presents, the judge looks first for precedents decided by the Fourth District Court of Appeal because San Diego is in the Fourth District.

The judge finds that the central point of law in the case has never been addressed by the Fourth District Court of Appeal. That doesn't mean the judge gets to make up her own mind about the issue, however. Instead, she must do further research to determine whether the courts of appeal in any of the five other districts has decided the question yet.

CHAPTER 1

It turns out that the First District Court of Appeal has established a precedent on the issue. The San Diego Superior Court judge must follow the First District precedent, even though San Diego is not in that district.

What if the judge had found two conflicting precedents, one from the First District and one from the Sixth District? She would choose between the two. That kind of conflict would eventually be cleared up by the highest court in the state system, the California Supreme Court.

c. California Supreme Court

The California Supreme Court is the state's highest court. It reviews cases decided by the Courts of Appeal.

The California Supreme Court consists of a chief justice and six associate justices. With limited exceptions, cases must go from Superior Court to a Court of Appeal before they can be appealed to the Supreme Court.

Death penalty appeals and disciplinary cases involving judges and lawyers go directly to the California Supreme Court and are not heard first in the Court of Appeal.

A petition for review to the California Supreme Court from a Court of Appeal decision is discretionary. The supreme court will grant a petition for review and hear the case if it presents a particularly important legal question, or if the Courts of Appeal have developed conflicting precedents.

The Supreme Court can resolve these conflicts because its decisions are binding on all other California state courts. One of the Supreme Court's most important functions is making the law uniform throughout the state. All Supreme Court opinions are published; they are the final word on California law.

The California Supreme Court receives over 5,400 petitions yearly seeking Court of Appeal decision reviews, and issues approximately 125 written opinions.

2. Federal Court System

www.uscourts.gov/districtcourts.html
www.courts.net/fed/index.html
www.diviacchi.com/courts.htm

Download Federal Cases Online from PACER

Federal courts only accept electronically filed cases. *PUBLIC ACCESS TO COURT ELECTRONIC RECORDS (PACER)* is an electronic public access service that allows users to obtain case and docket information from Federal Courts via the Internet.

The Federal Court System

U.S. Supreme Court

U.S. Court of Appeals
(11 Circuits + D.C. Circuit)

U.S. District Courts
(California: 4 District Courts, 39 Judges)

Specialized Courts

Tax Courts   **Federal Circuit**   **Bankruptcy Courts**

All federal judges are appointed by the president and confirmed by the Senate. The Constitution provides that they hold office "during good behavior," which generally means for life or until they retire.

a. Specialized Courts

There are a few specialized federal courts with narrow subject matter jurisdiction. The *U.S. TAX COURTS only hear cases involving the federal tax laws, the FEDERAL CIRCUIT COURT primarily hears appeals concerning patents or foreign trade, and the U.S. BANKRUPTCY COURTS hear nothing but bankruptcy cases.*

b. United States District Courts

The *U.S. DISTRICT COURTS are the main trial courts of the federal system.* There are 94 federal judicial districts, including at least one district in each state, the District of Columbia, and Puerto Rico. California has four district courts (39 judges): Northern (9 judges), Eastern (3), Central (21), and Southern (6).

A federal District Court judge's published decision is binding on other federal judges in the same district, but not on federal judges in other districts. A judge in the Eastern District of California must follow Eastern District precedents, but doesn't have to follow precedents decided in the Northern District of California.

U.S. District Courts have the power to hear cases ("subject matter jurisdiction") only if the cases fall into one of three categories:

1. The United States government is a party.

2. A federal question is presented.

3. There is diversity of citizenship, and the amount in controversy is more than $75,000.

CALIFORNIA'S FOUR FEDERAL COURT DISTRICTS

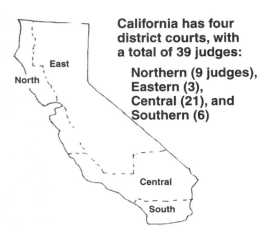

California has four district courts, with a total of 39 judges:

Northern (9 judges), Eastern (3), Central (21), and Southern (6)

In addition to subject matter jurisdiction, a court may hear a case only if there is an actual dispute (see the discussion of Cases or Controversies below) and if the plaintiff has standing (that is, must be a person aggrieved or legally harmed).

Cases in which the United States is a party include suits involving federal crimes: interstate car theft, racketeering, drug smuggling, and so forth. The U.S. can also be a party in a civil suit. For example, a defense contractor might sue the U.S. Army over a contract dispute. That case could be tried in a federal district court, since the army is a part of the U.S. government.

The District Courts also have jurisdiction over civil cases that present a federal question. A *FEDERAL QUESTION* is any issue regarding the application or interpretation of the U.S. Constitution, a federal statute, or a U.S. treaty. If a group of political protesters sues a city for interfering with their First Amendment right to freedom of speech, the case could be heard in a federal district court.

The third category of federal District Court jurisdiction covers civil cases in which there is diversity of citizenship and the amount in controversy is more than $75,000. There is *DIVERSITY OF CITIZENSHIP when the plaintiff and the defendant are not citizens of the same state. If a citizen of Alabama sues a citizen of California, or if a citizen of California sues a citizen of Brazil, the case can be heard in federal district court as long as more than $75,000 is at stake. This is called DIVERSITY JURISDICTION*.

The Federal Judicial Circuits

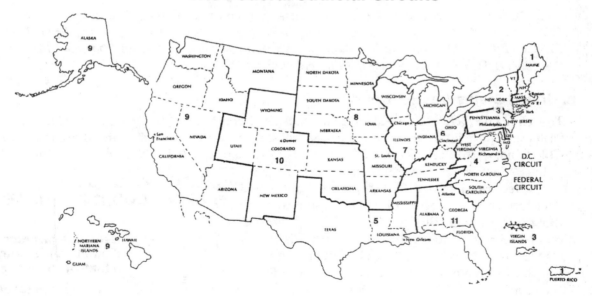

c. United States Court of Appeals

The result of a trial in a U.S. District Court can be appealed (by right) to one of the U.S. Courts of Appeals. There is a federal Court of Appeals for each of 11 numbered circuits; each circuit covers several states. There is an additional Court of Appeals in Washington, D.C., which is called the D.C. Circuit.

California is in the Ninth Circuit, along with Oregon, Washington, Montana, Idaho, Nevada, Arizona, Alaska, Hawaii, and Guam. The decision of a U.S. District Court of Appeals sitting in any of those states—for example, the District Court for the Eastern

District of California, or the Idaho District Court—could be appealed to the Ninth Circuit Court of Appeals.

There are 49 judges on the Ninth Circuit, which is the largest federal appeals court. Most appeals are heard by panels made up of three of the circuit's judges. A Ninth Circuit decision is a binding precedent for all the U.S. District Courts within the circuit.

> **Example:** A judge on the U.S. District Court for the Northern District of California rules in a published decision that a broker's hiring policies violated federal employment discrimination statutes. If a case involving similar hiring policies comes before the U.S. District Court for the Eastern District of Washington, the judge does not have to follow the Northern District of California's decision. He or she may decide that the hiring policy did not violate the federal statute. However, it's a different matter if the California broker appeals to the Ninth Circuit, and a three-judge panel affirms the California District Court's decision. Now a district court in Washington (or Hawaii, Arizona, or any Ninth Circuit state) is required to follow the Ninth Circuit's precedent and hold that the hiring policy violated the statute.

Other circuit courts of appeals do not have to follow the Ninth Circuit's precedent. District courts in other circuits—the District Court for the Western District of Kentucky, or for the Southern District of New York—are also free to ignore the Ninth Circuit's decision, but a decision by one of the U.S. Courts of Appeals may have persuasive value for other Courts of Appeals.

Not every opinion of the U.S. Courts of Appeal is published, but all the opinions that decide new issues or change old rules are.

d. United States Supreme Court

The U.S. Supreme Court is made up of the Chief Justice and Eight Associate Justices. Although it is the highest and most influential court in the country, its jurisdiction is limited, as jurisdiction is in the lower federal courts.

The Supreme Court has original jurisdiction in a few special types of cases: for example, a lawsuit involving officials of a foreign government, or a lawsuit filed by a state against a citizen of a different state. However, even though the Court is empowered to conduct the trials in these cases, they will usually take place in a U.S. District Court instead. The only trials that must take place in the Supreme Court are those where one state is suing another state.

The Supreme Court has appellate jurisdiction in all cases decided by the U.S. Courts of Appeal. Its decisions in these cases are binding precedents for all other courts. This gives the Supreme Court power to resolve conflicts between the decisions of U.S. Courts of Appeal in different circuits.

All appeals to the Supreme Court are discretionary. A losing party files a *PETITION FOR WRIT OF CERTIORARI, asking the Supreme Court to review the decision of a lower court.* It includes a list of the parties, a statement of the facts of the case, the legal questions presented for review, and arguments why the Court should grant the writ. Petitions are filed for thousands of cases each year, but the Court hears less than 5% of them. Although "I'll take my case all the way to the Supreme Court!" is a standard threat, it can rarely be carried out. The U.S. Court of Appeals is the end of the line for the overwhelming majority of federal cases.

C. RELATIONSHIP OF THE FEDERAL AND STATE COURTS

Because federal jurisdiction and state jurisdiction overlap, the relationship between the two court systems is complicated. We'll start with the simpler cases, those that must be heard in federal court and those that must be heard in state court—before moving on to the cases that can be heard in either one.

1. Exclusive Jurisdiction

In some federal statutes, Congress has included a requirement that lawsuits based on the statute can only be brought in federal court. For example, cases involving the Voting Rights Act of 1965 cannot be heard in state court. The same is true for suits regarding patents, copyrights, immigration, admiralty, and a number of other subjects that are controlled by federal statutes. Very few cases involving real property are in this category.

Any case that does not fall within the jurisdiction of the federal courts must be brought in state court. In other words, a case has to be heard in state court if:

1. the U.S. government is not a party,
2. no federal question is presented, and
3. there is no diversity of citizenship (or there is diversity, but the amount in controversy is $75,000 or less).

For example, most real estate cases must be brought in state court rather than federal court. In a typical real estate lawsuit, the plaintiff and the defendant are citizens of the same state, only questions of state law are involved, and the U.S. government is not a party.

2. Concurrent Jurisdiction

Concurrent jurisdiction means that both the state and federal court have jurisdiction.

The reason state and federal jurisdictions overlap is that most cases that may be brought in federal court do not have to be. A state court can hear a diversity case, even if the amount in controversy is over $75,000. A state court can also hear a federal question case, except if it concerns those subjects (like patents) that Congress has expressly reserved for the federal courts.

When a state trial court decides a federal question case, the decision can only be appealed in the state system. In other words, the case must be taken to one of the California Courts of Appeal rather than to the Ninth Circuit Court of Appeals. On a second appeal, it would go to the California Supreme Court.

From that point there is the possibility of a third appeal, to the U.S. Supreme Court. The U.S. Supreme Court will review the decision of a state Supreme Court if, and only if, the case presents an important federal question. It will not interfere in cases that only involve questions of state law.

a. Choosing Between Federal and State Court

When a case could be filed in either state or federal court, why does the plaintiff choose one over the other? The reasons aren't clear-cut.

Sometimes federal court is chosen just because the plaintiff's lawyer is accustomed to federal court and more familiar with federal court procedures. Some lawyers believe that federal court judges tend to be better qualified or more sophisticated since they are appointed rather than elected.

At times, the federal or state courts gain a reputation for favoring plaintiffs or defendants in a particular type of case. Civil rights cases are the most prominent example. In the 1960s (and later), state courts in southern states were seen as more likely to support racial segregation than the federal courts in those states. As a result, a southern plaintiff claiming that his or her right to equal protection was violated would almost invariably choose to bring the case in federal court.

D. LIMITATIONS ON ADJUDICATION

1. Case or Controversy Requirement

As a general rule, a lawsuit must involve an active conflict, not just a theoretical or potential conflict. Based on Article III of the U.S. Constitution, this is known as the CASE or CONTROVERSY REQUIREMENT.

Example: The landlord of a large new apartment building wonders if it is necessary to go to the expense of installing various security devices. If he doesn't install them, would he be liable if one of the apartments were burglarized? Could a tenant have them installed and then deduct the cost from the rent?

The landlord can consult a lawyer about these issues. The lawyer will give his or her opinion about what a court would probably decide if these cases arose.

However, a court would refuse to consider these hypothetical questions. A judge won't issue a binding decision on what this landlord's duty is unless one of the apartments is actually burglarized and the tenant sues the landlord, or unless a tenant actually deducts the installation costs and the landlord sues for the deducted portion of the rent.

In some situations, however, a court has discretion to grant *DECLARATORY RELIEF. Instead of requiring a problem to reach a crisis, the court will let the parties know in advance what their duties under a contract are, or what their property rights are.* A **quiet title action** is an example of declaratory relief. If there is a possible claim against a property holder's title (a boundary question, for example), he or she can ask a court to decide whether or not the claim is valid. The title holder does not have to wait for the potential claimant to sue. Without a quiet title action, the title holder might be reluctant to develop the property, since it could turn out to belong to someone else.

2. Statute of Limitations

The statute of limitations establishes the maximum time within which a lawsuit must be filed.

A defendant in a lawsuit may be able to raise a statute of limitations as a defense to the lawsuit if too much time has passed since the conflict arose. The reason for these time limits is that it becomes more and more difficult to prove or disprove a claim as years go by. Evidence is often lost, and witnesses' memories fade.

The time limits vary depending on the type of case. In California, personal injury lawsuits generally must be filed within two years after the harmful act occurred. Most written contract suits must be filed within four years after the breach occurred if the contract was in writing, or within two years if the contract was oral. A suit to recover possession of real property can't be filed more than five years after the plaintiff (or whoever transferred the property to the plaintiff) was last in possession.

In certain types of cases, the statute of limitations doesn't start running until the injury or loss is discovered, even if the wrongful act occurred much earlier. For example, California allows an action for fraud to be filed within three years of the time the victim discovers the fraud.

In some situations, the statute of limitations doesn't run against a minor or an incompetent person. When the minor reaches the age of majority, or if the incompetent person regains competence, the statute of limitations begins to run.

Anyone thinking about starting a lawsuit should find out the limitations period for that type of action, and keep it in mind. Once the statutory period has run out, legal remedy is lost for good.

3. Res Judicata

RES JUDICATA is a Latin phrase meaning "the thing has been decided." The doctrine of res judicata holds that once a dispute between two parties has been tried and a final judgment has been issued, the same dispute cannot be tried again. The dissatisfied party can't start a new lawsuit on the same question, hoping to find a more sympathetic judge or a more persuasive lawyer.

The purpose of the doctrine is simple: finality. It puts the case to rest, at least as far as the court system is concerned. Without *res judicata*, some parties would go on suing each other over the same matter forever. That would make the courts even more crowded than they already are.

VII. A Civil Lawsuit

Now we'll take a closer look at the litigation process. This section follows a simple civil lawsuit from its filing to the enforcement of the final judgment. The entire process would probably take at least several months; in some cases, it takes years.

A. THE DISPUTE: PREFILING

Henry Palermo has lived in the Grass River Valley in northern California for many years. The lot to the west of his property had always been vacant until Claire Mulligan bought it six months ago. Mulligan has had the lot cleared and regraded in preparation for construction of a house.

Recently there were very heavy rains, and Palermo's house was flooded. There was considerable damage to the house and yard, and many of Palermo's belongings were ruined, including expensive stereo recording equipment and a large record collection. Palermo discovers that his homeowner's insurance policy lapsed two months earlier.

There are essentially six steps relating to a lawsuit:

1. Prefiling,
2. Filing the lawsuit,
3. Pretrial discovery,
4. Pretrial,
5. Trial, and
6. Post-trial

Since his house was never flooded before, Palermo believes Mulligan's clearing and regrading next door changed the pattern of runoff and caused the flooding. He explains this to Mulligan, and says she should help pay for the damage.

Mulligan is furious. She tells Palermo his property flooded simply because it rained so hard. The changes she made in her property had nothing to do with it. In the course of a ten-minute conversation, the neighbors become enemies.

Palermo consults a lawyer. The lawyer evaluates Palermo's claim by researching the law (looking up statutes and case law) about drainage onto adjoining property. He decides Palermo has a fairly strong case. California law holds that a landowner who disturbs the natural flow of surface waters may be liable for resulting damage to adjacent property.

Mulligan also hires a lawyer to look into the matter. Her lawyer concludes that it would be difficult for Palermo to prove that Mulligan's clearing caused his property to flood. Unless Palermo can prove that in court, Mulligan will not be held liable for the damage. The two lawyers discuss their clients' positions. Palermo's lawyer says that unless Mulligan pays Palermo $30,000, Palermo will sue her. Mulligan's lawyer says that Mulligan won't pay Palermo a nickel because the damage was not her fault.

B. FILING THE LAWSUIT

Palermo and his lawyer decide to proceed with a lawsuit. Palermo's lawyer starts the suit (*Palermo v. Mulligan*) by filing a complaint in the Superior Court of the county where Mulligan and Palermo live and where the property is located. The complaint outlines the dispute, explains how the plaintiff (Palermo) believes his legal rights have been violated by the defendant (Mulligan), and asks the court to grant judgment in the plaintiff's favor. Palermo asks the court to order Mulligan to prevent any future flooding and pay him $30,000.

1. Choosing a Court

What kind of court a lawsuit takes place in depends on the jurisdictional issues that were introduced earlier. The case must come within the court's jurisdictional limits—geographical, subject matter, and monetary limits.

Palermo's lawyer didn't have a choice as to what kind of court to bring this suit in. It had to be in state Superior Court because Mulligan and Palermo are both citizens of California, and the case does not involve any federal laws (the laws concerning drainage and flooding are state laws).

CHAPTER 1

2. Personal Jurisdiction

Even when a case is within a particular court's jurisdictional limits (geographical, subject matter, and monetary limits), that court can only hear the case if it has authority over the defendant. That authority is referred to as PERSONAL JURISDICTION.

A court ordinarily acquires personal jurisdiction over a defendant by service of process. *SERVICE OF PROCESS means delivery of a summons and a copy of the complaint to the defendant. The SUMMONS is simply a notice telling the defendant that the complaint has been filed, and that he or she must file a response with the court within specified time (30 days).*

Service of process usually must take place in the state where the court sits. In most cases, the plaintiff has a process server take the summons and complaint to the defendant's home or business and hand it directly to the defendant. If the defendant tries to evade the process server, service can be accomplished by mail or publication, or through an agent of the defendant.

3. Jurisdiction Over Property

A court must also have jurisdiction over any property at issue in a lawsuit. California courts have jurisdiction over all real and personal property within the state's boundaries.

4. The Defendant's Answer

A summons and complaint was served on Mulligan at her home. Now her lawyer has 30 days to prepare an answer and file it with the court.

In the *ANSWER, a defendant may challenge the court's jurisdiction. The defendant may also deny the plaintiff's allegations, discuss facts that the plaintiff left out of the complaint, or make a cross-complaint against the plaintiff.* Mulligan's answer simply denies that the clearing and regrading on her property were the cause of Palermo's flood damage.

If a defendant fails to respond to the complaint, the plaintiff can win the case by default. The court may enter a **default judgment** against the defendant.

The complaint, the answer, and any additional documents filed with the court are called PLEADINGS.

C. PRETRIAL DISCOVERY

Once a lawsuit has been started, both the plaintiff and the defendant are given an opportunity to find out more about the disputed facts through the **discovery process**. *The rules of DISCOVERY require each side to provide the other with information upon request.* They also enable a litigant to obtain information from reluctant witnesses.

One method of acquiring information during discovery is a deposition. In a *DEPOSITION, one party's lawyer questions the other party or a witness about the case.* The *DEPONENT (the person responding to the lawyer's questions)* is under oath, just as if he or she were testifying in court. A word-for-word transcript of the deposition can be used as evidence in the trial.

Interrogatories are another important discovery tool. *INTERROGATORIES are like a deposition conducted by mail instead of in person.* One party's lawyer sends a series of questions to the other party; the other party must send back answers. Interrogatories are also answered under oath.

Palermo's lawyer sends Mulligan interrogatories asking about the clearing and grading process, and about what measures were taken regarding runoff. Mulligan's lawyer sends Palermo interrogatories asking about the extent of the water damage, and about flooding in previous years. In addition, each side deposes the other party about the facts of the dispute. If Mulligan and Palermo fail to show up for their depositions or fail to answer the interrogatories, they may be sanctioned by the court.

D. PRETRIAL (Settle or Proceed to Trial)

Litigation is almost always expensive, time consuming, and unpleasant. Both parties must weigh those costs against what they stand to gain, and how likely they are to win if the case goes to trial.

Throughout the litigation process, Palermo's and Mulligan's lawyers negotiate to settle the case. In a *SETTLEMENT, the defendant pays the plaintiff a sum of money (or agrees to do something or refrain from doing something) so the plaintiff will end the lawsuit.*

Soon after the action is filed, on the advice of her lawyer, Mulligan offers to pay Palermo $2,000 and install a culvert to rechannel runoff if he will drop the suit. On the advice of his lawyer, Palermo refuses this offer; he will take the case to trial unless Mulligan pays him $25,000 and rechannels the runoff.

As each lawyer learns more about the facts of the case through the discovery process, he reevaluates his client's claim. Palermo's lawyer may realize that it will be much more difficult than he first thought to prove that it was Mulligan's clearing and grading that caused Palermo's property to be flooded. On the other hand, Mulligan's lawyer may realize that it may be much easier to prove that than he thought.

On the basis of these reevaluations, the gap narrows between the parties' settlement offers. As the trial date approaches, Palermo is only asking $17,000 to settle, and Mulligan is offering $8,000.

It is extremely likely that Palermo and Mulligan will come to an agreement. Over 95% of civil cases settle before a judgment. Most settle before the trial even begins.

In some cases, however, the parties are unable to settle. It may be the facts of the case are really unclear, or that the laws governing the case are ambiguous. It may be that the litigants are unusually stubborn or extremely angry with one another.

We'll assume that for some combination of these reasons, Palermo and Mulligan do not settle and the case proceeds to trial.

1. Judge or Jury

The U.S. Constitution and the California Constitution guarantee litigants the right to trial by jury. That right applies in most civil cases, but some cases (and certain issues within some cases) cannot be tried by a jury. It depends on the remedies requested by the plaintiff.

a. Remedies at Law and Equitable Remedies

The remedies awarded in civil cases are classified either as remedies at law or as equitable remedies. A *REMEDY AT LAW is generally an award of money (damages).* An *EQUITABLE REMEDY, on the other hand, usually involves an* **INJUNCTION** *(an order to refrain from doing something) or* **SPECIFIC PERFORMANCE** *(an order to do what was promised in the contract).*

Example: If the court ordered Mulligan to install a culvert and replant protective vegetation, that is an equitable remedy. If Mulligan were ordered to pay Palermo $30,000 in damages, that is a remedy at law.

Equitable remedies can only be awarded when money would not adequately correct the problem. Specific performance and contract reformation (see Chapter 7), foreclosure, and quiet title are all equitable remedies.

For historical reasons, a jury is not allowed to decide equitable issues. If a plaintiff is asking only for an equitable remedy (such as foreclosure), the case cannot be heard by a jury. If a plaintiff is asking for both types of remedies (such as damages and an injunction), a jury may hear the case. The jury will decide on the remedy at law, but the judge will decide on the equitable remedy.

2. Choosing a Jury

Even when a lawsuit does not involve any equitable issues, a jury isn't automatically assigned to the case. One or both of the parties must request a jury. If neither party does, the judge will decide the questions of fact as well as the questions of law.

When should a litigant request a jury? It's an intuitive choice rather than a scientific one. Juries are supposed to be more sympathetic than judges in some cases. A jury hearing a personal injury suit may be more likely to feel compassion for the plaintiff than a judge, who might have heard dozens of similar cases. A jury may tend to side with the underdog or favor an individual over a corporation.

On the other hand, if a litigant's case is based on a complicated legal argument or detailed technical or scientific evidence, a jury might have a hard time understanding it—and jury trials take longer and are more expensive than nonjury trials.

Although Palermo's lawyer thinks that a jury would feel sorry for his client because of the property damage, he decides not to request a jury. Palermo's case depends too much on technical proof that Mulligan's changes caused the flooding. Mulligan's lawyer decides to request a jury. He hopes the jury will feel that Mulligan did nothing unreasonable, and that it is unfair to hold her responsible for Palermo's misfortune.

Jurors are taken from a pool of citizens chosen at random from the county voter registration lists and DMV records. Both lawyers have an opportunity to question the potential jurors, to learn about their backgrounds and discover their personal prejudices. Those who seem biased against or in favor of one of the parties may be eliminated from the jury.

There are ordinarily 12 people on a jury in California. **In civil cases and cases involving misdemeanor crimes, the parties can agree to have fewer than 12 jurors.** Once the jury has been chosen, the trial begins.

E. TRIAL

The plaintiff's case is presented first. The plaintiff's lawyer makes an *OPENING STATEMENT, telling his or her client's version of the events that gave rise to the lawsuit*. This explanation helps the judge and jurors understand the point of the evidence and testimony the lawyer is about to present. The defendant's lawyer can then also make an opening statement, or wait until after the plaintiff's case has been fully presented.

The plaintiff's lawyer examines witnesses whose testimony supports his or her client's version of the facts. There are two types of witnesses.

A *LAY (Fact) WITNESS is someone who had an opportunity to observe events connected with the dispute*. For example, Palermo's lawyer has some of his client's neighbors testify that there were even heavier rains three years earlier, yet Palermo's property wasn't flooded

---

The Trial

1. Opening statement
2. Presentation of the evidence (plaintiff goes first):
   – Fact witnesses
   – Expert witnesses
   – Physical or documentary evidence
3. Closing arguments
4. Jury instructions
5. The decision

---

then. A fact witness describes events he or she personally observed, and may offer opinions rationally based on the perception of the witness, provided the testimony is helpful to a clear understanding of the witness testimony.

An *EXPERT WITNESS is someone who has expert knowledge of a subject, either through experience or education.* Litigants hire expert witnesses to evaluate their claims. If the expert's opinion supports the litigant's case, the expert is paid to testify at the trial. Palermo's lawyer calls two engineering consultants to testify about the effect of Mulligan's clearing and grading on her property's drainage. The lawyer also examines an appraiser, who testifies about how much it will cost to repair or replace the water-damaged property.

The initial questioning of witnesses by the lawyer who called them to testify is the DIRECT EXAMINATION. Immediately after the direct examination of a witness, the opposing lawyer has a chance to cross-examine that witness. In the *CROSS-EXAMINATION, the opposing lawyer tries to cast doubt on the witness's testimony and bring out any facts that are unfavorable to the other side.* The first lawyer then has a chance to repair any damage done on cross-examination by redirect examination of the witness. Sometimes the opposing lawyer will cross-examine the witness a second time.

Court rules provide that some testimony (or documentary or physical evidence) cannot be used in court because it is considered unreliable or unfair. It is INADMISSIBLE.

> **Example:** Testimony must be relevant to the issues involved in the dispute. If a neighbor testifying on behalf of Palermo says, "Mrs. Mulligan struck me as a troublemaker," Mulligan's lawyer can **object**. The witness's impression of Mulligan has no bearing on whether or not her activities caused Palermo's property to flood. The witness's comment is irrelevant and therefore inadmissible.

A lawyer can object to a witness's testimony or to the other lawyer's questioning on a variety of grounds. For example, a fact witness is giving an opinion; a physician is being asked to divulge confidential information about a patient; the other lawyer is leading the witness (asking yes or no questions, rather than getting the witness to describe the events in his or her own words).

If the judge agrees with the objecting lawyer that the questioning is improper, the judge will tell the witness not to answer. If the judge agrees that testimony already given is inadmissible, he or she will tell the jury to disregard the witness's remarks, and may have them stricken from the trial record.

When the plaintiff's lawyer has finished presenting evidence, it is the defense lawyer's turn. The same procedure is repeated: direct and cross examination of the defendant's witnesses, with objections from the lawyers and ruling on admissibility by the judge. The plaintiff's lawyer then has a chance to present additional evidence to rebut the defendant's case. Finally, each lawyer makes a closing argument, explaining how all the evidence fits together.

1. Jury Instructions

The jury instructions include an explanation of the **burden of proof**. Here, as in most cases, the plaintiff has the burden of proof. That is, it was up to Palermo to prove that Mulligan's clearing and regrading were the cause of the damage. Mulligan was not required to prove that her changes did not cause the damage.

The judge will also explain that the plaintiff must have proven his claim by a **preponderance of the evidence**. In other words, the jury doesn't have to be absolutely certain that Mulligan's changes caused the damage. It is enough if Palermo has convinced the jury that it is more likely than not that Mulligan's changes were the cause. This is the burden of proof used in nearly all civil cases.

Clear and convincing evidence requires that the evidence "be sufficiently strong so as to command the assent of every reasonable mind."

(In criminal cases, where the defendant has so much at stake, a stricter standard of proof is applied: the prosecution must prove its case **beyond a reasonable doubt**.)

Either before or after the closing arguments by the lawyers, the judge will explain the law that applies to the case to the jurors by issuing written jury instructions.

Example: The judge explains that California law does not hold a landowner responsible for damage caused by the natural flow of surface water from his or her property onto adjoining property. However, if the landowner changes the natural pattern of drainage, he or she is liable for resulting damage. The judge points out that this liability does not depend on whether the defendant intended to cause damage.

2. The Decision

Under the California Constitution, three-fourths of the jury may render a verdict in a civil case.

A unanimous verdict is not necessary in a civil case in California; if three-quarters of the jury agrees, that's enough. (Unanimity is required in criminal cases, however.) If there is a *HUNG JURY, that is, the jury cannot agree on a verdict after deliberating for a long time*, the case must be tried all over again before a new jury.

The jury in *Palermo v. Mulligan* votes 10 to 2 in favor of the plaintiff. Most of the jurors found Palermo's expert witnesses more convincing than Mulligan's expert witnesses. The jurors concluded that the flooding would not have occurred if Mulligan had not cleared and regraded her lot.

The jury awards Palermo $22,000 to repair and replace his water-damaged property. This is significantly less than the $30,000 he requested. The jury wasn't willing to believe that Palermo's stereo equipment and record collection were worth what the appraiser testified. The lower award may also reflect sympathy for Mulligan.

In addition to the jury's damages award, the judge issues an injunction ordering Mulligan to install a culvert that will rechannel runoff. Based on the experts' testimony, the judge specifies changes that will prevent future flooding of Palermo's property without damaging Mulligan's property.

In hindsight, Mulligan and her lawyer appear to have miscalculated. Mulligan would have been better off accepting Palermo's $17,000 settlement offer, instead of going through with the trial in the hope of avoiding liability altogether.

The Losing Party. One thing further: unless the law provides that the winner receives reasonable attorney's fees from the loser (or the parties have so provided in the contract), attorney fees are absorbed by each party. Therefore, if Palermo's attorney cost $6,000, the net is $16,000.

Normally, the winning party is also allowed to add court costs to the judgment.

F. POST TRIAL

1. Appeal

Both Mulligan and Palermo have a right to appeal the Superior Court decision to the California Court of Appeal for the First District. After the lower court's judgment has been entered, there is a limited period (usually 60 days) for filing a notice of appeal.

If Mulligan were to appeal, she would be the **appellant**, and Palermo would be the **appellee** or **respondent**. If Palermo were to appeal, he would be the appellant, and Mulligan would be the appellee or respondent. Both of them decide not to appeal, however. Since the jury's fact conclusions can't be challenged on appeal, neither Palermo nor Mulligan could expect to gain much, and they are both very tired of the whole business.

2. Collecting a Judgment

Before filing a lawsuit, a plaintiff should determine if a judgment can be collected. If the defendant's financial condition makes collection unlikely or dischargeable by bankruptcy, it will be a waste of the plaintiff's time and money.

Just because the jury has awarded Palermo $22,000 doesn't mean Mulligan will take out her checkbook and pay him on the spot. It can take a long time to collect a judgment; some are never collected.

a. Judgment Liens

Mulligan (**judgment debtor**) doesn't pay the judgment immediately, so Palermo (**judgment creditor**) secures his interest by claiming a **lien** against Mulligan's real property. The lien attaches after Palermo obtains an **abstract of judgment** from the court clerk and files it with the county recorder. If Mulligan never pays, Palermo can foreclose on the lien, hoping to collect his $22,000 from the proceeds of a forced sale of the property. (Liens are discussed in Chapter 3.)

Judgment liens can also attach to some personal property, such as business equipment and inventory. However, many types of personal property are exempt from judgment liens, including the debtor's household furnishings and clothing.

b. Garnishment

When a judgment debtor is a wage earner, the judgment creditor can use **wage garnishment** to collect the judgment in installments. An earnings withholding order is served on the debtor's employer, who must set aside the debtor's earnings for the creditor. An amount necessary for the support of the debtor and his or her family is exempt from garnishment (usually 75%).

These collection devices are cumbersome and they aren't always successful. Some defendants turn out to be "judgment-proof": they have no wages and no assets, or their assets are either exempt from judgment liens or already heavily encumbered with other liens. In addition, the judgment debtor may file bankruptcy and discharge the entire debt. Inability to collect a judgment may be a real hardship for a judgment creditor who owes his or her own lawyer a substantial fee. That can make winning a lawsuit a hollow victory.

VIII. CHAPTER SUMMARY

1. The law is a system of rights and duties established and enforced by a government. It maintains order, resolves disputes, enforces promises, and prevents exploitation.

2. Substantive law defines rights and duties, while procedural law sets out the methods for enforcing substantive rights.

The government brings a criminal action to punish a wrongdoer and protect society. In a civil action, on the other hand, an injured party sues for compensation. Some wrongful acts can lead to both criminal and civil penalties.

Contracts, torts, and property are the fundamental concepts of civil law. Contract law concerns voluntarily assumed duties; tort law concerns the duties of reasonable conduct imposed by law; property law concerns the duties inherent in ownership.

3. Federal and state constitutions, legislatures, courts, and administrative agencies are the sources of law in the United States.

Constitutions protect individual rights by limiting government power. Within those constitutional limits, legislative and administrative bodies issue general rules in the form of statutes, ordinances, and regulations.

Courts apply these rules to resolve lawsuits. In interpreting the rules, judges develop case law. The doctrine of stare decisis requires judges to follow established precedents so that the law will be evenhanded and predictable.

4. A court system is a hierarchy of trial courts and appellate courts. An appeal is not a second trial. The appellate court reviews the trial record for prejudicial errors, focusing primarily on questions of law rather than fact.

The federal and state court systems are independent with overlapping jurisdictions. Federal jurisdiction is limited to cases involving federal questions, diversity of citizenship, or the U.S. government. State courts can hear any case except those that Congress has reserved for the federal courts.

The case or controversy requirement, statutes of limitation, and the doctrine of *res judicata* limit access to the courts. The court systems are severely overcrowded in spite of these rules. Many judges now require the parties to attend arbitration or mediation before hearing the case in court.

5. A civil suit begins when the plaintiff files a complaint with the court. The pretrial discovery process gives each side access to information the other might prefer to conceal. The parties' lawyers try to negotiate a settlement, to save the expense and trouble of a trial.

Litigants have a right to trial by jury on most issues that do not involve an equitable remedy. In the trial, each side presents testimony and other evidence favorable to its case. Evidence is only admissible if it meets established standards of reliability and fairness.

If the plaintiff wins, he or she may have to resort to garnishment or lien foreclosure to collect the judgment.

IX. KEY TERMS

act/statute/ordinance/bill	equitable/remedy law	remand
affirm/modify/reverse	remedies	*res judicata*
appellant/appellee	exhibit	service of process
arbitration	fact witness/expert witness	settlement
bench trial	federal question	specific performance
burden of proof	garnishment	standard of proof
case law	injunction	*stare decisis*
case or controversy	judicial review	state action
codification	jurisdiction	statute of limitations
common law	jury instructions	statutory construction
court of appeal(s)	mediation	subject matter jurisdiction
criminal/civil damages	opinion	substantive/procedural
declaratory relief	personal jurisdiction	summons/complaint/answer
deposition/interrogatories	plaintiff/defendant	tort
direct/cross examination	precedent	trial record
diversity jurisdiction	prejudicial error	trier of fact
due process	pretrial discovery	unconstitutional
equal protection	question of fact/of law	veto/override

X. CHAPTER QUIZ

1. The main historical influence on law in the United States was:

    a. Spanish law.
    b. feudal law.
    c. European law.
    d. English law.

2. When one individual sues another, the lawsuit is called:

    a. a civil action.
    b. an equitable suit.
    c. declaratory relief.
    d. criminal litigation.

3. The primary purpose of most civil lawsuits is to:

    a. punish a wrongdoer.
    b. compensate a person who has been harmed.
    c. protect society.
    d. deter crime.

4. A person who commits a tort:

    a. will be prosecuted by the government.
    b. will be held liable for breach of contract.
    c. has violated the standards of reasonable conduct imposed by law.
    d. must serve a jail term.

5. Which of the following would be more likely to issue an ordinance?

    a. The Pasadena City Council
    b. The Coastal Commission
    c. The California Assembly
    d. The Los Angeles County Superior Court

6. Codification refers to:

    a. reviewing statutes or regulations to determine whether they are constitutional.
    b. enforcing substantive rights.
    c. combining scattered, piecemeal laws into a comprehensive compendium (or collection) of laws called a code.
    d. interpretation of a contract by an appellate court.

7. When the California legislature adopts a new statute, the new law:

    a. is automatically reviewed by the state supreme court to determine whether it is constitutional.
    b. may change rules that were developed in earlier court decisions.
    c. must be approved by a majority vote of state citizens.
    d. none of the above.

8. Which of the following is a question of law?

    a. Was the broker required to put the earnest money in a trust account?
    b. Did the tenant inform the landlord that the railing was broken?
    c. Did the real estate agent inspect the attic?
    d. Was the buyer told that the agent was representing the seller?

9. Which of the following can limit a court's jurisdiction?

    a. Geographical boundaries
    b. Subject matter of the case
    c. Amount of money at issue in the case
    d. All of the above

10. A fact witness:

    a. testifies during the appeal.
    b. can state his/her opinions while testifying, if the testimony is helpful.
    c. may not be cross-examined.
    d. all of the above.

ANSWERS: 1. d; 2. a; 3. b; 4. c; 5. a; 6. c; 7. b; 8. a; 9. d; 10. b

CHAPTER 2
Nature of Real Property

CHAPTER OVERVIEW

This chapter describes the difference between real property and personal property and why they are important to the sale of real estate. The Civil Code defines **REAL PROPERTY** *as land; that which is affixed to land; that which is incidental or appurtenant to land; and that which is immovable by law.* Real property also includes mineral rights below the surface and the air space above the land. Airspace is subject to limitations, and rights in the use of airspace granted, by law. On the other hand, **PERSONAL PROPERTY** *is defined as every kind of property that is not real property, and is generally moveable.*

I. Land Description

The legal description of a piece of real property determines its boundaries. Boundary disputes are one of the most common sources of real estate lawsuits. Neighbors often disagree about where one's property ends and the other's begins. Buyers often discover that the property they bought isn't the property they thought they were buying.

Sellers are usually held liable for misrepresenting the location of their property boundaries, even if the misrepresentation was innocent as they are presumed to know the character and attributes of the property they are conveying. If they make an erroneous representation about the boundaries, they can be held liable. In the following example, the court found that the Stones had committed fraud in the sale to the Farnells and upheld an award of $15,000 in damages and the cancellation of the seller carryback loan of approximately $11,000.

> **Case Example:** The Stones sold their home in Beverly Hills to the Farnells for $38,000. Before the sale agreement was signed, Mrs. Stone took the Farnells around the property and pointed out its boundaries. Several months after the sale, the property was surveyed. The Farnells learned that the carport, the guest house, portions of the yard and driveway, and about one-third of the main house were not actually on the property described in their deed. Instead, they were on land owned by the city of Los Angeles, designated as part of Mulholland Drive. *Stone v. Farnell*, 239 F.2d 750 (9th Cir. 1956).

CHAPTER 2

CHAPTER OUTLINE

California courts have defined real estate agents' duty to visually inspect residential property (see Chapter 6), and what limits the agents' liability in connection with boundary problems.

A. METHODS OF DESCRIPTION

An accurate legal description of a property can usually be found in a recorded deed, trust deed, or lease. It's extremely important for these documents to contain accurate descriptions; an ambiguous or uncertain description is not legally adequate and may invalidate the document.

There are many methods for describing property, but the three most commonly used systems of land description are:

1. metes and bounds,
2. government survey, and
3. lot and block.

www.firstam.com/faf/dimensions/metes.html
Legal Descriptions of Property – Metes and Bounds

1. Metes and Bounds

> **Metes and Bounds** – identifies a parcel of land by boundaries including monuments, courses, and distances.
>
> **Government Survey** – divides the land into a series of rectangular grids called principal meridians and baselines.
>
> **Lot and Block** – legal description used for platted property stating a property's lot number and block number in a particular subdivision.

The **METES** *(measurements)* and **BOUNDS** *(boundaries)* system is the oldest method of describing land. British settlers used it in the thirteen colonies. The method is still frequently used in rural areas and is especially common in eastern states.

The metes and bounds method identifies a parcel of land by describing its outline or boundaries. The boundaries are fixed by reference to three things:

1. **monuments**, which may be natural objects such as rivers or trees, or man-made objects such as roads or survey markers;
2. **courses** (directions), in the form of compass readings, and
3. **distances**, measured in any convenient unit of length.

A metes and bounds description states a starting point and then proceeds around the boundary by listing a series of courses and distances. The description continues until the boundary has been described all the way around, back to the starting point.

A tract of land in Calaveras County is described as follows: Beginning at the old oak tree, thence south 15° east, 200 feet, thence north 90° west, 310 feet more or less to the center line of Smith Creek, thence northwesterly along the center line of Smith Creek to a point directly west of the old oak tree, thence north 90° east, 430 feet more or less to the point of beginning (see **Figure 2-1**).

Figure 2-1

a. Point of Beginning (POB)

A metes and bounds description must always start at a convenient and well-defined point that can be easily identified (such as the old oak tree in the example). *The starting point is referred to as the POINT OF BEGINNING (POB).* The point of beginning is always described by reference to a monument.

Example: "The SW corner of the intersection of 1st Ave. and Bridd St.," or "200 feet due north of the old oak tree."

Note that the point of beginning does not have to be a monument itself; it must simply be defined in relation to a monument. In the example, the oak tree is a monument and the point of beginning is 200 feet north of the tree.

Older metes and bounds descriptions often used natural monuments such as "the old oak tree." That created some problems, however, since a tree can be chopped down and a boulder can be moved. Modern metes and bounds descriptions generally use government survey lines as monuments.

b. Compass Bearings

In a metes and bounds description, a direction is described by reference to a compass point. The compass directions are stated in terms of the degree of deviation from north or south. Thus, northwest (or 315°) is written as north 45° west since it is a deviation of 45° to the west of north. Similarly, southeast (or 157.5°) is written as south 45° east, since it is a deviation of 22.5° to the east of south. East and west are both written relative to north: north 90° east and north 90° west, respectively.

Compass bearings in metes and bounds descriptions are given by reference to a line running north and south.

c. Order of Preference

Sometimes there are discrepancies between the various elements of a metes and bounds description. This is usually because the original surveyor made a mistake. For instance, if the description says "320 feet in a northerly direction to the corner of the Porter farmhouse," but the Porter farmhouse is really in a northwesterly direction, there's a discrepancy between the course (northerly) and the monument (the farmhouse). To help surveyors resolve this type of conflict, the following order of priority has been established:

1. natural monuments (Scrubfish Creek) have first priority,
2. then man-made monuments (Avondale Road),
3. then courses (south 8° east),
4. then distances (310 feet),
5. then names (the Holden Ranch),
6. then the area or amount of acreage (80 acres).

Example: A description reads "east 380 feet to the midpoint of Scrubfish Creek." It is actually 385 feet to the midpoint of Scrubfish Creek. The reference to Scrubfish Creek takes precedence over the distance. The property line extends clear to the midpoint of the creek, not just 380 feet.

2. Government Survey

A second method of land description is the **government survey**. This method was developed shortly after the American Revolution when the federal government owned vast tracts of undeveloped land. Land speculators and settlers were moving into the territories, and Congress was anxious to sell some of the land in order to increase revenues and diminish the national debt. It wasn't feasible to use the metes and bounds method for all of this property, so the government survey system was created. Government survey descriptions are mainly used in states west of the Mississippi.

http://nationalatlas.gov/articles/boundaries/a_plss.html
The Public Land Survey System

The government survey system is also called the **rectangular survey method** because it divides the land into a series of rectangular grids. Each grid is composed of two sets of lines, one set running north/south and the other east/west.

The main north/south line in each grid is called the PRINCIPAL MERIDIAN, and the main east/west line is the BASE LINE. There are 35 principal meridians and 32 base lines across the country. Each principal meridian has its own name, and these are used to identify the different grids.

California has three principal meridians: the Humboldt Meridian, the Mt. Diablo Meridian, and the San Bernardino Meridian.

NORTH/SOUTH LINES	EAST/WEST LINES
principal meridian	base line
guide meridians	correction lines
range lines	township lines
ranges	township tiers

Additional east/west lines, called **CORRECTION LINES**, run parallel to the base lines at intervals of 24 miles. Additional north/south lines, called **GUIDE MERIDIANS**, are also established at 24-mile intervals. Because of the curvature of the earth, all true north/south lines converge as they approach the North Pole. Therefore, each guide meridian only runs as far as the next correction line. A new interval of 24 miles is then measured and a new guide meridian is run. This way the guide meridians remain approximately the same distance apart and do not converge.

The large squares created by the intersection of guide meridians and correction lines are further divided into smaller tracts of land by additional north/south lines running at six-mile intervals that are called **RANGE LINES**. The range lines divide the land into columns called **RANGES**. Additional east/west lines run at six-mile intervals from the correction lines and are called **TOWNSHIP LINES**. They divide the land into rows or tiers called **TOWNSHIP TIERS**.

The square of land located at the intersection of a range and a township tier is called a **TOWNSHIP**. It is identified by its position relative to the principal meridian and base line.

Example: The township located in the fourth tier north of the base line and the third range east of the principal meridian is called "township 4 north, range 3 east" or "T4N, R3E."

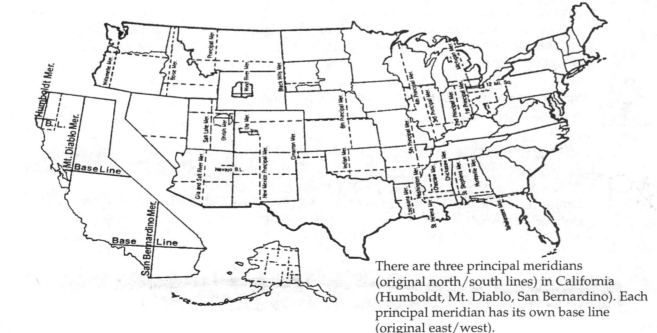

There are three principal meridians (original north/south lines) in California (Humboldt, Mt. Diablo, San Bernardino). Each principal meridian has its own base line (original east/west).

Each township measures 36 square miles. A township is divided into 36 sections, one square mile each. The sections are always numbered 1 through 36 in a specified sequence. (The diagram on the next page shows the numbering pattern.) Parcels of land smaller than sections can be identified by reference to sections and partial sections.

Example: "The northwest quarter of the southwest quarter of section 12, township 4 north, range 3 east." (In abbreviated form, "the NW 1/4 of the SW 1/4 of section 12, T4N, R3E.")

Since the grid systems are identical across the country, the description has to include the name of the principal meridian to identify the particular grid. It's also a good idea to mention the county and state where the land is located.

Example: A complete description of a township would be: "T4N, R3E of the Mt. Diablo meridian, Sacramento County, California."

www.outfitters.com/genealogy/land/twprangemap.html
Graphic Display of Federal Township and Range System

a. Government Lots

Because of the curvature of the earth, the convergence of range lines, and human surveying errors, it is impossible to keep all sections exactly one mile square. Any deficiency or surplus is placed in the north and west sections of a township. *These irregular sections are called* **GOVERNMENT LOTS** *and are referred to by a lot number.* A government lot also results when a body of water or some other obstacle makes it impossible to survey an accurate square-mile section.

3. Lot and Block (Final Subdivision Map)

In terms of surface area, more land in the United States is described by the rectangular survey method than by any other land description system. In terms of number of properties, the lot and block or recorded map system is the most important land description method. It's the method used most frequently in metropolitan areas.

Under this system, land is described by reference to a map called a **FINAL SUBDIVISION MAP,** recorded in the county where the land is located. Based on a survey of the subdivision, the subdivision map shows the dimensions and boundaries of each lot. Each lot and each block (a group of lots surrounded by streets) is numbered. After the map is recorded, reference to a lot number and block number on the specified map is a sufficient legal description of that lot.

Example: "Lot 2, Block 4 of Hilliard's Division, in the city of Eureka, county of Humboldt, state of California, as shown on the map recorded in book 22, page 36, of Maps, in the office of the recorder of said county."

Since a detailed description of the lot is already on file in the recorder's office, that description may be incorporated into any legal document simply by reference. To find out specific information about the lot, you look in the map book at the county recorder's office.

Basic Components of The Government Survey System

			RANGE LINES		NOTE OFFSET AT		

A diagram of the Government Survey System showing township and range grid with labels:

- RANGE LINES, 6 MI., RANGE, NOTE OFFSET AT CORRECTION LINE
- STANDARD PARALLEL (CORRECTION LINE)
- T5N, T4N, T3N, T2N, T1N
- TOWNSHIP LINES
- BASE LINE
- GUIDE MERIDIAN, 24 MI
- PRINCIPAL MERIDIAN
- R4W, R3W, R2W, R1W, R1E, R2E, R3E, R4E
- T1S, T2S, T3S, T4S
- STANDARD PARALLEL CORRECTION LINE
- 24 MI.
- 6 MI., A TOWNSHIP

Section numbering within a township:
31 32 33 34 35 36
1 | 6 5 4 3 2 1 | 6
12 | 7 8 9 10 11 12 | 7
13 | 18 17 16 15 14 13 | 18
24 | 19 20 21 22 23 24 | 19
25 | 30 29 28 27 26 25 | 30
36 | 31 32 33 34 35 36 | 31
6 5 4 3 2 1

A tract is
24 MI. x 24 MI. AND
INCLUDES 16 TOWNSHIPS

IMPORTANT POINTS TO NOTE ON THIS DIAGRAM

1) TRACT = 24 x 24 MI. = 16 TOWNSHIPS
2) TOWNSHIP = 6 x 6 MI. = 36 SECTIONS
3) SECTION = 1 x 1 MI. = 640 ACRES
4) NOTE NUMBERING SEQUENCE OF SECTIONS

Subdivision maps frequently contain a considerable amount of information in addition to the detailed description of property boundaries. Many subdivision maps include this information:

1. measurements of area,
2. easement locations and dimensions,
3. location of survey markers,
4. location of sewer lines and underground wiring,
5. subdivision restrictions,
6. topographical details such as elevation, and
7. school sites and recreational areas.

Township 4 North, Range 3 East

6	5	4	3	2	1
7	8	9	10	11	12
18	17	16	15	14	13
19	20	21	22	23	24
30	29	28	27	26	25
31	32	33	34	35	36

A township contains 36 sections, numbered in this sequence.

A section can be divided into smaller parcels.

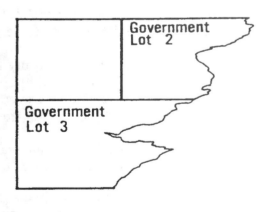

Government lots may be the result of a body of water intruding into a section.

Subdivision Map

Examining a subdivision map isn't a substitute for a thorough title search.

4. Other Methods of Description

There are other ways of describing land besides the three major methods previously discussed. Popular names (such as "the Bar Z Ranch") and blanket statements ("my six lots") can be legally sufficient descriptions if they make it possible to definitely determine what property is being described. However, a lawsuit would likely be needed to provide marketable title to the property described in one of these other methods.

Example: A grant of "all of my lands in San Diego County" is adequate because it's possible to determine from the public record what property the grantor owned when the deed was executed. However, a grant of "one of my lots in San Diego County" is not acceptable; there's no way to determine which lot is being referred to.

A lazy but legally adequate way of describing property is simply by referring to the description in an earlier recorded document.

Example: "I hereby grant all the property described in that deed of trust recorded in San Luis Obispo County on March 26, 1983; under recording number 8303260002..."

B. AIR SPACE (Lots)

Not all real property can be described simply by reference to a position on the face of the earth. Some types of property (such as a second-story unit in a condominium) also need to be described in terms of elevation above the ground. When describing the location of a condominium unit or other air space, you can't simply measure the height from the ground because the ground isn't a stable and precise legal marker.

The United States Geodetic Survey has established datums and bench marks as legal reference points. Most large cities have also established their own official datum and bench marks. A *DATUM is an artificial horizontal plane of elevation, established in reference to sea level. At certain locations, subsidiary reference points, called BENCH MARKS, are established.* A bench mark is a point whose position relative to a datum has been accurately measured. A bench mark may be a metal or concrete marker (often placed in a sidewalk or other stable position) that states the location relative to the datum.

www.crawls.archive.org/katrina/20051031172827/http://www.lib.noaa.gov/edocs/function.html
Functions of the Coast and Geodetic Survey

Bench Mark

Example: A metal disk in the sidewalk at the corner of Oak and Elm streets has the following words engraved on it: "Bench Mark No. 96, 17 feet above River City Datum."

Surveyors use the datum or a bench mark as a reference point in describing air (space) lots.

Example: A surveyor plotting a condominium unit on the 16th floor of a new building being built on Elm Street calculates that the floor of the unit will be 230 feet above the sidewalk. He therefore shows in his survey that the floor of the unit is 247 feet above the River City Datum as established by Bench Mark No. 96, because Bench Mark No. 96 is 17 feet above the datum.

C. DESCRIPTION PROBLEMS

1. Erroneous Descriptions

When the West was originally surveyed for the federal government, the surveyors often worked under harsh conditions with equipment that is considered inadequate today. As a result, there are errors in the government survey, and these create errors in property descriptions that are revealed by modern surveys. A court called upon to interpret this type of erroneous description will try to carry out the original surveyor's intentions.

Other description errors are simply the result of mistakes in transcription. Often the property description on a deed is copied off of the previous deed, and in the copying process, a lot of things can go wrong. A typographical error might transpose two numbers, so that "912 feet" winds up as "192 feet." Or part of the description might be left out altogether: the deed says only "Lot 3, Colvina Heights," but the subdivision has 22 blocks and there's a Lot 3 on each block.

When this kind of mistake is discovered, it may be possible to ask the person who transferred the property to execute a new deed with a corrected description. If that isn't possible, *the new owner can ask a court to issue an order correcting the description. This is called* **REFORMATION OF THE DOCUMENT.**

Statutory Rules of Land Description

- If A deeds property to B that states that a road or highway is the boundary for the property, it is presumed that the boundary goes to the center of the road unless shown to the contrary in the deed.

- If the grant describes the boundary as running a specified distance from a road, the boundary runs from the edge of the road and not from the center.

- When permanent and visible or ascertained boundaries or monuments are inconsistent with the measurement of either lines, angles, or surfaces, the boundaries or monuments are paramount.

- If in a lawsuit there is a dispute about the boundary of land patented or otherwise granted by the state or the validity of a state patent or grant dated before 1950, all parties must disclose to each other all relevant nonprivileged written evidence known and available about the property and the boundaries.

- When the boundaries have been disturbed by earth movements such as slides, subsidence, lateral or vertical displacements, or similar disasters, the land is in a different location. The **Culled Earthquake Act** provides a procedure to equitably reestablish boundaries and quiet title to the land within those boundaries.

- Water boundaries are discussed later in this chapter.

---

2. Ambiguous Descriptions

When a deed's description is ambiguous, the deed is technically invalid. This problem can be cured simply by possession.

Example: John Alvarez owns a ranch in Merced County and a ranch in Mariposa County, and each is known locally as "the Alvarez Ranch." Alvarez conveys one of the ranches to Maria Swanson. The deed identifies the property simply as "the Alvarez Ranch," without specifying in which county the land is located.

If Swanson occupies the ranch in Merced County, the deed can be held valid. Swanson's possession of the Merced County ranch makes it clear which ranch the deed referred to.

D. BOUNDARY DISPUTES

1. Agreed Boundary

Often a boundary described in a deed doesn't match up with the line that has actually been treated as the boundary on the property. One neighbor may want to reassert the true legal description, while the other wants to stick with the established physical boundary.

Many of these disputes are resolved by the *DOCTRINE OF AGREED BOUNDARY, which states that it is necessary to show that there was an uncertainty as to the true boundary line; an agreement, express or implied, between the conterminous (adjacent) owners fixing the line; and either acceptance and acquiescence in the line for a period of time determined by the statute of limitation, or that changing of its position would cause substantial loss.* The Doctrine of Agreed Boundary is not applicable to resolve boundary disputes where available legal records provide a reasonable basis for fixing a boundary, and the party relying upon the doctrine fails to establish that uncertainty as to location of the true boundary led to an agreement between landowners to create a boundary at an agreed-upon location.

An agreed boundary must be marked or be otherwise discernible on the property to give new owners notice of its location. Usually the agreed boundary must be accepted or acquiesced to for at least five years before it becomes the true boundary. If one of the parties would suffer a substantial loss if the original boundary were enforced, the five-year requirement does not apply.

CASE EXAMPLE: The Brandenburgers owned lot 57 of a subdivision that was surveyed in 1909 and recorded in 1910. Currently, the Bryants own the west one-half of lot 57 and the Blevins own the east one-half. The Blevins believed the fence line was the boundary line. The Bryants had their property surveyed shortly after buying it. The fence that covered the property was 11 to 42 feet off the true boundary, which resulted in a shortage of .4 acres. The Bryants sued to recover possession of the disputed line, and the Blevins cross-complained to establish title by the doctrine of agreed boundaries.

On appeal, the California Supreme Court held that there was no evidence that the fence was erected to resolve uncertainty as to the location of the property line. More importantly, the doctrine of agreed boundary is not to be used when the true boundary can be determined from existing legal descriptions and recordings as it undermines the significance of legal descriptions and encourages litigation.

It should only be used in instances in which existing legal records are inadequate to settle a boundary dispute. *Bryant v. Blevins*, 9 Cal. 4th 47; 36 Cal. Rptr. 2d 86 (1994).

II. Land

Once you know the boundaries of the real property included in the sale, you need to be familiar with what items and property rights are part of the real property. As noted before, the Civil Code provides that real property consists of land, things affixed to land, things appurtenant to land, and things immovable by law. The first of these elements is land. The Civil Code defines land as material of the earth, including soil, rock, or other substances, and the free or occupied space for an indefinite distance upwards as well as downwards, subject to limitations upon the use of airspace imposed by law.

One of the best ways to understand the rights that accompany real property is to imagine the property as an **inverted pyramid** with its tip at the center of the earth and its base extending out into the sky. A property owner has rights to the surface land within the boundaries of the property, plus everything under or over the surface that falls within the pyramid. This includes rights to oil and minerals beneath the surface, plus certain air and water rights.

The Inverted Pyramid

A. AIR RIGHTS

According to the inverted pyramid concept, a property owner's rights extend to the upper limits of the sky. However, through the Air Commerce Act of 1926 and the Civil Aeronautics Act of 1938, Congress declared that the United States government has almost complete control over America's air space.

1. Use of Air Space

Although the government imposes restricted air rights, property owners still have the exclusive right to use the lower reaches of air space over their property, as long as they do nothing to interfere with air traffic. Property owners also have the right not to be harmed by use of the air space above their property.

Example: The classic example is an airport built near a chicken farm. The noise of the airplanes flying over the farm causes the chickens to stop laying eggs. The farmer may be able to recover damages for the resulting loss of income.

2. Sale of Air Space

A property owner may sell rights to the air space over the property separately from the land. As the population increases and real estate prices rise, the sale of air space has become more common, especially in large urban areas.

Example: The New York Central and the New Haven Railroads had tracks running across real estate in a prime location. They sold rights to the air space above the tracks for an enormous sum. The purchasers acquired the air space plus a surface easement to allow for the construction and support of buildings. The Park Avenue Development (a large complex of commercial buildings) was later built above the tracks.

A more common example is an ordinary condominium sale. Someone who buys a condominium unit in a high-rise building purchases not just the physical apartment, but also the rights to the air space in which the unit is situated.

B. MINERAL RIGHTS

Minerals are considered real property until they are extracted, when they become personal property.

Standard Methods of Dividing Mineral Rights

1. **Mineral Deed** – a mineral deed transfers all rights to the minerals, and also grants the rights necessary to conduct mining operations to obtain the minerals. This usually includes the rights of access, development, processing, and transportation.
2. **Mineral Reservation** – a mineral reservation is similar to a mineral deed except that the owner sells or transfers the surface property and retains the mineral rights for himself or herself.
3. **Mineral Lease** – under a mineral lease, the lessee is given the right to mine and has title to the minerals obtained, but the lessor (the property owner) will regain the mineral rights when the lease expires. The lessor is usually compensated by royalty payments based on a percentage of the value of the extracted minerals.
4. **Mineral Rights Option** – a mineral rights option grants the right to explore for the presence of minerals. After exploration, the mining company decides whether or not to exercise its option to lease or purchase the mineral rights on the terms stated in the option agreement.

A landowner generally owns all minerals located in or under his or her property. *A landowner may sell mineral rights separately from the land. This type of sale is sometimes called a* **HORIZONTAL DIVISION.** The right to own and use the surface property is divided from rights to the subsurface minerals.

The owner of mineral rights must give a **written notice** to the owner of the property (and any public utility with a recorded interest in the property if there will be a excavation of the utility interest) of an intention to explore or mine before the first entry upon the property. The notice must state the extent and location of prospecting, mining, or extraction and the approximate times of entry and exit.

It was very common in California's past for a person selling property to reserve the mineral rights to the property, even though there was no foreseeable possibility that these rights would ever be used. Over time, these "dormant" mineral rights can affect the development of the land and the marketability of the property. California statutes now allow the lessor of an abandoned or expired mineral lease to demand a quitclaim deed or other document from the lessee showing abandonment. Failure of the lessee to do so may cause a lawsuit to clear the title and makes the lessee liable for the lessor's actual damages, attorney's fees, court costs, and $150. The owner of a mineral right may preserve the right by recording a **notice of intent** to preserve the mineral right. This shows nondormancy and nonabandonment.

An owner of property subject to a dormant mineral right can sue to terminate the right. A *DORMANT MINERAL RIGHT is one that goes back 20 years from the filing of the lawsuit.* During this period, there can have been no mining or exploration activities on the property; no separate tax assessment on the right or no taxes paid if assessed, and there can be no recorded document showing the mineral right. The court must allow the recording of a notice to preserve the mineral right if the right holder pays the property owner's litigation expenses, including attorney's fees.

The following case considers whether geothermal steam is a "mineral" for the purposes of a mineral reservation.

Case Example: The plaintiffs are the current landowners of property located in Sonoma and Lake Counties, title to which originated as patents from the State of California issued between 1949 and 1956. The patents reserved to the State of California "all oil, gas, oil shale, coal, phosphate, sodium, gold, silver, and all other mineral deposits contained in said land…" The property in this area, of which the plaintiffs' property is a part, is generally referred to as "The Geysers." The Geysers' geothermal reservoir system extends under the property in question. The geothermal system manifests itself in the form of hot springs and steam vents at the surface, although none are located on this property. The plaintiffs brought a quiet title and declaratory relief action to determine whether the geothermal resources were "mineral deposits" and "mineral water" reserved to the state in the patents. The trial court concluded that they were reserved to the state. The plaintiffs appealed.

At the time the patents were issued, neither the state nor the patentees had any knowledge of geothermal resources underlying the patented lands, no thought was given to the potential development of electricity through the use of the then undiscovered geothermal resources, and there was no specific intention by either party as to geothermal resources. The term "mineral water" has no precise scientific or legal definition. It is a vernacular term that includes water or steam valued for medicinal or therapeutic uses because of its chemical composition or its heat content. The controversy focuses on the meaning of "all other mineral deposits."

The purpose of a patent with a mineral reservation is to grant only a limited estate to the patentees. As a general rule, a grant or reservation of all minerals includes all minerals found on the premises whether or not known to exist. Additionally, California law provides that a grant by a public officer or body to a private person is to be interpreted in favor of the grantor. After the commencement of this case, the California Legislature changed the law, which expanded mineral deposits reserved to the State to include geothermal resources. This appears to be a clarification of what mineral deposits were meant to cover in the past. Therefore, the geothermal steam is reserved to the State as "mineral waters," and the geothermal resource beneath the property, including steam, is a "mineral deposit" reserved to the State by its patent reservation. The judgment is affirmed. *Pariani v. The State of California*, 105 Cal. App. 3d 923; Cal. Rptr. 683 (1980).

III. Attachments

You've decided to buy a particular property. You checked the legal description so you have a clear idea of what piece of land is being conveyed. Of course, the legal description doesn't mention the house, but you're sure that it's included in the sale. What about the kitchen appliances inside the house, the hot tub and the water fountain in the back yard, or the poplar trees and the rose garden?

Whenever land is transferred, it's necessary to distinguish between real property and personal property. Unless otherwise agreed, all the real property is included in the transfer, but the personal property is not. Buyers and sellers, landlords and tenants, owners and foreclosing creditors often disagree about whether an item is personal property or part of the realty. These disagreements can lead to lawsuits.

> **Example:** A homebuyer sues the seller in small claims court because the seller took the satellite dish with him, and the buyer assumed it was included in the purchase price.

When there's a conflict like this, the real estate agent may end up paying for the disputed item out of his or her own pocket to keep the peace. It's important for everyone involved in a transaction to know what things are included in the sale of the real property.

People tend to think of the actual land when they hear the term "real property," but real property is more than just rocks and dirt. *Things built on the land (like houses and fences) and things growing on the land (like trees and shrubs) are called **ATTACHMENTS**.* Attachments are considered part of the real property.

There are two main categories of attachments:

1. natural attachments, and
2. man-made attachments (or fixtures).

A. NATURAL ATTACHMENTS

NATURAL ATTACHMENTS are plants growing on the land. There are two types of natural attachments:

1. ***FRUCTUS NATURALES*** *(or "fruits of nature") are all naturally occurring trees and plants.*
2. ***FRUCTUS INDUSTRIALES*** *(or "fruits of industry") are planted and cultivated by people.*

www.farmlandinfo.org
Farmland Information

Both types of natural attachments are generally considered part of the real property.

When natural attachments are severed, mortgaged, or sold, they become personal property.

> **Example:** A stand of timber growing on the land is part of the real property. Once the trees have been felled, however, they are personal property.

Natural attachments may be considered personal property even before they are actually severed from the land, if they are sold separately from the land.

Example: A farmer sells the timber on his east 40 acres to a lumber company. The sale contract provides that the trees are to be cut in the next year. The lumber company owns the trees as of the date of the contract. They are considered personal property from that date forward, even though they are still attached to the land.

The crops produced by fructus naturales (the berries on wild blackberry bushes, for example) are part of the realty until they are picked or sold separately from the land. The crops produced by fructus industriales (such as the apples in a cultivated orchard), on the other hand, are treated as personal property, even before they've been harvested. However, between a seller and a buyer of land, crops produced by fructus industriales are part of the real property.

Example: Z lives on a small farm with an apple orchard and rampant wild blackberry bushes. The apple trees are fructus industriales, and the blackberry bushes are fructus naturales.

If Z mortgages her real property, the mortgage lien will attach to her land, the apple trees, the blackberry bushes, and the blackberries. It won't attach to the apples, though, because they are personal property, not part of the realty.

However, if Z sells her farm to A, the apples will be treated as part of the realty. They will be included in the sale unless Z specifically excludes them from it in the sale agreement.

Young plants or trees (nursery stock) temporarily placed in the soil pending sale and not intended to permanently grow in that location are personal property.

1. Doctrine of Emblements

A special rule called the **DOCTRINE OF EMBLEMENTS** *applies to crops planted by tenant farmers.* When a tenancy is for an indefinite period of time, and the tenancy is terminated (through no fault of the tenant) before the annual crop is ready for harvest, the tenant has the right to reenter the land and harvest the crop.

Example: For several years, a farmer has been renting a large field from his neighbor. They have a year-to-year lease; it is automatically renewed each June until one of the parties gives the other notice of termination.

In April, the neighbor tells the farmer the lease will end in June because she's planning to sell her land. The farmer has the right to enter the property in the autumn to harvest the crops he planted, even though the lease has ended.

To fall within this rule, the crop must be produced by the labor and industry of the farmer. For example, if the crop is wild mushrooms that grow naturally and were not planted or cultivated by the farmer, the rule does not apply. If the crops are an annual product of perennial plants, such as apples or strawberries, the right to reenter and harvest applies only to the first crop that matures after the tenancy has ended.

B. FIXTURES

*Man-made attachments are called **FIXTURES**.* They are items that were once personal property, but are now connected to the land in such a way that they are considered part of the real property. For instance, a pile of lumber and a batch of nails are personal property, but they become fixtures when they're used to build a barn.

Whether a particular item is a fixture or personal property is a question that real estate agents deal with constantly. Earlier, we referred to a dispute over a satellite dish. Is this a fixture? What about a tool shed? A swing set? Imported goldfish in a garden pond?

To avoid controversy over this issue, a real estate agent should discuss these kinds of items with the seller and buyer, making sure that both agree about what is and is not included in the sale. Of course, the agent must know what is ordinarily considered a fixture and what is considered personal property.

The courts have come up with a series of tests to determine when an item is a fixture.

Fixture Tests Take Into Account:

- The method of attachment,
- Adaptation to the realty,
- The intention of the annexor,
- The relationship of the parties, and
- Any written agreement.

MARIA

1. Method of Attachment

When an item is permanently attached to the land, it becomes part of the real estate. An attachment is considered permanent when the item is:

1. permanently resting on the land (such as large buildings like houses and barns);
2. affixed to the land by roots (as with trees and shrubs);
3. embedded in the earth (like sewer lines or septic tanks); or
4. attached by any enduring method (such as cement, plaster, nails, bolts, or screws).

Note that an item can be considered a fixture even when it isn't actually physically attached to the land. Attachment by the force of gravity may be sufficient, as in the case of a building without a foundation. *An item may also be considered a fixture when it's enclosed within a room or building in such a way that it cannot be removed without dismantling it or tearing down part of the building. In any of these situations, there is said to be **ACTUAL ANNEXATION**.*

*Some completely moveable items are regarded as so strongly connected with the property that they are considered fixtures, even though they are in no way actually attached to the realty. This is called the doctrine of **CONSTRUCTIVE ANNEXATION**.*

Example: A firm that manufactures widgets sells its main processing plant. The widget-making machine weighs twelve tons and is bolted to the floor. It is clearly a fixture. The key that turns on the widget maker and specialized tools for repairing the machine are also considered fixtures, although they are easily moved.

CHAPTER 2

The doctrine of constructive annexation also applies to fixtures that have been temporarily removed from the real property for servicing or repair.

Example: A sells his house to B. At the time of the sale, the built-in dishwasher is at a repair shop. Even so, the dishwasher is included in the sale, and its ownership transfers to B when she takes title to the house.

2. Adaptation to the Realty

If an item was specially designed or adapted for use in a particular building or is essential to the use of the building, it is probably a fixture. For example, wall-to-wall carpeting cut to fit a particular room would probably be treated as a fixture, even if it wasn't tacked down.

3. Intention

While the method of attachment test and the adaptation test are important, courts consider the key test to be the "intention" of the annexor.

The **ANNEXOR** *is the person who owned the item as personal property and brought it onto the real property.* Did the annexor intend for the item to become part of the realty or to remain personal property?

There must be objective evidence of intent. It isn't enough for the annexor to claim that he or she always intended to remove the item. The method of attachment and the adaptation of the item to the realty are viewed as objective evidence of intent.

Example: S puts a bird bath in his back yard, embedding it in concrete. Two years later, he sells his house to B. Their contract says nothing about the bird bath. When S moves out, he digs up the bird bath and takes it with him. B objects, arguing that the bird bath was a fixture and therefore was included in the sale.

S protests that he never intended the bird bath to be a fixture. This claim is inadequate since it isn't backed up by objective evidence. A court would interpret the method of attachment that S used (concrete) as evidence of an intent to make the bird bath a permanent part of the real property.

The California Supreme Court stated that classification of an item as a fixture "should turn on whether a reasonable person would consider the item a permanent part of the host real property, taking into account annexation, adaptation, and other objective manifestations of permanence" (*Crocker Nat'l Bank v. San Francisco*, 49 Cal. 3d 881, 264 Cal. Rptr. 139 [1989]).

4. Relationship of the Parties

Another factor considered in resolving a dispute over whether an item is a fixture is the relationship of the parties: seller and buyer, borrower and secured lender, landlord and tenant.

Between a seller and a buyer of real property, the rules for determining what is a fixture are interpreted in favor of the buyer.

Example: A homeowner screws a chandelier into his dining room ceiling. Several months later, he sells his house. The chandelier is considered a fixture and is included in the sale, even though it could easily be removed.

Between a trustor (trust deed borrower) and beneficiary (trust deed lender), the rules are interpreted in favor of the beneficiary. The chandelier is part of the realty, so it is covered by the beneficiary's lien.

Between a landlord and a tenant, the rules are interpreted in favor of the tenant. If a tenant installs a chandelier (or any other ornamental or domestic item), he or she will be allowed to remove it at the end of the lease. These rules tie in with the intention test: the law presumes that a homeowner intends to improve real property, but that a tenant intends to remove the items he or she installs.

The rule favoring the tenant extends to *TRADE FIXTURES*, *equipment installed for use in the tenant's business*. A tenant who operated a beauty parlor can remove the shampoo basins, lighted mirrors, and adjustable chairs, even though they are affixed to the walls or floors. The tenant is responsible for repairing any damage to the premises caused by the removal.

Allowing tenants to remove trade fixtures encourages efficiency in business. Tenants are more likely to install new equipment if they know they can take it with them when they leave. However, if the trade fixtures have become an integral part of the building, they cannot be removed. For example, a marble store front and plate glass windows become an integral part of the building and may not be removed.

Trade fixtures that aren't removed when the tenant leaves automatically become the property of the landlord.

The trade fixtures rule is not always applied to items that tenants have installed for farming purposes. **Agricultural fixtures** (a silo, for example) can't necessarily be removed by tenant farmers when they leave the property.

5. Written Agreement

Regardless of any of the previously discussed considerations, if there is a written agreement between the parties stipulating how a particular item is to be treated, a court will enforce the agreement and it is binding on third parties with notice of it.

When a seller wants to remove things that might be considered fixtures, he or she should inform the buyer, and include a statement in the purchase agreement specifying which items are excluded from the sale. Natural attachments (shrubs or rosebushes, for example) can be excluded in the same way.

6. Other Fixture Tests: Manufactured Housing

Manufactured housing is classified as personal property until it is permanently attached to the real property by removing the wheels and mounting the unit on a foundation. As personal property, manufactured housing may be sold without a real estate license, and the sales are subject to sales tax laws.

CHAPTER 2

7. Other Fixture Tests: Secured Financing and Fixtures

When personal property is purchased on credit or used as collateral, a creditor often takes a security interest in the property. What happens to that security interest if the personal property becomes attached to real property—in other words, when it becomes a fixture?

A creditor with a security interest in a fixture should record a financing statement in the county where the real property is located.

This is called "perfecting" the security interest. The recorded financing statement gives constructive notice of the creditor's interest to prospective lienholders or purchasers of the real property. If the debtor defaults, the secured creditor will be able to repossess the fixture.

Example: Q buys a small apartment building with a loan from Vault Savings, and the loan is secured by a trust deed on the property. Q purchases a central air conditioning unit on credit, and the air conditioner company files a financing statement to give notice of its security interest in the unit. Q has the air conditioner installed in his apartment building.

Later, Q defaults on the trust deed and on his air conditioner payments. Vault Savings forecloses on the trust deed and takes title to the building. Because the air conditioner is a fixture, the bank would ordinarily acquire ownership of the unit as part of the real property. However, because the air conditioner company perfected its security interest, it can repossess the unit rather than losing it to the bank.

Recorded financing statements are indexed according to the last name of the debtor. As part of a title search, a title insurance company routinely checks to determine whether there are perfected security interests in any of the fixtures on a property about to be sold or used as security for a loan.

IV. Appurtenances

Once you know the boundaries of the real property and what items are included in the sale, you also need to become familiar with what property rights are transferred along with the property. *A right that goes along with real property upon sale or other transfer is called an APPURTENANCE.* One basic type of appurtenance is the right to take or use something that is in or on the land, such as water, air, or minerals. When real property is transferred, appurtenant rights are ordinarily considered part of the real property and are transferred along with it. They can be sold separately, however, and may be limited by past transactions.

A. WATER RIGHTS

Water is vital for farming, industry, and day-to-day living. Because it is so scarce in many parts of California, water has been the source of a lot of legislation and litigation in this state. The statutes and lawsuits concern the right to use the water, ownership of the water, and ownership of lake or stream beds.

Under the Water Code, all water within the state is the property of "the people of the state."

Such ownership, however, is ownership in a regulatory, supervisory sense, rather than in a possessory, proprietary sense (*State of California v. Superior Court* [Underwriters at Lloyd's of London] [2000] 78 Cal. App. 4th 1019, 1027-1032, 93 Cal. Rptr. 2d 276, 283-287).

The two main types of water rights are:

1. riparian rights and
2. appropriative rights.

www.ca.water.usgs.gov
USGS - California Water Resources

1. Riparian Rights

Riparian rights are tied to land ownership. *Any land that is adjacent to or crossed by water, or contains a body of water within its boundaries, is* **RIPARIAN LAND**. **RIPARIAN RIGHTS** *attach to a natural water course not concrete aqueducts or canals used to move water from one location to another.* Even the federal government has riparian rights on federal land in California. Under the riparian rights system, every riparian landowner has an equal right to use the water that touches his or her property.

All riparian owners may use the water for swimming, boating, or other recreational purposes. They all have the right to take water for domestic uses such as drinking, washing, and watering a garden. They may use the water in any other way that is "reasonable and beneficial"—that is, not wasteful. **This right is not lost by nonuse**. According to the California Civil Code, domestic use is the highest use of water, and irrigation is the second highest.

However the water is used, it must be used on the riparian land, the land that adjoins the body of water. A riparian landowner is not allowed to divert water for use on nonriparian land.

> **Example:** C owns two lots, one adjoining the river and another across the road, which is landlocked. C channels irrigating water to her landlocked lot. The landlocked lot is not bordered by a stream or river and is not riparian land.

A riparian owner is also not allowed to use the water in a way that impairs other riparian owners' rights. In a time of water shortage, all the riparian owners must reduce their use. During a drought, a use that is ordinarily considered reasonable might be prohibited.

Landowners above an underground aquifer are said to have **OVERLYING RIGHTS**. These are very similar to riparian rights; most of the same rules apply.

2. Appropriative Rights

There are vast tracts of arid land in California where the riparian system won't work. To make that land habitable and productive, water must be transported from other areas. This use of water is controlled by the prior appropriation system.

Anyone can apply to the State Water Resources Control Board for an appropriation permit. If the application is approved, the permit holder is granted the right to take water from a particular lake, river, stream, or aquifer for a specified reasonable and beneficial use. The water does not have to be used on riparian land.

Under the **PRIOR APPROPRIATION SYSTEM**, *if two parties both have appropriation permits for the same body of water, first in time is first in right*. This means that the party who obtained a permit first can use as much water as the permit specifies, even if that leaves too little water for the people with later permits. However, appropriation for city inhabitants is first in right and does not have to be first in time.

The rights of the riparian landowners on a lake or river are taken into account when a permit to appropriate water from that lake or river is issued. Riparian rights are paramount, and appropriative rights must not interfere with them.

Example: A and B own land along the Almond River. C and D each have an appropriation permit for the river. C's permit was issued before D's. Usually the Almond River contains enough water to serve all four individuals. This spring, however, the river is very low. The riparian owners, A and B, have first claim on the water, as long as their use is reasonable under the circumstances. C is next in line. C can take all the water allocated in the appropriation permit, even though this means there won't be enough water left over to meet D's needs. (Again, C's use must be reasonable under the circumstances.)

An appropriative right is lost if it isn't used for 5 years or it is abandoned. In the example above, if C went for a long time without taking any water from the river, C would lose the right to do so. C could obtain a new permit, but then C would have a lower priority than D and other appropriators.

A prescriptive right to water can be acquired by a user either under claim of right or color of title by taking the water for 5 years. The amount of the water acquired by prescriptive right is a fixed amount based on current beneficial use. This prescriptive right can be lost by nonuse.

3. Navigable Waters

All navigable waterways in California are owned and controlled by the state government. When property borders on the ocean (or on a bay connected to it), the property owner only owns the land above the mean high water mark. When property borders on a navigable stream or lake, the property owner owns the land to the low water mark. Beyond those limits, coastal land and the beds of navigable lakes and rivers are owned by the government.

The government holds the state's navigable waters in trust for the public. The public has the right to use the waterways for transportation and recreation. Although landowners on a navigable lake own the land to the low water mark, their ownership of the land between the high water mark and the low water mark is subject to the public trust. They may not use that portion of their property in a way that would interfere with the public's rights. This rule significantly restricts development of many riparian properties.

The case below involves the taking by a water district by appropriation, but without the permission of the landowner.

Case Example: The Santa Clarita Water Company (company) sought to condemn a strip of property owned by Lyons and sent a draft for Lyons to sign. Lyons never signed or returned the document. Despite this fact, several years later the company installed a subsurface pipeline on the property. Subsequent to that, the company constructed a water well on the property to remove subsurface water and sold the water to its customers. The company never applied to the State Water Resources Board for the required permit. Approximately two years later, upon learning of this, Lyons immediately protested to the water company and the company sued to condemn the easement on the property. Lyons sued for, among other things, damages for trespass. In litigation, the company abandoned its condemnation action. With regard to damages, the court awarded Lyons $146,501 in compensatory damages for the value of the water taken by the company. The expert witness for Lyons determined that the company had taken 4,636.3 acre feet of water from the well (this would cover a square mile of land with approximately 7.4 feet of water). The court also concluded that the company was a "negligent trespasser" and that it had not acquired any prescriptive rights by reason of its occupancy of Lyons' land. The company appealed on several grounds.

The Court of Appeal agreed that the company committed a substantial trespass over a long period of time and had taken water for which it charged customers, but for which it had not paid. The company was not appropriate, or in the traditional sense of the word, merely a negligent trespasser. The compensatory damages portion of the judgment is affirmed. *Santa Clarita Water Company v. Lyons*, 161 Cal. App. 3d 450, 207 Cal. Rptr. 698 (1984).

4. Nonnavigable Waters

A nonnavigable lake is private property. If a small lake is completely within the boundaries of one landowner's property, the landowner owns the lake bed. If several different people own land around a nonnavigable lake or stream, ownership of the lake bed or stream bed is generally divided by tracing lines from each property boundary to the center of the lake or the center of a stream (thread of the stream) measured at its lowest point. Each owner has title to the parcel of the lake bed or stream bed adjoining his or her land. All owners also have the riparian right to the reasonable use of the entire surface of the lake or stream for recreational purposes (see **Figure 2-1**).

B. OIL AND GAS RIGHTS

In their natural state, oil and gas lie trapped beneath the surface of the earth under great pressure. Once an oil or gas reservoir has been tapped, the oil and gas begin to flow towards the point where the reservoir was pierced by the well as this is the area of lowest pressure. By drilling a well, a property owner can drain an oil or gas reservoir that lies beneath his or her own property and beneath several neighbors' properties as well.

Because of their migratory nature, oil and gas are covered by the *RULE OF CAPTURE*. *Under this rule, oil and gas in its natural state is not owned until it is "captured" by drilling and brought to the surface. With the rule of capture, the owner of land has the exclusive right on his land to drill for and produce oil, even though it may have migrated from under a neighbor's land.* This rule stimulates oil and gas production. If the neighbors want to protect their interests in the oil or gas beneath their property, they must drill **offset wells** to keep all of the oil or gas from migrating to one well. As a result, more oil and gas is produced in a shorter amount of time because more wells are drilled.

CHAPTER 2

Figure 2-1

Small
Nonnavigable
Lake

The right to drill for and produce oil and gas is a valuable right which a surface owner may transfer by deed or lease under both the Unruh Act and FEHA as of 1/1/2012.

Since most landowners don't have the necessary skill, experience, or equipment to drill for oil or gas themselves, they usually enter into lease agreements with oil or gas companies to drill the wells and extract the oil or gas. There is no standard lease form (fictitious oil and gas leases may be recorded), but oil and gas leases generally involve an initial cash amount paid for granting the lease and royalties paid to the landowner based on the amount of oil or gas actually extracted. The lease is granted for a specified period and ordinarily provides for an extension of time if necessary. No lease can last more than 99 years after it starts.

C. SUPPORT RIGHTS

A piece of land is supported by the other land that surrounds it. A landowner has the right to the natural support provided by the land beside and beneath his or her property.

1. Lateral Support

LATERAL SUPPORT is support from adjacent land. A neighbor's excavations might make your land shift and settle. Traditionally, the neighbor would have been held liable for damage that resulted from the excavations, no matter how carefully they were carried out. This rule has been modified, however. Now, unless the excavations are unusually deep, the neighbor will only be held liable for damage if he or she fails to follow the procedures prescribed by statute.

Among other provisions, the statute requires a landowner planning excavations to notify neighboring landowners. This gives them the opportunity to protect their property.

Example: J and K own adjacent lots. J's lot is vacant, but K's has a house and other improvements on it.

J plans to build a house, so he's going to excavate for the foundation. He gives K proper notice of when, where, and how deep he's going to dig. He takes reasonable precautions to sustain the adjoining land. K does nothing to protect her property.

When J carries out his excavation, K's land shifts, her foundation cracks, and the house tilts. As long as J complied with the statute and used ordinary care and skill in excavating, he is not liable for this damage. J would be liable if he failed to give notice or was negligent in excavating.

If the excavation is deeper than the foundations of the adjoining building and will endanger it, the owner must be given a 30-day notice to protect the property and is allowed access to the excavated property to do so. If the excavation is deeper than 9 feet below curb level and so is the adjoining building, then the excavator must support the land and building without cost to the owner, and is liable for any damage except minor settlement cracks.

2. Subjacent Support

SUBJACENT SUPPORT is support from the underlying earth. The right to subjacent support is important when a landowner transfers rights to the underlying minerals to someone else. The mineral rights owner will be held liable for surface damage caused by underground excavation, even if it was performed carefully. Liability is absolute, unless the weight of structures added on the surface contributed to the subsidence.

D. OTHER APPURTENANT RIGHTS

Easements and restrictive covenants also create rights that are appurtenant to real property. These types of appurtenances are discussed in Chapter 3 and Chapter 13, respectively.

V. CHAPTER SUMMARY

1. Real property is land; that which is affixed to the land; that which is incidental or appurtenant to the land; and that which is immovable by law. Personal property is moveable, and is defined as every kind of property that is not real property.

2. Knowing the correct property boundaries is important to everyone involved in a real estate transaction. A seller may be held liable for innocently misrepresenting property boundaries. A broker would probably not be held liable for an innocent misrepresentation, but will be held liable if he/she knows of the misrepresentation.

3. The three main methods of land description are metes and bounds, government (rectangular) survey, and lot and block. The lot and block method is the system used most frequently in metropolitan areas.

4. Attachments to real property are part of the real property. Unless otherwise agreed, they are transferred along with the land; personal property is not. The two types of attachments to real property are natural attachments and man-made attachments (fixtures). In deciding whether an item is a fixture, a court tries to determine the intention of the annexor. The court takes into account the method of attachment, adaptation to the realty, the relationship of the parties, and any written agreement.

5. An appurtenance is a right that goes along with or relates to real property, including air, water, oil, mineral, and support rights. These rights are ordinarily transferred with the land, but they may be severed from it and sold separately.

6. The right to use water is either a riparian right or an appropriative right. All landowners whose property adjoins a body of water have riparian rights. To acquire an appropriative right, you must obtain a permit from the government. Under the riparian system, the water must be used on riparian land. Under the prior appropriation system, the water may be used on nonriparian land.

VI. KEY TERMS

adaptation	fixture	nonnavigable waters
air lot	fructus faturales/industriales	personal property
appropriative rights	fructus naturales	point of beginning
appurtenance	horizontal rights	principal meridian
attachment	government survey	prior appropriation
base line	government lot	range
bench mark	guide meridian	real property
common grantor	intention	reformation
constructive annexation	inverted pyramid	relationship to the parties
correction line	land patent	riparian
course	lateral/subjacent support	rule of capture
datum	metes and bounds	section
doctrine of agreed boundary	method of attachment	township
doctrine of emblements	mineral rights	township tier
financing statement	monument	trade fixture
final subdivision map	navigable waters	water rights

VII. CHAPTER QUIZ

1. The boundaries in a metes and bounds description are fixed by reference to three things. Which of the following is not one of the three?

    a. Distances
    b. Monuments
    c. Triangles
    d. Courses

2. In a metes and bounds description, the term "courses" refers to:

    a. whether the direction goes uphill or downhill.
    b. compass readings.
    c. elevation.
    d. the natural pathway of a river or stream.

3. Compass directions are stated in terms of the degree of deviation from:

    a. north or south.
    b. north only.
    c. east and west.
    d. none of the above.

4. The government survey system is also called the:

    a. metes and bounds survey method.
    b. meridian survey method.
    c. agreed boundary survey method.
    d. rectangular survey method.

5. Range lines run:

    a. north/south at 4-mile intervals.
    b. north/south at 6-mile intervals.
    c. east/west at 4-mile intervals.
    d. east/west at 6-mile intervals.

6. Township lines run:

    a. east/west.
    b. north/west.
    c. north/south.
    d. north by northwest.

7. The three principal meridians in California are:

    a. Humboldt, San Bernardino, Mt. Diablo.
    b. Humboldt, San Diego, Mt. Diablo.
    c. San Bernardino, Mt. Humboldt, San Diego.
    d. San Diego, San Luis Obispo, Humboldt.

8. Between a buyer and a seller of land, crops produced by "fructus industriales" are:

    a. personal property.
    b. part of the real property.
    c. naturally occurring trees and plants.
    d. organic.

9. Trade fixtures refer to:

    a. any items of personal property purchased at a trade show.
    b. any items of personal property permanently installed in a person's residence.
    c. restaurant cooking appliances such as a knife.
    d. equipment installed for use in a tenant's business.

10. The owner of 10 acres of land with a one-acre pond in its center has:

    a. riparian water rights.
    b. appropriative water rights.
    c. prescriptive water rights.
    d. water rights by the doctrine of attachments.

ANSWERS: 1. c; 2. b; 3. a; 4. d; 5. b; 6. a; 7. c; 8. a; 9. b; 10. a

WARNING

NEIGHBORHOOD WATCH

CITY OF LOS ANGELES
L.A.P.D.

4180   MS 90

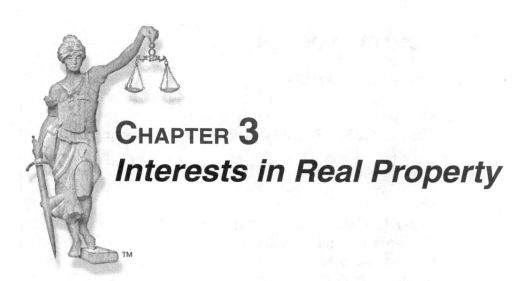

CHAPTER **3**
Interests in Real Property

CHAPTER OVERVIEW

*A person who has a property right or a claim against property is said to have an **INTEREST** in the property.* An interest might be an ownership right (such as a life estate), a right to use the property (such as an easement), or a financial claim against the title (such as a trust deed).

One of the most important steps in a real estate transaction is determining exactly what interest the seller holds in the property. You can only transfer the interest that you hold. If you're renting a house, you may be able to assign your lease to someone else, but you can't sell them the house.

A buyer also needs to know about other interests in the property. Do the neighbors have the right to swim in the pond whenever they want? Can Joe's Roofing foreclose if their bill isn't paid soon? Will ownership revert to the seller's uncle if the olive trees along the driveway are removed?

This chapter describes the various types of interests in real property. It explains how they are created and terminated, and how they affect the property.

www.megalaw.com/top/property.php
Legal Specialties: Real Property Law

I. Possessory Interests (Estates)

An ***ESTATE** is an interest in real property that is, will be, or may become **possessory**.* In other words, a person who has an estate either has the right to possess the property now, will have that right in the future, or may have that right in the future. *A right to immediate possession is called a **PRESENT INTEREST**. A right to possession in the future is called a **FUTURE INTEREST**.* Estates are classified according to the time of enjoyment (present or future), and also according to their duration.

A. FREEHOLD ESTATES

Under the feudal system in medieval England, all land was essentially owned by the king.

CHAPTER OUTLINE

The king parceled out land to his followers in return for their services. These men then could rent portions of their property to others. The modern U.S. system of ownership interests in real property grew out of English feudal law, and many of the legal terms still used to describe estates date back to the twelfth or thirteenth century.

The term "freehold" originally referred to the holdings of a freeman under the feudal/ English system. A freeman was allowed to sell his rights in the property, as long as the new owner agreed to give the same services to the lord or king, who held a higher interest in the property.

Today, a freehold estate can still be sold. A *FREEHOLD is a possessory interest of uncertain duration, which means that the length of time of ownership is unspecified and indefinite.* There are two main categories of freehold estates:

1. fee simple estates, and
2. life estates.

1. Fee Simple Estates

When a person is referred to as the "owner" of property, it usually means that he or she holds a fee simple estate. A *FEE SIMPLE ESTATE is the highest and largest interest that can exist in land.* A fee simple estate is:

1. inheritable,
2. transferable, and
3. perpetual. *#15 never-ending / changing*

An *INHERITABLE ESTATE is, quite simply, one that can be inherited.* Property held in fee simple may be left to someone in a will, or automatically passed to heirs if there is no will (by **intestate succession**). A fee simple estate is also freely transferable, which means that the owner can sell, divide, or even give away the property if he or she so desires. A fee simple is perpetual in that the owner has the right to possess the property for an unlimited period of time. In theory, the owner and his or her heirs could hold the fee simple estate forever.

In transferring a fee simple estate, the former owner may choose to qualify the new owner's title by including a condition or requirement in the deed. It could be a limitation on the use of the property (...on condition that the house is used as a museum...), or it might make title dependent on an event that has nothing to do with the property (... provided that the U.S. does not go to war with Mexico...). If the requirement is not met or maintained, the new owner could forfeit title to the property.

a. Fee Simple Absolute and Fee Simple Subject to a Condition Subsequent

*A fee simple estate that is not qualified or subject to any conditions is called a **FEE SIMPLE ABSOLUTE**. A fee simple estate that is subject to a condition is called a **FEE SIMPLE SUBJECT TO A CONDITION SUBSEQUENT**, a type of a defeasible fee estate* (Defeasible coming from a Latin word meaning "undo").

Nearly all ordinary residential property is held in fee simple absolute. And in a typical home sale, the real estate agent and the buyer probably assume the seller owns the property in fee simple absolute. But it's very important to check that assumption. Otherwise, the buyer might end up unable to use the property as planned (as a home instead of a museum), or could even lose the property because of an event beyond his or her control (war with Mexico).

With a defeasible fee estate, a deed or will transferring property contains a condition on ownership or use of the property and provides that the ownership and right to possess the property is forfeited if the stated condition is breached. Ownership and the right to possession would then return to the original grantor or that grantor's successors. Historically, California recognized several types of defeasible fee estates, including those that terminated automatically and those that required court action to terminate. But in 1982, the California legislature abolished the defeasible fee estates that terminated automatically with the passage of the Marketable Record Title Act. Now, the only type of defeasible fee recognized in California is a Fee Simple Subject to a Condition Subsequent. The Fee Simple Subject to a Condition Subsequent is a present estate that is subject to a stated condition. When a Fee Simple Subject to a Condition Subsequent is created (by deed or will), a future estate held by the grantor (and called a **Power of Termination**) is created at the same time. If the condition in the present estate is never met, the present interest of the Fee Simple Subject to a Condition Subsequent continues. However, if the condition isn't met, the grantor (or grantor's heirs or successor) has the right to terminate the Fee Simple Subject to a Condition Subsequent and retake ownership and possession of the property. But termination of the Fee Simple Subject to a Condition Subsequent interest is not automatic. The grantor (or grantor's heirs or successor) holding the Power of Termination must file a lawsuit against the to terminate the present interest and get the property back.

Example: K owned some property next door to Palabra Elementary School. In 1966, K transferred her property as a gift to the Mountain View School District. The deed granted it to the school district "provided that it is used for school purposes." For many years the property was used as a playground by the children at Palabra School.

In 1990, due to population changes and financial trouble, the Mountain View District closes down Palabra School, and K's property is no longer used for school purposes. K (or K's heirs, if she has died in the meanwhile) can take legal action to terminate the school district's interest in the property.

www.direct.business.com/directory/law/practice_areas/commercial_law/real_property_law/weblistings.asp
Sources of Property Law and Rights in the U.S.

Whenever a Fee Simple Subject to a Condition Subsequent present estate exists, there will be also be a Power of Termination future estate. Both estates are inheritable, transferable, and potentially perpetual, as with Fee Simple Absolute. If a person holding a Fee Simple Subject to a Condition Subsequent transfers this interest, the successors hold the same present interest subject to the stated condition. If the power of termination is transferred, the successor to that future interest have the same right to regain ownership if the condition is breached. However, the Marketable Record Title Act placed limits on exercise of the power of termination. A power of termination cannot be exercised if more than five years have passed since the deed condition was broken.

A power of termination expires 30 years after the deed granting the conditional fee was recorded, unless the power is preserved. The grantor (or grantor's heirs) can record a notice of intent to preserve the power of termination before it expires. That extends the power for another 30 years. This process can be repeated every 30 years, preserving the power of termination indefinitely. But if the power of termination is allowed to expire, the grantee's title is no longer subject to the condition. The grantee then owns the property in fee simple absolute.

The courts see forfeiture of the grantee's title as a harsh outcome that should be avoided. As a result, if the language in a deed can possibly be interpreted as a covenant rather than a condition, a court is likely to treat it as a covenant. A covenant is a legally binding promise (see Chapter 13). If a covenant in a deed is broken, the grantee may have to pay damages, but he or she will not forfeit title. This is the result courts prefer, but they are required to interpret a deed according to the language used.

> **Case Example:** In 1908 and 1916, Elizabeth Kraft and her son Edward granted to the city of Red Bluff their property to be used as a public library. The grant provided that if the property ceased to be used as a library, then it shall revert to the grantor or the heirs. In 1986, the books were removed. In 1988, Walton, the only surviving heir, sued to acquire the title. The Court of Appeal held that title reverted to Walton. Although the 1982 Marketable Record Title Act required Walton to record his notice to preserve the power of termination within 5 years of the enactment of the Act or within 30 years of the recording of the original deed, he did neither. This being the case, title should have stayed with the city. However, the attorney for Red Bluff failed to raise Walton's inaction as a defense and, therefore, Walton won. *Walton v. City of Red Bluff*, 2 Cal. App. 4th 177, 3 Cal. Rptr. 2d 275 (1991).

Thus, though it doesn't happen often, the owner of a fee simple subject to a condition subsequent may end up losing the property.

2. Life Estates

Unlike a fee simple estate, the duration of a life estate is limited. *The duration of a LIFE ESTATE is based on the length of someone's lifetime.* For example, property formerly owned by President Lyndon Johnson and his wife, Ladybird, has been donated to the public as a National Historical Site. President Johnson died in 1969, but Ladybird Johnson has a life estate in the property. She has the right to possess and occupy the property for the rest of her life. When she dies, the life estate terminates.

Life estates are often used to simplify the division of property in a will, or to avoid the expense of probate. *An owner can transfer property to another, but create a life estate in the property for himself or herself, called EXPRESS RESERVATION of a life estate.*

Example: To avoid probate expenses, B deeds his property to his son S, but reserves a life estate for himself. B has the right to use and occupy the property for the rest of his life, but upon his death, ownership will automatically pass to S.

An owner may also create a life estate for someone else by express grant.

Example: In his will, H left his second wife, W, a life estate in certain property, with the remainder interest to his son, S. W has the right to use and occupy the property for the rest of her life, and when she dies the property will automatically pass to S. H has expressly granted a life estate to W.

The holder of a life estate is called the LIFE TENANT. In all of the previous examples, the life estate's duration is measured by the lifetime of the life tenant: the life tenant may possess the property for the rest of his or her life. But a life estate may also be based on the lifetime of someone other than the life tenant. This is called a life estate *PUR AUTRE VIE (for another's life)*. This type of estate is sometimes used to create security for ailing parents or disabled children who are unable to provide for themselves.

Example: A's mother, M, is afflicted with Alzheimer's disease and can't take care of herself. A's brother B has been taking care of their mother. A deeds his property to B "for the life of M, and then to S." B has a life estate based on his mother's life. B has the right to use and occupy the property only as long as his mother is still alive. When the mother dies, the property automatically passes to A's son, S.

The mother's life is the MEASURING LIFE. The life estate lasts only as long as the mother's lifetime.

A life tenant has an ownership interest in the land that can be sold, leased, or mortgaged. Remember, however, that a person can only sell, lease, or mortgage the interest that he or she owns. If a life tenant sells his or her interest in the property, the buyers have only purchased a life estate. The buyer's interest ends at the end of the measuring life; in the example just given, it would end when M died.

3. Future Interests

When a life estate is granted, another interest is created at the same time: the interest of the person who will receive the property when the life estate ends. He or she will have the right to possess the property, but not until sometime in the future (when the measuring life ends). Thus, that person has a future interest. There are two types of future interests:

1. estates in remainder, and
2. estates in reversion.

In the previous example, the son, S, holds an *ESTATE IN REMAINDER; although he doesn't have the right to possess the property right now, he currently has an interest in the remainder of the estate (the estate left over after the life estate).* S is called the remainderman. When B's life estate ends (on M's death), S will take title to the property in fee simple absolute.

When the property is slated to return to the original grantor at the end of the life estate, the grantor has an ESTATE IN REVERSION (or reversionary interest).

Example: Q owns a house in fee simple absolute. He deeds the property to his mother for her lifetime. The deed says, "From Q to M for life, and then to Q." When M dies, Q will regain title in fee simple absolute.

The property would also revert to Q if the deed had simply said, "From Q to M for life," and nothing more. If a remainderman isn't specified in the deed, it is presumed to create an estate in reversion.

A life tenant has certain duties towards the property. He or she may not use or abuse the property in any way that would permanently damage it or reduce its market value. Such abuse is called **waste**. The term "waste" implies neglect or misconduct, and does not include the ordinary depreciation of property due to time and normal use.

A life tenant must allow for reasonable inspection of the property by the holder of the future interest (the remainderman or the grantor). If he or she discovers waste, the holder of the future interest may sue the life tenant for damages. If the waste isn't discovered until after the life tenant's death, the lawsuit can be brought against the life tenant's estate.

4. Trusts

Life estates aren't used very often anymore. A living trust can provide the same benefits as a life estate, and has a number of advantages. When a living trust is created, a trustee is given legal title to the property for the life of the beneficiary. The beneficiary has the right to use and occupy the property under the trustee's supervision. When the beneficiary dies, the property is disposed of according to instructions in the document that created the trust. (Trusts are discussed again in Chapter 4.)

B. LEASEHOLD ESTATES

A leasehold estate is a more limited interest in property than a freehold estate. *The holder of a leasehold estate is called the LESSEE (tenant).* A tenant does not own the property but merely

CHAPTER 3

leases or rents it. He or she has the right to exclusive possession of the property, but only for a limited time.

*An owner who leases property to a tenant is called the **LESSOR** (or landlord).* During the lease period, the landlord has a reversionary interest in the property, as possession will revert to the landlord when the lease ends.

The rules that govern landlord/tenant relationships are presented in Chapter 15. Here we will just describe the basic characteristics of leasehold estates. In California, the four kinds of recognized leasehold estates include:

1. tenancy for a fixed term (estate for years),
2. periodic tenancy (estate from period-to-period),
3. tenancy at will (estate at will), and
4. tenancy at sufferance (estate at sufferance).

1. Tenancy for a Fixed Term (Estate for Years)

A term *TENANCY is a leasehold estate for a fixed time period.* It is sometimes called an **estate for years**, but the term doesn't have to be a year or a period of years. It may be for three months, six months and five days, two years, or any fixed rental period with a specific beginning and ending date and no provision for automatic renewal.

Example: T is a college student renting an apartment for one semester. The lease gives him the right to possess the apartment from August 20 through December 31. This is an estate for years or term tenancy.

To end a term tenancy, neither the lessor nor the lessee is required to give the other party notice. The lease terminates automatically at the end of the specified rental period. If the parties want to terminate the lease sooner, they may do so only by mutual consent. *Ending a term tenancy by mutual consent is called **SURRENDER**.*

Unless expressly prohibited in the lease, a term tenancy is *ASSIGNABLE, meaning that the tenant may assign his or her interest in the property to another person.* Assignment and subleasing are discussed in Chapter 15.

86

2. Periodic Tenancy (Estate from Period-to-Period)

*The duration of a **PERIODIC TENANCY** is not limited to a specific term—it continues from period-to-period until the lessor or lessee gives the other party notice of termination.* The period may be any length of time that the parties agree on. Month-to-month tenancies are the most common. A month-to-month tenancy automatically renews itself at the end of each month, unless one of the parties terminates it. (The requirements for notice of termination are explained in Chapter 15.) Like a term tenancy, a periodic tenancy is assignable unless the lease says it isn't.

3. Tenancy at Will (Estate at Will)

Under a ***TENANCY AT WILL**, the tenant is in possession of the property with the owner's permission, but without any rental agreement.* A tenancy at will has no specified termination date and no regular time period. Usually no rent is paid, or else rent is given in some form that has no reference to periods of time.

> **Example:** P occupies a house in return for maintaining and repairing the property. This is considered a tenancy at will because it is for an indefinite time and P is not required to pay periodic rent.

www.dca.ca.gov/publications/landlordbook/before-rent.shtml
Rental Agreements – General Information

To end a tenancy at will, the landlord must give the tenant at least a 30-day notice in writing, or the tenant must give the landlord a 30-day notice if vacating.

A tenancy at will is most likely to arise at the end of a fixed-term tenancy. The term has expired, but the tenant has stayed on, and the landlord hasn't asked the tenant to leave. However, this is only a tenancy at will until the tenant starts paying rent on a regular basis. If the tenant gives the landlord a check every month, a month-to-month tenancy is established by implication.

Unlike a fixed-term tenancy or a periodic tenancy, a tenancy at will cannot be assigned to someone else. Also, a tenancy at will automatically ends upon the death of either the landlord or the tenant. The death of a month-to-month tenant usually terminates the tenancy at the end of month in which the death occurred. With an estate for years, on the other hand, the deceased tenant's heirs may take over the tenancy for the remainder of the term.

4. Tenancy at Sufferance (Estate at Sufferance)

*If the tenant who was in lawful possession wrongfully remains without the landlord's permission and without payment of rent, the tenancy is called a **TENANCY AT SUFFERANCE**.* No notice is required to terminate a tenancy at sufferance. However, when the landlord wants the tenant removed, an eviction process must be started.

II. Nonpossessory Interests (Encumbrances)

A freehold estate is a possessory interest in real property with ownership rights, and a leasehold estate is a possessory interest in real property without ownership rights. The third type of interest in real property is a nonpossessory interest. Someone who holds a nonpossessory interest has a claim or right concerning the property, but does not have the right to possess the property. Nonpossessory interests are also called encumbrances; they encumber or burden the title.

The two categories of nonpossessory interests discussed in this chapter are:

1. easements, and
2. liens.

Restrictive covenants also create nonpossessory interests. They are discussed in Chapter 13.

 www.homebuying.about.com/cs/easementsrow/a/easement_faq.htm
Facts About Easements and Rights of Way

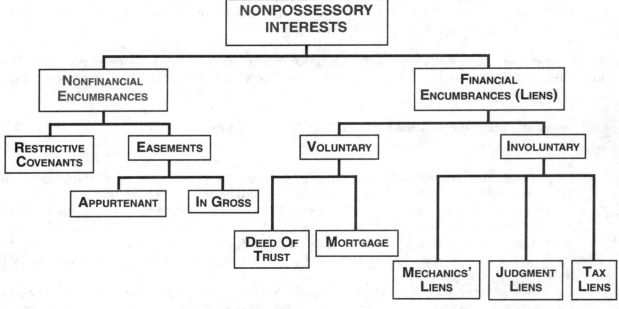

A. EASEMENTS ↗ *share driveway*

An **EASEMENT** *is a right held by one person to use the real property of another for a particular purpose.* The California Civil Code lists a wide variety of possible easements, ranging from the right to gather wood on another's land to the right of burial on another's land or from a solar easement to gather sunlight for heating to a conservation easement to preserve natural wonders.

1. Types of Easements

Easements affect the use and the value of property, so real estate agents and prospective buyers should find out whether a property is subject to any easements. A standard title insurance report will list the recorded easements, but usually won't list unrecorded easements. Agents and buyers should ask the seller about easements (particularly unrecorded easements), and should also keep an eye out for indications that the property is used by other people besides the seller (the neighbors, for instance).

a. Positive and Negative Easements

An easement can be either positive or negative. A **POSITIVE EASEMENT** *gives someone other than the owner a right to do something on the land or take something from the land.* The most common example of a positive easement is the right to cross another's land, often called a right-of-way or an access easement.

Example: D has an easement that allows her to cut across the corner of her neighbor's property to reach her mailbox, instead of having to go the long way around by the road. D has a positive easement over her neighbor's land.

A **NEGATIVE EASEMENT**, *on the other hand, prohibits a landowner from doing something on his or her own property.*

A negative easement is essentially the same thing as a restrictive covenant: both restrict the landowner's use of the property. The two terms are often used interchangeably.

Case Example: Mary Petersen and the Friedmans owned adjoining lots in San Francisco. Petersen had an easement against the Friedmans' property, entitling her to light, air, and an unobstructed view. It prohibited the Friedmans from erecting any structure on their lot that was over 28 feet high.

The Friedmans put up a TV antenna that exceeded the height limit. The court ruled that this violated Petersen's right to an unobstructed view, and ordered the Friedmans to take the antenna down. *Petersen v. Friedman*, 162 Cal. App. 2d 245, 328 P.2d 264 (1958).

In addition to being either positive or negative, an easement is either appurtenant or in gross.

b. Easement Appurtenant

An easement is said to burden a piece of land—it is an encumbrance on the property. An **EASEMENT APPURTENANT** *burdens one piece of land for the benefit of another piece of land.* In the case example above, the Friedmans' property was burdened with an easement that benefited Petersen's property.

The land benefited by an easement appurtenant (like Petersen's land) is called the **DOMINANT TENEMENT**. ("Tenement" is an old legal term that refers to the property held by freehold and all of the rights that go along with the land.) *The land burdened by that easement (like the Friedmans' land) is called the* **SERVIENT TENEMENT**. *The owner of the dominant tenement is called the* **DOMINANT TENANT**, *and the owner of the servient tenement is called the* **SERVIENT TENANT**. In the case example, Petersen is the dominant tenant and the Friedmans are the servient tenants.

An easement appurtenant ordinarily **RUNS WITH THE LAND**, *meaning if the dominant tenement is transferred (sold, willed, or given away), the easement is also transferred.* An easement appurtenant cannot be sold separately from the property. Whoever owns the dominant tenement also owns the easement.

Example: Diaz's easement allows her to drive across the west 30 feet of Sanchez property to get back and forth between her own property and the main road. The easement is appurtenant to Diaz's land (the dominant tenement). If Diaz sells her land to Chang,

Chang automatically acquires the easement. Sanchez must allow Chang to cross his land (the servient tenement).

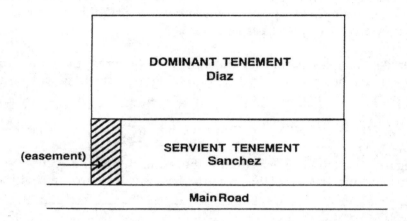

But what if the servient tenement is sold—what if Sanchez sells his land to Sullivan? Is the burden of an easement transferred to the new owner of the servient tenement? Yes, as long as the new owner has notice of the easement at the time of the transfer. Sullivan would be held to have notice of Chang's easement if someone told her about it, or if there was a recorded document that mentioned the easement, or even if an inspection of the property would have indicated that there might be an easement. Even if Sullivan didn't actually inspect the property or know about the recorded document, she would be required to let Chang use the easement. (See the discussion of actual and constructive notice in Chapter 10.)

If the dominant tenement is subdivided, the easement will usually run with all of the new lots.

Example: Continuing the previous example, suppose Chang divides the dominant tenement and sells half of it to Hernandez. Both Hernandez and Chang would have a right to use the easement over Sullivan's property. (Hernandez also has an easement over Chang's property.)

There's a limit to this rule, however: use of the easement cannot be increased so much that it increases the burden on the servient tenement. If Chang subdivided her property into 50 lots, a court would probably not permit all of the new owners to use the easement across Sullivan's land. The subdivider would have to make other arrangements for access to and from the 50 lots.

When landowners share easement rights to a right of way (for example, if A, B, C, and D use a private road crossing Z's lot to get to their lots), they must also share the cost of maintaining the easement. Unless otherwise agreed, each pays a share proportionate to how much he or she uses the road. If Z (the servient tenant—that is, the owner of the burdened property) doesn't use the road, he doesn't have an obligation to maintain or repair it for the easement holders.

c. Easements in Gross

Like an easement appurtenant, an easement in gross is a right that burdens another's land. *But unlike an easement appurtenant, an EASEMENT IN GROSS does not benefit a piece of land. There is a servient tenement (the land burdened by the easement in gross), but there is no dominant tenement.*

Example: F lives five miles away from G. G grants F an easement in gross to enter G's property and fish in the small lake there.

F's easement isn't appurtenant to his land. If F sells his property, the new owner does not gain the right to fish on G's land. The easement belongs to F personally, wherever he lives. But the easement in gross does run with G's land: if G sells his land to H, F will still have the right to fish in the lake.

An easement in gross that belongs to an individual (like F's right to fish) is called a **PERSONAL EASEMENT IN GROSS**. In many states, a personal easement in gross cannot be transferred, and is extinguished if the easement holder dies. But in California, a personal easement in gross may be sold or inherited unless the grantor expressly limited it to a particular individual.

Most easements in gross belong to commercial enterprises (such as public utilities) rather than individuals and are called **COMMERCIAL EASEMENTS IN GROSS**, and they are generally freely assignable.

Example: The Greentown Electric Company has an easement in gross that allows its employees to enter C's property to install and service power lines. When MegaElectric buys the Greentown Electric Company, it also purchases the easement in gross.

Note, however, that a commercial easement for a specific purpose cannot ordinarily be sold for another purpose. The electric company could not sell its power line easement to the local sewer district so that sewer lines could be laid in the easement.

When showing property to prospective buyers, a real estate agent should be able to explain any utility easements affecting the property. A typical residence may be subject to easements for the water company, the electric company, the gas company, a cable television company, and the telephone company. Sometimes these easements have an impact on the value of the property.

Example: The electric company has an easement running through your back yard. If the company installs unsightly power lines, the value of the property could drop sharply.

d. Solar Easement

The California Legislature Enacted the California Solar Rights Act to encourage the use of this renewable, nonpolluting energy source. A *SOLAR EASEMENT is the right to receive sunlight across property of another for a solar energy system.* A solar easement is a type of negative easement.

e. Conservation Easement

The California Legislature found that the preservation of land in its natural, scenic, agricultural, the store, forested, or open space condition is very important. Therefore, it is in the public interest to encourage the voluntary conveyance of conservation easements to qualified nonprofit organizations. A *CONSERVATION EASEMENT is an easement created by the property owner and is binding on successive owners of the land the purpose of which is to retain land in a condition mentioned above.* The easement is perpetual induration. The Legislature provides the process for the creation of the easement.

2. Creation of Easements

An easement may be by:

1. express agreement,
2. implication,
3. estoppel, or
4. prescription.

a. Express Easements

An easement can be expressly created in the deed that passes title to the dominant or servient property, or in a separate document that conveys only the easement. Because an express easement is an interest in real property, an oral agreement isn't enough—it must be in writing. (The requirements for a valid deed are explained in Chapter 10. Most of the same rules apply to a document creating an easement.)

Examples: D and S are neighbors. D asks S for an access easement allowing D to cross S's property. S agrees, but they never put it in writing. Six months later, S changes his mind and tells D to keep off his land. D can't enforce his easement right because it was only an oral agreement.

But suppose S signed a document granting D the easement. Now if S changes his mind, D has an enforceable right. D should record the document to make sure that anyone who buys the servient tenement from S will have notice of his easement.

A document creating an express easement usually states the purpose of the easement and describes its boundaries.

A deed may create an easement by express grant or express reservation. *An easement is created by* **EXPRESS GRANT** *when the grantor states in the deed that the grantee has a right to use the grantor's property for a particular purpose.*

Example: A sells the west half of his property to B. In the deed, A expressly grants to B the right to use the private road located on the east half of the property (which A still owns).

A deed creates an easement by **EXPRESS RESERVATION** *when the grantor reserves for him or herself (or for a third party) a right to use the grantee's property.*

Example: A sells the west half of his property to B. In the deed, A expressly reserves to himself the right to use the private road that is located on the west half of the property (which B now owns).

Another way that express easements are created is by plat maps. When a landowner subdivides land and sells it according to a recorded plat, anyone who buys a lot in the subdivision acquires the right to use the roads and alleys shown on the plat, even though these easements aren't mentioned in the deed.

b. Easement By Implication

An *EASEMENT BY IMPLICATION (or implied easement) is not written down in a deed or other document.* As a general rule, an easement by implication (or implied easement) can only arise when a tract of land was originally held by one owner and then was divided into two or more parcels. At the time of the division, the use giving rise to the easement must have been going on for a long time, and it must be apparent from a visual inspection of the property. The use must also be reasonably necessary for the enjoyment of the dominant tenement.

Case Example: Ms. Fischer owned lots 18 and 19 in a Los Angeles subdivision. The back yard of lot 18 sloped so that surface water flowed down onto lot 19. Fischer installed a drain on the boundary between the two lots.

Several years later, Fischer sold lot 18 to the Hendlers, but retained lot 19 herself. For more than two years after the sale, she continued to allow water to flow from lot 18 into the drain on the boundary. Then she closed off the drain. ▼

With the drain closed, the Hendlers' yard and four-car garage were repeatedly flooded. They sued Fischer to establish their right to use the drain. The court ruled that the Hendlers had an easement by implication. Lot 18's use of the drain was well established and obvious at the time of the sale, and the drain was reasonably necessary for the enjoyment of the property. *Fischer v. Hendler*, 49 Cal. App. 2d 319 (1942).

California courts distinguish easement by necessity from implied easements. An *EASEMENT BY NECESSITY is created when: 1) there is a strict necessity for the right-of-way as when the claimant's property is landlocked and 2) the dominant and servient tenements were under the same ownership at the time of the conveyance giving rise to the necessity.*

Note from the Case Example below that for an easement by necessity, the claimant does not have to prove that the use was long established and obvious at the time of the sale. But the claimant must prove that the easement is strictly necessary (not just reasonably necessary) for the use of the property. The easement continues only as long as the necessity.

Case Example: Dr. Clark owned two parcels of property. He sold one to the Sparlings. This left the other parcel landlocked, with no access to a public road.

Although nothing was said about an easement at the time of the sale, a court ruled that Dr. Clark acquired an easement by necessity across the Sparlings' parcel for access to and from his parcel. Otherwise his parcel would have been useless. *Roemer v. Pappas*, 249 Cal. Rptr. 743 (1988).

c. Easement by Estoppel

The term *ESTOPPEL refers to a legal doctrine that prevents a person from asserting rights or making claims that are contrary to his or her previous acts or conduct.*

Easements may be created by estoppel if the seller of land actually or constructively makes representations about the existence of an easement appurtenant upon which the buyer relied. An easement by estoppel is an equitable remedy. It recognizes that when a landowner induces another to change position in reliance upon his/her promise, he/she is estopped from then denying the existence of the rights simply because they did not meet the conveyance rule formalities.

Example: B owns and lives on several acres of land out in the country. Her house is connected to a large septic tank capable of serving several houses. B divides her property and sells half to C. No mention is made of the septic tank at the time of the sale.

C builds a house on his property. B watches but makes no objection when C hooks up his plumbing to the septic tank on her property.

An easement has been created by estoppel. Because of her failure to object, B cannot later claim that C has no right to use the septic tank.

d. Easement by Prescription

An *EASEMENT BY PRESCRIPTION (also called a prescriptive easement) is created when someone makes long and continuous use of another's property without the permission of the owner.*

Case Example: The plaintiffs purchased property in Fortuna in June 2000. The only access to public roads over their property is a one half mile long steep driveway the use of which stopped 20 years before. Current access to the property is a paved private road, known as the Texaco Road, that crosses the adjoining property owned by the defendants. The defendants moved onto the property in 1999. The Texaco Road was built in 1982, has been maintained by Texaco and resulted from a 1934 lease which provided the right for Texaco to gain access to prospect for and maintained wells on adjacent properties. Since the Texaco Road is easy access to public roads the previous occupants of the plaintiff's property used it for nearly 20 years without complaint. Shortly after the plaintiffs began using the road the defendants sought to the stop access. In 1990 and 1993 Texaco posted "permission to pass" signs authorized by Civil Code section 1008. Defendants posted a property in1999. When the property that the plaintiffs purchased went on the market, the defendants notified the sellers they were revoking permission to use the Texaco Road.

When the plaintiffs were shown the property they were aware of the road dispute and used the old driveway for access. The plaintiffs sued the defendants for, in essence, an easement by prescription on the Texaco Road. The trial court decided the case for plaintiffs and the defendants appealed.

A requirement for a prescriptive easement is that the use of the property has been open, notorious, continuous and adverse for an uninterrupted five years. Adverse means that the property was used without permission of the owner. The plaintiff's seller purchased the property in 1989 and used the Texaco Road never requesting permission from anyone for at least five years from 1990 to 1995. Therefore, the sellers obtained an easement by prescription, which can be transferred to the plaintiffs, unless the posting of the signs by Texaco gave legal permission to use the road.

The Civil Code section 1008 provides that a person cannot acquire a prescriptive easement if the "owner" posts the required signs. In this case, Texaco is not the owner of the land and therefore was unable to give permission and the signs were of no effect. The posting by the defendants was too late. Judgment affirmed. *Aaron v. Dunham*, 137 Cal. App. 4th 1244; 41 Cal. Rptr. 3d 32 (2006).

For a prescriptive easement to develop, use of the other person's land must be **OPEN and NOTORIOUS**, *meaning that the use must be obvious and unconcealed so that if the landowner keeps reasonably well informed about the property, he or she will be aware of the use.*

The use must also be **HOSTILE or ADVERSE**, *Meaning it is without the permission of the owner and against the owner's interests.* An owner may acquiesce to the use, but may not give permission. In other words, the owner is aware of the use and does not object, but also doesn't say that it's okay. If the owner gives permission, a license has been granted (see the discussion of licenses below), and a prescriptive easement can't develop.

In California, the use must be **continuous** and **uninterrupted** for five years. To be considered continuous, the use doesn't have to be constant, but only a regular use that is normal for the type of property in question.

Example: R and G both own summer cottages on a cliff above a beach. Steps cut into the cliff on R's property lead down to the beach. Every summer for the last eight years, G has used these steps to get to the beach. This is a continuous use even though G never uses the steps in winter time.

A continuous and uninterrupted use does not necessarily mean a use by only one person.

Example: Drummond and Saragossa own adjoining property. For two years, Drummond drives across a corner of Saragossa's property without Saragossa's permission. Drummond then sells his property to Digby. For another two years Digby drives across the same corner. Then Digby sells to Dillinger. Dillinger drives across Saragossa's property for another year.

Dillinger may be able to claim a prescriptive easement. *The time periods in which Drummond, Digby, and Dillinger drove across the property can be added together to make up the required five years. This is called TACKING.*

In California, a landowner can prevent anyone from acquiring an easement by prescription, either by posting signs on the property or recording a notice. If a recorded notice is used instead of signs, a copy of the notice must be sent by registered mail to the person who is using the property. The signs or notice must state (in language specified in the Civil Code) that use of the property is by permission and subject to the control of the owner. Since use is by permission, it can't be hostile or adverse. As a result, no prescriptive easement can develop against the property. The owner can later revoke permission and prevent the use.

Note that a prescriptive easement can never be acquired against government property or against property owned by a public utility.

RECORDED NOTICE is the right of the public or any person to make any use whatsoever of the described land or any portion thereof (other than any use expressly allowed by a written or recorded map, agreement, deed, or dedication) is by permission and subject to control of the owner (Section 813 of the Civil Code).

POSTED NOTICE is the right to pass by permission and subject to control of the owner (Section 1008 of the Civil Code).

3. Termination of Easements

There are several ways in which easements may be terminated or cease to exist. These roughly correspond to the ways in which easements are created.

1. Express termination
2. Implied termination:
   – through merger,
   – by abandonment,
   – when the necessity ends,
   – when the purpose of the easement fails, or
   – upon destruction of the servient tenement
3. Termination by estoppel
4. Termination by prescription

a. Express Termination

Most easements are granted for an indefinite period. If the grant of the easement specifies a limited term, the easement expires automatically at the end of that period. An easement may be granted for life. This type of easement automatically terminates upon the death of the person who was the measuring life.

Even when an easement is originally granted for an indefinite period, the parties (or subsequent owners of the dominant and servient tenements) may later agree to terminate it. The easement holder must then execute a written release, giving up his or her interest in the servient property.

Another way that an easement can be expressly terminated is by condemnation. That's when the state takes private property for a public use (see Chapter 10). If the state condemns either the dominant or the servient property, the easement will be terminated. The easement holder is entitled to compensation for the value of the easement.

Example: A has an easement to maintain a billboard on B's land. The state condemns B's property in order to build a new highway across it. The state has to compensate B for the value of his property, and must also compensate A for loss of the value of his easement.

b. Implied Termination

An easement may be terminated without any express agreement, either by actions of the parties or by circumstances beyond their control.

Merger or unity of title. When one person becomes the owner of both the dominant tenement and the servient tenement, the easement is extinguished by merger. You can't have an easement in your own property, since an easement is defined as an interest in another's land.

Necessity ends. If an easement was created by necessity, it terminates automatically when it is no longer necessary.

Abandonment. An easement ceases to exist if the easement holder abandons it. Failure to use the easement is not, by itself, abandonment; there usually must be an act or statement that clearly expresses an intent to abandon it.

California law presumes an easement has been abandoned and terminates the easement holder's rights when, during the last 20 years:

1. the easement has not been used at any time;
2. no separate property tax was made for the easement or, if so, none was paid, and
3. no instrument creating, reserving, transferring or otherwise evidencing the easement is recorded.

The easement holder can prevent that by recording a notice of intent to preserve the easement, or any other document indicating the existence of the easement (a deed transferring the dominant tenement and the easement, for example). The recording will protect the easement rights for another 20 years.

There is a special rule for easements created by prescription: a court may rule that a prescriptive easement has been abandoned after only five years of nonuse.

Failure of purpose. If an easement has been created for a particular purpose, it terminates when the purpose ceases or has been fulfilled. For example, a railroad's easement for train tracks across a farmer's property would terminate if the railroad discontinued that line and removed the tracks.

Destruction of servient tenement. When an easement exists in a building rather than in the land, the accidental destruction of the building terminates the easement. It won't revive automatically if the building is rebuilt.

Just as easements can be created by estoppel or prescription, they may also be terminated by estoppel or prescription.

c. Estoppel

If the easement holder's conduct leads the servient property owner to assume that the easement holder doesn't intend to use the easement, and the property owner takes some action in reliance on this, the easement holder may be prevented from later trying to enforce the easement.

Example: D sold half of his property to S but reserved an easement for himself so he could walk across the corner of S's property to get to his mailbox. After several years, D put up a high wooden fence that blocked off the path to the mailbox.

S naturally assumed that D was no longer going to use the path, so she planted a large garden in that corner of the property, plowing up the path. D was aware of S's work and said nothing at that time. But a year later he took down the fence and told S he was going to use his easement again, even though he'd be stomping right through her vegetables.

By building the fence, D led S to believe that he didn't intend to use the easement anymore. S reasonably relied on his conduct when she planted the garden. D is now estopped from claiming the right to use the easement.

d. Prescription

Actions by the owner of the servient property that interfere with the easement could extinguish the easement by prescription. There must be an open, adverse, continuous, and uninterrupted interference with the easement for five years.

Example: Consider the example just above. Now suppose it was S (the owner of the servient property) who built the fence across the easement without D's consent. The fence has been in place blocking off the path for five years. D's easement has been terminated by prescription.

4. The Distinction Between Easements and Licenses

☆18 Like an easement, a *LICENSE grants permission to enter another's property for a specific purpose. A license does not create an interest in the property.*

There are several differences between easements and licenses. Easements are often for an indefinite period of time, but licenses are usually temporary. Easements are created by written agreement or through action of law (implication, estoppel, or prescription), while licenses may be created by oral agreement. Easements appurtenant run with the land, and easements in gross can be assigned, **but a license is a purely personal right**. A license can't be sold or transferred, and becomes invalid if the licensee dies.

Perhaps the most important distinction is that an easement can't be revoked whereas a license may be revoked at any time.

> **Example:** A owns a large pasture right next to the freeway. For $500, A agreed to allow Z to put up a billboard in one corner of the pasture. Z has a license to enter the pasture and put up the billboard.
> A never asked Z what the billboard was going to say. It turns out to be an ad for an X-rated movie theater, and A strongly disapproves. A tells Z to take the billboard down immediately. Z's license is revoked; he no longer has the right to enter the property. Of course, A has to return the money Z paid for the license.

In some cases, however, a license becomes irrevocable. This can happen by estoppel, when the licensee makes a substantial financial commitment in reliance on the license.

> **Case Example:** The Stewarts bought Lot 11 in a new subdivision in San Pedro. Lot 12 sloped down toward Lot 11, and the boundary between the two properties was at the bottom of the slope. To make their yard more private, the Stewarts wanted to build a wall at the top of the slope (on Lot 12) instead of at the bottom.
> Lot 12 was owned by Mr. Jett. The Stewarts asked Jett for an easement allowing them to build their wall at the top of the slope, and he agreed. He never got around to writing up a grant of easement, however.
> The Stewarts went ahead and built their wall at the top of the slope. Afterwards, Jett sold Lot 12 to the Noronhas. Eight months later, the Noronhas demanded that the Stewarts tear down their wall.
> The court held that although Jett had not fulfilled the requirements for creating an easement, he had granted the Stewarts a license. Because the Stewarts spent a considerable amount of money in reliance on the license, the Noronhas could not revoke it. *Noronha v. Stewart*, 199 Cal. App. 3d 485, 245 Cal. Rptr. 94 (1988).

B. LIENS (Financial Encumbrances)

A *LIEN is a financial interest in property. It is security for a debt, giving the creditor (the lienholder) the right to foreclose on the debtor's property if the debt is not paid.* The property is sold, and the lienholder collects the amount of the debt from the proceeds of the foreclosure sale.

A lienholder doesn't own or have a right to possess the property. Liens usually do not affect the use of the property, but they do affect the title.

The fact that there are liens against a property does not prevent its transfer or sale, but the transfer doesn't eliminate the liens. The new owner takes the property subject to the liens. It is extremely important for a buyer to know what liens are attached to the property before purchasing; otherwise, the buyer could end up forced to pay off the seller's debts to prevent foreclosure. In most real estate transactions, the seller is required to clear the title of liens before closing.

1. Voluntary Liens

VOLUNTARY LIENS are liens that a property owner chooses to have placed against his or her property, usually to obtain a loan. There are only two kinds of voluntary liens: mortgages and deeds of trust (trust deeds).

Example: A real property owner borrows money using the property as collateral. The owner voluntarily signs a trust deed, which gives the lender the right to foreclose if the money is not repaid.

2. Involuntary Liens

INVOLUNTARY LIENS (sometimes called statutory liens) arise through operation of law without the property owner's consent. Involuntary liens are created to protect those who have valid financial claims against the owner.

Example: When property taxes are assessed, a tax lien arises against the property. If the taxes aren't paid, the property can be sold to satisfy the lien.

Liens are also classified as either general or specific. A *GENERAL LIEN attaches to all of the debtor's property.* A judgment lien is an example of a general lien. Judgment liens attach to all property owned by the judgment debtor in the county, as noted below. A *SPECIFIC LIEN attaches only to a particular piece of property.* A trust deed is an example of a specific lien. It attaches only to the particular property offered as security for the loan. The most common types of liens against real estate are:

1. deeds of trust,
2. mortgages,
3. mechanics' liens,
4. judgment liens, and
5. tax liens.

a. Deeds of Trust and Mortgages

Deeds of trust and mortgages are discussed in detail in Chapter 12. For now, it's enough to know that both are voluntary, specific liens, most often used to secure a purchase money loan—a loan that enables the borrower to purchase the property the lien attaches to. *The parties to a mortgage are the MORTGAGOR (the borrower) and the MORTGAGEE (the lender). The parties to a trust deed are the TRUSTOR (the borrower), the BENEFICIARY (the lender), and the TRUSTEE (a neutral third party).* The chief differences between mortgages and trust deeds have to do with the procedures for foreclosure. In California, deeds of trust are far more common than mortgages.

b. Mechanic's Lien

When construction or improvement work is performed on real property, the property stands as security for the payment of the labor and materials costs. *A worker or a materials supplier who isn't paid may obtain an involuntary, specific lien against the property. This is called a MECHANIC'S LIEN.* It gives the worker or supplier the power to force the sale of the property to collect the debt owed.

Virtually everyone connected with a construction project is entitled to a mechanic's lien: a general contractor, an architect, a landscaper, a carpenter, a plumbing supply company, and so on. The *MECHANIC'S LIEN LAW divides claimants into four groups: original contractors, subcontractors, laborers, and materialmen.*

An *ORIGINAL CONTRACTOR is a licensed independent contractor who has a direct contract with the property owner (or other person who requested the work).* In many cases, the original contractor is a *GENERAL CONTRACTOR who has charge of the whole project and hires subcontractors.* In other cases, there is no general contractor; the owner hires an electrician, a carpenter, and others directly, and then each of those workers is regarded as an original contractor.

SUBCONTRACTORS are licensed independent contractors hired by an original contractor. LABORERS are employees who work for wages under the control of an original contractor, a subcontractor, or the owner. A MATERIALMAN is anyone who supplies construction materials or equipment for the project. Each of these groups is treated slightly differently under the mechanic's lien law.

Claiming a Lien. To claim a lien, subcontractors and materialmen are required to serve a **preliminary 20-day notice** on the property owner, their original contractor, and the construction lender. Original contractors only have to serve this notice on the construction lender, and laborers aren't required to prepare one at all. The notice warns that a lien may be claimed and provides an estimate of the cost. A copy of the notice should be filed at the county recorder's office, although it won't actually be recorded.

The preliminary notice is usually served within 20 days after the contractor or materialman begins working or supplying materials for the project. If the notice isn't sent until later, the mechanic's lien will not cover the work done or materials supplied more than 20 days before the notice was served. (The contractor or materialman is still entitled to be paid for that part of the job, but the bill for that part won't be secured by the lien.)

The next step is to have a **claim of lien** recorded. Most claims can be filed for record as soon as the claimant stops working on the project. An original contractor can't file a claim until he or she has completed the contract, however. As a general rule, no claims can be filed later than 90 days after all work (not just the individual claimant's work) on the project has stopped.

If a claim of lien isn't recorded within that 90-day period, the lien rights are lost. The claimant may still be able to sue the property owner for breach of contract, but that is a more uncertain and time-consuming process than foreclosing on a lien.

A property owner can shorten the period in which lien claims can be filed for a particular project, by recording a **notice of cessation** or a **notice of completion**. The owner can file a notice of cessation if for any reason work on the project has been stopped for at least 30 days. A notice of completion can only be recorded within 15 days after the project is completed. Once either kind of notice has been recorded, a subcontractor, laborer, or materialman has only 30 days in which to file his or her claim of lien, and an original contractor has 60 days. An owner that records a notice of completion or notice of cessation is required to give a copy of the notice, within 10 days of recording, to contractors and any other person who gave a preliminary notice to the owner.

Foreclosure. If the property owner doesn't pay, the claimant can foreclose on the lien by filing a lawsuit. The suit must be filed in superior court. The foreclosure suit ordinarily must be filed within 90 days after the claim of lien was recorded. Otherwise the lien is void.

Example: New plumbing is being installed in an apartment building. K is the materialman who supplied the new pipes. The last load of pipes was delivered on June 15. K still had not been paid by August 1, so he filed a claim of lien against the property.

On November 15, K filed a legal action to foreclose on his lien. The lawsuit was dismissed, however, because it had been more than 90 days since the claim of lien was recorded.

Case Example: BBIC Investors, (Investors) owned a warehouse in Oakland and leased space to 360 networks (USA) inc. (360). 360 retained Howard S. Wright Construction Co. (Wright) to do necessary construction work for the facility. Investors posted and recorded a notice of nonresponsibility at the premises. Wright began work in March but by May 360's project manager notified Wright to put the work on hold and do what was necessary to secure the site. Wright agreed to do the additional work for $194,950. On June 18, 360 advised Wright that they were not going to pay any more money. This was confirmed by a letter on June 19 from Wright which asked for assurances of payment from which there was no response. On June 19 Wright's laborers and tradesmen left the construction site. On June 20 Wright recorded its claim of mechanic's lien for $2,452,412. Wright's job diary indicated that it moved some ductwork on June 26 and a closeout inspection meeting took place that day. Litigation ensued regarding the validity of the mechanics lien which the trial court determined was invalid. Wright appealed.

The main issue involves Civil Code section 3115 which provides that a lien must be filed after the contractor has completed the contract. The trial court concluded that the lien recordation was premature because the work ceased on June 26. Wright maintains that a contractor also completes the contract when, by some event before full performance, it no longer has any further obligations under the contract and this occurred on June 19 when 360 unquestionably repudiated its contract obligations. Anticipatory repudiation of a contract ends the contractor's obligation and this occurred on June 19. Recording of the mechanics lien on the 20th was valid. Judgment reversed. *Wright v. BBIC Investors*, LLC; 136 Cal. App. 4th 228; 38 Cal. Rptr 3d 769 (2006).

Termination of a Mechanic's Lien. A properly recorded mechanic's lien is usually terminated by payment of the debt that the lien is based on. The owner should obtain and record a **release of lien** after paying the claimant. But what if an owner believes that a particular claim is invalid, and intends to contest it in court? The owner can obtain a release of lien by putting up a bond for one and a half times the amount of the claim.

When this release is recorded, the lien is removed from the title, even though the lawsuit over the claim hasn't been resolved yet.

c. Judgment Lien

Judgment liens were discussed briefly in Chapter 1. At the end of a civil lawsuit, if the judge or jury determines that one of the parties owes money to the other, a judgment is entered against the losing party. The winner (the **judgment creditor**) may claim a lien against the loser's (the **judgment debtor's**) real property.

To claim a lien, the judgment creditor must obtain an abstract of judgment from the court clerk and record it in the county where the debtor's real property is located. The lien attaches to all of the debtor's real property in that county. (There is an exception if the debtor has filed a declaration of homestead. See the discussion of the homestead law later in this chapter.) Thus, a judgment lien is an involuntary, general lien.

If the debtor owns property in other counties, the judgment creditor may file an abstract of judgment in the other counties, and the lien attaches to those additional properties. The judgment lien also attaches to any real property in those counties that the debtor acquires during the lien period.

Example: B owns two acres of land in Shasta County. B lost a lawsuit, and a judgment was entered against him. The judgment creditor filed an abstract of judgment with the Shasta County recorder, and a lien was attached to B's two-acre property. Three months later, B's father died, leaving B a five-acre property, which is also in Shasta County. The judgment lien also attaches to this newly acquired property.

Once a judgment lien is on the real property, the debtor must pay the judgment in order to free the property from the lien. Unless the lien is paid, a transferee acquires the property subject to the lien. If it is not paid, the judgment creditor can file suit to foreclose on the debtor's property.

In California, a judgment lien is only valid for ten years after the date the judgment was entered, unless the judgment is renewed. The judgment creditor can renew the judgment for another ten years by filing an application for renewal with the court. The application can be filed at any time before the judgment expires, as long as at least five years have passed since the last time the judgment was renewed. Notice of the renewal must be served on the debtor and the debtor has an opportunity to object at a hearing. To extend the lien on real property, a certified copy of the application for renewal must be recorded in the county where the abstract was recorded.

If a transferee purchased the property subject to the lien and recorded the transfer, a judgment creditor wanting to renew the lien must serve the transferee with a copy of the application for renewal and file proof of the service within 90 days after the filing of the application for renewal. A lien can be removed by recording a satisfaction of judgment or a release of judgment lien signed by the judgment creditor.

3. Property Taxes in California

The annual ad valorem taxes imposed on real property are called GENERAL PROPERTY TAXES. They're described as "general" to distinguish them from special assessments. That's

CHAPTER 3

slightly confusing, since a property tax lien is a specific lien, attaching only to the taxed property, not a general lien attaching to everything the taxpayer owns. (See Chapter 3.)

California's first general property tax law was enacted in 1850, right after it became a state. The property tax was originally the main source of revenue for both state and local governments. In 1910, the general property tax was abandoned as a source of revenue for the state government, but it has remained local government's primary source of support. There are currently over 6,000 government entities or agencies in California that levy (impose) property taxes, or for which property taxes are levied. These include counties, cities, school districts, irrigation districts, and other special-purpose taxing districts.

Under the state constitution, all property is subject to taxation unless it's specifically exempted. Property can be exempted from taxation by the state constitution itself, by a California statute, by the U.S. Constitution, or a federal law.

Taxpayers and local governments often get into disputes over whether the taxpayer has a taxable property interest. Once that's settled, they argue about whether that interest is taxable as real property or personal property. Many tax questions depend on that distinction. For example, under state law, banks are required to pay real property taxes, but not personal property taxes.

www.taxlawsb.com/resources/PptyTax.htm
Resources Pertaining to California Property Taxation

Case Example: The city classified computer components in a bank building as fixtures and taxed them as real property. The bank sued, claiming that the computers were personal property.

The city argued that the computers were an essential part of the building in question; structural changes had been made so the building could accommodate the computers and serve as the bank's data processing center. The bank argued that the computers were standard office equipment that had not been designed or modified for the building and were not permanently attached to it.

The trial court ruled in the city's favor, holding that the computer components were fixtures. The bank appealed, but the court of appeal affirmed the trial court's decision. The bank appealed again, and the state supreme court reversed the lower court's decision: the computers were not fixtures and therefore could not be taxed as real property. *Crocker National Bank v. City and County of San Francisco*, 49 Cal. 3d 881, 264 Cal. Rptr. 139 (1990).

---

a. Proposition 13 and Property Tax Assessment

Proposition 13 (the Jarvis-Gann Initiative) was approved by California voters in 1978, leading to amendment of the state constitution (Article XIIIA). The amendment completely revised both the method of assessing real property and the tax rates imposed. *ASSESSMENT is the process of determining the value of property for tax purposes.*

b. Assessment and Tax Rates

Before Proposition 13, property was generally assessed at 25% of its full value and property taxes were very high. In other words, the amount of tax to be paid was calculated by applying the tax rate to 25% of the property's value. Tax rates varied depending on the county and city where the property was located.

www.leginfo.ca.gov/.const/.article_13A
California State Constitution, Article 13 – Tax Limitation

Property is now assessed at its full **cash value**. That's more or less the same thing as market value. The California Revenue and Taxation Code defines full cash value as the purchase price of the property, unless it can be shown that the property would not have been sold at that price on the open market. As a general rule, the tax rate now may not exceed one percent of the full cash value.

The Effects of Proposition 13

✔ Tax rate limited to 1% of the assessed value
✔ Assessed Value = Full Cash Value
(unless ownership hasn't changed since March 1975)
✔ Property reassessed on change of ownership
✔ Assessed value can't be increased more than 2% per year
(unless there's a new owner or improvements)

---

c. Limits on Assessment

Proposition 13 specifies certain limits on assessment to protect homeowners, who stay in the same home, from drastic tax increases when their homes appreciate in value. If there hasn't been a change in ownership since March 1, 1975, the property's 1975 value is *the starting point for assessment—the **BASE VALUE***. As long as the same person owns the property and no improvements are made, the assessed value can't be increased more than 2% per year. If the owner improves the property (by building a deck, for example), the assessed value may be increased by the amount the improvements added to the actual value.

The assessment is increased to the current full cash value only if there's a new owner or, as noted above, increased assessed value attributable to new construction on the property. When the property is sold or otherwise transferred, the new owner must file a **change in ownership statement** with the county recorder or assessor within 45 days. Unless the transaction is exempt from reassessment on change in ownership, the assessed value may be stepped up to the price paid or to the fair market value at the time of the transfer. That becomes the new base value.

To alleviate the harsh consequences of increased assessments following transfers of title when the property hasn't been sold or traded for profit, the law exempts several types of transfers from reassessment. These include:

1. transfers where the method of holding title is changed but the ownership isn't.
2. adding a joint tenant to a joint tenancy.
3. most transfers between parents and children, grandparents and grandchildren.
4. transfers between spouses to create or terminate community property or joint tenancy interests.

Propositions 60 and 90. California voters approved Proposition 60 in 1987. Under Proposition 60, when a senior citizen (over 55) sells his or her home and replaces it with another home in the same county, the assessed value of the old home can be used as the assessed value of the new home. The market value of the new home must be equal to or less than the market value of the old home, and the new home must be purchased within two years after the sale of the old one.

Example: M is 60 years old. She has lived in the same home in San Jose since the early 1970s. Because of Proposition 13, the assessed value of her home is only $85,000, even though it's now worth about $150,000. Her property taxes are around $850 per year.

M would like to move to a smaller home in a quieter place. She finds a condominium in a suburb that she likes; like San Jose, it's in Santa Clara County. So M sells her old home and buys a condo unit for $135,000.

Before Proposition 60, M's condo would have been assessed at its full cash value ($135,000). That would have made her property taxes about $1,350 per year. But because of Proposition 60, she can transfer the low assessed value of her old home ($85,000) to her condo, and save about $500 per year on her property taxes.

In 1988, the voters approved Proposition 90. It works the same way as Proposition 60, only it applies when a senior citizen buys a replacement home in a different county. The new law doesn't require all counties to allow senior citizens from other counties to keep their previous assessed value. However, many counties have decided to do so, to attract new residents. If M's new condo were in some other county besides Santa Clara County, she might or might not get to use her previous assessed value there.

The benefits of Propositions 60 and 90 were extended to severely and permanently disabled homeowners in 1990.

Proposition 193. Under Proposition 193 passed in 1996, a person who inherits property from a grandparent would receive the additional windfall of paying low property taxes based on the grandparent's old assessment.

Property Tax Exemptions. Although the general rule is that all property is taxed at full cash value, there are many total or partial exemptions. Property owned by the federal, state, and local governments is totally exempt from taxation; so is property used for religious, scientific, educational, charitable, or welfare purposes.

Of course, there's a lot of litigation over whether particular property qualifies for an exemption or not (see Case Example below).

There's a partial tax exemption for homeowners. The first $7,000 of the assessed value of an owner-occupied property is exempt from taxation. (In other words $7,000 is subtracted from the assessed value and only the remainder is taxed.) This exemption isn't automatic—the taxpayer has to apply for it. Once the exemption has been granted, it remains in effect until terminated; it isn't necessary to reapply each year.

Case Example: A church acquired property that had been used as a private tennis and swimming club. It included a building with meeting rooms, a sauna, a swimming pool, and five tennis courts. The church issued a statement of policy explaining that the facility was to be used for the nurture of persons within the church and to extend the gospel to other members of the community. ▼

> The church argued that the property should be exempt from taxation because the facilities were an important part of its evangelical mission. They also gave the church a way of serving the community.
>
> The court ruled against the church. Although the property didn't have to be used exclusively for religious purposes to qualify for the exemption, that had to be its primary use. That wasn't the case here. The recreational facilities were mostly used by dues-paying members of a "boosters" club. The pool and tennis courts had been used for religious purposes only three times: two baptisms and one dramatic presentation. It appeared to the court that the church was using the property in the same way the previous owner had, as a tennis and swimming club. *Peninsula Covenant Church v. City of San Mateo*, 94 Cal. App. 3d 383, 156 Cal. Rptr. 431 (1979).

Appealing an Assessment. A property owner who is dissatisfied with the assessment of his or her property may appeal to the county board of equalization. The county board of supervisors either appoints a board of equalization or plays that role itself. A board of equalization has the power to adjust the assessed value of property.

d. Calculating Property Taxes

The tax on a parcel of real estate is calculated by multiplying the tax rate by the assessed value. Because of Proposition 13, the tax rate is ordinarily close to 1%. The 1% limit may be exceeded to pay for a local government's bonded indebtedness, if the voters approved the bond issue before Proposition 13 was passed, or if the bond issue raised funds for the government's acquisition or improvement of real property.

Example: A single-family home has a market value of $500,000. Taking into account Proposition 13's limits on assessed value, the full cash value of the home is $480,000. The homeowner is entitled to a $7,000 exemption. The tax rate is 1.02% (including pre-1978 bonded indebtedness).

$480,000.00	Full cash value
-$7,000.00	Homeowner's exemption
$473,000.00	Taxable value

$473,000.00   x .0102 = $4,824.60 Annual property tax

e. The Levy and Collection Procedure

Property taxes are levied annually, on or before September 1 for each tax year. The tax year runs from July 1 through June 30 of the next calendar year. *Fiscal Year*

> The lien for the taxes attaches to the property on the previous January 1. The lien for the July 2020 – June 2021 tax year attached January 1, 2020. Since the taxes aren't actually levied until sometime later, the specific amount of the tax lien isn't known at the time the lien attaches.

Property tax liens have priority over all other liens except special assessment liens (discussed later in this chapter). Property tax liens have **parity** with special assessment liens—both types of liens have equal priority. A property tax lien continues for 30 years, or until the taxes are paid or the property is sold for delinquent taxes.

The county assessor completes and delivers the local tax roll to the county auditor on or before July 1. Before delivering the local roll to the county auditor, the assessor must notify each property owner of the value of the property as it will appear on the tax roll. The assessor is also required to give either individual or public notice of the time and place of the board of equalization hearings where the owner may appeal the assessment.

The county board of supervisors must fix the tax rates and levy county, school, and district taxes on or before September 1. Since the equalization process often isn't complete at that time, the taxes can be adjusted if there's a change in the valuation of property. After the taxes are levied, the county auditor computes them and enters them on the assessment roll. The roll is then delivered to the county tax collector for collection.

f. Payment of Taxes

NO DARN FOOLING AROUND

Property taxes may be paid in two installments. The first installment is due November 1 and is delinquent if not paid by 5:00 PM on December 10. The second installment is due February 1 and is delinquent if not paid by 5:00 PM on April 10. You can't pay the second installment until you've paid the first installment. A 10% penalty is added to any delinquent amount.

The tax collector has discretion to accept payment by electronic fund transfers. The board of supervisors can authorize payment by the use of credit card and add a fee to cover any costs related to the use of a credit card. Probably because of the nuisance of it, the tax collector can refuse payment of the tax in coins.

When property is reassessed because of a change in ownership, the new owner usually owes supplemental taxes, in addition to the taxes already billed for that year. This extra amount becomes due on the date the change of ownership occurs.

g. Enforcement of the Property Tax Laws

When property taxes aren't paid, the tax collector forecloses on the tax liens against the property. First a notice of impending default is published, then there's a five-year redemption period, and finally the property is sold to satisfy the taxes.

Property Tax Year: July 1 - June 30

Lien attaches	previous January 1
Tax rate determined	by September 1
Tax bill mailed	by November 1
First installment due	November 1
First installment delinquent	December 10
Second installment due	February 1
Second installment delinquent	April 10

---

h. Default

On or before June 8, the tax collector publishes a list of properties for which the property taxes are delinquent. The notice states that these properties will be in default if the taxes aren't paid by 5:00 PM on June 30. The notice also lists the amount due, and warns that the property may be sold to satisfy the tax lien if the taxes, penalties, and fees aren't paid.

On July 1 at 12:01 AM, all properties for which the taxes have not been paid are in default by operation of law. On or before September 8, the tax collector publishes a list of the properties for which taxes were not paid by the deadline. These are referred to as **tax defaulted properties**.

 www.boe.ca.gov/proptaxes/assessors.htm
Listing of County Assessors – State Board of Equalization

i. Redemption

Tax defaulted property may be redeemed by paying:

1. the amount of delinquent taxes,
2. the delinquency penalty and costs (a 10% delinquency penalty, and costs associated with publishing the notices),
3. the redemption penalty, and
4. the redemption fee.

Redemption fees and penalties vary depending on when the default occurred. The redemption penalty is 1.5% of the delinquent taxes for each month since the default occurred. The redemption fee covers the administrative costs of redemption; it's generally quite low (usually $15).

The total amount necessary for redemption may be paid in a lump sum or in installments. To redeem under an installment plan, the property owner must make the payments on time. Otherwise the property again becomes subject to the power of sale.

j. Tax Sale

If residential property isn't redeemed within five years after it becomes tax defaulted, it may be sold to pay the delinquent taxes, fees, and penalties. Nonresidential property can be sold for unpaid taxes after three years. *On or before June 8, the tax collector publishes a list of the properties which have been tax defaulted for five years and will be subject to sale after June 30. This is called a* **NOTICE OF POWER AND INTENT TO SELL**. The notice is also sent by registered mail to the property owner (or other taxpayer) at his or her last known address.

If the property isn't redeemed (either by full payment or by starting an installment plan) by June 30 five years after default, the property is subject to sale. The tax collector is supposed to make a good faith effort to sell the property within two years after it becomes subject to sale. If no acceptable bids are received at the attempted sale, the tax collector may discontinue the sale and try to sell the property again later on. The tax collector is required to attempt to sell the property at least once every four years until it's sold. Nonresidential property can be sold for unpaid taxes after three years.

At least 45 days (but not more than 60 days) before the sale, the tax collector must send a **notice of sale** by registered mail to the owner (or other taxpayer) and other persons having an interest in the property. The notice shows, among other things, the time and date set for the proposed sale and the minimum acceptable bid. If the property is the owner's residence, the tax collector must make a reasonable effort to contact the owner personally not less than 10 days (but not more than 60 days) prior to the sale date. Up to $100 can be added to the redemption amount to cover personal contact costs. The minimum bid is the amount that covers the delinquent taxes and penalties and the costs of advertising the sale.

The notice of sale must also be published in a newspaper, distributed in the county or judicial district, at least once a week for the three weeks preceding the sale. (If there isn't a newspaper, the notice has to be posted in three public places in the county or district.) If authorized by the county board of supervisors, the tax collector may advertise the sale by other means.

Tax sales are generally made to the highest bidder at public auction. (There are a few exceptions where the statute requires a sealed bid procedure.) The sale purchaser is given a **tax deed**.

Sometimes tax-defaulted property can be sold to a government agency or nonprofit organization rather than at public auction. The agency or organization must file an objection to the sale of the property. A government agency has to claim that a portion of property is needed for public use. A nonprofit organization has to agree to rehabilitate residential property and sell it to low-income persons, or to dedicate vacant land for public use.

Sale of the property terminates the right of redemption. If the sale proceeds exceed the amount needed to pay all delinquent taxes, penalties, fees, and costs of sale, the surplus is used to pay any remaining assessments or taxes. Any remaining funds may be claimed by the former owner, or anyone else having an interest in the property, within one year after the recording of the tax deed.

k. Sale Without Actual Notice

What if the owner never actually receives notice of the default or the sale? Is the tax sale still valid? As a general rule, yes. A number of California court decisions have held that the method of notice prescribed by the tax code (by registered mail to the last known owner, and publication in a newspaper or posting in a public place) is legally sufficient notice. A property owner is expected to know that the property taxes are due every year. If the owner hasn't been paying the taxes, he or she should know that they are delinquent and that the property may be lost. However, as the following case shows, the general rule doesn't always apply.

l. Tax Deeds

A tax deed conveys title to the purchaser free of almost all encumbrances that existed before the foreclosure sale. There are a few specific exceptions: certain tax and special assessment liens and easements, water rights, and restrictions of record. Aside from those, even liens or interests that were acquired or recorded before the tax lien are extinguished. As a result, a tax sale purchaser may receive better title than an ordinary buyer, who takes title subject to any earlier recorded liens or deeds.

Notice that in this respect, tax foreclosure differs from mortgage or deed of trust foreclosure. Those foreclosures eliminate only liens, encumbrances, and interests that were recorded after the lien being foreclosed. They have no effect on liens or interests recorded before the foreclosed lien.

m. Special Assessments

Special assessments are taxes used to pay for a public improvement in a particular neighborhood, such as the paving of a road or installation of sewer lines. The property owners that benefit from the improvement are required to pay their share of its cost. A special assessment creates an involuntary, specific lien against those owners' properties.

Case Example: Mr. and Mrs. Banas bought a home that happened to have been built partly on one lot and partly on another. Their deed only described one of the lots.

After moving in, the Banases received and paid tax bills for their residence and the one lot described in their deed. The tax bills for the other lot were apparently sent to the former owners, who never paid them. Accordingly, that lot was eventually sold for tax delinquency.

The Banases first learned of the problem after the tax sale, when the lot had already been transferred by tax deed. They sued to have the tax sale invalidated and the tax deed set aside, claiming that their property had been taken without due process of law.

The Banases argued that the notice procedures prescribed by law weren't adequate to give them notice that the taxes were delinquent. Since they received and paid a tax bill every year, they had no reason to suspect that the taxes weren't being paid on part of the land underneath their house.

The court agreed. An effective method of notification was available to the tax collector at reasonable cost: posting a notice at the property itself. Posting at the property would serve to give notice to owners who were in possession but who were not the legal owners of record. *Banas v. Transamerica Title Ins. Co.*, 133 Cal. App. 3d 845, 184 Cal. Rptr. 262 (1982).

---

n. Income Tax Liens

If state or federal income taxes aren't paid, another type of tax lien arises. Income tax liens are involuntary and general. A claim of lien is recorded, attaching to all of the taxpayer's personal and real property.

o. State Tax Lien Law

The state tax lien law provides that any state tax liabilities create a general lien against all real property owned by the taxpayer and located in California. In other words, the lien attaches to property other than the property subject to the tax. For example, if someone fails to pay sales tax on the sale of personal property, that tax liability can create a state tax lien on that person's home.

A state tax lien doesn't have the same priority as a property tax lien. A property tax lien is senior to all other liens; but a state tax lien is junior to the interest of:

1. a subsequent purchaser without notice of the state tax lien,
2. a mortgage or trust deed lender,
3. a mechanic's lienholder, or
4. a judgment lien creditor.

In each case, the interest must have been recorded before the state tax lien was recorded.

CHAPTER 3

4. Lien Priority

It's not at all unusual for a piece of property to have several liens against it at the same time. It may be subject to a trust deed, a mechanic's lien, and a property tax lien, for example. Sometimes, the total amount of the liens is more than the property will bring at a forced sale. Then not all of the liens can be paid in full. It is therefore necessary to establish an order of priority for paying off the liens after foreclosure.

Liens				
	Voluntary	**Involuntary**	**General**	**Specific**
IRS Lien		X	X	
Property Tax Lien		X		X
Special Assessment		X		X
Deed of Trust	X			X
Judgment Lien		X	X	
Mechanic's Lien		X		X
2nd Trust Deed	X			X

As a general rule, liens are given priority according to the order in which they attached to the property. For most liens, the attachment date is the date the lien was recorded. In other words, the lien recorded first has first priority for payment.

There are important exceptions to this rule, however. Property tax liens and special assessment liens are superior to all other liens against the property. Thus, these liens have priority even over liens that attached before they did.

The priority of a mechanic's lien is determined by the date work first started on the project, rather than the date the lien was recorded. All mechanics' liens from the same project have the same priority, regardless of when the individual mechanic or materialman performed his or her work or recorded a claim of lien. If the proceeds from the foreclosure sale aren't enough to cover all the mechanics' liens, the mechanics' lienholders receive prorated shares of the money.

You've seen that once an abstract of judgment is recorded, the judgment lien automatically attaches to any real property the debtor later acquires. If the judgment debtor took out a loan to buy the new property, the purchase money trust deed has priority over the judgment lien.

Example: D loses a lawsuit and a judgment is entered against her. The judgment creditor records an abstract of judgment to create a lien.

A year later, D buys a house. She borrows the money for the purchase and gives the lender a trust deed on the house. The trust deed is recorded on the same day D takes title to the property.

Technically, the judgment lien attached to the house at the instant D took title, but because the trust deed is for a purchase money loan, that lien has priority over the judgment lien.

Here's an example that shows how the different rules for lien priority work out after a foreclosure sale.

Example: Q's property has the following liens against it: a judgment lien that attached when Q took title on October 1; a purchase money deed of trust that was recorded October 1; a second deed of trust (not for a purchase money loan) that was recorded November 12; a mechanic's lien filed January 10 (but work on the project started on October 15); a mechanic's lien filed January 14 (from the same project); and a property tax lien that attached January 1.

If Q's property is sold at a foreclosure sale, the liens will be paid out of the sale proceeds in the following order: the property tax lien, the purchase money deed of trust, the judgment lien, both mechanics' liens (prorated shares, if necessary), and the second deed of trust.

If the sale only brings enough to pay the property tax lien, the other lienholders will receive nothing. If there's only enough to pay the tax lien and part of the trust deed, the rest will receive nothing.

5. The Homestead Law

Homestead laws give owner-occupied homes limited protection from foreclosure. California's homestead law protects only against judgment lien foreclosures, giving no protection against foreclosure of a mortgage, deed of trust, tax lien, or mechanic's lien. It also doesn't protect against foreclosure of a judgment lien when the judgment is for delinquent spousal or child support payments.

A *HOMESTEAD is the dwelling of the property owner or the owner's spouse, together with its land and outbuildings.* It can be a single-family home, a condo unit, or any other building, as long as the owner, or his or her spouse, lives there. The homestead law establishes an exemption, an amount of money that is exempt from judgment creditors' claims. The basic exemption is $75,000. The exemption is $100,000 if a family lives in the homestead and at least one member of the family owns no interest in it or only a community property interest in it.

Examples: The judgment debtor is a single parent, living in the homestead with one child. Since the child doesn't own any interest in the property, the exemption is $100,000.

Suppose the judgment debtor is married and childless, and the homestead is community property. Again, the exemption is $100,000.

Now suppose the debtor and his brother own the homestead and live there by themselves. The debtor's exemption amount is only $75,000. (The brother has a separate $75,000 exemption for claims against his interest.)

The exemption is $175,000 if the debtor (or the debtor's spouse) is 65 or older, or unable to work because of a disability, or 55 or older with an income of not more than $15,000 (if unmarried) or $20,000 (if married).

There are two types of homestead exemptions in California: a declared homestead exemption and an automatic homestead exemption. A *DECLARED HOMESTEAD*

EXEMPTION is established by recording a declaration of homestead. The owner or his or her spouse must be living on the property when the declaration is recorded.

Once a declaration of homestead has been recorded, if a judgment creditor later records an abstract of judgment, the lien does not attach to the debtor's entire interest in the homestead property, as it otherwise would. Instead, the judgment lien only attaches if the value of the homestead is greater than the amount of all existing liens against it plus the amount of the homestead exemption. The amount by which the value exceeds the liens and the exemption is called the surplus of equity, and the creditor's judgment lien can attach only to that surplus. If there is no surplus—if the value of the homestead does not exceed the amount of the liens and the exemption—then the judgment lien cannot attach.

Example: Currier records a declaration of homestead, and she's entitled to a $100,000 family exemption. The property is worth $365,000, but there's a deed of trust against the title and Currier still owes $302,000 on it.

Currier loses a lawsuit and a judgment is entered against her. The judgment creditor records an abstract of judgment. But the judgment lien won't attach to Currier's homestead because there isn't a surplus of equity: the amount of the deed of trust plus the exemption is more than the value of the homestead.

$302,000 (deed of trust)
+100,000 (exemption)
$402,000 (which is greater than $365,000, the property value)

Of course, a judgment lien will attach to a judgment debtor's home if no declaration of homestead has been filed. *Yet even in that case, the debtor can claim a homestead exemption in court during a proceeding to foreclose the judgment lien. This is the **AUTOMATIC HOMESTEAD EXEMPTION**, sometimes called the dwelling house exemption.*

Whether the debtor relies on the automatic exemption or on a declaration of homestead, the property cannot be sold unless there is a surplus of equity. The amount bid for the homestead at the foreclosure sale must be greater than the amount of all existing liens against the property (including the judgment lien) plus the amount of the homestead exemption. As a general rule, the sale bid must also be for at least 90% of the property's fair market value.

When a homestead is foreclosed, the sale proceeds are applied in the following order: first, to pay all liens not subject to the homestead exemption; second, to the homestead claimant for the exemption amount ($75,000, $100,000, or $175,000); third, to pay the costs of the sale; fourth, to pay the judgment creditor's court costs; fifth, to the judgment creditor to satisfy the debt. If there is any money left over, if goes to the homestead claimant.

After foreclosure, whatever money the claimant received as a result of the exemption (up to $75,000, $100,000, or $175,000) is still exempt for six months. This gives the claimant a chance to reinvest that money in another homestead.

One of the advantages of a declared homestead (compared to the automatic homestead exemption) is that the same six-month protection period applies to the proceeds of a voluntary sale. If the claimant sells the homestead, the exemption amount is protected from creditors for six months after closing. Another advantage is that the protection of a declared homestead continues even when the owners have stopped living on the property, as long as they don't record a declaration of homestead for some other property.

Example: Suppose after Currier recorded her declaration of homestead, she and her children moved to another city where she rented an apartment. In the meantime, she leased her homestead property to someone else. The homestead is still protected against Currier's creditors. It would not be if Currier was relying on the automatic homestead exemption. The automatic exemption can only be claimed by an owner who is living on the homestead when the judgment lien attaches.

A declaration of homestead terminates if the homestead claimant sells the property, records a declaration of abandonment, or records a declaration of homestead for another property. The declaration does not terminate if the claimant dies, however. It continues for the benefit of family members still living on the property.

III. CHAPTER SUMMARY

1. An estate is an interest in property that is, will, or may become possessory. There are freehold estates and leasehold estates.

2. The highest estate is the fee simple absolute, which is of unlimited duration. The duration of a fee simple defeasible estate is also unlimited, except that title may revert to the grantor if certain events occur.

3. The duration of a life estate is measured by someone's lifetime. The measuring life is usually the life tenant's, but it may be someone else's (a life estate "pur autre vie"). During a life estate, the grantor holds an estate in reversion, or else a remainderman holds an estate in remainder. These estates are called future interests.

4. There are four types of leasehold estates: the tenancy for a fixed term (estate for years), the periodic tenancy (estate from period-to-period), tenancy at will (estate at will), and tenancy at sufferance (estate at sufferance).

A leasehold tenant has a temporary possessory interest in the property, but does not hold title.

5. Easements and liens are nonpossessory interests, also called encumbrances. An easement is the right to use another's property for a particular purpose. Easements are either appurtenant or in gross. They can be created or terminated expressly, by implication, by estoppel, or by prescription.

6. Local governments levy ad valorem property taxes, taxing the value of real property. Proposition 13 limits the tax rate to 1% of the property's full cash value. Assessed value can't be increased more than 2% per year, unless there's a change in ownership or improvements.

7. The property tax year runs from July 1 through June 30. A property tax lien attaches on January 1, before the tax year begins. If the current year's property taxes haven't been paid by June 30, the property is tax defaulted. Tax defaulted property may be redeemed within five years. After five years, the property may be sold. Nonresidential property can be sold for unpaid taxes after three years.

8. The purchaser at a tax sale is given a tax deed. The tax deed conveys title free of all prior encumbrances and interests, except for some tax liens and special assessment liens, and easements, water rights, and restrictions of record.

9. Unpaid state taxes (sales taxes, use taxes, state income taxes, etc.) create a state tax lien against all of the taxpayer's real property in California.

10. A lien is a financial encumbrance. A lien gives a creditor the right to foreclose on the property and have the debt paid out of the sale proceeds. A lien is either specific or general, and either voluntary or involuntary. The most common liens are trust deeds, mechanics' liens, judgment liens, and tax liens. The homestead exemption gives a homeowner protection against judgment lien foreclosure.

IV. CASE PROBLEM

Masin v. La Marche, 136 Cal. App. 3d 687, 186 Cal. Rptr. 619 (1982)

The Thomases owned a large tract of land in Montecito. They subdivided it, and in 1971 sold some one-acre parcels, retaining 34 acres themselves. In the deeds to the one-acre parcels, the Thomases reserved an easement to provide access to their 34 acres. The deeds were recorded. This included the deed to parcel C, which they sold to Mr. La Marche.

La Marche moved onto parcel C. In 1972, he stretched a heavy rope attached to two poles across the access easement where it entered the dominant tenement (the 34-acre tract). He hung up a sign forbidding use of the easement road, but the sign disappeared after one week. Later, he erected a barrier made of a four-by-four and some two-by-fours in the middle of the road. La Marche took that barrier down in 1973, and began using the road as a storage area. From 1973 to 1979, he stored the walls of a dismantled cabin there; from 1975 to 1977, he stored a 20-foot trailer there.

Meanwhile, the Thomases sold the 34-acre dominant tenement, and after that the property changed hands a number of times. The access easement was not mentioned in any of these deeds. In 1978, the Masins purchased the 34 acres. Again, the deed did not refer to the easement.

There were other access routes onto the 34-acre property besides the easement across La Marche's lot. None of the people who owned the 34 acres before the Masins attempted to use the easement. The Masins, however, thought that the easement would be more convenient than the other routes. In 1979, they asked La Marche to move the cabin walls and other things that were blocking the easement road. He refused, and the Masins sued to establish their right to use the easement. Did the Masins have that right? Why or why not?

V. KEY TERMS

abandonment
absolute/defeasible
ad valorem
assessment
base value
board of equalization
condition subsequent
deed of trust
dominant tenement
dominant tenant
easement appurtenant
easement in gross
easement by necessity
encumbrance
estate
estoppel
exemption
fee simple
freehold/leasehold
full cash value
future interest

general property taxes
homestead
implied easement
judgment lien
levy
license
lien priority
lien
life estate pur autre vie
life estate
life tenant
measuring life
mechanic's lien
merger
mortgage
mortgagor/mortgagee
periodic tenancy
possessory/nonpossessory
power of termination
prescriptive easement
Proposition 60

Proposition 90
Proposition 13
purchase money loan
remainder/reversion
remainderman
reservation/grant
runs with the land
servient tenement
servient tenant
special assessment
surrender
tacking
tax lien
tenancy at will
tenant at sufferance
term tenancy (estate for years)
trust
trustor/beneficiary/trustee
waste

VI. CHAPTER QUIZ

1. A grant deed contains a condition regarding the use of the property which if broken returns the title to the previous owner or heirs. The condition has been broken and the previous owner must exercise the power of termination within what period of time?

    a. Five years from the date the deed was recorded
    b. Five years from the date the condition was broken
    c. Before the previous owner dies
    d. There is no time limitation

2. If a life estate is based on the lifetime of someone other than the life tenant, it is called :

    a. a life estate in remainder.
    b. a life estate pur autre vie.
    c. a fee simple absolute.
    d. none of the above are correct answers.

3. A life tenant:

    a. owes no duty to the property being occupied.
    b. may not use or abuse the property in any way that would permanently damage it.
    c. may not use or abuse the property in any way that we reduce its market value.
    d. answers b and c are correct.

4. Carlos is kicked out of the house by his wife. Lawrence, who is very understanding, tells Carlos that he can move into Lawrence's empty vacation cabin. Carlos and Lawrence had no discussion regarding whether Lawrence was to pay rent. This is called a(n):

    a. tenancy at will.
    b. periodic tenancy.
    c. tenancy at sufferance.
    d. estate for days.

5. An easement that burdens one piece of land for the benefit of another piece of land is called a(n):

    a. servient easement.
    b. easement appurtenant.
    c. easement in gross.
    d. pur autre vie.

6. Regarding real property taxes, with no change in ownership or new construction, the assessed value cannot be increased by more than what percent per year?

    a. 1
    b. 2
    c. 2.5
    d. 10

7. Regarding real property taxes, the basic tax rate is limited to what percent of the assessed value?

    a. 1
    b. 2
    c. 5
    d. 10

8. A person who acquires title by tax deed purchases the property:

    a. subject to all liens or interest that existed before the tax lien.
    b. and must wait two years to see if the delinquent owner chooses to redeem the property.
    c. free from most liens or interests that were recorded before the tax lien.
    d. must wait five years before recording the tax deed.

9. A single person 65 years of age or older owning and occupying a resident as a homestead exemption of:

    a. $20,000.
    b. $50,000.
    c. $75,000.
    d. $150,000.

10. If a property owner chooses to redeem the property by paying delinquent property taxes before June 30 of that tax year; the delinquent penalty is:

    a. $150.
    b. $500.
    c. 1.5%.
    d. 10%.

ANSWERS: 1. b; 2. b; 3. d; 4. a; 5. b; 6. b; 7. a; 8. c; 9. c; 10. d

CHAPTER 4
Co-Ownership of Real Property

CHAPTER OVERVIEW

Ownership of real property is frequently shared by more than one person. Two, ten, or two hundred people can be co-owners of the same piece of property at the same time (concurrently). This chapter explains the forms that concurrent ownership can take. The topic has three overlapping aspects. The first section of the chapter focuses on the various ways co-owners can hold title, such as tenancy in common. The second part of the chapter describes ownership by associations of two or more persons, such as partnerships. The third section looks briefly at condominiums and other properties specially developed for concurrent ownership.

I. Forms of Co-Ownership

ownership by one person

When property is owned by one individual, he or she holds title in **SEVERALTY** *(severalty coming from Latin word, meaning "separate," and used in the same manner as the word "sever").* In California, when property is owned by more than one individual, they can hold title in one of five ways:

1. tenancy in common,
2. joint tenancy,
3. community property,
4. community property with right of survivorship, or
5. tenancy in partnership.

Many prospective co-owners are unaware of these various forms of co-ownership, and wind up with one or another by accident. But the way title is held is very important. It determines how control of the property is shared. It can also have dramatic consequences when co-ownership ends, whether voluntarily or through dissolution or death. Co-owners need to understand these effects and make a deliberate choice.

A real estate agent should make sure that buyers realize the importance of the form of co-ownership. When an agent raises the subject, the buyers often ask for help in choosing how to take title. At that point, the agent must tell them to consult a lawyer. A well-intentioned agent

CHAPTER OUTLINE

who gives buyers friendly advice may end up charged with the unauthorized practice of law (see Chapter 6). Not only that, if buyers make the wrong choice based on the agent's advice, the agent could be liable for damages.

Even though real estate agents should avoid advising their customers about the forms of co-ownership, an agent needs a general understanding of the subject. Whenever a legal document is executed, the agent has to know whether only one co-owner may sign, or whether all the co-owners must sign. For the parties, it can mean the difference between an effective sale and a void transaction. For the agent, it can mean the difference between a commission and a lawsuit.

 www.investopedia.com/articles/mortgages-real-estate/08/title-ownership-property. asp#axzz2Jbmd5A6r
Options for Holding Title

A. TENANCY IN COMMON

TENANCY IN COMMON is the most basic form of concurrent ownership. It is the residual category: co-ownership that doesn't fit into any of the other three categories is a tenancy in common by default. If a deed transferring land to two unmarried individuals doesn't specify how they are taking title, they take title as tenants in common.

Co-owners who choose tenancy in common should make that clear in the deed, by adding "as tenants in common" after their names. If they own unequal shares in the property, that should be stated in the deed.

Example: When B and C bought A's tract of land, they decided to take title as tenants in common. B came up with two-thirds of the purchase price, and C contributed one-third. Their deed reads: "B, a single woman, with an undivided 2/3 interest, and C, a single woman, with an undivided 1/3 interest, as tenants in common."

When a deed does not state each co-tenant's fraction of interest, the law presumes that the interests are equal. In a lawsuit, a tenant in common can overcome that legal presumption by submitting evidence that the parties do not own equal interest, such as the contributions to the purchase price were unequal.

Example: B paid two-thirds of the purchase price and C paid one-third. Their deed simply says: "B, a single woman, and C, a single woman, as tenants in common."

Later B and C have a serious disagreement, and they take each other to court over the property. Because the deed doesn't state what fractional interest each of them owns, the judge presumes that each has a 1/2 interest.

B presents evidence (her canceled check) showing that she paid two-thirds of the price. This establishes that B has a 2/3 interest in the property, and C only has a 1/3 interest.

1. Unity of Possession

In principle, there's no limit to how many tenants in common can share a property. There are also no restrictions on how they divide up the ownership. One tenant in common might own a 1/2 interest in the property and 50 others might each own a 1/100 interest.

Whether tenants in common have equal interests or unequal interests, their interests are always *UNDIVIDED, meaning each tenant has a right to possess and occupy the whole property, no matter how small his or her share in the ownership is. This is referred to as UNITY OF POSSESSION*. The concept is best illustrated by contrasting tenancy in common with ownership in severalty.

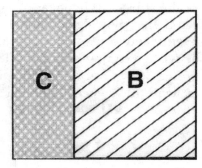

OWNERSHIP IN SEVERALTY
B owns the east 2/3
C owns the west 1/3

TENANCY IN COMMON
B has an undivided 2/3 interest in
the whole property
C has an undivided 1/3 interest
in the whole property

Example: A owns a large tract of land. She deeds the east two-thirds of it to B, and the west third to C.

B and C each own their portion of the tract in severalty. They are not co-owners; they are sole owners of two separate properties. Each has the right to exclude all others from his portion. B can exclude C from the east two-thirds, and C can exclude B from the west third.

On the other hand, suppose A deeded her entire tract to B and C as tenants in common, with B taking an undivided 2/3 interest and C taking an undivided 1/3 interest. Now they are co-owners of a single property. Both have the right to possess and occupy the whole tract; neither can exclude the other from any part of it. Even though B's interest in the property is twice as great as C's, B can't fence off two-thirds of the property and tell C to keep out.

a. Rents and Profits

Each tenant in common has a right to a share of any products or income generated by the property. Each tenant's share of the rents and profits is proportionate to his or her ownership interest, unless otherwise agreed. Diamonds from a mine or apples from an orchard belong to all the tenants in common. If they lease the property to someone else, the tenants in common share the rent they collect.

However, one tenant in common ordinarily doesn't have a right to charge another tenant in common rent. If tenant in common A chooses to live on the property and tenant in common B chooses not to, A is not required to pay rent to B, unless otherwise agreed. Tenant A is also not required to give tenant B a share of what the property produces as a result of A's labor.

b. Contribution

All tenants in common are required to share the property's expenses: maintenance, insurance, taxes, trust deed payments, and so forth. Unless otherwise agreed, each tenant's share is proportionate to his or her ownership interest. If tenant in common A has an undivided 2/3 interest and tenant in common B has an undivided 1/3 interest, A is liable for 2/3 of the expenses, and B is liable for 1/3 of the expenses.

A co-tenant who pays more than his or her share of the expenses can demand reimbursement from the other tenants in common. This is called the **RIGHT TO CONTRIBUTION**.

The right to contribution also applies to property improvements, but only when the other tenants in common have agreed to the improvement.

Example: A, B, and C own a house as tenants in common. A and B want to add a deck, but C is opposed to the project.

A pays a carpenter to build the deck. A is entitled to reimbursement from B, but not from C.

As you might guess, this rule often leads to disputes over whether a particular project (a new cedar roof, for example) was an improvement or necessary maintenance. When one or more of the tenants in common does not agree to contribute to the cost of an improvement, the contributing tenants in common are entitled to recover the value added by the improvement from any sales proceeds before the remaining profits from the sale are divided.

CHAPTER 4

The right to contribution gives a paying tenant in common an equitable lien against a nonpaying tenant's interest, but it can cost so much to enforce the lien that it may not be worthwhile to pay the tenants.

c. Waste

A tenant in common is liable to the other tenants for any **waste** he or she commits on the property (just as a life tenant is liable to a remainderman). If tenant in common A drives a car through the garage wall or kills the apple orchard, he will have to compensate tenant in common B for the damage.

2. Transfer and Encumbrance

A tenant in common is free to sell, will, or encumber his or her undivided interest without the consent of the other tenant(s). A tenant in common's interest can also be transferred involuntarily by foreclosure or bankruptcy. The transferee takes the interest subject to any liens or debts.

Example: A, B, and C are tenants in common. A takes out a loan and gives the bank a trust deed on her undivided 1/3 interest, but that trust deed doesn't encumber B's or C's interest.

A dies, leaving all her property to her friend D. Now B, C, and D are tenants in common, and D's undivided 1/3 interest is encumbered by the trust deed.

D can't make the trust deed payments, so eventually the bank forecloses. E purchases D's 1/3 interest at the foreclosure sale. Now B, C, and E are tenants in common.

To transfer or encumber the whole property, all the tenants in common must sign the deed, trust deed, or other document.

Example: A, B, C, and D are tenants in common. Z offers them a great deal of money for their land. A, B, and C leap at the offer, but D (who holds an undivided 1/16 interest) turns it down because of his sentimental attachment to the property.

A, B, and C can sell their combined undivided 15/16 interest in the property without D's consent, but they can't sell the whole. Z insists on all or nothing, since she wouldn't be able to carry out her plans for development with D still living there. The other co-owners plead with D, but he won't budge. Z withdraws her offer.

3. Terminating a Tenancy in Common (Partition)

a. Voluntary Partition

A tenancy in common can be terminated by the agreement of all the tenants. They can agree to change to one of the other forms of concurrent ownership (joint tenancy, community property, or tenancy in partnership), if any of those are applicable. *Or they can agree to divide their property, so that each owns a portion of it in severalty. This division by agreement is called VOLUNTARY PARTITION.*

Example: A wills 20 acres of vacant land to B and C as tenants in common. After A's death, B and C agree that they'd each rather have half the property instead of sharing the whole.

They have the land surveyed and divided into two ten-acre parcels. B deeds her undivided 1/2 interest in the east ten acres to C, and C deeds his undivided 1/2 interest in the west ten acres to B. Now each owns a ten-acre tract in severalty.

b. Judicial Partition

A tenancy in common can also be terminated by the unilateral action of one of the tenants without the consent of the others. If X wants to end the tenancy in common and the other tenants don't, X can file a **partition action** in superior court.

Everyone with a recorded interest in the property (co-tenants, lienholders) is brought into the partition suit as a defendant. The judge determines the status and priority of all the liens against the property and what interest each party holds, then terminates the tenancy in common by partitioning the property. Each former co-tenant is granted a share proportionate to his or her ownership interest.

Whenever possible, the judge will order the property to be physically divided, but physical division often won't work. For example, if A and B own a house as tenants in common, it would not be practical to divide the house itself in two.

Any time physical partition would be impractical or inequitable, the judge can order the property sold. The sale proceeds are then divided among the former co-tenants according to their ownership interests. In some cases, a judge will order part of the property sold and part of it physically divided.

A tenant in common in a partition suit may oppose a physical division of the property. He or she can present evidence (an appraisal) comparing the value of the divided property with the amount that a sale of the whole property would bring. If the divided property would be worth substantially less than the whole, the judge should order the property sold instead of physically divided.

B. JOINT TENANCY

JOINT TENANCY occurs when two or more people have identical interests in the whole property with the same right of possession and the right of survivorship. As long as joint tenants are alive and well, their relationship is similar to that of tenants in common: each joint tenant has an undivided interest and shares possession of the whole property.

The distinguishing feature of joint tenancy—the **right of survivorship**— comes into play if one of the joint tenants dies. When a joint tenant dies, his or her interest in the property passes automatically to the surviving joint tenant(s).

Example: (See chart on next page) A, B, and C buy a vacation home together. Sometime later, C dies. If A, B, and C were tenants in common, C's undivided interest would go to his heir, D. Then B, C, and D would own the property as tenants in common.

But A, B, and C were joint tenants. From the moment of C's death, A and B own the whole property. As a result of the right of survivorship, D does not acquire an interest in it.

1. Creating a Joint Tenancy

Since joint tenancy can have such a radical effect on the disposition of property, it isn't something co-owners slip into by default. There are specific rules for creating a joint tenancy and for maintaining one. If these rules aren't followed when the property is

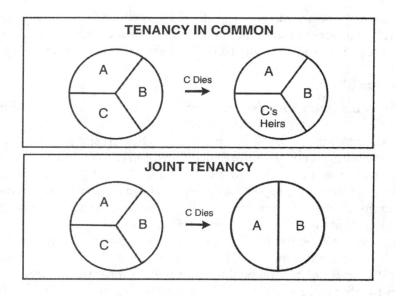

acquired, or if they are broken during the period of ownership, the joint tenancy fails and the right of survivorship is lost. Instead of a joint tenancy, the co-owners will either have a tenancy in common or (if they're a married couple) community property.

2. Requirements for Joint Tenancy

a. Four Unities (Possession, Interest, Time, and Title)

Joint tenancy requires four unities:

1. Unity of possession
2. Unity of interest
3. Unity of time
4. Unity of title

UNITY OF POSSESSION allows all co-tenants to have the right to possess the whole property at the same time.

UNITY OF INTEREST means that all the joint tenants must have an equal interest in the property. If there are two joint tenants, each must have a 1/2 interest; if there are three, each must have a 1/3 interest; if there are 20, each must have a 1/20 interest. If A has a 1/4 interest and B has a 3/4 interest, they aren't joint tenants.

UNITY OF TIME means that all of the joint tenants must acquire their interests in the property at the same moment.

UNITY OF TITLE means that they all must have taken title through the same deed or will.

Example: A deeds an undivided 1/2 interest in his property to B. Two months later, A deeds an undivided 1/2 interest in the same property to C.

B and C cannot be joint tenants because they acquired title at two different times, through two different deeds. Although there is unity of interest and unity of possession, there is no unity of time and no unity of title. As a result, there is no joint tenancy.

As a general rule, when any one of the four unities is missing (at the outset or at any time during the period of co-ownership) the joint tenancy fails. In California, the legislature has created a statutory exception to the four unities rule. An owner in severalty may create a joint tenancy by deeding the property to him or herself and others.

Example: A has owned some land for many years. When her children, B and C, reach adulthood, A deeds the property "to A, B, and C, as joint tenants."
This new deed satisfies the unity of time and title requirements, even though A originally acquired the property long before and through a different deed than B and C.

The unity of possession requirement is not rigidly applied. Joint tenants may agree among themselves to give one joint tenant exclusive possession of the property. Such an agreement does not destroy the joint tenancy. The agreement can even be entered into at the same time the co-owners acquire the property, without preventing creation of a joint tenancy.

b. Written Declaration of Joint Tenancy

A joint tenancy can only be created in writing (even in the case of personal property). The deed or will must expressly state the intention to create a joint tenancy. To be on the safe side, it should say either "as joint tenants" or "in joint tenancy." Courts have disagreed over whether any other language is sufficient evidence of intent to create a joint tenancy. The phrase "with the right of survivorship" will not create a joint tenancy by itself.

3. Rights and Duties of Joint Tenants

If co-owners manage to avoid all the pitfalls and establish a joint tenancy, they have basically the same rights and duties as tenants in common: the right to contribution, and to the products and rents from the property; the duty to not commit waste. A joint tenant can also encumber his or her own interest without the others' consent. However, a joint tenant in sole possession of the property does not have to share the profits of the property.
But in addition, joint tenants have a right that tenants in common don't have: the right of survivorship.

a. Right of Survivorship

As explained earlier, when a joint tenant dies, his or her interest in the joint tenancy property passes directly to the surviving joint tenants automatically, by operation of law. A joint tenancy interest cannot be willed or inherited because it no longer belongs to the joint tenant at the moment of his or her death. As a result, the joint tenancy property does not have to go through the probate process. This can spare the surviving joint tenants considerable expense and delay. (However, joint tenancy property doesn't escape federal estate taxes. The deceased joint tenant's interest is treated as part of his or her estate for tax purposes.)
Another result of the right of survivorship is that any liens against the deceased joint tenant's interest (for example, a judgment lien) are extinguished. The surviving joint tenants take the interest free and clear of the deceased joint tenant's deed of trust, judgment lien, or other debts. (Compare this to tenancy in common, where the deceased tenant's heir takes the interest subject to any liens and debts.)

Because a lien against one joint tenant's interest is so easily lost, few creditors are willing to accept such an interest as security. A lien against the entire property—a deed of trust signed by all the joint tenants, for example—is not lost if one or more of the joint tenants dies.

Making the Title Marketable. Although surviving joint tenants acquire the deceased joint tenant's interest automatically at the moment of death, they must take steps to clear their title because a person searching the real property records has no way to determine that a joint tenant died.

This can be accomplished by recording proof of the death, such as a court decree or a certified copy of the death certificate. When a death certificate is used instead of a court decree, the survivors should also record a sworn statement (an affidavit) that includes a description of the joint tenancy property, identifies the deceased as one of the joint tenants, and identifies the surviving joint tenants. It may also be necessary to record a certificate of inheritance tax release.

Until these steps have been taken, the surviving joint tenants' title is not marketable. That means the public record presents some question about the validity of their title.

A title company will refuse to insure a title unless it is marketable. Here again, however, a real estate agent shouldn't rely absolutely on the title company. The agent needs to know the rules and doublecheck to make sure they've been followed. When surviving joint tenants sell property, the buyer should not go through with the transaction until the proof of death, affidavit, and tax release have been recorded.

www.mlshomequest.com/content/view/11/27/
Understanding Common Ways of Holding Title

Simultaneous Death. If all the joint tenants die at once, each tenant's interest in the joint tenancy property is probated separately. The heirs of each joint tenant will receive his or her interest, and all the heirs will share ownership as tenants in common.

Example: A and B own property as joint tenants. They are killed at virtually the same moment when a tornado hits their house.

A's undivided 1/2 interest in the property passes to his heirs, X and Y, by intestate succession. B had written a will leaving all her property to her friend Z, so Z takes B's undivided 1/2 interest in the joint tenancy property.

After the probate process is completed, X, Y, and Z are tenants in common. X and Y each have an undivided 1/4 interest, and Z has an undivided 1/2 interest.

Note that although a joint tenancy interest can't usually be willed, it does pass according to will when there are no surviving joint tenants.

4. Terminating a Joint Tenancy

a. Partition

Just like tenants in common, joint tenants can agree to partition their property, or one joint tenant can bring suit for judicial partition. Either way, partition eliminates the right of survivorship and ends the co-ownership.

Merely filing a partition action does not terminate the joint tenancy. It ends only when the court's partition judgment is entered. If one of the joint tenants dies during the trial, the right of survivorship is still effective.

There is always the problem regardless of what type of tenancy exists, that one co-tenant occupies the property exclusively and refuses to allow the other co-tenant to share occupancy. Whether such an "ouster" exists will involve a review of many facts if it is disputed. One clear and simple way to establish an ouster is to use California Civil Code Section 843. Under this section, the tenant out of possession serves a written demand on the tenant in possession for concurrent possession. If the tenant in possession does not provide unconditional concurrent possession to the requesting tenant within 60 days after service of the demand, an ouster is established. The ousted tenant may now sue for possession, partition or any other appropriate remedy. This section cannot be used if the tenant out of possession is not entitled to possession, or a specific remedy is provided in an existing cotenancy agreement.

b. Severance

A joint tenancy is also terminated when it is **severed**, which can occur in a number of different ways. Severance ends the joint tenancy and eliminates the right of survivorship, but unlike partition, it does not terminate the co-ownership. Instead, severance changes a joint tenancy into a tenancy in common.

Each joint tenant has the power to sever the joint tenancy by transferring his or her interest. Transfer severs a joint tenancy by breaking the unities of time and title.

Example: A and B own some land as joint tenants. B sells her undivided 1/2 interest in the property to C. Now A and C each own an undivided 1/2 interest, but they are tenants in common, not joint tenants.

Involuntary transfer of a joint tenant's interest also severs the joint tenancy. This includes bankruptcy or foreclosure (see Chapter 12).

Transfer (either voluntary or involuntary) severs the joint tenancy only in regard to the transferred interest. When there are just two joint tenants, that ends the joint tenancy altogether. When there are more than two joint tenants, however, the co-owners who did not transfer their interests remain joint tenants in relation to one another.

Example: (See chart on next page) A, B, and C are joint tenants. C deeds her interest to her friend Z. This severs the joint tenancy as far as C's undivided 1/3 interest is concerned, so Z is not a joint tenant. Z is a tenant in common in relation to A and B. But A and B are still joint tenants in relation to one another.

If Z were to die, his interest would pass to his heirs, since the right of survivorship does not apply to him.

If instead it's B that dies, A (rather than B's heirs) takes B's interest. The right of survivorship was still effective between A and B. After B's death, A has an undivided 2/3 interest, and Z still has an undivided 1/3 interest. A and Z are tenants in common.

What if a joint tenant wants to sever the joint tenancy but still keep an ownership interest in the property? This problem arises when a joint tenant wants to eliminate the right of survivorship in order to will his or her interest in the property.

Until fairly recently, the law didn't allow a person to deed property to himself or herself, so the severing joint tenant had to deed his or her interest to an intermediary

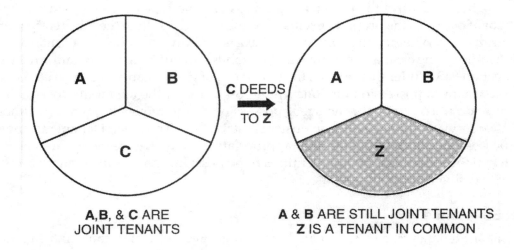

A,B, & C ARE JOINT TENANTS

C DEEDS TO Z

A & B ARE STILL JOINT TENANTS Z IS A TENANT IN COMMON

called a "strawman." Like any other transfer, this severed the joint tenancy. The strawman would then deed the property back to the former joint tenant, who would take title as a tenant in common.

In California, this straw transaction is no longer necessary. A joint tenant may sever the joint tenancy simply by deeding his or her interest in the property to him or herself.

Case Example: Mr. and Mrs. Riddle owned some real property as joint tenants. Mrs. Riddle retained a lawyer to plan her estate. The lawyer explained to her that the joint tenancy property would go to her husband upon her death.

Mrs. Riddle wanted to terminate the joint tenancy so that she could dispose of the property by will. The lawyer prepared a deed by which Mrs. Riddle granted her 1/2 interest in the property to herself. He also helped Mrs. Riddle write a will leaving her 1/2 interest to someone other than her husband. Mrs. Riddle died a few weeks after executing these documents.

When he discovered what his wife had done, Mr. Riddle sued Mrs. Riddle's estate. Following an established precedent, the trial court held that Mrs. Riddle's deed to herself had not severed the joint tenancy. By right of survivorship, Mr. Riddle now owned the entire property in severalty.

But this decision was reversed on appeal. Overruling the then existing precedent, the appellate court held that the deed had severed the joint tenancy. Mrs. Riddle's 1/2 interest passed according to her will, not by the right of survivorship. *Riddle v. Harmon*, 102 Cal. App. 3d 524 (1980). (California enacted a statute [Civil Code, sec. 683.2] in 1984 adopting the rule coming out of the *Riddle v. Harmon* decision.)

Transferring the property is not the only way to sever a joint tenancy. One of the co-owners can simply make a written declaration that the joint tenancy is severed. Not only that, executing any written instrument that shows an intention to sever the joint tenancy may be held to sever it.

Example: A and B own a house as joint tenants. They enter a written agreement stating that B is to have exclusive possession of the property.

This agreement suggests an intention to sever the joint tenancy, since unity of possession is one of the basic characteristics of a joint tenancy. For that reason, a court might hold that the agreement caused a severance.

However, if A and B state in their agreement that B can have exclusive possession on condition that the joint tenancy is unaffected, then it will not be severed. The joint tenants' actual intentions control in these situations.

A joint tenant's attempt to will the joint tenancy property does not automatically cause a severance. It may be used as evidence of intent to sever.

Recording Requirement. A deed, declaration, or other document severing a joint tenancy must be recorded for the severance to be effective. If the severance document is not recorded when the severing joint tenant dies, the property will still go to the surviving joint tenants. An exception is made if the severance document was executed no more than three days before the death, and is recorded within seven days after the death.

When all joint tenants have agreed to a severance, it isn't necessary to record the agreement. Recording is also unnecessary for severance when one joint tenant deeds his or her interest to another joint tenant.

Mutual Consent Agreement. Joint tenants may agree among themselves that their joint tenancy can only be severed by mutual consent, and not by the unilateral action of one tenant. If one joint tenant later deeds his or her interest to someone else, the transfer will not be effective, and the joint tenancy won't be severed.

Example: A and B agree that their joint tenancy can only be severed by mutual consent. Later, A deeds his undivided 1/2 interest to C. Because of the mutual consent agreement, the deed to C is invalid, and the joint tenancy is not severed.

There's an important exception to this rule, however. If C was a good faith purchaser for value (not someone in collusion with A or receiving the deed as a gift) and was not aware of the mutual consent agreement, the deed is valid and the joint tenancy is broken. To avoid this result, A and B could have recorded the mutual consent agreement, and then C (and everyone else) has constructive notice of the agreement.

There's one other situation in which a mutual consent agreement does not prevent severance. If one joint tenant murders another joint tenant, the joint tenancy is severed. This prevents the murderer from gaining the victim's interest in the property through the right of survivorship. The rule applies to voluntary manslaughter (killing under extreme provocation) as well as to premeditated murder.

5. Advantages and Disadvantages of Joint Tenancy

Co-owners who take title as joint tenants usually choose that form of ownership so the property won't have to be probated, and so the surviving tenant can take the property free of the other's liens and debts. These are substantial advantages, if in fact one of the parties dies during the period of co-ownership.

The right of survivorship is very easily lost through severance. Although a severance document must be recorded to be effective, a co-owner who has no reason to suspect that the joint tenancy has been severed is not likely to check the public record. He or she may be in for a shock if the other co-owner dies and wills an interest in the property to someone else.

CHAPTER 4

Co-owners can prevent this kind of surprise by agreeing that their joint tenancy cannot be severed except by mutual consent. This arrangement can create the opposite problem, by making it difficult to get out of the joint tenancy. If one of the joint tenants is unwilling to consent to a severance, the other(s) must file a partition action. Like any lawsuit, a partition action can be expensive, time consuming, and stressful.

C. COMMUNITY PROPERTY

In California, all property owned by married people is classified either as the **separate property** of one spouse, or as the **community property** of both spouses. These classifications determine a couple's rights and duties in regard to the property.

Outside of California, only Arizona, Idaho, Louisiana, Nevada, New Mexico, Texas, Washington, and Wisconsin have community property systems. In some other states, married couples co-own property as **tenants by the entirety**, which is similar to joint tenancy. In other states, there is no special form of ownership for married couples.

> **Case Example:** Juan Vargas lived a double life. He married Mildred in 1929. Sixteen years later, he married Josephine. Josephine believed that Juan had previously divorced Mildred. Since Juan had not, his marriage to Josephine was invalid. When Juan died, he had been married to Mildred for 40 years, and putatively married to Josephine for 24 years. Because Josephine had believed in good faith that she was validly married, the probate court divided Juan's estate equally between the two women. *Estate of Vargas*, 36 Cal. App. 3d 714 (1974).

The concept of community property is based in Spanish law, which is how it became established in California. The Treaty of Guadalupe Hidalgo (by which Mexico ceded California and other land to the United States in 1848) required the U.S. to respect the property rights of Mexican nationals living in the ceded territory. As a result, the California state constitution (1850) included a provision recognizing the separate property rights of wives. Subsequent legislation built on the distinction between separate property and community property.

In 1970, the California legislature passed the Family Law Act, which codified the community property system. Amendments to the act adopted over the next few years significantly revised the respective rights of husband and wife. Earlier law had given the husband management and control of the community property, but as of January 1, 1975, husband and wife share management and control.

1. When Community Property Rules Apply

Community property exists only in the context of a marriage and in the context of registered domestic partners. *REGISTERED DOMESTIC PARTNERS are persons of the same sex or persons of opposite sex over the age of 62 who have filed a Declaration of Domestic Partnership with the California Secretary of State and meet the other criteria set forth in the Family Code.* The Family Law Act's codified community property rules do not apply to nonmarital relationships, except for registered domestic partners.

This was confirmed in the famous "palimony" case, *Marvin v. Marvin*, 18 Cal. 3d 660, 134 Cal. Rptr. 815 (1976). Lee Marvin and Michelle Triola lived together for seven years without marrying. When their relationship ended, Triola sued Marvin for support and half the property the couple had acquired. The California Supreme Court ruled that an unmarried cohabitant may have a financial claim against an ex-partner, but the claim is not based on community property rights. The plaintiff must be able to prove that there was an agreement to share property or income, or some other basis for recovery.

However, if a couple is not validly married, but one or both partners believed in good faith that they were, their property will be divided as if they had been married.

2. Classifying the Property

The idea behind the community property system is that a marriage is a partnership. Husband and wife each work for the good of the partnership. Any money or property acquired through the skill or labor of either spouse during marriage belongs to the marital community, not just to the individual who earned it.

In addition, anything purchased with community funds or with community credit (such as a credit card issued to both spouses) is community property. Property may belong to the community even when title is held in the name of only one spouse.

On the other hand, everything an individual owns before marriage remains his or her separate property after marriage, provided it is kept separate and not mixed (commingled) with community property. This includes money accumulated before marriage.

Example: W earns her living as a bus driver. While she was single, she was able to save $8,000 out of her wages. After her marriage to H, that $8,000 remains W's separate property. The wages she earns during the marriage are community property, however.

Anything purchased with separate property funds is also separate property. So if W uses her $8,000 to buy a car during her marriage, the car is her separate property.

Property or money acquired by gift, will, or inheritance is separate property, even if it is received after marriage. It is not community property because it isn't earned by skill or labor. A gift purchased by one spouse for the other with community funds is the recipient's separate property.

To be separate property, a gift received during marriage must be a true gift. That is, it must not have been given in exchange for services rendered, either in the past or in the future.

Example: H is a married man. H's elderly mother gives H her sailboat. It is understood between them that the sailboat is H's compensation for helping his mother with housekeeping and other chores. The sailboat is not a true gift. Because H has earned it (or will earn it), the sailboat is community property rather than separate property.

Any appreciation in separate property, and any rents or profits generated by separate property, ordinarily are also separate property. However, if the appreciation, rents, or profits are the result of a spouse's effort, skill, or labor, they are community property instead.

Example: H owns an apartment building as his separate property. If he hires a property management company and is not actively involved in managing the building himself, the rents it generates will be his separate property. But if he spends time and energy on maintaining the building and leasing the apartments, the rents may be considered community property.

The rules change when a married couple is living separately or if a decree of separation has been issued. Then the income and property each spouse acquires is his or her separate property. If a separated spouse has a minor child living with him or her, the child's earnings are also that spouse's separate property.

When a married person wins a personal injury suit, the damage award is community property if it is received while the couple is living together. If the couple is living apart however, the award is the separate property of the injured spouse. If the cause of action arose after entry of judgment of dissolution or separation, or while the parties were living separately, the acquired property is separate property. However, a different rule applies if the personal injury was inflicted by the other spouse rather than a third party. Then the damages award is the injured spouse's separate property even while the couple is still living together.

Community Property	Separate Property
● Acquired through skill or labor during marriage ● Purchased with community funds or community credit	● Acquired before marriage ● Gift or Inheritance ● Purchased with separate funds or separate credit ● Appreciation, profits, or proceeds from separate property ● Earnings after separation ● Personal injury cause of action after separation

a. Mixed Separate and Community Property

Sometimes there are both separate and community interests in a single piece of property. This can occur either when the property is paid for over time, or when it is improved during the marriage.

When property is paid for over time (as with a deed of trust or an installment contract), some payments may be made with separate funds and some with community funds. This is especially likely to occur with a major purchase, such as a home.

Example: H and W purchased a residence for $150,000. They used W's separate funds to make the $30,000 downpayment. Their $120,000 deed of trust is a community obligation; that is, both H and W signed the loan documents. They also use community funds to make the monthly payments on the loan.

The home is considered community property, but W has a separate property interest in it.

The party making a contribution from his or her separate funds is entitled to be reimbursed for that contribution. However, the separate property contribution does not earn interest and, if the property value increases, the appreciation is all community property. If the property value decreases, the reimbursement cannot exceed the value of the property.

The same process works for separate property contributions made to community property. Let's say W's mother left her $10,000, and she used those separate funds to improve the home she and H own as community property. Then W would have a separate interest in the home along with the community's interest.

Community property—either community funds, or the time, skill, and labor of one of the spouses—is often used to improve separate property. That gives the marital community an interest in the property.

Example: W inherits a house from her mother. This is her separate property. Since H and W already have a home, W decides to lease the inherited house.

In preparing the house for rental, W spends $10,000 in community funds on repairs and improvements. The house is still W's separate property, but H and W's marital community has an interest in it. Although most of the rent generated by the property will be W's separate property, a portion will be H and W's community property.

When community property is contributed to separate property, the community is entitled to reimbursement for the community property contributions. However, for community contributions to separate property, the community obtains a proportionate ownership share of the property and shares in any property appreciation.

There's a complication, however. When one spouse makes a community contribution to the other's separate property as a gift, the community does not acquire an interest in the separate property. When one spouse makes a gift of separate property to the community, he or she does not acquire a separate interest in the community property.

Sometimes it is unclear whether or not a particular contribution was a gift. A court will apply legal presumptions to decide the question. In certain circumstances the law presumes a contribution was a gift, and in others it presumes a contribution was not a gift. For this reason, it can be difficult to tell whether there are mixed separate and community interests in a piece of property. (The presumption that a court in a dissolution proceeding will apply to separate property contributions that were used to acquire community property is discussed below.)

3. Consequences of Classification

Each spouse owns his or her separate property in severalty. Each has an undivided 1/2 interest in all of the couple's community property.

The couple's rights and duties in regard to the community property are different than those they'd have if they owned the property as tenants in common, joint tenants, or community property with the right of survivorship. For example, community property is not subject to judicial partition. It can only be divided by agreement, or when the marriage is dissolved.

a. Management and Control

Under the Family Law Act, husband and wife have equal control over community property. The only exception: when one spouse operates a business, the other spouse has no right to interfere in its management, even though the business is community property. Equal control of community property is the general rule. Equal control means that either spouse can act unilaterally without the other's consent.

Example: H and W own a car as community property. One day a passerby offers H $5,000 for the car. That strikes H as a very good price, so he accepts the offer without consulting W.

When H tells W he sold the car, she's very annoyed. But it's too late to do anything about it; H's unilateral action was legally binding.

 www.divorcenet.com/states/california/cafaq03
Califoria Community Property FAQ

However, there are several important limitations on this kind of unilateral action. These are called ***JOINDER REQUIREMENTS***: *both husband and wife must join in the transaction.* One spouse can't give away community property without the other's consent. (If H had given away the car, W could demand it back.) One spouse can't sell, lease, or encumber the couple's household furnishings without the other's consent. And one spouse can't sell the other spouse's clothing, or a minor child's clothing, even when these are community property.

For real estate agents, one joinder requirement is crucial: any transfer or encumbrance of community real property requires the signature of both husband and wife.

There are very few exceptions to this rule. It does not apply to a lease of real property that will end within one year from the date of execution. (So W can lease the couple's summer home for six months without H's consent; his signature is not necessary.) Joinder is also not required if estoppel applies. (If a neighbor builds a garage over the property line because H said it was okay, both H and W are estopped from objecting to the encroachment, even though W didn't give her approval.)

In any other real estate transaction—lease, encumbrance, or transfer—the consent and signatures of both husband and wife are essential.

Remedies for an Unauthorized Action. When only one spouse takes an action regarding community real property that requires the consent and signature of both, the transaction is not binding on the other spouse. The nonconsenting spouse may void the transfer or encumbrance, even when the buyer or lienholder acted in good faith. Any payment received from the buyer or lienholder must be refunded.

When title is in the signing spouse's name alone and the buyer is not aware the seller is married, the nonconsenting spouse must take action to void the transfer within one year after the deed or lien is recorded. If the instrument is never recorded, or the buyer knew the seller was married, this statute of limitations doesn't apply.

For real estate agents, buyers, and lenders, the rule is simple: always determine whether the grantor is married. If he or she is, the safest course is to have the spouse:

1. sign a quitclaim deed transferring any interest he or she might have in the property to the grantor spouse, or
2. co-sign all the documents involved in the transaction (the listing agreement, purchase agreement, and grant deed).

These steps are not legally necessary if the property is the grantor's separate property. The grantee is taking a big risk if the grantor's spouse doesn't sign. If it turns out that the community has an interest in the property, the grantee could lose the property.

b. Liability for Debts

Creditors' rights against a married person's property are determined by its classification as separate or community property.

One spouse's separate property is shielded from liability for the other spouse's premarital debts.

Example: At the time of H and W's marriage, W already owned a home. H owed a large judgment in connection with a car accident. Since the home is W's separate property, the judgment cannot become a lien against it.

Separate property is also protected from debts the other spouse incurs during the marriage, unless they were incurred for necessities such as food and clothing. So if H's car accident had happened during the marriage, W's separate property still could not be reached by the judgment creditor.

Community property, on the other hand, can be reached by the premarital creditor of either spouse. The nondebtor spouse can protect his or her earnings by keeping them apart from all other community funds in an account that the debtor spouse has no access to. This won't shield the earnings against debts the other spouse contracts during the marriage, however.

All community property is liable for the debts either spouse incurs during the marriage. Referring back to the previous example, if the home were community property, the judgment lien against H would attach to it, even though W had nothing to do with the car accident.

Separate Property vs. Community Property Debt		
	Other Spouses Premarital Debt	**Debt Incurred During Marriage**
Separate Property	SAFE	SAFE unless debt is for necessities
Community Property	LIABLE unless earnings kept in a separate account	LIABLE

c. Division of Property on Dissolution

At the end of a marriage, the court presiding over the dissolution has the power to divide and award the couple's community property. Separate property is excluded from this process. The court cannot award one spouse's separate property to the other spouse. (However, the spouse who owns the separate property may request that the court include it in the property settlement.)

As a general rule, the community property will be divided equally, but the court can distribute it differently if that would be more equitable.

In determining whether property is separate or community property, the court relies on legal presumptions that favor community property. One important presumption is

CHAPTER 4

that all property acquired during marriage in joint form is presumed to be community property. That presumption is applied even if the deed states the property is held in some other way, such as tenancy in common or joint tenancy. The presumption can be rebutted if the deed or a separate written agreement states that the husband and wife hold their interests as separate property.

Case Example: Robert and Joyce Hilke held the title to their house as "husband and wife, as joint tenants." Joyce filed for divorce, judgment was entered but she died before the property was distributed by the judge, who reserved the right to do so. Robert claimed the house as surviving joint tenant. Joyce's estate claims the house was community property.

The California Supreme Court held that Civil Code Section 4800.1 (now Family Code Section 22580) presumes that joint tenancy property is community property and the property should be sold with the proceeds split equally between the estate and Robert. *In Re Marriage of Hilke*, 4 Cal. 4th 215, 14 Cal. Rptr. 2d 371 (1992).

This presumption applies only in a dissolution, not when a married couple sells their property or when a spouse dies. Reconsidering the Hilke case, suppose the couple stayed married, but Joyce died a few years after they bought the land. In distributing her estate, the probate court would presume the land was joint tenancy property, not community property (see below).

In a dissolution, to prove that something is separate property, it is often necessary to trace the source of the funds that were used to purchase it. This can be a very complicated process, especially when separate property has changed form during the marriage (from a grand piano to cash to a motorcycle), or when separate funds have been commingled with community funds.

When there are both separate and community interests in the same piece of property, the court will order some form of reimbursement. A spouse must reimburse the community for contributions to his or her separate property, and the community must reimburse either spouse for separate contributions to community property. If the court holds that a contribution was a gift, however, reimbursement is not required.

If separate property was used to acquire community property (as when one spouse's separate funds were used to make the down payment on the couple's home), the contribution won't be treated as a gift unless the contributing spouse signed a waiver giving up the right to reimbursement or some other document that had the effect of a waiver. The amount reimbursed will be the amount originally contributed, without any adjustment due to a change in the property's value.

d. Disposition of Property at Death

When a married person dies, the probate court determines what part of the estate is separate property and what part is community property. The property is then distributed according to the will, or if there is no will, according to the rules of intestate succession. (See Chapter 10 for more information about wills and intestate succession.)

A married person is free to will separate property to anyone he or she chooses. In addition, husband and wife each have the right to will an undivided 1/2 interest in any community property to someone other than the spouse.

140

Example: H and W own a home as community property. W wills her 1/2 interest in the property to her friend A. When W dies, H and A each own an undivided 1/2 interest in the property as tenants in common. (H and A must be tenants in common rather than joint tenants since they don't share unity of time or title.)

If a married person dies without having made a valid will, all the community property vests in the surviving spouse.

Example: H and W had three children. H never got around to writing a will. On his death, W takes full title to their home, car, furniture, and everything else that was community property. She now owns all of this in severalty, and the children have no rights in it.

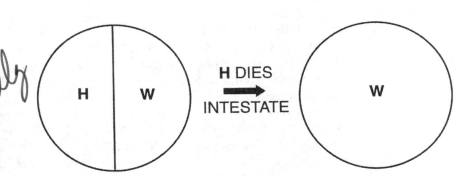

On the other hand, the intestate spouse's separate property is divided between the surviving spouse and the deceased's children. If there is one child, the spouse receives an undivided 1/2 interest and the child receives an undivided 1/2 interest. If there is more than one child, the spouse takes an undivided 1/3 interest, and the remaining 2/3 interest is apportioned equally among the children. All of these interests are, of course, held as tenants in common.

Example: W owns some land as her separate property. H and W have one daughter, D. When W dies intestate, H and D each take an undivided 1/2 interest in the land.

Suppose H and W had four children, A, B, C, and D. Then if W died intestate, H would have an undivided 1/3 interest in the land. A, B, C, and D would each have an undivided 1/6 interest in it (a 2/3 interest divided among four children).

When a married person dies, it isn't always necessary for the estate to go through the probate process. Property that passes to the surviving spouse (either by will or through intestacy) generally doesn't have to be probated. If it isn't probated, the surviving spouse will be liable to creditors for the deceased spouse's debts (up to the value of the property acquired). The surviving spouse may choose to have the probate court administer the entire estate and discharge the creditors' claims.

If the deceased's share of the community property was willed to someone other than the surviving spouse, that beneficiary should record a notice claiming an interest in the property. The notice must be recorded within 40 days after the death. After 40 days (unless a notice has been filed), the surviving spouse has full power to sell, lease, or encumber the community property. A buyer, lessee, or secured lender will be safe from the claims of beneficiaries and creditors.

D. COMMUNITY PROPERTY WITH RIGHT OF SURVIVORSHIP

In addition to holding property as community property, joint tenants, or tenants in common, a husband and wife may enjoy the potential income tax benefits of both community property and the survivorship benefits of joint tenancy benefits by tranferring jointly held property by deed to themselves as **community property with right of survivorship**.

If a couple held title as ordinary community property and one spouse died, there was a "stepped-up basis" for both halves of the property, which would provide a significant capital gains income tax advantage when the property was sold. That is because the income tax basis for the decedent's property is the fair market value of the property on the date of the decedent's death, not the original purchase basis. The transfer of title was not automatic.

If a couple held title as joint tenants with a right of survivorship and one spouse died, only the decedent spouse's portion of the property received a "stepped-up" basis (on only 1/2 of the fair market value on the date of the decedent's death), because the surviving spouse already owned 1/2 of the property (1/2 of the original purchase basis). But the transfer of title was automatic. On the death of a co-owner of joint tenancy property, title automatically transfers to the surviving owners on the death of one of the owners.

	Joint Tenancy	Tenancy in Common	Community Property	Community Property w/Right of Survivorship
Creation Presumed		X	X	
Equal Right to Possession	X	X	X	X
Equla Interests	X		X	X
Right of Survivorship	X			X
Each Co-Owner can convey undivided interest	X	X		
Each Co-Owner can wiil undivided interest		X	X	

E. CHOOSING A DIFFERENT FORM OF CO-OWNERSHIP

Husband and wife may share title to property as: 1) joint tenants, 2) tenants in common, or 3) community property with right of survivorship rather than holding it as community property. Each spouse's undivided interest in a joint tenancy or tenancy in common is his or her separate property. A married couple often chooses joint tenancy because the right of survivorship will allow the surviving spouse to avoid some creditors' claims.

As you've seen, in dissolution proceedings, property held in joint tenancy is presumed to be community property. The court will only treat the property as a joint tenancy if the deed or a later agreement between the spouses explicitly states not only that it is a joint tenancy, but also that it is separate property. A joint tenancy between husband and wife is not automatically severed by dissolution of the marriage. Either spouse may ask the court to partition the property during the dissolution proceedings, however.

In other types of legal proceedings involving property owned by a married couple, the court will not apply the community property presumption. On the contrary, if the deed says "as joint tenants," the court will presume the property is held in joint tenancy. Even so, the court may consider evidence that the property in question is community property.

In spite of the language in the deed, creditors, relatives, or other litigants who want the property to be treated as a community asset might argue that one or both of the spouses did not understand joint tenancy. The court will try to determine if the couple actually intended to hold the property in joint tenancy and not as community property. Unless they expressly agreed to alter the community character of the property, the court may decide that it is community property.

> **Example:** The deed to H and W's home says, "H and W, in joint tenancy." H dies, leaving a will. The will divided H's undivided 1/2 interest in the home to D, his daughter by a previous marriage.
>
> If the home was truly owned as a joint tenancy, H's interest in it couldn't be willed. The right of survivorship would vest H's interest in W automatically. H's attempt to will his interest to D would not sever the joint tenancy.
>
> But D wants to establish that the home was really held as community property, not in joint tenancy. In the probate court, she may argue that H and W didn't really understand what a joint tenancy was, and didn't intend to create one. D can use her father's attempt to will his interest to her as evidence that there wasn't a joint tenancy.
>
> If D succeeds in proving that the home was community property, the court will award her H's undivided 1/2 interest, in accordance with his will. D and W would then own the home as tenants in common.

Once a couple has established a joint tenancy, they may later agree to change the property to community property. This is called a **TRANSMUTATION AGREEMENT***.* (A transmutation agreement may be used to change any separate property into community property, or to change community property into separate property.) Any transmutation agreement must be in writing to be valid.

F. TENANCY IN PARTNERSHIP

The fifth type of concurrent title recognized in California is tenancy in partnership. Co-ownership takes this form when a business organized as a general or limited partnership owns property.

CHAPTER 4

Partnerships are described in the next section of this chapter. The rights and duties of tenants in partnership are outlined in that discussion.

II. Ownership by Associations

The second aspect of co-ownership is ownership by associations—businesses, nonprofit groups, and other organizations—rather than individuals. Depending on its form, an association may be a legal entity separate from its individual members or owners. Title to property can be held in an association's name.

Ownership by associations overlaps with the different forms of co-ownership discussed in the first part of the chapter. For example, a business organization may hold property in severalty, or it may be a tenant in common with other organizations or individuals.

An association can't be a joint tenant, however, since the right of survivorship is the key trait of a joint tenancy. Artificial entities such as corporations have a potentially perpetual existence. That would prevent a co-tenant from acquiring any genuine survivorship right.

A real estate agent should understand when and how an association can hold title to real property. Most importantly, he or she needs to know who can sign and who must sign on behalf of an association to enter contracts and transfer property.

Property can be owned by:

✔ Corporations,
✔ General Partnerships,
✔ Limited Liability Companies (LLCs),
✔ Real Estate Investment Trusts (REITs), and
✔ Unincorporated Associations.

A. CORPORATIONS

The most sophisticated form of association is the corporation.

The ownership interests in a corporation are divided into shares. The corporation is owned by shareholders, individuals who purchase shares in the company as an investment. The money invested provides the corporation with operating capital.

A corporation may have only a few shareholders, or it may have hundreds. The **CORPORATION** *is legally a separate entity from its shareholders. The law treats it as an artificial individual; it can enter contracts, own property, incur debts, sue and be sued.* Because of this special legal status, corporations are closely regulated by state and federal laws.

1. Creation

To start a corporation in California, its organizers (the **incorporators**) file **articles of incorporation** with the California Secretary of State's office. The articles establish the corporation's name, list the name and address of the principal agents, explain the share structure, and include a general statement of purpose. In order to sell stock, the incorporators must obtain a permit from the state Corporations Commissioner and comply with securities laws.

144

In California, a **DOMESTIC CORPORATION** *is one organized in compliance with California law.* A **FOREIGN CORPORATION** *is one organized under the laws of another state, or in another country.* A foreign corporation involved in California real estate transactions must be certified to do business here by the California Secretary of State's office.

☆26

2. Management

A corporation's shareholders have very little direct involvement in its management. They receive an annual report and have the right to inspect the corporate records; they may attend an annual meeting and vote on some major issues (one vote per share owned).

The real power behind a corporation is its **BOARD OF DIRECTORS**, *who govern the corporation's affairs in accordance with its bylaws.* They appoint corporate officers—the president or chief executive officer (CEO), vice presidents, the treasurer or chief financial officer, and the corporate secretary—who run the business on a day-to-day basis. In some small corporations, one person fills more than one corporate office; for example, the president and treasurer might be the same person.

The officers are not automatically authorized to convey or encumber the corporation's real property. These actions must be expressly authorized by a resolution of the board. A title company will usually require proof of the authorization before insuring a transaction, although that requirement is sometimes waived. The proof takes the form of a certificate signed by the corporate secretary stating that the transaction is authorized.

If all (or nearly all) of a corporation's assets are being transferred, the transaction usually must be approved by the shareholders as well as the board. As a general rule, however, the board may execute a trust deed on all of the corporation's assets without shareholder approval.

3. Liability

The primary advantage of the corporate form of organization is that shareholders are protected from liability for the corporation's debts.

> **Example:** A few years ago, Z spent $3,000 on stock in the ABC Corporation. Her shares are now worth $3,600.
>
> The ABC Corporation is found liable for an injury caused by a defective product it manufactured, and a $100,000 judgment is entered against the corporation. The judgment creditor can file a lien against the corporation's assets if the judgment is not paid.
>
> However, the creditor cannot proceed against Z to collect the judgment. Her home, bank accounts, and other property are protected from liability because the corporation is a separate legal entity.

In theory, all shareholders have this protection from liability, but in fact, creditors often require the personal guaranties of the major shareholders before they will make large loans to a corporation.

4. Taxation

The chief drawback to the corporate form of organization is double taxation. First the corporation must pay corporate income taxes on any profits it generates. Then if the profits are distributed to the shareholders as **dividends**, the same money is taxed again as the personal income of the shareholders.

Business investors can avoid double taxation by choosing a different form of organization, such as a partnership. But, as you'll see, other forms have disadvantages of their own.

B. GENERAL PARTNERSHIPS

A *GENERAL PARTNERSHIP is simply an association of two or more individuals as co-owners of a business run for profit*. It doesn't have the formal structure of a corporation. Although a general partnership can own property, for most other purposes (taxation, liability) the law does not recognize a general partnership as an entity independent from its members.

General partnerships are usually created by express agreement (either oral or written). But they can be created by implied agreement, based on the actions of the parties.

Having a common interest in a business transaction doesn't automatically create a partnership, however. The parties must intend to carry on a definite, ongoing business as co-owners, sharing the management and profits. When that is their intention, they have a partnership, whether they call it that or not.

1. Management and Profits

A general partnership agreement can provide for almost any allocation of rights and duties between the partners. But if the agreement doesn't address an issue (or if it is an implied agreement), then the allocation will be according to statute. The rules outlined here are the statutory rules; most of them can be altered in the partnership agreement.

All general partners have an equal voice in the management and control of the business. The partnership is legally bound by the actions of one partner, as long as the partner is acting within the scope of his or her authority. (Each partner is an agent and a fiduciary of the partnership, so the agency rules explained in Chapter 5 apply.)

Unless otherwise agreed, the partners all share in the profits equally, even if their contributions to the business were unequal. (Some partners may only contribute skill or labor, without making any capital contribution.) Partners usually divide losses in the same way they share in the profits.

2. Liability

General partners have unlimited liability for the acts of the partnership. Each partner can be made to pay the partnership's debts out of his or her own pocket.

Example: P, Q, and R own the PQR Company, a general partnership. The PQR Company and the individual partners are sued for breach of a construction contract, and a judgment is entered against them for $95,000. The company has no assets. P, Q, and R don't pay the judgment, so the judgment creditor claims a lien against Q's home. Q ends up paying the entire $95,000 to protect his home from foreclosure.

Q can then demand reimbursement from P and R for their share of the judgment, and can sue them if they don't pay. But this personal liability is the main disadvantage of a general partnership. It contrasts with the protection a corporate shareholder enjoys.

3. Tenancy in Partnership

All property that general partners bring into the business at the outset, and all that they later acquire (with partnership funds) for the business, is partnership property.

TENANCY IN PARTNERSHIP *arises when personal (moveable) and real property is held in the name of a partnership as opposed to individual names.*

Unless otherwise agreed, each partner has a right to possess all partnership property for partnership purposes. A partner has no right to possess partnership property for any other purpose, except with the consent of the other partners.

It's necessary to distinguish between a partner's undivided interest in partnership property and his or her interest in the partnership itself. For example, if a partner is married, that partner's interest in the partnership may be treated as community property, but his or her interest in partnership property cannot be community property.

A partner can't transfer an interest in a piece of partnership property to someone outside the partnership, except when all of the partners assign the whole property. But (unless otherwise agreed) one partner may assign his or her interest in the partnership itself to an outsider. That gives the assignee a right to share in the partnership's profits. It does not make the assignee a partner, however, or give the assignee the right to interfere in the management of the business.

Example: A and B own the A & B Company, a general partnership. They also own a building as partnership property.

B is involved in a car accident, and a judgment is entered against her. The judgment creditor cannot claim a lien against the A & B Company's building. (The creditor could claim a lien if the judgment were against the partnership rather than B.)

But B's interest in the partnership itself can be reached by her judgment creditor: the creditor can garnish B's share of the profits.

When a partner dies, his or her interest in partnership property vests in the surviving partners. The deceased partner's estate has a right to an accounting and a share of the partnership profits, but it does not have an interest in the partnership property.

Title Held in the Partnership's Name. To transact business using a partnership name (rather than the names of all the individual partners), the partners must publish and record a **fictitious business name certificate** in the county where their principal place of business is located. The certificate lists the names and addresses of all the partners, and must be signed by all of them. This prevents them from concealing their identities from creditors and from the public.

Once the partners have recorded a fictitious business name certificate, title to property can be held in the partnership's name. To convey property held in the partnership's name, it is generally also necessary to record a **statement of partnership** in the county where the property is located. Title insurance companies require this before they will insure a conveyance of property held in a partnership's name. The statement lists the partnership name and the names of all the partners. It must be signed and acknowledged by at least two of the partners.

Keep in mind that neither of these steps is necessary for the creation of partnership property. Property can be partnership property if the title is held in the names of the individual partners, and even if it is held in the name of only one of the partners.

When title is held in the partnership's name, the property can be encumbered or conveyed by the signature of any authorized partner. If any of the partners are married, their spouses' signatures are not required. When there are several partners and they live in different cities, this can save a lot of trouble.

Holding title in the partnership's name is not just a matter of convenience, however. It can also protect the partnership from a partner's unauthorized action.

Although ordinarily a partner who exceeds his or her authority can't bind the partnership, there's an important exception. If the partner conveys partnership property to a good faith purchaser who doesn't realize that the partner is not authorized to sell it, the partnership can't recover the property.

Example: J, K, and L own JKL Enterprises, a general partnership. They also own some land as partnership property. Title to the land is in K's name.

K sells the land to Z without his partners' consent. Because Z believes that K has authority to sell the land, the partnership will be bound by the sale. J and L can sue K for violating his duties to the partnership, but they can't get the land back from Z.

If title is in the partnership's name, the partnership can protect itself from this. The statement of partnership can then include restrictions on the individual partners' authority to convey partnership real property. That gives everyone—including good faith purchasers like Z—constructive notice of the restrictions. If JKL Enterprises held the land in its own name and included restrictions in its statement of partnership, it could recover the land even from a good faith purchaser.

Both for convenience and protection, it is advisable for partnership property to be held in the partnership's name. Anyone purchasing partnership property should check the statement of partnership to make sure the conveyance is authorized. If there's any doubt, all the partners should be asked to join in the conveyance.

C. LIMITED PARTNERSHIPS

A **LIMITED PARTNERSHIP**, *like a general partnership, is an association of two or more persons as co-owners of a business, but a limited partnership has one or more general partners, plus one or more limited partners*. The rights and duties of general partners in a limited partnership are the same as in a general partnership. The limited partners, however, have limited liability and a limited role in management.

You can think of a limited partnership as a compromise between a general partnership and a corporation. Limited partners cannot participate in management of the business to the extent that general partners do, although they can have a greater role than corporate shareholders. Like corporate shareholders, limited partners are protected from the business's debts. As a result, limited partnerships are more strictly regulated than general partnerships.

A limited partnership avoids the double taxation problem that corporations suffer from.

Like general partnerships, limited partnerships do not have to pay tax on the partnership's income. The profits are taxed only once as the personal income of the partners.

A limited partnership can only be created by a written partnership agreement. A **certificate of limited partnership** must be filed with the California Secretary of State's office. The certificate should also be recorded in any county where the limited partnership owns real property.

The certificate of limited partnership authorizes the general partner(s) to sell, lease, or encumber property vested in the name of the limited partnership. As a result, the limited partners' signatures are not required on the conveyance documents. However, like a statement of partnership, a certificate of limited partnership may contain restrictions on the general partners' authority to convey partnership property.

A limited partner has no ownership interest in the partnership property. The partnership property is controlled by the general partners just as in a general partnership.

www.en.wikipedia.org/wiki/Limited_partnership
Limited Partnerships

D. LIMITED LIABILITY COMPANIES (LLCs)

The **Beverly-Killea Limited Liability Company Act** (Corporations Code Section 17000-17705) became effective on September 30, 1994 and California followed 45 other states that had previously enacted such legislation. A limited liability company (LLC) allows its members to enjoy the limited liability of corporate shareholders and the tax advantage of a partnership. An LLC can engage in any lawful business activity, except banking, insurance, trust company business, or profession that requires a license, registration or certification.

It is relatively simple to form an LLC since it involves completion of forms prepared by the secretary of state. There must be **one** or more members, which may be individuals, partnerships, corporations, or other entities. Form LLC-1 (Limited Liability Company Articles of Organization) is completed and filed with the California Secretary of State along with the filing fee, and at that moment the LLC begins. The name of an LLC must end with the words "LLC", "Limited Liability Company," or "Ltd. Liability Co." Each LLC must have an operating agreement dealing with the manner in which business is to be conducted, but it does not have to be filed with the secretary of state. The LLC must also pay an annual minimum state tax.

An ownership interest in an LLC is either a membership interest or an economic interest. The membership interest has full economic, management and voting rights, but unless otherwise provided in the article or operating agreement, may be assigned only with unanimous consent of the other members. An economic interest has no management or voting rights and is freely assignable.

An LLC shall be dissolved and its affairs wound up on the happening of the first to occur of: 1) if any time is stated in its articles of organization; 2) when an event happens specified in the articles of organization or written operating agreement; 3) on the vote of a majority in interest of the members or a greater percentage of voting interests if specified; 4) by decree of judicial dissolution in a court action initiated by a manager or member.

The California Secretary of State has provided numerous other forms for future LLC use, such as an amendment of the articles, a correction of previously filed documents, certificates to dissolve, continue, cancel, or merge LLCs, and an annual information statement. A foreign LLC (from another state) must file with the secretary of state an application for registration along with a certificate of good standing from the state where the LLC was formed before transacting intrastate business in California. An unregistered LLC transacting business in California risks daily penalties for each day unauthorized business is conducted.

E. TRUSTS

An increasingly popular method of property ownership in California is in a form of trust, particularly the **REVOCABLE LIVING (INTER VIVOS) TRUST**, *Which is effective during the life of the owner rather than upon his or her death*. The major advantages of holding title in a trust include avoiding probate, thus reducing costs, time, trouble, and public disclosure, and there are significant estate tax planning advantages.

Living Trust		
Trustor	**Trustee Successor Trustee(s)**	**Beneficiary**
– Creator(s) of the trust maintain control – Usually primary Beneficiary	– Administers the trust pursuant to trust provisions – Distributes balance of trust upon Trustor's death or termination	– Named by Trustor – Usually the Trustor for life—then balance to Beneficiary

Revocable or irrevocable, testamentary or living, the A-B trust, A-B-C trust, family limited partnership trusts (FLIP), charitable lead trust, charitable remainder unitrust, or annuity trust are some of the most frequently created forms of trusts. The determination of which type of trust is appropriate will depend on the individual circumstances of the trustor's estate.

The most common trust for an individual with an estate under $600,000, or a couple with an estate under $1,200,000 is the revocable living (inter vivos) trust. The creator of the trust is the trustor, or settlor. The trustee administers the trust, and the beneficiary receives the trust assets, without probate, upon the death of the trustors(s), or upon the termination for the trust.

Example: Revocable inter vivos trust (living trust). Elizabeth and Robert Martin, are a married couple, and they each have two children from a former marriage. Their total estate has a value of $900,000 consisting of a home, two rental properties, and savings. Their goals are (1) to ensure that these assets will be available to both Elizabeth and Robert for life, as needed (2) to be certain the four children will equally receive the balance of the estate without the time and expense of probate, and (3) to eliminate estate taxes.

Elizabeth and Robert created the Martin family revocable living trust, dated October 1, 2XXX. They transfer title to the home, the rental units, and the savings accounts to "Elizabeth and Robert Martin, co-trustees of the Martin Revocable Trust, dated October 1, 2XXX". During Elizabeth and Robert's joint lifetime, they will manage the trust assets and will equally enjoy and benefit from the trust estate. During their joint lifetime, Elizabeth and Robert may revoke or amend the trust to correspond with their changing needs and goals.

Upon the first trustor's death, the assets will be divided 50/50, with 50% going into the A trust and 50% into the B trust. The surviving trustor will continue to have full control and benefit of the A trust, the same as he or she would have as the sole owner of these assets. The surviving trustor will also be the primary beneficiary of the assets in the B trust, if needed. The survivor will continue to administer the trust as the successor co-trustee.

Upon the survivor's death, the successor trustee(s) will distribute the remaining trust assets to the beneficiaries who were named by the trustors as the beneficiaries of the trust assets. In this example, the trust assets will pass equally to Elizabeth's two children and to Robert's two children without the time and expense of probate. There will be no estate tax due on this estate.

This method of holding title, and estate planning has the advantages of allowing the trustors to keep control, keeping the family secrets private, eliminating the time and expense of the probate, and eliminating estate taxes.

F. REAL ESTATE INVESTMENT TRUSTS (REITs)

The federal **Real Estate Investment Trust Act of 1960** extended tax benefits to real estate investors who organize in accordance with its terms. The act was intended to encourage substantial investments in real estate under strict regulation.

A REAL ESTATE INVESTMENT TRUST (REIT) is a real estate investment business with at least 100 investors, organized as a trust.

To obtain the act's tax benefits, a real estate investment business must be organized as a **trust**. In a trust, one or more persons (the **trustees**) manage property for the benefit of others (the **beneficiaries**). A written trust instrument vests the property in the trustees. The trustees have only those powers expressly granted to them in the trust instrument. The beneficiaries have no legal interest in the property, only the power to enforce performance of the trust.

A real estate investment trust (REIT) must have at least 100 investors. The investors are the trust's beneficiaries. The trustees use the money invested in the business to purchase property or real estate securities (mortgages or deeds of trust). They hold title to the property or securities, and manage them for the benefit of the investors.

The advantage of an REIT is that it has the conveniences of a corporation, but can avoid double taxation. If an REIT distributes at least 95% of its income to its investors, it only pays corporate taxes on the income it retains. So 95% (or more) of the earnings are taxed only as the investors' personal income, and not as the REIT's income. The investors, like corporate shareholders, are shielded from liability for the REIT's debts.

www.reit.com
National Association of Real Estate Investment Trusts

G. UNINCORPORATED ASSOCIATIONS

The designation "unincorporated association" can be used by any group that agrees to adopt it. An *UNINCORPORATED ASSOCIATION is not a legal entity separate from its members.*

CHAPTER 4

However, title to property can be held in the association's name, as long as the property is necessary to the association's business.

For title to be held in the association's name, its members must prepare a statement listing the names of those who are authorized to execute conveyances on behalf of the association. The statement should be recorded in any county where the association owns real property. This enables the unincorporated association to encumber and convey its property without having all the members sign every document.

H. JOINT VENTURES

A JOINT VENTURE is similar to a partnership, but is formed for a single transaction or a related series of transactions, not as an ongoing business. There are no formal requirements for the creation of a joint venture. The parties simply agree to work together on a project and to share the profits or losses.

A joint venture is not an entity separate from its individual members. Title to property cannot be held in the joint venture's name, unless the ventures designate their business an unincorporated association, as described above.

1. Syndicates

A SYNDICATE is not a recognized legal entity. Like "company," the term "syndicate" can be used to refer to virtually any business organization. The XYZ Syndicate might be a corporation, partnership, trust, or unincorporated association, and it would hold title accordingly.

III. Common Interest Developments (CIDs)

A COMMON INTEREST DEVELOPMENT (CID) is a form of property ownership in a project which combines ownership of a separate lot, unit, or exclusive right of possession with co-ownership of the common area in the project that is held in undivided interests by all of the owners of the separate interests. Normally, a non-profit association of the owners manages the common area.

As cities have grown more crowded, single-family homes have become harder to find and more expensive to buy and maintain. Condominiums and other multifamily housing have become popular ownership alternatives. California law refers to these as common interest developments. They are structured (physically and legally) to combine individual ownership with concurrent ownership. See Chapter 13 for more details about common interest developments.

A. CONDOMINIUMS

Office buildings and retail centers have been developed as condominiums, but most condominiums were designed for residential use. A typical condominium looks like an apartment building. A *CONDOMINIUM isn't owned by a landlord who rents out apartment units to tenants. Instead, it is owned by its residents.*

Each resident (or family of residents) has exclusive ownership of one of the units. The other parts of the property—*the grounds, the parking lot, the recreational facilities, the building's lobby, elevators, and hallways—are called the COMMON AREAS.* These are owned by all of the

152

residents as tenants in common. Thus, each condominium owner has a separate interest in his or her unit, plus an undivided interest in the common areas.

> **Example:** J bought a unit in a 30-unit condominium. The deed describes her property as "Unit 14 in Pearl Hill, a condominium, together with an undivided 1/30 interest in the common areas of said condominium."

Unless otherwise agreed, one unit's undivided interest in the common areas is equal to the other units' undivided interests. Each unit in J's building has an undivided 1/30 interest in the common areas, even the larger and more expensive units. An undivided interest in the common areas cannot be conveyed separately from the unit to which it attaches.

1. Creation

Property can be developed as a condominium in the first place, or an existing building can be converted to a condominium. In either case, condominium status is established by recording a **CONDOMINIUM DECLARATION**, *which describes the project and lists any restrictions on residents' use of the units and common areas.*

At the same time, the developers must record a **CONDOMINIUM PLAN**, *which consists of a survey map of the land, floor plans for the building, and a certificate of consent.* The certificate is signed by all record owners of the property, indicating that they consent to the plan. It must also be signed by anyone holding a recorded security interest in the property.

Condominiums are considered subdivisions, so in most cases, the developer will be required to comply with state and local subdivision laws (see Chapter 13). After complying with those laws and recording the declaration and plan, the developer may the sell units.

A unit's deed doesn't have to include a complete property description of the project; it may just specify the unit number and refer to the condominium plan (just as platted property can be described by its lot and block numbers). The restrictions governing use of the property must be included in the deed by reference to the condominium declaration.

2. Management

A *condominium is controlled by a* **COMMUNITY ASSOCIATION (called Homeowner's Association - HOA)** *made up of all the unit owners.* The association's members elect a board of directors from among themselves. The board is responsible for managing the common areas of the condominium: maintenance, utility bills, repairs, taxes, insurance, and improvements. Some issues are referred back to the association as a whole for a vote. The board is required to keep the members informed about the association's finances.

The association has the power to levy regular and special assessments to pay for common area expenses. Local water-efficient landscape ordinances or water conservation measures cannot be restricted or prohibited by HOA governing documents. HOAs must annually distribute an "Assessment and Reserve Funding Disclosure Summary."

3. Encumbrance and Transfer

Each owner may give a lender a deed of trust on his or her unit and its accompanying undivided interest in the common areas, and each owner's creditors can claim a lien against his or her unit and undivided interest. If a lienholder forecloses, only that unit and its

CHAPTER 4

undivided interest are affected. The lienholder can't foreclose on the entire condominium. Property taxes are also levied against each unit separately, so a tax lien foreclosure won't affect the whole property.

When a condominium unit is conveyed, an undivided interest in the common areas and membership in the community association are automatically conveyed, too. The seller must provide the buyer with a copy of the condominium declaration, the association's articles of incorporation, bylaws, and most recent financial statement, and a statement concerning any unpaid assessments.

B. STOCK COOPERATIVES

Like condominiums, *STOCK COOPERATIVES are usually residential buildings. Title to a cooperative building is held by a corporation formed for that purpose. A person who wants to live in the building buys shares of stock in the corporation, instead of renting or buying a unit.* The building's residents are the corporation's shareholders. The corporation owns the building, but the residents own the corporation.

A cooperative shareholder is usually given a proprietary lease to a unit in the building, along with the right to use the common areas. A *PROPRIETARY LEASE has a longer term than most ordinary leases and gives the shareholder more rights than an ordinary tenant would have.*

To establish a cooperative, the developer must take the same steps required for any corporation—filing articles of incorporation, and so forth. In addition, just as with a condominium, the developer must file a declaration and plan, and comply with the subdivision laws.

A cooperative shareholder pays a pro rata share of the building's expenses. This generally includes a contribution toward payments on a **blanket trust deed**. Since each apartment isn't separately owned, they aren't separately financed. Instead, the corporation gives the lender a trust deed that covers the whole building. The expenses also include property taxes levied against the whole building. If any resident fails to pay his or her share of the expenses, the entire cooperative may be threatened with foreclosure.

To transfer an interest in a cooperative, a shareholder must convey his or her shares of stock and assign the proprietary lease to the new shareholder. Because one shareholder's financial instability can jeopardize the whole cooperative, the cooperative agreement may provide that a shareholder can't transfer an interest without the other shareholders' consent.

Consent provisions of this kind, in addition to the drawbacks of blanket trust deeds and blanket property taxes, can lead to serious conflicts among the shareholders. As a result, cooperatives have been much less popular than condominiums in California.

C. COMMUNITY APARTMENT PROJECTS (CAPs)

In a *COMMUNITY APARTMENT PROJECT (CAP), the residents own the whole property as tenants in common, but the deed assigns each owner an exclusive right to occupy a particular apartment unit.* Community apartment projects are sometimes called tenant in common units, or TICs, or as "own your own." A recorded declaration and plan are required to establish a CAP, and in some cases it is also necessary to comply with subdivision laws. A CAP is usually governed by a community association.

D. PLANNED DEVELOPMENTS (PDs)

In a *PLANNED DEVELOPMENT (PD), each resident has separate ownership of his or her house and the lot that it's located on.* How is it different from a standard subdivision of single-family homes? A planned development includes areas or facilities that are either owned by all the homeowners as tenants in common, or that are owned by a community association and maintained for the use of the homeowners.

Like the other forms of common interest projects, a planned development project is established by a recorded declaration and plan.

IV. Timeshares

*In a **TIMESHARING** arrangement, buyers purchase the exclusive right to possession of the property for specified periods each year.*

Example: B bought a timeshare in a condominium unit in Palm Springs. B's interest gives her the right to use the unit from December 1 through December 15 each year.

C, D, E, F, and so on have similar rights in the same unit, each for a different annual period. Of course, each timeshare costs only a fraction of what it would cost to buy the unit outright. A timesharing arrangement could be developed for any kind of housing, but it has been most commonly used for resort condominiums.

*Not every timeshare project actually involves co-ownership. In some cases, individuals purchase only a license to use the property, rather than an interest in the property. This is called a **TIMESHARE USE**.* When a timesharing arrangement does involve the purchase of an interest in the property, that interest is called a timeshare estate.

Because timesharing arrangements are complex, with many potential problems and abuses, the sale of timeshares is now strictly regulated. See the Real Estate Commissioner's Regulations, sections 2810-2813.13.

CHAPTER 4

V. CHAPTER SUMMARY

1. A tenancy in common is the most basic form of co-ownership. Tenants in common may have unequal interests; their interests are undivided, and they share possession of the whole property. A tenant in common's interest can be freely transferred or willed. A tenancy in common may be terminated by partition, either voluntarily or by court order.

2. A joint tenancy requires the four unities (time, title, interest, and possession). The key characteristic of joint tenancy is the right of survivorship; it prevents a joint tenant from willing his or her interest, but makes probate of the property unnecessary. The transfer of a joint tenant's interest severs the joint tenancy by breaking the unities of time and title. Severance does not terminate the co-ownership, but changes it to tenancy in common.

3. Property owned by a married couple is either the separate property of one spouse or the community property of both. Husband and wife have equal control over community property. The joinder requirement prevents transfer or encumbrance of community real property without the signature of both spouses. An unauthorized transfer is voidable by the nonconsenting spouse.

4. A revocable living trust may be created by an individual or a married couple who wish to maintain control, keep family secrets private, eliminate the time and expense of probate, and eliminate or reduce estate taxes.

5. Title to real property can be held by associations of individuals: corporations, general and limited partnerships, REITs, and unincorporated associations. Each form of organization has advantages and disadvantages in terms of management, taxation, regulation, and liability.

6. In a general partnership, the partners own property as tenants in partnership, whether or not title is in the partnership's name. They have equal rights of possession and control of partnership property. One partner cannot transfer or encumber his or her undivided interest in the property separately from the other partners' interests.

7. In a limited liability company(LLC), the one or more members have the limited liability of a corporate shareholder and the tax advantage of a partner in a partnership. An LLC can be an individual.

8. The owner of a condominium unit has a separate interest in his or her unit, plus an undivided interest in the common areas. A stock cooperative is owned by a corporation; each shareholder has a proprietary lease for one of the units. The owners of a CAP own the whole property as tenants in common, but each owner has the exclusive right to occupy a particular unit. In a planned development, a homeowner has separate title to a single-family home and lot, and shares title to common areas or facilities with the neighbors.

VI. CASE PROBLEM

Estate of Baumann, 247 Cal. Rptr. 532 (4th Dist. 1988)

When Leola Baumann purchased a condominium unit, she took title in joint tenancy with her son, John. This was done so Leola could qualify for a purchase money loan, and so the property would not have to be probated when she died.

Sometime later, John defaulted on some large business loans, and his creditors sued him. To protect the condo unit, John used a quitclaim deed to transfer his undivided 1/2 interest in it to Leola. John's creditors proceeded with their lawsuit and eventually obtained a judgment against him.

Leola died a few months later. In her will, she left the condo unit to John's two sons, Chris and Jeff (her grandsons). John's creditors claimed a judgment lien against the unit.

The creditors argued that the quitclaim deed from John to Leola was void, because its purpose was to defraud the creditors. Therefore, John and his mother still owned the unit in joint tenancy at the time of her death. As a result, the entire property vested in John by the right of survivorship.

John argued that the quitclaim had been effective so that Leola owned the condo in severalty and had the power to will it to her two grandsons. Since John no longer owned the property, the judgment lien could not attach to it.

The court agreed with the creditors that the quitclaim deed was void and had not been effective to transfer John's interest to Leola, but the court held that the quitclaim had severed the joint tenancy. As a result of this ruling, who owns the condo unit? How is title held? Can John's judgment creditors claim a lien against the unit? How does all of this affect the other unit owners in the condominium?

VII. KEY TERMS

blanket trust deed	ouster	stock cooperative
common areas	partition	syndicate
community property	partnership	tenancy in common
condominium	(general/limited)	tenancy in partnership
corporation	partnership property	the four unities
joinder requirements	planned development	timeshare
joint venture	REIT	trust
joint tenancy	right of survivorship	undivided interest
limited liability company	separate property	unincorporated association
living trust	severalty	
marketable title	severance	

CHAPTER 4

VIII. CHAPTER QUIZ

1. A and B own a house in San Francisco. A has an undivided 3/4 interest in the property and B has an undivided 1/4 interest. They hold the property as:

    a. a tenancy in common.
    b. a joint tenancy.
    c. a tenancy by the entirety.
    d. community property.

2. In California, a married person cannot hold title to real property as:

    a. his or her separate property.
    b. a tenant in partnership.
    c. a tenant by the entirety.
    d. a joint tenant.

3. When title to property is held in severalty:

    a. the property cannot be transferred or encumbered without the consent of a majority of the co-owners.
    b. the property is owned by one individual.
    c. none of the owners can be a corporation.
    d. the property cannot be willed.

4. The only one of the four unities required for a tenancy in common is the unity of:

    a. time.
    b. title.
    c. interest.
    d. possession.

5. When A and B took title to the house as joint tenants, they agreed that only B would live there. What effect did this agreement have on the joint tenancy?

    a. It severed the joint tenancy; unity of possession is essential.
    b. It did not sever the joint tenancy if A and B stated that they did not intend to sever it.
    c. It did not sever the joint tenancy as long as A is charging B rent.
    d. It severed the joint tenancy by partitioning the property.

6. A, B, and C own some land as joint tenants. When C dies, A and B each have a 1/2 interest because of:

    a. the right of survivorship.
    b. unity of possession.
    c. the rules of intestate succession.
    d. the doctrine of severalty.

7. A, B, and C own a house as joint tenants. B takes out a loan, giving the lender a trust deed on her interest in the property. Which of the following is true?

    a. If B defaults on her trust deed, the lender can foreclose on the entire property.
    b. The trust deed is void.
    c. The trust deed severs the joint tenancy.
    d. If B dies before A and C, the lender loses its lien against the property.

8. H and W are a married couple; they own some land as community property. H wills all his property to A. When H dies, who owns the land?

    a. W owns the land in severalty.
    b. W has an undivided 2/3 interest and A has an undivided 1/3 interest.
    c. W and A each have an undivided 1/2 interest.
    d. W, A, and H's minor child each have an undivided 1/3 interest.

9. The ZAP Corporation owns some land in severalty. In order to sell the land, who must sign the sale documents?

    a. The CEO and at least one member of the board of directors
    b. A majority of the directors
    c. A majority of the stockholders
    d. Corporate officers authorized to sell it by a resolution of the board of directors

10. Which of these statements about condominiums is false in most cases?

    a. Each unit owner has an undivided interest in the common areas.
    b. Property taxes are assessed separately for each unit.
    c. A blanket trust deed covers the entire condominium property.
    d. The association can levy assessments to pay for maintenance.

ANSWERS: 1. a; 2. c; 3. b; 4. d; 5. b; 6. a; 7. d; 8. c; 9. d; 10. c

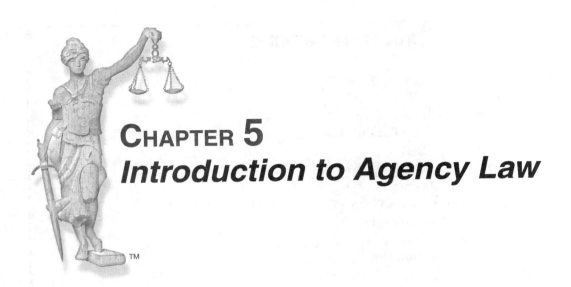

CHAPTER 5
Introduction to Agency Law

CHAPTER OVERVIEW

This chapter describes the agency relationships between real estate brokers and salespersons and their clients. It explains the different ways an agency relationship can be created and terminated. It also discusses the duties imposed on brokers and salespersons by the California Real Estate Law in regard to licensing, record keeping, and trust fund accounts. Other agency duties are discussed in Chapter 6.

I. Agency

"Real estate agent" is a very familiar term, but few people stop to think about what the word "agent" means. An *AGENT is someone who is authorized to represent or act for another person (the PRINCIPAL) in dealings with third parties.* Agency is a special legal relationship. The agent's authorized actions are legally binding on the principal. For example, suppose a principal authorizes her agent to negotiate and sign a contract with a third party on her behalf. The agent's signature on the contract binds the principal to the terms of the agreement, just as though the principal had signed it herself.

Another important characteristic of an agency relationship is that the knowledge of the agent can be imputed to the principal. If a third party discloses something to the agent, the principal may be held to have known it—whether or not the agent actually passed the information on to the principal.

Not only that, an agent's wrongful acts can be imputed to the principal, so that the principal is legally responsible for them. If the agent in the example above had lied to the third party to persuade him to sign the contract, the third party could sue the principal as well as the agent for fraud. The principal might be held liable even though she did not direct her agent to lie. The principal could, in turn, sue the agent, and might recover from the agent what she paid to satisfy the third party's judgment. The issue of the agent's liability to the principal generally would not affect the principal's liability to the third parties. *THIRD PARTIES are others who are involved in a contract with the principal and agent.*

CHAPTER 5

CHAPTER OUTLINE

Agency is a Special Legal Relationship

An **agent** is one who is authorized to represent or act for another person (principal).
The **principal** is the person who hires an agent to represent him or her.
Third parties are others involved in a contract with the principal and agent.

A. AGENT'S AUTHORITY

#29

An agent's authority always comes from the principal. *Authority intentionally given to the agent by the principal is called ACTUAL AUTHORITY.* Actual authority is usually express or sometimes it may be implied by the conduct of the principal.

EXPRESS AUTHORITY is expressly communicated by the principal to the agent either orally or in writing. IMPLIED AUTHORITY is inferred by the conduct of the principal indicating his or her intent to confer it or causing the agent to believe he or she possesses it. For example, a seller gives a real estate agent express authority to find a buyer for the property. This is generally understood to give the agent implied authority to advertise the property, put up "For Sale" signs, show the property, and negotiate with prospective buyers.

Sometimes a person may simply appear to be the agent of another. This is called OSTENSIBLE AGENCY. Although the principal has not granted actual authority to the agent, a third party is led to believe by the principal not objecting, that the ostensible agent is acting as though he or she has authority. The ostensible agent is acting as though he or she is authorized, and the principal's words or conduct seem to back that up. In this situation, the principal may be bound by the acts of the ostensible agent, even though they weren't actually authorized. Ostensible agency created by estoppel will be discussed later in the chapter.

Unlike most agencies, real estate agents appointed to find a buyer for a seller's property lack the authority to bind the principal (the seller) to a contract.

B. TYPES OF AGENTS

Agents are classified according to the scope of authority the principal has conferred on them. An agent may be general or special.

A *GENERAL AGENT has authority to handle all matters for the principal in a specified area.*

Example: A property manager is a general agent if he or she has authority to market and maintain the property, hire and fire maintenance personnel, enter lease agreements on the owner's behalf, and take full responsibility for managing the property.

A *SPECIAL AGENT has limited authority to do a specific thing or conduct a specific transaction.* Most real estate brokers are special agents. Their authority is usually limited to a single transaction, such as the sale of a particular house. An agent should keep the limits of his or her authority in mind and be careful not to go beyond them. As a general rule, the principal isn't bound by or liable for the agent's acts if they exceed the scope of the authority granted.

"Real estate agents hired to find a buyer for a single property are special agents.

II. How an Agency is Created

The principal's liability and the agent's duties arise as soon as an agency relationship is established. It's important to understand how and when an agency is created.

An Agency Must Be Created By:

- Express Agreement,
- Ratification, or
- Estoppel (Ostensible)

A. EXPRESS AGREEMENT

An express agency relationship can be created by oral or written agreement. In some cases the principal signs a *POWER OF ATTORNEY—a document that appoints another person as an agent and defines the scope of the agent's authority*. In most cases it is created in an employment contract, usually verbal but sometimes written. Any person having the capacity to contract may appoint an agent; and any person may be an agent.

In real estate, an agency relationship between a real estate broker and a seller is usually created with a **written listing agreement**. The broker is the agent and the seller is the principal. The listing agreement sets forth the duties of both parties.

A written listing agreement is required if the broker is to collect a commission. However, even if the agreement is only oral, the broker is still held to the same degree of responsibility and must perform all duties owed to the principal. If the broker doesn't carry out these duties or performs them negligently, the principal may sue the broker for damages even without a written agreement.

> **Example:** A seller orally agrees to pay a real estate broker a 5.5% commission if he finds a buyer for her property. The broker receives an offer of $152,000, but he's extremely busy, so he doesn't pass the offer on to the seller right away. The next day, before the broker has told the seller about the offer, it is withdrawn.
>
> To the broker's relief, another prospective buyer makes an offer a few days later. But this one is only for $145,000. The broker informs the seller of this offer, the seller accepts it, and the sale closes.
>
> Afterwards, the seller refuses to pay the broker his commission. The broker can't sue for the commission because he never had a written agreement with the seller.
>
> Later the seller finds out about the first (and higher) offer. She sues the broker for negligence and breach of duty for failing to transmit the offer to her promptly. She has a right to sue even though there was no written agency agreement.

This is a bit one-sided, but for a good reason. The law protects the public in their dealings with professionals. When an agency relationship is established, a real estate agent assumes certain responsibilities. The client's failure to pay doesn't excuse the agent from carrying out these responsibilities competently. And a real estate agent can protect him or herself very easily, by requiring the client to sign a written listing agreement.

Even without an express contract, an agency can be implied from the words and conduct of the individuals as well as the circumstances surrounding the activities of the parties. Whether or not there is an agency may have to be decided by the courts based on the facts.

www.lendingtree.com/real-estate/advice/finding-a-realtor/what-to-expect-of-listing-agents/
www.homebuying.about.com/cs/dealingagents/a/agentdisclosure_2.htm
www.sacramentorealestatevoice.com/sellers-do-you-know-what-you-should-expect/
What to Expect from Your REALTOR®

B. RATIFICATION

Sometimes one person acts on another's behalf without agency authorization because either there is no agency or the act exceeds the agent's authority. *If the other person (principal) later approves these actions, he or she is said to have* **RATIFIED** *them.* The unauthorized act may be ratified either by an express approval by the principal or by the principal's acceptance of the benefits of the unauthorized act. Additionally, for ratification to take place the ratifying party must have knowledge of all material facts in order to ratify the act. When agency relationship is created by ratification the legal consequences are just the same as if the actions had been authorized beforehand. Additionally, the third party may resent or cancel the transaction at any time prior to ratification without any reason since there is no contract.

If a certain type of agency can only be expressly created in writing, it can only be ratified in writing. For other types of agency, the ratification does not have to take a particular form. The principal simply has to say or do something that indicates an intent to adopt the agent's actions as the principal's own. If the principal accepts the benefit of the agent's actions, that's considered ratification, as long as the principal has full knowledge of the facts.

Example: X and Y are neighbors. X happens to be a real estate broker. Y casually mentions to X that he would consider selling his house if the price were right. X begins to take prospective buyers to Y's house to show them the property. She receives two offers on the property and relays them to Y. Y accepts one of the offers.

A court could rule that although Y never expressly authorized X to act as his agent, he ratified the agency relationship by accepting the benefit of her actions.

The most common method of ratifying an unauthorized act is by accepting the benefits of that unauthorized act.

Even if a real estate broker's unauthorized actions have been ratified by the seller, the broker isn't legally entitled to a commission unless the ratification is in writing. In the example above, although an agency relationship has been established by ratification, X could not sue Y if he refused to pay her for her services.

If the seller signs a purchase agreement containing a provision stating that the seller has employed the broker and agrees to pay a commission, he or she has ratified the agency relationship in writing and will be liable for the commission even if there was no written listing.

www.dre.ca.gov/Consumers/InformationForHomebuyers.html
Information for Home Buyers

C. ESTOPPEL (OSTENSIBLE) AGENCY

An agency relationship may also be created by estoppel, also known as an ostensible agency. As noted in Chapter 3, the term estoppel refers to a legal doctrine that a person is not permitted to deny the existence of a fact or relationship which that person has, by his or her acts or negligence, allowed another person to believe to be true. In most agency by estoppel situations, there is no express agency relationship; that is no principal who has actually authorized another person to act as an agent. However, if a person intentionally or negligently causes a third person to believe that someone is acting as an agent, that person is estopped (prevented) from denying the existence of an agency relationship and will be held to be a principal (and thus responsible for the acts of the "agent"). Estoppel may also occur when a person has actually appointed an agent and that agent exceeds the agent's authority. If the principal intentionally or negligently allowed a third person to believe that the agent did have authority for the unauthorized act, the principal will be bound by the agent's act just as if the principal had given authority to the agent. The agent is said to have ostensible authority and the principal is estopped from asserting that the agent did not have authority.

The purpose of ostensible agency is to protect innocent third parties who have reasonably assumed that a person had authority to act for the principal. The principal is held responsible because he or she led the third party to believe that the apparent agent was acting without authority. Ostensible agency is only created by conduct or acts of the principal, not the conduct or actions of the supposed agent.

> **Example:** F owns several pieces of property. In the past, his daughter, D, has handled real estate sales for him. D gives a broker an exclusive listing for one of F's properties. F doesn't protest when the broker places a "For Sale" sign on the property and shows the property to prospective purchasers. F sells the property to one of the broker's customers, but refuses to pay a commission to the broker. F claims that D was not his agent and had no authority to contract with the broker.
>
> Since F, negligently or deliberately, allowed the broker to believe in and rely on D's ostensible authority, a court could hold that F was estopped from denying responsibility.

Note that a third party has a duty to make a reasonable effort to discover whether or not a person is an agent and, if so, whether or not the agent's acts are authorized. When an agent acts without actual authority, the third party can't hold the principal liable unless the principal's conduct indicated approval or acceptance of the agent's acts.

A third party should always verify that anyone representing himself or herself as an agent is, in fact, an agent and has the authority to act in the capacity expected by the third party.

III. Real Estate Agency Relationships

There is more than one agency relationship in a typical real estate transaction. In addition to the listing broker, the transaction is likely to involve at least one real estate salesperson, and it may also involve other brokers. Whose agents are they? The answer isn't simple.

A. SALESPERSON: THE BROKER'S AGENT

It is the standard practice for a real estate broker to hire licensed salespersons. A salesperson often handles nearly every aspect of a particular listing—advising the seller, negotiating with buyers, filling out the purchase agreement form, and so on. The seller is likely to think of the salesperson as "my real estate agent." Yet in strict legal terms, the salesperson is not the seller's agent but the broker's agent.

Under California law, a real estate salesperson can only work for a broker.

Broker/Salesperson employment agreements are explained fully in Chapter 8. A salesperson cannot work directly for a member of the public in a real estate transaction. Thus, the salesperson is legally the broker's agent, not the seller's agent. The salesperson can't continue to represent the seller if the broker tells her to stop, and the salesperson can't sue the seller for a commission, except through the broker.

1. Liabilities to Third Parties

Even though the salesperson is not the seller's agent, the seller as well as the broker may be held liable if the salesperson does something wrong in the real estate transaction. First the salesperson's action is imputed to the salesperson's principal, the broker. Then, depending on the circumstances, the action might be imputed to the broker's principal, the seller. The agency relationships create a chain of liability.

 www.realestateabc.com/glossary/
Real Estate Terms

2. Employee or Independent Contractor

A real estate salesperson is his or her broker's agent. For some purposes, the law also classifies the salesperson either as the broker's employee or as an independent contractor. (Any agent is either the principal's employee or an independent contractor. An employee or an independent contractor is not necessarily an agent, however. Only someone authorized to represent the principal in dealings with third parties is an agent.) All Department of Real Estate regulations obligating the broker to supervise the broker's salespersons apply whether the broker-salesperson relationship is treated as an employer/employee relationship or independent contractor relationship for other purposes.

Certain employment laws apply only to the relationship between an employer and an employee, and do not apply when someone hires an independent contractor. For example, minimum wage laws apply only to employees. The distinction also affects liability: an employer is legally responsible for torts committed by an employee in the course of and within the scope of his or her employment. A buyer or seller who hires an independent contractor generally isn't liable for the contractor's torts.

Since most real estate salespeople work independently, have flexible schedules, and are paid by commission, they are independent contractors for minimum wage purposes. There's a complication, however. California law requires real estate brokers to supervise the salespersons who work for them. Failure to adequately supervise a salesperson is grounds for suspension or revocation of the broker's license. In this sense, the salesperson is the broker's employee, not an independent contractor, as a matter of law. It doesn't matter how they structure their working relationship or what terms they use to describe it in their contract; the broker can't avoid the duty to supervise the salesperson's work.

A broker may be able to treat a real estate salesperson as an independent contractor for the purposes of income tax laws, social security, and unemployment taxes. The Internal Revenue Service considers a real estate salesperson to be an independent contractor if:

1. he or she is a licensed real estate agent,
2. compensation is directly related to sales rather than to hours worked, and
3. the services are performed pursuant to a written contract that states that the individual will not be treated as an employee for tax purposes.

If these three criteria are met, the broker is not required to withhold taxes and social security contributions from the salesperson's compensation. Similarly, if a salesperson is paid only by commission (with no base wage or salary), the broker is not required to pay unemployment taxes, and the salesperson is not eligible to receive unemployment compensation. A salesperson may be eligible for worker's compensation if injured on the job, however.

B. COOPERATING BROKERS

A **COOPERATING BROKER** *is a non-listing broker with whom the listing broker agrees to share a commission (not necessarily ½ and ½) if the non-listing broker sells the property.*

Real estate brokers often belong to a Multiple Listing Service (MLS). Under the terms of MLS membership, when a broker obtains a listing he or she submits it to the MLS. That permits other brokers who belong to the MLS to help find buyer for the listed property. In relation to the listing broker, these other brokers are known as Cooperating Brokers.

An exclusive listing, posted on an MLS, encourages participation in the sale by numerous brokers, resulting in the most market exposure and the highest possible selling price. Cooperating brokers then share the commission, as agreed. If a seller does NOT wish to be listed in an MLS, he or she must indicate so in writing.

An **ASSOCIATE LICENSEE** *means a person who is licensed as a real estate broker or salesperson who is either licensed under a broker or has entered into a written contract with a broker to act as the broker's licensee in connection with acts requiring a real estate license and to function under the broker's supervision in the capacity of an associate licensee.*

A subagent is a person to whom an agent delegates agency powers. However, it doesn't include an associate licensee who is acting under the supervision of an agent in a real property transaction.

Because of liability issues (responsiblity for the actions, error and omissions), subagency is an outdated practice, all but dead in most states. Most real estate forms and MLS agreements focus on cooperating brokers.

A broker represents a seller when taking a listing. A salesperson or broker working under that listing broker (in the same firm) who is acting as the broker's agent is an associate licensee. A broker who does not work for the same firm, but helps find a buyer is a cooperating broker. A cooperating broker also may have associate licensees representing him or her.

If the listing broker is placed in the MLS, the listing broker is offering to share the commission with any cooperating broker who procures a buyer for the property.

www.realtor.com/realestateagents/
Find a REALTOR®

IV. Terminating an Agency

An agent's authority ends when the agency ends. There are two categories of ways in which an agency may be terminated. The first is by actions of the parties to the agency contract. This consist of revocation of the agency by the principal; renunciation of the agency by the agent; accomplishment of the purpose the parties agreed to in the agency contract; expiration of the agency term as provided in the contract; or by the mutual agreement of both the principal and agent. The second way the agency can terminate is by operation of the law. This means that legislation has provided situations where the agency is terminated.

A. ACCOMPLISHMENT OF PURPOSE

Perhaps the most common reason for termination is that the purpose of the agency has been accomplished.

> **Example:** An owner hires a real estate broker to help her sell some property. Once the property is sold and all of the details are taken care of, the agency relationship terminates.

B. EXPIRATION

When an agency agreement specifies that the agency is for a limited term, the agency ends automatically when the term expires. In California, a listing agreement must include a specific termination date. (One exception: an open listing doesn't have to have a termination date. The different types of listings are discussed at the end of this chapter.)

> **Example:** An owner hires a real estate broker to help him sell some property. He signs an exclusive listing agreement that provides the agency will last through March 30. When this date passes, the agency terminates.

C. MUTUAL AGREEMENT

An agency is a consensual relationship, which means that it is based on the written consent of both parties. If both the principal and the agent want to end the agency, they can agree to terminate it at any point. When an agency is terminated by mutual agreement, neither party is liable to the other for damages.

D. RENUNCIATION (Agent) fire you as a client,

Because of the consensual nature of agency, each party in an agency relationship has the power to terminate it unilaterally. The agent may **renounce** his or her agency at any time. If the agency agreement is open-ended, without a specific termination date, the agent will not have any further obligation to the principal. If there is a termination date, the agent may be liable to the principal for damages resulting from breach of contract.

CHAPTER 5

An agency agreement is a personal services contract: a real estate agent (for example) agrees to provide services for a seller. A court can't force a person to perform personal services because that would violate the constitutional prohibition against involuntary servitude (slavery). So when an agent breaches an agency contract, the principal can't demand specific performance—that is, the principal can't require the agent to provide the services as originally agreed. Instead, an award of money damages (if proved) is usually the principal's only remedy. (See Chapter 7 for further discussion of specific performance and other remedies for breach of contract.)

E. REVOCATION (Principal)

A principal can **revoke** the grant of agency powers at any time by firing the agent. If the agency agreement is open-ended, the principal may have to reimburse the agent for expenses already incurred, but will not be liable to the agent for damages. However, if the agency agreement has a specific termination date (so that the revocation is a breach of contract), the principal may be liable for any damages suffered by the agent because of the breach.

> **Example:** C is planning to sell his house. He signs a 90-day exclusive listing agreement with B, a real estate broker. Two weeks later, C starts dating a real estate salesperson who convinces him to change the listing to her brokerage. C tells B that her agency is revoked because he's changing to a different broker.
>
> C has the power to revoke, but the revocation is a breach of contract, so he's liable for the consequences. He may be required to pay B's damages, which will probably be the full amount of the commission she might have earned if C hadn't ended the agency. (C's new agent may also be in trouble. She interfered with another agent's exclusive listing, and convinced C to breach his agreement. This type of problem is discussed in Chapter 8.)

F. OPERATION OF LAW

An agency relationship may also be terminated by operation of law. This means that the agency ends automatically if certain events occur because the law says so. An agency is terminated by operation of law if:

1. either party dies or becomes incapacitated,
2. either party goes bankrupt,
3. the property that is the subject of the agency is destroyed or condemned,
4. the agent loses his or her license, or
5. a conflict of interest arises between the parties.

> **Example:** A hires B (broker) to help him sell some commercial property. B happens to be part owner of a gas station located across the street from A's property. One of the potential buyers for A's property turns out to be a rival oil company that wants to build a station there.
>
> As A's agent, B must act in his principal's best interest. It may be in A's best interest to sell the property to the rival gas station. However, B has a conflict of interest, since the sale to a competing oil company could cut into B's profits from the existing gas station. B should inform A of the conflict and withdraw from the agency relationship. If B doesn't, a court might later decide the conflict of interest was so substantial that the agency terminated by operation of law.

Termination of Agency

Acts of the Parties	Operation of Law
1. Accomplishment of purpose	1. Death or incapacity
2. Expiration of agency term	2. Bankruptcy
3. Mutual agreement	3. Property destroyed
4. Agent renounces	4. Agent loses license
5. Principal revokes	5. Conflict of interests

G. AGENCY COUPLED WITH AN INTEREST

There's an exception to the rule that a principal can revoke an agency agreement: the principal does not have the power to revoke if the agency is coupled with an interest. An agency is coupled with an interest when the agent has a financial or ownership interest in the property that is the subject of the agency. In that case, the principal can't revoke the agency, and the death, incompetency, or bankruptcy of the principal doesn't terminate the agency.

Example: A broker loans funds to a contractor to complete the building of a home. As a means of repaying the loan, the contractor gives the broker an exclusive right to sell the property when the home is completed.

Before the home is sold, the contractor dies. The agency is not automatically terminated by the contractor's death, because the broker has an interest in the property.

V. The California Real Estate Law

As you've seen, general agency law applies to a real estate agent's relationships with clients and customers. In addition, the California Real Estate Law governs many aspects of those relationships. The Real Estate Law can be found in the **Business and Professions Code**, starting at section 10000.

The primary purpose of the Real Estate Law is to protect the public in real estate transactions. Toward this goal, it provides detailed rules concerning licensing, record keeping, and client trust funds. These are outlined below. The law also includes rules about unethical and illegal conduct and disciplinary proceedings, which are the focus of the next chapter.

A. LICENSING

In general, anyone who represents another person in a real estate transaction and is paid or expects to be paid for those services must have a valid real estate license. But if you don't expect to be paid and in fact are not paid, a license isn't necessary.

Example: As a favor, A helped her friend B sell his house. A did not expect to be paid for her services, and B did not pay or offer her any compensation. This isn't a violation of the Real Estate Law, although A was not licensed.

Even when you are paid, it isn't necessary to be licensed if you have some other legal authorization to act for the other person. For example, if you are a lawyer, an executor, or a trustee, you may be allowed to represent another person without a license. A person having a power of attorney giving authority to act for another person may also be exempt from the license requirement. However, a power of attorney can't be used on an ongoing basis to get around the licensing requirements.

Case Example: The Leins gave Ms. Sheetz a power of attorney to manage 23 residential and commercial properties, including soliciting tenants, negotiating leases, and collecting rents. The DRE charged Sheetz with acting as a real estate broker without a license. On appeal, the court held that the power of attorney exception to the licensing requirements was only intended to apply to isolated transactions, not to someone engaged in the real estate business. *Sheetz v. Edmonds*, 201 Cal. App. 3d 1432, 247 Cal. Rptr. 776 (1988).

A person found guilty of acting as a broker or salesperson without a license can be sentenced to up to six months in jail and fined up to $10,000.

Brokers are permitted by law to conduct brokerage services through various entities, including corporations and partnerships, or under a fictitious business name. Importantly, the type of business entity under which the broker operates may affect his or her liability for wrongs committed by the salespersons.

1. Obtaining and Maintaining a License

To obtain a real estate salesperson license, you must be at least 18 years old, successfully complete the required Real Estate Principles, Real Estate Practice, and an additional approved real estate class, as well as pay application and examination fees and then pass the salesperson's exam to obtain a salesperson's license. For a broker's license, you must have at least two years' active experience as a salesperson (or experience that the Real Estate Commissioner considers equivalent), or have a degree with a major or minor in real estate from a four-year college. You must also complete required courses, pay application and examination fees, and pass the broker's exam.

Real estate licenses must be renewed every four years. Ordinarily, a renewal applicant must show he or she has completed 45-clock hours of continuing education courses during the previous four-year period. Of the 45 hours, there must be a three-hour course in each of the following: ethics, agency, trust funds, fair housing, and risk management. Risk management was added as a required course for licensees renewing on or after July 1, 2007. The first time a salesperson or broker applies for renewal, he or she must have completed a three-hour course in all five topics. The broker must also complete a minimum of 18 hours of consumer protection courses and the remaining 12 hours in either consumer protection or customer service.

For subsequent renewals, all real estate brokers and salespersons must complete 45 clock hours consisting of: an 8-hour survey course that covers the mandatory topics of ethics, agency, trust funds, fair housing and risk management; 18 hours of consumer protection courses; with the remaining hours in either consumer service or consumer protection courses.

IMPORTANT: ALL LICENSEES RENEWING FOR THE FIRST TIME ON OR AFTER JULY 1, 2007 MUST TAKE AN INDIVIDUAL THREE-HOUR COURSE IN RISK MANAGEMENT. SUBSEQUENT RENEWALS CAN BE ACCOMPLISHED WITH THE EIGHT-HOUR SURVEY COURSE.

A broker keeps the licenses of all his or her salespersons and associate brokers. These licenses, and the broker's own license, must be available for inspection by a representative from the Commissioner's office. A licensee whose business address changes should notify the DRE and write the new address on his or her license.

Whenever a salesperson joins or leaves his or her staff, a broker is required to notify the Commissioner in writing, within 5 days of hiring or 10 days of terminating a salesperson. A salesperson changing brokerages must transfer his or her license to the new office, writing the new address and broker's name on the face of the license.

B. RECORD KEEPING

The Real Estate Law requires a broker to keep a record of each transaction he or she is involved in. This should include a copy of the listing, the purchase agreement, canceled checks, trust fund records (see below), and any other documents connected with the transaction.

Real estate records must be retained for at least three years from the closing date or the listing date if the transaction was never completed.

It's a good idea to retain the records for even longer than three years. Statutes of limitations require many lawsuits to be brought within two or three years after the wrong occurred, but suits involving an accusation of fraud can be filed up to three years after the fraud was discovered. That could be many years after the transaction took place. Clear records can be an important part of a defense against such charges.

C. TRUST FUNDS

Trust funds are money (or other things of value) that a real estate agent receives on behalf of the principal or any other person involved in a transaction.

Mishandling of trust funds is probably the most common reason for suspension or revocation of real estate licenses.

When a broker receives trust funds, he or she must place them into a neutral escrow depository, the hands of the principal, or a trust fund account. This must be done no later than the third business day (first business day if broker is also the escrow agent for the transaction) following receipt of the funds. If a salesperson receives trust funds, he or she must immediately turn them over to the broker, or at the broker's request, deposit them in escrow or a trust account or give them to the principal.

The trust funds that real estate brokers handle most often are earnest money deposits, tendered by prospective buyers when they make an offer to purchase property. For earnest money, there is an exception to the general rules regarding broker's trust funds. Under written instructions from the buyer, a broker may hold onto an earnest money check without cashing the check until the offer has been accepted, as long as the broker informs the seller (before or at the time the offer is presented) that the check is being held. Once the seller has accepted the offer, the broker normally must place the earnest money check in the trust account or a neutral escrow **within three business days**, or by the next business day if the broker is also acting as escrow for the transaction.

A broker should make it clear to his/her licensees that deposits must be immediately turned over to the broker—or what office procedure is required if the broker is unavailable.

A trust account can be opened at a bank, savings bank, or other financial institution. The institution must be in California, with a few exceptions. The account should be in the name of the broker as trustee. It must be a demand-deposit account—one that allows withdrawal without advance notice.

Trust funds can't be withdrawn except by the broker, or (if authorized in writing by the broker) by a salesperson employed by the broker, or a bonded employee of the broker.

No matter who is authorized to make withdrawals, the broker is responsible for the funds at all times. If a salesperson or employee mishandles the funds, the broker is liable.

At the request of the owner of the trust funds or the parties to a transaction, the trust account may be a separate, interest-bearing, federally insured account. The account must be in the name of the broker as trustee for the owner, and a full disclosure of any fees and calculations must be made to the owner. None of the interest may benefit the broker or salesperson. In their contract or in a separate agreement, the parties must specify whom the interest is to be paid or credited to.

A separate account for each transaction is required if the account is interest-bearing. A broker must keep a trust account record for each transaction, accounting for all deposits and disbursements.

It's especially important for a broker to avoid *COMMINGLING—mixing his or her personal money in with trust funds*. Trust funds *must never* be placed in the broker's general account, no matter how briefly. The Real Estate Commissioner allows a broker to keep up to $200 of his or her own money in the trust account to cover the bank's service charges, but it's better to have the service charges on a trust account paid out of the broker's general account.

When a broker has earned a commission that is to be paid out of a trust account, the broker must transfer the amount of the commission to his or her own account within 25 days of the time it was earned. This doesn't mean a broker can transfer trust funds whenever a client owes the broker money. The funds must have been earmarked for the broker (either as the commission or as reimbursement for expenses).

Example: A buyer gives a broker $10,000 as a deposit; the broker puts it in a trust account for the seller. The buyer and seller reach an agreement, and the broker has earned a $12,000 commission.

The seller later refuses to pay the broker, claiming that she didn't do enough to earn that much. Although the broker is in the right about her commission, she can't transfer the $10,000 from the trust fund account to her general account without the seller's permission. The funds in a trust account are never the property of the broker.

Trust account records are subject to examination by the Commissioner, and may be audited. If the audit uncovers a violation of the trust fund rules, the broker will be charged for the cost of the audit in addition to other penalties.

VI. Commissions

Although many people enjoy selling real estate, nearly everyone would admit that the main reason they do it is to make money. As you've seen, to be paid for representing another person in a real estate transaction, you must be properly licensed. To be able to sue to collect a commission, you must have a written agreement with the principal and it must be signed by the principal.

The written agreement between broker and principal doesn't have to be detailed to be enforceable.

If the parties never agreed on an amount, the court will determine the reasonable value of the broker's services. Of course, they should always put the terms of employment in writing rather than having to take the matter to court. A written listing agreement should clearly set forth the amount of the commission and explain under what circumstances the broker will be entitled to receive it.

Always put the agreed to commission in writing and have both parties sign the document.

> **Case Example:** Mr. Davinroy, a broker, represented the Thompsons in an exchange of real property. The only written agreement regarding Davinroy's employment was a provision in the exchange agreement itself. It listed Davinroy as one of the brokers involved in the transaction and said merely, "Commissions are to be settled and paid for outside of the escrow."
>
> The Thompsons had orally agreed to pay Davinroy $30,000, but they only paid him $1,710. Davinroy sued.
>
> The court ruled that a broker can sue for a commission as long as there is some written memorandum showing that he or she was employed in the transaction. Evidence of an oral agreement can be used to establish the amount of the commission. *Davinroy v. Thompson*, 169 Cal. App. 2d 63, 336 P.2d 1028 (1959).

A. COMMISSION AMOUNT

The amount or rate of commission is set through the agreement of the principal and the broker. It is a violation of state and federal antitrust laws for brokers to set uniform commission rates. Any discussion of commission rates among members of competing firms could give rise to a charge of price-fixing.

There's a special rule that applies to listing agreements for residential property with four units or less and for manufactured homes. If the broker uses a preprinted form for the agreement, it must state, in not less than 10-point boldface type immediately before the compensation amount, that the amount or rate of the commission is not fixed by law and may be negotiable. The commission rate or amount cannot be printed in the form—it must be filled in for each transaction.

Notice: The amount or rate of real estate commissions is not fixed by law. They are set by each broker individually and may be negotiable between the seller and broker.

B. EARNING A COMMISSION

Payment of a broker's commission may be made dependent on any lawful condition. A listing agreement may specify that the commission is due at the time of acceptance of an offer, on approval of financing, at closing, or out of the proceeds of the sale. When the stated conditions have been met, the broker has earned the commission.

A broker is usually hired to find a buyer who is **ready, willing, and able** to purchase on the terms established by the seller. A buyer is considered ready and willing if he or she makes an offer that meets the seller's terms. A buyer is considered able if he or she has the financial ability to complete the purchase. This means that the buyer must have one of the following:

1. enough cash to complete the sale,
2. a strong credit rating and enough personal assets to ensure that he or she can complete the sale, or
3. a binding commitment for a loan to finance the purchase.

In most cases, once the agent has procured a ready, willing, and able buyer, he or she has earned the commission even if the sale is never completed. Many factors may prevent the sale from being completed without canceling the agent's right to a commission. For a seller's agent, these include:

1. the seller's decision not to sell after all,
2. defects in the seller's title,
3. the seller's inability to deliver possession, or
4. mutual agreement of the seller and buyer to cancel their agreement.

Earning a Commission

✔ Agent is properly licensed
✔ Valid, written listing agreement
✔ Ready, willing, and able buyer
✔ Parties agree on essential terms of sale

Example: K hires a broker to sell her house because she's planning to get married and move into the home of her fiancé. The broker finds a ready, willing, and able buyer who meets all of the terms specified in the listing agreement. Meanwhile, K has broken off her engagement so she no longer wants to sell her house. Although she can refuse to accept the buyer's offer, she is still required to pay the broker his commission.

If a prospective buyer's offer doesn't precisely match the terms specified by the seller in the listing, the broker isn't entitled to a commission if the seller refuses to contract.

Example: A seller lists her house for $292,500. She specifies that she wants 20% cash at closing, with the rest to be paid to her in equal monthly installments for 20 years at 9% annual interest.

The broker obtains an offer of $292,500 in cash. The seller refuses to accept this offer. The broker isn't entitled to a commission, since the offer didn't match the terms specified by the seller.

The standard language in the California Association of Realtors® Exclusive Authorization and Right to Sell listing form reproduced in Chapter 8 provides that the listing broker is entitled to a commission if a buyer makes an offer to purchase the seller's property on the price and terms described in the listing agreement or on any other price and terms that the seller subsequently accepts.

However, the listing agreement may provide that no commission is payable unless escrow closes or some other condition that may restrict when the commission is payable is satisfied.

Case Example: Herald Shilberg (seller) signed a contract to sell Thomas Horning (buyer) a multi-unit property in Imperial Beach for $715,000. In the CAR® purchase contract prepared by the buyer, a real estate broker representing himself, the seller agreed to pay buyer a commission as "compensation for services" of 3% of the purchase price at the close of escrow. The buyer failed to to deliver prequalification letter due on December 24 and on January 2 seller canceled the contract. About one year later, seller eventually sold the property for $920,000. The buyer sued for, among other things, $21,450 for the agreed commission and $205,000 as the difference between the purchase price and the subsequent sale price. Ultimately, the trial court found that the seller had breached the contract, but the buyer had suffered no damages because a broker acting as a principal is not entitled to recover a commission and that, under the law, the buyer suffered no damages with regard to the breach of the purchase contract. As a result, the seller was determined to be the prevailing party and was entitled to attorney's fees and costs. The court awarded the seller $80,373 in attorney's fees and $5,558.72 as cost. The buyer appealed.

The appellate court noted that a person is a broker only if acting (1) for compensation and (2) on behalf of someone else. A licensee acting on his or her own behalf is not a broker within the meaning of this definition. A broker's commission is predicated on an agency relationship with a third party. In this case there is no agency and therefore no entitlement to a commission. Any agreement to pay a purported "commission" or compensation to a broker purchasing property on his or her own behalf is, in essence, an agreement to a reduction in the purchase price.

If the buyer is entitled to any damages at all it would be measured by the difference between the purchase price and the fair market value of the property as of the date of the breach of contract (the market price-contract price differential, Civil Code Section 3306), plus any consequential damages according to proof. However, at trial, the buyer presented no evidence of the value of the property on the date of the breach. Thus, the damages equaled zero. Judgment affirmed. *Horning v. Shilberg*, 130 Cal. App. 4th 197, 29 Cal. Rptr. 3d 717 (2005).

Listing Agreements and Broker's Right to a Commission

Exclusive Right to Sell	Exclusive Agency	Open
(No matter who sells)	(Anyone except the seller sells)	(Procuring cause)
Requires a termination date	**Requires a termination date**	

---

1. Types of Listing Agreements

A broker's right to a commission also depends on the type of listing agreement used. Under an *EXCLUSIVE RIGHT TO SELL agreement, the broker is entitled to the commission if the property is sold during the listing term, no matter who sells it.* Under an *EXCLUSIVE AGENCY agreement, the seller owes the broker the commission if the property is sold during the listing term, unless the seller finds a buyer by him or herself.* The California Real Estate Commissioner requires that both types of exclusive listings (right to sell and agency) have a definite determinable termination date to be valid, but with an *OPEN LISTING, a broker is not entitled to a commission unless he or she is the **procuring cause** of the sale.*

To be the procuring cause, the broker must be primarily responsible for the parties' agreement, or the broker's actions must start a chain of events that results in an agreement or a signed sales contract. Sometimes two brokers contribute to a particular sale and they agree to divide the commission.

Unfortunately, in some cases brokers end up arguing over who was the procuring cause of a sale. That's one of the chief disadvantages of an open listing.

Example: A principal gave open listings to five brokers, A, B, C, D, and E. A and B both showed the property to the same buyer. A brought the buyer to the property for the first time, but it was B who successfully negotiated the offer that the principal accepted.

A claims she should receive part of the commission, but the agent who effected the sale is the procuring cause, so B is entitled to the commission.

www.realtor.org/mempolweb.nsf/pages/code
National Association of REALTORS® Code of Ethics

Regardless of the type of listing used, if the buyer and seller sign an agreement before the listing expires, the broker has earned the commission even if the sale does not close until after the listing's expiration date.

Many listing agreements contain an extender clause (also called a protective clause, carryover clause, or safety clause). An *EXTENDER CLAUSE provides that the broker is still entitled to a commission if the property is sold within a certain period after the listing expires, and the buyer is someone the broker negotiated with during the listing term* (see Chapter 8).

The extender clause usually requires the agent to deliver a written list of prospective purchasers, that the agent worked with, to the seller within a stated period of time in order to claim the commission.

178

C. SALESPERSONS' COMMISSIONS

A salesperson may only receive a commission or other compensation directly from the salesperson's supervising broker. The salesperson must not accept any compensation from any other broker or agent, or directly from the seller.

1. Finder's Fee (Exception to License Law)

A *FINDER'S FEE is compensation paid for bringing two parties together, such as the introduction of a prospective buyer to the seller.* The finder does not have to be licensed and, of course, can perform no services for which a license is required.

One who merely introduces two parties to a real estate transaction, whether or not he or she solicits those persons, does not need to be as knowledgeable about the real estate transactions as a licensed broker, unless he or she participated in the transaction.

In general, an unlicensed individual may recover an agreed compensation where he or she merely found a buyer, seller, lender, or borrower. But, if in addition to finding such a person, he or she goes further and helps to conclude the transaction by taking part in negotiating the details of the transaction, compromising or composing differences between the parties by way of example, he or she may not recover the agreed compensation.

RESPA also prohibits all "settlement service providers" from paying or receiving referral fees. This include real estate licensees, escrow, title, lenders, appraisers, pest control inspectors, surveyors, attorneys, credit reporting agencies, etc.

Case Example: Irma Kellogg was interested in selling her ranch in Santa Barbara County. She orally agreed to pay her musician friend Sullivan a commission of 5% of the purchase price if he could find a buyer. Sullivan contacted an attorney friend in Denver who interested two clients, Stegall and Hopkins, in the ranch. When the attorney, Stegall, and Hopkins came to Santa Barbara, Sullivan introduced them to Kellogg and her attorney Crawford. Both Kellogg and her attorney, Crawford, assumed Sullivan was a real estate broker. Sullivan did not participate in the negotiations, but on occasion helped out by collecting information available to the public when requested by the parties. A written sales contract was entered into, selling the ranch for $1,700,000 and providing that the buyers would pay the $85,000 commission that Kellogg was originally obligated to pay. Subsequently, the buyers refused to pay the commission, claiming that Sullivan had to be a licensed real estate broker to collect a commission. Sullivan claimed he was a finder and could receive a fee without being licensed.

The United States Court of Appeals stated that a finder receives a fee for bringing the parties together with no involvement in negotiating the price or any of the other terms of the transaction. Sullivan was simply obligated to bring the buyer and seller together to earn his fee. *Sullivan v. Hopkins*, 435 F.2d 1128 (1970).

VII. CHAPTER SUMMARY

1. A principal authorizes an agent to act for him or her. An agent may have express or implied authority. An agent without actual or implied authority may be found to have ostensible authority if the principal's acts or neglect leads others to believe that the agent has this authority. An agent may be general or special. Most real estate agents are special agents.

2. An agency relationship can be created by express agreement, implied by conduct, ratification, or by estoppel (ostensible). Most real estate agency relationships are created by express listing agreements. A real estate agent can't sue to collect a commission without a written agreement with the principal.

3. A broker must have a written employment agreement with each salesperson or broker on staff, covering duties, supervision, compensation, and termination.

4. A salesperson is his or her broker's agent, not the seller's agent. Sometimes the seller and broker can be held liable for the salesperson's wrongful acts. The broker is required to supervise the salesperson. A salesperson may be considered an independent contractor for income tax purposes.

5. A cooperating broker is a non-listing broker with whom the listing broker agrees to share a commission if the non-listing broker sells the property. An associate licensee is licensed as a real estate broker or salesperson who is either licensed under a broker or has entered into a written contract with a broker to act as the broker's licensee in connection with acts requiring a real estate license and to function under the supervision in the capacity of an associate licensee.

6. An agency may be terminated by accomplishment of purpose, expiration of the term, operation of law, mutual agreement, renunciation, or revocation. An agent who renounces or a principal who revokes an agency may be liable to the other party for damages. An agency coupled with an interest can't be revoked, and isn't terminated by the death, incapacity, or bankruptcy of the principal.

7. The California Real Estate Law includes rules regarding licensing, record keeping, and trust funds. After receiving trust funds, a broker has until the end of the third business day (first business day if broker is also the escrow agent for the transaction) to deposit them in a trust account or an escrow account, or deliver them to the principal. A broker must never commingle trust funds with his or her own money.

8. Generally, only a properly licensed real estate agent may be paid for representing another in a real estate transaction. A listing agreement for residential property with 1-4 units must contain a statement that the commission is not set by law but may be negotiable between the broker and the seller. A broker is ordinarily entitled to a commission after the seller and a ready, willing, and able buyer agree on the essential terms of the sale. The type of listing agreement also affects whether a broker is entitled to a commission. A salesperson may only receive a commission from his or her own broker.

VIII. CASE PROBLEM

Charles V. Webster Real Estate v. Rickard, 21 Cal. App. 3d 612, 98 Cal. Rptr. 559 (1971)

In May 1967, Dr. Moore listed his 156-acre vineyard with Watson Realty for $234,000. The exclusive right to sell agreement, which provided for a 5% commission, specified that the agency would terminate on December 31, 1968.

Dr. Moore later gave written consent to have the listing transferred from Watson Realty to Webster Real Estate. The list price was reduced to $187,200.

In June 1968, Dr. Moore died. Without any help from the real estate agents, the executor of Dr. Moore's estate sold the vineyard in November for $152,000.

Believing they were entitled to their commission under the exclusive right to sell agreement, Webster Real Estate filed a claim against Dr. Moore's estate for $7,600 (5% of the sale price). The executor rejected the claim, so Webster Real Estate sued the estate.

Was Webster Real Estate entitled to its commission? Were they entitled to damages for breach of contract? Why or why not? What if Webster Real Estate had been the procuring cause of the November sale?

IX. KEY TERMS

agency	estoppel	power of attorney
agency coupled with an interest	exclusive right to sell	principal
	exclusive agency	procuring cause
agent	extender clause	ratification
associate licensee	finder's fee	ready, willing, and able
attorney in fact	implied authority	renunciation
commingling	independent contractor	revocation
conflict of interest	open listing	trust funds
cooperating broker	ostensible authority	

CHAPTER 5

X. CHAPTER QUIZ

1. Most real estate agents are considered:
    a. general agents.
    b. universal agents.
    c. special agents.
    d. none of the above.

2. An agency is terminated when:
    a. both parties agree to end it.
    b. the agent renounces it.
    c. the principal revokes it.
    d. any of the above.

3. A real estate agency is terminated by operation of law if:
    a. the principal fires the broker.
    b. the broker goes bankrupt.
    c. there is no extender clause.
    d. the broker hires a cooperating broker without the principal's permission.

4. Which of the following three-unit courses is a requirement for first renewal of a real estate license?
    a. Discrimination
    b. Trust Funds
    c. Salesmanship
    d. Commercial Property

5. The Real Estate Law requires brokers to keep adequate records of real estate transactions and retain these records:
    a. for one year.
    b. for three years.
    c. for ten years.
    d. until the transaction has closed.

6. Generally, trust funds received by a broker must be deposited in a trust account or an escrow account:
    a. the same day they're received.
    b. the next business day if he/she is not acting as escrow.
    c. within three business days after receipt.
    d. as soon as reasonably possible.

7. A broker may hold a buyer's check for an earnest money deposit without depositing it in escrow or the broker's trust fund account if:

    a. the buyer instructs the broker to hold the check until the buyer's offer is accepted.
    b. the seller is informed that the check has not been cashed.
    c. the check is properly deposited within 3 business days from acceptance.
    d. all of the above are true.

8. A real estate broker's trust fund accounts must be:

    a. interest-bearing accounts.
    b. demand-deposit accounts.
    c. uninsured accounts.
    d. all of the above.

9. A salesperson may be paid a commission:

    a. by his or her own broker.
    b. by the seller directly.
    c. by any licensed broker.
    d. any of the above.

10. The amount of the commission paid to the broker by the seller:

    a. is 6% of the sale price.
    b. is set by the Board of Realtors in each county.
    c. is agreed upon between the broker and the seller.
    d. must be the same for all brokers.

ANSWERS: 1. c; 2. d; 3. b; 4. d; 5. b; 6. c; 7. c; 8. b; 9. a; 10. c

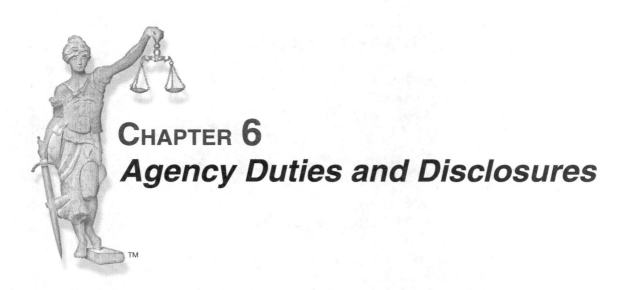

CHAPTER 6
Agency Duties and Disclosures

CHAPTER OVERVIEW

The last chapter explained what an agent is, and how an agency relationship is created and terminated. This chapter describes the real estate agent's duties. It also discusses the agent's liability—the penalties for failing to carry out those duties.

It also covers the obligations of the seller and the agents to disclose material information to a buyer regarding the defects and problems about the property and the surrounding area that a buyer should know before making a commitment to purchase the property.

A real estate agent's primary duties are owed to the principal, the person the agent is representing in a transaction. But the agent also owes duties to the other parties involved in the transaction. Fulfilling both responsibilities is the agent's duty.

Business cards, stationary, advertising materials, websites, email, and regular mail must include your real estate license (broker or salesperson) number and it must be disclosed at the first point of contact with a consumer, including any purchase agreements.

I. Agency Disclosure

In 1988, the California Legislature enacted an agency disclosure statute that applies to residential transactions involving 1-4 dwelling units or mobilehomes. Under the statute, a real estate agent owes a duty to both the seller and the buyer to let them know which party the agent is representing in the transaction.

www.leginfo.ca.gov/calaw.html
California Civil Code

So, if you are a real estate agent working with the seller or potential buyer, or you are a seller of real estate or a potential buyer, here's what you need to know about agency disclosure. The Legislature requires a written disclosure of potential agency relationships in a real estate transaction. Hopefully, this will help eliminate confusion and mystery as to exactly which agent represents which party (principal), and what agency duties and obligations exist. This legislation is contained in California Civil Code Sections 2079-2079.4, and can be found in the CAR® form

CHAPTER OUTLINE

Disclosure Regarding Real Estate Agency Relationships (Figure 6-1). To help with clarification, we will use the following definitions:

1. **Listing Agent.** A person who has obtained a listing of the real property acting as an agent of the seller for compensation.

2. **Selling Agent.** A listing agent who (a) acts alone, or (b) an agent who acts in cooperation with a listing agent and who sells or finds and obtains a buyer for the real property, or (c) an agent who locates property for a buyer or who finds a buyer for a property for which no listing exists and presents an offer to purchase to the seller.

3. **Buyer.** A person who (a) signs an offer to purchase real property from a seller or through an agent, or (b) who seeks the services of an agent in more than a casual, transitory, or preliminary manner with the object of entering into a real property transaction including a lessee.

4. **Associate Licensee.** A licensee who is (a) licensed under a broker or (b) has entered into a written contract with a broker to act as the broker's agent in real estate transactions and function under the broker's supervision as an associate licensee.

5. **Dual Agent.** An agent acting, either directly or through an associate licensee, as agent for both the seller and the buyer.

6. **Seller.** A person who sells the real property, including an owner who (a) listed the property with an agent, or (b) who receives an offer to purchase the property from an agent on behalf of another, and includes a lessor.

7. **Subagent.** A person to whom an agent delegates agency powers, but does not include an associate licensee who was acting under the supervision of an agent (broker).

Figure 6-1

CALIFORNIA
ASSOCIATION
OF REALTORS®

DISCLOSURE REGARDING
REAL ESTATE AGENCY RELATIONSHIP
(Listing Firm to Seller)
(As required by the Civil Code)
(C.A.R. Form AD, Revised 11/12)

☐ (If checked) This form is being provided in connection with a transaction for a leaseholder interest in a dwelling exceeding one year as per Civil Code section 2079.13(j) and (l).

When you enter into a discussion with a real estate agent regarding a real estate transaction, you should from the outset understand what type of agency relationship or representation you wish to have with the agent in the transaction.

SELLER'S AGENT
A Seller's agent under a listing agreement with the Seller acts as the agent for the Seller only. A Seller's agent or a subagent of that agent has the following affirmative obligations:
To the Seller: A Fiduciary duty of utmost care, integrity, honesty and loyalty in dealings with the Seller.
To the Buyer and the Seller:
    (a) Diligent exercise of reasonable skill and care in performance of the agent's duties.
    (b) A duty of honest and fair dealing and good faith.
    (c) A duty to disclose all facts known to the agent materially affecting the value or desirability of the property that are not known to, or within the diligent attention and observation of, the parties. An agent is not obligated to reveal to either party any confidential information obtained from the other party that does not involve the affirmative duties set forth above.

BUYER'S AGENT
A selling agent can, with a Buyer's consent, agree to act as agent for the Buyer only. In these situations, the agent is not the Seller's agent, even if by agreement the agent may receive compensation for services rendered, either in full or in part from the Seller. An agent acting only for a Buyer has the following affirmative obligations:
To the Buyer: A fiduciary duty of utmost care, integrity, honesty and loyalty in dealings with the Buyer.
To the Buyer and the Seller:
    (a) Diligent exercise of reasonable skill and care in performance of the agent's duties.
    (b) A duty of honest and fair dealing and good faith.
    (c) A duty to disclose all facts known to the agent materially affecting the value or desirability of the property that are not known to, or within the diligent attention and observation of, the parties.
An agent is not obligated to reveal to either party any confidential information obtained from the other party that does not involve the affirmative duties set forth above.

AGENT REPRESENTING BOTH SELLER AND BUYER
A real estate agent, either acting directly or through one or more associate licensees, can legally be the agent of both the Seller and the Buyer in a transaction, but only with the knowledge and consent of both the Seller and the Buyer.
In a dual agency situation, the agent has the following affirmative obligations to both the Seller and the Buyer:
    (a) A fiduciary duty of utmost care, integrity, honesty and loyalty in the dealings with either the Seller or the Buyer.
    (b) Other duties to the Seller and the Buyer as stated above in their respective sections.
In representing both Seller and Buyer, the agent may not, without the express permission of the respective party, disclose to the other party that the Seller will accept a price less than the listing price or that the Buyer will pay a price greater than the price offered.
The above duties of the agent in a real estate transaction do not relieve a Seller or Buyer from the responsibility to protect his or her own interests. You should carefully read all agreements to assure that they adequately express your understanding of the transaction. A real estate agent is a person qualified to advise about real estate. If legal or tax advice is desired, consult a competent professional.
Throughout your real property transaction you may receive more than one disclosure form, depending upon the number of agents assisting in the transaction. The law requires each agent with whom you have more than a casual relationship to present you with this disclosure form. You should read its contents each time it is presented to you, considering the relationship between you and the real estate agent in your specific transaction. **This disclosure form includes the provisions of Sections 2079.13 to 2079.24, inclusive, of the Civil Code set forth on page 2. Read it carefully. I/WE ACKNOWLEDGE RECEIPT OF A COPY OF THIS DISCLOSURE AND THE PORTIONS OF THE CIVIL CODE PRINTED ON THE BACK (OR A SEPARATE PAGE).**

☐ Buyer ☐ Seller ☐ Landlord ☐ Tenant _____ Date _____

☐ Buyer ☐ Seller ☐ Landlord ☐ Tenant _____ Date _____

Agent _____ DRE Lic. # _____
             Real Estate Broker (Firm)

By _____ DRE Lic. # _____ Date _____
    (Salesperson or Broker-Associate)

Agency Disclosure Compliance (Civil Code §2079.14):
- When the listing brokerage company also represents Buyer/Tenant: The Listing Agent shall have one AD form signed by Seller/Landlord and a different AD form signed by Buyer/Tenant.
- When Seller/Landlord and Buyer/Tenant are represented by different brokerage companies: (i) the Listing Agent shall have one AD form signed by Seller/Landlord and (ii) the Buyer's/Tenant's Agent shall have one AD form signed by Buyer/Tenant and either that same or a different AD form presented to Seller/Landlord for signature prior to presentation of the offer. If the same form is used, Seller may sign here:

(SELLER/LANDLORD: DO NOT SIGN HERE)	**(SELLER/LANDLORD: DO NOT SIGN HERE)**
Seller/Landlord Date	Seller/Landlord Date

Reviewed by _____ Date _____

EQUAL HOUSING
OPPORTUNITY

AD REVISED 11/12 (PAGE 1 OF 2)

DISCLOSURE REGARDING REAL ESTATE AGENCY RELATIONSHIP (AD PAGE 1 OF 2)

Agent: WALT HUBER	Phone:	Fax:	Prepared using zipForm® software
Broker:			

CIVIL CODE SECTIONS 2079.24 (2079.16 APPEARS ON THE FRONT)

2079.13 As used in Sections 2079.14 to 2079.24, inclusive, the following terms have the following meanings:
(a) "Agent" means a person acting under provisions of title 9 (commencing with Section 2295) in a real property transaction, and includes a person who is licensed as a real estate broker under Chapter 3 (commencing with Section 10130) of Part 1 of Division 4 of the Business and Professions Code, and under whose license a listing is executed or an offer to purchase is obtained. **(b)** "Associate licensee" means a person who is licensed as a real estate broker or salesperson under Chapter 3 (commencing with Section 10130) of Part 1 of Division 4 of the Business and Professions Code and who is either licensed under a broker or has entered into a written contract with a broker to act as the broker's agent in connection with acts requiring a real estate license and to function under the broker's supervision in the capacity of an associate licensee. The agent in the real property transaction bears responsibility for his or her associate licensees who perform as agents of the agent. When an associate licensee owes a duty to any principal, or to any buyer or seller who is not a principal, in a real property transaction, that duty is equivalent to the duty owed to that party by the broker for whom the associate licensee functions. **(c)** "Buyer" means a transferee in a real property transaction, and includes a person who executes an offer to purchase real property from a seller through an agent, or who seeks the services of an agent in more than a casual, transitory, or preliminary manner, with the object of entering into a real property transaction. "Buyer" includes vendee or lessee. **(d)** "Dual agent" means an agent acting, either directly or through an associate licensee, as agent for both the seller and the buyer in a real property transaction. **(e)** "Listing agreement" means a contract between an owner of real property and an agent, by which the agent has been authorized to sell the real property or to find or obtain a buyer. **(f)** "Listing agent" means a person who has obtained a listing of real property to act as an agent for compensation. **(g)** "Listing price" is the amount expressed in dollars specified in the listing for which the seller is willing to sell the real property through the listing agent. **(h)** "Offering price" is the amount expressed in dollars specified in an offer to purchase for which the buyer is willing to buy the real property. **(i)** "Offer to purchase" means a written contract executed by a buyer acting through a selling agent which becomes the contract for the sale of the real property upon acceptance by the seller. **(j)** "Real property" means any estate specified by subdivision (1) or (2) of Section 761 in property which constitutes one to four dwelling units, any leasehold in this type of property exceeding one year's duration, and mobile homes, when offered for sale or sold through an agent pursuant to the authority contained in Section 10131.6 of the Business and Professions Code. **(k)** "Real property transaction" means a transaction for the sale of real property in which an agent is employed by one or more of the principals to act in that transaction, and includes a listing or an offer to purchase. **(l)** "Sell," "sale," or "sold" refers to a transaction for the transfer of real property from the seller to the buyer, and includes exchanges of real property between the seller and buyer, transactions for the creation of a real property sales contract within the meaning of Section 2985, and transactions for the creation of a leasehold exceeding one year's duration. **(m)** "Seller" means the transferor in a real property transaction, and includes an owner who lists real property with an agent, whether or not a transfer results, or who receives an offer to purchase real property of which he or she is the owner from an agent on behalf of another. "Seller" includes both a vendor and a lessor. **(n)** "Selling agent" means a listing agent who acts alone, or an agent who acts in cooperation with a listing agent, and who sells or finds and obtains a buyer for the real property, or an agent who locates property for a buyer or who finds a buyer for a property for which no listing exists and presents an offer to purchase to the seller. **(o)** "Subagent" means a person to whom an agent delegates agency powers as provided in Article 5 (commencing with Section 2349) of Chapter 1 of Title 9. However, "subagent" does not include an associate licensee who is acting under the supervision of an agent in a real property transaction.
2079.14 Listing agents and selling agents shall provide the seller and buyer in a real property transaction with a copy of the disclosure form specified in Section 2079.16, and, except as provided in subdivision (c), shall obtain a signed acknowledgement of receipt from that seller or buyer, except as provided in this section or Section 2079.15, as follows: **(a)** The listing agent, if any, shall provide the disclosure form to the seller prior to entering into the listing agreement. **(b)** The selling agent shall provide the disclosure form to the seller as soon as practicable prior to presenting the seller with an offer to purchase, unless the selling agent previously provided the seller with a copy of the disclosure form pursuant to subdivision (a). **(c)** Where the selling agent does not deal on a face-to-face basis with the seller, the disclosure form prepared by the selling agent may be furnished to the seller (and acknowledgement of receipt obtained for the selling agent from the seller) by the listing agent, or the selling agent may deliver the disclosure form by certified mail addressed to the seller at his or her last known address, in which case no signed acknowledgement of receipt is required. **(d)** The selling agent shall provide the disclosure form to the buyer as soon as practicable prior to execution of the buyer's offer to purchase, except that if the offer to purchase is not prepared by the selling agent, the selling agent shall present the disclosure form to the buyer not later than the next business day after the selling agent receives the offer to purchase from the buyer.
2079.15 In any circumstance in which the seller or buyer refuses to sign an acknowledgement of receipt pursuant to Section 2079.14, the agent, or an associate licensee acting for an agent, shall set forth, sign, and date a written declaration of the facts of the refusal.
2079.16 Reproduced on Page 1 of this AD form.
2079.17 (a) As soon as practicable, the selling agent shall disclose to the buyer and seller whether the selling agent is acting in the real property transaction exclusively as the buyer's agent, exclusively as the seller's agent, or as a dual agent representing both the buyer and the seller. This relationship shall be confirmed in the contract to purchase and sell real property or in a separate writing executed or acknowledged by the seller, the buyer, and the selling agent prior to or coincident with execution of that contract by the buyer and the seller, respectively. **(b)** As soon as practicable, the listing agent shall disclose to the seller whether the listing agent is acting in the real property transaction exclusively as the seller's agent, or as a dual agent representing both the buyer and seller. This relationship shall be confirmed in the contract to purchase and sell real property or in a separate writing executed or acknowledged by the seller and the listing agent prior to or coincident with the execution of that contract by the seller.
(c) The confirmation required by subdivisions (a) and (b) shall be in the following form.

(DO NOT COMPLETE, SAMPLE ONLY) _____ is the agent of (check one) ☑ the seller exclusively; or ☐ both the buyer and seller.
(Name of Listing Agent)

(DO NOT COMPLETE, SAMPLE ONLY) _____ is the agent of (check one): ☑ the buyer exclusively; or ☐ the seller exclusively; or
(Name of Selling Agent if not the same as the Listing Agent) ☐ both the buyer and seller.

(d) The disclosures and confirmation required by this section shall be in addition to the disclosure required by Section 2079.14.
2079.18 No selling agent in a real property transaction may act as an agent for the buyer only, when the selling agent is also acting as the listing agent in the transaction.
2079.19 The payment of compensation or the obligation to pay compensation to an agent by the seller or buyer is not necessarily determinative of a particular agency relationship between an agent and the seller or buyer. A listing agent and a selling agent may agree to share any compensation or commission paid, or any right to any compensation or commission for which an obligation arises as the result of a real estate transaction, and the terms of any such agreement shall not necessarily be determinative of a particular relationship.
2079.20 Nothing in this article prevents an agent from selecting, as a condition of the agent's employment, a specific form of agency relationship not specifically prohibited by this article if the requirements of Section 2079.14 and Section 2079.17 are complied with.
2079.21 A dual agent shall not disclose to the buyer that the seller is willing to sell the property at a price less than the listing price, without the express written consent of the seller. A dual agent shall not disclose to the seller that the buyer is willing to pay a price greater than the offering price, without the express written consent of the buyer. This section does not alter in any way the duty or responsibility of a dual agent to any principal with respect to confidential information other than price.
2079.22 Nothing in this article precludes a listing agent from also being a selling agent, and the combination of these functions in one agent does not, of itself, make that agent a dual agent.
2079.23 A contract between the principal and agent may be modified or altered to change the agency relationship at any time before the performance of the act which is the object of the agency with the written consent of the parties to the agency relationship.
2079.24 Nothing in this article shall be construed to either diminish the duty of disclosure owed buyers and sellers by agents and their associate licensees, subagents, and employees or to relieve agents and their associate licensees, subagents, and employees from liability for their conduct in connection with acts governed by this article or for any breach of a fiduciary duty or a duty of disclosure.

Buyer's Initials (_____) (_____)   Seller's Initials (_____) (_____)

Published and Distributed by:
REAL ESTATE BUSINESS SERVICES, INC.
a subsidiary of the CALIFORNIA ASSOCIATION OF REALTORS®
525 South Virgil Avenue, Los Angeles, California 90020

AD REVISED 11/12 (PAGE 2 OF 2)

Reviewed by _____ Date _____

EQUAL HOUSING OPPORTUNITY

Untitled

DISCLOSURE REGARDING REAL ESTATE AGENCY RELATIONSHIP (AD PAGE 2 OF 2)

CHAPTER 6

Note that the term "Agent" as used in the statute always means the supervising broker, whether acting directly or through an associate licensee. As noted in the previous chapter, a salesperson or other associate licensee is never the direct agent of the principal (seller or buyer), but acts as an agent of the supervising broker.

A. AGENCY DISCLOSURE REQUIREMENTS

Agency disclosure is required in all real estate transactions involving a sale, exchange, or an installment sale, of one-to-four dwelling units, including a manufactured or mobilehome, or a lease with a term in excess of one year.

The disclosure is not required in a sale or lease of commercial or industrial property, loan transactions, or when a prospective buyer receives a public report in a subdivision transfer.

The agency disclosure process is a three step process—disclose, elect, and confirm. The first step is to deliver and explain a disclosure form containing specific language required by the statute. The second step is to choose (elect) a legally permissible agency relationship. The third step is to have the principals approve (confirm) the chosen agency relationships in writing. Details of these three steps follow.

1. Delivery of the Agency Disclosure Form

The listing agent must deliver the agency disclosure form to the seller prior to signing the listing agreement. The listing agent is not required to provide the agency disclosure form to the buyer, unless the listing agent is also the selling agent.

A selling agent must provide the disclosure form to the buyer as soon as practicable prior to the buyer signing the offer to purchase. However, if the offer is not prepared by the selling agent, the agent must present the disclosure form to the buyer not later than the next business day after the selling agent receives the offer to purchase from the buyer. The listing agreement is voidable if the real estate licensee fails to provide the sellers with the statutory agency disclosure statement. *Huijers v. deMarrais*, 11 Cal.App.4th 676 (1993).

The selling agent must provide the disclosure form to the seller as soon as practicable prior to presenting the seller with an offer, unless the selling agent previously provided the seller with the disclosure form. A listing agent who is also the selling agent does not have to give the seller a second disclosure form before presenting the offer.

In fulfilling agency duties, it's important to read through the form with the seller or buyer and discuss its ramifications.

If a seller or buyer refuses to sign the receipt of the disclosure form, the agent must prepare a written declaration stating the facts of the refusal and sign it. Frequently, the selling agent does not deal on a face-to-face basis with the seller. In that case, the listing agent can deliver the disclosure form and get it signed for the selling agent. In the alternative, the selling agent may send the disclosure form by certified mail to the seller, in which case no signed receipt is required. Notice that in the definition of "Buyer" above that a buyer is not a person who is looking in a casual, transitory, or preliminary manner with regard to real estate. People who stop by your office to ask a question about real estate, or that you chat with as they're looking at real estate postings on your window, or that attend an open house would generally not be considered a buyer and, therefore, are not entitled to an agency disclosure form.

If the agent is going to represent the buyer exclusively (buyer's listing) then the disclosure form must be delivered to the buyer before the buyer signs a buyer's agency agreement.

2. Agency Election

The beginning of the disclosure form states: "When you enter into a discussion with a real estate agent regarding a real estate transaction, you should from the outset understand what type of agency relationship or representation you wish to have with the agent to the transaction." The law requires that, as soon as practicable, **the listing agent must disclose to the seller whether the listing agent is acting exclusively as the seller's agent, or as a dual agent representing both the buyer and seller**. Additionally, as soon as practicable, the selling agent must disclose to the buyer and seller whether the selling agent is acting exclusively as the buyer's agent, exclusively as the seller's agent, or as a dual agent representing both the buyer and seller.

The legally possible agency relationships for the listing agent and selling agent are set out in the statute. A listing agent may act as the agent of the seller exclusively or may act as a dual agent representing both the seller and buyer. A selling agent may legally act as an agent of the seller exclusively, an agent of the buyer exclusively, or as a dual agent. From a practical standpoint, when the listing agent and selling agent are brokers at different firms, the listing agent (directly or through an associate licensee) will likely elect to act as an agent of the seller exclusively, and the selling agent (again directly or through an associate licensee) will elect to act as an agent of the buyer exclusively. A broker would typically only elect to act as a dual agent in an "in house" sale, where the broker has the listing and the broker or an associate licensee under the broker's supervision finds the buyer, and thus the broker is both the listing broker and selling broker. However, before electing to act as a dual agent, the broker must certain that the broker will be able to comply with all of the agency fiduciary duties owed to both the seller and the buyer in the transaction.

3. Agency Confirmation

While the agency elections by the listing agent and selling agent must be made "as soon as practicable," **there is a statutory deadline for making those elections**—the deadline imposed for confirming the elections. A selling agent, whether or not acting in a dual agency role, must confirm the relationship in the purchase contract or in a separate writing executed or acknowledged by the seller, the buyer, and the selling agent prior to or coincident with the signing of the purchase agreement. The listing agent is also required to confirm the listing agent's election prior to or at the time that the purchase contract is signed. The confirmation is typically in the purchase contract but may be in a separate document. The language of the agency confirmation, contained in the **California Residential Purchase Agreement and Joint Escrow Instructions**, is discussed in detail in Chapter 8, is shown at the top of the next page.

Remember, the "agents" named in the disclosure form and in the confirmation of agency are the brokers and not the sales licensees.

Also, just because the proper agency disclosure forms and confirmation have been signed doesn't necessarily make the agency relationship conclusive. The agents must

> 2. **AGENCY:**
>   A. **DISCLOSURE:** Buyer and Seller each acknowledge prior receipt of a "Disclosure Regarding Real Estate Agency Relationships" (C.A.R. Form AD).
>   B. **POTENTIALLY COMPETING BUYERS AND SELLERS:** Buyer and Seller each acknowledge receipt of a disclosure of the possibility of multiple representation by the Broker representing that principal. This disclosure may be part of a listing agreement, buyer representation agreement or separate document (C.A.R. Form DA). Buyer understands that Broker representing Buyer may also represent other potential buyers, who may consider, make offers on or ultimately acquire the Property. Seller understands that Broker representing Seller may also represent other sellers with competing properties of interest to this Buyer.
>   C. **CONFIRMATION:** The following agency relationships are hereby confirmed for this transaction:
>   Listing Agent _____ (Print Firm Name) is the agent of (check one):
>   ☐ the Seller exclusively; or ☐ both the Buyer and Seller.
>   Selling Agent _____ (Print Firm Name) (if not the same as the Listing Agent) is the agent of (check one): ☐ the Buyer exclusively; or ☐ the Seller exclusively; or ☐ both the Buyer and Seller. Real Estate Brokers are not parties to the Agreement between Buyer and Seller.

have actually performed, and continue to perform the part required by the disclosed relationship.

B. DUAL AGENCY

A broker who represents both the buyer and seller in a transaction is a **DUAL AGENT**. Dual agency situations also commonly occur when one associate licensees under the supervision a broker is working with the seller who listed property with the broker and another associate licensee supervised by the same broker is working with a buyer and that buyer makes an offer to purchase the listed property. The supervising real estate broker is both the listing agent and selling agent and may be a dual agent, with both associate licensees also acting as dual agents through their agency relationships with their supervising broker.

A dual agent owes fiduciary duties to both the buyer and seller at the same time. The dual agent must disclose to each party any information he/she learns from the other, with one exception: **A dual agent must not reveal to a buyer the lowest price the seller will accept, or to a seller, the maximum price a buyer is willing to pay**. As with all agency relationships, dual agency representation of a buyer and seller must be disclosed to and confirmed by the buyer and seller as soon as practicable, but no later than when the buyer or seller sign a purchase contract (*Brown v. FSR Brokerage, Inc.*, 62 Cal.App.4th 766 [1998]). The dual agent is forbidden from telling the buyer that the seller will accept anything less than the listing price, unless the seller gives written consent, and without the buyer's written permission, the agent cannot let the seller know that the buyer will pay a penny more than the amount offered.

Dual agency has drawbacks. Critics point out that there is an inherent conflict of interest in the arrangement. A seller is looking for the highest price, while the buyer is looking for the lowest price. It may be challenging to adequately represent these two opposing interests. There is also a conflict between the fiduciary duties of confidentiality and full disclosure that a dual agent owes to both the buyer and seller. A dual agent is required to not to disclose confidential information about a principal, but by not disclosing confidential information about one principal to the other principal, the agent may be breaching the duty of full disclosure owed to the other principal. The statute discussed in the next section provides that **a dual agent is not allowed to disclose confidential price information**; however, there is no statute that would excuse a dual agent from disclosing other confidential information or protect the dual agent if the agent did disclose one principal's confidential information to the other principal.

Dual agency also gives the agent an opportunity to manipulate one client in favor of the other. This is particularly likely to occur when the agent has an ongoing relationship with one party (a friend, relative, or established client), but not the other.

1. Legislation

California law provides the following:

a. A listing agent may also be a selling agent and the combination of these functions in one agent does not, of itself, make that agent a dual agent. However, no selling agent may act as an agent for only a buyer when the selling agent is also acting as the listing agent in the transaction.

b. A dual agent shall not disclose to the buyer that the seller is willing to sell the property at a price less than the listing price, without the express written consent of the seller. The dual agent shall not disclose to the seller that the buyer is willing to pay a price greater than the offering price, without the express written consent of the buyer. This does not alter in any way the duty or responsibility of a dual agent to any principal with respect to confidential information **other than price**.

c. Nothing in the law shall be construed to either diminish the duty of disclosure owed to buyers and sellers by agents and their associate licensees, subagents, and employees or to relieve agents and their associate licensees, subagents, and employees from liability for their conduct in connection with any breach of a fiduciary duty or duty of disclosure.

d. A contract between the principal and agent may be modified or altered to change the agency relationship at any time before the performance of the act that is the object of the agency with the written consent of the parties to the agency relationship.

Based on this legislation, an agent can act as a dual agent. Of course, this takes place when the agent is acting in an agency relationship with the buyer and the seller in the same transaction, has fully explained how this effects both parties, and has the written consent of both parties to do so. **(As long as the agent represents both principals fairly and makes a full disclosure of the material facts, other than price, involved in the transaction to each principal, the dual agency should be successful.)**

Dual agency requires written consent of both parties after a complete explanation and requires that the dual agent carry out fiduciary duties to both principals."

2. Inadvertent Dual Agency

There are potential problems creating a dual agency that an agent might not see.

Example: Listing agent L answers some general questions of X, who has entered the office inquiring about real estate for sale in the area. X decides to use L in an effort to locate property. In discussions between the two, X has revealed important personal information regarding price range, ability to get a loan and make payments, the most important and the least important criteria in a house, et cetera. L gives X an agency disclosure statement. Of course, X believes that L has been hired to perform real estate services for X: to give advice and counsel on available property, financing, property values, and to disclose all facts materially affecting the value and desirability of property they look at. They have looked at numerous properties and now prepare an offer for one of L's listings. Is L the agent of the buyer? X certainly thinks so. Or is there a dual agency? What does L tell X?

The above example illustrates a common problem where the initial understanding of the agency relationship between the listing agent and the seller may have to be changed and the confirmation of the agency will need to reflect the current relationship.

Case Example: A seller of property sued his agents alleging that the agents failed to disclose that they were representing both the purchaser and seller in a dual agency. The trial court granted the defendants' motion for summary judgment and the appellate court reversed.

The plaintiff/seller claimed that his agents told him during negotiations for the sale of his property that they were representing him exclusively, when in truth the agents represented both the buyer and seller. Defendants provided the court with an agency disclosure form disclosing that there was a dual agency, escrow instructions showing that the brokerage represented both the buyer and seller and commission instructions showing that the brokerage would receive the entire commission. All the documents were signed by the plaintiff. In response, the plaintiff claimed that he signed the documents without reading them and did not know that they contained such representations.

The court held that there was an issue of fact as to whether the disclosure of the dual agency was made to the plaintiff and that a jury should decide the issue. *Brown v. FSR Brokerage Inc.*, 62 Cal. App. 4th 766, 72 Cal. Rptr. 2d 828 (1998).

II. The Agent's Duties to the Principal

The relationship between an agent and a principal is a fiduciary relationship. A *FIDUCIARY is someone who acts for the benefit of another in a relationship founded on trust and confidence.* The law holds a fiduciary to high standards to prevent the fiduciary from disappointing or exploiting the other party's trust. Fiduciary duties require real estate agents to devote their energies and professional expertise to producing the results for their clients.

The basic fiduciary duties that an agent owes the principal are the duties of utmost care, integrity, honesty and loyalty, which includes a duty of confidentiality. The agent also owes the additional obligations of: (a) diligent exercise of reasonable skill and care and performance of the agent's duties; (b) a duty of honest and fair dealing and good faith; (c) a duty to disclose all facts known that to the agent materially affecting the value or desirability of the property that are not known to, or within the diligent attention and observation of, the parties.

The Real Estate Commissioner prepared and adopted Regulation §2773, which requires that the name and **eight (8) digit license number** of a broker or salesperson, when engaging in acts for which a license is required, be disclosed on materials intended to be the "first point of contact" with consumers.

A. REASONABLE SKILL AND CARE

In acting for their clients, real estate agents must use reasonable care and skill.

What is reasonable? It's the degree of care and skill ordinarily used by others competently engaged in the same business. When a court evaluates an agent's knowledge and performance, the agent will be compared with competent real estate agents, not with the average citizen.

Example: X is a real estate salesperson representing B, who is buying a house from Mr. and Mrs. S. Mrs. B and and Mrs. S sign the purchase agreement form. B asks X if it's okay that Mr. S didn't sign. X says it isn't necessary for him to sign because one spouse's signature binds the other spouse to the agreement.

The next day, Mr. S tells B they've received a better offer and are returning his deposit. B learns he can't enforce the purchase agreement because, contrary to what X told him, both spouses must sign any document transferring an interest in community real property.

Salesperson X misled B—she just didn't realize that both spouses (in community property states) have to sign the purchase agreement. Many people don't know that rule, but all competent real estate agents are expected to know it. X is required to meet the standard set by other real estate agents. Her failure to do so was a breach of her fiduciary duties to B.

A breach of fiduciary duty that causes harm to another is a tort (see Chapter 1). An act which involves recklessness or a breach of the standard of care is called negligence. In the previous example, X was negligent in advising B. In a civil lawsuit, X would be liable to B for any financial harm her negligence caused him.

1. Alleging Expertise

All real estate agents are held to a minimum standard of competence. An agent who claims to have expertise in a particular area—property management or appraisal, for example—is held to an even higher standard. You should never take on any special tasks beyond your ability, and never claim expertise in areas where you have no special training or skills. The claim may impress the client at first, but it might to lead to a lawsuit.

As an example, consider a property appraisal. Helping a client decide on a listing price is one thing; claiming to perform an expert valuation is another.

An agent should not claim expertise he/she does not have.

When an agent is not able to give accurate advice, he or she should say so and recommend that the client seek the advice of an attorney, accountant, appraiser, or other expert. In the following case, a broker was sued for failing to give accurate advice as to the income tax consequences of a particular transaction (see Case Example on next page).

CHAPTER 6

2. Unauthorized Practice of Law

Many aspects of real estate transactions raise legal questions or have legal consequences. Real estate agents need to remember and to remind their clients that agents are not attorneys and do not have the required license to practice law. **Agents should never give legal advice or perform any acts that might amount to the unauthorized practice of law.**

In California, a real estate agent is permitted to complete simple standard forms that have been approved by a lawyer, the California Bar Association, or CAR®. An agent may only fill out forms in connection with a real estate transaction that he or she is handling. The agent must not charge the client separately for completing the forms.

Even when filling in the blanks on standard forms in the ordinary course of business, an agent who inserts complicated clauses that require legal expertise is guilty of the unauthorized practice of law.

When in doubt, recommend your client seek legal advice and write a note that you did so.

The unauthorized practice of law is a criminal offense, a misdemeanor. The penalty may be a fine or even a jail term. Note that a real estate agent may be convicted of the unauthorized practice of law even if he or she gave accurate legal advice. If the advice was unsound, the clients who followed it can sue the agent for negligence to recover any damages they suffered.

Agent's Fiduciary Duties to The Principal

- Reasonable Care and Skill
- Diligence, Good Faith, and Loyalty
- Disclosure of Material Information

B. DILIGENCE, GOOD FAITH, AND LOYALTY

An agent owes the principal diligence, good faith, and loyalty.

The agent must faithfully carry out the principal's instructions, and may be held liable for any loss caused by failure to obey them.

1. Diligence

An agent who acts in good faith exercises diligence on behalf of the principal. In other words, an agent is supposed to make a reasonably diligent effort to achieve the principal's goals. As a general rule, the principal can terminate the agency without paying damages if the agent isn't trying to get the job done.

However, there are conflicting court decisions on whether a real estate broker is entitled to a commission under an exclusive listing agreement if he or she hasn't made a diligent effort to find a buyer.

2. Loyalty

The duty of loyalty means that the agent must put the principal's interests above all others, including the agent's own interests. In an agency relationship, the principal often discloses confidential information to the agent. Out of loyalty to the principal, the agent must not reveal this information to others, nor take advantage of it for his/her own benefit.

Example: S listed her house with broker X for $225,000, although she told X she'd accept as little as $200,000 for it. A prospective buyer, B, is very interested in the house, but can't afford more than $205,000.

X would like B to have the house. X also needs his commission as soon as possible, so he wants S's house to sell quickly. But if X hints to B that S would be willing to accept less than the listing price, he is violating his fiduciary duties to S.

California courts have consistently held that the agent's duty of loyalty is the same as the duty of loyalty that a trustee owes to the beneficiaries of a trust. This includes a duty not to use or deal with the principal's property for the agent's own profit or to take part in any transaction in the agent has or is representing someone who has interest adverse to the principal. A transaction between the principal and an agent is presumed to be a violation of the agent's duty of loyalty.

3. Disclosure of Material Information

An agent is required to disclose to his or her principal any material information that affects the subject matter of the agency.

CHAPTER 6

Any fact that could influence the principal's judgment or decision in the transaction is a material fact and should be brought to his or her attention. A real estate agent representing a seller should be especially careful to inform the principal about:

1. the value of the property, and anything that might affect its value;
2. all offers to purchase;
3. the identity of the purchaser;
4. the purchaser's financial condition;
5. any relationship between the purchaser and the broker, and
6. any commission splitting arrangements with other brokers.

a. Property Value

When trying to get a listing, a real estate agent may be tempted to exaggerate the market value of the property. A high value estimate might make the seller more willing to sign an exclusive listing agreement, but that's a breach of the agent's duty to act in good faith.

The agent is required to do his or her best to inform the seller of the property's value. Anything that affects the value should be pointed out, including the condition of the title or the condition of the property itself. Sometimes inexpensive repairs or improvements could make a big difference in the value, and the agent should suggest these to the seller. If the agent is aware of any recent or upcoming changes that may have an impact on the value, the agent should let the seller know.

This duty to inform the seller continues throughout the listing period. If the agent comes across new information (new comparable sales, for example) indicating that the original valuation was high or low, that must be passed along to the seller.

b. Present All Offers

Even if an offer seems totally unacceptable, the agent must present it to the principal. The principal, not the agent, decides which offer is acceptable. The agent must present an offer to the principal even if its acceptance would mean a smaller commission, because the agent's first duty is loyalty to the principal.

Example: A lists his property with Z. A tells Z he would prefer a cash sale, but is willing to consider an alternative if necessary. Z receives offers from two prospective buyers. Buyer #1 offers $180,000 cash. Buyer #2 offers $195,000 if A is willing to accept a trust deed with a balloon payment in five years.

Z's commission will be $900 less if A accepts Buyer #1's offer instead of Buyer #2's. Z decides not to present Buyer #1's offer at all. Rationalizing, he tells himself that Buyer #2 has an excellent credit rating, and A will be much better off in the long run with Buyer #2's offer. Whether or not that is true, Z has violated his fiduciary duties to A. Z has the duty to disclose all offers.

What about an offer the agent receives after the seller has already accepted an earlier offer? It should also be presented to the seller. However, the agent should not try to persuade the seller to breach the agreement with the first buyer. (The first buyer might sue the agent for interfering with a contractual relationship—see Chapter 7.) If the seller wants to accept the later offer, he or she should be advised to talk to a lawyer.

Agents must present all offers, even after an offer has been accepted.

c. Buyer's Financial Information

The seller's agent must disclose to the seller any material fact he or she knows about the buyer's financial position. As a general rule, a seller's agent does not lose the right to a commission simply because the buyer failed to perform under the contract. However, if the agent didn't disclose detrimental financial information about the buyer, the agent may lose the right to a commission because the agent didn't actually produce a buyer who was ready, willing, and financially able to complete the sale.

Financial information regarding the buyer is material if the seller might have refused to accept the offer if he or she had been aware of it. It could be negative information about the buyer's assets, income, or credit rating. Many cases concern the source of the down payment (a loan from a relative rather than savings, for example), or the form of the earnest money deposit.

4. Secret Profit and Self-Dealing

As you've seen, in some cases an agent conceals information from the principal just to complete a sale and get the commission. Sometimes, however, there's an extra motive behind the breach of duty: a secret profit.

A *SECRET PROFIT is any profit or financial benefit the agent obtains without the principal's authorization*. A common example is self-dealing. *SELF-DEALING occurs, for example, when the agent has his sisters buy the property for him, and then he sells it again for a profit.*

It isn't automatically improper for an agent to buy property from the principal, but the agent must disclose to the seller that he or she is the buyer. In addition, the courts will presume that any transaction between an agent and the agent's principal is a breach of the agent's duty of loyalty. The agent must also inform the seller if the buyer is the agent's relative or close friend, or a business entity in which the agent has an interest. This alerts the seller to a possible conflict of interest, and the seller may choose to find another agent.

An agent has the duty to advise the seller of any steps that could be taken to increase the selling price of the property, such as repairs, cleanup work, or minor modifications. If the agent buys the property without suggesting the improvements and then carries out these improvements, the agent has used a superior knowledge of real estate for his or her own profit instead of the principal's. This is a breach of the duty of loyalty and good faith.

Case Example: Plaintiff Jerry Roberts retained defendant Patricia Lomanto (agent) to sell the Cable Park Shopping Center. Roberts signed a purchase agreement selling the property to Lamanto for $11 million. While acting as Robert's agent, Lamanto assigned the purchase contract to a third-party buyer with Robert's required consent. She disclosed to Roberts that the third-party was paying her an assignment fee, but refused to disclose the amount or the price the buyer had agreed to pay for the property. After the deal finalized, Roberts learned that her assignment fee was $1.2 million and the buyer had paid $12.2 million for the property (including the assignment fee). Roberts sued his agent for breach of the fiduciary duty to disclose a secret profit. The trial court held for the agent. Roberts appealed.

The appellate court noted that the agent made an unsolicited offer to buy the shopping center from Roberts representing it was not worth more than $11 million. ▼

> She presented no other buyers to Roberts. Relying on the agent's expertise and trust that the property was worth no more than $11 million, he sold it to her. He agreed to the assignment based on express representation that the property was worth no more than $11 million.
>
> Roberts paid her $110,000 as her commission on the sale. The purchase agreement plainly stated that Patricia Lomanto is the seller's exclusive agent for selling of the property.
>
> A real estate agent who has undertaken to represent a principal in a transaction does not cease to be a fiduciary merely because she enters the transaction as a principal in her own right.
>
> Additionally, any licensee who takes a secret or undisclosed amount of compensation is subject to discipline by the Real Estate Commissioner. The ultimate purchaser paid Roberts' agent $1.2 million that was presumably available to pay Roberts as part of the purchase price.
>
> The agent clearly acted in her own best interest and not in the best interest of her principal, thereby breaching her fiduciary duty. The assignment fee of $1.2 million is a secret profit and the agent may not retain it. The fact that the transaction yielded Roberts his full asking price does not change that result.
>
> Judgment for Roberts on the $1.2 million assignment fee. The case is sent back to the trial court for determination on whether the agent deliberately intended to defraud Roberts, a necessary element for recovery of the commission paid. *Roberts v. Lomanto*, 112 Cal. App. 4th 1553, 5 Cal. Rptr. 3d 866 (2003).

If the seller's agent is going to "buy" the property, the agent must make a full disclosure to the seller.

III. The Agent's Duties to Third Parties

A. DISCLOSURE TO THE BUYER

In addition to a seller's agent's duties to the principal, the agent owes the buyer a duty of good faith and fair dealing.

An agent is not a fiduciary in relation to a third party. He or she is not required to advance the third party's interests; in fact, the agent's duty of loyalty to the principal will often prohibit this.

What is fair dealing? The law's view of this question has changed substantially in recent years. In the past, the rule of *CAVEAT EMPTOR* ("let the buyer beware") governed real estate transactions. The seller and the seller's agent had very few duties to the buyer. It was up to the buyer to inspect the property and ask questions about it. The seller and agent were required to answer questions truthfully, but were not required to disclose information if the buyer did not ask. That rule is no longer followed in most states, at least not in residential transactions. Especially in California, court decisions and statutes have expanded sellers' and real estate agents' duties in order to protect residential buyers. Now it's not enough to avoid misleading a buyer—there are affirmative duties to disclose certain facts and even to investigate on a buyer's behalf.

If the seller and agent know anything about the property that materially affects its value or desirability, they must tell the buyer, unless it is something the buyer could easily see or determine.

For example, as a fiduciary Seigal should not have advised his clients as to the size, subdivision possibilities, and boundaries of the property where he did not know that to be the case and the facts were material to the plaintiff's decision to purchase. While he was not required to investigate the sellers' representations or the truth of the description contained in the multiple listing service sheet, Seigal was at least required to tell plaintiffs that he had not verified the information; that he was simply relying upon the description provided by the sellers. *Salahutdin v. Valley of California, Inc.*, 24 Cal.App.4th 555 (1994).

Disclose facts even if you think they are obvious to the buyer.

1. Broker's Duty to Disclose Material Facts – Sources of Requirement

a. Easton v. Strassburger

Until *Easton v. Strassburger*, a seller's agent had no duty to try and find out more about the property then he or she already knew. If the seller didn't tell the agent about problems, the agent didn't have to go looking for them.

Case Example: Valley Realty was the listing broker representing the Strassburgers (sellers) in a sale of their residential property to Easton (buyer). Shortly after the May 1976 purchase, there were massive earth movements on the property because a portion of the property was fill that had not been properly engineered and compacted. The value of the property was $170,000 in an undamaged condition; the value of the damaged property was estimated to be as low as $20,000. Repair estimates ranged as high as $213,000. The evidence indicated that the agents had conducted a limited investigation of the property and that they were aware of "red flags" indicating erosion or settlement problems. But evidence indicated that one or both of the agents knew that the residence was built on fill and that settlement and erosion problems are commonly associated with such soil. The agents had seen netting on a slope of the property that had been placed there to repair a slide that occurred most recently prior to the sale. One of the agents had observed that the floor of the guest house on the property was not level, and the other agent knew uneven floors were a "red flag" indication of soil problems. Despite this information, the agents did not request a soils report be prepared, nor take any other significant steps to determine whether there had been slides or other soil problems. The sellers did not tell the agents anything about prior slides or the corrective action they had taken as a result thereof. No one told Easton this material information.

The issue is whether the agents were responsible for negligence regarding the inspection and disclosure to the buyers. Valley Realty argued that under current case law, a broker or agent is under no duty to disclose these facts to the buyer. In other words, a broker is only obliged to disclose known facts and has no duty to disclose facts that would benefit the buyer that should be known to him/her through a reasonably diligent inspection.

At trial, the jury apparently concluded that a reasonably competent and diligent inspection of the property would have uncovered the past history of soil problems.

The court concluded that the duty of disclosure of a real estate broker representing the seller included the affirmative duty to conduct a reasonably competent and diligent inspection of the residential property listed for sale and to disclose to the prospective buyer all the facts materially affecting the value or desirability of the property that such an investigation would reveal. *Easton v. Strassburger*, 152 Cal. App. 3d 90, 199 Cal. Rptr. 383 (1984).

CHAPTER 6

b. Transfer Disclosure Statement (TDS)

In addition to the previously mentioned duties of an agent to the principal in a real estate transaction and as a result of judicial decisions (see *Easton* above) requiring disclosures of material facts, legislation was passed to establish the framework for disclosures by real estate brokers involving specific real estate. Recall that the Transfer Disclosure Statement requires an agent to "disclose all facts known to the agent materially affecting the value or desirability of the property that are not known to, or within the diligent attention and observation of, the parties." Also recall that an agent is not obligated to reveal to either party any confidential information obtained from the other party that does not involve the affirmative duties of the agency.

If the seller does not provide a Transfer Disclosure Statement, the buyer may cancel the purchase contract. A buyer cannot waive the right to receive a Transfer Disclosure Statement. *Realmuto v. Gagnard*, 110 Cal.App.4th 193 (2003).

A real estate agent's duty may be established by the agreement of the parties as well as from obligations imposed by statute and implementing regulations. *Carleton v. Tortosa*, 14 Cal. App. 4th 745 (1994).

c. Agent's Duty of Inspection (Civil Code Sections 2079 - 2079.6)

Historically, a listing agent had to disclose all material facts to a buyer (and seller) that were known to that agent affecting the value or desirability of the property being sold. An agent would be guilty of fraud for a failure to disclose a known material fact. This duty was derived from court decisions, and it applied to all real property. Ultimately, *Easton v. Strassburger* imposed a new obligation on an agent, requiring the agent to inspect the property being sold and disclose material facts that the agent discovered or should have discovered upon a reasonable inspection. As a result, legislation (Civil Code Sections 2079-2079.6) was enacted to clarify the scope of an agent's duty of inspection of real property.

Sellers and listing brokers have no duty to explain to buyers the ramifications of disclosed facts. *Sweat v. Hollister*, 37 Cal.App.4th 603 (1995). A buyer's agent may have the duty to explain the significance and consequences of a disclosed fact or a duty to recommend that that buyer conduct additional investigations to ensure that the buyer is making an informed decision.

Conduct a reasonably competent and diligent visual inspection and disclose revealed material facts. Don't rely on what a seller tells you.

1. Property Covered by the Visual Inspection

The listing broker, the selling agent, and a cooperating broker have a duty to a buyer of used residential property comprising one-to-four dwelling units, or leases of that property, which include an option to purchase, or ground leases of land on which one-to-four dwelling units have been constructed, or the purchase of such property on an installment sales contract to conduct a reasonably competent and diligent visual inspection of the property and to disclose to the buyer all facts materially affecting the value or desirability of the property that a visual investigation would reveal. This inspection duty also applies to the sale of a used manufactured home or mobilehome. Therefore, all agents are going to do a visual inspection and disclosure. **Subdivision property sales that are required to be preceded by the furnishing of a copy of a public report are not covered by these disclosure provisions.**

2. Property Not Covered by the Visual Inspection

The visual inspection does not include:

a. Areas that are not reasonably and normally accessible to such an inspection,

b. Areas off the site of the subject property,

c. Public records or permits concerning the title or use of the property,

d. More than the unit offered for sale if located in a common interest development, provided the required development documents are delivered. Additionally, an agent is not required to ask the HOA if there are defects in the common areas or if any pending construction defect litigation exists.

3. Agent's Standard of Care

The standard of care owed by an agent conducting the visual inspection is that which a reasonably prudent real estate licensee would exercise and is measured by the degree of knowledge through education, experience, and examination required to obtain a license. If the agent fails to exercise that degree of skill, then the agent may have liability for negligence. The agent's duty to the principal also requires verification of the information received. **An agent has a duty either to verify the information received as being correct or tell the principal that it has not been verified and suggest that the principal may want to verify it.** If an agent does pass the information on to the principal, to be safe the agent needs a reasonable basis to believe the information is true and, if it is not, may be liable for negligent misrepresentation. Also, a visual inspection must be made even if the property is being sold "as is."

"As is" does not remove an agent's duty to inspect.

Nothing in this legislation requiring the visual inspection and disclosure relieves a buyer or prospective buyer of the duty to exercise reasonable care to protect himself or herself, including those facts which are known to or within the diligent attention and observation of the buyer or prospective buyer.

d. Transfer Disclosure Statement (TDS) (Civil Code Sections 1102 -1102.17)

1. The Statutory Form

The Legislature decided to help clarify the disclosures by legislating a specific transfer disclosure statement. **Read the form carefully (Figure 6-2).** This form is required in any transfer by sale, exchange, installment sales contract, a lease with an option to purchase, a ground lease coupled with improvements, or a residential stock cooperative consisting of not more than four used dwelling units. It is also required with regard to a used manufactured home or mobilehome. This legislation does not affect the existing obligations of the parties to a real estate contract, or

Figure 6-2

CALIFORNIA
ASSOCIATION
OF REALTORS®

REAL ESTATE TRANSFER DISCLOSURE STATEMENT
(CALIFORNIA CIVIL CODE §1102, ET SEQ.)
(C.A.R. Form TDS, Revised 11/12)

THIS DISCLOSURE STATEMENT CONCERNS THE REAL PROPERTY SITUATED IN THE CITY OF
_____Marina del Rey_____ , COUNTY OF _____ , STATE OF CALIFORNIA,
DESCRIBED AS _____ 123 Sail Avenue, Marina del Rey, CA 90292 _____ .
THIS STATEMENT IS A DISCLOSURE OF THE CONDITION OF THE ABOVE DESCRIBED PROPERTY IN
COMPLIANCE WITH SECTION 1102 OF THE CIVIL CODE AS OF (date) _____ . IT IS NOT A
WARRANTY OF ANY KIND BY THE SELLER(S) OR ANY AGENT(S) REPRESENTING ANY PRINCIPAL(S) IN THIS
TRANSACTION, AND IS NOT A SUBSTITUTE FOR ANY INSPECTIONS OR WARRANTIES THE PRINCIPAL(S) MAY
WISH TO OBTAIN.

I. COORDINATION WITH OTHER DISCLOSURE FORMS

This Real Estate Transfer Disclosure Statement is made pursuant to Section 1102 of the Civil Code. Other statutes require disclosures, depending upon the details of the particular real estate transaction (for example: special study zone and purchase-money liens on residential property).

Substituted Disclosures: The following disclosures and other disclosures required by law, including the Natural Hazard Disclosure Report/Statement that may include airport annoyances, earthquake, fire, flood, or special assessment information, have or will be made in connection with this real estate transfer, and are intended to satisfy the disclosure obligations on this form, where the subject matter is the same:

☐ Inspection reports completed pursuant to the contract of sale or receipt for deposit.
☐ Additional inspection reports or disclosures: _____

II. SELLER'S INFORMATION

The Seller discloses the following information with the knowledge that even though this is not a warranty, prospective Buyers may rely on this information in deciding whether and on what terms to purchase the subject property. Seller hereby authorizes any agent(s) representing any principal(s) in this transaction to provide a copy of this statement to any person or entity in connection with any actual or anticipated sale of the property.

THE FOLLOWING ARE REPRESENTATIONS MADE BY THE SELLER(S) AND ARE NOT THE REPRESENTATIONS OF THE AGENT(S), IF ANY. THIS INFORMATION IS A DISCLOSURE AND IS NOT INTENDED TO BE PART OF ANY CONTRACT BETWEEN THE BUYER AND SELLER.

Seller ☐ is ☐ is not occupying the property.
A. The subject property has the items checked below: *

☐ Range	☐ Wall/Window Air Conditioning	☐ Pool:
☐ Oven	☐ Sprinklers	☐ Child Resistant Barrier
☐ Microwave	☐ Public Sewer System	☐ Pool/Spa Heater:
☐ Dishwasher	☐ Septic Tank	☐ Gas ☐ Solar ☐ Electric
☐ Trash Compactor	☐ Sump Pump	☐ Water Heater:
☐ Garbage Disposal	☐ Water Softener	☐ Gas ☐ Solar ☐ Electric
☐ Washer/Dryer Hookups	☐ Patio/Decking	☐ Water Supply:
☐ Rain Gutters	☐ Built-in Barbecue	☐ City ☐ Well
☐ Burglar Alarms	☐ Gazebo	☐ Private Utility or
☐ Carbon Monoxide Device(s)	☐ Security Gate(s)	Other _____
☐ Smoke Detector(s)	☐ Garage:	☐ Gas Supply:
☐ Fire Alarm	☐ Attached ☐ Not Attached	☐ Utility ☐ Bottled (Tank)
☐ TV Antenna	☐ Carport	☐ Window Screens
☐ Satellite Dish	☐ Automatic Garage Door Opener(s)	☐ Window Security Bars
☐ Intercom	☐ Number Remote Controls _____	☐ Quick Release Mechanism on
☐ Central Heating	☐ Sauna	Bedroom Windows
☐ Central Air Conditioning	☐ Hot Tub/Spa:	☐ Water-Conserving Plumbing Fixtures
☐ Evaporator Cooler(s)	☐ Locking Safety Cover	

Exhaust Fan(s) in _____ 220 Volt Wiring in _____ Fireplace(s) in _____
☐ Gas Starter _____ ☐ Roof(s): Type: _____ Age: _____ (approx.)
☐ Other: _____

Are there, to the best of your (Seller's) knowledge, any of the above that are not in operating condition? ☐ Yes ☐ No. If yes, then describe. (Attach additional sheets if necessary): _____

(*see note on page 2)

Buyer's Initials (_____)(_____)   Seller's Initials (_____)(_____)

EQUAL HOUSING OPPORTUNITY

TDS REVISED 11/12 (PAGE 1 OF 3)   Reviewed by _____ Date _____
REAL ESTATE TRANSFER DISCLOSURE STATEMENT (TDS PAGE 1 OF 3)

Agent: WALT HUBER	Phone:	Fax:	Prepared using zipForm® software
Broker:			

The TDS from now contains a checkbox in Section IIA for a seller to disclose whether the property has water conserving plumbing fixtures (low-flow toilets, shower heads, and faucets).

123 Sail Avenue
Property Address: Marina del Rey, CA 90292 _____ Date: _____

B. Are you (Seller) aware of any significant defects/malfunctions in any of the following? ☐ Yes ☐ No. If yes, check appropriate space(s) below.

☐ Interior Walls ☐ Ceilings ☐ Floors ☐ Exterior Walls ☐ Insulation ☐ Roof(s) ☐ Windows ☐ Doors ☐ Foundation ☐ Slab(s)
☐ Driveways ☐ Sidewalks ☐ Walls/Fences ☐ Electrical Systems ☐ Plumbing/Sewers/Septics ☐ Other Structural Components
(Describe: _____
_____)

If any of the above is checked, explain. (Attach additional sheets if necessary.): _____
_____
_____

*Installation of a listed appliance, device, or amenity is not a precondition of sale or transfer of the dwelling. The carbon monoxide device, garage door opener, or child-resistant pool barrier may not be in compliance with the safety standards relating to, respectively, carbon monoxide device standards of Chapter 8 (commencing with Section 13260) of Part 2 of Division 12 of, automatic reversing device standards of Chapter 12.5 (commencing with Section 19890) of Part 3 of Division 13 of, or the pool safety standards of Article 2.5 (commencing with Section 115920) of Chapter 5 of Part 10 of Division 104 of, the Health and Safety Code. Window security bars may not have quick-release mechanisms in compliance with the 1995 edition of the California Building Standards Code. Section 1101.4 of the Civil Code requires all single-family residences built on or before January 1, 1994, to be equipped with water-conserving plumbing fixtures after January 1, 2017. Additionally, on and after January 1, 2014, a single-family residence built on or before January 1, 1994, that is altered or improved is required to be equipped with water-conserving plumbing fixtures as a condition of final approval. Fixtures in this dwelling may not comply with section 1101.4 of the Civil Code.

C. Are you (Seller) aware of any the following:

1. Substances, materials, or products which may be an environmental hazard such as, but not limited to, asbestos, formaldehyde, radon gas, lead-based paint, mold, fuel or chemical storage tanks, and contaminated soil or water on the subject property . . . . ☐ Yes ☐ No
2. Features of the property shared in common with adjoining landowners, such as walls, fences, and driveways, whose use or responsibility for maintenance may have an effect on the subject property . . . . ☐ Yes ☐ No
3. Any encroachments, easements or similar matters that may affect your interest in the subject property . . . . ☐ Yes ☐ No
4. Room additions, structural modifications, or other alterations or repairs made without necessary permits. . . . . . . ☐ Yes ☐ No
5. Room additions, structural modifications, or other alterations or repairs not in compliance with building codes. . . . ☐ Yes ☐ No
6. Fill (compacted or otherwise) on the property or any portion thereof . . . . ☐ Yes ☐ No
7. Any settling from any cause, or slippage, sliding, or other soil problems . . . . ☐ Yes ☐ No
8. Flooding, drainage or grading problems . . . . ☐ Yes ☐ No
9. Major damage to the property or any of the structures from fire, earthquake, floods, or landslides . . . . ☐ Yes ☐ No
10. Any zoning violations, nonconforming uses, violations of "setback" requirements . . . . ☐ Yes ☐ No
11. Neighborhood noise problems or other nuisances . . . . ☐ Yes ☐ No
12. CC&R's or other deed restrictions or obligations . . . . ☐ Yes ☐ No
13. Homeowners' Association which has any authority over the subject property . . . . ☐ Yes ☐ No
14. Any "common area" (facilities such as pools, tennis courts, walkways, or other areas co-owned in undivided interest with others) . . . . ☐ Yes ☐ No
15. Any notices of abatement or citations against the property . . . . ☐ Yes ☐ No
16. Any lawsuits by or against the Seller threatening to or affecting this real property, including any lawsuits alleging a defect or deficiency in this real property or "common areas" (facilities such as pools, tennis courts, walkways, or other areas, co-owned in undivided interest with others) . . . . ☐ Yes ☐ No

If the answer to any of these is yes, explain. (Attach additional sheets if necessary.): _____
_____
_____
_____

D. 1. The Seller certifies that the property, as of the close of escrow, will be in compliance with Section 13113.8 of the Health and Safety Code by having operable smoke detector(s) which are approved, listed, and installed in accordance with the State Fire Marshal's regulations and applicable local standards.
2. The Seller certifies that the property, as of the close of escrow, will be in compliance with Section 19211 of the Health and Safety Code by having the water heater tank(s) braced, anchored, or strapped in place in accordance with applicable law.

Seller certifies that the information herein is true and correct to the best of the Seller's knowledge as of the date signed by the Seller.

Seller _____ Date _____

Seller _____ Date _____

Buyer's Initials (_____) (_____)

TDS REVISED 11/12 (PAGE 2 OF 3)

| Reviewed by _____ Date _____ |
| EQUAL HOUSING OPPORTUNITY |

REAL ESTATE TRANSFER DISCLOSURE STATEMENT (TDS PAGE 2 OF 3)   Untitled

CHAPTER 6

Property Address: *123 Sail Avenue*
Marina del Rey, CA 90292 _____ Date: _____

III. AGENT'S INSPECTION DISCLOSURE
(To be completed only if the Seller is represented by an agent in this transaction.)

THE UNDERSIGNED, BASED ON THE ABOVE INQUIRY OF THE SELLER(S) AS TO THE CONDITION OF THE PROPERTY AND BASED ON A REASONABLY COMPETENT AND DILIGENT VISUAL INSPECTION OF THE ACCESSIBLE AREAS OF THE PROPERTY IN CONJUNCTION WITH THAT INQUIRY, STATES THE FOLLOWING:

☐ See attached Agent Visual Inspection Disclosure (AVID Form)
☐ Agent notes no items for disclosure.
☐ Agent notes the following items: _____

_____
_____
_____

Agent (Broker Representing Seller) _____ By _____ Date _____
            (Please Print)   (Associate Licensee or Broker Signature)

IV. AGENT'S INSPECTION DISCLOSURE
(To be completed only if the agent who has obtained the offer is other than the agent above.)

THE UNDERSIGNED, BASED ON A REASONABLY COMPETENT AND DILIGENT VISUAL INSPECTION OF THE ACCESSIBLE AREAS OF THE PROPERTY, STATES THE FOLLOWING:

☐ See attached Agent Visual Inspection Disclosure (AVID Form)
☐ Agent notes no items for disclosure.
☐ Agent notes the following items: _____

_____
_____
_____

Agent (Broker Obtaining the Offer) _____ By _____ Date _____
            (Please Print)   (Associate Licensee or Broker Signature)

V. BUYER(S) AND SELLER(S) MAY WISH TO OBTAIN PROFESSIONAL ADVICE AND/OR INSPECTIONS OF THE PROPERTY AND TO PROVIDE FOR APPROPRIATE PROVISIONS IN A CONTRACT BETWEEN BUYER AND SELLER(S) WITH RESPECT TO ANY ADVICE/INSPECTIONS/DEFECTS.

I/WE ACKNOWLEDGE RECEIPT OF A COPY OF THIS STATEMENT.

Seller _____ Date _____ Buyer _____ Date _____

Seller _____ Date _____ Buyer _____ Date _____

Agent (Broker Representing Seller) _____ By _____ Date _____
      (Please Print)   (Associate Licensee or Broker Signature)

Agent (Broker Obtaining the Offer) _____ By _____ Date _____
      (Please Print)   (Associate Licensee or Broker Signature)

SECTION 1102.3 OF THE CIVIL CODE PROVIDES A BUYER WITH THE RIGHT TO RESCIND A PURCHASE CONTRACT FOR AT LEAST THREE DAYS AFTER THE DELIVERY OF THIS DISCLOSURE IF DELIVERY OCCURS AFTER THE SIGNING OF AN OFFER TO PURCHASE. IF YOU WISH TO RESCIND THE CONTRACT, YOU MUST ACT WITHIN THE PRESCRIBED PERIOD.

A REAL ESTATE BROKER IS QUALIFIED TO ADVISE ON REAL ESTATE. IF YOU DESIRE LEGAL ADVICE, CONSULT YOUR ATTORNEY.

THIS FORM HAS BEEN APPROVED BY THE CALIFORNIA ASSOCIATION OF REALTORS®. NO REPRESENTATION IS MADE AS TO THE LEGAL VALIDITY OR ADEQUACY OF ANY PROVISION IN ANY SPECIFIC TRANSACTION. A REAL ESTATE BROKER IS THE PERSON QUALIFIED TO ADVISE ON REAL ESTATE TRANSACTIONS. IF YOU DESIRE LEGAL OR TAX ADVICE, CONSULT AN APPROPRIATE PROFESSIONAL.
This form is available for use by the entire real estate industry. It is not intended to identify the user as a REALTOR®. REALTOR® is a registered collective membership mark which may be used only by members of the NATIONAL ASSOCIATION OF REALTORS® who subscribe to its Code of Ethics.

Published and Distributed by:
REAL ESTATE BUSINESS SERVICES, INC.
a subsidiary of the California Association of REALTORS®
525 South Virgil Avenue, Los Angeles, California 90020

Reviewed by _____ Date _____

EQUAL HOUSING OPPORTUNITY

TDS REVISED 11/12 (PAGE 3 OF 3)

REAL ESTATE TRANSFER DISCLOSURE STATEMENT (TDS PAGE 3 OF 3)

Untitled

their agents, to disclose any fact materially affecting the value and desirability of the property (as mentioned above). Additionally, the delivery of the real estate transfer disclosure statement may not be waived, even in an "as is" sale. Also, local county or city ordinances may require particular disclosures and also must be in writing and can be on a form provided by a local ordinance.

Read and complete the transfer disclosure statement (TDS) form carefully.

The purpose of the CAR® form *SELLER PROPERTY QUESTIONNAIRE (SPQ) is to provide additional information when a TDS is completed. It is not a substitute for the TDS.*

2. When Transfer Disclosure Statement Is Not Required

The transfer disclosure statement is not required in the following:

a. Transfers pursuant to court order, which includes transfers in probate court, transfers pursuant to a writ of execution, foreclosure sales, bankruptcy sales, eminent domain, and a court decree of specific performance.

b. Default sales.

c. Transfers by a fiduciary in the course of the administration of the decedent's estate, guardianship, conservatorship, or trust.

d. Transfers that are required to be preceded by the furnishing of a public report (the first sale of a new home in a subdivision).

e. Transfers from one co-owner to another.

f. Transfers made to a spouse or family member.

g. Transfers made from one spouse to another as a result of a judgment of dissolution of marriage.

h. Transfers made by the Controller of California.

i. Transfers made under the authority of the Revenue and Taxation Code.

j. Transfers or exchanges to or from any government entity.

3. The Procedure

The seller will use the transfer disclosure statement to make the required disclosure to the buyer. The **listing agent** is required to disclose the facts discovered by the required visual inspection in the transfer disclosure statement by either stating that there are no further items to disclose other than those already disclosed by the seller, or listing specific items the seller did not disclose. The **selling agent** also has the same obligation of disclosure on the form. Both the listing agent and the selling agent sign their disclosures (usually on behalf of the broker). At the end of the form, both the seller and buyer sign and there is a place for acknowledgment of receipt of a copy.

If you are not completely sure of your disclosure, you can use an approximation, but you must say it is an approximation.

4. Delivery and Confirmation

The transfer disclosure statement must be delivered to the prospective buyer as soon as practicable before the transfer of title.

If the transfer is pursuant to an installment sales contract by a lease with an option to purchase, or a ground lease coupled with improvements, it must be delivered as soon as practicable before the signing of the contract. Additionally, evidence of the transferor's compliance must be included in the purchase agreement, real property sales contract, lease or any addendum attached thereto or on a separate document. If the delivery of the transfer disclosure statement occurs after the signing of the purchase agreement, the buyer has three days after delivery in person or five days after delivery by deposit in the mail, to terminate the offer by the delivery of a written notice of termination to the seller or the seller's agent. If the transaction involves a manufactured home or mobilehome, the delivery of the transfer disclosure statement must be as soon as practicable, but no later than the close of escrow.

Case Example: Realmuto (seller) sued Gagnard and Savoy (buyer) for specific performance and for breach of contract to purchase seller's residence in Alpine, California. The seller never provided the required Transfer Disclosure Statement to the buyers. The seller claimed the buyers did not ask him to provide a disclosure statement during the escrow period. The buyers never completed their purchase of the seller's property. The court's review of the Transfer Disclosure Statement legislation shows that the seller's delivery of a disclosure statement is a nonwaivable condition precedent to the buyer's performance. By mandating delivery of the disclosure statement "before transfer of title" the Legislature plainly contemplated the buyers would never be irrevocably committed to performing the contract without having received the required disclosures. The seller's performance of this condition also gives rise to a statutory right of rescission by the buyer. The seller's failure to deliver a Transfer Disclosure Statement precludes this action against the buyers for specific performance and breach of contract. *Realmuto v. Gagnard*, 110 Cal. App.4th 193, 1 Cal. Rptr. 3d 569 (2003).

If more than one broker is acting as an agent regarding the sale of the property, the broker who obtained the offer shall deliver the transfer disclosure statement to the buyer unless the seller has given other written instructions for delivery. If that broker cannot obtain the transfer disclosure statement and does not have written assurance from the buyer that the disclosure statement has been received, the broker must advise the buyer in writing of his or her rights to the disclosure. No transfers shall be invalidated solely because of the failure of a person to comply with the disclosure requirements. However, any person who willfully or negligently violates or fails to perform any duty required of them shall be liable in the amount of actual damages suffered by a buyer.

Give the transfer disclosure statement to a prospective buyer at the earliest possible moment.

5. Protection from Liability

Neither the seller nor any listing or selling agent is liable for any error, inaccuracy, or omission of any information delivered if the error, inaccuracy or omission was not within the personal knowledge of the seller or agent, or was based on information timely provided by public agencies and ordinary care was exercised in obtaining and transmitting it. The seller or agents have no further duty or liability if a document delivered pursuant to the disclosure requirement was prepared by a public agency or by an expert regarding matters within the scope of a professional license or expertise.

The real estate licensee sued for failure to disclose the property's defects may seek equitable indemnity from the property inspectors who negligently failed to discover or disclose defects in the property. *Leko v. Comersione Home Inspection* 86 Cal.App.4th 1109 (2001).

6. Other Required Disclosures Unrelated Directly to Structure or Land

A seller or agent with knowledge must disclose to a purchaser deaths of an occupant that occurred on the property within three years prior to the date the purchaser offers to purchase the property. **No disclosures are required regarding the death or manner of death of an occupant if it occurred more than three years prior to the offer to purchase**. No disclosure is required at all if the occupant died from AIDS or HIV or was afflicted with AIDS or HIV. However, the seller or an agent may be liable for making an intentional misrepresentation in response to the direct inquiry concerning deaths on the property. In other words, if the seller or agent is asked about deaths, regardless of when a death may have occurred, an honest and full disclosure must be made. AIDS and the HIV virus are considered handicaps under the Federal Fair Housing Act and discrimination against persons with AIDS or HIV is a violation of federal law. For this reason, the California Association of REALTORS® legal staff has suggested that the response to a buyer's question about AIDS or HIV be **"The information is considered to be confidential and protected from disclosure by state or federal law."**

Also note that **the transfer disclosure statement requires disclosures about annoyances or nuisances on adjoining property**. For example, a dog that barks all night or neighbors who play loud music or have loud all-night parties must be disclosed.

Case Example: The Court of Appeal noted that the statutory disclosure form requires disclosure of "neighborhood noise problems or other nuisances" to buyers. The case involved the McKnights whose tree trimming business operated out of the home and used a noisy tree chipper machine. There were late-night noisy activities, too many cars on the property, a deck constructed without a building permit, and a cabana that violated the covenants, conditions, and restrictions on the property. The court held that it would be tortuous not to disclose a negative fact when it is reasonably foreseeable that it has a depressing effect on the property's value. This disclosure is required even though the court has ordered abatement. *Alexander v. McKnight*, 7 Cal. App. 4th 973, 9 Cal. Rptr. 2d 453 (1992).

7. No Warranty to Buyer

Although the transfer disclosure statement includes very specific lists of problems, the lists are not necessarily complete. The old non-statutory disclosure rule still stands: if the seller or agent is aware of anything that materially affects the value or desirability of the property, it must be disclosed to the buyer. **One final thing: it is very important that the buyer realize that the transfer disclosure statement is not a warranty by the seller, nor is it intended to be part of the sales contract**.

The transfer disclosure statement is not a warranty to the buyer.

B. STATUTE OF LIMITATIONS

If a lawsuit is brought against a broker for breach of the duty to visually inspect and disclose (negligence), the statute of limitations is two years from the date of possession, which means the date of recordation, the date of close of escrow, or the date of occupancy, whichever occurs first. However, if the lawsuit is brought on the basis of intentional fraud, the statute of limitations is three years and starts with the date of discovery of the fraud.

The statute of limitations is two years for negligent visual inspection and three years for breach of fiduciary duty or intentional fraud.

C. BUYER'S DUTY TO USE REASONABLE CARE

As mentioned before, the agent's duty of **visual inspection** and **disclosure** does not relieve the buyer of the duty to exercise reasonable care to protect himself or herself, including discovery of facts known to or within the diligent attention and observation of the buyer (Civil Code § 2079.5). A buyer is held to be aware of obvious and patent conditions.

Case Example: James Baum (seller) listed his mobilehome park for sale. He did not inform either the real estate broker or the agent who handled the transaction on his behalf about a pipeline easement or his temporary removal of five mobilehomes to allow work on the pipeline. The park has 44 spaces.

Ted and Alice Stevenson (buyers) bought the mobilehome park under a purchase contract, which provided that title is to be free of easements other than those of record. The buyers first reviewed a title report during the signing of escrow instructions that disclosed the existence of an oil company easement for ingress and egress, but did not disclose the pipeline location. The buyers interpreted the easement to mean only that the oil company could enter and travel across the property. The buyers never met or spoke with the seller before they took title to the park. After escrow closed, Chevron Pipeline Company informed the buyers that the mobilehomes in the park encroached on the easement and would have to be removed to allow access to the pipeline. The buyers sued the seller for failure to disclose that five of the spaces were constructed and laid out over a pipeline easement, and that they had to be removed in the past to permit work on the pipeline.

The buyers allege that they purchased only 39 spaces since five were unusable. The buyers introduced no evidence to show that the five spaces over the easement were unusable.

▼

The buyers assert that the seller had a duty to disclose the pipeline's existence, its actual location, and his prior removal of mobilehomes that encroached on the easement. The primary material fact that potentially affected the value the property was the underlying fact of the pipeline itself, a fact immediately ascertainable from public records. A reasonable person in the buyers' position, knowing that the oil company's easement was for pipeline purposes, would have realized that the holder might exercise its right of access to the pipeline at any time.

Moreover, it is undisputed that the recorded easement accurately describes where the pipeline was; thus if the Stevenson's had consulted the public records, they would have learned that the pipeline underlay the mobilehome spaces. By warning the buyers in the purchase contract that they took title subject to the easements of record, the seller put them on notice of the material facts, which satisfied his duty of disclosure. Because the seller did not breach that duty, the buyers cannot state a cause of action for fraudulent nondisclosure. Judgment for seller. *Stevenson v. Baum*, 65 Cal. App. 4th 159, 75 Cal. Rptr. 2d 904 (1998).

In addition, the seller's agent may provide the buyer with a **Buyer's Inspection Advisory (BIA)** form (**Figure 6-3**) as a substituted disclosure under Item I of the Transfer Disclosure Statement. The form clearly states in bold print that:

"YOU ARE STRONGLY ADVISED TO INVESTIGATE THE CONDITION AND SUITABILITY OF ALL ASPECTS OF THE PROPERTY. IF YOU DO NOT DO SO, YOU ARE ACTING AGAINST THE ADVICE OF BROKERS."

D. STATEWIDE BUYER AND SELLER ADVISORY (SBSA)

The CAR© *STATEWIDE BUYER AND SELLER ADVISORY (SBSA) form (Figure 6-4) advises both buyer and seller of various factors that may affect the decision to buy, different types of inspections that can be obtained, and questions to ask about or research and information to be disclosed.* The Buyer is advised in each particular section to contact appropriate professionals for concerns. This form is designed to work in conjunction with local disclosure addenda. This form is not mandated by statute or contract.

The latest updated form added underground gas pipelines to the items that a Buyer may consider to be material facts in a residential transaction.

In the SBSA, among the usual hazard advisories—zone disclosures for earthquake faults, seismic hazards, wildland fires, 100-year floodplains, supplemental property taxes, and Megan's Law—a new paragraph has been added regarding Underground Pipelines and Utilities.

This updated form acknowledges the growing concern among real estate consumers about living near a natural gas transmission pipeline. In September 2010, a Pacific Gas and Electric (PG&E) pipeline exploded in a residential neighborhood on the San Francisco Peninsula, killing eight people and destroying 38 homes and damaging 61 others. In the aftermath, the utility formally took the extraordinary act of notifying millions of California residents that they reside within 2,000 feet of a PG&E gas transmission pipeline. The State of California also enacted five new laws to strengthen transmission pipeline safety. However, newly mandated testing of existing pipelines continues to expose dangerous leaks in old buried pipelines.

Figure 6-3

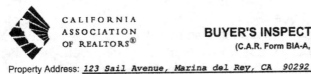

CALIFORNIA
ASSOCIATION
OF REALTORS®

BUYER'S INSPECTION ADVISORY
(C.A.R. Form BIA-A, Revised 10/02)

Property Address: *123 Sail Avenue, Marina del Rey, CA 90292* ("Property").

A. IMPORTANCE OF PROPERTY INVESTIGATION: The physical condition of the land and improvements being purchased is not guaranteed by either Seller or Brokers. For this reason, you should conduct thorough investigations of the Property personally and with professionals who should provide written reports of their investigations. A general physical inspection typically does not cover all aspects of the Property nor items affecting the Property that are not physically located on the Property. If the professionals recommend further investigations, including a recommendation by a pest control operator to inspect inaccessible areas of the Property, you should contact qualified experts to conduct such additional investigations.

B. BUYER RIGHTS AND DUTIES: You have an affirmative duty to exercise reasonable care to protect yourself, including discovery of the legal, practical and technical implications of disclosed facts, and the investigation and verification of information and facts that you know or that are within your diligent attention and observation. The purchase agreement gives you the right to investigate the Property. If you exercise this right, and you should, you must do so in accordance with the terms of that agreement. This is the best way for you to protect yourself. It is extremely important for you to read all written reports provided by professionals and to discuss the results of inspections with the professional who conducted the inspection. You have the right to request that Seller make repairs, corrections or take other action based upon items discovered in your investigations or disclosed by Seller. If Seller is unwilling or unable to satisfy your requests, or you do not want to purchase the Property in its disclosed and discovered condition, you have the right to cancel the agreement if you act within specific time periods. If you do not cancel the agreement in a timely and proper manner, you may be in breach of contract.

C. SELLER RIGHTS AND DUTIES: Seller is required to disclose to you material facts known to him/her that affect the value or desirability of the Property. However, Seller may not be aware of some Property defects or conditions. Seller does not have an obligation to inspect the Property for your benefit nor is Seller obligated to repair, correct or otherwise cure known defects that are disclosed to you or previously unknown defects that are discovered by you or your inspectors during escrow. The purchase agreement obligates Seller to make the Property available to you for investigations.

D. BROKER OBLIGATIONS: Brokers do not have expertise in all areas and therefore cannot advise you on many items, such as soil stability, geologic or environmental conditions, hazardous or illegal controlled substances, structural conditions of the foundation or other improvements, or the condition of the roof, plumbing, heating, air conditioning, electrical, sewer, septic, waste disposal, or other system. The only way to accurately determine the condition of the Property is through an inspection by an appropriate professional selected by you. If Broker gives you referrals to such professionals, Broker does not guarantee their performance. You may select any professional of your choosing. In sales involving residential dwellings with no more than four units, Brokers have a duty to make a diligent visual inspection of the accessible areas of the Property and to disclose the results of that inspection. However, as some Property defects or conditions may not be discoverable from a visual inspection, it is possible Brokers are not aware of them. If you have entered into a written agreement with a Broker, the specific terms of that agreement will determine the nature and extent of that Broker's duty to you. **YOU ARE STRONGLY ADVISED TO INVESTIGATE THE CONDITION AND SUITABILITY OF ALL ASPECTS OF THE PROPERTY. IF YOU DO NOT DO SO, YOU ARE ACTING AGAINST THE ADVICE OF BROKERS.**

E. YOU ARE ADVISED TO CONDUCT INVESTIGATIONS OF THE ENTIRE PROPERTY, INCLUDING, BUT NOT LIMITED TO THE FOLLOWING:
1. **GENERAL CONDITION OF THE PROPERTY, ITS SYSTEMS AND COMPONENTS:** Foundation, roof, plumbing, heating, air conditioning, electrical, mechanical, security, pool/spa, other structural and non-structural systems and components, fixtures, built-in appliances, any personal property included in the sale, and energy efficiency of the Property. (Structural engineers are best suited to determine possible design or construction defects, and whether improvements are structurally sound.)
2. **SQUARE FOOTAGE, AGE, BOUNDARIES:** Square footage, room dimensions, lot size, age of improvements and boundaries. Any numerical statements regarding these items are APPROXIMATIONS ONLY and have not been verified by Seller and cannot be verified by Brokers. Fences, hedges, walls, retaining walls and other natural or constructed barriers or markers do not necessarily identify true Property boundaries. (Professionals such as appraisers, architects, surveyors and civil engineers are best suited to determine square footage, dimensions and boundaries of the Property.)
3. **WOOD DESTROYING PESTS:** Presence of, or conditions likely to lead to the presence of wood destroying pests and organisms and other infestation or infection. Inspection reports covering these items can be separated into two sections: Section 1 identifies areas where infestation or infection is evident. Section 2 identifies areas where there are conditions likely to lead to infestation or infection. A registered structural pest control company is best suited to perform these inspections.
4. **SOIL STABILITY:** Existence of fill or compacted soil, expansive or contracting soil, susceptibility to slippage, settling or movement, and the adequacy of drainage. (Geotechnical engineers are best suited to determine such conditions, causes and remedies.)

Buyer's Initials (_____) (_____)
Seller's Initials (_____) (_____)

Reviewed by	Date

EQUAL HOUSING
OPPORTUNITY

BIA-A REVISED 10/02 (PAGE 1 OF 2)

BUYER'S INSPECTION ADVISORY (BIA-A PAGE 1 OF 2)

Agent: WALT HUBER	Phone:	Fax:	Prepared using zipForm® software
Broker:			

Property Address: _123 Sail Avenue, Marina del Rey, CA 90292_ _____ Date: _____

5. **ROOF:** Present condition, age, leaks, and remaining useful life. (Roofing contractors are best suited to determine these conditions.)

6. **POOL/SPA:** Cracks, leaks or operational problems. (Pool contractors are best suited to determine these conditions.)

7. **WASTE DISPOSAL:** Type, size, adequacy, capacity and condition of sewer and septic systems and components, connection to sewer, and applicable fees.

8. **WATER AND UTILITES; WELL SYSTEMS AND COMPONENTS:** Water and utility availability, use restrictions and costs. Water quality, adequacy, condition, and performance of well systems and components.

9. **ENVIRONMENTAL HAZARDS:** Potential environmental hazards, including, but not limited to, asbestos, lead-based paint and other lead contamination, radon, methane, other gases, fuel oil or chemical storage tanks, contaminated soil or water, hazardous waste, waste disposal sites, electromagnetic fields, nuclear sources, and other substances, materials, products, or conditions (including mold (airborne, toxic or otherwise), fungus or similar contaminants). (For more information on these items, you may consult an appropriate professional or read the booklets "Environmental Hazards: A Guide for Homeowners, Buyers, Landlords and Tenants," "Protect Your Family From Lead in Your Home" or both.)

10. **EARTHQUAKES AND FLOODING:** Susceptibility of the Property to earthquake/seismic hazards and propensity of the Property to flood. (A Geologist or Geotechnical Engineer is best suited to provide information on these conditions.)

11. **FIRE, HAZARD AND OTHER INSURANCE:** The availability and cost of necessary or desired insurance may vary. The location of the Property in a seismic, flood or fire hazard zone, and other conditions, such as the age of the Property and the claims history of the Property and Buyer, may affect the availability and need for certain types of insurance. Buyer should explore insurance options early as this information may affect other decisions, including the removal of loan and inspection contingencies. (An insurance agent is best suited to provide information on these conditions.)

12. **BUILDING PERMITS, ZONING AND GOVERNMENTAL REQUIREMENTS:** Permits, inspections, certificates, zoning, other governmental limitations, restrictions, and requirements affecting the current or future use of the Property, its development or size. (Such information is available from appropriate governmental agencies and private information providers. Brokers are not qualified to review or interpret any such information.)

13. **RENTAL PROPERTY RESTRICTIONS:** Some cities and counties impose restrictions that limit the amount of rent that can be charged, the maximum number of occupants; and the right of a landlord to terminate a tenancy. Deadbolt or other locks and security systems for doors and windows, including window bars, should be examined to determine whether they satisfy legal requirements. (Government agencies can provide information about these restrictions and other requirements.)

14. **SECURITY AND SAFETY:** State and local Law may require the installation of barriers, access alarms, self-latching mechanisms and/or other measures to decrease the risk to children and other persons of existing swimming pools and hot tubs, as well as various fire safety and other measures concerning other features of the Property. Compliance requirements differ from city to city and county to county. Unless specifically agreed, the Property may not be in compliance with these requirements. (Local government agencies can provide information about these restrictions and other requirements.)

15. **NEIGHBORHOOD, AREA, SUBDIVISION CONDITIONS; PERSONAL FACTORS:** Neighborhood or area conditions, including schools, proximity and adequacy of law enforcement, crime statistics, the proximity of registered felons or offenders, fire protection, other government services, availability, adequacy and cost of any speed-wired, wireless internet connections or other telecommunications or other technology services and installations, proximity to commercial, industrial or agricultural activities, existing and proposed transportation, construction and development that may affect noise, view, or traffic, airport noise, noise or odor from any source, wild and domestic animals, other nuisances, hazards, or circumstances, protected species, wetland properties, botanical diseases, historic or other governmentally protected sites or improvements, cemeteries, facilities and condition of common areas of common interest subdivisions, and possible lack of compliance with any governing documents or Homeowners' Association requirements, conditions and influences of significance to certain cultures and/or religions, and personal needs, requirements and preferences of Buyer.

Buyer and Seller acknowledge and agree that Broker: **(i)** Does not decide what price Buyer should pay or Seller should accept; **(ii)** Does not guarantee the condition of the Property; **(iii)** Does not guarantee the performance, adequacy or completeness of inspections, services, products or repairs provided or made by Seller or others; **(iv)** Does not have an obligation to conduct an inspection of common areas or areas off the site of the Property; **(v)** Shall not be responsible for identifying defects on the Property, in common areas, or offsite unless such defects are visually observable by an inspection of reasonably accessible areas of the Property or are known to Broker; **(vi)** Shall not be responsible for inspecting public records or permits concerning the title or use of Property; **(vii)** Shall not be responsible for identifying the location of boundary lines or other items affecting title; **(viii)** Shall not be responsible for verifying square footage, representations of others or information contained in Investigation reports, Multiple Listing Service, advertisements, flyers or other promotional material; **(ix)** Shall not be responsible for providing legal or tax advice regarding any aspect of a transaction entered into by Buyer or Seller; and **(x)** Shall not be responsible for providing other advice or information that exceeds the knowledge, education and experience required to perform real estate licensed activity. Buyer and Seller agree to seek legal, tax, insurance, title and other desired assistance from appropriate professionals.

By signing below, Buyer and Seller each acknowledge that they have read, understand, accept and have received a Copy of this Advisory. Buyer is encouraged to read it carefully.

Buyer Signature	Date	Buyer Signature	Date

Seller Signature	Date	Seller Signature	Date

| Reviewed by _____ Date _____ |

BIA-A REVISED 10/02 (PAGE 2 OF 2)

BUYER'S INSPECTION ADVISORY (BIA-A PAGE 2 OF 2)

Untitled

Figure 6-4

CALIFORNIA
ASSOCIATION
OF REALTORS®

STATEWIDE BUYER AND SELLER ADVISORY
(This Form Does Not Replace Local Condition Disclosures.
Additional Addenda May Be Attached to This Advisory. See Paragraph 51)
(C.A.R. Form SBSA, Revised 11/12)

Property Address *123 Sail Avenue Marina del Rey, CA 90292*_____ Date: _____

BUYER RIGHTS AND DUTIES:
- The physical condition of the land and improvements being purchased are not guaranteed by Seller or Brokers.
- You should conduct thorough investigations of the Property both personally and with appropriate professionals.
- If professionals recommend further inspections, you should contact qualified experts to conduct such inspections.
- You should retain your own professional even if Seller or Broker has provided you with existing reports.
- You should read all written reports given to you and discuss those reports with the persons who prepared them.
- You have the right to request that the Seller make repairs or corrections or take other actions based on inspections or disclosures, but the Seller is not obligated to make any such repairs, corrections or other requested actions.
- If the Seller is unwilling or unable to satisfy your requests, and you act within certain time periods, you may have the right to cancel the Agreement (the Purchase Agreement and any Counter Offer and Addenda together are the "Agreement"). If you cancel outside of these periods, you may be in breach of the Agreement and your deposit might be at risk.
- The terms of the purchase agreement and any counter offers and addenda establish your rights and responsibilities.

YOU ARE STRONGLY ADVISED TO INVESTIGATE THE CONDITION AND SUITABILITY OF ALL ASPECTS OF THE PROPERTY. IF YOU DO NOT DO SO, YOU ARE ACTING AGAINST THE ADVICE OF BROKERS.

SELLER RIGHTS AND DUTIES:
- You have a duty to disclose material facts known to you that affect the value or desirability of the Property.
- You are obligated to make the Property available to the Buyer and have utilities on for inspections as allowed by the Agreement.
- This form is not a substitute for completing a Real Estate Transfer Disclosure Statement, if required, and any other property-specific questionnaires or disclosures.
- The terms of the Agreement establish your rights and responsibilities.

BROKER RIGHTS AND DUTIES:
- Brokers do not have expertise in all areas and matters affecting the Property or your evaluation of it.
- For most sales of residential properties with no more than four units, Brokers have a duty to make a reasonably competent and diligent visual inspection of the accessible areas of the Property and disclose to you material facts or defects that the inspection reveals.
- Many defects and conditions may not be discoverable by a Broker's visual inspection.
- If Brokers give a referral to another professional, Brokers do not guarantee that person's performance. You may select any professional of your own choosing.
- Any written agreement between a Broker and either Buyer or Seller or both establishes the rights and responsibilities of those parties.

1. **INSPECTIONS:** Buyer and Seller are advised that Buyer has the right to obtain various inspections of the Property under most residential purchase agreements. Buyer is advised to have the Property inspected by a professional property inspection service within Buyer's inspection contingency period. A licensed building contractor or other professional may perform these services. The inspector generally does not look behind walls or under carpets, or take equipment apart. Certain items on the Property, such as chimneys and spark arresters, plumbing, heating, air conditioning, electrical wiring, pool and spa, septic system, well, roof, foundation and structural items may need to be inspected by another professional, such as a chimney sweep, plumber, electrician, pool and spa service, septic or well company or roofer. A general physical inspection typically will not test for mold, wood destroying pests, lead-based paint, radon, asbestos and other environmental hazards, geologic conditions, age, remaining useful life or water-tightness of roof, cracks, leaks or operational problems associated with a pool or spa or connection of the Property to a sewer system. If Buyer wants further information on any aspect of the Property, Broker recommends that Buyer have a discussion with the professional property inspector and that Buyer hire an appropriate professional for the area of concern to Buyer. Brokers do not have expertise in these areas. Brokers do not verify the results of any such inspection or guarantee the performance of any such inspector or service. Any election by Buyer to waive the right to a physical inspection of the Property or to rely on somebody other than an appropriate professional is against the advice of Brokers. Not all inspectors are licensed and licenses are not available for all types of inspection activities.

Buyer's Initials (_____) (_____)   Seller's Initials (_____) (_____)

Reviewed by _____ Date _____

SBSA REVISED 11/12 (PAGE 1 OF 11)

STATEWIDE BUYER AND SELLER ADVISORY (SBSA PAGE 1 OF 11)

Agent: WALT HUBER	Phone:	Fax:	Prepared using zipForm® software
Broker:			

Property Address: *123 Sail Avenue*
Marina del Rey, CA 90292 _____ Date: _____

2. SQUARE FOOTAGE, LOT SIZE, BOUNDARIES AND SURVEYS: Buyer and Seller are advised that only an appraiser or land surveyor, as applicable, can reliably confirm square footage, lot size, Property corners and exact boundaries of the Property. Representations regarding these items that are made in a Multiple Listing Service, advertisements, and from property tax assessor records are often approximations, or based upon inaccurate or incomplete records. Fences, hedges, walls or other barriers may not represent actual boundary lines. Unless otherwise specified by Broker in writing, Brokers have not verified any such boundary lines or any representations made by Seller or others. Brokers do not have expertise in this area. Standard title insurance does not insure the boundaries of the Property. If Buyer wants information about the exact square footage, lot size or location of Property corners or boundaries, Broker recommends that Buyer hire an appraiser or licensed surveyor to investigate these matters or to prepare a survey of the property during Buyer's inspection contingency period.

3. SOIL AND GEOLOGIC CONDITIONS: Buyer and Seller are advised that real estate in California is subject to settling, slippage, contraction, expansion erosion, subsidence, earthquakes and other land movement. The Property may be constructed on fill or improperly compacted soil and may have inadequate drainage capability. Any of these matters can cause structural problems to improvements on the Property. Civil or geo-technical engineers are best suited to evaluate soil stability, grading, drainage and other soil conditions. Additionally, the Property may contain known or unknown mines, mills, caves or wells. Brokers do not have expertise in this area. If Buyer wants further information, Broker recommends that Buyer hire an appropriate professional. Not all inspectors are licensed and licenses are not available for all types of inspections.

4. GEOLOGIC HAZARDS: Buyer and Seller are advised that California has experienced earthquakes in the past, and there is always a potential of future earthquakes. Damage caused by an earthquake may not be discoverable by a visual inspection of Buyer(s) or Broker(s). Inspection by a licensed, qualified professional is strongly recommended to determine the structural integrity and safety of all structures and improvements on the Property. If the Property is a condominium, or located in a planned unit development or in a common interest subdivision, Buyer is advised to contact the homeowners association about earthquake repairs and retrofit work and the possibility of an increased or special assessment to defray the costs of earthquake repairs or retrofit work. Buyer is encouraged to obtain and read the booklet entitled, "The Homeowner's Guide to Earthquake Safety." In most cases a questionnaire within the booklet must be completed by Seller and the entire booklet given to the Buyer if the Property was built prior to 1960. If the Property was built before 1975, and contains structures constructed of masonry or precast (tilt up) concrete walls, with wood frame floors or roof, or if the building has unreinforced masonry walls, then Seller must provide Buyer a pamphlet entitled "The Commercial Property Owner's Guide to Earthquake Safety." Many areas have a wide range of geologic problems and numerous studies have been made of these conditions. Some of this information is available for public review at city and county planning departments. Buyer is encouraged to review the public maps and reports and/or obtain a geologist's inspection report. Brokers do not have expertise in this area. Buyer may be able to obtain earthquake insurance to protect their interest in the Property. Sellers who agree to provide financing should also consider requiring Buyers to obtain such insurance naming Seller(s) as insured lien holder(s).

5. ENVIRONMENTAL HAZARDS: Buyer and Seller are advised that the presence of certain kinds of organisms, toxins and contaminants, including, but not limited to, mold (airborne, toxic or otherwise), fungi, mildew, lead-based paint and other lead contamination, asbestos, formaldehyde, radon, pcb's, methane, other gases, fuel oil or chemical storage tanks, contaminated soil or water, hazardous waste, waste disposal sites, electromagnetic fields, nuclear sources, urea formaldehyde, or other materials may adversely affect the Property and the health of individuals who live on or work at the property as well as pets. If Buyer wants further information, Buyer is advised and Broker(s) recommends, that Buyer have the Property inspected for the existence of such conditions and organisms, and conditions that may lead to their formation. Not all inspectors are licensed and licenses are not available for all types of inspection activities. Buyer is also advised to consult with appropriate experts regarding this topic during Buyer's inspection contingency period. Brokers do not have expertise in this area. Broker recommends that Buyer and Seller read the booklets titled "Residential Environmental Hazards: A Guide for Homeowners, Homebuyers, Landlords and Tenants," and "Protect Your Family From Lead In Your Home."

6. EPA's LEAD-BASED PAINT RENOVATION, REPAIR AND PAINTING RULE: The new rule requires that contractors and maintenance professionals working in pre-1978 housing, child care facilities, and schools with lead-based paint be certified; that their employees be trained; and that they follow protective work practice standards. The rule applies to renovation, repair, or painting activities affecting more than six square feet of lead-based paint in a room or more than 20 square feet of lead-based paint on the exterior. Enforcement of the rule begins October 1, 2010. See the EPA website at www.epa.gov/lead for more information. Buyer and Seller are advised to consult an appropriate professional.

7. FORMALDEHYDE: Formaldehyde is a substance known to the State of California to cause cancer. Exposure to formaldehyde may be caused by materials used in the construction of homes. The United States Environmental Protection Agency, the California Air Resources Board, and other agencies have measured the presence of formaldehyde in the indoor air of select homes in California. Levels of formaldehyde that present a significant cancer risk have been measured in most homes that were tested. Formaldehyde is present in the air because it is emitted by a variety of building materials and home products used in construction. The materials include carpeting, pressed wood products, insulation, plastics, and glues. Most homes that have been tested elsewhere do contain formaldehyde, although the concentrations vary from home

Buyer's Initials (_____) (_____)

SBSA REVISED 11/12 (PAGE 2 OF 11)

Seller's Initials (_____) (_____)

Reviewed by _____ Date _____

EQUAL HOUSING
OPPORTUNITY

STATEWIDE BUYER AND SELLER ADVISORY (SBSA PAGE 2 OF 11)   SBSA 11-11 cha

Property Address: 123 Sail Avenue
Marina del Rey, CA 90292   Date: _____

to home with no obvious explanation for the differences. One of the problems is that many suppliers of building materials and home products do not provide information on chemical ingredients to builders. Buyers may have further questions about these issues. Buyer is advised to consult with appropriate experts regarding this topic during Buyer's investigation period. Brokers do not have expertise in this area. Broker(s) recommend that Buyer and Seller read the booklet titled "Residential Environmental Hazards: A Guide for Homeowners, Homebuyers, Landlords and Tenants."

8. MOLD: Buyer and Seller are advised that the presence of certain kinds of mold, fungi, mildew and other organisms, sometimes referred to as "toxic mold" (collectively "Mold"), may adversely affect the Property and the health of individuals who live on or work at the Property as well as pets. Mold does not affect all people the same way, and may not affect some people at all. Mold may be caused by water leaks or other sources of moisture such as, but not limited to, flooding, and leaks in windows, pipes and roof. Seller is advised to disclose the existence of any such conditions of which he or she is aware. Buyer should carefully review all of Seller's disclosures for any indication that any of these conditions exist. It is, however, possible that Mold may be hidden and that Seller is completely unaware of its existence. In addition, Mold is often undetectable from a visual inspection, a professional general property inspection and even a structural pest control inspection. Brokers do not have expertise in this area. If Buyer wants further information, Broker recommends that Buyer have the Property tested for Mold by an environmental hygienist or other appropriate professional during Buyer's inspection contingency period. Not all inspectors are licensed and licenses are not available for all types of inspection activities.

9. WATER INTRUSION: Buyer and Seller are advised that many homes suffer from water intrusion or leakage. The causes of water intrusion are varied, and can include defective construction, faulty grading, deterioration of building materials and absence of waterproof barriers. Water intrusion can cause serious damage to the Property. This damage can consist of wood rot, mold, mildew and even damage to the structural integrity of the Property. The cost of repairing and remediating water intrusion damage and its causes can be very significant. The existence and cause of water intrusion is often difficult to detect. Because you, your Broker or a general home inspector cannot visually observe any effects of water intrusion, Buyer and Seller should not assume that such intrusion does not exist. Broker recommends that Buyer have the Property inspected for water intrusion by an appropriate professional. Brokers do not have expertise in this area.

10. SEPTIC SYSTEMS: Buyer and Seller are advised that a property may be served by one or more septic systems even though adjoining properties are connected to a sewer line. Buyer and Seller are also advised that some septic tanks and systems may have been abandoned or have leaked into ground water sources. Buyer is advised to contact the appropriate government agency to verify that the Property is connected to a sewer or served by a septic system. If the Property is served by a septic system, it may consist of a septic tank, cesspool, pits, leach lines or a combination of such mechanisms ("collectively, System"). No representation or warranty is made by Seller or Broker concerning the condition, operability, size, capacity or future expansion of a System, nor whether a System is adequate for use by the intended occupants of the Property. A change in the number of occupants or the quantity, composition or methods of depositing waste may affect the efficiency of the System. In addition, the amount of rainfall and ground water table may also affect the efficiency of the System. Many factors including, but not limited to, natural forces, age, deterioration of materials and the load imposed on a System can cause the System to fail at any time. Broker recommends that Buyer obtain an independent evaluation of any System by a qualified sanitation professional during Buyer's inspection contingency period. Brokers do not have expertise in this area. Buyer should consult with their sanitation professional to determine if their report includes the tank only, or other additional components of the System such as pits and leach fields. Not all inspectors are licensed and licenses are not available for all types of inspection activities. In some cases, Buyer's lender as well as local government agencies may require System inspection. System-related maintenance costs may include, but not be limited to, locating, pumping or providing outlets to ground level. Brokers are unable to advise Buyer or Seller regarding System-related issues or associated costs, which may be significant. If Buyer and Seller agree to obtain a System inspection, Buyer and Seller are cautioned that the inspection cost may include, but not be limited to, the costs of locating, pumping or providing outlets to ground level.

11. WELL AND WATER SYSTEM(S): Buyer and Seller are advised that the Property may be served by one or more water wells, springs, or private community or public water systems. Any of these private or public water systems may contain bacteria, chemicals, minerals and metals, such as chromium. Well(s) may have been abandoned on the Property. Buyer is advised to have both the quality and the quantity of water evaluated, and to obtain an analysis of the quality of any domestic and agricultural water in use, or to be used at the Property, from whatever source. Water quality tests can include not only tests for bacteria, such as coliform, but also tests for organic and inorganic chemicals, metals, mineral content and gross alpha testing for radioactivity. Broker recommends that Buyer consult with a licensed, qualified well and pump company and local government agency to determine whether any well/spring or water system will adequately serve Buyer's intended use and that Buyer have a well consultant perform an extended well output test for this purpose. Water well or spring capacity, quantity output and quality may change at any time. There are no guarantees as to the future water quality, quantity or duration of any well or spring. If Buyer wants further information, Broker(s) recommend that Buyer obtain an inspection of the condition, age, adequacy and performance of all components of the well/spring and any water system during Buyer's inspection contingency period. Brokers do not have expertise in this area.

Buyer's Initials (_____) (_____)

Seller's Initials (_____) (_____)

| Reviewed by _____ Date _____ |

EQUAL HOUSING OPPORTUNITY

STATEWIDE BUYER AND SELLER ADVISORY (SBSA PAGE 3 OF 11)   SBSA 11-11 cha

Property Address: *123 Sail Avenue*
Marina del Rey, CA 90292 _____ Date: _____

12. WOOD DESTROYING PESTS: Buyer and Seller are advised that the presence of, or conditions likely to lead to the presence of infestation or infection of wood destroying pests and organisms may adversely affect the Property. Inspection reports covering these items can be separated into two sections: Section 1 identifies areas where infestation or infection is evident. Section 2 identifies areas where there are conditions likely to lead to infestation or infection. Brokers do not have expertise in this area. If Buyer wants further information, Buyer is advised and Broker recommends that Buyer have the Property inspected for the existence of such conditions and organisms, and conditions that may lead to their formation, by a registered structural pest control company during Buyer's inspection contingency period.

13. EASEMENTS, ACCESS AND ENCROACHMENTS: Buyer and Seller are advised that confirming the exact location of easements, shared or private driveways or roadways, and encroachments on or to the Property may be possible only by conducting a survey. There may be unrecorded easements, access rights, encroachments and other agreements affecting the Property that may not be disclosed by a survey. Representations regarding these items that are made in a Multiple Listing Service or advertisements, or plotted by a title company are often approximations, or based upon inaccurate or incomplete records. Unless otherwise specified by Broker in writing, Brokers have not verified any such matters or any representations made by Seller(s) or others. If Buyer wants further information, Buyer is advised and Broker(s) recommend that Buyer hire a licensed surveyor during Buyer's inspection contingency period. Brokers do not have expertise in this area.

14. EARTHQUAKE FAULT ZONES AND SEISMIC HAZARD ZONES: Buyer and Seller are advised that California Public Resources Code Sections 2622 and 2696 require the delineation and mapping of "Earthquake Fault Zones" along known active faults and "Seismic Hazard Zones" in California. Affected cities and counties must regulate certain development projects within these zones. Construction or development on affected properties may be subject to the findings of a geological report prepared by a registered California geologist. Generally, Seller must disclose if the Property is in such a zone and can use a research company to aid in the process. If Buyer wants further information, Broker recommends that, during Buyer's inspection contingency period, Buyer make independent inquiries with such research companies or with appropriate government agencies concerning the use and improvement of the Property. Brokers do not have expertise in this area. Buyer is advised that there is a potential for earthquakes and seismic hazards even outside designated zones.

15. FIRE HAZARDS: Buyer and Seller are advised that fires annually cause the destruction of thousands of homes. Due to varied climate and topography, certain areas have higher risks of fires than others. Certain types of materials used in home construction create a greater risk of fire than others. If the Property is located within a State Fire Responsibility Area or a Very High Fire Hazard Zone, generally Seller must disclose that fact to Buyer under California Public Resources Code Section 4136 and California Government Code Sections 51178 and 51183.5, and may use a research company to aid in the process. Owners of property may be assessed a fire prevention fee of up to $150.00 per structure on each parcel in such zones. The fee may be adjusted annually commencing July 1, 2013. If Buyer wants further information, Broker recommends that, during Buyer's inspection contingency period, Buyer contact the local fire department and Buyer's insurance agent regarding the risk of fire. Brokers do not have expertise in this area. Buyer is advised that there is a potential for fires even outside designated zones.

16. FLOOD HAZARDS: Buyer and Seller are advised that if the Property is located within a Special Flood Hazard Area, as designated by the Federal Emergency Management Agency (FEMA), or an area of Potential Flooding pursuant to California Government Code Section 8589.3, generally Seller must disclose this fact to Buyer and may use a research company to aid in the process. The National Flood Insurance Program was established to identify all flood plain areas and establish flood-risk zones within those areas. The program mandates flood insurance for properties within high-risk zones if loans are obtained from a federally-regulated financial institution or are insured by any agency of the United States Government. The extent of coverage and costs may vary. If Buyer wants further information, Broker(s) recommend that Buyer consult his or her lender and/or insurance agent during Buyer's inspection contingency period. Brokers do not have expertise in this area. Buyer is advised that there is a potential for flooding even outside designated zones.

17. ZONE MAPS MAY CHANGE: Maps that designate, among other things, Earthquake Fault Zones, Seismic Hazard Zones, State Fire Responsibility Areas, Very High Fire Hazard Zones, Special Flood Hazard Areas, and Potential Flooding Areas are occasionally redrawn by the applicable Government Agency. Properties that are currently designated in a specified zone or area could be removed and properties that are not now designated in a specified zone or area could be placed in one or more such zones or areas in the future. A property owner may dispute a FEMA flood hazard location by submitting an application to FEMA.

18. BUILDING PERMITS, ZONING AND CODE COMPLIANCE: Buyer and Seller are advised that any structure on the Property, including the original structure and any addition, modification, remodel or improvement may have been built without permits, not according to building codes, or in violation of zoning laws. Further, even if such structure was built according to the then-existing code or zoning requirement, it may not be in compliance with current building standards or local zoning. It is also possible that local law may not permit structures that now exist to be rebuilt in the event of damage or destruction. Buyer is advised to check with appropriate government agencies or third party professionals to verify permits and legal requirements and the effect of such requirements on current and future use of the Property, its development and size. If Buyer wants further information, Broker(s) recommend that Buyer discuss the issue with an appropriate professional during Buyer's inspection contingency period. Brokers do not have expertise in this area.

Buyer's Initials (_____) (_____)   Seller's Initials (_____) (_____)

SBSA REVISED 11/12 (PAGE 4 OF 11)

Reviewed by _____ Date _____

EQUAL HOUSING OPPORTUNITY

STATEWIDE BUYER AND SELLER ADVISORY (SBSA PAGE 4 OF 11)   SBSA 11-11 cha

CHAPTER 6

123 Sail Avenue
Property Address: **Marina del Rey, CA   90292** _____ Date: _____

19. VIEWS: Buyer and Seller are advised that present views from the Property may be affected by future development or growth of trees and vegetation on adjacent properties and any other property within the line of sight of the Property. Brokers make no representation regarding the preservation of existing views. If Buyer wants further information, Broker(s) recommend that Buyer review covenants, conditions and restrictions, if any, and contact neighboring property owners, government agencies and homeowner associations, if any, during Buyer's inspection contingency period. Brokers do not have expertise in this area.

20. FUTURE REPAIRS, REPLACEMENTS AND REMODELS: Buyer and Seller are advised that replacement or repairs of certain systems or rebuilding or remodeling of all or a portion of the Property may trigger requirements that homeowners comply with laws and regulations that either come into effect after Close of Escrow or are not required to be complied with until the replacement, repair, rebuild or remodel has occurred. Permit or code requirements or building standards may change after Close of Escrow, resulting in increasing costs to repair existing features. In particular, changes to state and federal energy efficiency regulations impact the installation, replacement and some repairs of heating and air conditioning units (HVAC). Federal regulations now require manufacturers of HVAC units to produce only units meeting a new higher Seasonal Energy Efficiency Rating (SEER). This will likely impact repairs and replacements of existing HVAC units. State regulations now require that when installing or replacing HVAC units, with some exceptions, duct work must be tested for leaks. Duct work leaking more than 15 percent must be repaired to reduce leaks. The average existing duct work typically leaks 30 percent. More information is available at the California Energy Commission's website http://www.energy.ca.gov/title24/changeout. Home warranty policies may not cover such inspections or repairs. If Buyer wants further information, Broker recommends that Buyer discuss the issue with an appropriate professional during Buyer's inspection contingency period. Brokers do not have expertise in this area.

21. GOLF COURSE DISCLOSURES: Buyer and Seller are advised that if the Property is located adjacent to or near a golf course the following may apply: **(i)** Stray golf balls – Any residence near a golf course may be affected by errant golf balls, resulting in personal injury or destruction to property. Golfers may attempt to trespass on adjacent property to retrieve golf balls even though the project restrictions may expressly prohibit such retrieval. **(ii)** Noise and lighting – The noise of lawn mowers irrigation systems and utility vehicles may create disturbances to homeowners. Maintenance operations may occur in the early morning hours. Residents living near the clubhouse may be affected by extra lighting, noise, and traffic. **(iii)** Pesticides and fertilizer use – A golf course may be heavily fertilized, as well as subjected to other chemicals during certain periods of the year. **(iv)** Irrigation system – Golf course sprinkler systems may cause water overspray upon adjacent property and structures. Also the irrigation system of a golf course may use reclaimed and retreated wastewater. **(v)** Golf carts – Certain lots may be affected more than others by the use of golf carts. Lots adjacent to a tee or putting green may be subject to noise disturbances and loss of privacy. **(vi)** Access to golf course from residences – It is likely that most residences will not have direct access from their lots to the golf course. The project restrictions may disclaim any right of access or other easements from a resident's lot onto the golf course. **(vii)** View obstruction – Residents living near a golf course may have their views over the golf course impacted by maturing trees and landscaping or by changes to the course's configuration. **(viii)** Water restrictions – As some municipalities face water shortages, the continued availability of water to the golf course may be restricted or otherwise reduced by the local water agency. If Buyer wants further information, Broker(s) recommend that Buyer contact the local water agency regarding this matter.

22. SCHOOLS: Buyer and Seller are advised that children living in the Property may not, for numerous reasons, be permitted to attend the school nearest the Property. Various factors including, but not limited to, open enrollment policies, busing, overcrowding and class size reductions may affect which public school serves the Property. School district boundaries are subject to change. Buyer is advised to verify whether the Property is now, and at the Close of Escrow will be, in the school district Buyer understands it to be in and whether residing in the Property entitles a person to attend any specific school in which that Buyer is interested. Broker(s) recommend that Buyer contact the local school or school district for additional information during Buyer's inspection contingency period. Brokers do not have expertise in this area.

23. NEIGHBORHOOD NOISE SOURCES: Buyer and Seller are advised that even if the Property is not in an identified airport noise influence area, the Property may still be subject to noise and air disturbances resulting from airplanes and other aircraft, commercial or military or both, flying overhead. Other common sources of noise include nearby commercial districts, schools, traffic on streets, highways and freeways, trains and general neighborhood noise from people, dogs and other animals. Noise levels and types of noise that bother one person may be acceptable to others. Buyer is advised to satisfy him/herself with regard to any sources of and amounts of noise at different times of day and night. Brokers do not have expertise in this area.

24. PETS AND ANIMALS: Buyer and Seller are advised that the current or previous owner(s) may have had domesticated or other pets and animals at the Property. Odors from animal urine or other contamination may be dormant for long periods of time and then become active because of heat, humidity or other factors and might not be eliminated by cleaning or replacing carpets or other cleaning methods. Pet urine and feces can also damage hardwood floors and other floor coverings. Additionally, an animal may have had fleas, ticks and other pests that remain on the Property after the animal has been removed. If Buyer wants further information, Broker(s) recommend that Buyer discuss the issue with an appropriate professional during Buyer's inspection contingency period. Brokers do not have expertise in this area.

25. SWIMMING POOL, SECURITY AND SAFETY: Buyer and Seller are advised that state and local Law may require the installation of barriers, anti-entrapment grates, access alarms, self-latching mechanisms and/or other measures to decrease the risk to children and other persons of existing swimming pools and hot tubs, as well as various fire safety and other measures concerning other features of the Property. Compliance requirements differ from city to city and county to county.

Buyer's Initials (_____) (_____)   Seller's Initials (_____) (_____)

Copyright © 2004-2012, CALIFORNIA ASSOCIATION OF REALTORS®, INC.

SBSA REVISED 11/12 (PAGE 5 OF 11)

Reviewed by _____ Date _____

STATEWIDE BUYER AND SELLER ADVISORY (SBSA PAGE 5 OF 11)   SBSA 11-11 cha

218

Property Address: *123 Sail Avenue*
*Marina del Rey, CA 90292*_____ Date: _____

Unless specifically agreed, the Property may not be in compliance with these requirements. Brokers do not have expertise in this area. If Buyer wants further information, Broker(s) recommend that Buyer contact local government agencies about these restrictions and other requirements.

26. RETROFIT, BUILDING REQUIREMENTS, AND POINT OF SALE REQUIREMENTS: Buyer and Seller are advised that state and local Law may require **(i)** the installation of operable smoke detectors, **(ii)** bracing or strapping of water heaters, and **(iii)** upon sale completion of a corresponding written statement of compliance that is delivered to Buyer. Although not a point of sale or retrofit obligation, state law may require the property to have operable carbon monoxide detection devices. Additionally, some city and county governments may impose additional retrofit standards at time of sale including, but not limited to, installing low-flow toilets and showerheads, gas shut-off valves, and tempered glass. Brokers do not have expertise in this area. Broker(s) recommend that Buyer and Seller consult with the appropriate government agencies, inspectors, and other professionals to determine the retrofit standards for the Property, the extent to which the Property complies with such standards, and the costs, if any, of compliance.

27. WATER SHORTAGES AND CONSERVATION: Buyer and Seller are advised that the Property may be located in an area that could experience water shortages. The policies of local water districts and the city or county in which the Property is located can result in the occurrence of any or all of the following: **(i)** limitations on the amount of water available to the Property, **(ii)** restrictions on the use of water, and **(iii)** an increasingly graduated cost per unit of water use, including, but not limited to, penalties for excess usage. For further information, Broker recommends that Buyer contact the supplier of water to the Property regarding the supplier's current or anticipated policies on water usage and to determine the extent to which those policies may affect Buyer's intended use of the Property. If the Property is serviced by a private well, Buyer is advised that drought conditions and/or a low water table may make it necessary to arrange, through a private supplier, for delivery of water to the Property. Buyers should contact water truck companies for the costs involved. Brokers do not have expertise in this area.

28. NEIGHBORHOOD, AREA, PERSONAL FACTORS, HIGH SPEED RAILS, AND SMOKING RESTRICTIONS: Buyer and Seller are advised that the following may affect the Property or Buyer's intended use of it: neighborhood or area conditions, including schools, proximity and adequacy of law enforcement, crime, fire protection, other government services, availability, adequacy and cost of any speed-wired, wireless internet connections or other telecommunications or other technology services and installations, proximity to medical marijuana growing or distribution locations, cell phone towers, manufacturing, commercial, industrial, airport or agricultural activities or military ordnance locations, existing and proposed transportation, construction, and development, any other source that may affect noise, view, traffic, or odor, wild and domestic animals, other nuisances, hazards, or circumstances, protected species, wetland properties, botanical diseases, historic or other governmentally-protected sites or improvements, cemeteries, conditions and influences of significance to certain cultures and/or religions, and personal needs, requirements and preferences of Buyer. California is potentially moving toward high speed rail service between Northern and Southern California. This rail line could have an impact on the Property if it is located nearby. More information on the timing of the project and routes is available from the California High-Speed Rail Authority at http://cahighspeedrail.ca.gov. The State of California has long-standing no smoking laws in place restricting smoking in most business and some public spaces. Local jurisdictions may enact laws that are more restrictive than state law. Many California cities have enacted restrictions on smoking in parks, public sidewalks, beaches and shopping areas. Some jurisdictions have restrictions entirely banning smoking inside privately owned apartments and condominiums as well as in the common areas of such structures, or limiting smoking to certain designated areas. If Buyer wants further information, Broker(s) recommend that Buyer contact local government agencies about these restrictions.

29. UNDERGROUND PIPELINES AND UTILITIES: Throughout California underground pipelines transport natural gas, liquid fuel and other potentially hazardous materials. These pipelines may or may not provide utility services to the Property. Information about the location of some of the pipelines may be available from a company that also provides disclosures of natural and other hazards or from other sources of public maps or records. Proximity to underground pipelines, in and of itself, does not affirmatively establish the risk or safety of the property. If Buyer wants further information about these underground pipelines and utilities, Buyer is advised to consult with appropriate experts during Buyer's investigation contingency period. Brokers do not have expertise in this area.

30. MARIJUANA AND METHAMPHETAMINE LABS: Buyer and Seller are advised that California law permits individual patients to cultivate, possess and use marijuana for medical purposes. Furthermore, California law permits primary caregivers, lawfully organized cooperatives, and collectives to cultivate, distribute and possess marijuana for medicinal purposes. California's medical marijuana law is in direct conflict with federal law which recognizes no lawful use for marijuana and has no exemptions for medical use. Federal criminal penalties, some of which mandate prison time, remain in effect for the possession, cultivation and distribution of marijuana. Buyer and Seller are strongly advised to seek legal counsel as to the legal risks and issues surrounding owning or purchasing a property where medical or any other marijuana activity is taking place. Marijuana storage, cultivation and processing carry the risk of causing mold, fungus or moisture damage to a property, additionally, some properties where marijuana has been cultivated have had alterations to the structure or the electrical system which may not have been done to code or with permits and may affect the safety of the structure or the safe operation of the electrical system. Buyer is strongly advised to retain an environmental hygienist contractor and other appropriate professionals to inspect a property where medical or any other marijuana activity has taken place. Broker recommends that Buyer and Seller involved with a property where there is medical marijuana activity or where it may take place review the California Attorney General's Guidelines for the "Security and Non-Diversion of Marijuana Grown for Medical Use" (http://ag.ca.gov/cms_attachments/press/pdfs/n1601_medicalmarijuanaguidelines.pdf) and the U.S. Department of Justice memo regarding marijuana prosecutions at http://www.justice.gov.opa/documents/medicalmarijuana.pdf. Brokers do not have expertise in this area. While no state law permits the private production of

Buyer's Initials (_____) (_____)   Seller's Initials (_____) (_____)

Copyright © 2004-2012, CALIFORNIA ASSOCIATION OF REALTORS®, INC.
SBSA REVISED 11/12 (PAGE 6 OF 11)

| Reviewed by _____ Date _____ |

STATEWIDE BUYER AND SELLER ADVISORY (SBSA PAGE 6 OF 11)   SBSA 11-11 cha

Property Address: 123 Sail Avenue
Marina del Rey, CA 90292 _____ Date: _____

methamphetamine, some properties have been the site of an illegal methamphetamine laboratory. State law imposes an obligation to notify occupants, a ban on occupying the property and clean up requirements when authorities identify a property as being contaminated by methamphetamine. Buyer is advised that a property where methamphetamine has been produced may pose a very serious health risk to occupants. Buyer is strongly advised to retain an environmental hygienist contractor or other appropriate professionals to inspect the property if methamphetamine production is suspected to have taken place. Brokers do not have expertise in this area.

31. INSURANCE AND TITLE INSURANCE AFTER FORECLOSURE: Buyer and Seller are advised that Buyer may have difficulty obtaining insurance regarding the Property if there has been a prior insurance claim affecting the Property or made by Buyer but unrelated to the Property. Seller is required by C.A.R. Form RPA to disclose known insurance claims made during the past five years (C.A.R. Form SPQ or SSD). Sellers may not be aware of claims prior to their ownership. If Buyer wants further information, Broker(s) recommend that, during Buyer's inspection contingency period, Buyer conduct his or her own investigation for past claims. Buyer may need to obtain Seller's consent in order to have access to certain investigation reports. If the Property is a condominium, or is located in a planned unit development or other common interest subdivision, Buyer and Seller are advised to determine if the individual unit is covered by the Homeowner Association Insurance. Broker(s) recommend that Buyer consult Buyer's insurance agents during Buyer's inspection contingency period to determine the need, availability and possibility of securing any and all forms of other insurance or coverage or any conditions imposed by insurer as a requirement of issuing insurance. If Buyer does any repairs to the property during the escrow period or Buyer takes possession prior to Close of Escrow or Seller remains in possession after Close of Escrow, whether for a limited or extended period of time, Broker(s) recommend that Buyer and Seller each consult with their own insurance agent regarding insurance or coverage that could protect them in the transaction (including but not limited to: personal property, flood, earthquake, umbrella and renter's). Buyer and Seller are advised that traditional title insurance generally protects Buyer's title acquired through the sale of the property. While all title insurance policies, as do all insurance policies, contain some exclusions, some title insurance policies contain exclusions for any liability arising from a previous foreclosure. This can occur when a short sale has occurred but the lender mistakenly has also proceeded with a foreclosure. Buyer is strongly advised to consult with a title insurer to satisfy themselves that the policy to be provided adequately protects their title to the property against other possible claimants. Brokers do not have expertise in this area.

32. CALIFORNIA FAIR PLAN: Buyer and Seller are advised that insurance for certain hillside, oceanfront and brush properties may be available only from the California Fair Plan. This may increase the cost of insurance for such properties and coverage may be limited. Broker(s) recommend that Buyer consult with Buyer's own insurance agent during Buyer's inspection contingency period regarding the availability of coverage under the California Fair Plan and the length of time it may take for processing of a California Fair Plan application. Brokers do not have expertise in this area.

33. HISTORICAL DESIGNATION, COASTAL COMMISSION, ARCHITECTURAL, LANDSCAPE, AGRICULTURAL OR OPEN SPACE AND OTHER RESTRICTIONS ON BUILDINGS OR IMPROVEMENTS: Buyer and Seller are advised that the Property may be: **(i)** designated as a historical landmark, **(ii)** protected by a historical conservancy, **(iii)** subject to an architectural or landscaping review process, **(iv)** within the jurisdiction of the California Coastal Commission or other government agency, or **(v)** subject to a contract preserving use of all or part of the Property for agriculture or open space. If the Property is so designated or within the jurisdiction of any such, or similar, government agency, then there may be restrictions on Buyer's ability to develop, remove or trim trees or other landscaping, remodel, make improvements to and build on or rebuild the Property. Broker(s) recommend that Buyer satisfy him/herself during Buyer's inspection contingency period if any of these issues are of concern to Buyer. Brokers do not have expertise in this area.

34. 1915 IMPROVEMENT BOND MELLO-ROOS COMMUNITY DISTRICT, AND OTHER ASSESSMENT DISTRICTS: Buyer and Seller are advised that the Property may be subject to an improvement bond assessment under the Improvement Bond Act of 1915, a levy of a special tax pursuant to a Mello-Roos Community Facilities district, and/or a contractual assessment as provided in Section 5898.24 of the Streets And Highways Code or other assessment districts. Seller is generally required to make a good faith effort to obtain a disclosure notice from any local agency collecting such taxes and deliver such notice to Buyers. Brokers do not have expertise in this area.

35. HOMEOWNER ASSOCIATIONS AND COVENANTS, CONDITIONS AND RESTRICTIONS ("CC&Rs"); CHARGING STATIONS: Buyer and Seller are advised that if the Property is a condominium, or located in a planned unit development, or in a common interest subdivision, there are typically restrictions on use of the Property and rules that must be followed. Restrictions and rules are commonly found in Declarations and other governing documents. Further there is likely to be a homeowner association (HOA) that has the authority to affect the Property and its use. Whether or not there is a HOA, the Property may still be subject to CC&Rs restricting use of the Property. The HOA typically has the authority to enforce the rules of the association, assess monetary payments (both regular monthly dues and special assessments) to provide for the upkeep and maintenance of the common areas, and enforce the rules and assessment obligations. If you fail to abide by the rules or pay monies owed to the HOA, the HOA may put a lien against your Property. Additionally, if an electric vehicle charging station is installed in a common area or an exclusive use common area, each Seller whose parking space is on or near that charging station must disclose its existence and that the Buyer will have the responsibilities set forth in California Civil Code §1353.9. The law requires the Seller to provide the Buyer with the CC&Rs and other governing documents, as well as a copy of the HOA's current financial statement and operating budget, among other documents. Buyer is advised to carefully review all HOA documents provided by Seller and the CC&Rs, if any, and satisfy him/herself regarding the use and restrictions of the Property, the amount of monthly dues and/or assessments, the adequacy of reserves, current and past insurance coverage and claims, and the possibility of any legal action that may be taken by or against the HOA. The HOA may not have insurance or may not cover personal property belonging to the owner of the unit in the condominium, common interest or planned unit development. See paragraph 31 for further information regarding insurance. See C.A.R.'s Common Interest Development Basic Information Guide on ePUBS® in zipForm®6 for further information. Brokers do not have expertise in this area.

Buyer's Initials (_____) (_____)   Seller's Initials (_____) (_____)

| Reviewed by _____ Date _____ |

STATEWIDE BUYER AND SELLER ADVISORY (SBSA PAGE 7 OF 11)   SBSA 11-11 cha

123 Sail Avenue
Property Address: Marina del Rey, CA 90292   Date: _____

36. LEGAL ACTION: Buyer and Seller are advised that if Seller or a previous owner was involved in a legal action (litigation or arbitration) affecting the Property, Buyer should obtain and review public and other available records regarding the legal action to determine: (i) whether the legal action or any resolution of it affects Buyer and the Property, (ii) if any rights against any parties involved in the legal action survive the legal action or have been terminated or waived as a result of the legal action, whether or not involving the same issue as in the legal action, and (iii) if any recommendations or requirements resulting from the legal action have been fulfilled and, if so, that Buyer is satisfied with any such action. Buyer should seek legal advice regarding these matters.

37. COMMUNITY ENHANCEMENT AND PRIVATE TRANSFER FEES: Buyer and Seller are advised that some areas or communities may have enhancement fees or user-type fees, or private transfer taxes and fees, over and above any stated fees. The Federal Housing Finance Agency has issued a rule that prohibits Fannie Mae and Freddie Mac from purchasing loans made on properties with private transfer fees if those fees were established on or after February 8, 2011. See title 12 Code of Federal Regulations Section 1228 for more information and exceptions. Private transfer fees: (i) may last for a fixed period of time or in perpetuity, (ii) are typically calculated as a percentage of the sales price, and (iii) may have private parties, charitable organizations or interest-based groups as their recipients who may use the funds for social issues unrelated to the property. Brokers do not have expertise in this area.

38. GENERAL RECALL/DEFECTIVE PRODUCT/CLASS ACTION INFORMATION: Buyer and Seller are advised that government entities and manufacturers may at any time issue recall notices and/or warnings about products that may be present in the Property, and that these notices or warnings can change. The following nonexclusive, non-exhaustive list contains examples of recalled/defective products/class action information: horizontal furnaces, Whirlpool Microwave Hood Combination; RE-Con Building products roof tiles; Central Sprinkler Company Fire Sprinklers; Robert Shaw Water Heater Gas Control Valves; Trex Decking; water heaters; aluminum wiring; galvanized, abs, polybutylene and copper pipe; and dry wall manufactured in China. There is no single, all-inclusive source of information on product recalls, defective products or class actions; however, the U.S. Consumer Product Safety Commission (CPSC) maintains a website that contains useful information. If Buyer wants further information regarding the items listed above, Broker(s) recommend that Buyer review the CPSC website at http://www.cpsc.gov during Buyer's inspection contingency period. Another source affiliated with the CPSC is Saferproducts.gov which allows a Buyer to search by product type or product name. Buyers may also search using the various search engines on the Internet for the specified product or products in question. Brokers recommend that Buyers satisfy themselves regarding recalled or defective products. Brokers do not have expertise in this area and Brokers will not determine if any aspect of the Property is subject to a recall or is affected by a class action lawsuit.

39. RENTAL PROPERTY RESTRICTIONS: Buyer and Seller are advised that some cities and counties impose restrictions that limit the rent that can be charged to a tenant, the maximum number of tenants who can occupy the property and the right of a landlord to terminate a tenancy and the costs to do so. If Buyer wants further information, Broker(s) recommend that Buyer investigate the issue with an appropriate government authority during Buyer's inspection contingency period. Brokers do not have expertise in this area.

40. LAND LEASE: Buyer and Seller are advised that certain developments are built on leased land. This means that: (i) Buyer does not own the land, (ii) the right to occupy the land will terminate at some point in time, (iii) the cost to lease the land may increase at some point in the future, and (iv) Buyer may not be able to obtain title insurance or may have to obtain a different type of title insurance. If Buyer wants further information, Broker recommends that Buyer discuss the issue with an attorney or other appropriate professional. Brokers do not have expertise in this area.

41. HOME WARRANTY: Buyer and Seller are advised that Buyer and Seller can purchase home warranty plans covering certain standard systems of the Property both before and after Close of Escrow. Seller can obtain coverage for the Property during the listing period. For an additional premium, an upgraded policy providing additional coverage for air conditioning, pool and spa and other features can be purchased. Home warranties do not cover every aspect of the Property and may not cover inspections or upgrades for repairs required by state or federal laws or pre-existing conditions. Broker(s) recommend that Buyer review the policy for details. Brokers do not have expertise in this area.

42. INTERNET ADVERTISING; INTERNET BLOGS; SOCIAL MEDIA: Buyer and Seller are advised that Broker may employ a service to provide a "virtual tour" or Internet marketing of the Property, permitting potential buyers to view the Property over the Internet. Additionally, some Internet sites and other social media provide formats for comments or opinions of value of properties that are for sale. Neither the service provider nor Brokers have control over who will obtain access to such services or what action such persons might take. Buyer and Seller are advised that Brokers have no control over how long the information concerning the Property will be available on the Internet or through social media. Brokers do not have expertise in this area.

43. ESCROW FUNDS: Buyer and Seller are advised that California Insurance Code Section 12413.1 provides that escrow companies cannot disburse funds unless there are sufficient "good funds" to cover the disbursement. "Good funds" are defined as cash, wire transfers and cashiers' or certified checks drawn on California depositories. Escrow companies vary in their own definitions of "good funds." Broker(s) recommend that Buyer and Seller ask the escrow company regarding its treatment of "good funds." All samples and out-of-state checks are subject to waiting periods and do not constitute "good funds" until the money is physically transferred to and received by the escrow holder. Brokers do not have expertise in this area.

44. NOTICE OF YOUR "SUPPLEMENTAL" PROPERTY TAX BILL: Buyer and Seller are advised that pursuant to Civil Code § 1102.6(c), Seller, or his or her agent is required to provide the following "Notice of Your 'Supplemental' Property Tax Bill" to the Buyer:

"California property tax law requires the Assessor to revalue real property at the time the ownership of property changes. Because of this law, you may receive one or two supplemental tax bills, depending on when your loan closes.

The supplemental tax bills are not mailed to your lender. If you have arranged for your property tax responsibility payments to be paid through an impound account, the supplemental tax bills will not be paid by your lender. It is your

Buyer's Initials (_____) (_____)

SBSA REVISED 11/12 (PAGE 8 OF 11)

Seller's Initials (_____) (_____)

Reviewed by _____ Date _____

EQUAL HOUSING OPPORTUNITY

STATEWIDE BUYER AND SELLER ADVISORY (SBSA PAGE 8 OF 11)   SBSA 11-11 cha

Property Address: *123 Sail Avenue*
Marina del Rey, CA 90292 _____ Date: _____

responsibility to pay these supplemental bills directly to the Tax Collector. If you have any questions concerning this matter, please call your Tax Collector's Office."

Although the notice refers to loan closing as a trigger, it is actually the change of ownership which triggers this reassessment of property taxes. Therefore, the Property can be reassessed even if there is no loan involved in the purchase of the Property. The Purchase Agreement may allocate supplemental tax bills received after the Close of Escrow to the Buyer. If Buyer wants further information concerning these matters, Broker(s) recommend that Buyer discuss the issue with the County Assessor or Tax Collector or their own tax or legal advisor. Brokers do not have expertise in this area.

45. NON CONFIDENTIALITY OF OFFERS: Buyer is advised that Seller or Listing Agent may disclose the existence, terms, or conditions of Buyer's offer, unless all parties and their agent have signed a written confidentiality agreement (such as C.A.R. Form CND). Whether any such information is actually disclosed depends on many factors, such as current market conditions, the prevailing practice in the real estate community, the Listing Agent's marketing strategy and the instructions of the Seller.

46. FIRPTA/CALIFORNIA WITHHOLDING: Buyer and Seller are advised that: (i) Internal Revenue Code Section 1445 requires a Buyer to withhold and to remit to the Internal Revenue Service 10% of the purchase price of the property if the Seller is a non-resident alien, unless an express exemption applies. Seller may avoid withholding by providing Buyer a statement of non-foreign status. The statement must be signed by Seller under penalty of perjury and must include Seller's tax identification number. Buyer can also avoid having to withhold Federal taxes from Seller's Proceeds if the property price is $300,000 or less, and the Buyer signs an affidavit stating Buyer intends to occupy the property as a principal residence. (ii) California Revenue and Taxation Code Section 18662 requires that a Buyer withhold and remit to the California Franchise Tax Board 3 1/3% of the purchase price of the property unless the Seller signs an affidavit that the property was the Seller's (or the decedent's, if a trust or probate sale) principal residence or that the sales price is $100,000 or less or another express exemption applies. Exemptions from withholding also apply to legal entities such as corporations, LLCs, and partnerships. Brokers cannot give tax or legal advice. Broker recommends that Buyer and Seller seek advice from a CPA, attorney or taxing authority. Brokers do not have expertise in this area.

47. LIQUIDATED DAMAGES: Buyer and Seller are advised that a liquidated damages clause is a provision Buyer and Seller can use to agree in advance to the amount of damages that a seller will receive if a buyer breaches the Agreement. The clause usually provides that a seller will retain a buyer's initial deposit paid if a buyer breaches the agreement, and generally must be separately initialed by both parties and meet other statutory requirements to be enforceable. For any additional deposits to be covered by the liquidated damages clause, there generally must be another separately signed or initialed agreement (see C.A.R. Form RID). However, if the Property contains from 1 to 4 units, one of which a buyer intends to occupy, California Civil Code Section 1675 limits the amount of the deposit subject to liquidated damages to 3% of the purchase price. Even though both parties have agreed to a liquidated damages clause, an escrow company will usually require either a judge's or arbitrator's decision or instructions signed by both parties in order to release a buyer's deposit to a seller. Buyers and Sellers must decide on their own, or with the advice of legal counsel, whether to agree to a liquidated damages clause. Brokers do not have expertise in this area.

48. MEDIATION: Buyer and Seller are advised that mediation is a process by which the parties hire a neutral person to facilitate discussion and negotiation between the parties with the goal of helping them reach a settlement of their dispute. The parties generally share in the cost of this confidential, non-binding negotiation. If no agreement is reached, either party can pursue further legal action. Under C.A.R. Form RPA-CA: (i) the parties must mediate any dispute arising out of their agreement (with a few limited exceptions, such as matters within the jurisdiction of a small claims court) before they resort to arbitration or court, and (ii) if a party proceeds to arbitration or court without having first attempted to mediate the dispute, that party risks losing the right to recover attorney fees and costs even if he or she prevails.

49. ARBITRATION: Buyer and Seller are advised that arbitration is a process by which the disputing parties hire a neutral person to render a binding decision. Generally, arbitration is faster and less expensive than resolving disputes by litigating in court. The rules are usually less formal than in court, and it is a private process not a matter of public record. By agreeing to arbitration, the parties give up the right to a jury trial and to appeal the arbitrator's decision. Arbitration decisions have been upheld even when arbitrators have made a mistake as to the law or the facts. If the parties agree to arbitration, then after first attempting to settle the dispute through mediation, any dispute arising out of their agreement (with a few limited exceptions) must be submitted to binding arbitration. Buyer and Seller must weigh the benefits of a potentially quicker and less expensive arbitration against giving up the right to a jury trial and the right to appeal. Brokers cannot give legal advice regarding these matters. Buyers and Sellers must decide on their own, or with the advice of legal counsel, whether to agree to arbitration. Brokers do not have expertise in this area.

Buyer's Initials (_____) (_____)

Seller's Initials (_____) (_____)

Copyright © 2004-2012, CALIFORNIA ASSOCIATION OF REALTORS®, INC.
SBSA REVISED 11/12 (PAGE 9 OF 11)

Reviewed by _____ Date _____

STATEWIDE BUYER AND SELLER ADVISORY (SBSA PAGE 9 OF 11)   SBSA 11-11 cha

Property Address: *123 Sail Avenue*
Marina del Rey, CA 90292 _____ Date: _____

50. MEGAN'S LAW DATABASE DISCLOSURE: Notice: Pursuant to Section 290.46 of the Penal Code, information about specific registered sex offenders is made available to the public via an Internet Web site maintained by the Department of Justice at www.meganslaw.ca.gov. Depending on an offender's criminal history, this information will include either the address at which the offender resides or the community of residence and ZIP Code in which he or she resides. (Neither Seller nor Brokers are required to check this website. If Buyer wants further information, Broker recommends that Buyer obtain information from this website during Buyer's inspection contingency period. Brokers do not have expertise in this area.)

51. DEATH ON THE PROPERTY: California Civil Code Section 1710.2 protects a seller from: (i) failing to disclose a death on the property that occurred more than 3 years before a buyer has made an offer on a property; and (ii) failing to disclose if an occupant of a property was afflicted with HIV/AIDS, regardless of whether a death occurred or if so, when. Section 1710.2 does not protect a seller from making a misrepresentation in response to a direct inquiry. If the Buyer has any concerns about whether a death occurred on the Property or the manner, location, details or timing of a death, the buyer should direct any specific questions to the Seller in writing.

52. LOCAL ADDENDA (IF CHECKED):
The following local disclosures or addenda are attached:

A. ☐ _____
B. ☐ _____
C. ☐ _____
D. ☐ _____

Buyer and Seller acknowledge and agree that Brokers: **(i)** do not decide what price Buyer should pay or Seller should accept; **(ii)** do not guarantee the condition of the Property; **(iii)** do not guarantee the performance, adequacy or completeness of inspections, services, products or repairs provided or made by Seller or others; **(iv)** do not have any obligation to conduct an inspection of common areas or areas off the site of the Property **(v)** shall not be responsible for identifying defects on the Property, in common areas, or offsite unless such defects are visually observable by an inspection of reasonably accessible areas of the Property or are known to Brokers; **(vi)** shall not be responsible for inspecting public records or permits concerning the title or use of Property; **(vii)** shall not be responsible for identifying the location of boundary lines or other items affecting title; **(viii)** shall not be responsible for verifying square footage, representations of others or information contained in investigation reports, Multiple Listing Service, advertisements, flyers or other promotional material; **(ix)** shall not be responsible for providing legal or tax advice regarding any aspect of a transaction entered into by Buyer or Seller; and **(x)** shall not be responsible for providing other advice or information that exceeds the knowledge, education and experience required to perform real estate licensed activity. Buyer and Seller agree to seek legal, tax, insurance, title and other desired assistance from appropriate professionals.

Buyer's Initials (_____) (_____)   Seller's Initials (_____) (_____)

Reviewed by _____ Date _____

EQUAL HOUSING OPPORTUNITY

SBSA REVISED 11/12 (PAGE 10 OF 11)

STATEWIDE BUYER AND SELLER ADVISORY (SBSA PAGE 10 OF 11)   SBSA 11-11 cha

Property Address: _123 Sail Avenue_
Marina del Rey, CA 90292 _____ Date: _____

Buyer and Seller are encouraged to read this Advisory carefully. By signing below, Buyer and Seller acknowledge that each has read, understands and received a copy of this Advisory.

Date _____   Date _____

BUYER _____   BUYER _____

(Print name) _____   (Print name) _____

(Address) _____

Date _____   Date _____

SELLER _____   SELLER _____

(Print name) _____   (Print name) _____

(Address) _____

Real Estate Broker (Selling Firm) _____ DRE Lic. # _____

By _____ DRE Lic. # _____ Date _____

Address _____ City _____ State ____ Zip _____

Telephone _____ Fax _____ Email _____

Real Estate Broker (Listing Firm) _____ DRE Lic. # _____

By _____ DRE Lic. # _____ Date _____

Address _____ City _____ State ____ Zip _____

Telephone _____ Fax _____ Email _____

 Published and Distributed by:
REAL ESTATE BUSINESS SERVICES, INC.
a subsidiary of the California Association of REALTORS®
525 South Virgil Avenue, Los Angeles, California 90020

Reviewed by _____ Date _____

SBSA REVISED 11/12 (PAGE 11 OF 11)

STATEWIDE BUYER AND SELLER ADVISORY (SBSA PAGE 11 OF 11)   SBSA 11-11 cha

The SBSA explains to the consumer that underground pipelines transporting natural gas, liquid fuel, and other potentially hazardous materials exist throughout California. The form also directs the consumer to hazard disclosure companies and other public sources that can provide detailed information as to the location of existing pipelines with respect to a specific property.

The SBSA defines what the buyer and seller can expect, and what their mutual and exclusive rights and duties are. Sellers will see it at the time of the listing, and buyers may review it before an offer is made. The SBSA covers the following areas.

A. Buyer Rights and Duties
B. Seller Rights and Duties
C. Broker Rights and Duties

1. Inspections
2. Square Footage, Lot Size, Boundaries, and Surveys
3. Soil and Geologic Conditions
4. Geologic Hazards
5. Environmental Hazards
6. EPA's Lead-Based Paint Renovation, Repair, and Painting Rule
7. Formaldehyde
8. Mold
9. Water Intrusion
10. Septic System
11. Well and Water System(s)
12. Wood Destroying Pests
13. Easements, Access, and Encroachments
14. Earthquake Fault Zones and Seismic Hazard Zones
15. Fire Hazards
16. Flood Hazards
17. Zone Maps May Change
18. Building Permits, Zoning, and Code Compliance
19. Views
20. Future Repairs, Replacements, and Remodels
21. Golf Course Disclosures
22. Schools
23. Neighborhood Noise Sources
24. Pets and Animals
25. Swimming Pool, Security, and Safety
26. Retrofit, Building Requirements, and Point of Sale Requirements
27. Water Shortages and Conservation
28. Neighborhood, Area, Personal Factors, High Speed Rails, and Smoking Restrictions
29. Underground Pipelines and Utilities
30. Marijuana and Methamphetamine Labs
31. Insurance and Title Insurance After Foreclosure
32. California Fair Plan
33. Historical Designation, Coastal Commission, Architectural, Landscape, Agricultural or Open Space, and Other Restrictions on Buildings or Improvements
34. 1915 Improvement Bond Mello-Roos Community District, and Other Assessment Districts

CHAPTER 6

E. FRAUD

Failing to disclose information that you're required to disclose is a form of fraud. Fraud can also take the form of making false or misleading statements (misrepresentation).

1. Actual Fraud

In California, fraud is classified as actual or constructive. *ACTUAL FRAUD includes intentional misrepresentation, concealment, and negligent misrepresentation. NEGLIGENT MISREPRESENTATION means making a false assertion without reasonable grounds for believing that it's true—even if the speaker does in fact believe that it's true.* The falsehood is the result of carelessness or negligence, rather than an intention to deceive.

The following case involves allegations of negligent and intentional misrepresentations based on the failure to disclose structural defects in the house and soil.

Case Example: Helm and Grossman owned and lived in a house that Helm, an architect, designed and built. The property was listed for sale with Prudential California Realty and its agent, Stubbs. On the transfer disclosure statement, the sellers represented they were unaware of any significant defects in the foundation, exterior walls, windows, ceilings or other components of the home. Stubbs' inspection noted hairline cracks in the stucco, which Helm assured him were only cosmetic. On the transfer disclosure statement, Stubbs wrote "property appears to be in good condition ... I see nothing to contradict what the seller has mentioned ..." The Robinsons looked at the home several times and noted the stucco cracks. Their agent, Maier, recommended a professional home inspection. The Robinsons agreed to purchase the property and the sellers provided a copy of a geological report, which assured that "the house was very well built, ... and was not going anyplace ..." Stubbs sent a letter to the Robinsons advising that the stucco cracks were cosmetic in nature and were patched with a stucco and glue mixture. Escrow closed. ▼

226

> Subsequently, buyers' swimming pool excavation collapsed and they sued alleging the land suffered geotechnical and soils distress and the house contained numerous defects that were known, but not disclosed by the defendants. At trial, the jury found for Prudential and Stubbs, and that they did not breach their professional standard of care. As to negligent misrepresentation, the jury found a misrepresentation of a past or existing material fact, but the misrepresentation was not made without a reasonable ground for believing it to be true. The buyers appealed.
>
> The appellate court noted that an agent representing a seller must also complete his or her portion of the transfer disclosure statement form, and that the disclosure must be made in good faith. The court found no support for Robinsons' argument that the agent's disclosure duty included a duty to independently verify or disclaim the accuracy of the seller's (Helm) representations. Once the sellers and their agent make the required disclosures, it is incumbent upon the potential buyers to investigate and make an informed decision based on the disclosures. The sellers' agent is required only to act in good faith and not convey the sellers' representations without a reasonable basis for believing them to be true. Additionally, the Robinsons had actual knowledge of potential structural problems well before escrow closed.
>
> Both Stubbs and Maier encouraged the Robinsons to obtain their own independent inspections to verify the causes of the potential problems. The Robinsons failed to obtain a geotechnical inspection and their home inspector confirmed the sellers' representations. The Robinsons have shown no detrimental reliance on anything the sellers' agents disclosed or failed to disclose. It was only after the escrow that the Robinsons began complaining. The sellers' agents have no post-escrow duty to make any disclosures to the Robinsons about new information acquired. The trial court judgment in favor of the sellers' agents is affirmed. *Robinson v. Grossman*, 57 Cal. App. 4th 634, 67 Cal. Rptr. 2d 380 (1997).

To sue for actual fraud, the plaintiff generally must be able to prove five elements:

1. A person makes a false statement of a material fact or fails to disclose a material fact that he or she has a legal duty to disclose.
2. In regard to a misrepresentation, the person making the statement knows that it is false (intentional) or does not know if it is true, and has no reasonable basis for believing it is (negligent).
3. The statement or concealment is made with intent of inducing entry into a transaction.
4. The other person relies on the statement or lack of knowledge of the concealed information.
5. The other person is harmed as a result of entering the transaction.

Actual Fraud

● Intentional Misrepresentation   ● Negligent Misrepresentation   ● Concealment

---

2. Constructive Fraud

CONSTRUCTIVE FRAUD comprises any act, omission, or concealment involving a breach of legal or equitable duty, trust or confidence that results in damage to another even though the conduct is not otherwise fraudulent.

The distinction between a negligent misrepresentation (actual fraud) and constructive fraud is somewhat fuzzy. An agent's carelessness or misstatement could be construed as either. Generally, if the agent's action or failure to act constitutes a breach of a fiduciary duty to the principal, that will most likely be constructive fraud. If the action or failure to act is a breach of a duty owed to another party, that will most likely be negligent misrepresentation. Ultimately, if there is litigation, the court will decide.

A buyer's damages for fraud are limited to the difference between what the buyer had expended and the value of the property. *Cory v. Villa Properties*, 180 Cal.App.3d 592 (1986).

3. Opinion, Prediction, and Puffing (Not Fraud)

Generally, a seller or agent can't be sued for misrepresentation if his or her statements were merely opinions, predictions, or puffing (exaggeration).

> **Opinion:** "I think this is an excellent buy."
> **Prediction:** "That roof should last for another seven years."
> **Puffing:** "This is a dream house; it has an incredible view."

To prove fraud based on a misrepresentation, it's necessary to show that you relied on the misrepresentation. Because of their nonfactual or exaggerated nature, opinions, predictions, and puffing are not considered the type of statements a reasonable person would rely on in making a decision to buy property.

Example: The broker tells a buyer: "This is a great little house. You'll be very happy here." After purchasing the house, the buyer is not happy. He discovers several problems and decides it is not a great little house at all.

Even if it is, in fact, not a great house, the broker is not liable for his statement. It was just puffing—an exaggeration made to induce the purchaser to buy, but not relating any specific material fact.

However, an agent should be very cautious about making unsubstantiated opinions or predictions. If it is considered a professional or expert opinion, the agent may be held liable. A court may allow recovery based on opinions given by:

1. an expert hired to give advice,
2. a person who has superior knowledge and is acting in a fiduciary relationship, or
3. someone who states an opinion that he or she does not actually hold.

Case Example: The real estate agents told the buyers that the condominium units were "luxurious" and had "outstanding investment potential." In fact, the agents knew the construction was substandard and violated the minimum requirements of the building code.

The buyers sued the agents (along with the architects and developers). The court held that if it were shown that the agents could not reasonably have believed the opinions they expressed, they would be liable for fraud. *Cooper v. Jevne*, 56 Cal. App. 3d 860, 128 Cal. Rptr. 724 (1976).

---

4. "As is" Clause

An "as is" clause in a purchase agreement usually states that the buyer has inspected the property and agrees to accept it "as is"—in its current condition. There may be additional statements to the effect that the seller makes no warranties concerning the condition of the property. When there is an "as is" clause, the buyer takes the property subject to any defects that he or she could discover through a reasonably thorough visual inspection. This would include broken windows, cracks in walls, and other obvious flaws, such as peeling paint.

However, an "as is" clause cannot relieve a seller or agent from liability for fraud. If there are known hidden defects in the property that the seller and agent had a duty to disclose, a court will not enforce the "as is" clause.

as is = no repairs to property but ~~buyer~~ agent must still disclose buyer.

"As is" still requires inspection and disclosure by the agent and seller.

IV. Penalties for Breach of Agent's Duty

When a real estate agent breaches a duty to the principal or to a third party, there are several possible consequences. These include expulsion from professional associations, disciplinary action by the Department of Real Estate, and a civil lawsuit brought by the injured party. In particularly serious cases, a breach of duty can give rise to criminal charges against the agent.

A. ACTION BY PROFESSIONAL ASSOCIATIONS

A *CODE OF ETHICS is a system of moral standards and rules of conduct.* Many professional organizations for real estate brokers and salespersons (like NAHREP and NAREB) have adopted a code of ethics to set standards for members' conduct toward the public, clients, and other members of the profession.

The most widely recognized code is the National Association of REALTORS® Code of Ethics. The NAR's Code of Ethics is not legally binding, but all NAR members agree to follow it. A member who violates the code may be expelled from the organization. That kind of censure can be professionally disastrous, especially in a small community. **In addition, every four years REALTORS® are required to take three hours of ethical training.**

In deciding cases involving real estate agents, judges sometimes refer to the NAR's Code of Ethics as evidence of prevailing industry standards for ethical and competent agents. A judge may use the code as a basis for finding negligence or incompetence on the part of an agent.

Examples of National Real Estate Organizations

NAR. The National Association of REALTORS® is the national trade association for all the state associations and local boards of REALTORS® in the U.S. (**realtor.com**)

NAREB. The National Association of Real Estate Brokers, or "Realtist," is an organization of brokers with a predominance of African-American members. (**nareb.org/index.htm**)

NAHREP. The National Association of Hispanic Real Estate Professionals is a non-profit trade association made up primarily of Hispanic members. (**nahrep.com**)

CHAPTER 6

B. CIVIL LAWSUITS

As the case examples throughout this chapter show, a real estate agent who breaches a duty may be sued by a client or customer. These lawsuits are tort suits, since breach of a legal duty is a tort. If the plaintiff is able to prove that he or she suffered harm as the result of the breach of duty, the agent will be held liable.

Liability for the wrongful acts of the salesperson may also be imposed only on a corporation form of brokerage ownership (which has limited liability) if the broker license is as a corporation. **Fortunately, such liability is not imposed on the individual owner or officer of that corporation.** (*Meyer v. Holley*, 537 US 280, 123 S.Ct. at 824, 829 [2003])

1. Compensatory (Actual) Damages –

An agent who is found liable may be required to pay *COMPENSATORY (ACTUAL) DAMAGES, where the injured party is compensated for any monetary loss resulting from the breach of duty.* When the plaintiff is a client, that damage may include the transaction commission. If secret proits are involved, damage may include forfeiting the secret profits.

2. Punitive (Exemplary) Damages –

A court may separately award punitive damages if there is fraud, oppression, or malice. *PUNITIVE DAMAGES, unlike compensatory damages, are intended to punish the wrongdoer and deter others from similar acts.* (They are also called exemplary damages.)

The following case will show how damages can be computed in a court of law against an agent and the employing broker.

Case Example: On August 5, 1999, John Strebel (buyer) contracted to buy a house in Sonoma County from the Steels (sellers) for $420,000. Unbeknownst to the buyer, the house was encumbered with tax liens and judgments that exceeded the purchase price. Haya Smith was acting as dual agent and employed by Brenlar Investments, Inc., DBA Frank Howard Allan (broker). Smith was aware of the liens, but concealed that information from the buyer. The sellers wrote to Smith explaining they had made a compromise offer to the IRS to reduce the tax liens, but if the offer was rejected they would be unable to transfer title to the buyer. Smith did not inform the buyer. When the buyer learned of the tax liens, Smith told the buyer that the sellers were working on reducing the liens, which would not be a problem. Three days later, Smith again reassured the buyer that the sellers were "taking care of it and escrow would close; they were moving forward with the transaction."

The buyer had sold his San Bruno property for $424,950 with the sale contingent on the Sonoma escrow proceeding. Based on what Smith said, the buyer closed the San Bruno escrow on schedule and moved his personal property into a storage unit in Sonoma. The buyer netted approximately $321,000 from the sale. The IRS rejected the sellers' compromise on October 4, 1999. The buyer placed the proceeds in a bank account at 4% interest and for over one year searched unsuccessfully for additional property in Sonoma. By September 2001, he was still unable to find a suitable replacement and began to conclude that he had priced himself out of the Sonoma County real estate market. ▼

On June 27, 2000, the buyer sued Smith and the broker alleging, among other things, fraud, negligence, and breach of fiduciary duty. The jury awarded the buyer a total of $300,000 finding that Smith and the broker had intentionally concealed material facts with intent to defraud the buyer and also that they were liable for negligence. The negligence verdict added an additional $50,000 for noneconomic damages (emotional distress). The jury also found in the buyer's favor for breach of contract against the sellers. It appears the court deducted a 5% comparable fault from the $350,000 that the jury attributed to the buyer and an additional amount received by the buyer for some other related claims against another party making a total judgment of $305,000.

Smith and the broker appealed, contesting the computation of damages. The buyer's expert witness subtracted the 1999 sale price of the San Bruno property from his opinion of the then current fair market value of the house based on a study of comparable sales at the time of trial in 2003. He then reduced the gross amount by the estimated closing cost based on current fair market value to reach a net loss appreciation of $183,427. The expert calculated buyer's loss of use damages for the San Bruno home by subtracting the costs associated with living in his house, mortgage interest, taxes and insurance, from the cost of renting a similar house in San Bruno. This difference was $66,046. Adding this amount to the lost appreciation produced a total of $247,273.

The fact that the buyer received what was the fair market value for this house at the time he sold it did not eliminate financial loss from the premature sale of the property.

The buyer did not attempt to profit from an unreasonable delay in filing the lawsuit. He filed the complaint within a year of the fraud and for over a year after that continued to look for a suitable replacement property. In addition to the testimony of the expert witness, the jury also made adjustments for other amounts such as a reduction from the damage award for the 4% interest earned by the buyer in arriving at a judgment of $305,000. The buyer was unable to prove punitive damages for the intentional fraud.

The Court of Appeal affirmed the judgment of the trial court but reduced it by the $50,000 awarded for emotional distress and an additional $52,727 for unproven damages. The total judgment against Smith and the broker was $202,273. *Strebel v. Brenlar Investments, Inc.*, 135 Cal. App. 4th 740, 37 Cal. Rptr. 3d 699 (2006).

3. Real Estate Recovery Account

If a client or customer is awarded damages against a real estate agent, but is unable to collect the judgment from the agent, he or she may be entitled to payment out of the **Real Estate Recovery Account**. The judgment must be based on the agent's intentional fraud, misrepresentation, deceit, or conversion of trust funds. The Recovery Account is administered by the Department of Real Estate and funded by fees charged to all agents at the time of licensing or license renewal. **Payment to judgment creditors out of the Recovery Account is limited to $50,000 for liability arising from any one transaction, and $250,000 for the misconduct of any one agent.**

C. CRIMINAL PROSECUTION

A serious and intentional breach of duty may not only lead to civil liability, but may also be a crime. An agent who willfully violates (or knowingly participates in a violation of) the Real Estate Law is guilty of a misdemeanor. He or she may be fined up to $10,000, imprisoned for up to six months, or both. The agent's conduct may also be the basis for a felony conviction, with more severe penalties.

D. ACTION BY THE REAL ESTATE COMMISSIONER

A real estate agent's breach of duty is often a violation of the Real Estate Law. An agent who violates the Real Estate Law is subject to disciplinary action by the Commissioner of Real Estate, whether or not a client or customer sues the agent. The Real Estate Law establishes specific grounds for disciplinary action. This topic will be discussed in more detail in Chapter 9.

V. Disclosures Required of a Seller and/or a Broker/Agent

A. DISCLOSURES UPON TRANSFER OF RESIDENTIAL PROPERTY

The requirement for a seller to provide the Transfer Disclosure Statement (TDS) to a buyer is discussed earlier in the Chapter. California Civil Code sections 1102-1102.17 and 1103-1103.14 also require other disclosures that must be given to the buyer. With limited exceptions, these disclosures apply to the transfer of residential property with one-to-four units.

1. Local Option Real Estate Transfer Disclosure Statement

The seller may be required by a city or county to provide specific information about the neighborhood or community in the transfer disclosure statement.

2. Natural Hazards Disclosure

The seller or his/her real estate agent is required to provide prospective buyers with a revised Natural Hazard Disclosure statement disclosing the property is located within one or more of the six specified natural hazard zones, including:

1. Special Flood Hazard Area
2. Area of Potential Flooding
3. Very High Fire Hazard Area
4. Designated Wildland Area (State Responsibility Zone)
5. Earthquake Fault Zone
6. Seismic Hazard Zone

3. Mello-Roos Bonds and Taxes

If the property is subject to a continuing lien securing the levy of special taxes to finance designated public facilities and services under the Mello-Roos Community Facilities Act, the seller must attempt to obtain a notice from the appropriate local taxing agency disclosing details of the tax and deliver it to the buyer.

4. Property Taxes

The seller or his or her agent is required to deliver to the prospective purchaser a disclosure notice that includes both of the following:

(1) A notice, in at least 12-point type (not shown in 12 pt. type here) or a contrasting color, as follows:

> "California property tax law requires the Assessor to revalue real property at the time the ownership of the property changes. Because of this law, you may receive one or two supplemental tax bills, depending on when your loan closes.
>
> The supplemental tax bills are not mailed to your lender. If you have arranged for your property tax payments to be paid through an impound account, the supplemental tax bills will not be paid by your lender. It is your responsibility to pay these supplemental bills directly to the Tax Collector.
>
> If you have any question concerning this matter, please call your local Tax Collector's Office."

(2) A title must be included in at least 14-point type (not shown in 14 pt. type here) or a contrasting color that reads as follows:

> "Notice of Your 'Supplemental' Property Tax Bill."
>
> The disclosure notice requirements of this section may be satisfied by including the required information in the Mello-Roos disclosure (see Part I, Section I, Subsection A, Item 5 – Mello-Roos Bonds and Taxes). Supplemental taxes may be assessed whether a new loan is obtained or an existing loan is assumed to accomplish the purchase of the property, or whether the property is purchased without financing.

5. Ordnance Location

Seller must give written notice of any knowledge of former state or federal ordnance (of military munitions) locations within 1 mile of the property.

6. Window Security Bars

Seller must disclose the existence of window security bars and safety release mechanisms in the transfer disclosure statement.

7. Industrial Uses

A seller who has actual knowledge must disclose on the transfer disclosure statement, or if mandated on the local option transfer disclosure statement, should the property be adjacent to or zoned to allow an industrial use (Cal. Civ. § 1102.17).

B. EARTHQUAKE GUIDES

Seller and agent provide a transferee with a copy of the *Homeowner's Guide to Earthquake Safety*, from the Seismic Safety Commission. Important: If a buyer receives a copy of the booklet, neither the seller nor the agent are required to provide additional information regarding geological and seismic hazards other than those listed herein or actually known.

Seller and agent must also disclose that a property is in an earthquake zone as indicated on maps from the California Division of Mines and Geology where the maps are locally unavailable.

C. SMOKE DETECTOR STATEMENT OF COMPLIANCE

Seller must provide buyer with a written statement that the property complies with the California smoke detector's law.

D. DISCLOSURE REGARDING LEAD-BASED PAINT HAZARDS

Seller must disclose the presence of the lead-based paint or lead-based hazards and any known information and reports about them, such as location and condition of painted surfaces. Buyer of property built prior to 1978 must receive the EPA booklet *Protect Your Family from Lead in Your Home*. Buyer has 10 days to conduct inspection.

E. CALIFORNIA'S ENVIRONMENTAL HAZARD'S PAMPHLET

The Real Estate Transfer Disclosure Statement (TDS) provided to the buyer by the seller and his/her real estate agent must specify environmental hazards of which the seller or agent are aware. If the buyer is given a pamphlet entitled *Environmental Hazards: a Guide for Homeowners, Buyers, Landlords, and Tenants*, neither the seller nor his real estate agent is required to furnish any more information concerning such hazards unless the seller or agent has actual knowledge of the existence of an environmental hazard on or affecting the property. **The pamphlet includes a chapter on mold and will include information regarding carbon monoxide.**

F. DELIVERY OF STRUCTURAL PEST CONTROL INSPECTION AND CERTIFICATION REPORTS

If required by contract or by the lender, the seller or his/her agent must deliver to the buyer, before transfer of title, a report and written certification of completion of work by a registered structural pest control company, regarding the presence of wood-destroying organisms. Buyer's broker must ensure delivery to buyer. If nondelivery, agent must inform buyer of right to get previous pest reports from the state.

G. ENERGY CONSERVATION RETROFIT AND THERMAL INSULATION DISCLOSURES

State law prescribes minimum energy conservation standards for all new construction. Some local governments also have ordinances that impose additional energy conservation measures on new and/or existing homes. These local ordinances may impose energy retrofitting as a condition of the sale of an existing home. The seller and/or the seller's agent(s) are to disclose to a prospective buyer the requirements of the various ordinances, as well as who is responsible for compliance.

Federal law requires that a "new home" seller (including a subdivider) disclose in every sales contract the type, thickness, and R-value of the insulation which has been or will be installed. However, if the buyer signs a sales contract before it is known what type of insulation will be installed, or if there is a change in the contract regarding insulation, the seller shall give the buyer the required information as soon as it is available.

H. FOREIGN INVESTMENT IN REAL PROPERTY TAX

A buyer of real property must withhold and sent to the IRS 10% of the gross sales price if the seller is a "foreign person."

I. NOTICE AND DISCLOSURE TO BUYER OF STATE TAX WITHHOLDING ON DISPOSITION OF CALIFORNIA REAL PROPERTY

The buyer must withhold 3.333 percent of the total sales price as state income tax in certain transactions.

J. FURNISHING CONTROLLING DOCUMENTS AND A FINANCIAL STATEMENT FOR COMMON INTEREST DEVELOPMENTS

A prospective buyer must receive the following: (a) copy of governing documents of development; the (b) copy of the most recent financial statement of the homeowner's association; (c) a written statement from the association specifying the amount of the current, regular, and special assessments and any unpaid assessments.

K. NOTICE REGARDING THE ADVISABILITY OF TITLE INSURANCE

Where no title insurance is to be issued, the buyer must receive and sign or acknowledge a statutory notice regarding the advisability of obtaining title insurance with the close of escrow; check to determine if escrow officer gives notice.

L. CERTIFICATION REGARDING WATER HEATER'S SECURITY AGAINST EARTHQUAKE

A seller must certify in writing to the prospective buyer that a water heater has been braced, anchored, or strapped to resist the movement due to earthquake motion.

M. DATABASE REGARDING LOCATION OF REGISTERED SEX OFFENDERS (Megan's Law)

A statutorily defined notice regarding the existence of public access to database information regarding sex offenders is required in every real property sales contract.

N. GAS TRANSMISSION PIPELINES

California Civil Code Section 2079.10.5 requires that contracts for the sale of residential real property entered into on or after July 1, 2013, contain the following notice, in not less than 8-point type:

**NOTICE REGARDING GAS AND
HAZARDOUS LIQUID TRANSMISSION PIPELINES**

This notice is being provided simply to inform you that information about the general location of gas and hazardous liquid transmission pipelines is available to the public via the National Pipeline Mapping System (NPMS) Internet Web site maintained by the United States Department of Transportation at **www.npms.phmsa.dot.gov**. To seek further information about possible transmission pipelines near the property, you may contact your local gas utility or other pipeline operators in the area. Contact information for pipeline operators is searchable by ZIP Code and county on the NPMS Internet Web site.

CHAPTER 6

VI. CHAPTER SUMMARY

1. A broker must print his or her real estate license number on all advertising, including business cards, stationary, websites, email etc, so it is disclosed at the first point of contact with a consumer.

2. The agency disclosure law requires an agent in a residential transaction to have both the buyer and the seller sign an agency disclosure form (explaining agency duties) and an agency confirmation statement (explaining which party the agent represents).

3. An agent owes fiduciary duties to the principal. These include the duty to use reasonable care and skill, obedience, utmost good faith, and loyalty. An agent should not disclose confidential information to third parties, or conceal material information from the principal. The agent must avoid undisclosed self-dealing, secret profits, and the unauthorized practice of law.

4. Dual agency is legal as long as it is disclosed to and approved by the buyer and seller, but the dual agent owes fiduciary duties to both parties making it difficult to adequately represent both parties.

5. An agent doesn't owe fiduciary duties to third parties, but must deal fairly with them. Both the seller and the agent are required to disclose anything they're aware of that materially affects the value or desirability of the property. An agent has to conduct a diligent visual inspection of residential property and disclose any problems he or she discovers. The seller and agent must fill out a Real Estate Transfer Disclosure Statement (TDS) for the buyer.

6. Actual fraud is intentional misrepresentation or concealment, or negligent misrepresentation. Constructive fraud is a breach of duty that misleads another, without an intention to deceive. Opinions, predictions, and puffing usually aren't actionable fraud, but an expert opinion may be. An "as is" clause doesn't shield a seller or broker from liability for fraud.

7. A client or customer can sue a real estate agent for breach of duty. The agent may be required to forfeit the commission or pay compensatory and punitive damages. In cases involving intentional fraud or conversion of trust funds, a judgment creditor, who is unable to collect from the agent, may be paid out of the Real Estate Recovery Fund. An agent accused of a serious breach of duty may be subject to criminal prosecution as well as civil suits.

8. A breach of duty may also be a violation subject to action by the Real Estate Commissioner.

VII. KEY TERMS

"as is" clause	desist and refrain order	restricted license
actionable fraud	dual agency	secret profits
actual fraud	fiduciary	self-dealing
caveat emptor	misrepresentation	seller property questionnaire
code of ethics	negligence	(SPQ)
compensatory (actual)	puffing	summary suspension
damages	punitive (exemplary)	
constructive fraud	damages	

VIII. CHAPTER QUIZ

1. A person who has obtained a listing of the real property acting as an agent for compensation is a(n):

    a. selling agent.
    b. associate licensee.
    c. listing agent.
    d. subagent.

2. A selling agent must provide the agency disclosure form to the buyer:

    a. as soon as practicable before the buyer signs an offer.
    b. after the close of escrow.
    c. as soon as practicable before the seller signs the buyer's offer.
    d. as soon as practicable before the buyer's offer is presented.

3. The selling agent must provide the agency disclosure form to the seller:

    a. before escrow closes.
    b. any time before the seller signs of the offer.
    c. as soon as practicable before presenting the seller with a buyer's offer.
    d. before signing escrow instructions.

4. Real estate agents must confirm their agency relationships:

    a. only in the purchase contract.
    b. only in a separate writing.
    c. only on a form approved by the California Association of REALTORS®.
    d. in either the purchase contract or a separate writing.

5. An agent has a duty to disclose material facts based on an inspection that includes:

    a. a reasonably competent and diligent visual inspection of the property.
    b. areas that are reasonably and normally inaccessible to visual inspection.
    c. areas off the site of the subject property.
    d. public records or permits concerning the title or use of the property.

6. With regard to a transfer disclosure statement on residential property:

    a. filling out the form is optional with the seller.
    b. if the seller has an agent, only the agent is required to complete the form.
    c. the transfer disclosure statement is not required on residential property.
    d. the seller, listing agent, and selling agent all sign the form.

7. Residential property being sold "as is":

    a. is illegal in California.
    b. does not require a transfer disclosure statement.
    c. does not relieve the seller from disclosing known property defects.
    d. constitutes a waiver of the requirement for a transfer disclosure statement.

CHAPTER 6

8. If husband Bob is conveying his ownership interest in their residence to his wife Mary:

    a. a transfer disclosure statement is required.

    b. a transfer disclosure statement is not required.

    c. a transfer disclosure statement is required only if the value of the interest being conveyed to Mary is more than $500,000.

    d. a transfer disclosure statement is required only if it is a gift to Mary.

9. The statute of limitations for a lawsuit brought against a broker is:

    a. two years for negligent inspection.

    b. three years for intentional fraud.

    c. five years for either negligent or intentional fraud.

    d. both a and b are correct.

10. Which of the following is not a disclosure required to be given to the buyer upon transfer of residential property of one-to-four units?

    a. Natural Hazards Disclosure

    b. Misdemeanor Conviction Status Disclosure

    c. Mello-Roos Bonds and Taxes Disclosure

    d. Ordnance Location Disclosure

ANSWERS: 1. c; 2. a; 3. c; 4. d; 5. a; 6. d; 7. c; 8. b; 9. d; 10. b

238

1725

SANTA MONICA
COUNTY
BUILDING

Priority Entrance for

EMPLOYEES
AND
JURORS ONLY

Identification is Required

CHAPTER 7
Contract Law

CHAPTER OVERVIEW

A **CONTRACT** *is an agreement between two or more parties to do (or not do) a certain thing, which the court will enforce.* It doesn't have to be a ten-page legal document; it could be a spoken promise, a bus pass, or a movie ticket. They are all examples of contracts. To be enforced by a court, an agreement must be made according to the rules of contract law. These rules are designed to protect the parties against misunderstandings and false claims.

A sale of real property often involves a number of contracts: an employment agreement between a broker and a salesperson, a listing agreement, a purchase agreement, a title insurance policy, and an escrow agreement. As a result, it's essential for a real estate agent to understand basic contract law.

This chapter describes how a valid contract is formed and the possible remedies when a contract is not fulfilled (breach). The next chapter covers in more detail the types of contracts you're likely to encounter in real estate transactions.

I. Contract Classifications

There are four fundamental ways of classifying all contracts:

1. express or implied,   *oral/written or actions*
2. unilateral or bilateral,   *exp promise or if*
3. executory or executed, and   *fully performed or to be done by one party*
4. valid, voidable, void, or unenforceable.

An **EXPRESS CONTRACT** *is an agreement that has been made in words, whether spoken or written.* An **IMPLIED CONTRACT**, *on the other hand, hasn't been put into words. Instead, the agreement is implied from the actions of the parties.* An implied contract is often based on custom, or on an established course of dealing between the parties. Some contracts are partly express and partly implied. When you order a meal in a restaurant, it's understood that you agree to pay the price on the menu, although you don't actually say that to the waiter.

CHAPTER 7

A ***BILATERAL CONTRACT*** *exists when each party makes a binding promise to the other; the contract is formed by the exchange of promises.* For example, a buyer promises to pay a seller $329,000 for his house, and the seller promises to transfer title to the buyer in exchange for the money. Both parties are legally obligated to fulfill their promises. Most contracts are bilateral.

A ***UNILATERAL CONTRACT*** *exists when one party promises something if the other party performs a certain action, but the other party does not promise to perform it.* The contract is formed only if the other party actually performs the requested action.

> **Example:** An offer of a reward is a unilateral contract. If Pedro offers a reward for the return of his lost textbook, he is making a promise in return for a specified act. Pedro is not asking for anyone to promise to find and return his book, and no one is making a promise to do so. The offer of the reward becomes binding if someone actually finds the textbook and returns it to Pedro. At that point, Pedro is obligated to pay the reward.

An ***EXECUTED CONTRACT*** *is one that has been fully performed.* An ***EXECUTORY CONTRACT*** *refers to a contract where something remains to be done by one party.* One or all of the parties have not begun to carry out their promises, or are in the process of carrying them out. Most contracts start out executory and end up executed.

In addition to being express or implied, unilateral or bilateral, and executory or executed, a contract is either valid, void, voidable, or unenforceable. A ***VALID CONTRACT*** *is an agreement that meets all the legal requirements for contract formation* outlined in the next section of this chapter. *If one of the parties doesn't fulfill his or her side of the bargain (**BREACHES** the contract),* the other can sue to have the contract enforced.

*Many agreements don't meet one or more of the requirements for contract formation. These agreements are usually considered legally **VOID**.* The term "void contract" is a contradiction in terms, because

243

EXPRESS Written or Oral	OR	IMPLIED Conduct of the Parties
UNILATERAL Promise for an act	OR	BILATERAL Mutual Promises for Acts
EXECUTED Fully Performed	OR	EXECUTORY Not Yet Fully Performed

no contract is actually formed. Neither party has an obligation to perform and neither party can enforce the other party's promise in court. It would be more exact to say that there is a void agreement, because no contract has been created.

If one party breaches and the other sues, the judge may rule that no contract was formed, and will refuse to enforce the agreement.

Example: A owns a vacant lot on the east side of town and B owns a vacant lot on the south side of town. Just before teeing off for their usual Saturday golf game, B bets his lot against A's lot that B will shoot a lower score than A. A accepts the bet. A shoots a 78 and B an 80, and A demands the deed to B's lot. B refuses to deliver and A sues B for the deed. Since gambling is illegal in California, this betting agreement is void and cannot be enforced.

CONTRACT TYPE	LEGAL EFFECT	EXAMPLE
VOID	No contract at all	An agreement for which there is no consideration
VOIDABLE	Valid unless rejected by one party	A contingency in a contract not met
UNENFORCEABLE	Neither party may sue for performance	A contract after the statute of limitations has expired
VALID or ENFORCEABLE	Binding and enforceable	An agreement that meets all requirements of a contract

Sometimes, even though an agreement doesn't comply with all the rules, it is not void. An otherwise valid contract may be declared *VOIDABLE if one of the parties has the right to either rescind or affirm the contract.* This generally happens when one of the parties has taken advantage of the other in some way. The injured party can choose whether or not to go through with the contract. If he or she decides against it, the injured party can *DISAFFIRM the contract—that is, ask a court to terminate it.* The situations in which a contract is voidable (rather than void) are explained in the next section.

Finally, some contracts are **unenforceable** even when they are not void or voidable. *A contract that may be valid in all respects except that it cannot be enforced in a court of law is an UNENFORCEABLE CONTRACT.* For example, a valid contract becomes unenforceable when the statute of limitations runs out. Or, maybe all the requirements for contract formation were met, but there isn't proper evidence to prove it in court. (This problem often comes up with oral contracts.) A contract is also likely to be unenforceable if it is vaguely worded.

II. Contract Formation

There are four essential elements for a valid contract:

1. capacity to contract,
2. mutual consent,
3. consideration, and
4. a lawful purpose.

> **The Statute of Frauds requires that certain contracts be in writing.**

These requirements apply to all contracts. In addition, certain contracts (especially real estate contracts) must be in **writing** and signed to be enforceable.

www.real-estate-public-records.com
Real Estate Public Records Search

A. CAPACITY TO CONTRACT

To have **capacity** to make a valid contract, a person must be at least **18 years of age** and must also be of **sound mind**. This requirement protects minors and the mentally ill who might enter into contracts without understanding the consequences. As noted in the next section, there are some exceptions in which a person under the age of 18 may be able to make a contract.

1. Minors

When a minor makes an agreement concerning real property, the agreement is void. Neither the minor nor the other party can sue to enforce the agreement.

> **Example:** M is only 17. He signs a purchase agreement, agreeing to buy S's house. If either M or S breaches this agreement, the other cannot enforce it because it is void.

Most other types of contracts are **voidable** only at the election of the minor, meaning the minor can decide whether he or she wants to afirm the transaction. If not, the minor can go to court to disaffirm the contract. If the minor does want to go through with it, the other party is bound.

> **Example:** Suppose M bought S's car instead of her house. A week later, M decides he doesn't like the color. This contract is voidable by M, so he may ask a court to terminate it. M will return the car, and S will have to return whatever M paid her for it. This is true even if the car was destroyed in a fire and all M can return is burned, twisted metal.

A minor must disaffirm a voidable contract before he or she turns 18, or within a reasonable time after turning 18. What is a reasonable period of time is determined on a case-by-case basis. There is an additional issue called **ratification**. If after turning 18, the individual does something that indicates an intention to be bound by the contract entered

CHAPTER 7

into while a minor, the contract is binding even though the individual acted within a reasonable amount of time. It is inconsistent to attempt to avoid a contract once having indicated an intention to be bound by it.

www.dre.ca.gov/Publications/RealEstateLaw.html
Department of Real Estate - Real Estate Law

Example: M bought S's car and paid $500.00 down and is paying $100.00 per month until it is paid for. Six days after turning 18, M makes another monthly payment. Seven days later, M chooses to avoid the car purchase contract made while a minor. Assuming that 13 days is within a reasonable time after turning 18, M is bound by the contract. Making a monthly payment after acquiring mental capacity (turning 18) resulted in the ratification of the contract made while a minor, and it became a binding contract.

Even if the minor misrepresents his or her age when buying or selling something, the contract can still be disaffirmed. Consequently, verifying that the other party to a contract is 18 or older is very important. If you determine the person is under 18, consider your choices:

1. Decline to enter into the contact because the risk is too great (having to return money received from the minor and get back nothing if the item has been destroyed, or receive it in a damaged condition with no way to recover for the damage).

2. Enter into the contract and wait for the reasonable period after turning 18, or hope for ratification after 18.

3. Enter into the contract, but only if the minor provides a competent adult to cosign the contract.

www.lawyers.com
Real Estate Law Internet Sites

There are four major areas where minors may enter into valid (binding and enforceable in court) contracts.

a. Emancipation

Once a minor becomes emancipated, he or she has the capacity to "buy, sell, lease, encumber, exchange, or transfer an interest in real or personal property..." under Family Code Section 7050. An emancipated minor is a person under 18 who:

1. is or has been married,
2. is on active duty with armed forces, or
3. has received a court declaration of emancipation.

To petition the superior court for a Declaration of Emancipation, the minor:

1. must be at least 14 years old;
2. is willingly living separate and apart from his or her parents or guardian with the consent or acquiescence of the minor's parents or guardian;

3. is managing his or her own financial affairs (an income and expense declaration is required);
4. cannot be receiving income from a criminal activity.

Once the court determines it is in the best interest of the minor, the court issues a Declaration of Emancipation. The court can rescind the declaration at a later time if necessary. The emancipated minor can receive a California identification card for an emancipated minor from the Department of Motor Vehicles.

b. Necessities (Necessary Purchases)

Contracts entered into by minors for necessities (such as food or medicine) may be valid. However, since most minor's necessities are provided by parents with the minor living at home, most of the minor's other contracts are voidable since the parents are providing the necessities. Additionally, what is a necessity for one minor may or may not be a necessity for another minor. Family Code Section 6712 covers necessities and provides:

"A contract, otherwise valid, entered into during minority, may not be disaffirmed on that ground either during the actual minority of the person entering into the contract, or at any time thereafter, if all of the following requirements are satisfied:

1. The contract is to pay the reasonable value of things necessary for the support of the minor or the minor's family.
2. These things have been actually furnished to the minor or to the minor's family.
3. The contract is entered into by the minor when not under the care of a parent or guardian able to provide for the minor or the minor's family."

It's difficult to find a situation for a binding necessity contract as most minors live with their parents; so the minor will generally be living on his/her own.

c. Art, Entertainment, Sports

A minor's contract in art, entertainment, or professional sports is also valid under California law. To be binding, these contracts must be approved by a superior court judge. Additionally, the judge must set aside 15% of the minor's gross earnings under the contract in a trust fund for the future benefit of the minor. The court may require an amount in excess of 15% be set aside if requested by the parent, guardian, or minor. Recent legislation specifies that all earnings from such entertainment and sports contracts belong to the minor (typically controlled by the parent or guardian), but all other earnings of minors remain the property of the parents. The minor's earnings must be used to pay liabilities of the minor under the contract. The amount in trust will be turned over upon turning 18 years of age.

d. Medical Services

Minors were having problems getting medical treatment without parental consent. The legislature responded with a variety of situations where the minor can receive medical treatment, some without parental consent, knowledge, or liability for payment. For example, Family Code Section 6926 provides:

1. A minor who is 12 years of age or older and who may have come into contact with an infectious, contagious, or communicable disease may consent to medical care related to the diagnosis or treatment of the disease, if the disease or condition is one that is required by law, or regulation adopted pursuant to law to be reported to the local health officer, or is a related sexually transmitted disease, as may be determined by the State Director of Health Services.

2. The minor's parents or guardian are not liable for payment for medical care provided pursuant to this section.

There are other sections involving consent by a minor to treatment for rape, assault, pregnancy and prevention thereof, and drug or alcohol abuse.

2. Mental Incompetence

MENTAL INCOMPETENCE is the inability of a person to make or carry out important decisions regarding his/her affairs.

The Civil Code provides that a person "of unsound mind" does not have the capacity to enter into a valid contract. *UNSOUND MIND means a failure to understand the nature and consequences of the transaction.* After a person has been declared incompetent by a court (because of mental illness, retardation, or senility), any contract he or she enters into is void. Also, if the person made a contract before the Declaration of Incompetence, but while of unsound mind, a court-appointed conservator can ask the court to have that contract set aside.

In a few cases, if a person was under the influence of alcohol or other drugs at the time of entering into a contract, it may be voidable. To disaffirm, the person must prove that he or she was of unsound mind at the time of the contract or the other party had reason to know of the lack of capacity caused by drugs or alcohol.

B. MUTUAL CONSENT

For a contract to be a binding obligation, all the parties must consent to its terms and their consent must be freely given. Mutual consent is achieved through the process of **offer** and **acceptance**.

1. Offer

The *OFFER is the proposal, typically made by the buyer (offeror), which if accepted (by the offeree), will result in the formation of a contract.* To be the basis for a contract, an offer must be communicated to the offeree and must:

1. express an intent to contract, and
2. have definite terms.

a. Intent to Contract

The intent requirement is concerned with *OBJECTIVE INTENT (what the offeror says and does)* rather than *SUBJECTIVE INTENT (what the offeror is actually thinking)*. If you say or do something a reasonable person could interpret as a serious expression of an intent to make a contract ("I'll sell you a dozen roses for $15"), it may be a legally binding offer—even if you don't have any roses and never really intended to come up with them.

On the other hand, a casual remark or a joke is not a binding offer. Because of the nature of the remark, the tone of voice, or the situation, a reasonable person would not understand the statement as a serious offer.

Example: Z paid $20,000 for a sports car. After it breaks down for the second time in a week, Z tells Q, "I'm so tired of this piece of junk I'd sell it for ten bucks." Q pulls out her wallet and hands Z a ten-dollar bill.

Z is not required to sell Q the car for ten dollars because his statement was not a binding offer. A reasonable person would not have interpreted his remark as a serious expression of an intent to contract.

Note that a real estate listing is not considered a property owner's offer to sell. It is the authorization of a broker to find a buyer or renter for the owner's property.

A buyer doesn't create a contract by accepting the seller's listing. Instead, a prospective buyer makes an offer to purchase, and the seller accepts or rejects the offer. (The listing agreement is an employment contract for personal service between the seller and a real estate broker that creates an agency relationship, not part of the contract between the seller and buyer.)

b. Definite Terms

An offer must have definite terms—it isn't binding if it's too vague. It should state, at least, such basic terms as the subject matter, the time for performance, and the price. In some commercial cases, usually involving a sale of goods, a court may fill in the blanks with a reasonable time or a reasonable price. If too many terms are left unspecified, the terms are not definite. A salesperson should never make an offer without a stated price. Preliminary negotiations for a contract do not constitute a binding offer.

Case Example: Two developers needed financing for a hotel project near San Francisco. They applied for a loan from Coast Federal Savings. Coast prepared a conditional commitment letter for a $7,000,000 loan at 9% interest. The letter did not specify the security for the loan, the payment schedule, or the disbursement procedures, among other things.

After receiving the commitment letter, the developers went ahead with their project and didn't apply for financing from any other banks, but then Coast Federal decided against making the loan. The developers sued the S&L for breach of contract.

The court ruled in favor of Coast Federal. The conditional commitment letter left out too many important terms; it did not make a clear and unambiguous promise to commit to making a loan, so no contract had been formed. *Laks v. Coast Federal Savings & Loan Ass'n.*, 60 Cal. App. 3d 885, 131 Cal. Rptr. 836 (1976).

2. Termination of an Offer

Offers that are terminated before acceptance never result in the formation of a contract. Once they have been terminated they are legally dead.

Terminated offers can be classified into two general categories: (1) offers which are terminated by operation of law, and (2) offers terminated by acts of the parties.

a. Termination by Operation of Law

Figure 7-1 lists a variety of circumstances where offers can be terminated without any action whatsoever by the parties. These situations range from death of either of the parties to the case where performance of the contract would be considered to be illegal or impossible.

Figure 7-1

Offers Terminated by Operation of Law
(Where no action of the parties is necessary)

- Death or insanity of either offeror or offeree
- Destruction of the property to be sold
- Impossibility of performance
- Illegality of performance

With respect to the **destruction of the subject matter** of the contract, namely the house to be sold/purchased, the law treats this mishap a bit differently, depending on whether a contract has actually been formed.

Suppose, for example, that Henry Homebuyer presents an offer to purchase a particular property. Suppose further that the house burns to the ground. If the property is destroyed after a contract is formed, but before title is transferred, Henry may be able to terminate his contract obligation to purchase based on the seller's impossibility of performance. However, there may be situations where Henry would be obligated to complete the contract (such as when Henry took possession before closing or contract language provided that Henry accepted the risk that the property may be destroyed)."

Impossibility of performance terminates the offer in cases of physical impossibility, and cases of extreme impracticability of performance.

b. Termination by Act of the Parties

The four most common types of offer terminations by act of the parties themselves are listed in **Figure 7-2**. In each of these instances, the parties have acted (or not acted) in a way as to render the offer ineffective, thereby preventing the creation of a valid contract.

Figure 7-2

Offers Terminated by Act of the Parties

- Revocation by the offeror before the offer is accepted
- Rejection of any part of the offer by the offeree
- Counter offer by the offeree
- Lapse of time where "too much" time has passed

---

c. Revocation

If an offeror revokes the offer before it is accepted, it is terminated—the offeree has lost the chance to accept the offer. This is true even if the offer stated that it was irrevocable, or that it would not expire until a particular date.

> **Case Example:** Mrs. Moeller offered to exchange her orange grove for some property owned by Mr. Richardson. Her offer stated, "Unless this offer shall be accepted in writing within 10 days of the date hereof ... [it shall be void.] During said period, this offer shall be irrevocable."
>
> Moeller's real estate agent delivered the offer to Richardson on October 16, but the next day Moeller had second thoughts. She had her agent tell Richardson that nothing further should be done about the proposed exchange for the time being.
>
> On October 20, Richardson visited the orange grove and discussed the exchange with Moeller again. The next day, Richardson signed Moeller's offer and informed her that he had accepted it. When Moeller refused to go through with the exchange, Richardson sued her.
>
> The court held that no contract had been formed. Richardson's acceptance was ineffective · (even though it came well within the ten-day period) because Moeller revoked the offer the day after she made it. Moeller had the right to revoke the offer at any time, even though it stated that it was irrevocable. The broker, however, could sue Mrs. Moeller (the principal) for his or her commission. *Roth v. Moeller*, 185 Cal. 415, 197 P. 62 (1921).

The *Roth v. Moeller* case would have come out differently if Richardson had paid Moeller a sum of money to keep the offer open for those ten days. When a offeree pays or gives something (consideration) to the offeror in exchange for holding an offer open, the offer cannot be revoked during the specified period. (See the discussion of options in Chapter 9.) Without such a payment, an offer can be revoked at any time before it is accepted. Once it has been accepted, however, the offeror can no longer revoke it.

A revocation is effective as soon as it is communicated to the offeree.

In California, revocations are effective when sent. Thus, when a notice of revocation is mailed to the offeree, the offer is revoked the moment the revocation is mailed.

The ability to revoke an offer before it is accepted is not absolute. The right to buy or sell property at an agreed price may be purchased, and if the right is not exercised by a specific date, it is forfeited. In other words if an option contract exists, an offer may not be withdrawn or revoked during the time period in which the option may be exercised.

d. Rejection

An offer is also terminated when it is rejected by the offeree.

Rejections are effective to terminate the offer when received by the offeror. If I reject your offer on Monday, I can't change my mind and call back on Tuesday to accept it. If you're still interested in the deal, we can start the process of offer and acceptance over again. Your original offer was terminated by my rejection, and if you've lost interest, I can no longer hold you to your offer.

A *COUNTER OFFER is a new offer made in rejection of an offer from a buyer/seller with different terms from the original offer.* A counter offer terminates an original offer.

3. Acceptance

When an offer is accepted, a contract is formed.

Once an offer is accepted, the parties are legally bound. Neither can back out unless the other is willing to call off the contract. There are four basic requirements for acceptance:

1. An offer can only be accepted by the offeree.
2. An acceptance must be communicated to the offeror. ✓
3. An acceptance must be made in the manner specified. ✓
4. An acceptance must not vary the terms of the offer. ✓

a. Accepted by the Offeree

The first of these requirements—that an offer can only be accepted by the offeree—may sound obvious. It means that if A makes an offer to B and B decides not to accept it, C can't accept the offer and force A to deal with him/her. Of course, A may be willing to work with C, but any contract between A and C is based on a new offer, not on the offer A made to B.

b. Communicated to the Offeror

An acceptance must be communicated to the offeror: "You may already have decided to accept my offer, but until you let me know that you've accepted it, I can still revoke it."

> **Case Example:** Mr. Carr's agent told Mr. Lauritson that the frontage of Carr's property was 900 feet. On November 14, Lauritson signed a purchase agreement offering to buy the property, and the agent delivered it to Carr.
>
> A few days later, however, the agent told Lauritson that the frontage was actually only 581 feet. Lauritson said he could not go through with the purchase. Carr sued.
>
> Carr claimed that he signed the purchase agreement on November 15, the day after he received it. Since Carr didn't send the purchase agreement back to Lauritson, or communicate his acceptance in any other way before the offer was revoked, the court ruled that no contract was formed. *Carr v. Lauritson*, 41 Cal. App. 2d 31, 106 P. 2d 19 (1940).

When an acceptance is not communicated directly (in person or over the telephone), it is effective as soon as the message is posted (mailed), even though the offeror may not receive it immediately or at all. This is called the ***MAILBOX RULE**, where the acceptance creates a binding contract when the offeree drops it in the mailbox.*

c. Manner of Acceptance

As mentioned earlier, certain types of contracts (including most contracts concerning real property) are required by law to be in writing and signed. For those, only a written, signed acceptance binds the offeree.

Example: A writes B a letter offering to sell him her house for $200,000. It's an excellent offer, so B calls A on the phone and says he's accepting it.

Two hours later, B changes his mind. He can call A back and withdraw his acceptance because it wasn't in writing.

However, if no law requires that the contract be in writing, an acceptance does not necessarily have to be in writing to bind the offeror to the contract. Any reasonable method of acceptance will be effective, unless the offer specifies how it is to be accepted. If the offer does specify a particular method (such as "in writing," "by registered mail," or "by delivering a cashier's check"), the acceptance will not bind the offeror unless those instructions are followed.

> **Case Example:** Gladstone Holmes, Inc., offered to sell 75 acres near Pomona to the Moreland Development Company. The offer took the form of a purchase agreement filled out and signed by Gladstone and delivered to Moreland.
>
> Moreland decided to accept the offer, so the agreement was signed and sent to Gladstone by certified mail. Moreland claimed to have mailed the document by 4:45 p.m. on March 9.
>
> Gladstone had a messenger hand deliver a letter to Moreland's office at 5:00 p.m. on the same day. The letter stated that the offer was revoked. Since March 9 was a Friday, however, neither the acceptance nor the revocation was opened and read until Monday morning.
>
> The court in this case did not decide if a contract was formed. That question would turn on whether Moreland could prove that it mailed the acceptance before Gladstone's revocation was received. If Moreland was able to prove that, the acceptance was effective and a contract was formed—the offer was revoked too late. It doesn't matter that neither party actually learned of the other's action until Monday. *Moreland Devel. Co. v. Gladstone Holmes, Inc.*, 135 Cal. App. 3d 973, 186 Cal. Rptr. 6 (1982).

Example: A offers to sell his antique car to B. The offer states it is to be accepted by registered mail. B drops by A's office and tells him that she's accepting the offer. A can still revoke it.

Of course, an offeror can waive any express requirement of acceptance. If A chooses to treat B's spoken acceptance as effective, a contract is formed. Can silence be acceptance? Not as a general rule, because an acceptance must be communicated.

Example: X writes Z a letter offering to buy her sailboat for $2,000. The letter says, "If you have not rejected this offer by Saturday, I will consider it accepted." Z receives the letter but never replies.

X goes to Z's house with $2,000 and demands the boat. Z is not required to let him have it. Her silence in response to X's letter was not acceptance, and no contract was formed.

On the other hand, if the offeree accepts the benefits of the offer, silence may be construed as acceptance. If X had enclosed a $2,000 check with his letter and Z cashed it, she would be deemed to have accepted his offer and might be required to let him have the boat.

d. Acceptance Must Not Vary the Offer's Terms

To create a contract, the offeree must accept exactly those terms that he or she was offered. The offeree can't modify the terms of the offer or add any new terms (if so, it is a counter offer).

A counter offer terminates the original offer, just as a rejection would. If your counter offer is rejected, it's too late to go back and accept the original offer. You can start again with a new offer identical to the original offer. If the original offeror has had a change of heart, however, you can no longer hold him or her to the original offer. **It's important to keep this in mind, since a real estate transaction often involves a series of offers and counter offers.**

Each counter offer terminates the previous offer.

Case Example: James and Barbara Gibbs made an offer to purchase a Woodland Hills house owned by American Savings for $180,000. During the morning of June 6, 1985, American Savings delivered a counter offer to the Gibbs containing several additional terms, but it did not mention the price. The Gibbs signed the counter offer. Mrs. Gibbs placed the accepted counter offer in an envelope, prepared a certified mail tag, and before 10 a.m. handed it to the mail clerk at her office telling him to mail it for her. At approximately 11 a.m. that same morning, a representative of American Savings spoke on the telephone with Barbara Gibbs saying that the counter offer was in error since American Savings had intended to increase the sales price to $198,000. Consequently, due to the error, the counter offer was revoked.

American Savings took the position that no contract had been formed. The Gibbs insisted they had accepted the counter offer before it was revoked and that an enforceable contract therefore existed. The counter offer was postmarked on June 7, 1985. The Gibbs appealed from a judgment entered for American Savings.

Civil Code Section 1583 provides: "consent is deemed to be fully communicated between the parties as soon as the party accepting a proposal has put his acceptance in the course of transmission to the proposer..." This means that the acceptance must be placed out of control of the accepting party in order to be considered "in the course of transmission." California's mailbox rule means that an acceptance of an offer is effective and deemed communicated upon deposit in the mail. The postmark on the counter offer shows the deposit occurred on June 7, and not on June 6. The counter offer was not placed in the course of transmission beyond the control of the offeree when Barbara Gibbs gave it to the mail clerk in her office with instructions to deliver it to the post office. It was placed in the course of transmission when it was deposited with the Postal Service on June 7. Therefore, the counter offer was revoked on June 6, prior to the Gibbs' acceptance and no contract was formed. Judgment affirmed. *Gibbs v. American Savings and Loan Association*, 217 Cal. App. 3d 1372, 266 Cal. Rptr. 517 (2nd Dist. 1990).

4. Defenses to Mutual Consent

Even if there has been a valid offer and acceptance, the contract may still be void or voidable under certain conditions that show that there was no true, freely given consent.

a. Fraud and Misrepresentation

FRAUD AND MISREPRESENTATION is a deceptive promise or representation of fact made in order to gain an unfair advantage over another. A misrepresentation made by an offeror could not only render the contract voidable, but it may subject the wrongdoer to significant monetary damages.

b. Mutual Mistake of Fact

Under a **MUTUAL MISTAKE OF FACT**, where both parties are mistaken as to a material fact that is critical to the contract, either party may declare the contract voidable. This remedy is not available if only *one party is mistaken (known as a **UNILATERAL MISTAKE)**.

c. Duress or Menace

An offer accepted under **DURESS** *(an intentional, unlawful physical act against someone)* or **MENACE** *(the threat of a wrongful act)* may also render the contract void or voidable. The duress/menace must be measured in subjective terms, in other words, how the victim perceives the threat. For example, if a person accepts a contract in the presence of a gun-waving offeror, it makes no difference that the gun was not loaded so long as the unwilling offeree believed it was loaded.

d. Undue Influence

UNDUE INFLUENCE *refers to an overpowering influence that a person holding a dominant or fiduciary position holds over another.* A fiduciary is a person who owes another person special duties such as trust, loyalty and obedience, to name a few.

Acceptance of a contract offer by a person influenced by a dominant individual or a fiduciary may render the contract voidable.

Thus, a contract to purchase, for example, investment property, by an old sickly patient under the care of a strong willed nurse, whose husband sold investment property, might trigger suspicion that the contract acceptance was obtained through the overpowering influence of another.

Case Example: The Channells owned a 51-acre ranch in Fresno County. Because of financial difficulties, they were no longer able to make their mortgage payments or pay their property taxes. Afraid of foreclosure, they tried to sell the property. They listed it for $60,000, but the only offer was for $40,000. That seemed too low, and the Channells did not accept it.

Then Mr. Anthony, the nephew of a neighbor, came to the Channells' rescue. Anthony said he would protect the ranch from foreclosure.

Anthony wrote up an agreement under which he would purchase the ranch by assuming the mortgage and other liens, which totaled approximately $34,700. He told the Channells that this transfer of title was "just for show," to prevent foreclosure. After the property was in escrow, the agreement would be torn up.

The Channells would be able to continue living on the ranch. Anthony also said he would give Mr. Channell a job and would pay off all the Channells' bills. The Channells hesitated, but then signed the agreement.

After talking to their son and their bookkeeper, however, the Channells had second thoughts. Anthony opened an escrow, but when he asked the Channells to sign the escrow papers, they refused.

Then Anthony filed a lawsuit against the Channells to enforce the purchase agreement. The Channells were very upset; they couldn't afford to hire a lawyer. Anthony told them he'd drop the lawsuit if they signed the escrow papers. The Channells reluctantly agreed, and Anthony drove them to a notary's office. ▼

Neither of the Channells could read without glasses. They only owned one pair, which they shared, and they forgot to bring it with them to the notary's office. When the Channells signed the escrow instructions, they didn't realize they were also signing a grant deed that Anthony had slipped in among the other papers. Anthony told the Channells that he was going to keep his promises and take care of them.

Later, the Channells learned they had signed a deed transferring the ranch to Anthony. Shortly afterwards, Anthony had the Channells evicted from the property. The Channells sued.

The jury decided that the purchase agreement was voidable by the Channells because Anthony used fraud (promises he never intended to keep) to get them to sign it. The escrow agreement was voidable because of undue influence. Anthony pressured the Channells into signing it by taking unfair advantage of their distress about being sued. *Channell v. Anthony*, 58 Cal. App. 3d 290, 129 Cal. Rptr. 704 (1976).

Case Example: Rich & Whillock contracted with Ashton Development, Inc. to perform grading and excavating work. Bills were submitted for work as it was done, which were regularly paid. When the final bill for $72,286.45 was submitted, Rich and Whillock were in financial difficulty and faced bankruptcy if not paid. Ashton offered to pay $50,000 on a "take it or leave it" basis making it necessary for Rich and Whillock to bring a lawsuit to get the reminder of the money they were entitled to. After strenuously protesting Ashton's coercive tactics, the only way to avoid an economic disaster was to accept the compromise amount of $50,000, and they signed a release of the balance. Later, Rich and Whillock sued Ashton for the balance owed. Ashton defended that the claim was extinguished by the signed release. The court ruled that there is an increasing recognition of the law's role in correcting inequitable or unequal exchanges between parties of disproportionate bargaining power and a greater willingness not to enforce agreements which were entered into under coercive circumstances. Clearly, Ashton acted in bad faith and was liable for the $22,286.45 due under the contract. *Rich and Whillock, Inc. v. Ashton Development, Inc.*, 157 Cal. App. 3d 1154, 204 Cal. Rptr. 86 (1984).

Case Example: Ms. Williams leased the second floor of a building from Ms. Puccinelli. They agreed that Williams would open a restaurant in the space. Neither of them realized that under San Francisco's building code, substantial structural alterations to the whole building would be necessary before a restaurant could be operated on the second floor.

A month after signing the lease, Williams learned about the required alterations. She asked Puccinelli to have the alterations done, but Puccinelli said that wasn't her responsibility. Williams sued to disaffirm the contract.

The court ruled that the contract was voidable because it was based on a mutual mistake regarding the law. Both parties had mistakenly assumed that the second floor could be used for the designated purpose without structural changes in the rest of the building. *Williams v. Puccinelli*, 236 Cal. App. 2d 512, 46 Cal. Rptr. 285 (1965).

C. CONSIDERATION

In general terms, both parties must agree to do or give up something they are not obligated to do for consideration to exist.

[handwritten annotation: "① Does not have to be money"]

[handwritten annotation: "(wash car for house paint)"]

Even when parties who have the capacity to contract freely consent to an agreement, it isn't a valid contract unless it is supported by consideration. **CONSIDERATION** *is something of value exchanged by the parties.* A contract can't be a one-way street: each party must give something to the other in order to get something from the other. The exchange of consideration is what distinguishes a contractual promise from the promise of a gift.

> **Example:** If A promises B his sweater in exchange for B's promise to give A his wheelbarrow, they have a contract. Each has given the other some consideration: A gave B a promise, and B gave A a promise.
>
> If A promises B his sweater and B promises A nothing in return, there is no contract. The sweater is a gift.
>
> The distinction becomes important if, after making the promise, A fails to give B the sweater. In the first case, where A received consideration for his promise (namely, B's promise to give him the wheelbarrow), B can sue A to enforce the promise.
>
> In the second case, however, B can't sue A. The courts will not enforce a promise that is not supported by consideration. It wasn't very nice of A to break his promise, but since the sweater was a gift instead of a contractual obligation, the law won't get involved.

The consideration for most contracts is a promise to give something of value—whether a sweater, $10, or a split-level house. For this reason, the parties to a contract are sometimes referred to as the **PROMISOR** *(the one making a promise)* and the **PROMISEE** *(the one who is to receive the benefit of a promise).*

In a typical real estate purchase contract, the buyer promises to pay the seller money, and the seller promises to transfer title to the buyer. By exchanging promises, they create an executory contract; when they fulfill their promises (when the buyer actually pays the seller and the seller actually gives the buyer the deed), the contract is executed.

To provide consideration for a contract, a promisor must either do something that benefits the promisee, or give something up. Promising not to do something can be consideration—for example, promising to stop smoking, or a promise to never start smoking can be consideration.

An illusory empty promise is not consideration for a contract: if you've never smoked, promising to quit can't be consideration, and something that you've already done can't be consideration.

> **Example:** A quit smoking, and B is very pleased. B says to A, "Because you quit smoking, I'm going to buy you a yacht." This is not a contract since A had already quit smoking, he didn't really give B anything (or give up anything) in exchange for B's promise.

Also, promising to do something that you're already legally obligated to do (or promising to refrain from doing something that you're obligated to refrain from doing) is not consideration.

> **Example:** A contracts to build a house for B for $200,000. When the house is more than halfway completed, A says, "You're going to have to pay me another $30,000 if you want me to finish this project." B meekly agrees. This is not an enforceable contract—A can't sue B for the additional $30,000—because A was already obligated to finish the house.

CHAPTER 7

1. Adequacy

It's important to understand that the value of the consideration one party gives doesn't have to be equal to the value of what the other gives. In other words, even though one party struck a bad bargain, they still have an enforceable contract.

Example: Maura is 19 years of age and lives in a state where the legal age for drinking alcohol is 21. Maura's promise not to drink alcohol before she turns 21 would not be consideration since she is not legally entitled to drink alcohol.

Of course, when the consideration is grossly unequal, that may be a sign that there was fraud, undue influence, duress, menace, or a mistake involved in the contract negotiations. If mutual consent can be proven, however, the contract is enforceable. Grossly unequal consideration may also affect the types of remedies available for breach of contract. In the previous example, Z could sue for money damages, but not for an order of specific performance (discussed later in this Chapter).

D. LAWFUL PURPOSE

The purpose of a contract (sometimes called the "object" of the contract) must be lawful when the contract is made. If one person promises to pay another for committing an illegal act, their contract is void and cannot be enforced by a court. This may seem obvious; a hit man is unlikely to take his employer to court to collect his fee. But the requirement has a considerably broader application. For example, a listing agreement hiring someone who is not a licensed real estate broker is void. Also, according to the Civil Code, even when a contract's purpose does not violate an express provision of the law, it is unlawful if it is contrary to public policy or good morals.

Many contracts have more than one purpose, and they are often severable—one part can be enforced without the other. When part of a contract is legal and part is illegal, a court may set aside the illegal part and enforce the rest. When a contract has a single purpose, if any of the consideration given for that purpose is unlawful, the entire contract is void.

Example: A agreed to sell his house to B in exchange for $100,000 and a pound of cocaine. The whole contract is void. The court can't just ignore the cocaine and enforce a sale of the house for $100,000.

E. STATUTE OF FRAUDS

The provision of the Civil Code requiring certain contracts to be in writing and signed is known as the STATUTE OF FRAUDS. (The same name is used for similar laws in other states, too—it was adopted from common law.) As the name suggests, the writing requirement is intended to prevent fraudulent claims. The parties to an unwritten contract are more likely to later disagree about exactly what each agreed to do—or whether they agreed to do anything. Putting a contract in writing helps eliminate that kind of dispute because the document is solid evidence of the existence of an agreement and its essential terms.

 www.leginfo.ca.gov/cgi-bin/displaycode?section=civ&group=01001-02000&file=1619-1633
Civil Code - Statute of Frauds

1. What Contracts Must Be in Writing

The statute of frauds applies to any agreement that is not to be performed within one year from the time it is made, and any sale of goods for $500 or more. It applies to any contract that is not to be performed during the lifetime of the promisor. It also applies to a promise to pay another's debt, or guarantee payment of another's debt. Most importantly for our purposes, the statute of frauds applies to these contracts concerning real property:

1. An agreement for the sale, exchange, or an interest in real property.
2. A lease of real property that will expire more than one year after it was signed.
3. An agency agreement authorizing an agent to purchase or sell real property, or lease it for more than one year. (A power of attorney, for example.)
4. An agency agreement authorizing an agent to "procure, introduce, or find" a buyer or seller (or lessee or lessor, for a lease for more than one year), if the agent will receive compensation. (A listing agreement, for example.)
5. An assumption of a mortgage or deed of trust.

To be enforceable, any of these contracts must be in writing and signed.

Although any listing agreement or finder's contract must be in writing if the agent expects to be paid (#4 on the list above), the statute of frauds doesn't apply to a commission-splitting agreement between two brokers. If a listing broker orally agrees to share a commission with another broker, they have a valid contract. The cooperating broker can sue the listing broker to collect his or her share.

The statute of frauds doesn't explicitly mention mortgages or deeds of trust, but they are considered agreements for the sale of an interest in real property (#1 on the list above). In any case, a separate provision of the Civil Code requires them to be in writing and signed.

The statute of frauds also doesn't mention employment agreements between brokers and salespersons. Nonetheless, these agreements do have to be in writing and signed—it's required by the Real Estate Commissioner's Regulations.

2. What Kind of Writing Satisfies the Statute of Frauds

The writing required by the statute of frauds doesn't have to be a formal legal document. A note or memorandum is enough if it indicates there is an agreement between the parties and it is signed.

Case Example: Mr. Seck, a real estate broker, had known Mr. Foulks for a long time. Foulks asked Seck to help him sell his ranch in Sacramento County, and Seck agreed.

However, Foulks refused to give Seck a formal listing agreement. "You know doggone well you know me, I'm not going to cheat you out of a commission," Foulks said. But Seck took out one of his business cards and jotted down the basic terms of the listing on the back of the card. It looked like this: ▼

---

310 M/L	quarterly with int
2000 per acre	keep taxes up to date
1/2 down	1/2 mineral rights
bal. 5 years	6% comm
5% int	10/1/65

Seck asked Foulks to initial and date the card. Foulks wrote, "3/24/65 GWF."

Seck found a buyer for the ranch, but Foulks refused to pay Seck a commission. When Seck sued, Foulks argued that the notes on the business card weren't enough to comply with the statute of frauds. But the court disagreed. The court said that all Seck needed was some written, signed note indicating the fact of employment. This requirement was fulfilled by "6% comm" and Foulks's initials on the business card. *Seck v. Foulks*, 25 Cal. App. 3d 556, 102 Cal. Rptr. 170 (1972).

To comply with the statute of frauds, a contract only needs to have been signed by "the party to be charged"—that is, the one who's being sued. For example, it didn't matter that Seck hadn't signed the business card as long as Foulks had. A full signature is unnecessary; initials are enough. In fact, anything that the signer intends as a signature will do. However, it may be difficult to prove that a wavy line or an "X" was someone's signature if that person later denies it.

Once you've signed a contract, you're bound by its terms, even if you claim you never read it. Before signing, an illiterate person must ask someone trustworthy to explain all the terms of a written agreement. The same is true for a person signing a document written in a foreign language. (However, California law has a special rule for certain loan contracts and residential leases: when the contract was negotiated in Spanish but is written in English, the signer must be given a written translation of the document.) Of course, if someone convinces another person to sign a document by misrepresenting its contents, that's fraud, and the contract is voidable.

F. PROMISSORY ESTOPPEL

As you can see, there are many potential pitfalls in making a contract: the other party may lack capacity; the process of offer and acceptance may have gone wrong; consideration might be missing, or a signed writing might have been necessary. Many people aren't aware of these legal requirements, and they are often surprised to discover that a promise someone made them is unenforceable. The outcomes of some contract lawsuits seem very unfair.

To prevent unfairness in at least a few cases, the courts have developed the doctrine of **promissory estoppel** (also called the doctrine of **detrimental reliance**). *THE DOCTRINE OF PROMISSORY ESTOPPEL allows the courts to preclude the maker of false statements from denying them and treats them as promises, if the promisee relied on them in good faith and to his/her advantage.* Here's an outline of the kind of situation in which this doctrine is applied:

1. A makes a promise to B.

2. A should realize that the promise is likely to induce B to take some action.

3. B does, in fact, take action in reasonable reliance on A's promise.

4. If A is not required to fulfill the promise, B will suffer harm because of his or her reliance on it.

In such a case, a court may decide to enforce the promise, even though there was no consideration, no signed writing, or some other contractual defect.

Example: M is S's mother. M bought a large tract of land and promised to give it to S. S cleared and fenced the land. He built a house on it and moved in with his wife.

Two years later, M and S have a fight. M tells S and his wife to get off her property, but they refuse to leave. M sues to regain possession of her land.

Originally, M's promise to S was not enforceable since S did not give M any consideration in exchange for her promise, and there was no signed writing. But the court uses the doctrine of promissory estoppel to rule in S's favor. M should have realized that her promise would induce action by S, and she was, in fact, aware of all his work on the property. S's reliance on M's promise was reasonable, so the court rules that S and his wife are entitled to possession of the property.

It's important to remember that the doctrine of promissory estoppel will only be applied when the promisee's reliance on the promise was reasonable. In *Phillippe v. Shapell Industries, Inc.*, 43 Cal. 3d 1247, 241 Cal. Rptr. 22 (1987), the California Supreme Court ruled that a real estate broker without a written listing cannot use promissory estoppel to collect a commission. A broker is supposed to know that a written agreement is necessary. In effect, it is never reasonable for a broker to rely on a client's verbal promise.

However, promissory estoppel can be used in a broker's favor if the client fraudulently misled the broker into believing they had a valid written agreement.

Case Example: Mr. Owens, a broker, orally agreed to help the Foundation for Ocean Research (FOR) sell a large tract of land in San Diego. Owens began working after a lawyer representing the FOR told him a written listing agreement had been prepared and formally accepted by the board of directors, But, in fact, the board never accepted a written agreement, and the FOR later refused to pay a commission. Owens sued.

The court ruled that because the FOR fraudulently led Owens to believe there was a signed writing, it was estopped from using the writing requirement as a defense to his claim for a commission. *Owens v. Foundation for Ocean Research*, 107 Cal. App. 3d 179, 165 Cal. Rptr. 571 (1980).

Remember, too, that the statute of frauds only applies to an action for breach of contract. Even when a broker does not have a valid contract, he or she may be able to sue a client for fraud (which is a tort action, not a contract action).

III. Performance and Breach of Contract

If one party to a contract performs his or her side of the bargain, the other party is also required to perform. If one party fails to perform (breaches the contract), the other is not required to perform. If I contract to build you a house for $250,000 and I don't build the house, you don't owe me $250,000.

CHAPTER 7

In most cases, each party carries out the promised performance to the other's satisfaction. In some cases, one party clearly fails to do what he or she promised.

Sometimes, however, it's not so clear-cut. One party (A) does all of the things promised, but the other party (B) feels they were not done well. Or A does nearly everything promised, but some details aren't taken care of. Or A does everything promised, but takes longer to do it than agreed. In these cases, there is room for argument about whether or not the contract was breached. Is B required to perform his side of the bargain?

The answer to that question depends on whether there has been **substantial performance** or a **material breach**. If A hasn't fulfilled every detail of the contract, but has carried out its main objectives, that may be treated as substantial performance. Although B may be able to sue for damages because of the unfulfilled details, they don't excuse B from performing his side of the bargain.

On the other hand, if A fails to perform some important part of the contract, or performs very badly, it will be treated as a material breach. If A commits a material breach, B is excused from fulfilling his promises. If B doesn't perform, he won't be liable to A for breach of their contract because A already materially breached it. (If B has already fully performed, A will be required to pay him damages for breach of contract.)

What provisions of a contract are so important that failure to fulfill them amounts to a material breach? That depends on all the circumstances of each case. If the promisee emphasized to the promisor that a particular detail of the contract was especially important, failure to comply with that detail may be a material breach. On the other hand, if the promisee acted as though a detail was unimportant, failure to comply with it isn't a material breach.

> **Case Example:** Because of financial problems, Mrs. Fong put her house up for sale. Mr. and Mrs. Converse wanted to buy it, so they signed a purchase contract that called for a $5,000 deposit. The Converses could only come up with $3,000, but said they'd pay the other $2,000 soon. Then Mrs. Fong's children gave her some money so that she wouldn't have to sell the house. Fong tried to back out of her contract with the Converses, but they sued. Fong argued that their failure to pay the full deposit was a material breach, so she couldn't be required to sell them the house.
>
> The court disagreed. Fong had requested the deposit to show the State Franchise Tax Board the house would be sold, to delay a forced tax sale of the property. The Converses' $3,000 served that purpose, and Fong said nothing to indicate that it was urgent for them to pay her the remainder. Fong did not suffer any harm as a result of the delay in payment. It was not a material breach, and Fong had to go through with the sale. *Converse v. Fong*, 159 Cal. App. 3d 86, 205 Cal. Rptr. 242 (1984).

Many standard contract forms state that "**time is of the essence**." *TIME IS OF THE ESSENCE refers to acts described in a contract that must be performed within time limits described in the contract.* The purpose of including "time is of the essence" is to emphasize that timely performance is crucial. This makes failure to meet a deadline a material breach. Otherwise, a delay isn't a material breach as long as performance is completed within a reasonable time after the deadline. It is often a printed clause in a standard "fill-in-the-blanks" contract form.

A. CONDITIONS

#47

Contracts often include one or more conditions (sometimes called contingency clauses). A *CONDITION makes the promisor's obligation dependent on the occurrence of a particular event.* If the event does not occur, the promisor can withdraw without liability for breach of contract. For example, many purchase agreements are contingent on whether the buyers qualify for financing, or on the results of an appraisal, termite inspection, or soil test.

When a contract is conditional, the promisor must make a good faith effort to fulfill the condition. He or she can't deliberately prevent its fulfillment to get out of the contract.

> **Case Example:** The contract provided that the buyer had the right to review and approve certain reports as a condition to the close of escrow, within 28 days of their receipt. Within that time, the buyer disapproved of the reports and proposed some novel ways to keep the "deal alive." Having not heard from the seller, 60 days later, the buyer wrote the seller that the objections were waived and to proceed and close escrow. The seller then canceled escrow. The buyer refused to cancel escrow and sued for specific performance.
>
> The Court of Appeal held that the approval of the reports was a condition that had to occur before the buyer's duty to purchase arose (condition precedent). The disapproval was rejection of the reports, which therefore terminated the contract. The condition gave the buyer the option to terminate the contract, which the buyer did. Once the contract was terminated, it was impossible to revive it. The buyers were then unable to waive the objections to the reports. *Beverly Way Associates v. Barhan*, 226 Cal. App. 3d 49, 276 Cal. Rptr. 240 (1990).

A condition can be waived by the party it was intended to benefit or protect.

Example: The purchase agreement is contingent on a satisfactory termite inspection. It states that if the results of the inspection are unsatisfactory, the buyer can withdraw from the purchase unless the seller takes action to correct the problems revealed.

The inspection shows that the house is infested with termites. The seller informs the buyer that she is not going to correct the problem, but the buyer decides to go ahead with the purchase. The buyer has a right to waive the condition because it was included in the contract for his protection.

When a condition is included for the benefit of both parties, neither one can waive it without the other's consent.

Example: B has interviewed for a job with a certain company, but it will be another month before he hears whether they've hired him. L agrees to loan B some money on the condition that B gets the job. This condition protects both B and L: it prevents B from taking out a loan he won't be able repay, and it prevents L from lending to someone who's very likely to default.

Suppose B doesn't get the job after all, but he still wants to borrow the money. He'd like to waive the condition. B can't waive it unilaterally, however, as L must also agree to waive it, or the contract is void.

CHAPTER 7

B. TENDERING PERFORMANCE

In many cases, one party (A) has reason to believe that the other (B) is not going to fulfill the contract. The time for performance has arrived, and B hasn't taken any steps toward carrying out her side of the bargain. Before A can sue B for breach of contract, he is required to offer to perform his side of the bargain. *An offer of performance by one party is called a tender offer or simply a TENDER.*

> **Example:** B contracted to buy A's house, but A suspects B doesn't plan to go through with the purchase. On the agreed closing date, A must offer to deliver the deed to B as promised in their contract. If B refuses to pay A and accept the deed, B is in default, and A may sue.

A tender must be made in good faith. In other words, the tendering party must be willing and able to perform everything he or she promised, fully and immediately. The tender must be unconditional, unless the contract contained a condition that the other party hasn't fulfilled yet.

It is not necessary to tender performance when there has been an **anticipatory repudiation**. *ANTICIPATORY REPUDIATION is the unjustifiable denial by a party to a contract of any intention to perform contractual duties, which occurs prior to the time performance is due.* If B repudiates the contract by notifying A that she won't perform, A can file suit for breach without making a tender. (The tender would be a waste of time.) An anticipatory repudiation must be a clear, unequivocal statement. A can't infer repudiation from B's behavior or from a vague remark.

IV. Discharge of a Contract

A. MODIFICATION OF A CONTRACT

When both parties agree that their written contract contains an error or omission, they can replace it with a new written contract.

Oral modifications of written contracts must be supported by new consideration.

> **Example:** In March, A agrees to buy B's house for $150,000, and closing is set for April 30. A few days later, A realizes he's not going to have the money by then. He asks B if he'd be willing to modify their contract so that closing will take place on June 1. B agrees, just because he's a nice guy, but no new contract is written up.
>
> Then B discovers he absolutely has to have the sale proceeds by May 15. He asks A if closing can be moved back to May 14, but A refuses.
>
> B can enforce the contract as it was originally written (with an April 30 closing). The modification is unenforceable, because B did not receive any consideration for his promise to move the closing date to June 1.
>
> If A had provided consideration for the modification—for example, by promising to pay $150,500 instead of $150,000—then it would be enforceable, and B could not demand an April 30 closing.

There are exceptions to this consideration requirement. For example, when the parties' original contract was oral, it can be modified in writing without new consideration. Once a modification is executed rather than executory—in other words, the agreement as modified has already been performed—a lack of consideration for the modification doesn't matter.

An oral contract can be modified orally if new consideration is supplied. A written contract can also be modified orally if new consideration is supplied or if the oral agreement is executed, unless it says that it can only be modified in writing, or unless the contract as modified is subject to the statute of frauds. Thus, a modification of any purchase agreement or listing agreement must be in writing to be effective.

MODIFICATION

A modification must be supported by <u>new consideration</u> **unless**:

1. the original contract was oral and the modification is in writing; or
2. the modification is already executed (not executory).

A modification must be <u>in writing</u> **if**:

1. the original contract provides that it can only be modified in writing; or
2. the contract as modified is required to be in writing by the statute of frauds.

Otherwise, the modification may be oral, as long as it is supported by new consideration or the oral agreement has been executed.

---

1. Assignment

When one party to a contract transfers his or her contractual rights and duties to another person, it's called an ASSIGNMENT. Generally, a promisor can't assign his or her duties without the promisee's consent. As a general rule, however, a promisee may assign his or her rights without the promisor's consent unless the contract states that consent is required. In fact, many contracts do require consent to an assignment.

> **Example:** L and T sign a two-year residential lease. It provides that T, the tenant, cannot assign her rights under the lease (the right to live in the apartment) to anyone else without L's permission.
>
> However, the contract doesn't prevent L from assigning his rights to someone else without T's permission. L assigns the lease to C; L is the assignor and C is the assignee. Now T is required to pay rent to C.

Even without a provision prohibiting assignment, a contract for personal services can't be assigned without consent. If you hire me to play the piano at a birthday party, I can't send my sister over instead. (Listing agreements are considered personal services contracts.) A contract also can't be assigned without consent if the assignment would significantly change the other party's duties or increase his or her risks.

Even when the other party consents to an assignment, the assignor isn't relieved of liability under the contract. The assignor is secondarily liable, and can be required to pay the other party if the assignee doesn't.

> **Example:** L and T sign a two-year lease that prohibits T from assigning it without L's consent. A year later, T asks L for permission to assign the lease to X, and L agrees. T

moves out and X moves in, but X doesn't pay the rent. Not only can L sue X, L can still sue T. If X turns out to be judgment-proof, L can collect the judgment from T.

2. Novation

To avoid secondary liability, a party who wants to withdraw from a contract should request a novation instead of an assignment. In a *NOVATION, a new person takes the place of one of the parties, and the withdrawing party is completely relieved of liability connected with the contract.*

A novation can only be arranged with the other original party's consent.

A novation is essentially a new contract, so it must comply with all the rules for contract formation, including the mutual consent requirement.

Note that the term "novation" doesn't necessarily refer to the substitution of a new party. It can also refer to the substitution of a new obligation in place of the original one. If the original parties tear up a two-year lease and execute a five-year lease, that's a novation.

3. Accord and Satisfaction

Sometimes, especially when there is a good faith dispute over contract performance, a promisee agrees to accept something different or less than what the original contract required the promisor to provide. This kind of agreement is called an ACCORD; it does not have to be supported by separate consideration. To extinguish the promisor's original obligation, the promisee executes a *SATISFACTION, which is a document expressly stating that the promisor's performance has been accepted in satisfaction of the obligation.*

4. Release

A contractual obligation can be eliminated altogether if the promisee grants the promisor a **release**. An oral release is valid if the promisee receives some new consideration; a written release doesn't have to be supported by new consideration. When the contract has to be in writing because of the statute of frauds, the release should also be in writing.

V. Remedies for Breach of Contract

When a promisor has performed badly, or has refused to perform at all (either by anticipatory repudiation or by rejecting the tender offer), he or she has breached the contract. The promisee can then turn to the legal system for help in enforcing the contract.

A. ARBITRATION

As we discussed in Chapter 1, the courts are overflowing with litigation, and it can take years for a case to get to trial. Because of these long delays, more and more contracts include arbitration provisions. These provisions will be discussed in Chapter 9.

ARBITRATION is an alternative to the court system. To save time and money, the parties to a dispute can agree to submit to arbitration instead of going to court. They hire an arbitrator to perform the functions of a judge: reviewing the evidence and resolving the dispute. When an arbitration provision is initialed in a real estate purchase contract, the parties agree in advance to arbitrate if a dispute arises.

Arbitration is usually much more informal than a trial; the discovery process is limited and the rules of evidence are relaxed. Unless otherwise agreed, the arbitrator's decision will be legally binding on the parties—the loser can't just shrug it off. Often they don't even have a right to appeal the decision to the court system. In their effort to save time and money, the parties agree to give that up.

As you can see, an arbitration provision in a contract has a significant effect on the parties' rights in the event of a breach. There was concern that many people involved in real estate transactions sign contracts containing arbitration provisions without understanding the legal consequences. As a result, the California legislature adopted a statute requiring real estate contracts with binding arbitration provisions to include a warning in large, boldface type. The warning states in part:

YOU ARE GIVING UP ANY RIGHTS YOU MIGHT POSSESS TO HAVE THE DISPUTE LITIGATED IN A COURT OR JURY TRIAL... YOU ARE GIVING UP YOUR JUDICIAL RIGHTS TO DISCOVERY AND APPEAL, UNLESS THOSE RIGHTS ARE SPECIFICALLY INCLUDED... IF YOU REFUSE TO SUBMIT TO ARBITRATION AFTER AGREEING TO THIS PROVISION, YOU MAY BE COMPELLED TO ARBITRATE...

This statute applies to any contract containing an arbitration clause that conveys real property or concerns a possible future conveyance of real property. This includes marketing contracts, purchase agreements, installment land contracts, and leases with options to purchase. It also applies to any agreement between a principal and an agent in a real property sale, such as a listing agreement.

www.rereader.com/alanslaw/alanslaw13.html
Arbitration Clauses in Real Estate Contracts

B. CONTRACT LAWSUIT

1. Statute of Limitations

In California, a lawsuit based on a written contract generally must be filed within four years after the breach occurred. For some oral contracts (such as an oral employment contract, or an oral six-month lease), suit must be filed within two years after the breach. However, suit can be filed within four years in the case of any contract (oral or written) for the sale of goods—that is, a sale of personal property, not real property.

The parties to a contract can agree to a shorter limitation period than the one prescribed by statute, but the period must not be unreasonably short. In a contract for the sale of goods, the parties can agree to shorten the limitation period to one year, but not less.

These limitation periods apply even when the suing party was not aware of the breach at the time it occurred. However, suit can be filed within four years in the case of any contract (oral or written) for the sale of goods—that is, a sale of most types of tangible personal property, not real property or intangible personal property (such as corporate stock or copyrights).

CHAPTER 7

2. Interpretation of the Contract

To decide whether a contract has been performed or breached, the court must interpret the parties' agreement. The court tries to give effect to what the parties intended when they entered the contract.

When the contract is in writing, the court is supposed to determine the parties' intention from the written document alone, if possible. If the document is unclear or ambiguous, the judge will let the parties testify about their negotiations in drawing up the contract, to shed light on the intended meaning of the document. When the language in the document is clear and unambiguous, the judge should refuse to admit evidence about negotiations or oral agreements that contradict the terms of the written agreement.

Example: T is going to lease a townhouse from L for nine months. The written lease form clearly states that rent is due on the first of each month. Before signing the lease, T asks L if she can pay the rent on the 15th of each month instead, and L agrees. They don't change the lease form to reflect this agreement, however.

Later, T and L wind up in court. T wants to testify that L agreed to accept the rent on the 15th of each month, but the judge may decide to exclude this testimony. The written contract is clear about the 1st, and there was no new consideration agreed to for a change to the 15th.

This is known as the **parol evidence rule**. ("Parol" is a legal term that means "spoken.") The parol evidence rule states that when parties intend a written contract to be the final expression of their agreement, the written terms cannot be contradicted by evidence of any prior oral or written agreement or any oral agreement that was made at the same time as the written agreement (called a contemporaneous oral agreement).

Case Example: In June 1988, EPA Real Estate Partnership signed a listing agreement with Feher Young and Associates Commercial Brokerage (Young) to sell its apartment complex for $2.5 million. The listing expired August 15, 1988 and included a 6% commission. On July 18 Kang submitted an offer directly to Jack Horton, one of the partners of EPA, for $2.45 million, which Horton declined because of the 6% commission to Young. Kang suggested signing a contract to sell the property to him at the expiration of the listing if it remained unsold at that time. Young said he would not do that because of the commission. Kang assured Horton that the contract would include a promise to indemnify EPA should it be obligated to pay the commission as a result of this sale. Later, Kang returned with the July 18 offer and a separate addendum that included the indemnity clause and Horton signed it.

On August 19, Kang presented a new sales agreement, which was signed. However, on September 30, the parties signed yet another new agreement for the sale of the apartment complex for $2.35 million. This agreement contained the following clause: "19. Entire Contract: Time is of the essence. All prior agreements between the parties are incorporated in this agreement which constitutes the entire contract. Its terms are intended by the parties as a final expression of their agreement with respect to such terms as are included herein and may not be contradicted by evidence of any prior agreement or contemporaneous oral agreement. The parties further intend that this agreement constitutes the complete and exclusive statement of its terms and that no extrinsic evidence whatsoever may be introduced in any judicial or arbitrary proceeding, if any, involving this agreement." ▼

The September 30 agreement did not contain an indemnity clause. After conveying title to Kang, Young sued EPA for its commission and demanded arbitration pursuant to the listing agreement. The arbitrator awarded Young $249,394.33, which EPA paid. EPA also incurred litigation cost of $41,739.26 in defending a Young's claim. EPA sued Kang after it was unsuccessful in seeking indemnity from Kang for the commission. Judgment for Kang. EPA appealed.

The parol evidence rule generally prohibits the introduction of extrinsic evidence, oral or written, to vary or contradict terms of an integrated written instrument. Had EPA wished to include an indemnity provision in the final contract of September 30, Horton should have expressly done so in the document or referred to it in any earlier document. The September 30 agreement superseded all prior understandings related to the sale of the property. Judgment affirmed. *EPA Real Estate Partnership v. Kang*, 12 Cal. App. 4th 171, 15 Cal. Rptr. 2d 209 (1992).

This rule, like the statute of frauds, is intended to cut down on false claims and prevent promisors from weaseling out of what they agreed to do. However, parol evidence is admissible to clarify an ambiguity or show fraud, mutual mistake, duress, forgery, or illegality of the subject matter. Parol evidence is admissable to show a subsequent agreement (modification), or that the parties did not intend a binding contract until a condition outside of the contract was satisfied (approval by an inspector).

Suppose that, in the previous example, T asked L several months after signing the lease to agree to accept rent payments on the 15th, and L verbally agreed. This modification agreement comes into court because it occurred after the written contract. However, T loses because there was no consideration to support the modification. T should have gotten L to agree in writing to payments on the 15th for consideration of $10 more rent each month.

3. Damages

Once the court has concluded there has been a breach of contract, it must decide on a remedy. The most common remedy for breach of contract is a *DAMAGES award, where the breaching party is ordered to pay a sum of money to the nonbreaching party.* How much? The award is supposed to be the amount that will put the nonbreaching party in the position he or she would have been in if the other party had fulfilled the contract.

Example: Perkins contracted to clear Hanawalt's property for $10,000, but he quit the project soon after starting. Hanawalt then hired Lopez to carry out the job. Lopez charged her $12,000.

Hanawalt sues Perkins for breach of contract, and Perkins is ordered to pay her $2,000. If Perkins had not breached the contract, it would only have cost Hanawalt $10,000 (rather than $12,000) to have her property cleared. The $2,000 judgment against Perkins represents the difference between what the job actually cost Hanawalt and what it would have cost her if Perkins hadn't breached: $12,000 - $10,000 = $2,000.

However, if Lopez had charged Hanawalt only $9,000 to clear the property, Hanawalt would actually have been better off as a result of Perkins's breach. The job would have cost her $1,000 less than it would have if Perkins had fulfilled the contract. In that case, Hanawalt

CHAPTER 7

would not be entitled to a judgment against Perkins because she wasn't damaged by his breach. The point of a contract lawsuit is to compensate the promisee for actual damages, not to punish the promisor for breaching. Punitive damages are generally only awarded in cases involving a tort (such as fraud), not for breach of contract. (See Chapter 6.)

4. Certainty Requirement

To be the basis for a damages award, a loss resulting from breach of contract must be proven with reasonable certainty. Occasionally, a contract lawsuit includes a claim for **lost profits**: "If Z hadn't breached the contract, I could have opened my store a month earlier, and I would have made at least $1,000 in profit during that month." In most cases, lost profits are considered too uncertain to be included in the judgment. Who knows whether the store would have turned a profit if it had been opened that month? It might even have lost money. Unless the evidence proves that there would have been a profit, and that it definitely would have been at least a certain amount, lost profits are not awarded. Certainly a business with a lengthy profit history stands a better chance of recovering lost profits than a new business.

5. Mitigation Requirement

The nonbreaching party in a contract dispute is required to *MITIGATE DAMAGES, which means the nonbreaching party must do what he or she can to cut down on losses resulting from the other party's breach.*

> **Example:** L leases an apartment to T for one year; T has agreed to pay $1,000 a month. Two months later, T decides she doesn't like the place, so she moves out and doesn't make any further rent payments. This is clearly a breach of contract.
>
> If L finds a new tenant for $1,000 per month, T will not be liable for any unpaid rent for the remaining term of the lease. However, T would be liable for unpaid rent for any period of time that the property was vacant before the new tenant began paying rent and for any expenses L incurred in renting the apartment again, such as costs of advertising.
>
> If L finds a new tenant for $1,000 a month, T will not be liable for any of her unpaid rent. However, T may be required to reimburse L for any expenses incurred in renting the apartment again, such as the cost of advertising.
>
> Suppose no one will rent the apartment for $1,000 a month, but someone rents it for $800 a month. Then T will be liable to L for the difference between what L actually collects and what she would have collected if T hadn't breached: $200 per month for 10 months. The damages award would be $2,000 ($200 x 10 = $2,000), plus expenses.

6. Liquidated Damages

To lessen the possibility of expensive litigation, some contracts include a *LIQUIDATED DAMAGES PROVISION, wherein the parties agree in advance that if there is a breach, the damages are set at a specified sum or calculated according to a specified formula.* The nonbreaching party will accept the liquidated damages instead of suing for actual damages.

$4n

failed to paint = $10

270

> **Case Example:** The Angells contracted to buy the Felicianos' home. To finance the purchase, the Angells executed a $30,000 deed of trust in favor of the Felicianos.
>
> The deed of trust had a liquidated damages provision: if the transaction was not closed by November 1, the Angells would pay the Felicianos $22 per day until it did close. That amount was intended to cover the trust deed interest that the Felicianos would lose because of the delay.
>
> As it turned out, closing was several days late because the Angells had some trouble selling their previous home. The Angells had to pay the Felicianos $261 in liquidated damages. *Angell v. Rowlands*, 85 Cal. App. 3d 536, 149 Cal. Rptr. 574 (1978).

As a general rule, a court will enforce a liquidated damages provision unless one of the parties proves that the amount agreed to was unreasonable at the time the contract was made. "Without the benefit of a valid liquidated damages clause, a seller of real estate may retain the deposit only to the extent that actual damages where incurred." *Kuish v. Smith*, 181 Cal.App.4th 1419 (2010).

There are also restrictions on liquidated damages for certain types of contracts. For residential leases, a liquidated damages clause is void unless it would be extremely difficult to calculate the actual damages after a breach. The same rule is true for consumer contracts for the retail purchase, or rental, of personal property. A liquidated damage provision in a residential lease or a consumer personal property purchase agreement is, therefore, rarely enforceable.

In a contract to purchase real property, the buyer and seller often agree to treat the buyer's deposit as liquidated damages. If they do, the seller is entitled to keep the deposit if the buyer breaches the contract. However, California has some statutory limits on use of the deposit as liquidated damages. These apply in a transaction involving residential property with up to four units if the buyer intends to occupy one of the units. If the amount paid under the contract's liquidated damages provision is 3% of the purchase price or less, the provision is presumed to be valid. The seller can keep that much of the deposit unless the buyer proves the amount is unreasonable under the circumstances. If the amount paid is more than 3% of the price, a court will regard the provision as invalid, unless the seller can prove that the amount is reasonable. In any case, the liquidated damages provision must appear in large, boldface type in the contract, and it must be separately initialed or signed by the parties.

7. Equitable Remedies

A damage award—a sum of money intended to compensate the nonbreaching party—is the standard remedy in a contract dispute, but money doesn't always do the trick. In some cases, alternative remedies are available.

a. Injunction

An **INJUNCTION** *is a court order directing a person to do something or refrain from doing something* (see Chapter 1). As a general rule, a court cannot issue an injunction to keep someone from breaching a contract. The law requires payment of damages for breach, but ordinarily does not prevent the breach.

The handful of exceptions to that rule rarely apply to cases involving real estate contracts. However, an injunction can be issued to prevent the breach of a restrictive covenant (see Chapter 13), if it can be shown that the breach will cause irreparable harm. Harm is considered irreparable if it can't be adequately redressed by a damages award.

b. Rescission

If someone has done wrong to you in a contract, you may not want to go through with the contract. Instead, you may just want to undo the contract, erase it, go back to square one. In that case, you may ask a court to rescind the contract. With *RESCISSION, each party returns any consideration the other has given (this is called RESTITUTION), all contractual obligations are terminated, and everthing is returned to its pre-contract state.*

Rescission is available under a variety of circumstances. Whenever a voidable contract is disaffirmed—because of lack of capacity, fraud, undue influence, duress, menace, or mistake—the court will rescind it. One party can request rescission if the other party failed to provide the promised consideration or if that consideration turns out to be void. A court will also rescind an unlawful contract (unless the unlawfulness was clear from the contract's terms and the parties were equally at fault—then a court will refuse to become involved in any way).

A contract can also be rescinded without going to court if both parties agree. In some situations, however, they may prefer to **cancel** their contract instead of rescinding it. When a contract is cancelled, all further obligations are terminated, but the parties aren't required to return what they've already received under the contract.

c. Specific Performance

Sometimes the nonbreaching party to a contract doesn't just want to be compensated for the harm that resulted from the other's breach. Instead, the nonbreaching party wants to make the other party do what he or she promised to do.

Think back to a case described earlier in this chapter, *Converse v. Fong*. Mrs. Fong put her house up for sale to prevent foreclosure, and the Converses contracted to buy it. Then Mrs. Fong's children gave her some money so that she wouldn't have to sell her house. Mrs. Fong tried to back out of her contract with the Converses, and they sued. The Converses didn't just want to be compensated for their expenses (the appraisal, inspections, and so forth); they wanted to make Mrs. Fong sell them her house. They had their hearts set on that particular house, and finding a comparable substitute wouldn't be the same. The court ordered Mrs. Fong to complete the sale to the Converses.

This is called *SPECIFIC PERFORMANCE, where the court orders the breaching party to carry out the performance he or she promised in the contract.* Specific performance is not available as a remedy when an award of damages would ~~not~~ be adequate to compensate the non-breaching party. For example, a car dealer won't be ordered to sell you a particular car when you could get an identical one from another dealer. (If you have to pay more at the second dealer, the first dealer is liable to you for the difference as a damages award.) The remedy of specific performance is usually only given when the contract involves unique property. If a contract is for a one of a kind item, then specific performance is an appropriate remedy. A damages award won't enable you to buy an identical one because there isn't another just like it.

Specific performance is most often used in enforcing real estate contracts because a piece of real property is unique—like Mrs. Fong's house. Under a California statute, there is a presumption that a damages award is not sufficient compensation for breach of an agreement to transfer real property. When the property in question is a single-family home that the nonbreaching party intended to occupy, this presumption is conclusive: if the nonbreaching party requests specific performance, the court may order it (some courts will not). When the case involves some other kind of real property, the breaching party is given an opportunity to rebut the presumption by proving that a damages award will be sufficient compensation.

1. When Specific Performance is Not Available

There are many circumstances in which a court cannot grant specific performance. It can never be a remedy for breach of a personal services contract: no one can be forced to work for someone or to employ someone. Specific performance also can't be ordered for an agreement to procure the act or consent of another person, such as when a husband has agreed to persuade his wife to sign a document.

You can't be ordered to perform a contract if it wasn't just and reasonable, or if you didn't receive legally adequate consideration. For example, if you agreed to sell your $350,000 house for $175,000, the contract is enforceable even though the consideration is inadequate. Although you may be required to pay damages to the buyer ($175,000 is likely), you can't be forced to complete the sale. On the other hand, a buyer can't be ordered to complete a purchase of real property when the seller doesn't have marketable title.

You also can't be ordered to perform if the other party hasn't fulfilled all the conditions he or she agreed to. And you can't be ordered to perform if your consent to the contract was obtained by misrepresentation or unfair practices, or if your consent was given because of mistake, misapprehension, or surprise.

In spite of all these restrictions, specific performance is a common remedy when a seller breaches a purchase agreement. Note that specific performance can be ordered even when the contract includes a liquidated damages provision.

C. INTERFERENCE WITH CONTRACTUAL RELATIONS

Sometimes one of the parties to a contract is persuaded to breach it by a third party, someone outside the contractual relationship. For example, another real estate agent might convince your client to breach the listing agreement he has with you, or might persuade a seller to breach a binding purchase agreement and accept a better offer.

These acts may constitute a tort called **interference with contractual relations**. *INTERFERENCE WITH CONTRACTUAL RELATIONS permits a plaintiff to recover damages based upon a claim that a defendant interfered with the plaintiffs contractual relations.* In this case, the nonbreaching party can file a tort lawsuit against the third party, in addition to filing a contract lawsuit against the breaching party. To win the tort suit, the plaintiff must show that the defendant (the third party) was aware of the contract and intentionally disrupted it. Because this is a tort suit instead of a contract suit, punitive damages may be awarded if the defendant's actions were malicious, that is, if they were designed to injure the plaintiff or were done with conscious disregard for the plaintiff's rights.

There is also a tort called *INTENTIONAL INTERFERENCE WITH PROSPECTIVE ECONOMIC ADVANTAGE, which is similar to interference with contractual relations but the plaintiff doesn't have to show that he/she had a binding contract with another person.* It's only necessary to prove that they had an economic relationship and the defendant was aware of that relationship. In *Buckaloo v. Johnson*, 14 Cal. 3d 815, 122 Cal. Rptr. 745 (1975), the California

CHAPTER 7

Supreme Court ruled that a seller's broker without a written listing agreement could sue a buyer and another broker for interference with prospective economic advantage.

In *Aas v. Superior Court (William Lyon Company)*, 24 Cal. 4th 627, 101 Cal. Rptr. 2d 718, 12 P.3d 1125 (2000), the California Supreme Court refused to permit a cause of action for interference with prospective economic advantage where homeowners and a homeowner's association sought to recover damages for negligence from the developer, contractor and subcontractors who built their dwellings for construction defects that had not caused property damage. In dissent, Chief Justice George stated, "In determining that a negligently constructed home must first collapse or be gutted by fire before a homeowner may sue in tort to collect costs necessary to repair negligently constructed shear walls or fire walls, the majority today embraces a ruling that offends both established common law and basic common sense." The majority stated that adopting a rule like that proposed by the Chief Justice was something for the Legislature to do.

VI. CHAPTER SUMMARY

1. A contract is an agreement to do or not do a certain thing. Every contract is either express or implied, unilateral or bilateral, executory or executed, and valid, void, voidable, or unenforceable.

2. A person lacks capacity to contract unless he or she is competent and at least 18 years old. A contract by an incompetent person is void. A contract by a minor is void if it concerns real property; otherwise, it is generally voidable. A contract may be valid if it involves necessities, medical services, art, entertainment or professional sports, or is entered into by an emancipated minor.

3. A valid contract is based on the parties' mutual consent, and achieved through offer and acceptance. Acceptances are effective when sent. An offer must express an objective intent to contract, and it must have definite terms. An offer can be revoked at any time until it has been accepted. Revocations are effective when sent. The offeree's acceptance isn't effective until it has been communicated (sent) to the offeror in the manner specified in the offer. If the offeree changes the terms of the offer, it's a counter offer (rejection), not an acceptance. Rejections are effective when sent

4. When one party has obtained the other's consent through fraud, undue influence, duress, menace, or mistake, the contract is voidable by the victim.

5. A contract generally isn't valid unless it is supported by consideration: each party must give something of value to the other. A contract is enforceable even though the consideration given by the parties is unequal.

6. A court will not enforce a contract unless its purpose is lawful.

7. The statute of frauds requires certain contracts to be in writing and signed by the party to be charged. This includes real estate purchase contracts, leases for more than one year, listing agreements, powers of attorney, and trust deed assumptions. Other laws also require mortgages, trust deeds, and broker/salesperson employment agreements to be in writing and signed.

274

8. A contract modification usually must be supported by new consideration. The modification may be oral unless the original contract stated that it could only be modified in writing, or unless the statute of frauds applies to the contract as modified. Assignment, novation, accord, and satisfaction are specific types of contract modifications.

9. If one party commits a material breach of contract, the other isn't required to fulfill his or her side of the bargain. When there is substantial performance by one party, the other is also required to perform. The nonbreaching party has to tender performance before he or she can sue for breach of contract unless there has been an anticipatory repudiation.

10. When a contract is conditional, the promisor can't get out of it by preventing the condition from being fulfilled. A condition may be waived by the party it was intended to benefit.

11. The most common remedy for breach of contract is compensatory damages; punitive damages are not awarded. The nonbreaching party is required to mitigate the damages. A liquidated damages provision states in advance how much one party will be entitled to collect in the event of a breach. Other remedies for breach of contract are rescission and specific performance.

VII. CASE PROBLEM
Hsu v. Abbara, 9 Cal. 4th 863, 39 Cal. Rptr 2d 824 (1995)

On June 5, 1987, the Abbaras listed their home for sale at $299,900 with Roy Rhino of Merrill Lynch Realty. The Hsus made an offer to purchase the home for $285,000 through their agent Ben Lin on June 8, 1987. The purchase agreement contained a provision for attorney's fees: "In any action between Broker, BUYER or SELLER arising out of this agreement, the prevailing party shall be entitled to reasonable attorney's fees and costs." On June 9, the Abbaras made a counter offer on a standard purchase agreement for $297,000, set to expire at 5 p.m. on June 10, and this counter offer incorporated the terms of the original offer. The Hsus viewed the property a second time and on the bottom of the counter offer wrote "All terms are accepted except price to be $292,000" and "this counter offer is good until 11 a.m. on June 10."

On the evening of June 9, Lin spoke with Rhino to see if the Abbaras would take a price under $297,000. Rhino said to present a new written offer. Lin called again to say that the Hsus were firm at $292,000. On June 10, Abbaras told Rhino no on $292,000 and to go back to $299,900.

The afternoon of June 10, Rhino received the Abbaras' counter offer ($297,000) with the "All terms are accepted except price to be $292,000" lined out. In its place was handwritten "offer terms are accepted." Rhino called the Abbaras to report that Hsus agreed on $297,000. Abbaras said anything less than full price was not acceptable. Rhino was unsuccessful in finding another house for the Abbaras, who then decided not to sell. Rhino prepared escrow instructions, which Hsus signed but Abbaras did not. On June 22, Hsus sued the Abbaras for specific performance.

Was there a contract?

CHAPTER 7

VIII. KEY TERMS

acceptance	express/implied	right of first refusal
accord and satisfaction	liquidated damages	severable
assignment	material breach	specific performance
breach	menace	statute of frauds
cancellation	mitigation	substantial performance
capacity	mutual mistake	tender offer
consideration	novation	undue influence
contingency clause	offer	unenforceable
counter offer	offeror/offeree	unilateral/bilateral
disaffirm	parol evidence rule	valid
duress	promisor/promisee	void
economic duress	promissory estoppel	voidable
executory/executed	rescission	

IX. CHAPTER QUIZ

1. A offers to pay B $2,000 to set fire to A's motor home so that she can collect money under her vehicle insurance policy. B accepts the offer. B sets fire to the motor home, completely destroying it. A now refuses to pay B. Will B be successful in a lawsuit against A to recover the contract price?

    a. Yes, because B fully performed this bilateral contract.

    b. Yes, this was a unilateral contract offer and B completed performance, thereby forming a unilateral contract.

    c. Yes, B can recover the agreed compensation, but may be prosecuted for a crime.

    d. No, this is not an enforceable contract because it requires an illegal act.

2. With regard to an emancipated minor:

    a. his/her contracts are voidable.

    b. his/her contracts are voidable only if the contracts involve necessities.

    c. his/her contracts are binding and enforceable.

    d. an emancipated minor cannot enter into a binding and enforceable contract for the purchase of real estate.

3. A unilateral mistake occurs when:

    a. one party to a contract makes the mistake.

    b. both parties to a contract make a mistake.

    c. a unicyclist makes a mistake.

    d. the government makes a mistake.

4. The statute of limitations:

    a. sets a maximum dollar amount that can be recovered in a judgment for breach of contract.

    b. sets the period of time in which a lawsuit may be brought.

    c. limits the way an offer may be accepted.

    d. limits the jurisdiction of the small claims court.

5. Punitive damages are:

    a. available to a prevailing plaintiff in a breach of contract lawsuit.
    b. only awarded in cases involving a tort (such as fraud), and not for breach of contract.
    c. awarded to place the victim of the breach in the position he or she would have been in if the breaching party had fulfilled the contract.
    d. none of the above.

6. In California, there is a presumption that a liquidated damages provision in a contract for the sale of residential property is valid if the amount of the liquidated damages is no more than what percent of the purchase price?

    a. 2%
    b. 3%
    c. 5%
    d. 6%

7. If the contract provides for the amount of damages in the event of a breach at the time the contract is signed, that provision is called a(n):

    a. bilateral provision.
    b. unilateral provision.
    c. liquidated damage.
    d. an illegal provision in California.

8. If the parol evidence rule applies:

    a. the evidence comes into court.
    b. the evidence does not come into court.
    c. the evidence is thrown out of court along with the attorney.
    d. the defendant will win the lawsuit.

9. If a person's obligation depends on the occurrence of a particular event, then that obligation is subject to:

    a. the statute of limitations.
    b. a condition.
    c. an accord.
    d. a satisfaction.

10. Technically, with regard to the statute of frauds:

    a. the contract must be signed by both parties to be enforceable in court.
    b. the contract does not have to be signed by either party.
    c. the contract must be signed by the person being sued.
    d. one of the parties to the contract has committed a fraud on the other party.

ANSWERS: 1. d; 2. c; 3. a; 4. b; 5. b; 6. b; 7. c; 8. b; 9. b; 10. c

STATE OF CALIFORNIA
· Department of Real Estate ·
· Department of Corrections ·

2201

CHAPTER 8
Real Estate Contracts

CHAPTER OVERVIEW

Now that you have a general understanding of the nature of contracts and the terms involved, it is time to explore specific contracts used by people in real estate: an employment contract between a broker and a salesperson, the listing contract between the property owner and the broker, the contracts between the seller and the buyer of the property (generally referred to as the purchase agreement), and options.

A real estate agent is expected to be familiar with several different kinds of contracts, but each contract is just a particular application of the basic rules of contract law that will be outlined in the first part of this chapter.

As you've seen, the statute of frauds requires many of the contracts used in a real estate transaction to be in writing. Even when a signed written contract isn't required by law, it's always wise to have one. The parties to a contract can draft a document for themselves, but it's much safer to use standard forms or (for a complex transaction) to have lawyers do the drafting. A real estate agent preparing a contract for others must use preprinted or prepared forms with minimal additions and changes, or risk liability for the unauthorized practice of law.

Whenever a document is executed in the course of a real estate transaction, the agent must see to it that each party receives a copy at the time of signing. This includes copies of any modifications of the agreements, too.

If a salesperson prepares documents, the salesperson's broker is required to review the documents as part of the broker's supervision responsibility. Remember: the broker must keep copies of all documents pertaining to a transaction for a minimum of three years. This includes copies of all listings, purchase agreement, canceled checks, and trust records.

Some of the contracts commonly used in real estate transactions will be discussed in this and later chapters, including title insurance policies (Chapter 10), escrow instructions (Chapter 11), deeds of trust, mortgages, and land contracts (Chapter 12), and leases (Chapter 15).

This section examines listing agreements, purchase agreements, and options. We've used the California Association of REALTORS® (CAR®) forms to illustrate typical provisions, but many other forms are available. Our use of the CAR® forms is not intended as an endorsement of them, nor as a criticism of any other forms. Keep in mind that the provisions discussed are not necessarily required by law; other forms may not include them, and the parties may choose to alter them.

CHAPTER 8

Mobile Technology and the Real Estate Industry

No chapter on real estate forms would be complete without discussing mobile technology and the effects it has on the industry. Most of the forms presented in this chapter are available for mobile download.

"Thanks to the immediacy of Internet transmissions, you can relieve customers anxieties by instantly generating offers, counter offers, acceptances, and rejections—three days wait time can be condensed into three minutes—saving your clients from sleepless nights."
– Walt Huber

The California Association of REALTORS® offers zipForms® free to their members. zipForms® are constantly upgraded forms that can be downloaded from the Internet (**www.car.org**). The forms you will find in this chapter are available for transactions "on the go" with zipForm® 6 Professional and zipForm® Mobile Web Edition.

zipForms® can now be downloaded to your iPad®, iPhone®, Blackberry®, and Android® devices (in addition to your desktop or laptop computers).

The following can be accomplished using the CAR zipForm® Mobile Web Edition:

1. Create a new transaction.
2. List the forms within a transaction.
3. Add forms from licensed libraries.
4. List and modify transactions by date and time.
5. Fill in all fields with the "edit" feature (and automatically use that information for all transaction file records).
6. Generate forms in PDF or PNG formats, and email forms in PDF format for comments.

More sophisticated tech-savvy users will find additional applications, including the following capabilities:

7. Send documents for electronic signature using the CAR® member benefit zipLogix Digital Ink® when your clients are not with you.
8. Signing directly on tablet devices with TouchSign® (*Tablets only*),
9. Automated email delivery of signed documents to participants;
10. Free faxing.
11. Create sticky notes on your forms (*Tablets only*).
12. Highlight important text on the forms.
13. Use the mortgage calculator.

An **ELECTRONIC SIGNATURE** *is (1) an electronic sound, symbol or process; (2) attached or associated with a contract or other document; and (3) adopted by a person with the intent to sign.* Not all real transactions are allowed to use electronic signatures, but good old-fashioned fax machines and computers with fax-accepting capabilities are still very much in use.

Mobile Tablets, like iPads, are lightening the load of real estate professionals and attorneys—forget about briefcases—a roomful of documents can fit on new mobile devices!

Using Craigslist to Get Ahead (www.craigslist.org)

In this era of social media and wireless communication, more and more REALTORS® are using Craigslist to advertise their properties for sale. You are able to post a picture of the house and even a virtual tour (though a hyperlinked image of your YouTube video. All new postings go to the top of Craigslist until the next one is posted. While classified newspaper ads are not exactly obsolete, it is becoming increasingly popular to check websites like Craigslist for home listings, even if it's just to get a feel for an area or an idea of what prices are going for these days.

While Craig's List is free for most amateur users, as a frequent business user you will eventually be charged a nominal fee for their services — well worth all the exposure your property will get. As with all documents, read the fine print before engaging in any business contract, and show common sense when meeting strangers for the first time in person!

Most real estate brokers take advantage of this free (to consumers) online publication. It gets the property on the market in a matter of minutes, not days and as we all know, "time is money." Interested parties can search the very latest additions to the website through mobile devices instead of waiting for the next day's newspaper.

Considering how prevalent Internet advertising is to the industry, no Real Estate Law textbook would be complete without the following information from the Statewide Buyer and Seller Advisory (SBSA) form (see Chapter 6):

42. INTERNET ADVERTISING; INTERNET BLOGS; SOCIAL MEDIA: Buyer and Seller are advised that Broker may employ a service to provide a "virtual tour" or Internet marketing of the Property, permitting potential buyers to view the Property over the Internet. Additionally, some Internet sites and other social media provide formats for comments or opinions of value of properties that are for sale. Neither the service provider nor Brokers have control over who will obtain access to such services or what action such persons might take. Buyer and Seller are advised that Brokers have no control over how long the information concerning the Property will be available on the Internet or through social media. Brokers do not have expertise in this area.

I. Broker/Salesperson Employment Agreements

The Real Estate Commissioner's Regulations require a broker to have a written employment agreement with each licensee who works for him or her. (This includes other brokers as well as salespersons.) The agreement must be dated and signed by both parties. The Commissioner's regulations require that the agreement cover material aspects of the relationship between the parties, including supervision of licensed activities, duties and compensation. Although brokers may use their own agreement forms to comply with this regulation, the California Association of REALTORS® has developed an agreement form, the **Independent Contractor Agreement (ICA)**, presented in **Figure 8-1**, that can be used by brokers.

Note that the CAR® Independent Contractor Agreement uses the term "Associate-Licensee" instead of salesperson. Associate-Licensee is used because persons who have a broker's license may choose to work under the supervision of another broker. For purposes of explaining this form, we will use the term salesperson instead of Associate-Licensee.

Recall the discussion of the distinctions between independent contractors and employees in Chapter 5. **Paragraph 3A** of the CAR® agreement provides that the salesperson will be treated as an independent contractor to the extent allowed by law, and includes language that allows the broker to treat the salesperson as an independent contractor requirements under IRS rules. However, the salesperson will always be treated as an agent or employee of the broker for supervision purposes, and the broker may be liable for salesperson's wrongful acts. **Paragraph 14** contains an indemnity clause, which allows the broker to pursue the salesperson for reimbursement of any claims or costs that the broker incurs as the result of the salesperson's actions.

In the CAR® form, the broker's control over the salesperson's work is limited to the supervision required by law (**Paragraph 3**). The broker does not have the right to order the salesperson to work on a particular listing, or to direct how the salesperson carries out the work. The broker agrees to provide the salesperson with current listings and the use of the office facilities (**Paragraph 4**). The salesperson agrees to work diligently to sell or lease properties listed with the broker, and to solicit new listings (**Paragraph 4-D-ii**). The broker's control over the salesperson's work is limited to the supervision required by law (**Paragraph 3**). The broker does not have the right to order the salesperson to work on a particular listing, or to direct how the salesperson carries out the work.

Compensation is covered in **Paragraph 8** of the CAR® agreement. **Paragraph 8A** is for the parties to describe the compensation that the broker expects in listing agreements or other agreements that the salesperson may obtain as the broker's agent. **Paragraph 8B** describes how the broker will compensate the salesperson when the salespersons efforts result in the broker being paid under a listing agreement or as a cooperating broker. Note the following language in Paragraph 8B: "Associate-licensee shall receive a share of compensation actually collected by broker,.... " Paragraph 8-B can create a problem when the broker does not pursue collection or chooses to "let the commission go." The conditions to the broker's obligation to pay the salesperson are set out in **Paragraph 8E**. The form states that the salesperson's share of the commission is payable "immediately or as soon thereafter as practicable" (**Paragraph 8-E-i**). This means the broker doesn't have to pay the salesperson unless the commission is collected. By law, the salesperson can only collect the commissions through the broker. Yet nothing in the contract requires the broker to sue the client for the commission or take any other steps to collect it.

The salesperson and broker agree to arbitrate any disputes through the local Association of REALTORS® (**Paragraph 10**). If the Association does not have an arbitration procedure or declines to hear the dispute, then it is arbitrated under the rules of the American Arbitration Association.

Figure 8-1

INDEPENDENT CONTRACTOR AGREEMENT
(Between Broker and Associate-Licensee)
(C.A.R. Form ICA, Revised 6/11)

This Agreement, dated _____ , is made between _____
_____ ("Broker") and
_____ ("Associate-Licensee").
In consideration of the covenants and representations contained in this Agreement, Broker and Associate-Licensee agree as follows:

1. **BROKER:** Broker represents that Broker is duly licensed as a real estate broker by the State of California, ☐ doing business as _____ (firm name), ☐ a sole proprietorship, ☐ a partnership, or ☐ a corporation. Broker is a member of the _____ Association(s) of REALTORS®, and a subscriber to the _____ Multiple Listing Service(s). Broker shall keep Broker's license current during the term of this Agreement.

2. **ASSOCIATE-LICENSEE:** Associate-Licensee represents that: **(i)** he/she is duly licensed by the State of California as a ☐ real estate broker, ☐ real estate salesperson, and **(ii)** he/she has not used any other names within the past five years, except _____ .
Associate-Licensee shall keep his/her license current during the term of this Agreement, including satisfying all applicable continuing education and provisional license requirements.

3. **INDEPENDENT CONTRACTOR RELATIONSHIP:**
   A. Broker and Associate-Licensee intend that, to the maximum extent permissible by law: **(i)** This Agreement does not constitute an employment agreement by either party; **(ii)** Broker and Associate-Licensee are independent contracting parties with respect to all services rendered under this Agreement; and **(iii)** This Agreement shall not be construed as a partnership.
   B. Broker shall not **(i)** restrict Associate-Licensee's activities to particular geographical areas, or **(ii)** dictate Associate-Licensee's activities with regard to hours, leads, open houses, opportunity or floor time, production, prospects, sales meetings, schedule, inventory, time off, vacation, or similar activities, except to the extent required by law.
   C. Associate-Licensee shall not be required to accept an assignment by Broker to service any particular current or prospective listing or parties.
   D. Except as required by law: **(i)** Associate-Licensee retains sole and absolute discretion and judgment in the methods, techniques, and procedures to be used in soliciting and obtaining listings, sales, exchanges, leases, rentals, or other transactions, and in carrying out Associate-Licensee's selling and soliciting activities; **(ii)** Associate-Licensee is under the control of Broker as to the results of Associate-Licensee's work only, and not as to the means by which those results are accomplished; **(iii)** Associate-Licensee has no authority to bind Broker by any promise or representation; and **(iv)** Broker shall not be liable for any obligation or liability incurred by Associate-Licensee.
   E. Associate-Licensee's only remuneration shall be the compensation specified in paragraph 8.
   F. Associate-Licensee who only performs as a real estate sales agent, shall not be treated as an employee for state and federal tax purposes. However, an Associate-Licensee who performs loan activity shall be treated as an employee for state and federal tax purposes unless the activity satisfies the legal requirements to establish an independent contractor relationship.
   G. The fact that Broker may carry workers' compensation insurance for Broker's own benefit and for the mutual benefit of Broker and licensees associated with Broker, including Associate-Licensee, shall not create an inference of employment.
   (Workers' Compensation Advisory:) Even though a Real Estate sales person may be treated as independent contractors for tax and other purposes, the California Labor and Workforce Development Agency considers them to be employees for workers' compensation purposes. According to that Agency: **(i)** Broker must obtain workers' compensation insurance for a Real Estate sales person and **(ii)** Broker, not a Real Estate sales person, must bear the cost of workers' compensation insurance. Penalties for failure to carry workers' compensation include, among others, the issuance of stop-work orders and fines of up to $1,000 per agent, not to exceed $100,000 per company.)

4. **LICENSED ACTIVITY:**
   A. All listings of property, and all agreements, acts or actions for performance of licensed acts, which are taken or performed in connection with this Agreement, shall be taken and performed in the name of Broker. Associate-Licensee agrees to and does hereby contribute all right and title to such listings to Broker for the benefit and use of Broker, Associate-Licensee, and other licensees associated with Broker.

Broker's Initials (_____) (_____)

ICA REVISED 6/11 (PAGE 1 OF 4)

Associate-Licensee's Initials (_____) (_____)

Reviewed by _____ Date _____

INDEPENDENT CONTRACTOR AGREEMENT (ICA PAGE 1 OF 4)

Agent: WALT HUBER	Phone:	Fax:	Prepared using zipForm® software
Broker:			

B. Broker shall make available to Associate-Licensee, equally with other licensees associated with Broker, all current listings in Broker's office, except any listing which Broker may choose to place in the exclusive servicing of Associate-Licensee or one or more other specific licensees associated with Broker.

C. Associate-Licensee shall provide and pay for all professional licenses, supplies, services, and other items required in connection with Associate-Licensee's activities under this Agreement, or any listing or transaction, without reimbursement from Broker except as required by law.

D. Associate-Licensee shall work diligently and with his/her best efforts to: **(i)** sell, exchange, lease, or rent properties listed with Broker or other cooperating Brokers; **(ii)** solicit additional listings, clients, and customers; and **(iii)** otherwise promote the business of serving the public in real estate transactions to the end that Broker and Associate-Licensee may derive the greatest benefit possible, in accordance with law.

E. Associate-Licensee shall not commit any unlawful act under federal, state or local law or regulation while conducting licensed activity. Associate-Licensee shall at all times be familiar, and comply, with all applicable federal, state and local laws, including, but not limited to, anti-discrimination laws and restrictions against the giving or accepting a fee, or other thing of value, for the referral of business to title companies, escrow companies, home inspection companies, pest control companies and other settlement service providers pursuant to the California Business and Professions Code and the Real Estate Settlement Procedures Acts (RESPA).

F. Broker shall make available for Associate-Licensee's use, along with other licensees associated with Broker, the facilities of the real estate office operated by Broker at _____ and the facilities of any other office locations made available by Broker pursuant to this Agreement.

G. **PROHIBITED ACTIVITIES:** Associate-Licensee agrees not to engage in any of the following Real Estate licensed activities without the express written consent of Broker:
☐ Property Management;
☐ Loan Brokerage
☐ _____ ;
☐ _____
However, if Associate-Licensee has a Real Estate Broker's License, Associate-Licensee may nonetheless engage in the following prohibited activity(ies) only: _____ provided that **(1)** such prohibited activities are not done under the Broker's License, **(2)** no facilities of Broker (including but not limited to phones, fax, computers, and office space) are used for any such prohibited activities, **(3)** Associate-Licensee shall not use any marketing, solicitation or contact information that include Broker's name (including business cards) for such prohibited activities, **(4)** Associate-Licensee informs any actual or intended Principal for whom Associate-Licensee performs or intends to perform such prohibited activities the name of the broker under whose license the prohibited activities are performed, and **(5)** if Associate-Licensee is performing other permitted licensed activity for that Principal under Broker's license, then Associate-Licensee shall inform any actual or intended Principal for whom the prohibited activities are performed that the prohibited activities are not performed under Broker's license.

5. **PROPRIETARY INFORMATION AND FILES:**
A. All files and documents pertaining to listings, leads and transactions are the property of Broker and shall be delivered to Broker by Associate-Licensee immediately upon request or termination of this Agreement.
B. Associate-Licensee acknowledges that Broker's method of conducting business is a protected trade secret.
C. Associate-Licensee shall not use to his/her own advantage, or the advantage of any other person, business, or entity, except as specifically agreed in writing, either during Associate-Licensee's association with Broker, or thereafter, any information gained for or from the business, or files of Broker.

6. **SUPERVISION:** Associate-Licensee, within 24 hours (or ☐ _____) after preparing, signing, or receiving same, shall submit to Broker, or Broker's designated licensee: **(i)** all documents which may have a material effect upon the rights and duties of principals in a transaction; **(ii)** any documents or other items connected with a transaction pursuant to this Agreement in the possession of or available to Associate-Licensee; and **(iii)** all documents associated with any real estate transaction in which Associate-Licensee is a principal.

7. **TRUST FUNDS:** All trust funds shall be handled in compliance with the Business and Professions Code, and other applicable laws.

8. **COMPENSATION:**
A. **TO BROKER:** Compensation shall be charged to parties who enter into listing or other agreements for services requiring a real estate license:
☐ as shown in "Exhibit A" attached, which is incorporated as a part of this Agreement by reference, or
☐ as follows: _____

Any deviation which is not approved in writing in advance by Broker, shall be: **(1)** deducted from Associate-Licensee's compensation, if lower than the amount or rate approved above; and, **(2)** subject to Broker approval, if higher than the amount approved above. Any permanent change in commission schedule shall be disseminated by Broker to Associate-Licensee.

Broker's Initials (_____) (_____)   Associate-Licensee's Initials (_____) (_____)

ICA REVISED 6/11 (PAGE 2 OF 4)   Reviewed by _____ Date _____

INDEPENDENT CONTRACTOR AGREEMENT (ICA PAGE 2 OF 4)   Untitled

B. **TO ASSOCIATE-LICENSEE:** Associate-Licensee shall receive a share of compensation actually collected by Broker, on listings or other agreements for services requiring a real estate license, which are solicited and obtained by Associate-Licensee, and on transactions of which Associate-Licensee's activities are the procuring cause, as follows:

☐ as shown in "Exhibit B" attached, which is incorporated as a part of this Agreement by reference, or

☐ other: _____

_____

_____

_____

C. **PARTNERS, TEAMS, AND AGREEMENTS WITH OTHER ASSOCIATE-LICENSEES IN OFFICE:** If Associate-Licensee and one or more other Associate-Licensees affiliated with Broker participate on the same side (either listing or selling) of a transaction, the commission allocated to their combined activities shall be divided by Broker and paid to them according to their written agreement. Broker shall have the right to withhold total compensation if there is a dispute between associate-licensees, or if there is no written agreement, or if no written agreement has been provided to Broker.

D. **EXPENSES AND OFFSETS:** If Broker elects to advance funds to pay expenses or liabilities of Associate-Licensee, or for an advance payment of, or draw upon, future compensation, Broker may deduct the full amount advanced from compensation payable to Associate-Licensee on any transaction without notice. If Associate-Licensee's compensation is subject to a lien, garnishment or other restriction on payment, Broker shall charge Associate-Licensee a fee for complying with such restriction.

E. **PAYMENT:** (i) All compensation collected by Broker and due to Associate-Licensee shall be paid to Associate-Licensee, after deduction of expenses and offsets, immediately or as soon thereafter as practicable, except as otherwise provided in this Agreement, or a separate written agreement between Broker and Associate-Licensee. (ii) Compensation shall not be paid to Associate-Licensee until both the transaction and file are complete. (iii) Broker is under no obligation to pursue collection of compensation from any person or entity responsible for payment. Associate-Licensee does not have the independent right to pursue collection of compensation for activities which require a real estate license which were done in the name of Broker. (iv) Expenses which are incurred in the attempt to collect compensation shall be paid by Broker and Associate-Licensee in the same proportion as set forth for the division of compensation (paragraph 8(B)). (v) If there is a known or pending claim against Broker or Associate-Licensee on transactions for which Associate-Licensee has not yet been paid, Broker may withhold from compensation due Associate-Licensee on that transaction amounts for which Associate-Licensee could be responsible under paragraph 14, until such claim is resolved. (vi) Associate-Licensee shall not be entitled to any advance payment from Broker upon future compensation.

F. **UPON OR AFTER TERMINATION:** If this Agreement is terminated while Associate-Licensee has listings or pending transactions that require further work normally rendered by Associate-Licensee, Broker shall make arrangements with another associate-licensee to perform the required work, or Broker shall perform the work him/herself. The licensee performing the work shall be reasonably compensated for completing work on those listings or transactions, and such reasonable compensation shall be deducted from Associate-Licensee's share of compensation. Except for such offset, Associate-Licensee shall receive the compensation due as specified above.

9. **TERMINATION OF RELATIONSHIP:** Broker or Associate-Licensee may terminate their relationship under this Agreement at any time, with or without cause. After termination, Associate-Licensee shall not solicit: (i) prospective or existing clients or customers based upon company-generated leads obtained during the time Associate-Licensee was affiliated with Broker; (ii) any principal with existing contractual obligations to Broker; or (iii) any principal with a contractual transactional obligation for which Broker is entitled to be compensated. Even after termination, this Agreement shall govern all disputes and claims between Broker and Associate-Licensee connected with their relationship under this Agreement, including obligations and liabilities arising from existing and completed listings, transactions, and services.

10. **DISPUTE RESOLUTION:**
Broker and Associate-Licensee agree to mediate all disputes and claims between them arising from or connected in any way with this Agreement before resorting to court action. If any dispute or claim is not resolved through mediation, or otherwise, instead of resolving the matter in court, Broker and Associate-Licensee may mutually agree to submit the dispute to arbitration at, and pursuant to the rules and bylaws of, the Association of REALTORS® to which both parties belong.

11. **AUTOMOBILE:** Associate-Licensee shall maintain automobile insurance coverage for liability and property damage in the following amounts $ _____ /$ _____ . Broker shall be named as an additional insured party on Associate-Licensee's policies. A copy of the endorsement showing Broker as an additional insured shall be provided to Broker.

Broker's Initials   (_____) (_____)

Associate-Licensee's Initials   (_____) (_____)

ICA REVISED 6/11 (PAGE 3 OF 4)

Reviewed by _____ Date _____

EQUAL HOUSING OPPORTUNITY

INDEPENDENT CONTRACTOR AGREEMENT (ICA PAGE 3 OF 4)

Untitled

12. **PERSONAL ASSISTANTS:** Associate-Licensee may make use of a personal assistant, provided the following requirements are satisfied. Associate-Licensee shall have a written agreement with the personal assistant which establishes the terms and responsibilities of the parties to the employment agreement, including, but not limited to, compensation, supervision and compliance with applicable law. The agreement shall be subject to Broker's review and approval. Unless otherwise agreed, if the personal assistant has a real estate license, that license must be provided to the Broker. Both Associate-Licensee and personal assistant must sign any agreement that Broker has established for such purposes.

13. **OFFICE POLICY MANUAL:** If Broker's office policy manual, now or as modified in the future, conflicts with or differs from the terms of this Agreement, the terms of the office policy manual shall govern the relationship between Broker and Associate-Licensee.

14. **INDEMNITY AND HOLD HARMLESS; NOTICE OF CLAIMS:**
   A. Regarding any action taken or omitted by Associate-Licensee, or others working through, or on behalf of Associate-Licensee in connection with services rendered or to be rendered pursuant to this Agreement or Real Estate licensed activity prohibited by this agreement: (i) Associate-Licensee agrees to indemnify, defend and hold Broker harmless from all claims, disputes, litigation, judgments, awards, costs and attorney's fees, arising therefrom and (ii) Associate-Licensee shall immediately notify Broker if Associate-Licensee is served with or becomes aware of a lawsuit or claim regarding any such action.
   B. Any such claims or costs payable pursuant to this Agreement, are due as follows:
   ☐ Paid in full by Associate-Licensee, who hereby agrees to indemnify and hold harmless Broker for all such sums, or
   ☐ In the same ratio as the compensation split as it existed at the time the compensation was earned by Associate-Licensee ☐ Other: _____

   Payment from Associate-Licensee is due at the time Broker makes such payment and can be offset from any compensation due Associate-Licensee as above. Broker retains the authority to settle claims or disputes, whether or not Associate-Licensee consents to such settlement.

15. **ADDITIONAL PROVISIONS:** _____
   _____
   _____

16. **DEFINITIONS:** As used in this Agreement, the following terms have the meanings indicated:
   A. "Listing" means an agreement with a property owner or other party to locate a buyer, exchange party, lessee, or other party to a transaction involving real property, a mobile home, or other property or transaction which may be brokered by a real estate licensee, or an agreement with a party to locate or negotiate for any such property or transaction.
   B. "Compensation" means compensation for acts requiring a real estate license, regardless of whether calculated as a percentage of transaction price, flat fee, hourly rate, or in any other manner.
   C. "Transaction" means a sale, exchange, lease, or rental of real property, a business opportunity, or a manufactured home, which may lawfully be brokered by a real estate licensee.

17. **ATTORNEY FEES:** In any action, proceeding, or arbitration between Broker and Associate-Licensee arising from or related to this Agreement, the prevailing Broker or Associate-Licensee shall be entitled to reasonable attorney fees and costs.

18. **ENTIRE AGREEMENT:** All prior agreements between the parties concerning their relationship as Broker and Associate-Licensee are incorporated in this Agreement, which constitutes the entire contract. Its terms are intended by the parties as a final and complete expression of their agreement with respect to its subject matter, and may not be contradicted by evidence of any prior agreement or contemporaneous oral agreement. This Agreement may not be amended, modified, altered, or changed except by a further agreement in writing executed by Broker and Associate-Licensee.

Broker: Associate-Licensee:

_____   _____
(Brokerage firm name)   (Signature)
By
Its ☐ Broker ☐ Office manager (check one)   _____
                                                             (Print name)
_____
(Print name)   _____
                                                             (Address)
_____
(Address)   _____
                                                             (City, State, Zip)
_____
(City, State, Zip)   _____
                                                             (Telephone)   (Fax)
_____
(Telephone)   (Fax)

THIS FORM HAS BEEN APPROVED BY THE CALIFORNIA ASSOCIATION OF REALTORS® (C.A.R.). NO REPRESENTATION IS MADE AS TO THE LEGAL VALIDITY OR ADEQUACY OF ANY PROVISION IN ANY SPECIFIC TRANSACTION. A REAL ESTATE BROKER IS THE PERSON QUALIFIED TO ADVISE ON REAL ESTATE TRANSACTIONS. IF YOU DESIRE LEGAL OR TAX ADVICE, CONSULT AN APPROPRIATE PROFESSIONAL.

This form is available for use by the entire real estate industry. It is not intended to identify the user as a REALTOR®. REALTOR® is a registered collective membership mark which may be used only by members of the NATIONAL ASSOCIATION OF REALTORS® who subscribe to its Code of Ethics.

Published and Distributed by:
REAL ESTATE BUSINESS SERVICES, INC.
a subsidiary of the California Association of REALTORS®
* 525 South Virgil Avenue, Los Angeles, California 90020

Reviewed by _____ Date _____

EQUAL HOUSING OPPORTUNITY

ICA REVISED 6/11 (PAGE 4 OF 4)

INDEPENDENT CONTRACTOR AGREEMENT (ICA PAGE 4 OF 4)

Untitled

This is an attempt to minimize the costs, fees, and time that would be necessary if litigation was used.

The contract also provides that in the event of any action, proceeding, or arbitration arising from the purchase agreement, the prevailing party is entitled to reasonable attorney fees and costs paid by the nonprevailing party (**Paragraph 17**). If the contract did not contain such a clause, each party would pay their own attorney fees and the prevailing party would not be able to recover fees from the loser. Attorney fees are generally not recoverable unless a state law allows for recovery or there is a recovery clause in the written contract.

The California Supreme Court case of *Hsu v. Abbara*, 9 Cal. 4th 863, 39 Cal. Rptr. 2d 824 (1995), which is at the end of Chapter 7, held that Abbara was the prevailing party in the lawsuit based on a purchase agreement offer that had an attorney fees clause in it. Abbara was entitled to attorney fees from Hsu even though there was not a binding contract providing for attorney fees. If Hsu had won and proved that a contract existed, Hsu would receive attorney fees from Abbara. Therefore, the court reasoned Abbara should receive attorney fees for successfully defending a lawsuit based on an alleged contract that contained an attorney fees clause.

Sometimes a party to a contract containing an attorney fees provision is motivated to bring a lawsuit since a victory will allow the recovery of reasonable attorney fees spent on the lawsuit from the losing defendant. However, as things progress the plaintiff may decide, for whatever reason, to dismiss the case prior to trial. Is the defendant entitled to attorney fees from the plaintiff? No, as the court of appeal stated in *Jue v. Patton*, 33 Cal. App. 4th 456, 39 Cal. Rptr. 2d 364 (1995), "Recovery of attorney fees based on a contract provision is not permitted when the action is voluntarily dismissed prior to trial."

The final paragraph (**Paragraph 18**) of the CAR® form states that *this document is the entire contract agreement between the parties. This is called an* **INTEGRATION CLAUSE**, and most standard contract forms include one. Basically, the integration clause is a way to state the parol evidence rule in the contract. When a contract contains an integration clause, neither party can rely on any oral promises or side agreements that the other makes. Any terms not included in the written document are unenforceable.

> **Example:** Z is a new salesperson. Before signing the employment contract, Z says he is concerned because his share of a commission won't be payable unless the commission is collected. The broker says, "Oh, don't worry about that. I always act fast to collect from any client who doesn't pay right away. You'll always get your money."
>
> As it turns out, the broker doesn't always take the trouble to collect from difficult clients. On one occasion, Z ended up with nothing to show for a lot of work.

If their employment agreement did not contain an integration clause, Z might have been able to treat the broker's statement as a contractual promise to take action to collect commissions. However, because the integration clause makes the written document the complete agreement between Z and the broker, the broker's statement is not an enforceable promise.

II. Listing Agreements

A listing agreement is another kind of employment contract, this time between a seller and a broker. The types of listing agreements and some of the requirements for listing agreements were covered in Chapter 5. As discussed in the Statute of Frauds section in Chapter 7, a broker cannot sue for a commission unless the listing is in writing and signed by the client. The case where the broker was able to enforce a listing agreement jotted on the back of a business card (described in a previous chapter) shows that the listing doesn't have to be a formal legal document. Remember, however, the Civil Code requires that the listing agreement be in writing for the seller's promise to pay a commission to the broker to be enforceable in court. This requirement can be satisfied with language in the listing agreement itself, or in a memorandum or note, stating that the signer is employing the broker.

Case Example: Mr. Franklin, a broker, agreed to help Mr. Hansen sell some residential property in Newport Beach. Hansen assured Franklin a written listing was unnecessary—his word was good.

Franklin obtained an offer and called Hansen in Los Angeles. Hansen decided to accept the offer, so Franklin asked him to send a telegram as a written authorization for the sale. Hansen sent Franklin a telegram that read, "This is to confirm that I will sell 608 South Bay Front, Balboa Island for $100,000 cash... Chas. P. Hansen."

Later, Hansen refused to sign the purchase agreement to complete the sale and refused to pay Franklin's commission. Franklin sued.

The court ruled that the telegram did not fulfill the written listing requirement. Even though it was addressed to Franklin, nothing in it indicated that Hansen was employing Franklin or planning to pay him a commission. It was simply an acceptance of the buyer's offer. *Franklin v. Hansen*, 59 Cal. 2d 570, 30 Cal. Rptr. 530 (1963).

Recall from the discussion in Chapter 5 that even when a broker does not have an enforceable promise to collect a commission, the broker nevertheless owes fiduciary duties to his or her principal. Those duties are based on agency law, not on contract law. They are in addition to, and independent of, the contractual duties the broker takes on in a listing agreement. If the client doesn't provide consideration (that is, doesn't pay the broker), the broker is not required to perform his or her contractual obligations, but can still be held liable for failing to carry out fiduciary duties. (See Chapter 6.)

Also, don't forget that for a residential transaction (one to four units), a broker must provide the seller with an agency disclosure addendum before the seller signs a listing agreement. This form was discussed in Chapter 6.

Because a listing agreement is a personal services contract, it can only be assigned to another broker with the client's consent. The assignment, like the original contract, must be in writing. It should be signed by the assignor and the assignee, as well as the client.

www.newhomesmatch.com
California New Homes For Sale

Case Example: Hartline and Neville (Sellers) signed a standard "Exclusive Authorization to Sell" listing agreement form with Spring Valley Lake Realty (Broker), which provided, among other things, that the sellers would pay a 6% commission upon sale of the property and authorize the Broker to cooperate with subagents. The property sold for $2,310,980 and Sellers paid the commission. Pursuant to the escrow instructions, 3% was paid to the Broker and 3% to Regal Realty under the "cooperate" clause. ▼

Prior to the close of escrow, real estate broker Niebuhr demanded Regal's 3% of the commission on the grounds that he was the procuring cause (for which he made a very strong case), not Regal. Niebuhr was not paid and sued Sellers for paying the wrong person.

The Court of Appeal held that the Sellers had no obligation to pay Niebuhr because there was no contract of employment between the Seller and Niebuhr, the cooperating broker. The listing authorized Broker to cooperate with subagents, but clearly provided that payment of a commission was to be made to the Broker. Niebuhr must sue the Broker for any commission due under the cooperating broker agreement. *Colbaugh v. Hartline*, 29 Cal. App. 4th 1516, 35 Cal. Rptr. 2d 213 (1994).

Case Example: Smith and Siegel (defendants) were the owners of a large tract of unimproved land in Ventura County and indicated orally to Wm. E. Doud Company Realtors (plaintiffs) that if plaintiffs located a prospective purchaser satisfactory to the defendants and negotiations were entered into, the plaintiffs would issue a written memorandum acknowledging that and agreeing to pay, upon consummation of the sale of the property to such prospective purchasers, a commission. Plaintiffs sent two prospective purchasers, Mark Kornwasser and Kaufman and Broad represented by Byron Laskey. The defendants sent a signed letter to the plaintiffs stating the amount of a commission to be paid if the land was "sold it to either of these buyers." Subsequently, Laskey ceased representing Kaufman and Broad and thereafter he and Harlan Lee agreed to purchase the property from the defendants. The plaintiffs sued for the commission and the trial court ultimately dismissed the case. Plaintiffs appealed.

The property in question was not sold to either Kaufman and Broad or to Mark Kornwasser. More explicit language could hardly have been used to state that the commission would become due only upon sale to either party. Since the plaintiffs are attempting to recover their real estate commission on an oral contract, the statute of frauds bars any recovery. *Wm. E. Doud & Co. Inc. v. Smith*, 256 Cal. App. 2d 552 64 Cal. Rptr. 222 (1967).

A. BASIC LISTING AGREEMENT ELEMENTS

One form of listing agreement, the CAR® **Residential Listing Agreement (Exclusive Authorization and Right to Sell)**, is shown as **Figure 8-2**. A listing agreement should identify the property to be sold or leased. The street address is generally useful, but it may not be enough to identify the property with certainty. This usually isn't an issue, but it can become one if the client decides not to sell and tries to avoid paying a commission. It's good practice to attach a legal description of the property to the contract as an exhibit. Any pages attached to a contract should be dated and initialed by the parties to show that the attachments were intended to be part of the agreement.

The exclusive right to sell agency and the exclusive agency listings (see Chapter 5) must contain a termination date and be kept by the broker for at least three years.

1. Provisions Affecting Liability for a Commission

A listing agreement ordinarily states the sales price and terms the client is willing to accept. In the CAR® form, the listing price and terms are found in Paragraph 3. As noted in Chapter 7, the listing price and terms in the listing agreement are not an offer by the

Figure 8-2

CALIFORNIA
ASSOCIATION
OF REALTORS®

RESIDENTIAL LISTING AGREEMENT
(Exclusive Authorization and Right to Sell)
(C.A.R. Form RLA, Revised 11/12)

1. **EXCLUSIVE RIGHT TO SELL:** _____ ("Seller")
   hereby employs and grants _____ ("Broker")
   beginning (date) _____ and ending at 11:59 P.M. on (date) _____ ("Listing Period")
   the exclusive and irrevocable right to sell or exchange the real property in the City of _____*Marina del Rey*_____ ,
   County of _____ , Assessor's Parcel No. _____
   California, described as: _____*123 Sail Avenue*_____ ("Property").

2. **ITEMS EXCLUDED AND INCLUDED:** Unless otherwise specified in a real estate purchase agreement, all fixtures and fittings that are attached to the Property are included, and personal property items are excluded, from the purchase price.
   ADDITIONAL ITEMS EXCLUDED: _____.
   ADDITIONAL ITEMS INCLUDED: _____.
   Seller intends that the above items be excluded or included in offering the Property for sale, but understands that: **(i)** the purchase agreement supersedes any intention expressed above and will ultimately determine which items are excluded and included in the sale; and **(ii)** Broker is not responsible for and does not guarantee that the above exclusions and/or inclusions will be in the purchase agreement.

3. **LISTING PRICE AND TERMS:**
   A. The listing price shall be: _____ Dollars ($ _____).
   B. Additional Terms: _____
   _____
   _____

4. **COMPENSATION TO BROKER:**
   Notice: The amount or rate of real estate commissions is not fixed by law. They are set by each Broker individually and may be negotiable between Seller and Broker (real estate commissions include all compensation and fees to Broker).
   A. Seller agrees to pay to Broker as compensation for services irrespective of agency relationship(s), either ☐ _____ percent of the listing price (or if a purchase agreement is entered into, of the purchase price), or ☐ $ _____ , AND _____ , as follows:
      (1) If during the Listing Period, or any extension, Broker, cooperating broker, Seller or any other person procures a buyer(s) who offers to purchase the Property on the above price and terms, or on any price or terms acceptable to Seller. (Broker is entitled to compensation whether any escrow resulting from such offer closes during or after the expiration of the Listing Period, or any extension).
   OR **(2)** If within _____ calendar days **(a)** after the end of the Listing Period or any extension; or **(b)** after any cancellation of this Agreement, unless otherwise agreed, Seller enters into a contract to sell, convey, lease or otherwise transfer the Property to anyone ("Prospective Buyer") or that person's related entity: **(i)** who physically entered and was shown the Property during the Listing Period or any extension by Broker or a cooperating broker; or **(ii)** for whom Broker or any cooperating broker submitted to Seller a signed, written offer to acquire, lease, exchange or obtain an option on the Property. Seller, however, shall have no obligation to Broker under paragraph 4A(2) unless, not later than **3 calendar days** after the end of the Listing Period or any extension or cancellation, Broker has given Seller a written notice of the names of such Prospective Buyers.
      (3) If, without Broker's prior written consent, the Property is withdrawn from sale, conveyed, leased, rented, otherwise transferred, or made unmarketable by a voluntary act of Seller during the Listing Period, or any extension.
   B. If completion of the sale is prevented by a party to the transaction other than Seller, then compensation due under paragraph 4A shall be payable only if and when Seller collects damages by suit, arbitration, settlement or otherwise, and then in an amount equal to the lesser of one-half of the damages recovered or the above compensation, after first deducting title and escrow expenses and the expenses of collection, if any.
   C. In addition, Seller agrees to pay Broker: _____
   D. Seller has been advised of Broker's policy regarding cooperation with, and the amount of compensation offered to, other brokers.
      (1) Broker is authorized to cooperate with and compensate brokers participating through the multiple listing service(s) ("MLS") by offering to MLS brokers out of Broker's compensation specified in 4A, either ☐ _____ percent of the purchase price, or ☐ $ _____
      (2) Broker is authorized to cooperate with and compensate brokers operating outside the MLS as per Broker's policy.
   E. Seller hereby irrevocably assigns to Broker the above compensation from Seller's funds and proceeds in escrow. Broker may submit this Agreement, as instructions to compensate Broker pursuant to paragraph 4A, to any escrow regarding the Property involving Seller and a buyer, Prospective Buyer or other transferee.
   F. **(1)** Seller represents that Seller has not previously entered into a listing agreement with another broker regarding the Property, unless specified as follows: _____
      (2) Seller warrants that Seller has no obligation to pay compensation to any other broker regarding the Property unless the Property is transferred to any of the following individuals or entities: _____
      _____
      (3) If the Property is sold to anyone listed above during the time Seller is obligated to compensate another broker: **(i)** Broker is not entitled to compensation under this Agreement; and **(ii)** Broker is not obligated to represent Seller in such transaction.

RLA REVISED 11/12 (PAGE 1 OF 4)

Seller's Initials (_____) (_____)

Reviewed by _____ Date _____

EQUAL HOUSING
OPPORTUNITY

RESIDENTIAL LISTING AGREEMENT - EXCLUSIVE (RLA PAGE 1 OF 4)

Agent: WALT HUBER	Phone:	Fax:	Prepared using zipForm® software
Broker:			

CHAPTER 8

Property Address: **123 Sail Avenue**
Marina del Rey, CA 90292 _____ Date: _____

5. **OWNERSHIP, TITLE AND AUTHORITY:** Seller warrants that: **(i)** Seller is the owner of the Property; **(ii)** no other persons or entities have title to the Property; and **(iii)** Seller has the authority to both execute this Agreement and sell the Property. Exceptions to ownership, title and authority are as follows: _____.

6. **MULTIPLE LISTING SERVICE:** All terms of the transaction, including financing, if applicable, will be provided to the selected MLS for publication, dissemination and use by persons and entities on terms approved by the MLS. Seller acknowledges that Broker is required to comply with all applicable MLS rules as a condition of entry of the listing into the MLS and Seller authorizes Broker to comply with all applicable MLS rules. MLS rules require that the listing sales price be reported to the MLS. MLS rules allow MLS data to be made available by the MLS to additional Internet sites unless Broker gives the MLS instructions to the contrary. MLS rules generally provide that residential real property and vacant lot listings be submitted to the MLS within 48 hours or some other period of time after all necessary signatures have been obtained on the listing agreement. However, Broker will not have to submit this listing to the MLS if, within that time, Broker submits to the MLS a form signed by Seller (C.A.R. Form SEL or the locally required form).
   Information that can be excluded:
   A. Internet Display:
   (1) Seller can instruct Broker to have the MLS not display the Property on the Internet. Seller understands that this would mean consumers searching for listings on the Internet may not see information about the Property in response to their search; **(2)** Seller can instruct Broker to have the MLS not display the Property address on the Internet. Seller understands that this would mean consumers searching for listings on the Internet may not see the Property's address in response to their search.
   B. Features on MLS Participant and Subscriber Websites:
   (1) Seller can instruct Broker to advise the MLS that Seller does not want visitors to MLS Participant or Subscriber Websites that display the Property listing to have **(i)** the ability to write comments or reviews about the Property on those sites; or **(ii)** the ability to hyperlink to another site containing such comments or reviews if the hyperlink is in immediate conjunction with the Property. Seller understands **(i)** that this opt-out applies only to Websites of MLS Participants and Subscribers who are real estate broker and agent members of the MLS; **(ii)** that other Internet sites may or may not have the features set forth herein; and **(iii)** that neither Broker nor the MLS may have the ability to control or block such features on other Internet sites. **(2)** Seller can instruct Broker to advise the MLS that Seller does not want MLS Participant or Subscriber Websites that display the Property listing to operate **(i)** an automated estimate of the market value of the Property; or **(ii)** have the ability to hyperlink to another site containing such automated estimate of value if the hyperlink is in immediate conjunction with the Property. Seller understands **(i)** that this opt-out applies only to Websites of MLS Participants and Subscribers who are real estate brokers and agent members of the MLS; **(ii)** that other Internet sites may or may not have the features set forth herein; and **(iii)** that neither Broker nor the MLS may have the ability to control or block such features on other Internet sites.
   Seller acknowledges that for any of the above opt-out instructions to be effective, Seller must make them on a separate instruction to Broker signed by Seller (C.A.R. Form SEL or the locally required form). Information about this listing will be provided to the MLS of Broker's selection unless a form instructing Broker to withhold the listing from the MLS is attached to this listing Agreement.

7. **SELLER REPRESENTATIONS:** Seller represents that, unless otherwise specified in writing, Seller is unaware of: **(i)** any Notice of Default recorded against the Property; **(ii)** any delinquent amounts due under any loan secured by, or other obligation affecting, the Property; **(iii)** any bankruptcy, insolvency or similar proceeding affecting the Property; **(iv)** any litigation, arbitration, administrative action, government investigation or other pending or threatened action that affects or may affect the Property or Seller's ability to transfer it; and **(v)** any current, pending or proposed special assessments affecting the Property. Seller shall promptly notify Broker in writing if Seller becomes aware of any of these items during the Listing Period or any extension thereof.

8. **BROKER'S AND SELLER'S DUTIES: (a)** Broker agrees to exercise reasonable effort and due diligence to achieve the purposes of this Agreement. Unless Seller gives Broker written instructions to the contrary, Broker is authorized to **(i)** order reports and disclosures necessary, **(ii)** advertise and market the Property by any method and in any medium selected by Broker, including MLS and the Internet, and, to the extent permitted by these media, control the dissemination of the information submitted to any medium; and **(iii)** disclose to any real estate licensee making an inquiry the receipt of any offers on the Property and the offering price of such offers. **(b)** Seller agrees to consider offers presented by Broker, and to act in good faith to accomplish the sale of the Property by, among other things, making the Property available for showing at reasonable times and referring to Broker all inquiries of any party interested in the Property. Seller is responsible for determining at what price to list and sell the Property. **Seller further agrees to indemnify, defend and hold Broker harmless from all claims, disputes, litigation, judgments attorney fees and costs arising from any incorrect information supplied by Seller, or from any material facts that Seller knows but fails to disclose.**

9. **DEPOSIT:** Broker is authorized to accept and hold on Seller's behalf any deposits to be applied toward the purchase price.

10. **AGENCY RELATIONSHIPS:**
    A. Disclosure: If the Property includes residential property with one-to-four dwelling units, Seller shall receive a "Disclosure Regarding Agency Relationships" (C.A.R. Form AD) prior to entering into this Agreement.
    B. Seller Representation: Broker shall represent Seller in any resulting transaction, except as specified in paragraph 4F.

Copyright © 1991-2012, CALIFORNIA ASSOCIATION OF REALTORS®, INC.
RLA REVISED 11/12 (PAGE 2 OF 4)

Seller's Initials (_____) (_____)
Reviewed by _____ Date _____

RESIDENTIAL LISTING AGREEMENT - EXCLUSIVE (RLA PAGE 2 OF 4)

Untitled

Property Address: *123 Sail Avenue*
Marina del Rey, CA 90292 _____ Date: _____

C. Possible Dual Agency With Buyer: Depending upon the circumstances, it may be necessary or appropriate for Broker to act as an agent for both Seller and buyer, exchange party, or one or more additional parties ("Buyer"). Broker shall, as soon as practicable, disclose to Seller any election to act as a dual agent representing both Seller and Buyer. If a Buyer is procured directly by Broker or an associate licensee in Broker's firm, Seller hereby consents to Broker acting as a dual agent for Seller and Buyer. In the event of an exchange, Seller hereby consents to Broker collecting compensation from additional parties for services rendered, provided there is disclosure to all parties of such agency and compensation. Seller understands and agrees that: **(i)** Broker, without the prior written consent of Seller, will not disclose to Buyer that Seller is willing to sell the Property at a price less than the listing price; **(ii)** Broker, without the prior written consent of Buyer, will not disclose to Seller that Buyer is willing to pay a price greater than the offered price; and **(iii)** except for (i) and (ii) above, a dual agent is obligated to disclose known facts materially affecting the value or desirability of the Property to both parties.

D. Other Sellers: Seller understands that Broker may have or obtain listings on other properties, and that potential buyers may consider, make offers on, or purchase through Broker, property the same as or similar to Seller's Property. Seller consents to Broker's representation of sellers and buyers of other properties before, during and after the end of this Agreement.

E. Confirmation: If the Property includes residential property with one-to-four dwelling units, Broker shall confirm the agency relationship described above, or as modified, in writing, prior to or concurrent with Seller's execution of a purchase agreement.

11. SECURITY AND INSURANCE: Broker is not responsible for loss of or damage to personal or real property, or person, whether attributable to use of a keysafe/lockbox, a showing of the Property, or otherwise. Third parties, including, but not limited to, appraisers, inspectors, brokers and prospective buyers, may have access to, and take videos and photographs of, the interior of the Property. Seller agrees: **(i)** to take reasonable precautions to safeguard and protect valuables that might be accessible during showings of the Property; and **(ii)** to obtain insurance to protect against these risks. Broker does not maintain insurance to protect Seller.

12. PHOTOGRAPHS AND INTERNET ADVERTISING:

A. In order to effectively market the Property for sale it is often necessary to provide photographs, virtual tours and other media to buyers. Seller agrees (or ☐ if checked, does not agree) that Broker may photograph or otherwise electronically capture images of the exterior and interior of the Property ("Images") for static and/or virtual tours of the Property by buyers and others on Broker's website, the MLS, and other marketing sites. Seller acknowledges that once Images are placed on the Internet neither Broker nor Seller has control over who can view such Images and what use viewers may make of the Images, or how long such Images may remain available on the Internet. Seller further agrees that such Images are the property of Broker and that Broker may use such Images for advertisement of Broker's business in the future.

B. Seller acknowledges that prospective buyers and/or other persons coming onto the Property may take photographs, videos or other images of the Property. Seller understands that Broker does not have the ability to control or block the taking and use of Images by any such persons. (If checked) ☐ Seller instructs Broker to publish in the MLS that taking of Images is limited to those persons preparing Appraisal or Inspection reports. Seller acknowledges that unauthorized persons may take images who do not have access to or have not read any limiting instruction in the MLS or who take images regardless of any limiting instruction in the MLS. Once Images are taken and/or put into electronic display on the Internet or otherwise, neither Broker nor Seller has control over who views such Images nor what use viewers may make of the Images.

13. KEYSAFE/LOCKBOX: A keysafe/lockbox is designed to hold a key to the Property to permit access to the Property by Broker, cooperating brokers, MLS participants, their authorized licensees and representatives, authorized inspectors, and accompanied prospective buyers. Broker, cooperating brokers, MLS and Associations/Boards of REALTORS® are **not** insurers against injury, theft, loss, vandalism or damage attributed to the use of a keysafe/lockbox. Seller does (or if checked ☐ does not) authorize Broker to install a keysafe/lockbox. If Seller does not occupy the Property, Seller shall be responsible for obtaining occupant(s)' written permission for use of a keysafe/lockbox (C.A.R. Form KLA).

14. SIGN: Seller does (or if checked ☐ does not) authorize Broker to install a FOR SALE/SOLD sign on the Property.

15. EQUAL HOUSING OPPORTUNITY: The Property is offered in compliance with federal, state and local anti-discrimination laws.

16. ATTORNEY FEES: In any action, proceeding or arbitration between Seller and Broker regarding the obligation to pay compensation under this Agreement, the prevailing Seller or Broker shall be entitled to reasonable attorney fees and costs from the non-prevailing Seller or Broker, except as provided in paragraph 20A.

17. ADDITIONAL TERMS: ☐ REO Advisory Listing (C.A.R. Form REOL) ☐ Short Sale Information and Advisory (C.A.R. Form SSIA)

_____
_____
_____
_____
_____

18. MANAGEMENT APPROVAL: If an associate-licensee in Broker's office (salesperson or broker-associate) enters into this Agreement on Broker's behalf, and Broker or Manager does not approve of its terms, Broker or Manager has the right to cancel this Agreement, in writing, within **5 Days** After its execution.

19. SUCCESSORS AND ASSIGNS: This Agreement shall be binding upon Seller and Seller's successors and assigns.

RLA REVISED 11/12 (PAGE 3 OF 4)

Seller's Initials (_____) (_____)
Reviewed by _____ Date _____

RESIDENTIAL LISTING AGREEMENT - EXCLUSIVE (RLA PAGE 3 OF 4)

Untitled

Property Address: **123 Sail Avenue**
Marina del Rey, CA 90292 _____ Date: _____

20. DISPUTE RESOLUTION:

A. MEDIATION: Seller and Broker agree to mediate any dispute or claim arising between them out of this Agreement, or any resulting transaction, before resorting to arbitration or court action. Mediation fees, if any, shall be divided equally among the parties involved. If, for any dispute or claim to which this paragraph applies, any party (i) commences an action without first attempting to resolve the matter through mediation, or (ii) before comencement of an action, refuses to mediate after a request has been made, then that party shall not be entitled to recover attorney fees, even if they would otherwise be available to that party in any such action. THIS MEDIATION PROVISION APPLIES WHETHER OR NOT THE ARBITRATION PROVISION IS INITIALED. **Exclusions from this mediation agreement are specified in paragraph 20C.**

B. ARBITRATION OF DISPUTES:

Seller and Broker agree that any dispute or claim in Law or equity arising between them regarding the obligation to pay compensation under this Agreement, which is not settled through mediation, shall be decided by neutral, binding arbitration. The arbitrator shall be a retired judge or justice, or an attorney with at least 5 years of residential real estate Law experience, unless the parties mutually agree to a different arbitrator. The parties shall have the right to discovery in accordance with Code of Civil Procedure §1283.05. In all other respects, the arbitration shall be conducted in accordance with Title 9 of Part 3 of the Code of Civil Procedure. Judgment upon the award of the arbitrator(s) may be entered into any court having jurisdiction. Enforcement of this agreement to arbitrate shall be governed by the Federal Arbitration Act. **Exclusions from this arbitration agreement are specified in paragraph 20C.**

"NOTICE: BY INITIALING IN THE SPACE BELOW YOU ARE AGREEING TO HAVE ANY DISPUTE ARISING OUT OF THE MATTERS INCLUDED IN THE 'ARBITRATION OF DISPUTES' PROVISION DECIDED BY NEUTRAL ARBITRATION AS PROVIDED BY CALIFORNIA LAW AND YOU ARE GIVING UP ANY RIGHTS YOU MIGHT POSSESS TO HAVE THE DISPUTE LITIGATED IN A COURT OR JURY TRIAL. BY INITIALING IN THE SPACE BELOW YOU ARE GIVING UP YOUR JUDICIAL RIGHTS TO DISCOVERY AND APPEAL, UNLESS THOSE RIGHTS ARE SPECIFICALLY INCLUDED IN THE 'ARBITRATION OF DISPUTES' PROVISION. IF YOU REFUSE TO SUBMIT TO ARBITRATION AFTER AGREEING TO THIS PROVISION, YOU MAY BE COMPELLED TO ARBITRATE UNDER THE AUTHORITY OF THE CALIFORNIA CODE OF CIVIL PROCEDURE. YOUR AGREEMENT TO THIS ARBITRATION PROVISION IS VOLUNTARY."

"WE HAVE READ AND UNDERSTAND THE FOREGOING AND AGREE TO SUBMIT DISPUTES ARISING OUT OF THE MATTERS INCLUDED IN THE 'ARBITRATION OF DISPUTES' PROVISION TO NEUTRAL ARBITRATION."

| Seller's Initials _____ / _____ | Broker's Initials _____ / _____ |

C. ADDITIONAL MEDIATION AND ARBITRATION TERMS: The following matters shall be excluded from mediation and arbitration: (i) a judicial or non-judicial foreclosure or other action or proceeding to enforce a deed of trust, mortgage or installment land sale contract as defined in Civil Code §2985; (ii) an unlawful detainer action; (iii) the filing or enforcement of a mechanic's lien; and (iv) any matter that is within the jurisdiction of a probate, small claims or bankruptcy court. The filing of a court action to enable the recording of a notice of pending action, for order of attachment, receivership, injunction, or other provisional remedies, shall not constitute a waiver or violation of the mediation and arbitration provisions.

21. ENTIRE AGREEMENT: All prior discussions, negotiations and agreements between the parties concerning the subject matter of this Agreement are superseded by this Agreement, which constitutes the entire contract and a complete and exclusive expression of their agreement, and may not be contradicted by evidence of any prior agreement or contemporaneous oral agreement. If any provision of this Agreement is held to be ineffective or invalid, the remaining provisions will nevertheless be given full force and effect. This Agreement and any supplement, addendum or modification, including any photocopy or facsimile, may be executed in counterparts.

By signing below, Seller acknowledges that Seller has read, understands, received a copy of and agrees to the terms of this Agreement.

Seller _____ Date _____
Address _____ City _____ State _____ Zip _____
Telephone _____ Fax _____ Email _____

Seller _____ Date _____
Address _____ City _____ State _____ Zip _____
Telephone _____ Fax _____ Email _____

Real Estate Broker (Firm) _____ DRE Lic. # _____
By (Agent) _____ DRE Lic. # _____ Date _____
Address _____ City _____ State _____ Zip _____
Telephone _____ Fax _____ Email _____

RLA REVISED 11/12 (PAGE 4 OF 4)

RESIDENTIAL LISTING AGREEMENT - EXCLUSIVE (RLA PAGE 4 OF 4)   Untitled seller to sell the property to any potential buyer. Even if a buyer makes an offer that exactly matches the terms in the listing agreement, the seller is not obligated to sell. However, if a buyer makes an offer that exactly matches the price and terms in the listing agreement, the seller would likely be obligated to pay a commission to the listing broker, even if the seller rejects the buyer's offer. The client can refuse any offer that doesn't meet these terms without being liable for a commission. It is, therefore, very important for the price and terms to be set forth clearly and fully in the listing. (Any personal property included in the sale should be specified, since this affects the price. See **Paragraph 2** of the CAR® form.) Of course, if the broker presents an offer that doesn't meet the listing terms and the client accepts it anyway, he or she is liable for the commission.

A provision stating the amount or rate of the broker's compensation is another key part of every listing agreement. Recall from Chapter 5 that there are special rules that apply to listing agreements for residential property with four or fewer units and mobilehomes. The agreement must contain a statement that the amount or rate of commission is not set by law but may be negotiable between the seller and buyer. See **Paragraph 4** in Figure 8-2. Also, the agreement cannot have the amount or rate of commission preprinted in the form. See **Paragraph 4A** in Figure 8-2.

The listing agreement in Figure 8-2 is a type of exclusive right to sell listing. **Paragraph 4A-1** of this agreement provides that the listing broker is entitled to a commission if a buyer makes an offer on the listing price and terms, or on any other price and terms accepted by the seller, whether that buyer is procured by the listing broker, any other broker, the seller, or any other person. Under the terms of most listing agreement forms, the broker is entitled to a commission even if the transaction never closes, as long as the client and a ready, willing, and able buyer have agreed on the essential terms of a sale (see Chapter 5). It doesn't have to work that way, however. The seller can add a condition to the listing agreement, making liability for the commission depend on the sale actually closing or on some other event.

If the broker is not doing what he or she promised in the exclusive right to sell listing, then the seller can terminate the listing agreement. Reviewing the listing agreement, it appears that the seller is making all the promises and the broker is not making any promises. However, Paragraph 8 of Figure 8-2 contains a very important promise by the broker—that the broker will use reasonable efforts and due diligence to complete the purpose of the agreement (finding a buyer). Even in absence of such an express promise, the courts would likely imply a term in a listing agreement that the listing broker use diligence to find a buyer. If the broker does not use diligence, the seller may terminate the listing. If the broker sues for a commission, the court will decide if the broker exercised diligence or not. It may be in the best interest of the seller to impose a specific obligation on the part of the broker by including what is agreed to in the listing. This obligation could cover topics like how many open houses and how often and what kind of advertising.

If the seller is really concerned about the "diligence" that the broker will use, the seller should insist on an "Exclusive Agency," allowing the seller to compete against the broker in finding a purchaser. Of course the broker will want an arrangement to advise the seller of the people with whom the broker has dealt so that the seller could not sell to one of them and avoid paying a commission.

A seller may spend considerable time trying to personally sell the property to two potential buyers and later decide to list the property with a broker. If he/she doesn't want to pay the broker a commission if the property is sold to either potential buyer, the seller could include a clause that no commission (or a reduced commission) will be paid to the broker if the property is sold to either potential buyer.

Even under a standard listing agreement, however, if the buyer/seller contract is **conditional** (contingent on the results of an inspection, for example), the seller isn't liable for a commission unless the condition is either fulfilled or waived by the parties.

2. Extender Clause and Withdrawal Clause

Exclusive listing forms usually include an extender clause (also called a safety clause or carryover clause). An *EXTENDER CLAUSE (see **Paragraph 4-A-2**) makes the client liable for a commission during a specified period after the listing expires if the property is sold to someone the broker showed the property to during the listing term.* This makes it more difficult for a buyer and seller to conspire to deprive the broker of a commission by waiting until the listing expires before signing a purchase agreement.

The extender clauses in some forms require: (1) the client to pay the commission if the broker merely introduced the buyer to the property during the listing term, or (2) that the client doesn't have to pay the commission unless the broker was the procuring cause of the sale. The CAR® form extender clause makes the client liable for a commission if the property is sold to a buyer the broker negotiated with before the listing expired, provided the client received a written notice of the names of prospective purchasers before or at the time of termination of the listing. For listing purposes, is everyone the broker "had negotiations" with the same as a "prospective purchaser"?

There may be situations where a seller is reluctant to sign a listing agreement because another broker may claim that the seller is obligate to pay a commission and sue the seller if not paid. This situation could occur when the seller signed a listing agreement with another broker and that listing agreement expired, but had an extender clause (discussed below). The CAR® form in Figure 8-2 has provisions, Paragraph 4F-1 and 4F2, to specify that the seller is not obligated to pay a commission to the new listing broker under this situation. A seller should use **Paragraph 4F-2** and list the names of Prospective Buyers received from a former broker (named in **Paragraph 4F-1**) with whom the property was listed so that the new listing broker knows that there is potential commission liability for those whose names are listed. This safeguards a seller from having to pay two commissions.

Most exclusive listing forms make the client liable for a commission if he or she withdraws the property from sale or does anything to make it unmarketable. The CAR® agreement in Figure 8-2 has this type of provision in **Paragraph 4A-3**. This section also obligates the seller to pay a commission if the seller makes the property unmarketable, such as by renting the property out because the property is not selling as quickly as the seller anticipated.

3. Other Provisions

Other clauses of interest to the seller are:

6 – MULTIPLE LISTING SERVICE. Some sellers may not be familiar with how the multiple listing service operates. The broker should make sure the seller understands what is in this paragraph and how will affect the seller.

12 – KEYSAFE/LOCKBOX. Since there is no way of knowing how many people have access to the lockbox, there is always a risk of unauthorized entry into the structure, snooping around inside, and theft of personal property, especially when the owner is away from the property. Those who have access to the property do not want to assume the risk that they bring with that access, and have eliminated liability in **Paragraph 11**. Consequently, the listing broker needs to explain that insurance may be appropriate to cover the risk (checking the sellers' homeowner's insurance for coverage may be a good idea). The seller may wish to strike out **Paragraph 11** and allow access only when personally on the property or, if not on the property, allow access to others only when accompanied by the listing broker.

13 – SIGN. The agent needs to discuss with the seller when the for sale sign will be erected on the property and how long it will stay there. Typically, sellers want the "for sale" sign up as soon as possible. The issue then becomes when will the sign be removed and if a "sold" sign will be placed on it. For example, a seller may want the sign removed on the day the purchase agreement is signed and the agent may want to leave the sign on the property until the close of escrow. A broker and the client may wish to clarify this with some exact dates and place them on the margin of the contract or in **Paragraph 16** with both initialing this addition.

19A – MEDIATION OF DISPUTES. If there is a dispute between the broker and seller, both agree to mediate claims before resorting to arbitration or court action. See Chapter 9 on alternatives to dispute resolution.

19B – ARBITRATION OF DISPUTES. If initialed by broker and seller, both agree to binding arbitration of disputes and no court action is possible.

20 – ENTIRE AGREEMENT (Integration Clause). This clause is the parol evidence rule in written form. Therefore, both parties must make sure the listing states everything agreed to. The friendly broker who says "Trust me, we don't need to clutter up the contract with that stuff" should be an alarm that causes everything agreed to outside the writing to now be included in the listing agreement.

III. The Purchase Agreement

The general name for a contract between a buyer and seller of real property is a "purchase agreement," "purchase and sale agreement," or something similar. In most transactions, the buyers put up an earnest money deposit (although it is not legally required) at the same time they make an offer to purchase. The standard form used as a written offer also serves as the buyer's receipt for the deposit. If the seller decides to accept the offer, he or she signs the form, and it becomes the parties' contract. A copy of the 8-page **CAR® Residential Purchase Agreement and Joint Escrow Instructions** form (RPA-CA) is shown in **Figure 8-3**.

A. ELEMENTS OF A PURCHASE AGREEMENT

The Residential Purchase Agreement and Joint Escrow Instructions is a multi-functional form and contains:

CHAPTER 8

Figure 8-3

CALIFORNIA
ASSOCIATION
OF REALTORS®

CALIFORNIA
RESIDENTIAL PURCHASE AGREEMENT
AND JOINT ESCROW INSTRUCTIONS
For Use With Single Family Residential Property — Attached or Detached
(C.A.R. Form RPA-CA, Revised 4/10)

Date *June 14, 20xx*

1. **OFFER:**
   A. **THIS IS AN OFFER FROM** *Walter   Buyer, Debbie   Buyer* ("Buyer").
   B. **THE REAL PROPERTY TO BE ACQUIRED** is described as *264 Beach Lane, Costa Mesa CA 92627*
   , Assessor's Parcel No. , situated in
   Costa Mesa, County of *Orange*, California, ("Property").
   C. **THE PURCHASE PRICE** offered is *Eight Hundred Thousand*
   (Dollars $ *800,000.00*).
   D. **CLOSE OF ESCROW** shall occur on _____ (date) (or ☒ *90* **Days** After Acceptance).

2. **AGENCY:**
   A. **DISCLOSURE:** Buyer and Seller each acknowledge prior receipt of a "Disclosure Regarding Real Estate Agency Relationships" (C.A.R. Form AD).
   B. **POTENTIALLY COMPETING BUYERS AND SELLERS:** Buyer and Seller each acknowledge receipt of a disclosure of the possibility of multiple representation by the Broker representing that principal. This disclosure may be part of a listing agreement, buyer representation agreement or separate document (C.A.R. Form DA). Buyer understands that Broker representing Buyer may also represent other potential buyers, who may consider, make offers on or ultimately acquire the Property. Seller understands that Broker representing Seller may also represent other sellers with competing properties of interest to this Buyer.
   C. **CONFIRMATION:** The following agency relationships are hereby confirmed for this transaction:
   Listing Agent *Sail Realty* (Print Firm Name) is the agent
   of (check one): ☒ the Seller exclusively; or ☐ both the Buyer and Seller.
   Selling Agent *Ramos Realty* (Print Firm Name) (if not the same as the
   Listing Agent) is the agent of (check one): ☒ the Buyer exclusively; or ☐ the Seller exclusively; or ☐ both the Buyer and Seller. Real Estate Brokers are not parties to the Agreement between Buyer and Seller.

3. **FINANCE TERMS:** Buyer represents that funds will be good when deposited with Escrow Holder.
   A. **INITIAL DEPOSIT:** Deposit shall be in the amount of . . . . $ *10,000.00*
   (1) Buyer shall deliver deposit directly to Escrow Holder by personal check, ☐ electronic funds transfer, ☐ Other _____ within 3 business days after acceptance (or ☐ Other _____);
   OR (2) (If checked) ☒ Buyer has given the deposit by personal check (or ☐ _____)
   to the agent submitting the offer (or to ☒ _____),
   made payable to *ABC Escrow* . The deposit shall be held
   uncashed until Acceptance and then deposited with Escrow Holder (or ☐ into Broker's trust account) within **3** business days after Acceptance (or ☐ Other _____).
   B. **INCREASED DEPOSIT:** Buyer shall deposit with Escrow Holder an increased deposit in the amount of . . . . $ _____
   within _____ **Days** After Acceptance, or ☐ _____
   If a liquidated damages clause is incorporated into this Agreement, Buyer and Seller shall sign a separate liquidated damages clause (C.A.R. Form RID) for any increased deposit at the time it is deposited.
   C. **LOAN(S):**
   (1) **FIRST LOAN:** in the amount of . . . . $ *640,000.00*
   This loan will be conventional financing or, if checked, ☐ FHA, ☐ VA, ☐ Seller (C.A.R. Form SFA), ☐ assumed financing (C.A.R. Form PAA), ☐ Other _____ . This loan shall be at a fixed rate not to exceed *8.000* % or, ☐ an adjustable rate loan with initial rate not to exceed _____ %. Regardless of the type of loan, Buyer shall pay points not to exceed *2.00* % of the loan amount.
   (2) ☐ **SECOND LOAN:** in the amount of . . . . $ _____
   This loan will be conventional financing or, if checked, ☐ Seller (C.A.R. Form SFA), ☐ assumed financing (C.A.R. Form PAA), ☐ Other _____ . This loan shall be at a fixed rate not to exceed _____ % or, ☐ an adjustable rate loan with initial rate not to exceed _____ %. Regardless of the type of loan, Buyer shall pay points not to exceed _____ % of the loan amount.
   (3) **FHA/VA:** For any FHA or VA loan specified above, Buyer has **17 (or ☐ _____) Days** After Acceptance to Deliver to Seller written notice (C.A.R. Form FVA) of any lender-required repairs or costs that Buyer requests Seller to pay for or repair. Seller has no obligation to pay for repairs or satisfy lender requirements unless otherwise agreed in writing.
   D. **ADDITIONAL FINANCING TERMS:** _____

   E. **BALANCE OF PURCHASE PRICE OR DOWN PAYMENT:** in the amount of . . . . $ *150,000.00*
   to be deposited with Escrow Holder within sufficient time to close escrow.
   F. **PURCHASE PRICE (TOTAL):** . . . . $ *800,000.00*

Buyer's Initials (_____) (_____)   Seller's Initials (_____) (_____)

RPA-CA REVISED 4/10 (PAGE 1 OF 8)

Reviewed by _____ Date _____

CALIFORNIA RESIDENTIAL PURCHASE AGREEMENT (RPA-CA PAGE 1 OF 8)

Agent: WALT HUBER   Phone: Fax: Prepared using zipForm® software
Broker: WALT HUBER REALTOR

Property Address: *264 Beach Lane*
Costa Mesa, CA 92627   Date: *June 14, 20xx*

G. VERIFICATION OF DOWN PAYMENT AND CLOSING COSTS: Buyer (or Buyer's lender or loan broker pursuant to 3H(1)) shall, within **7 (or** ☐ _____ **) Days** After Acceptance, Deliver to Seller written verification of Buyer's down payment and closing costs. (If checked, ☐ verification attached.)

H. LOAN TERMS:

    (1) LOAN APPLICATIONS: Within **7 (or** ☐ _____ **) Days** After Acceptance, Buyer shall Deliver to Seller a letter from lender or loan broker stating that, based on a review of Buyer's written application and credit report, Buyer is prequalified or preapproved for any NEW loan specified in 3C above. (If checked, ☐ letter attached.)

    (2) LOAN CONTINGENCY: Buyer shall act diligently and in good faith to obtain the designated loan(s). Obtaining the loan(s) specified above **is a contingency** of this Agreement unless otherwise agreed in writing. Buyer's contractual obligations to obtain and provide deposit, balance of down payment and closing costs **are not contingencies** of this Agreement.

    (3) LOAN CONTINGENCY REMOVAL:

        (i) Within **17 (or** ☐ _____ **) Days** After Acceptance, Buyer shall, as specified in paragraph 14, in writing remove the loan contingency or cancel this Agreement;

        OR (ii) (if checked) ☐ the loan contingency shall remain in effect until the designated loans are funded.

    (4) ☐ **NO LOAN CONTINGENCY** (If checked): Obtaining any loan specified above is NOT a contingency of this Agreement. If Buyer does not obtain the loan and as a result Buyer does not purchase the Property, Seller may be entitled to Buyer's deposit or other legal remedies.

I. APPRAISAL CONTINGENCY AND REMOVAL: This Agreement is (**or, if checked,** ☐ **is NOT**) contingent upon a written appraisal of the Property by a licensed or certified appraiser at no less than the specified purchase price. If there is a loan contingency, Buyer's removal of the loan contingency shall be deemed removal of this appraisal contingency (**or,** ☐ if checked, Buyer shall, as specified in paragraph 14B(3), in writing remove the appraisal contingency or cancel this Agreement within **17 (or** _____ **) Days** After Acceptance). If there is no loan contingency, Buyer shall, as specified in paragraph 14B(3), in writing remove the appraisal contingency or cancel this Agreement within **17 (or** _____ **) Days** After Acceptance.

J. ☐ **ALL CASH OFFER** (If checked): Buyer shall, within **7 (or** ☐ _____ **) Days** After Acceptance, Deliver to Seller written verification of sufficient funds to close this transaction. (If checked, ☐ verification attached.)

K. BUYER STATED FINANCING: Seller has relied on Buyer's representation of the type of financing specified (including but not limited to, as applicable, amount of down payment, contingent or non contingent loan, or all cash). If Buyer seeks alternate financing, (i) Seller has no obligation to cooperate with Buyer's efforts to obtain such financing, and (ii) Buyer shall also pursue the financing method specified in this Agreement. Buyer's failure to secure alternate financing does not excuse Buyer from the obligation to purchase the Property and close escrow as specified in this Agreement.

4. ALLOCATION OF COSTS (If checked): Unless otherwise specified in writing, **this paragraph** only determines who is to pay for the inspection, test or service ("Report") mentioned; it **does not determine who is to pay for any work recommended or identified in the Report.**

    A. INSPECTIONS AND REPORTS:

        (1) ☐ Buyer ☒ Seller shall pay for an inspection and report for wood destroying pests and organisms ("Wood Pest Report") prepared by *Bug B Gone* a registered structural pest control company.

        (2) ☐ Buyer ☐ Seller shall pay to have septic or private sewage disposal systems pumped and inspected _____ .

        (3) ☐ Buyer ☐ Seller shall pay to have domestic wells tested for water potability and productivity _____ .

        (4) ☐ Buyer ☐ Seller shall pay for a natural hazard zone disclosure report prepared by _____ .

        (5) ☐ Buyer ☐ Seller shall pay for the following inspection or report _____ .

        (6) ☐ Buyer ☐ Seller shall pay for the following inspection or report _____ .

    B. GOVERNMENT REQUIREMENTS AND RETROFIT:

        (1) ☐ Buyer ☒ Seller shall pay for smoke detector installation and/or water heater bracing, if required by Law. Prior to Close Of Escrow, Seller shall provide Buyer written statement(s) of compliance in accordance with state and local Law, unless exempt.

        (2) ☐ Buyer ☐ Seller shall pay the cost of compliance with any other minimum mandatory government retrofit standards, inspections and reports if required as a condition of closing escrow under any Law. _____ .

    C. ESCROW AND TITLE:

        (1) ☒ Buyer ☒ Seller shall pay escrow fee *50%/50%*
        Escrow Holder shall be *ABC Escrow*

        (2) ☒ Buyer ☐ Seller shall pay for **owner's** title insurance policy specified in paragraph 12E
        Owner's title policy to be issued by _____
        (Buyer shall pay for any title insurance policy insuring Buyer's **lender**, unless otherwise agreed in writing.)

    D. OTHER COSTS:

        (1) ☐ Buyer ☐ Seller shall pay County transfer tax or fee _____ .

        (2) ☐ Buyer ☐ Seller shall pay City transfer tax or fee _____ .

        (3) ☐ Buyer ☐ Seller shall pay Homeowner's Association ("HOA") transfer fee _____ .

        (4) ☐ Buyer ☐ Seller shall pay HOA document preparation fees _____ .

        (5) ☐ Buyer ☐ Seller shall pay for any private transfer fee _____ .

        (6) ☐ Buyer ☐ Seller shall pay the cost, not to exceed $ _____ , of a one-year home warranty plan, issued by _____ , with the following optional coverages:
        ☐ Air Conditioner ☐ Pool/Spa ☐ Code and Permit upgrade ☐ Other: _____
        Buyer is informed that home warranty plans have many optional coverages in addition to those listed above. Buyer is advised to investigate these coverages to determine those that may be suitable for Buyer.

        (7) ☐ Buyer ☐ Seller shall pay for _____ .

        (8) ☐ Buyer ☐ Seller shall pay for _____ .

Buyer's Initials (_____) (_____)

Seller's Initials (_____) (_____)

RPA-CA REVISED 4/10 (PAGE 2 OF 8)

Reviewed by _____ Date _____

EQUAL HOUSING OPPORTUNITY

CALIFORNIA RESIDENTIAL PURCHASE AGREEMENT (RPA-CA PAGE 2 OF 8)

Cal Principles -

Property Address: **264 Beach Lane**
Costa Mesa, CA   92627 _____   Date: *June 14, 20xx* _____

5. **CLOSING AND POSSESSION:**
   A. Buyer intends (or ☐ does not intend) to occupy the Property as Buyer's primary residence.
   B. **Seller-occupied or vacant property:** Possession shall be delivered to Buyer at 5 PM or (☒ *11* ☒ AM ☐ PM), on the date of Close Of Escrow; ☐ on _____ ; or ☐ no later than _____ **Days** After Close Of Escrow. If transfer of title and possession do not occur at the same time, Buyer and Seller are advised to: **(i)** enter into a written occupancy agreement (C.A.R. Form PAA, paragraph 2); and **(ii)** consult with their insurance and legal advisors.
   C. **Tenant-occupied property:**
      (i) Property shall be vacant at least **5 (or ☐ _____) Days** Prior to Close Of Escrow, unless otherwise agreed in writing. **Note to Seller: If you are unable to deliver Property vacant in accordance with rent control and other applicable Law, you may be in breach of this Agreement.**
      OR **(ii)** (if checked) ☐ **Tenant to remain in possession.** (C.A.R. Form PAA, paragraph 3)
   D. At Close Of Escrow, **(i)** Seller assigns to Buyer any assignable warranty rights for items included in the sale, and **(ii)** Seller shall Deliver to Buyer available Copies of warranties. Brokers cannot and will not determine the assignability of any warranties.
   E. At Close Of Escrow, unless otherwise agreed in writing, Seller shall provide keys and/or means to operate all locks, mailboxes, security systems, alarms and garage door openers. If Property is a condominium or located in a common interest subdivision, Buyer may be required to pay a deposit to the Homeowners' Association ("HOA") to obtain keys to accessible HOA facilities.

6. **STATUTORY DISCLOSURES (INCLUDING LEAD-BASED PAINT HAZARD DISCLOSURES) AND CANCELLATION RIGHTS:**
   A. **(1)** Seller shall, within the time specified in paragraph 14A, Deliver to Buyer, if required by Law: **(i)** Federal Lead-Based Paint Disclosures (C.A.R. Form FLD) and pamphlet ("Lead Disclosures"); and **(ii)** disclosures or notices required by sections 1102 et. seq. and 1103 et. seq. of the Civil Code ("Statutory Disclosures"). Statutory Disclosures include, but are not limited to, a Real Estate Transfer Disclosure Statement ("TDS"), Natural Hazard Disclosure Statement ("NHD"), notice or actual knowledge of release of illegal controlled substance, notice of special tax and/or assessments (or, if allowed, substantially equivalent notice regarding the Mello-Roos Community Facilities Act and Improvement Bond Act of 1915) and, if Seller has actual knowledge, of industrial use and military ordinance location (C.A.R. Form SPQ or SSD).
      (2) Buyer shall, within the time specified in paragraph 14B(1), return Signed Copies of the Statutory and Lead Disclosures to Seller.
      (3) In the event Seller, prior to Close Of Escrow, becomes aware of adverse conditions materially affecting the Property, or any material inaccuracy in disclosures, information or representations previously provided to Buyer, Seller shall promptly provide a subsequent or amended disclosure or notice, in writing, covering those items. **However, a subsequent or amended disclosure shall not be required for conditions and material inaccuracies** of which Buyer is otherwise aware, or which are **disclosed in reports provided to or obtained by Buyer or ordered and paid for by Buyer.**
      (4) If any disclosure or notice specified in 6A(1), or subsequent or amended disclosure or notice is Delivered to Buyer after the offer is Signed, Buyer shall have the right to cancel this Agreement within **3 Days** After Delivery in person, or **5 Days** After Delivery by deposit in the mail, by giving written notice of cancellation to Seller or Seller's agent.
      (5) Note to Buyer and Seller: Waiver of Statutory and Lead Disclosures is prohibited by Law.
   B. **NATURAL AND ENVIRONMENTAL HAZARDS:** Within the time specified in paragraph 14A, Seller shall, if required by Law: **(i)** Deliver to Buyer earthquake guides (and questionnaire) and environmental hazards booklet; **(ii)** even if exempt from the obligation to provide a NHD, disclose if the Property is located in a Special Flood Hazard Area; Potential Flooding (Inundation) Area; Very High Fire Hazard Zone; State Fire Responsibility Area; Earthquake Fault Zone; Seismic Hazard Zone; and **(iii)** disclose any other zone as required by Law and provide any other information required for those zones.
   C. **WITHHOLDING TAXES:** Within the time specified in paragraph 14A, to avoid required withholding, Seller shall Deliver to Buyer or qualified substitute, an affidavit sufficient to comply with federal (FIRPTA) and California withholding Law, (C.A.R. Form AS or QS).
   D. **MEGAN'S LAW DATABASE DISCLOSURE:** Notice: Pursuant to Section 290.46 of the Penal Code, information about specified registered sex offenders is made available to the public via an Internet Web site maintained by the Department of Justice at www.meganslaw.ca.gov. Depending on an offender's criminal history, this information will include either the address at which the offender resides or the community of residence and ZIP Code in which he or she resides. (Neither Seller nor Brokers are required to check this website. If Buyer wants further information, Broker recommends that Buyer obtain information from this website during Buyer's inspection contingency period. Brokers do not have expertise in this area.)

7. **CONDOMINIUM/PLANNED DEVELOPMENT DISCLOSURES:**
   A. **SELLER HAS: 7 (or ☐ _____) Days** After Acceptance to disclose to Buyer whether the Property is a condominium, or is located in a planned development or other common interest subdivision (C.A.R. Form SPQ or SSD).
   B. If the Property is a condominium or is located in a planned development or other common interest subdivision, Seller has **3 (or ☐ _____) Days** After Acceptance to request from the HOA (C.A.R. Form HOA): **(i)** Copies of any documents required by Law; **(ii)** disclosure of any pending or anticipated claim or litigation by or against the HOA; **(iii)** a statement containing the location and number of designated parking and storage spaces; **(iv)** Copies of the most recent 12 months of HOA minutes for regular and special meetings; and **(v)** the names and contact information of all HOAs governing the Property (collectively, "CI Disclosures"). Seller shall itemize and Deliver to Buyer all CI Disclosures received from the HOA and any CI Disclosures in Seller's possession. Buyer's approval of CI Disclosures is a contingency of this Agreement as specified in paragraph 14B(3).

8. **ITEMS INCLUDED IN AND EXCLUDED FROM PURCHASE PRICE:**
   A. **NOTE TO BUYER AND SELLER:** Items listed as included or excluded in the MLS, flyers or marketing materials are not included in the purchase price or excluded from the sale unless specified in 8B or C.
   B. **ITEMS INCLUDED IN SALE:**
      (1) All EXISTING fixtures and fittings that are attached to the Property;
      (2) EXISTING electrical, mechanical, lighting, plumbing and heating fixtures, ceiling fans, fireplace inserts, gas logs and grates, solar systems, built-in appliances, window and door screens, awnings, shutters, window coverings, attached floor coverings, television antennas, satellite dishes, private integrated telephone systems, air coolers/conditioners, pool/spa equipment, garage door openers/remote controls, mailbox, in-ground landscaping, trees/shrubs, water softeners, water purifiers, security systems/alarms; (If checked ☐ stove(s), ☐ refrigerator(s); and
      (3) The following additional items: _____
      (4) Seller represents that all items included in the purchase price, unless otherwise specified, are owned by Seller.
      (5) All items included shall be transferred free of liens and without Seller warranty.
   C. **ITEMS EXCLUDED FROM SALE:** Unless otherwise specified, audio and video components (such as flat screen TVs and speakers) are excluded if any such item is not itself attached to the Property, even if a bracket or other mechanism attached to the component is attached to the Property; and _____

Buyer's Initials (_____)(_____)

Copyright © 1991-2010, CALIFORNIA ASSOCIATION OF REALTORS®, INC.
RPA-CA REVISED 4/10 (PAGE 3 OF 8)

Seller's Initials (_____)(_____)

Reviewed by _____ Date _____

CALIFORNIA RESIDENTIAL PURCHASE AGREEMENT (RPA-CA PAGE 3 OF 8)   Cal Principles -

Property Address: *264 Beach Lane*
Costa Mesa, CA   92627   Date: *June 14, 20xx*

9. **CONDITION OF PROPERTY:** Unless otherwise agreed: (i) the Property is sold (a) in its PRESENT physical ("as-is") condition as of the date of Acceptance and (b) subject to Buyer's Investigation rights; (ii) the Property, including pool, spa, landscaping and grounds, is to be maintained in substantially the same condition as on the date of Acceptance; and (iii) all debris and personal property not included in the sale shall be removed by Seller by Close Of Escrow.
   A. Seller shall, within the time specified in paragraph 14A, DISCLOSE KNOWN MATERIAL FACTS AND DEFECTS affecting the Property, including known insurance claims within the past five years, and make any and all other disclosures required by law.
   B. Buyer has the right to inspect the Property and, as specified in paragraph 14B, based upon information discovered in those inspections: (i) cancel this Agreement; or (ii) request that Seller make Repairs or take other action.
   C. **Buyer is strongly advised to conduct investigations of the entire Property in order to determine its present condition. Seller may not be aware of all defects affecting the Property or other factors that Buyer considers important. Property improvements may not be built according to code, in compliance with current Law, or have had permits issued.**
10. **BUYER'S INVESTIGATION OF PROPERTY AND MATTERS AFFECTING PROPERTY:**
   A. Buyer's acceptance of the condition of, and any other matter affecting the Property, is a contingency of this Agreement as specified in this paragraph and paragraph 14B. Within the time specified in paragraph 14B(1), Buyer shall have the right, at Buyer's expense unless otherwise agreed, to conduct inspections, investigations, tests, surveys and other studies ("Buyer Investigations"), including, but not limited to, the right to: (i) inspect for lead-based paint and other lead-based paint hazards; (ii) inspect for wood destroying pests and organisms; (iii) review the registered sex offender database; (iv) confirm the insurability of Buyer and the Property; and (v) satisfy Buyer as to any matter specified in the attached Buyer's Inspection Advisory (C.A.R. Form BIA). Without Seller's prior written consent, Buyer shall neither make nor cause to be made: (i) invasive or destructive Buyer Investigations; or (ii) inspections by any governmental building or zoning inspector or government employee, unless required by Law.
   B. Seller shall make the Property available for all Buyer Investigations. Buyer shall (i) as specified in paragraph 14B, complete Buyer Investigations and, either remove the contingency or cancel this Agreement, and (ii) give Seller, at no cost, complete Copies of all Investigation reports obtained by Buyer, which obligation shall survive the termination of this Agreement.
   C. Seller shall have water, gas, electricity and all operable pilot lights on for Buyer's Investigations and through the date possession is made available to Buyer.
   D. **Buyer indemnity and Seller protection for entry upon property:** Buyer shall: (i) keep the Property free and clear of liens; (ii) repair all damage arising from Buyer Investigations; and (iii) indemnify and hold Seller harmless from all resulting liability, claims, demands, damages and costs of Buyer's investigations. Buyer shall carry, or Buyer shall require anyone acting on Buyer's behalf to carry, policies of liability, workers' compensation and other applicable insurance, defending and protecting Seller from liability for any injuries to persons or property occurring during any Buyer Investigations or work done on the Property at Buyer's direction prior to Close Of Escrow. Seller is advised that certain protections may be afforded Seller by recording a "Notice of Non-responsibility" (C.A.R. Form NNR) for Buyer Investigations and work done on the Property at Buyer's direction. Buyer's obligations under this paragraph shall survive the termination or cancellation of this Agreement and Close of Escrow.
11. **SELLER DISCLOSURES; ADDENDA; ADVISORIES; OTHER TERMS:**
   A. **Seller Disclosures (if checked):** Seller shall, within the time specified in paragraph 14A, complete and provide Buyer with a:
      ☒ Seller Property Questionnaire (C.A.R. Form SPQ)   OR   ☐ Supplemental Contractual and Statutory Disclosure (C.A.R. Form SSD)
   B. **Addenda (if checked):**   ☐ Addendum #_____ (C.A.R. Form ADM)
      ☐ Wood Destroying Pest Inspection and Allocation of Cost Addendum (C.A.R. Form WPA)
      ☒ Purchase Agreement Addendum (C.A.R Form PAA)   ☒ Septic, Well and Property Monument Addendum (C.A.R. Form SWPI)
      ☐ Short Sale Addendum (C.A.R. Form SSA)   ☐ Other
   C. **Advisories (if checked):**   ☒ Buyer's Inspection Advisory (C.A.R. Form BIA)
      ☐ Probate Advisory (C.A.R. Form PAK)   ☒ Statewide Buyer and Seller Advisory (C.A.R. Form SBSA)
      ☐ Trust Advisory (C.A.R. Form TA)   ☐ REO Advisory (C.A.R. Form REO)
   D. **Other Terms:**
12. **TITLE AND VESTING:**
   A. Within the time specified in paragraph 14, Buyer shall be provided a current preliminary title report, which shall include a search of the General Index. Seller shall within 7 Days After Acceptance give Escrow Holder a completed Statement of Information. The preliminary report is only an offer by the title insurer to issue a policy of title insurance and may not contain every item affecting title. Buyer's review of the preliminary report and any other matters which may affect title are a contingency of this Agreement as specified in paragraph 14B.
   B. Title is taken in its present condition subject to all encumbrances, easements, covenants, conditions, restrictions, rights and other matters, whether of record or not, as of the date of Acceptance except: (i) monetary liens of record unless Buyer is assuming those obligations or taking the Property subject to those obligations; and (ii) those matters which Seller has agreed to remove in writing.
   C. Within the time specified in paragraph 14A, Seller has a duty to disclose to Buyer all matters known to Seller affecting title, whether of record or not.
   D. At Close Of Escrow, Buyer shall receive a grant deed conveying title (or, for stock cooperative or long-term lease, an assignment of stock certificate or of Seller's leasehold interest), including oil, mineral and water rights if currently owned by Seller. Title shall vest as designated in Buyer's supplemental escrow instructions. THE MANNER OF TAKING TITLE MAY HAVE SIGNIFICANT LEGAL AND TAX CONSEQUENCES. CONSULT AN APPROPRIATE PROFESSIONAL.
   E. Buyer shall receive a CLTA/ALTA Homeowner's Policy of Title Insurance. A title company, at Buyer's request, can provide information about the availability, desirability, coverage, survey requirements, and cost of various title insurance coverages and endorsements. If Buyer desires title coverage other than that required by this paragraph, Buyer shall instruct Escrow Holder in writing and pay any increase in cost.
13. **SALE OF BUYER'S PROPERTY:**
   A. This Agreement is NOT contingent upon the sale of any property owned by Buyer.
   OR B. ☐ (If checked): The attached addendum (C.A.R. Form COP) regarding the contingency for the sale of property owned by Buyer is incorporated into this Agreement.

Buyer's Initials (_____) (_____)   Seller's Initials (_____) (_____)

RPA-CA REVISED 4/10 (PAGE 4 OF 8)   Reviewed by _____ Date _____

CALIFORNIA RESIDENTIAL PURCHASE AGREEMENT (RPA-CA PAGE 4 OF 8)   Cal Principles -

264 Beach Lane
Property Address: *Costa Mesa, CA 92627*   Date: *June 14, 20xx*

14. TIME PERIODS; REMOVAL OF CONTINGENCIES; CANCELLATION RIGHTS: The following time periods may only be extended, altered, modified or changed by mutual written agreement. Any removal of contingencies or cancellation under this paragraph by either Buyer or Seller must be exercised in good faith and in writing (C.A.R. Form CR or CC).

A. **SELLER HAS: 7 (or ☐ _____) Days** After Acceptance to Deliver to Buyer all Reports, disclosures and information for which Seller is responsible under paragraphs 4, 6A, B and C, 7A, 9A, 11A and B, and 12. Buyer may give Seller a Notice to Seller to Perform (C.A.R. Form NSP) if Seller has not Delivered the items within the time specified.

B. **(1) BUYER HAS: 17 (or ☐ _____) Days** After Acceptance, unless otherwise agreed in writing, to:
   (i) complete all Buyer Investigations; approve all disclosures, reports and other applicable information, which Buyer receives from Seller; and approve all other matters affecting the Property; and
   (ii) Deliver to Seller Signed Copies of Statutory and Lead Disclosures Delivered by Seller in accordance with paragraph 6A.

     (2) Within the time specified in 14B(1), Buyer may request that Seller make repairs or take any other action regarding the Property (C.A.R. Form RR). Seller has no obligation to agree to or respond to Buyer's requests.

     (3) Within the time specified in 14B(1) (or as otherwise specified in this Agreement), Buyer shall Deliver to Seller either (i) a removal of the applicable contingency (C.A.R. Form CR), or (ii) a cancellation (C.A.R. Form CC) of this Agreement based upon a contingency or Seller's failure to Deliver the specified items. However, if any report, disclosure or information for which Seller is responsible is not Delivered within the time specified in 14A, then Buyer has **5 (or ☐ _____) Days** After Delivery of any such items, or the time specified in 14B(1), whichever is later, to Deliver to Seller a removal of the applicable contingency or cancellation of this Agreement.

     (4) Continuation of Contingency: Even after the end of the time specified in 14B(1) and before Seller cancels this Agreement, if at all, pursuant to 14C, Buyer retains the right to either (i) in writing remove remaining contingencies, or (ii) cancel this Agreement based upon a remaining contingency or Seller's failure to Deliver the specified terms. Once Buyer's written removal of all contingencies is Delivered to Seller, Seller may not cancel this Agreement pursuant to 14C(1).

C. **SELLER RIGHT TO CANCEL:**
   (1) Seller right to Cancel; Buyer Contingencies: If, within time specified in this Agreement, Buyer does not, in writing, Deliver to Seller a removal of the applicable contingency or cancellation of this Agreement then Seller, after first Delivering to Buyer a Notice to Buyer to Perform (C.A.R. Form NBP) may cancel this Agreement. In such event, Seller shall authorize return of Buyer's deposit.
   (2) Seller right to Cancel; Buyer Contract Obligations: Seller, after first Delivering to Buyer a NBP may cancel this Agreement for any of the following reasons: **(i)** if Buyer fails to deposit funds as required by 3A or 3B; **(ii)** if the funds deposited pursuant to 3A or 3B are not good when deposited; **(iii)** if Buyer fails to Deliver a notice of FHA or VA costs or terms as required by 3C(3) (C.A.R. Form FVA); **(iv)** if Buyer fails to Deliver a letter as required by 3H; **(v)** if Buyer fails to Deliver verification as required by 3G or 3J; **(vi)** if Seller reasonably disapproves of the verification provided by 3G or 3J; **(vii)** if Buyer fails to return Statutory and Lead Disclosures as required by paragraph 6A(2); or **(viii)** if Buyer fails to sign or initial a separate liquidated damage form for an increased deposit as required by paragraphs 3B and 25. In such event, Seller shall authorize return of Buyer's deposit.
   (3) Notice To Buyer To Perform: The NBP shall: **(i)** be in writing; **(ii)** be signed by Seller; and **(iii)** give Buyer at least **2 (or ☐ _____) Days** After Delivery (or until the time specified in the applicable paragraph, whichever occurs last) to take the applicable action. A NBP may not be Delivered any earlier than **2 Days** Prior to the expiration of the applicable time for Buyer to remove a contingency or cancel this Agreement or meet an obligation specified in 14C(2).

D. **EFFECT OF BUYER'S REMOVAL OF CONTINGENCIES:** If Buyer removes, in writing, any contingency or cancellation rights, unless otherwise specified in a separate written agreement between Buyer and Seller, Buyer shall with regard to that contingency or cancellation right conclusively be deemed to have: (i) completed all Buyer Investigations, and review of reports and other applicable information and disclosures; (ii) elected to proceed with the transaction; and (iii) assumed all liability, responsibility and expense for Repairs or corrections or for inability to obtain financing.

E. **CLOSE OF ESCROW:** Before Seller or Buyer may cancel this Agreement for failure of the other party to close escrow pursuant to this Agreement, Seller or Buyer must first give the other a demand to close escrow (C.A.R. Form DCE).

F. **EFFECT OF CANCELLATION ON DEPOSITS:** If Buyer or Seller gives written notice of cancellation pursuant to rights duly exercised under the terms of this Agreement, Buyer and Seller agree to Sign mutual instructions to cancel the sale and escrow and release deposits, if any, to the party entitled to the funds, less fees and costs incurred by that party. Fees and costs may be payable to service providers and vendors for services and products provided during escrow. **Release of funds will require mutual Signed release instructions from Buyer and Seller, judicial decision or arbitration award. A Buyer or Seller may be subject to a civil penalty of up to $1,000 for refusal to sign such instructions if no good faith dispute exists as to who is entitled to the deposited funds (Civil Code §1057.3).**

15. REPAIRS: Repairs shall be completed prior to final verification of condition unless otherwise agreed in writing. Repairs to be performed at Seller's expense may be performed by Seller or through others, provided that the work complies with applicable Law, including governmental permit, inspection and approval requirements. Repairs shall be performed in a good, skillful manner with materials of quality and appearance comparable to existing materials. It is understood that exact restoration of appearance or cosmetic items following all Repairs may not be possible. Seller shall: **(i)** obtain receipts for Repairs performed by others; **(ii)** prepare a written statement indicating the Repairs performed by Seller and the date of such Repairs; and **(iii)** provide Copies of receipts and statements to Buyer prior to final verification of condition.

16. FINAL VERIFICATION OF CONDITION: Buyer shall have the right to make a final inspection of the Property within **5 (or _____) Days** Prior to Close Of Escrow, **NOT AS A CONTINGENCY OF THE SALE,** but solely to confirm: **(i)** the Property is maintained pursuant to paragraph 9; **(ii)** Repairs have been completed as agreed; and **(iii)** Seller has complied with Seller's other obligations under this Agreement (C.A.R. Form VP).

17. PRORATIONS OF PROPERTY TAXES AND OTHER ITEMS: Unless otherwise agreed in writing, the following items shall be PAID CURRENT and prorated between Buyer and Seller as of Close Of Escrow: real property taxes and assessments, interest, rents, HOA regular, special, and emergency dues and assessments imposed prior to Close Of Escrow, premiums on insurance assumed by Buyer, payments on bonds and assessments assumed by Buyer, and payments on Mello-Roos and other Special Assessment District bonds and assessments that are a current lien. The following items shall be assumed by Buyer WITHOUT CREDIT toward the purchase price: prorated payments on Mello-Roos and other Special Assessment District bonds and assessments and HOA special assessments that are a current lien but not yet due. Property will be reassessed upon change of ownership. Any supplemental tax bills shall be paid as follows: **(i)** for periods after Close Of Escrow, by Buyer; and **(ii)** for periods prior to Close Of Escrow, by Seller (see C.A.R. Form SPT or SBSA for further information). **TAX BILLS ISSUED AFTER CLOSE OF ESCROW SHALL BE HANDLED DIRECTLY BETWEEN BUYER AND SELLER.** Prorations shall be made based on a 30-day month.

Buyer's Initials (_____) (_____)   Seller's Initials (_____) (_____)

RPA-CA REVISED 4/10 (PAGE 5 OF 8)

Reviewed by _____ Date _____

CALIFORNIA RESIDENTIAL PURCHASE AGREEMENT (RPA-CA PAGE 5 OF 8)   Cal Principles -

Property Address: *264 Beach Lane*
Costa Mesa, CA 92627   Date: *June 14, 20xx*

18. SELECTION OF SERVICE PROVIDERS: Brokers do not guarantee the performance of any vendors, service or product providers ("Providers"), whether referred by Broker or selected by Buyer, Seller or other person. Buyer and Seller may select ANY Providers of their own choosing.

19. MULTIPLE LISTING SERVICE ("MLS"): Brokers are authorized to report to the MLS a pending sale and, upon Close Of Escrow, the sales price and other terms of this transaction shall be provided to the MLS to be published and disseminated to persons and entities authorized to use the information on terms approved by the MLS.

20. EQUAL HOUSING OPPORTUNITY: The Property is sold in compliance with federal, state and local anti-discrimination Laws.

21. ATTORNEY FEES: In any action, proceeding, or arbitration between Buyer and Seller arising out of this Agreement, the prevailing Buyer or Seller shall be entitled to reasonable attorney fees and costs from the non-prevailing Buyer or Seller, except as provided in paragraph 26A.

22. DEFINITIONS: As used in this Agreement:
   A. **"Acceptance"** means the time the offer or final counter offer is accepted in writing by a party and is delivered to and personally received by the other party or that party's authorized agent in accordance with the terms of this offer or a final counter offer.
   B. **"C.A.R. Form"** means the specific form referenced or another comparable form agreed to by the parties.
   C. **"Close Of Escrow"** means the date the grant deed, or other evidence of transfer of title, is recorded.
   D. **"Copy"** means copy by any means including photocopy, NCR, facsimile and electronic.
   E. **"Days"** means calendar days. However, After Acceptance, the last **Day** for performance of any act required by this Agreement (including Close Of Escrow) shall not include any Saturday, Sunday, or legal holiday and shall instead be the next Day.
   F. **"Days After"** means the specified number of calendar days after the occurrence of the event specified, not counting the calendar date on which the specified event occurs. and ending at 11:59PM on the final day.
   G. **"Days Prior"** means the specified number of calendar days before the occurrence of the event specified, not counting the calendar date on which the specified event is scheduled to occur.
   H. **"Deliver", "Delivered" or "Delivery",** regardless of the method used (i.e. messenger, mail, email, fax, other), means and shall be effective upon (i) personal receipt by Buyer or Seller or the individual Real Estate Licensee for that principal as specified in paragraph D of the section titled Real Estate Brokers on page 8; OR (ii) if checked, ☐ per the attached addendum (C.A.R. Form RDN).
   I. **"Electronic Copy" or "Electronic Signature"** means, as applicable, an electronic copy or signature complying with California Law. Buyer and Seller agree that electronic means will not be used by either party to modify or alter the content or integrity of this Agreement without the knowledge and consent of the other party.
   J. **"Law"** means any law, code, statute, ordinance, regulation, rule or order, which is adopted by a controlling city, county, state or federal legislative, judicial or executive body or agency.
   K. **"Repairs"** means any repairs (including pest control), alterations, replacements, modifications or retrofitting of the Property provided for under this Agreement.
   L. **"Signed"** means either a handwritten or electronic signature on an original document, Copy or any counterpart.

23. BROKER COMPENSATION: Seller or Buyer, or both, as applicable, agrees to pay compensation to Broker as specified in a separate written agreement between Broker and that Seller or Buyer. Compensation is payable upon Close Of Escrow, or if escrow does not close, as otherwise specified in the agreement between Broker and that Seller or Buyer.

24. JOINT ESCROW INSTRUCTIONS TO ESCROW HOLDER:
   A. **The following paragraphs, or applicable portions thereof, of this Agreement constitute the joint escrow instructions of Buyer and Seller to Escrow Holder,** which Escrow Holder is to use along with any related counter offers and addenda, and any additional mutual instructions to close the escrow: 1, 3, 4, 6C, 11B and D, 12, 13B, 14F, 17, 22, 23, 24, 28, 30, and paragraph D of the section titled Real Estate Brokers on page 8. If a Copy of the separate compensation agreement(s) provided for in paragraph 23, or paragraph D of the section titled Real Estate Brokers on page 8 is deposited with Escrow Holder by Broker, Escrow Holder shall accept such agreement(s) and pay out of Buyer's or Seller's funds, or both, as applicable, the respective Broker's compensation provided for in such agreement(s). The terms and conditions of this Agreement not specifically referenced above, in the specified paragraphs are additional matters for the information of Escrow Holder, but about which Escrow Holder need not be concerned. Buyer and Seller will receive Escrow Holder's general provisions directly from Escrow Holder and will execute such provisions upon Escrow Holder's request. To the extent the general provisions are inconsistent or conflict with this Agreement, the general provisions will control as to the duties and obligations of Escrow Holder only. Buyer and Seller will execute additional instructions, documents and forms provided by Escrow Holder that are reasonably necessary to close the escrow.
   B. A Copy of this Agreement shall be delivered to Escrow Holder within **3** business days after Acceptance (or ☐ _____). Escrow Holder shall provide Seller's Statement of Information to Title company when received from Seller. Buyer and Seller authorize Escrow Holder to accept and rely on Copies and Signatures as defined in this Agreement as originals, to open escrow and for other purposes of escrow. The validity of this Agreement as between Buyer and Seller is not affected by whether or when Escrow Holder Signs this Agreement.
   C. Brokers are a party to the escrow for the sole purpose of compensation pursuant to paragraphs 23 and paragraph D of the section titled Real Estate Brokers on page 8. Buyer and Seller irrevocably assign to Brokers compensation specified in paragraphs 23, respectively, and irrevocably instruct Escrow Holder to disburse those funds to Brokers at Close Of Escrow or pursuant to any other mutually executed cancellation agreement. Compensation instructions can be amended or revoked only with the written consent of Brokers. Buyer and Seller shall release and hold harmless Escrow Holder from any liability resulting from Escrow Holder's payment to Broker(s) of compensation pursuant to this Agreement. Escrow Holder shall immediately notify Brokers: **(i)** if Buyer's initial or any additional deposit is not made pursuant to this Agreement, or is not good at time of deposit with Escrow Holder; or **(ii)** if either Buyer or Seller instruct Escrow Holder to cancel escrow.
   D. A Copy of any amendment that affects any paragraph of this Agreement for which Escrow Holder is responsible shall be delivered to Escrow Holder within **2** business days after mutual execution of the amendment.

Buyer's Initials (_____) (_____)   Seller's Initials (_____) (_____)

RPA-CA REVISED 4/10 (PAGE 6 OF 8) Print Date

Reviewed by _____ Date _____

CALIFORNIA RESIDENTIAL PURCHASE AGREEMENT (RPA-CA PAGE 6 OF 8)   Cal Principles -

Property Address: *264 Beach Lane*
Costa Mesa, CA 92627   Date: *June 14, 20xx*

25. LIQUIDATED DAMAGES: If Buyer fails to complete this purchase because of Buyer's default, Seller shall retain, as liquidated damages, the deposit actually paid. If the Property is a dwelling with no more than four units, one of which Buyer intends to occupy, then the amount retained shall be no more than 3% of the purchase price. Any excess shall be returned to Buyer. Release of funds will require mutual, Signed release instructions from both Buyer and Seller, judicial decision or arbitration award. **AT TIME OF THE INCREASED DEPOSIT BUYER AND SELLER SHALL SIGN A SEPARATE LIQUIDATED DAMAGES PROVISION FOR ANY INCREASED DEPOSIT. (C.A.R. FORM RID).**

Buyer's Initials	/	Seller's Initials	/

26. DISPUTE RESOLUTION:

A. **MEDIATION:** Buyer and Seller agree to mediate any dispute or claim arising between them out of this Agreement, or any resulting transaction, before resorting to arbitration or court action. **Buyer and Seller also agree to mediate any disputes or claims with Broker(s), who, in writing, agree to such mediation prior to, or within a reasonable time after, the dispute or claim is presented to the Broker.** Mediation fees, if any, shall be divided equally among the parties involved. If, for any dispute or claim to which this paragraph applies, any party (i) commences an action without first attempting to resolve the matter through mediation, or (ii) before commencement of an action, refuses to mediate after a request has been made, then that party shall not be entitled to recover attorney fees, even if they would otherwise be available to that party in any such action. THIS MEDIATION PROVISION APPLIES WHETHER OR NOT THE ARBITRATION PROVISION IS INITIALED. **Exclusions from this mediation agreement are specified in paragraph 26C.**

B. **ARBITRATION OF DISPUTES:**

Buyer and Seller agree that any dispute or claim in Law or equity arising between them out of this Agreement or any resulting transaction, which is not settled through mediation, shall be decided by neutral, binding arbitration. Buyer and Seller also agree to arbitrate any disputes or claims with Broker(s), who, in writing, agree to such arbitration prior to, or within a reasonable time after, the dispute or claim is presented to the Broker. The arbitrator shall be a retired judge or justice, or an attorney with at least 5 years of residential real estate Law experience, unless the parties mutually agree to a different arbitrator. The parties shall have the right to discovery in accordance with Code of Civil Procedure §1283.05. In all other respects, the arbitration shall be conducted in accordance with Title 9 of Part 3 of the Code of Civil Procedure. Judgment upon the award of the arbitrator(s) may be entered into any court having jurisdiction. Enforcement of this agreement to arbitrate shall be governed by the Federal Arbitration Act. **Exclusions from this arbitration agreement are specified in paragraph 26C.**

"NOTICE: BY INITIALING IN THE SPACE BELOW YOU ARE AGREEING TO HAVE ANY DISPUTE ARISING OUT OF THE MATTERS INCLUDED IN THE 'ARBITRATION OF DISPUTES' PROVISION DECIDED BY NEUTRAL ARBITRATION AS PROVIDED BY CALIFORNIA LAW AND YOU ARE GIVING UP ANY RIGHTS YOU MIGHT POSSESS TO HAVE THE DISPUTE LITIGATED IN A COURT OR JURY TRIAL. BY INITIALING IN THE SPACE BELOW YOU ARE GIVING UP YOUR JUDICIAL RIGHTS TO DISCOVERY AND APPEAL, UNLESS THOSE RIGHTS ARE SPECIFICALLY INCLUDED IN THE 'ARBITRATION OF DISPUTES' PROVISION. IF YOU REFUSE TO SUBMIT TO ARBITRATION AFTER AGREEING TO THIS PROVISION, YOU MAY BE COMPELLED TO ARBITRATE UNDER THE AUTHORITY OF THE CALIFORNIA CODE OF CIVIL PROCEDURE. YOUR AGREEMENT TO THIS ARBITRATION PROVISION IS VOLUNTARY."

"WE HAVE READ AND UNDERSTAND THE FOREGOING AND AGREE TO SUBMIT DISPUTES ARISING OUT OF THE MATTERS INCLUDED IN THE 'ARBITRATION OF DISPUTES' PROVISION TO NEUTRAL ARBITRATION."

Buyer's Initials	Seller's Initials	/

C. ADDITIONAL MEDIATION AND ARBITRATION TERMS:

(1) **EXCLUSIONS:** The following matters shall be excluded from mediation and arbitration: (i) a judicial or non-judicial foreclosure or other action or proceeding to enforce a deed of trust, mortgage or installment land sale contract as defined in Civil Code §2985; (ii) an unlawful detainer action; (iii) the filing or enforcement of a mechanic's lien; and (iv) any matter that is within the jurisdiction of a probate, small claims or bankruptcy court. The filing of a court action to enable the recording of a notice of pending action, for order of attachment, receivership, injunction, or other provisional remedies, shall not constitute a waiver or violation of the mediation and arbitration provisions.

(2) **BROKERS:** Brokers shall not be obligated or compelled to mediate or arbitrate unless they agree to do so in writing. Any Broker(s) participating in mediation or arbitration shall not be deemed a party to the Agreement.

27. TERMS AND CONDITIONS OF OFFER:

This is an offer to purchase the Property on the above terms and conditions. The liquidated damages paragraph or the arbitration of disputes paragraph is incorporated in this Agreement if initialed by all parties or if incorporated by mutual agreement in a counter offer or addendum. If at least one but not all parties initial such paragraph(s), a counter offer is required until agreement is reached. Seller has the right to continue to offer the Property for sale and to accept any other offer at any time prior to notification of Acceptance. If this offer is accepted and Buyer subsequently defaults, Buyer may be responsible for payment of Brokers' compensation. This Agreement and any supplement, addendum or modification, including any Copy, may be Signed in two or more counterparts, all of which shall constitute one and the same writing.

28. TIME OF ESSENCE; ENTIRE CONTRACT; CHANGES: Time is of the essence. All understandings between the parties are incorporated in this Agreement. Its terms are intended by the parties as a final, complete and exclusive expression of their Agreement with respect to its subject matter, and may not be contradicted by evidence of any prior agreement or contemporaneous oral agreement. If any provision of this Agreement is held to be ineffective or invalid, the remaining provisions will nevertheless be given full force and effect. Except as otherwise specified, this Agreement shall be interpreted and disputes shall be resolved in accordance with the laws of the State of California. **Neither this Agreement nor any provision in it may be extended, amended, modified, altered or changed, except in writing Signed by Buyer and Seller.**

Buyer's Initials (_____) (_____)   Seller's Initials (_____) (_____)

RPA-CA REVISED 4/10 (PAGE 7 OF 8)

Reviewed by	Date

CALIFORNIA RESIDENTIAL PURCHASE AGREEMENT (RPA-CA PAGE 7 OF 8)   Cal Principles -

Property Address: *264 Beach Lane*
Costa Mesa, CA 92627   Date: *June 14, 20xx*

29. EXPIRATION OF OFFER: This offer shall be deemed revoked and the deposit shall be returned unless the offer is Signed by Seller and a Copy of the Signed offer is personally received by Buyer, or by _____, who is authorized to receive it, by 5:00 PM on the third Day after this offer is signed by Buyer (or, if checked, ☐ by ☐ AM ☐ PM, on _____ (date)).

Buyer has read and acknowledges receipt of a Copy of the offer and agrees to the above confirmation of agency relationships.

Date *June 14, 20xx*   Date *June 14, 20xx*

BUYER _____   BUYER _____
Walter   Buyer   *Debbie   Buyer*
(Print name)   **(Print name)**
100 Boat Avenue, Marina del Rey CA 90292
(Address)
☐ Additional Signature Addendum attached (C.A.R. Form ASA).

30. ACCEPTANCE OF OFFER: Seller warrants that Seller is the owner of the Property, or has the authority to execute this Agreement. Seller accepts the above offer, agrees to sell the Property on the above terms and conditions, and agrees to the above confirmation of agency relationships. Seller has read and acknowledges receipt of a Copy of this Agreement, and authorizes Broker to Deliver a Signed Copy to Buyer.

☐ (If checked) **SUBJECT TO ATTACHED COUNTER OFFER (C.A.R. Form CO) DATED:** _____

Date *June 15, 20xx*   Date *June 15, 20xx*

SELLER _____   SELLER _____
Tony   Seller   *Ramona J.   Seller*
(Print name)   **(Print name)**
264 Beach Lane, Costa Mesa, CA 92627
(Address)
☐ Additional Signature Addendum attached (C.A.R. Form ASA).

(_____ / _____) **CONFIRMATION OF ACCEPTANCE:** A Copy of Signed Acceptance was personally received by Buyer or Buyer's authorized
(Initials) agent on (date) *June 15, 20xx* at *11* ☒ AM ☐ PM. A binding Agreement is created when a Copy of Signed Acceptance is personally received by Buyer or Buyer's authorized agent whether or not confirmed in this document. Completion of this confirmation is not legally required in order to create a binding Agreement. It is solely intended to evidence the date that Confirmation of Acceptance has occurred.

REAL ESTATE BROKERS:
A. Real Estate Brokers are not parties to the Agreement between Buyer and Seller.
B. Agency relationships are confirmed as stated in paragraph 2.
C. If specified in paragraph 3A(2), Agent who submitted the offer for Buyer acknowledges receipt of deposit.
D. COOPERATING BROKER COMPENSATION: Listing Broker agrees to pay Cooperating Broker **(Selling Firm)** and Cooperating Broker agrees to accept, out of Listing Broker's proceeds in escrow: (i) the amount specified in the MLS, provided Cooperating Broker is a Participant of the MLS in which the Property is offered for sale or a reciprocal MLS; or (ii) ☐ (if checked) the amount specified in a separate written agreement (C.A.R. Form CBC) between Listing Broker and Cooperating Broker. Declaration of License and Tax (C.A.R. Form DLT) may be used to document that tax reporting will be required or that an exemption exits.

Real Estate Broker (Selling Firm) *Ramos Realty* _____ DRE Lic. # *00 000 000*
By *Joseph Ramos* DRE Lic. # *00 000 000* Date *06/14/20xx*
Address *777 Newport Blvd.* City *Newport Beach* State *CA* Zip *92663*
Telephone *(714)647-0000* Fax *(714)647-0001* E-mail *jr@ramosrealty.com*

Real Estate Broker (Listing Firm) *Sail Realty* _____ DRE Lic. # *00 000 000*
By *Carmen Capo* DRE Lic. # *00 000 000* Date *06/15/20xx*
Address *227 Harbor Blvd.* City *Costa Mesa* State *CA* Zip *92627*
Telephone *(714)626-2828* Fax *(714)626-2829* E-mail *carmen@sailrealty.com*

ESCROW HOLDER ACKNOWLEDGMENT:
Escrow Holder acknowledges receipt of a Copy of this Agreement, (if checked, ☐ a deposit in the amount of $ _____),
counter offer numbered _____, ☐ Seller's Statement of Information and ☐ Other _____
_____, and agrees to act as Escrow Holder subject to paragraph 24 of this Agreement. any supplemental escrow instructions and the terms of Escrow Holder's general provisions if any.
Escrow Holder is advised that the date of Confirmation of Acceptance of the Agreement as between Buyer and Seller is _____

Escrow Holder _____ Escrow # _____
By _____ Date _____
Address _____
Phone/Fax/E-mail _____
Escrow Holder is licensed by the California Department of ☐ Corporations, ☐ Insurance, ☐ Real Estate. License # _____

PRESENTATION OF OFFER: (_____) Listing Broker presented this offer to Seller on _____ (date).
Broker or Designee Initials

REJECTION OF OFFER: (_____) (_____) No counter offer is being made. This offer was rejected by Seller on _____ (date).
Seller's Initials

Reviewed by _____
Broker or Designee _____ Date _____

REVISION DATE 4/10

CALIFORNIA RESIDENTIAL PURCHASE AGREEMENT (RPA-CA PAGE 8 OF 8)   Cal Principles -

CHAPTER 8

1. an offer to purchase real property,
2. a completed contract when accepted and signed by the buyer and seller,
3. a receipt for the good faith earnest money,
4. joint escrow instructions,
5. the seller's agreement to pay listing broker's compensation,
6. a mediation and arbitration agreement,
7. a confirmation of the agency relationships, and
8. an irrevocable assignment of compensation to brokers.

This CAR® form is detailed enough to address most issues involving the sale of real property. While modifications may be made to insure that all of the terms of parties' agreement are accurate and clear, it should be noted that extensive modification or drafting of additional paragraphs may be considered to be the the unauthorized practice of law and should be avoided.

Escrow is open when the escrow holder signs an acknowledgment of receipt of the this completed form. Unless otherwise agreed, the parties have three days to deliver the agreement to the escrow holder—usually at the same time as the deposit is placed in escrow. However, failing to submit the agreement to escrow will not invalidate the agreement between buyer and seller.

The buyer and seller may receive additional instructions directly from the escrow holder and agree to sign reasonable forms to complete the transactions. The escrow instructions also include the compensation being paid to the broker in the agreement.

1. The Parties

There are two key questions to ask regarding the parties to a purchase agreement:

1. Does everyone who is signing have the capacity to contract?
2. Is everyone with an ownership interest signing?

If any of the parties is underage or incompetent, the contract will be void. Also, unless everyone with an ownership interest in the property signs, the buyer won't be able to compel conveyance of the whole property.

2. Conditions

Most agreements between buyers and sellers are conditional. Any conditions must be spelled out in the purchase agreement. It should state exactly what must occur to fulfill each condition and should explain how one party is to notify the other when a condition has been fulfilled or waived. It should also state a time limit: if the condition is not fulfilled by the designated date, the contract will be terminated or the condition waived. Finally, it should explain the parties' rights in the event that the condition is not met or waived.

If a real estate agent believes that a contingency clause in a purchase agreement may affect the date of closing or the time that the buyer can take possession of the property, the agent is required to explain that to the parties. Failure to do so is a violation of the Real Estate Law, and may lead to suspension or revocation of the agent's license. Here are two of the more important areas involving conditions:

a. Financing

Nearly all residential transactions are contingent on whether the buyer is able to obtain financing. This is why it's particularly important to describe the financing arrangements in detail. In the CAR® Agreement in Figure 8-3, the terms of the financing that the buyer will use to purchase the property are described in Paragraphs 3C and D. Paragraph 3H of the CAR® agreement provides that the buyer's obligation to purchase is contingent upon the buyer obtaining any loans described in the agreement, unless the box in Paragraph 3H(4) or Paragraph 3J is checked. The buyer is required to make a diligent, good faith effort to obtain financing on the terms stated in the purchase agreement. If no lenders are willing to loan on those terms, the buyer can back out without forfeiting the deposit.

Case Example: Mr. Fry wanted to buy the Millers' house. His written offer stated that it was "conditioned upon the buyer obtaining a $20,000 loan at 5% for 20 years." The Millers accepted the offer immediately, and Fry made a $4,250 deposit.

The Millers had previously mortgaged the house to Western Mortgage Company. Fry was advised that although most banks wouldn't be willing to make him a 20-year, $20,000 loan at 5% interest, Western Mortgage Company would be willing to refinance on those terms.

Fry applied for the loan at two banks, but both turned him down. Fry never contacted Western Mortgage, although the Millers and their broker urged him to on a number of occasions.

Eventually, Fry told the Millers that the deal was off, since he wasn't able to obtain the loan that their contract was conditioned on. The Millers refused to return Fry's deposit, so Fry sued.

The court held that Fry wasn't entitled to the deposit. If he had applied to Western Mortgage, they would have granted him a loan that would have fulfilled the condition. Fry avoided contacting Western Mortgage because, in fact, he had lost interest in the Millers' house. By failing to make a good faith effort to fulfill the condition, Fry breached the contract. *Fry v. George Eikins Co.*, 162 Cal. App. 2d 256, 327 P.2d 905 (1958).

b. Sale of Buyer's Home

Many purchases are contingent on the buyer's ability to sell his or her current home. In fact, even when that isn't an express condition, it may be a hidden condition. Often a buyer won't have enough money for a down payment unless the current home is sold. As a result, he or she can't qualify for a loan without selling the current home.

If the buyer cannot obtain financing unless his or her current home is sold, it's best to make the sale of the current home an express condition in the purchase agreement (**Paragraph 13-B**). Otherwise, the seller may be misled into believing that the buyer has a much better chance of obtaining the necessary loan than he or she actually has. Note that an attached addendum to **Paragraph 13** (CAR® form Contingency For Sale or Purchase of Other Property - COP) enables the seller to keep the property on the market pending fulfillment of the condition. If the seller receives another offer before the buyer's home is sold, the seller can demand that the buyer waive the condition and verify funds to close escrow, or cancel their contract.

c. Other Contigencies

The CAR® agreement has other contingencies for the benefit of the buyer. There are contingencies relating to appraisal of the property (**Paragraph 3 I**), delivery of required disclosures (**Paragraph 6A**), inspection of the property (**Paragraph 10**), and review of a preliminary report from the title company selected by the parties (**Paragraph 12**). The time periods and procedure for satisfying or waiving these conditions are described in Paragraph 14 of the CAR® purchase agreement.

d. Release of Contract

When one transaction fails because a condition is not met, the seller may want to enter into another agreement with a second buyer. In this situation, it's advisable for the seller to include an express condition in the second purchase agreement, making it contingent on the failure of the first agreement and on the first buyer's release of all claims. The seller and new buyer should not proceed with the second transaction without first clearly establishing that the first agreement is terminated and the first buyer has no right to enforce it. The best way to accomplish this is by asking the first buyer to execute a release of contract form.

3. Deposit

The buyer's deposit is an expression of good faith and a serious intention to buy the property. Under the terms of the CAR® form, the buyer may hold the check and deposit the check directly with escrow if the buyer's offer is accepted (**Paragraph 3A-1**), or the buyer may give the check to the broker with instructions to hold the check uncashed until the buyer's offer is accepted (**Paragraph 3A-2**). If the buyer gives the deposit check to the broker and the buyer's offer is accepted, then broker has 3 business days to deposit the check into escrow or into the broker's trust fund account, as directed in Paragraph 3A-2.

The purchase agreement should not only acknowledge receipt of the deposit, it should explain the circumstances in which the deposit will be refunded or forfeited. The parties have the option of treating the deposit as liquidated damages by initialing the blanks in **Paragraph 25**. When the buyer and seller initial in the appropriate space, if the buyer defaults, the seller will keep the deposit as liquidated damages instead of suing for actual damages. For a residential transaction (where the property has up to four units and the buyer intends to occupy one of them), a liquidated damages provision must be in boldface type and initialed by the parties, as in the CAR® form. The liquidated damages may not exceed 3% of the purchase price, so if the deposit was more than 3%, the seller will have to return part of it.

Be cautioned that funds deposited in escrow are not released automatically if there is a dispute. If the seller wants to retain the deposit as liquidated damages, the escrowee will usually not release that money to the seller without the buyer's consent. It may be necessary to sue or submit the matter to arbitration to establish the buyer's default and that the seller is entitled to liquidated damages (see **Paragraph 25**).

4. Agency Confirmation

As discussed in Chapter 6, the listing broker and selling broker are required to have their agency elections confirmed by the seller and buyer either in the purchase contract or in a separate written agreement signed before or at the same time that the purchase contract is signed. **Paragraph 2** of the CAR® form has blanks for the listing broker and selling broker to make their elections and get the confirmation of those elections. Note that the form has language, (Print Firm Name), to remind the licensee who completes the form that the listing agent and selling agent will always be a supervising broker, and never be a salesperson.

5. Mediation and Arbitration

Paragraph 26 of the CAR® agreement has provisions relating to dispute resolution. Note that in **Paragraph 26A** of this agreement, the seller and buyer agree to mediate their disputes as a required first step, before proceeding to arbitration or court. If the buyer and seller want to go to arbitration as a second step, they need to initial the spaces provided in **Paragraph 26B**. If they do not initial these spaces, then Paragraph 26B does not become part of their agreement. Mediation and arbitration are discussed in more detail in Chapter 9.

6. Broker's Compensation

The final section of the CAR® purchase agreement (**Paragraph 30**) is headed "ACCEPTANCE OF OFFER." Here the seller accepts the buyer's offer as set forth in the rest of the document. In **Paragraph 23**, the seller, buyer, or both agreed to compensate the broker. In most cases, this is merely a reaffirmation of the commission agreement in an earlier written listing. Because up to this point the broker has taken the risk of operating under an oral or implied listing agreement, this provision will satisfy the statute of frauds. If the purchase agreement provides for a different commission amount than the listing agreement, the purchase agreement is controlling since it was entered into at a more recent date.

Under the compensation provision of the CAR® purchase agreement, if the buyer defaults the broker is entitled to half of the damages the seller receives.

In practice, this generally means that the broker will take half of the forfeited deposit if the parties initialed the liquidated damage clause. However, the broker is not allowed to receive more in damages than he or she would have received as a commission if the transaction had closed.

IV. Counter Offers and the Purchase Agreement

Often a seller is unwilling to accept the buyer's offer as written, but would accept slightly different terms. Remember that when an offeree varies any terms in an offer, it's a counter offer instead of an acceptance. The original offeror (the buyer) is not bound unless he or she chooses to accept the seller's counter offer.

When a seller wants to make a counter offer, some agents simply cross out the appropriate terms on the buyer's purchase agreement and replace them with the seller's new terms. The seller signs the purchase agreement and initials and dates the changes. Then, if the buyer is willing to accept the counter offer, he or she also initials and dates the changes. This approach may work if the changes are minor and there is enough space to indicate them clearly. However, the agreement may become difficult to read (especially if the buyer makes another change). Worse, sometimes an agent fails to get every change initialed, so that it isn't clear whether the parties ever reached an agreement on all the terms.

CHAPTER 8

It's clearer and more professional to write any counter offer on another form or a separate attachment. There are forms specifically designed for the purpose of making changes to the purchase agreement, such as the CAR® **Counter Offer** form (**Figure 8-4**) to change or alter the terms of the purchase agreement form, or the CAR® **Purchase Agreement Addendum** form (**Figure 8-5**) to incorporate additional terms that are not in the purchase agreement form.

V. Options

An OPTION is a contract giving one party the right to do something without obligating him or her to do it. In real estate, the most common type of option is an option to purchase at a specific price. An option to purchase gives one party (the **optionee**) the right to buy the property of the other (the **optioner**) at a specified price for a limited time. Within that period, the optionee may choose to exercise the option—that is, enter into a contract to buy the property, but the optionee is under no obligation to exercise the option.

Example: Sullivan is interested in buying Hubbard's house, but hasn't quite made up his mind. He asks Hubbard to grant him an option to purchase the house for $250,000. Hubbard agrees, and writes up a legal option agreement that will expire in two weeks.

A week later, while Sullivan is still making up his mind, he hears that Pirandello is planning to offer Hubbard $275,000 for the house. Sullivan decides he does want to buy the house, so he exercises his option. Hubbard is bound to sell her house to Sullivan for $250,000 instead of selling it to Pirandello for $275,000.

Note that an option to purchase real property must be in writing and signed. The written option agreement should be as specific as possible, identifying the parties, the consideration, the property, and stating all the terms of the potential sale. The option must also be exercised in writing.

A. CONSIDERATION FOR AN OPTION

To be enforceable, an option must be supported by consideration. An option that is not supported by consideration is merely an offer that can be revoked

Without consideration, an option is just an offer to sell, which can only be accepted by exercising the option. In this case, the optionor can revoke the option at any time until it is exercised (just as if it were merely an offer to sell). In the previous example, Sullivan didn't give Hubbard any consideration for the option. If Hubbard had managed to revoke the option before Sullivan exercised it, she would have been free to sell her house to Pirandello. This is true, even though she originally granted the option for two weeks.

However, if Sullivan had provided consideration for the option—for example, if he had paid Hubbard $200 to keep the option open for two weeks—then Hubbard would not have a right to revoke it during that period. To make an option irrevocable, very little consideration is necessary. If the consideration is not "legally adequate," however, the optionee will not be able to sue for specific performance, which will limit recovery.

Figure 8-4

CALIFORNIA ASSOCIATION OF REALTORS®

COUNTER OFFER No. _____
For use by Seller or Buyer. May be used for Multiple Counter Offer.
(C.A.R. Form CO, Revised 11/10)

Date _____

This is a counter offer to the: ☐ California Residential Purchase Agreement, ☐ Counter Offer, or ☐ Other _____ ("Offer"),
dated _____, on property known as _____123 Sail Avenue_____ ("Property"),
between _____ ("Buyer") and
_____ ("Seller").

1. **TERMS:** The terms and conditions of the above referenced document are **accepted subject to the following:**
   A. **Paragraphs in the Offer that require initials by all parties, but are not initialed by all parties, are excluded from the final agreement unless specifically referenced for inclusion in paragraph 1C of this or another Counter Offer.**
   B. **Unless otherwise agreed in writing, down payment and loan amount(s) will be adjusted in the same proportion as in the original Offer.**
   C. _____
   _____
   _____
   _____
   _____
   _____
   _____
   _____

   D. **The following attached addenda are incorporated into this Counter Offer:** ☐ Addendum No. _____
   ☐ _____ ☐ _____

2. **RIGHT TO ACCEPT OTHER OFFERS:** If this is a Seller Counter Offer, (i) Seller has the right to continue to offer the Property for sale or for another transaction, and to accept any other offer at any time prior to Acceptance, as described in paragraph 3 and (ii) Seller's acceptance of another offer prior to Buyer's Acceptance of this Counter Offer, shall revoke this Counter Offer.

3. **EXPIRATION:** This Counter Offer shall be deemed revoked and the deposits, if any, shall be returned unless this Counter Offer is signed by the Buyer or Seller to whom it is sent and a Copy of the signed Counter Offer is personally received by the person making this Counter Offer or by _____, who is authorized to receive it, by 5:00 PM on the third Day After the later date specified in paragraph 5 or, (if checked) by ☐ _____ (date), at _____ ☐ AM ☐ PM. This Counter Offer may be executed in counterparts.

4. ☐ **(If checked:) MULTIPLE COUNTER OFFER:** Seller is making a Counter Offer(s) to another prospective buyer(s) on terms that may or may not be the same as in this Counter Offer. Acceptance of this Counter Offer by Buyer shall **not** be binding unless and until it is subsequently re-Signed by Seller in paragraph 7 below and a Copy of the Counter Offer Signed in paragraph 7 is personally received by Buyer or by _____, who is authorized to receive it, by 5:00 PM on the third Day After the later date specified in paragraph 5 or (if checked) by ☐ _____ (date), at _____ ☐ AM ☐ PM. Prior to the completion of all of these events, Buyer and Seller shall have no duties or obligations for the purchase or sale of the Property. **NOTE TO SELLER: Sign and date in paragraph 5 to make this Counter Offer.**

5. **OFFER:** ☐ **BUYER OR** ☐ **SELLER MAKES THIS COUNTER OFFER ON THE TERMS ABOVE AND ACKNOWLEDGES RECEIPT OF A COPY.**
   _____ Date _____
   _____ Date _____

6. **ACCEPTANCE: I/WE** accept the above Counter Offer (**If checked** ☐ **SUBJECT TO THE ATTACHED COUNTER OFFER**) and acknowledge receipt of a Copy.
   _____ Date _____ Time _____ ☐ AM ☐ PM
   _____ Date _____ Time _____ ☐ AM ☐ PM

7. **MULTIPLE COUNTER OFFER SIGNATURE LINE:** By signing below, Seller accepts this Multiple Counter Offer.
   NOTE TO SELLER: Do NOT sign in this box until after Buyer signs in paragraph 6. (Paragraph 7 applies only if paragraph 4 is checked.)
   _____ Date _____ Time _____ ☐ AM ☐ PM
   _____ Date _____ Time _____ ☐ AM ☐ PM

8. (_____ / _____) (Initials) **Confirmation of Acceptance:** A Copy of Signed Acceptance was personally received by the maker of the Counter Offer, or that person's authorized agent as specified in paragraph 3 (or, if this is a Multiple Counter Offer, the Buyer or Buyer's authorized agent as specified in paragraph 4) on (date) _____ at _____ ☐ AM ☐ PM. A binding Agreement is created when a Copy of Signed Acceptance is personally received by the the maker of the Counter Offer, or that person's authorized agent (or, if this is a Multiple Counter Offer, the Buyer or Buyer's authorized agent) whether or not confirmed in this document. Completion of this confirmation is not legally required in order to create a binding Agreement; it is solely intended to evidence the date that Acceptance has occurred.

Published and Distributed by:
REAL ESTATE BUSINESS SERVICES, INC.
a subsidiary of the California Association of REALTORS®
525 South Virgil Avenue, Los Angeles, California 90020

Reviewed by _____ Date _____

EQUAL HOUSING OPPORTUNITY

CO REVISED 11/10 (PAGE 1 OF 1)

COUNTER OFFER (CO PAGE 1 OF 1)

Agent:	WALT HUBER	Phone:	Fax:	Prepared using zipForm® software
Broker:				

CHAPTER 8

Figure 8-5

CALIFORNIA
ASSOCIATION
OF REALTORS®

PURCHASE AGREEMENT ADDENDUM No. _____
(May Also Be Used With Counter Offer)
(C.A.R. Form PAA, Revised 4/11)

This is an addendum to the ☐ California Residential Purchase Agreement, ☐ Counter Offer No. _____, ☐ Other _____
_____, ("Agreement"), dated _____, on
property known as _____123 Sail Avenue, Marina del Rey, CA 90292_____ ("Property"),
between _____ ("Buyer"),
and _____ ("Seller").
(The definitions in the California Residential Purchase Agreement are applicable to this Purchase Agreement Addendum.)

1. ☐ **CANCELLATION OF PRIOR SALE; BACK-UP OFFER** (If checked): This Agreement is in back-up position number _____, and is contingent upon written cancellation of any prior contracts and related escrows ("Prior Contracts") between Seller and other buyers. Seller and other buyers may mutually agree to modify or amend the terms of Prior Contracts. Buyer may cancel this Agreement in writing at any time before Seller provides Buyer Copies of written cancellations of Prior Contracts Signed by all parties to those contracts. If Seller is unable to provide such written Signed cancellations to Buyer by _____ (date), then either Buyer or Seller may cancel the Agreement in writing.
   A. **BUYER'S DEPOSIT CHECK** shall be: (i) held uncashed until Copies of the written cancellations Signed by all parties to the Prior Contracts are provided to Buyer; OR (ii) (if checked) ☐ immediately handled as provided in the Agreement.
   B. **TIME PERIODS** in the Agreement for investigations, contingencies, covenants and other obligations (i) shall begin on the Day After Seller provides Buyer Copies of Signed cancellations of Prior Contracts; OR (ii) (if checked) ☐ all time periods shall begin as provided in this Agreement. However, if the date for Close Of Escrow is a specific calendar date, that date shall NOT be extended, unless agreed to in writing by Buyer and Seller.

2. ☐ **SELLER TO REMAIN IN POSSESSION AFTER CLOSE OF ESCROW** (If checked): This provision is intended for short-term occupancy (i.e. less than 30 Days). If occupancy is intended to be for 30 Days or longer, use Residential Lease After Sale (C.A.R. Form RLAS). **Note: Local rent control or other Law regarding tenant's rights may impact Buyer's and Seller's rights and obligations.**
   A. **TERM:** Seller to remain in possession of Property for _____ **Days** After Close Of Escrow (or ☐ _____). Seller has no right to remain in possession beyond this term and may be responsible for court awarded damages if Seller does remain.
   B. **COMPENSATION:** Seller agrees to pay Buyer (i) for the term specified in 2A, $ _____ per Day (or ☐ _____) and (ii) a security deposit in the amount of $ _____. Seller shall deposit such funds with escrow holder prior to Close Of Escrow or such funds shall be withheld from Seller's proceeds. At Close Of Escrow, compensation and security deposit will be released to Buyer (or ☐ held in escrow).
   C. **LATE CHARGE/NSF CHECKS:** If any payment from Seller is required outside of escrow, and any such payment is not received by Buyer within **5 (or ☐ _____) Days** After date due, Seller shall pay to Buyer an additional sum of $ _____ as a Late Charge. If a check is returned for non-sufficient funds ("NSF"), Seller shall pay to Buyer $25.00 as an NSF charge. Seller and Buyer agree that these charges represent a fair and reasonable estimate of the costs Buyer may incur by reason of Seller's late or NSF payment. Buyer's acceptance of any Late Charge or NSF fee shall not constitute a waiver as to any default by Seller.
   D. **UTILITIES:** Seller agrees to pay for all utilities and services, and the following charges: _____ except _____, which shall be paid for by Buyer.
   E. **ENTRY:** Seller shall make Property available to Buyer for the purpose of entering to make necessary or agreed repairs, or to supply necessary or agreed services, or to show Property to prospective or actual purchasers, tenants, mortgagees, lenders, appraisers or contractors. Buyer and Seller agree that 24 hours notice (oral or written) shall be reasonable and sufficient notice. In an emergency, Buyer may enter Property at any time without prior notice.
   F. **MAINTENANCE:** Seller shall maintain the Property, including pool, spa, landscaping and grounds, and all personal property included in the sale in substantially the same condition as on the date of Acceptance of the Agreement. Except as provided in the Agreement, Seller shall not make alterations to the Property without Buyer's written consent.
   G. **ASSIGNMENT; SUBLETTING:** Seller shall not assign or sublet all or any part of the Property, or assign or transfer the right to occupy the Property. Any assignment, subletting or transfer of the Property by voluntary act of Seller, by operation of Law or otherwise, without Buyer's prior written consent shall give Buyer the right to terminate Seller's right to possession.
   H. **SELLER'S OBLIGATIONS UPON DELIVERY OF POSSESSION:** Upon delivery of possession to Buyer, Seller shall deliver the Property in the condition and on the terms provided in the Agreement.
   I. **INSURANCE:** Seller's personal property (including vehicles) is not insured by Buyer, and, if applicable, owner's association, against loss or damage due to fire, theft, vandalism, rain, water, criminal or negligent acts of others, or any other cause. Seller is to carry Seller's own insurance to protect Seller from such loss.
   J. **WAIVER:** The waiver of any breach shall not be construed as a continuing waiver of the same or any subsequent breach.
   K. **OTHER TERMS AND CONDITIONS/SUPPLEMENTS:** _____

Buyer's Initials (_____) (_____)
Seller's Initials (_____) (_____)
Reviewed by _____ Date _____

PAA REVISED 4/11 (PAGE 1 OF 2)

PURCHASE AGREEMENT ADDENDUM (PAA PAGE 1 OF 2)

Agent: WALT HUBER   Phone: Fax: Prepared using WINForms® software
Broker:

Property Address: _123 Sail Avenue, Marina del Rey, CA 90292_ _____ Date: _____

3. ☐ **TENANT TO REMAIN IN POSSESSION** (If checked): Buyer shall take Property subject to the rights of existing tenants. Seller shall, within **7 (or ☐ _____) Days** After Acceptance, deliver to Buyer Copies of all: estoppel certificates sent to and received back from tenants; leases; rental agreements; and current income and expense statements ("Rental Documents"). Seller shall give Buyer written notice of any changes to existing leases or tenancies or new agreements to lease or rent ("Proposed Changes") at least **7 (or ☐ _____) Days** prior to any Proposed Changes. Buyer's approval of the Rental Documents and Proposed Changes is a contingency of the Agreement. Buyer shall, within **5 (or ☐ _____) Days** After receipt of Rental Documents or Proposed Changes remove the applicable contingency or cancel the Agreement. Seller shall transfer to Buyer, through escrow, all unused tenant deposits. No warranty is made concerning compliance with governmental restrictions, if any, limiting the amount of rent that can lawfully be charged, and/or the maximum number of persons who can lawfully occupy the Property, unless otherwise agreed in writing.

4. ☐ **SECONDARY OR ASSUMED LOAN** (If checked): Obtaining the secondary loan or assumption below, and Buyer's approval of such assumed financing, is a contingency of this Agreement. Buyer shall act diligently and in good faith to obtain the designated financing.
   A. ☐ **SECONDARY LOAN:**
      (1) The loan shall be conventional financing or, if checked, ☐ SELLER FINANCING, ☐ OTHER. The loan shall be at a fixed rate not to exceed _____ %, or ☐ an adjustable rate loan with an initial rate not to exceed _____ %. Regardless of the type of loan, Buyer shall pay points not to exceed _____ % of the loan amount.
      (2) (i) Within **17 (or ☐ _____) Days** After Acceptance, Buyer shall, as specified in the Agreement, remove this contingency or cancel this Agreement.
      OR (ii) (If checked) ☐ secondary loan contingency shall remain in effect until the loan is funded.
   B. ☐ **ASSUMPTION OF EXISTING LOAN:**
      (1) Buyer will assume an existing note and deed of trust. Seller shall, within **5 (or _____) Days** After Acceptance, request from Lender, and upon receipt provide to Buyer, Copies of all applicable notes and deeds of trust, loan balances and current interest rates. Differences between estimated and actual loan balances shall be adjusted at Close Of Escrow by cash down payment. Impound accounts, if any, shall be assigned and charged to Buyer and credited to Seller. If this is an assumption of a VA Loan, the sale is contingent upon Seller being provided a release of liability and substitution of eligibility, unless otherwise agreed in writing.
      (2) (i) Within **17 (or ☐ _____) Days** After Acceptance, Buyer shall, as specified in the Agreement, remove this contingency or cancel this Agreement. However, if the assumed loan documents are not provided to Buyer within **7 Days After Acceptance,** Buyer has **5 (or ☐ _____) Days** After receipt of these documents, or the fixed time specified in 4B(2), whichever occurs last, to remove this contingency or cancel the Agreement.
      OR (ii) (If checked) ☐ assumed loan contingency shall remain in effect until the assumption is approved.

5. ☐ **COURT CONFIRMATION** (If checked): This Agreement is contingent upon court confirmation on or before _____ (date). If court confirmation is not obtained by that date, Buyer may cancel this Agreement in writing. Court confirmation may be required in probate, conservatorship, guardianship, receivership, bankruptcy or other proceedings. The court may allow open, competitive bidding, resulting in Property being sold to the highest bidder. Broker recommends that Buyer appear at the court confirmation hearing. Buyer understands that **(i)** Broker and others may continue to market the Property and **(ii)** Broker may represent other competitive bidders prior to and at the court confirmation.

By signing below Buyer and Seller acknowledge that each has read, understands, received a copy of and agrees to the terms of this Purchase Agreement Addendum.

Date _____ Date _____

Buyer _____ Seller _____

Buyer _____ Seller _____

Published and Distributed by:
REAL ESTATE BUSINESS SERVICES, INC.
a subsidiary of the California Association of REALTORS®
525 South Virgil Avenue, Los Angeles, California 90020

PAA REVISED 4/11 (PAGE 2 OF 2)

Reviewed by _____ Date _____

PURCHASE AGREEMENT ADDENDUM (PAA PAGE 2 OF 2)

Untitled

Example: Hubbard granted Sullivan an option to purchase her house for $350,000. Sullivan gave Hubbard $15 to keep the option open for two weeks. During that period, Pirandello offers Hubbard $375,000 for the house. Hubbard can't revoke Sullivan's option because he gave her consideration.

However, Hubbard decides to breach the option contract and sell the house to Pirandello. When Sullivan sues Hubbard for breach of contract, the court rules that $15 was not adequate consideration for a two-week option on a $350,000 house. Sullivan is entitled to damages for breach of contract (probably $25,000), but not specific performance. The court cannot order Hubbard to sell the house to Sullivan for $350,000.

The consideration paid for an option contract is not refundable. If the optionee decides not to exercise the option, he or she can't demand that the optionor return the consideration. It is also not considered to be a portion of the price of the property under the option agreement, it merely bought the time in which to exercise the option.

B. RELATION BACK

When an option is exercised, the interest the optionee acquires in the property relates back to the time the option was granted. In the eyes of the law, it's as though the optionee purchased the property when the option was granted, rather than when the option was exercised.

> **Case Example:** In November 1969, the Enzlers gave C/H Realty an exclusive listing agreement that was to expire on May 15, 1970. An extender clause entitled C/H Realty to a commission if the property was sold before August 15, 1970, to anyone C/H Realty introduced to the Enzlers as a prospective buyer.
>
> In December 1969, C/H Realty showed the property to the Armtrouts. In June 1970, the Enzlers granted the Armtrouts an option to purchase, but the Enzlers and the Armtrouts agreed that the option would not be exercised until after C/H Realty's safety period expired. That way the Enzlers wouldn't have to pay the broker's commission. Therefore, the Armtrouts did not exercise their option until September 4, 1970.
>
> C/H Realty sued for its commission. The court ruled that the Enzlers were required to pay the broker. When the Armtrouts exercised their option, their interest in the property related back to the time the option was granted (June 1970). In effect, they were held to have purchased the property in June rather than in September. Since the safety period didn't expire until August, C/H Realty was entitled to the commission. *Anthony v. Enzler*, 61 Cal. App. 3d 872, 132 Cal. Rptr. 553 (1976).

This rule makes it particularly important for a real estate purchaser to check the public record for any options recorded against the property he or she intends to buy. When an option is exercised, any rights acquired since the option was granted are cut off if the person who acquired the rights had actual or constructive knowledge of the option.

Example: Dunn buys Schauer's property in March. Dunn doesn't know that Nguyen has an option to purchase the property that won't expire until June. Since Nguyen recorded her option in February, Dunn is charged with constructive knowledge of the option. Without realizing it, Dunn has taken the property subject to Nguyen's option.

In May, Nguyen decides to exercise the option. She can require Dunn to convey the property to her, just as if it were still owned by Schauer.

However, keep in mind that until an option is exercised, it is only a contract right, not an interest in the property. Therefore, an option can't be used as security for a deed of trust, and it isn't a lien.

C. ASSIGNMENT OF AN OPTION

An option agreement generally can be assigned, unless the contract states that assignment is prohibited. There's an exception, however, when the consideration paid by the optionee is an unsecured promissory note. In that case, the option can't be assigned without the written consent of the optionor.

An option to purchase is often included in a lease. If the lease is assigned, the option is assigned too, even when the assignment doesn't specifically mention the option.

D. TERMINATION OF AN OPTION

When an optionee has given consideration for the option, the death of the optionor does not terminate the option. The option contract is binding on the optionor's heirs, and the optionee can still exercise it.

An option terminates automatically if it is not exercised before its expiration date. If the option agreement was recorded, however, it can still be a cloud on the title after it has expired. A title insurance company will not simply ignore a recorded option after its expiration date—they can't be sure that the optionor didn't grant an extension. Therefore, when a recorded option is no longer effective, a document canceling the option should be recorded. To make absolutely sure the optionee doesn't have any claim on the property, title insurers often require a quitclaim deed from the optionee to the optionor.

However, this precaution isn't necessary six months after the option expires. The Civil Code provides that a recorded option no longer gives constructive notice of the optionee's interest if no instrument extending or exercising it has been recorded six months after it expires. Also, if the option doesn't state an expiration date, it no longer gives constructive notice six months after it was recorded.

Case Example: Defendants leased property to the plaintiff for a term expiring October 1, 1963 with an option to renew for two successive one-year terms. Plaintiff exercised the renewal option extending the least to October 31, 1965. The lease granted the plaintiff in option to purchase the property on specific terms including the assumption of an existing trust deed and payment to the defendants under a second trust deed at a rate of $75 per month and interest at 6% per annum. The option to purchase had to be exercised within 30 days of the termination of the lease or any option of renewal on the lease. On September 13, 1965, plaintiff opened in escrow for the purchase of the property. The escrow officer mailed the signed instructions by the plaintiff together a deed to defendants to sign and return. The defendants received the documents on September 30 and failed to sign or return them. On October 18, the escrow officer telephone defendants and was told that the defendants were going out of town and would call on the 25th.

On October 25, the defendant called saying the documents would not be signed and refused to reveal to why. The plaintiff sued for specific performance. Defendants contend that the escrow instructions differed from the option agreement and therefore the plaintiff failed to exercise the option in accordance with its terms within the specified period. Judgment for plaintiff. Defendants appeal. ▼

Any tender of performance, including the exercised an option, is ineffective if it imposes conditions upon its acceptance. However, the imposition of such conditions is waived by the giver of the option if he does not specifically point out the alleged defects in the tender of the option. First, a reasonable construction of the words "within 30 days of the termination of this Lease" is that the phrase was intended to mean the 30 day period immediately preceding the expiration of the term. Therefore the option was exercised in a timely manner. Second, the fact that the exercise of the option contained variances (being that the proposed escrow provided for refinancing the existing loan and also for payments of $75 per month principal and interest included) these variances were corrected when the plaintiff filed a second amended complaint agreeing to comply with the option agreement. Judgment affirmed. *Riverside Fence Co. Inc. v. Novak*, 273 Cal. App. 2d 656, 78 Cal. Rptr. 536 (1969).

E. RIGHT OF PREEMPTION

A *RIGHT OF PREEMPTION* (sometimes called a *right of first refusal*) is not the same thing as an option. Someone who holds a preemption right has the right to buy the property only if and when the owner decides to sell it. The owner can't be required to sell the property against his/her will, unlike an optionor.

Preemption rights are often included in leases for office space. If adjacent space on the same floor becomes vacant, the lessor must offer the lessee the chance to expand into that space before it can be offered to a new tenant. Co-owners of property sometimes grant each other preemption rights: if one co-owner decides to sell his or her share, the other has the right to buy it instead of letting it go to a stranger.

VI. CHAPTER SUMMARY

1. To sue for a commission, a real estate broker must have a signed writing by the client that indicates the fact of employment. A listing agreement should state the terms of sale the seller is willing to accept and should specify when the broker will be entitled to the commission. Most exclusive listing agreements include an extender clause.

2. The purchase agreement should set forth all the terms of the agreement between the buyer and seller. Most purchase agreements contain conditions, making the purchase contingent on the buyer's ability to obtain financing, sell current home, or the results of an appraisal or inspection. A buyer's deposit may be treated as liquidated damages, but in a residential transaction, the seller may not keep more than 3% of the agreed purchase price.

3. Most contracts entered into with licensed agents are on standard preprinted forms and blanks are filled in. The preprinted forms can avoid the problem of practicing law without a license.

4. The standard forms contain an attorney fee provision allowing the prevailing party to recover reasonable attorney fees from the loser. Without such a clause, the winner would have to absorb the fees.

5. The standard forms also contain an integration clause, which insures that the document being signed represents the final expression of the bargain, and any future modification must be in writing.

6. An option to purchase gives the optionee a right to buy the property at a specified price without requiring him or her to buy it. An option can be revoked unless it is supported by consideration. When an option is exercised, the optionee's ownership relates back to the time the option was granted. A recorded option is a cloud on the title until six months after its expiration date.

7. A right of preemption (right of first refusal) is not an option; the holder has a right to purchase the property only if the owner decides to sell.

VII. CASE PROBLEM
Niles v. Hancock, 140 Cal. 157, 73 Pac. 840 (1903)

On March 27, plaintiff wrote to defendant, asking if he would sell specific property. On April 30, defendant wrote to plaintiff stating that, among other things, if he should conclude to sell it would want to sell the entire property. On May 5, plaintiff wrote defendant saying he would be pleased to buy the entire property and asking for the best price for it. On May 14, the defendant replied stating his price was $100 per acre and to inform him if he want it at that price. On May 22, plaintiff offered $65 an acre. On June 1, defendant replied saying the price was too low. On June 9, plaintiff wrote saying the price was too high and that he would make one more offer which amounted to slightly over $80 per acre and the defendant should telegram him at once if he accepted this offer. This letter was received by the defendant on June 15. Defendant made no reply. On June 18, plaintiff telegram that he accepted the offer to buy the property at $100 per acre. On June 19, the defendant wrote the plaintiff confirming that he had telegrammed his acceptance and was sending appropriate paperwork. On June 26, the defendant wrote the plaintiff returning the unsigned paperwork. Plaintiff sued for specific performance of the purchase contract. Was there an offer? Was there acceptance? Why or why not?

VIII. KEY TERMS

counter offer form	integration clause	optionor
employment form	listing agreement	purchase agreement
(broker/salesperson)	option form	right of preemption
extender clause	optionee	

CHAPTER 8

IX. CHAPTER QUIZ

1. The agreement between a broker and salesperson must contain a provision relating to:

    a. compensation.
    b. supervision.
    c. duties of the broker and salesperson.
    d. all of the above.

2. A clause in a contract that states this written document is the entire contract agreement between the parties is referred to as a(n):

    a. interpretation clause.
    b. integration clause.
    c. explanation clause.
    d. closing clause.

3. Regarding a listing agreement for a home, the broker must provide the seller with an agency disclosure addendum:

    a. before the seller signs the listing agreement.
    b. within three days after the seller signs the listing agreement.
    c. within five days after the seller signs the listing agreement.
    d. the broker is not required to provide the seller with this form.

4. Which of the following listings must contain a termination date?

    a. Exclusive Agency
    b. Exclusive Right to Sell Agency
    c. Open Listing
    d. Both a and b are correct

5. If a broker has an exclusive right to sell listing it must be kept on file by the broker for at least:

    a. one year.
    b. two years.
    c. three years.
    d. six months.

6. Regarding the California Association of REALTORS® Purchase Agreement, in order for arbitration to be a required method of resolving any disputes between the buyer and seller:

    a. both the buyer and seller must initial the arbitration provision.
    b. only the seller needs to initial the arbitration provision.
    c. only the buyer needs to initial the arbitration provision.
    d. the arbitration provision is binding whether it is initialed or not.

7. Regarding the California Association of REALTORS® Purchase Agreement, in order for mediation to be a required method of resolving any disputes between the buyer and seller:

    a. both the buyer and seller must initial the mediation provision.
    b. only the seller needs to initial the mediation provision.
    c. only the buyer needs to initial the mediation provision.
    d. the mediation provision is binding whether it is initialed or not.

8. Regarding an offer for the purchase of property:

    a. an earnest money deposit of at least 10% of the purchase price offered is required.
    b. an earnest money deposit of at least $1,000 is required.
    c. an earnest money deposit of 20% of the purchase price offered is required.
    d. an earnest money deposit is not required to make an offer of purchase.

9. A provision in a purchase contract that provides that the seller is entitled to a specified dollar amount in the event that the buyer breaches the contract is known as a(n):

    a. penalty clause.
    b. fair compensation clause.
    c. equity clause.
    d. liquidated damages clause.

10. The right of preemption is also referred to as a:

    a. right of first refusal.
    b. buyer's option.
    c. seller's option.
    d. refusal option.

ANSWERS: 1. d; 2. b; 3. a; 4. d; 5. c; 6. a; 7. d; 8. d; 9. d; 10. a

CHAPTER 9
Alternatives to Litigation

CHAPTER OVERVIEW

Today, litigation is only one of the ways used to resolve different types of controversies. Not only are contractual rights being decided outside of the courts, but also certain types of property rights.

I. Alternative Dispute Resolution (ADR)

Before they'll hear a case, California court judges routinely require litigants to go to negotiation, mediation or arbitration, sometimes more than once. This saves judges time and taxpayers money.

Conflict between people is increasingly being resolved through the use of **Alternative Dispute Resolution (ADR)**. People and businesses dissatisfied with the time and expense of litigation are looking for alternatives to resolve their disputes. Negotiation, mediation and arbitration are three types of ADR that are being utilized to avoid litigation when controversies surrounding contracts and property rights arise. Administrative hearings are used by the Department of Real Estate to avoid the use of courts when deciding issues surrounding real estate licensees.

ADR is a catchall term used to describe out-of court methods to resolve disputes, including negotiation, arbitration, and mediation, among other methods.

Alternative Dispute Resolution (ADR)

- **Negotiation**
- **Mediation**
- **Arbitration**

In fact, California has indicated its support of ADR in the real estate industry by amending the **California Arbitration Act** (Code of Civil Procedure Sections 1298-1298.8) to **specifically address arbitration clauses in real estate contracts**.

Additionally, the Legislature has found that approaching dispute resolution from an adversarial position "can be unnecessarily costly, time-consuming, and complex when achieved through formal court proceedings." It therefore strongly encourages the parties to resolve their disputes outside of the judicial process. There are definite potential advantages to alternative dispute resolution when compared to litigation. Not all the advantages will be present in every situation. Among these advantages are:

1. **Speedier.** With the crowded court calendars, it may be years before the dispute is actually heard by the court.

2. **Less expensive.** Taking less time reduces the expense of resolving the dispute. Normally there is limited discovery (see Chapter 1), which is the process of determining what evidence exists prior to trial.

3. **Use of an expert as the decision maker.** In most of the ADR processes, the parties are able to select the decision maker by agreement. This gives them the opportunity to have an expert knowledgeable in the field make a decision.

4. **Proceedings are confidential.** Most of the ADR processes are private affairs and closed to the public. Negotiations and decisions are confidential and not available for public inspection unless the parties approve.

5. **Decisions are final and not appealable.** Decisions reached through most of the ADR processes are final and binding upon the parties. This finality reduces the expense and time. However, there are very limited grounds for appeal that will be discussed later.

6. **Less formal.** ADR uses the parties themselves to determine how the process will run. The formalities of judicial procedures are not a normal aspect of many ADR processes.

Arbitration is also seen to have several disadvantages, including:

1. Less formal (little or no right to discovery if a party would benefit from discovery).

2. Arbitrator's decision may not be supported by law or facts.

3. Parties must pay arbitrator.

4. Party may need to go to court to establish arbitration rules, to pick arbitrator, to force arbitration, or to enforce award.

5. Decision cannot be appealed.

6. Possibility of a "split forum" requiring both arbitration and a separate court action when some parties necessary to resolve the dispute did not agree to arbitrate.

A. NONADJUDICATIVE AND ADJUDICATIVE ALTERNATIVES

Alternatives to the judicial process may be classified into two categories: nonadjudicative and adjudicative. In the *NONADJUDICATIVE alternatives, the parties are encouraged to voluntarily enter into agreements that settle the controversy.* Many times the parties will use a neutral third party to assist in reaching an agreement among themselves. The *ADJUDICATIVE alternatives of dispute resolution mirror the judicial process in that a third party decides the controversy, much as a judge does in court.* The adjudicative processes may be concerned with settling controversies among private parties or between regulatory agencies and individuals.

Nonadjudicative means attempting a voluntary resolution. Adjudicative means a third party decides the controversy.

II. Negotiation

Although arbitration receives much of the focus in the ADR literature, negotiation continues to serve as the primary method by which conflicts are resolved. *NEGOTIATION is a voluntary process where parties attempt to settle their conflicts in a peaceful manner.*

Example: Peters is upset that some shrubbery was damaged by his neighbor Sharon during a remodel project. Peters politely tells Sharon how upset he is over the damaged shrubbery and that it is going to cost $75 to replace it. Sharon had failed to notice she had damaged Peters' shrubs and was embarrassed she had not been more careful. Sharon offered to replace the shrubs if Peters would wait until the remodel work was completed. This was acceptable to Peters and once Sharon had finished her remodel project, she paid to replace Peters' shrubs.

To successfully negotiate, it is necessary to move beyond positions on issues and negotiate about the person's interests or needs. Looking past positions on issues can be hard for many people, yet, it is helpful to focus on underlying interests or needs if agreement is to be reached. By asking yourself "why" a person is taking a certain position, you can often determine what his or her true interests or needs are and then be better prepared to offer solutions that will lead to an agreement.

Example: With only one orange between them, two sisters argue over who gets the orange. Each sister takes the position that she deserves the orange more than the other. Eventually they split the orange, with each only getting one-half of what they desired. Had they known the interest behind each other's position they would have discovered that one sister wanted the orange to make juice with, while the other sister desired the peel for use in making a cake. (Adapted from Fisher, Ury, and Patton's book *Getting to Yes: Negotiating Agreement Without Giving In* (1991).)

A. DISTRIBUTIVE NEGOTIATION (Win-Lose)

Negotiations may be either distributive or integrative. *DISTRIBUTIVE NEGOTIATION (win-lose or competitive) is where the goals of the parties are interdependent but not compatible.* It occurs when one person wins and the other person loses. If a seller of a house lowers the selling price, the buyer gains by paying a lower price. The seller loses and the buyer wins.

Distributive negotiators focus on their own personal situation and do not give credence to the other party's situation unless it helps to maximize the distributive negotiator's own return. To a distributive negotiator, a win occurs when the other party is defeated. A major contributor to the success of a distributive negotiator is the other party's desire to avoid the pain of litigation, i.e., time, money, and emotional strain involved in taking the dispute through the judicial process.

B. INTEGRATIVE NEGOTIATION (WIn-Win)

INTEGRATIVE NEGOTIATION (problem-solving) occurs when both parties win. The negotiators seek to achieve mutual gains and they focus on the needs and interests of both parties. This means the negotiators look past their individual positions ("their" solution to the dispute) and identify "why" those solutions are being sought by each party. This form of negotiating works best when the parties view the negotiations as part of a long-term relationship. The example with the sisters and the orange exemplifies a situation where integrative bargaining can lead to both parties' needs being met. Instead of seeing a situation where there are only limited resources, the negotiators see varied options for apportioning those resources.

"I win and you lose" is the purpose of a distributive negotiation. "I win and you win" is the purpose of an integrative negotiation.

C. BEST ALTERNATIVE TO A NEGOTIATED AGREEMENT (BATNA)

No matter which approach to negotiation is used, there are three basic stages to the negotiation process: 1) preparation, 2) actual negotiations, and 3) conclusion of negotiations. Each stage is important but the better prepared a person is, the more likely their success in negotiations. During the preparation stage, a person should attempt to determine what needs and interests are behind not only their goals, but also those of the other party. Roger Fisher, William Ury, and Bruce Patton, in their original book, *Getting To Yes: Negotiating Agreement Without Giving In* (1991), suggest developing your Best Alternative to a Negotiated Agreement (BATNA) at this stage so you will know when to walk away from the negotiations.

A *BEST ALTERNATIVE TO A NEGOTIATED AGREEMENT (BATNA) is developed by identifying what actions you could take if no agreement is reached, developing the best of those possible actions into viable alternatives, and then selecting the best alternative you have developed.* With your BATNA you can now better judge whether to reach an agreement or to simply walk away from the negotiations. It is also important that you try to identify your opponent's BATNA as you prepare for the negotiations.

The case in Chapter 1 between Palermo and Mulligan illustrates how negotiation is a continual part of dispute resolution. Even though Palermo and Mulligan are litigating their dispute, there is opportunity for settlement discussions throughout the process. These discussions on possible settlement involve the process of negotiation. They illustrate how negotiation is a continuing process that evolves until either an agreement is reached by the parties or they realize only a third party is capable of settling the dispute.

III. Mediation (A Neutral Third Party)

In *MEDIATION, a neutral third party assists the parties in voluntarily negotiating a settlement to their dispute by helping them recognize their interests involved, developing choices, and analyzing the alternatives.* The goal is to overcome the problems and negotiate a mutually satisfying agreement.

Because mediation is voluntary, the parties must agree to the use of mediation in attempting to resolve the dispute. A **mediation clause** may be included in the contract the parties are executing. If there is an existing dispute but no contractually agreed-to clause to mediate the dispute, the parties may stipulate to mediating the dispute. As noted in Chapter 8, the California Association of REALTORS® listing agreement and purchase contract both have contract clauses that require the parties to first try to resolve their disputes by mediation. The mediation clause in the Dispute Resolution paragraph of the California Residential Purchase Agreement states in part:

> "**MEDIATION. Buyer and seller agree to mediate any dispute or claim arising between them out of this Agreement, or any resulting transaction, before resorting to arbitration or court action ...**"

A. ADVANTAGES TO MEDIATION

The most obvious advantage to mediation is that parties maintain an active role, even if they have an attorney. And a neutral party assists to identify, develop, and explore viable settlement alternatives. Mediation is likely to produce a settlement faster than litigation.

Mediation may be preferred to arbitration for a number of reasons, such as:

1. parties retain greater control of proceeding;
2. parties know soon if the matter and issues may be resolved, and differences narrowed, and
3. the process is quicker and less expensive, if it is resolved.

Even though attorneys may be used in mediation, the parties are directly involved in the settlement process.

B. MEDIATOR'S ROLE

A *MEDIATOR facilitates the parties in reaching a voluntary agreement*. He or she does this by encouraging the parties to identify obstacles that stand in the way of an agreement and assisting them to overcome these obstacles. Mediators help the parties identify alternatives for resolving the dispute by getting them to focus on their interests and needs instead of their positions. *Many times the mediator will meet individually with each party to make this determination. This is called a CAUCUS.* It is important that the parties involved in mediation fully disclose relevant information to the mediator to enable the mediator to best perform his or her function.

> **Example:** The seller of a house does not believe the buyer has made a good faith effort to obtain financing as called for in the purchase agreement. Having agreed to try mediation, both parties meet with the mediator. After meeting jointly with both parties, the mediator has a caucus with each separately and determines that the seller only wants to punish the buyer. Because the sale price of the house has actually increased during the time the seller waited for the buyer to arrange financing, the seller will not suffer any monetary losses. The seller is simply upset that the buyer did not diligently pursue adequate financing and wants to teach the buyer a lesson. Knowing the interest of the seller in only wanting to punish the buyer will assist the mediator in guiding the negotiations.

An important aspect of mediation is that the mediator facilitates resolution of the conflict instead of imposing a decision. Mediation works because the parties themselves are able to settle the dispute with the assistance of the mediator. If the parties are unwilling to voluntarily settle the dispute, mediation will not be successful.

A mediator is a neutral third party who helps to resolve the dispute.

C. MEDIATION PROCESS

First Step. In the first step, the pre-session, the parties agree to use mediation as a means of resolving the dispute. As was discussed above, the parties may use a mediation clause in their contract or may stipulate to take an existing dispute to mediation.

Second Step. A second part of this stage is for the mediator to be selected. The mediation clause should describe the procedure to be used and, if a mediation service is referenced in the clause, the procedure established by that service will determine how the mediator is to be selected. After the mediator is selected by the parties, the mediator then communicates with both parties and begins the process of establishing a rapport with the parties.

Third Step. The mediation session itself is the next step in the process. The mediator begins by explaining the process to the parties and, with the agreement of the parties, guidelines are established. Throughout the actual mediation session, the mediator works to create and maintain a positive atmosphere. During the mediation session, the third stage occurs when the mediator gathers the facts behind the dispute. Once the facts have been gathered, the mediator helps the parties see beyond their positions and to clarify the "real" issues. After the parties have identified their interests and needs, the mediator attempts to determine the significance of each interest and to prioritize them if possible.

By asking questions of the parties, the mediator tries to get the parties to focus on the actual issues involved in the dispute. The mediator at this point starts developing a strategy to assist the parties in understanding the other party's interests and needs. The mediator will provide each party with an objective evaluation of the case in order to help them understand how the dispute looks to a neutral third party.

Fourth Step. Once the issues have been identified, the fourth step begins. The parties will need to start creating alternatives and options to resolve the dispute. The mediator will often caucus with each of the parties to develop these alternatives and options. The information given to the mediator during these caucuses is considered confidential and the mediator should not convey this information to one party without the consent of the other party.

Fifth Step. At the fifth stage, the parties either reach an agreement on an option that satisfies their needs and interests or they recognize that the dispute cannot be voluntarily resolved.

Sixth Step. If the parties have reached an agreement on an option, the final stage concludes by reducing the agreement to a writing, signed by both parties.

The parties to the mediation will share the costs of mediating the dispute unless they have agreed otherwise. Organizations that supply mediation services usually charge a filing fee to set up the file and then an hourly charge for the actual mediation. The hourly fees are compensation for both the service and the mediator. Some services will apply either all or part of the filing fee to the fee charged for arbitration if the dispute is not settled in mediation and the parties choose to arbitrate the dispute.

Generally, a mediator's fee is split equally between the parties.

327

CHAPTER 9

www.professionalmediator.org/
The Professional Mediation Association (PMA)

IV. Arbitration

In an *ARBITRATION, the parties agree to submit the dispute to a neutral third party for a final, and unless otherwise agreed to by the parties, binding decision*. The advantages of arbitration over litigation are many. It is a less formal process, it may be quicker, it may be less costly, the parties are able to have a knowledgeable expert arbitrate the dispute, and the process, including the decision, is not a public one. In an arbitration, formal pleadings are not used, discovery is normally quite limited, the rules of evidence do not apply, and should the parties so agree, the decision can be final and binding with no right to appeal the arbitrator's decision. As noted earlier in the chapter, arbitration may also have disadvantages, some of which may be the same as the advantages depending upon a party's perception (for example, no right to appeal is an advantage to the person who gets a favorable arbitration decision, but is a disadvantage to the other party, particularly if the decision is contrary to law).

Because of these advantages, both the federal government and the state of California have indicated their support for arbitration. The federal government has expressed a strong preference for arbitration and has enacted the **Federal Arbitration Act (9 USC Section 1 et seq.)**. California enacted the **California Arbitration Act (Code Civ. Proc., Section 1280 et seq.)** in 1961 and the courts have uniformly and vigorously promoted its goals.

While arbitrations are meant to be less formal than litigating the dispute, the parties may agree to be represented by attorneys. In such case, each party must pay for his or her own attorney fees unless the agreement provides for recovery of the fees by the prevailing party. If attorney fees are to be awarded by the arbitrator under the terms of the arbitration agreement, it is within the arbitrator's power to determine what amount of fees should be awarded.

Generally, the arbitrator makes a final resolution to the dispute.

A. TYPES OF ARBITRATION

1. Court-Ordered (Mandated) Arbitrations

Arbitrations may be judicial arbitrations (court-mandated arbitrations, often referred to as court-ordered arbitrations) that are required before a case may be heard by the trial courts, or they may be private arbitrations agreed to by the parties. Court-annexed arbitrations may be ordered by the superior court when there is less than $50,000 at stake or the parties stipulate to arbitration.

2. Private Arbitrations

Private arbitrations create a duty to arbitrate only when the parties have contractually created this duty. It is created when the parties have either an agreement that calls for submitting disputes to arbitration or, if there is no existing contract with an arbitration clause, the parties must enter into an agreement to take the dispute to arbitration.

3. Nonbinding or Binding

If the arbitration may be reviewed by the courts, or if the parties have agreed that it is not to be final, it is considered to be nonbinding. If the arbitration is binding, the arbitrator's award is final and, but for certain limited statutory exceptions, is not reviewable by the courts for errors of fact or law. The California Supreme Court has stated that "it is a general rule that parties to a private arbitration impliedly agree that the arbitrator's decision will be both binding and final" (*Moncharsh v. Heily & Blase et al.*, 3 Cal. 4th 1, 10 Cal. Rptr. 2d 183 (1992)).

Generally, most arbitration proceedings are binding.

Binding Arbitration – Not reviewable by the courts
Nonbinding Arbitration – Reviewable by the courts

---

4. California Arbitration Legislation

Because the parties are giving up their right to use the judicial system, arbitration clauses should be knowingly executed with informed consent. To help insure that a person does not unknowingly enter into a real estate contract containing an arbitration clause, California Code of Civil Procedure Section 1298 requires that contracts for the sale of real estate and listing agreements clearly title any clauses calling for the binding arbitration of disputes, **"ARBITRATION OF DISPUTES." The title must "be set out in at least 10-point bold type or in contrasting red in at least 8-point type"** and, when part of a typed contract, the entire title must be typed in capital letters. That code section further requires specific warning language with similar typeface requirements. This warning states:

NOTICE: "BY INITIALING IN THE SPACE BELOW YOU ARE AGREEING TO HAVE ANY DISPUTE ARISING OUT OF THE MATTERS INCLUDED IN THE 'ARBITRATION OF DISPUTES' PROVISION DECIDED BY NEUTRAL ARBITRATION AS PROVIDED BY CALIFORNIA LAW AND YOU ARE GIVING UP ANY RIGHT YOU MIGHT POSSESS TO HAVE THE DISPUTE LITIGATED IN A COURT OR JURY TRIAL. BY INITIALING IN THE SPACE BELOW YOU ARE GIVING UP YOUR JUDICIAL RIGHTS TO DISCOVERY AND APPEAL, UNLESS THOSE RIGHTS ARE SPECIFICALLY INCLUDED IN THE 'ARBITRATION OF DISPUTES' PROVISION. IF YOU REFUSE TO SUBMIT TO ARBITRATION AFTER AGREEING TO THIS PROVISION, YOU MAY BE COMPELLED TO ARBITRATE UNDER THE AUTHORITY OF THE CALIFORNIA CODE OF CIVIL PROCEDURE. YOUR AGREEMENT TO THIS ARBITRATION PROVISION IS VOLUNTARY."

WE HAVE READ AND UNDERSTAND THE FOREGOING AND AGREE TO SUBMIT DISPUTES ARISING OUT OF THE MATTERS INCLUDED IN THE 'ARBITRATION OF DISPUTES' PROVISION TO NEUTRAL ARBITRATION.

CHAPTER 9

The above notice is an important part of **Section 26B. DISPUTE RESOLUTION:, B. ARBITRATION OF DISPUTES** of the California Association of REALTORS® (CAR®) purchase agreement contained in Chapter 8. Please reread that section now.

For the arbitration clause to be valid in a real estate contract, the parties are required to initial the clause to show their willingness to arbitrate any disputes arising out of the contract.

A real estate agent needs to make certain that the principal has carefully read and understands the arbitration provision before initialing it.

Note that the requirements of Civil Code Section 1298 does not apply to disputes between a broker and salesperson under an employment agreement. For example, the CAR® Independent Contractor Agreement discussed in Chapter 8 has a mandatory arbitration provision (see paragraph 10B of Figure 8-1). The provision in this contract does not require the notices and initials that are required for real estate purchase contracts and listing agreements.

Additionally, California Code of Civil Procedure Section 1298.7 states that in the event that an arbitration provision is included in a contract or agreement, it shall not preclude nor limit any right of action for bodily injury or wrongful death. This section presented a problem in the following case.

Case Example: Plaintiffs, a married couple, bought a home using a California Association of Realtors® standard purchase agreement, which requires the arbitration of disputes arising out of the agreement or any resulting transaction. Both buyers and sellers agree to arbitration. The agreement excluded from arbitration "an action for bodily injury or wrongful death." Plaintiffs allege that as a result of the broker's failure to disclose termite and other damage rendering the home uninhabitable and the plaintiffs suffered severe emotional distress, worry, depression, anxiety, and fear. Additionally, the wife was pregnant at the time of the purchase and she was advised that, while on the property, she should wear a mask and special clothing to protect herself and her unborn child from exposure to dry rot, fungus, and other hazardous substances. Ultimately, the wife alleges that the emotional distress surrounding the purchase caused her to develop gestational diabetes. The plaintiffs never moved into the premises. The plaintiffs sued their brokers for failure to disclose the structural damage. The brokers moved to compel arbitration, but the trial court denied the motion on the ground that the action was for bodily injury which was excluded from arbitration according to the purchase agreement. The brokers appealed.

The Court of Appeals noted that California has a strong public policy in favor of arbitration, that arbitration agreements should be liberally interpreted, and arbitration should be ordered unless the agreement clearly does not apply to the dispute in question. We cannot say that the mere nondisclosure of termite damage, absent exposure to a real or tangible effect of the infestation (for example, a collapsible wall), threatens a buyer with physical injury. Rather, a breach of duty, as alleged in this case, directly affects only a property or financial interest. The plaintiffs could not reasonably have expected that a claim for emotional distress would exist against a broker under the circumstances here, much less that the claim would be one for bodily injury. ▼

If emotional distress were considered a bodily injury, the arbitration exclusion in the agreement could apply in virtually every dispute, rendering the arbitration provision a nullity. The arbitration exclusion for bodily injury does not include the plaintiffs' claims for emotional distress. *Gravillis v. Coldwell Banker Residential Brokerage Company*, 143 Cal. App. 4th 761, 49 Cal. Rptr. 3d 531 (2006).

B. PARTIES MAY AGREE TO SUBMIT THE DISPUTE TO ARBITRATION

If an arbitration clause has not been used, it is still possible for a dispute to be taken to arbitration. If the parties have a current controversy they would like to arbitrate and there is no previous contractually created duty, the parties may execute a *SUBMISSION AGREEMENT*, *whereby they agree to submit the dispute to arbitration.*

If no previous arbitration exists, the parties can sign a document called a submission agreement to arbitrate their dispute.

Because the duty to arbitrate is contractually created, the arbitration clause (or the submission agreement) determines the scope of the arbitration and what powers the arbitrator will have. Therefore, care must be taken to insure that all possible concerns are addressed regarding how the arbitration is to be conducted. Because it is hard to insure that all contingencies are covered in the arbitration clause, it is not uncommon to find the arbitration clause refer to the procedures of an arbitration service as controlling the arbitration process. If the clause does reference an arbitration service, that service's procedures determine exactly how the arbitration is to be conducted. In fact, indicating that the arbitration will be handled by the arbitration service incorporates, by reference, that service's procedures. An example of an arbitration service's rules is the American Arbitration Association's (AAA) "Residential Real Estate Dispute Resolution Rules."

Example: Ms. B signed a listing agreement with Broker. The listing agreement contained an arbitration clause that Ms. B initialed. The arbitration clause stated that any disputes arising out of the agreement are to be submitted to arbitration according to the rules of the American Arbitration Association. It is becoming more common to find that mere membership in a professional association may impose a duty to arbitrate disputes. As a condition of membership, some associations may require its members to submit disputes to arbitration. This requirement may be imposed by the organization's bylaws or by clauses on membership application forms. This is the type of arbitration requirement that is found in Article 17 of the **Code of Ethics and Standards of Practice for the National Association of REALTORS®**.

1. Controversy Between REALTORS® Shall Be Arbitrated – Article 17

In the event of contractual disputes or specific noncontractual disputes as defined in **Standard of Practice 17-4** between REALTORS® (principals) associated with different firms, arising out of their relationship as REALTORS®, the REALTORS® shall submit the dispute to arbitration in accordance with the regulations of their Board or Boards rather than litigate the matter.

In the event clients of REALTORS® wish to arbitrate contractual disputes arising out of real estate transactions, REALTORS® shall arbitrate those disputes in accordance with the regulations of their Board, provided the clients agree to be bound by the decision.

The obligation to participate in arbitration contemplated by this Article includes the obligation of REALTORS® (principals) to cause their firms to arbitrate and be bound by any award.

C. WHO IS IN CHARGE OF SELECTING THE ARBITRATOR?

Another important feature of arbitration is that the parties are able to choose who serves as the arbitrator. The method of selecting the arbitrator is up to the parties and should be part of the arbitration clause. If the parties have chosen an arbitration service, the arbitrator will be selected according to the procedures set out by that service's rules. Where the parties have failed to include how an arbitrator is to be selected and are unable to mutually agree on how to select an arbitrator, the court may be petitioned to appoint an arbitrator from a list of persons supplied jointly by the parties.

Effective 2010, an arbitrator must comply with the ethics standards adopted by the California Judicial Council. Those arbitrator ethics standards are not negotiable, and cannot be waived.

D. ARBITRATOR'S ROLE

The *ARBITRATOR is a neutral third party who makes a decision on the merits of the dispute after an informal hearing.* The arbitrator is interested in getting to the truth of the matter. To accomplish this, the arbitrator listens to the parties, their witnesses, reviews evidence offered by the parties, and then, by weighing both of these, determines what the facts of the dispute are. The arbitrator will analyze the facts and then render a decision.

It is the arbitrator's responsibility to maintain a proper decorum during the arbitration hearing. Both parties should be given the opportunity to present necessary evidence and arguments. The power to decide whether evidence is to be admitted into the hearing belongs solely to the arbitrator.

E. ARBITRATION PROCESS

If the arbitration clause is *SELF-EXECUTING, the parties do not need to petition the courts to compel arbitration.* On the other hand, if the arbitration clause is not self-executing, one of the parties must petition the court to compel arbitration.

A self-executing arbitration clause contains:

1. the method for selection of arbitrator;
2. the procedure for conducting arbitration; and
3. a provision for continuing arbitration if one party refuses to proceed.

Example: The American Arbitration Association "Residential Real Estate Dispute Resolution Rules" state in Section 30 under the "Arbitration Rules" that "... the arbitration may proceed in the absence of any party or representative who, after due notice, fails to be present or fails to obtain a postponement."

Where the agreement is self-executing, most arbitrations start with a written notice being sent by the claimant that indicates arbitration is being sought under the agreement. This written notice should include the nature of the dispute, the amount involved, and the remedy sought. The *party receiving the demand, the* **RESPONDENT**, may respond with a statement answering the demand.

1. Selection of the Arbitrator

The next step is to select the arbitrator. The method set out in the arbitration clause should be followed and if no method is stated in the clause, or if there is no arbitration clause, the parties should mutually agree on how to select the arbitrator. As was mentioned previously, if all else fails, the court will appoint an arbitrator for the parties.

If an arbitration service is used, it is likely that a **STRIKE LIST** *will be utilized, meaning the association sends each party a list of persons from the panel maintained by the association, and each party "strikes" from the list any unacceptable names.* The list is then sent back to the association where one of the acceptable names on the list is chosen to arbitrate the dispute.

Prior to the hearing, only limited discovery is permitted unless the agreement provides for extended discovery. By statute, if the dispute is over $50,000, the parties are only entitled to demand, in writing, a list of witnesses the other party intends to call, with expert witnesses noted, and a list of documents the other party intends to introduce at the hearing. The party making this demand must also include a list of their witnesses and a list of documents they intend to introduce at the time they make the demand of the other party.

The arbitrator should be neutral and have a good understanding of the subject matter of the controversy.

2. Power to Issue Subpoenas

The arbitrator has the power to issue subpoenas.

A **SUBPOENA** *may be issued to compel the attendance of a witness, and if books, records, or other documents are desired, a* **SUBPOENA DUCES TECUM** *may be issued.* It is solely up to the arbitrator to make the determination as to the issuance of the subpoenas.

3. Rules of Judicial Procedure

Even though an arbitration hearing usually mirrors the judicial process, there is no requirement that rules of judicial procedure be followed. However, it is common for the claimant to make an opening statement, present his or her side of the dispute, offer any witnesses he or she may have, and present whatever evidence he or she wants the arbitrator to use. After the claimant has finished, the respondent presents his or her side, also using any witnesses and evidence he or she may have. The parties, and any witnesses that testify, are subject to cross-examination. The arbitrator may ask questions of either party or witnesses. While the arbitrator has the ability to decide how the hearing will progress, the arbitrator must provide for a full and equal opportunity for each party to present relevant evidence.

After hearing all the evidence presented by the parties, the arbitrator analyzes the facts and issues the decision. If the arbitration is binding, the decision is final. Court review may only be made if there was corruption or misconduct by the arbitrator, the arbitrator improperly conducted the hearing or the arbitrator exceeded his or her powers in making

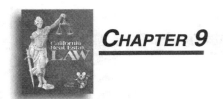

CHAPTER 9

the award. If the arbitration was nonbinding, either party may continue the dispute using the judicial process. Decisions rendered under binding arbitration may be enforced just as if a court had rendered the decision.

Remember that one party to the arbitration can have an attorney present, which is useful to determine if the arbitrator is acting properly and not exceeding his/her powers.

F. ARBITRATION AWARDS (Final Judgment)

When the arbitration clause or the procedures being followed provide that the *arbitrator's decision, called the AWARD*, is to be rendered within a certain time period, the award must be rendered within that time period or else it is void and unenforceable. The award must be in a signed writing that states what decision the arbitrator has reached.

One aspect of the parties agreeing to binding arbitration is that the courts recognize the arbitrator's award as being a final judgment in the dispute. The courts will normally overturn an arbitrator's award only if it was obtained through corruption, fraud, or other undue means. The courts will not delve into whether the arbitrator correctly determined the facts or arrived at the award by following precedents.

Additionally, where it can be shown that an arbitrator substantially prejudiced one of the party's rights by exceeding the powers vested in him or her, refusing to postpone a hearing, or in not accepting new relevant evidence, the courts will overturn the award. The courts will also overturn the award when an arbitrator has failed to disqualify himself or herself under the provisions applying to judges.

If the arbitration is not binding, the parties are not bound to accept the decision of the arbitrator as a conclusive disposition of the dispute, and may seek a *TRIAL DE NOVO (new trial)* to resolve the dispute in the superior court.

Once a final the award has been rendered and the parties comply with its ruling, there is no further judicial action to be taken. *If, however, one of the parties refuses to comply with the arbitration award, the other party may file with the court a PETITION TO CONFIRM the award.*

The following case shows what happens when there is a postarbitration litigation involving the attempt to confrm the arbitrator's award.

Case Example: Marcus & Millichap Real Estate Investment Brokerage Co. (Marcus) filed a demand for arbitration for payment of a commission pursuant to a listing agreement with Woodman Investments Group (Woodman). Woodman filed a cross-complaint in the arbitration proceeding for breach of fiduciary duty and constructive fraud. The listing agreement provided that in any litigation, arbitration or other legal proceeding the prevailing party shall be entitled to recover its costs, including cost of arbitration and reasonable attorney's fees. The arbitrator awarded approximately $300,000, including $70,000 for attorney's fees in favor of Marcus. Woodman's claims were denied. Marcus filed a petition in court to confirm the arbitration award. Woodman filed a cross-petition to vacate the arbitration award on the ground the arbitrator had exceeded her authorized powers. The court denied Marcus's petition to confirm and granted Woodman a cross-petition to vacate. Woodman then filed a motion to recover attorney's fees and costs pursuant to Section 1293.2, which authorizes the court to award costs in postarbitration judicial proceedings. ▼

The court granted Woodman's request for attorney's fees and costs, awarding $33,492.50 to Woodman as the prevailing party in the judicial proceedings. Marcus appealed.

The Court of Appeal noted that Woodman was entirely successful. Not only did they defeat Marcus & Millichap's effort to have the arbitration award confirmed, but they also persuaded the trial court to vacate the arbitration award against Woodman.

With respect to the postarbitration judicial proceedings, Woodman must be considered the prevailing party. Because no rehearing of the arbitration was ordered by the trial court its decision to vacate the original arbitration award is now final. In addition, the contract language requires postarbitration judicial proceedings to be considered a discrete "legal proceeding" for purposes of determining a party's right to an award of attorney fees. The order awarding attorney fees and costs is affirmed. *Marcus & Millichap Real Estate Investment Brokerage Co. v. Woodman Investment Group*, 129 Cal. App. 4th 508, 28 Cal. Rptr. 3d 584 (2005).

V. Resolving Disputes Concerning a Real Estate License

In Chapter 5 it is noted that it is unlawful to act in the capacity of a real estate broker or real estate salesperson without first obtaining a real estate license from the Department of Real Estate. Issues and disputes surrounding the issuance of a license, its revocation or suspension and hearing procedures involved are certainly areas of importance to real estate licensees. These problems are resolved through negotiation and, when that fails, an adjudicative process takes place.

A. COMMON REAL ESTATE LAW VIOLATIONS

Most of the common Real Estate Law violations are found in Section 10176 and Section 10177 of the Business and Professions Code. Section 10176 is the legal guideline for the licensee engaged in the practice and performance of any of the acts within the scope of the Real Estate Law. Section 10177 of the Real Estate Law applies to some situations where the person involved was not necessarily acting as an agent or as a licensee. Section 490 of the Business and Professions Code concerning criminal convictions is also included.

The vast majority of brokers and salespeople are honest and perform their services in a straightforward manner. Occasionally, a section of the Real Estate Law may be violated inadvertently and without intent. In such cases the Commissioner would most likely consider suspension of the real estate license. On the other hand, a flagrant violation would most likely cause a revocation of the license.

Business and Professions Code

Section 10176: A license may be temporarily suspended or permanently revoked by the Commissioner if the licensee has been guilty of any of the following:

a. Making any substantial misrepresentation. What is "substantial" will depend on the facts.
b. Making any false promise of a character likely to influence, persuade or induce.
c. A continued and flagrant course of misrepresentation or making false promises through real estate licensees. ▼

d. Acting for more than one party in a transaction without the knowledge or consent of all parties thereto.

e. Commingling with licensee's own money or property the money or property of others which is received and held by the licensee.

f. Claiming, demanding, or receiving a fee, compensation or commission under an exclusive agreement authorizing or employing a licensee to perform acts where the agreement does not contain a definite, specified date of final and complete termination.

g. A licensee claiming or taking of any secret or undisclosed compensation, or failing to reveal the full amount of compensation or profit to the person employing the licensee prior to entering into prior to entering into the contract. This can arise when the licensee makes a low offer, usually through a "dummy" purchaser, when the licensee already has a higher offer from another buyer. The difference between the dummy price and the resale price after the licensee purchases the property is the secret profit.

h. The use by a licensee of option to purchase the property contained in the listing agreement except when the licensee reveals in writing to the principal the full amount of the licensee's profit and obtains the written consent of the principal approving the amount of profit prior to or coincident with the exercise of the option.

i. Any other conduct, whether of the same or of a different character than specified in this section, which constitutes fraud or dishonest dealing. This is a "catch-all" that gives the Commissioner the latitude to interpret conduct and making a decision on fraud or dishonest dealing before taking action against the licensee.

j. Brokers must obtain the written authorization to sell (business opportunities) from an owner before securing the signature of a prospective purchaser to the agreement. This section eliminates what was once a common practice in some areas, or the prospective purchaser was forced to deal with the broker who furnished him or her with the listing.

k. Failing to distribute funds in accordance with a commitment to make a mortgage loan that is accepted by the applicant when the real estate broker represents to the applicant that the broker is either: (1) the lender, or (2) authorized to issue a commitment on the half of the lender.

l. Intentionally delaying the closing of a mortgage loan for the sole purpose of increasing interest, costs, fees, or charges payable by the borrower.

Section 10177; The Commissioner may suspend or revoke a license or may deny the issuance of a license if any of the following has occurred:

a. Procured, or attempted to procure the real estate license or license renewal for himself or herself or any salesperson by fraud, misrepresentation, or deceit or by making any material misstatement of fact on the application.

b. Entered a plea of guilty or nolo contendere to, or have been found guilty of or convicted of a felony or crime involving moral turpitude.

c. Knowingly authorized or aided in the publication, advertisement, distribution, or circulation of any material false statement or representation concerning the licensee's designation or certification of special-education, credential, trade organization membership, or business, or concerning any business opportunity or any land or subdivision offered for sale.

d. Violations by the licensee of any section of the Real Estate Law, the regulations of the Commissioner and the subdivision laws.

▼

e. Will fully use the term "realtor" or in a trade name or insignia of membership in any real estate organization of which the licensee is not a member.

f. Acted or conducted himself or herself in a matter that would have warranted the denial of a license or the person has had a government issued license suspended or revoked after receiving fair notice of the charges, an opportunity for a hearing, due process and only upon an express finding of a violation of the law.

g. Demonstrated negligence or incompetence in performing any act for which he or she is required to hold a license.

h. The holder of a broker license has failed exercise reasonable supervision over the activities of sales licensees or the officer designated by corporate broker failed to supervise activities of the corporation for which the license is required.

i. Has used his or her employment by government agency in a capacity having access to other than public records in a manner that violates the confidential nature of the records.

j. Engaged in any other conduct, whether of the same or different character than specified in this section, which constitutes fraud or dishonest dealing. Another "catch-all" for the benefit of the Commission.

k. Violated any of the terms or conditions contained in an order granting a restricted license.

l. Solicited or induce the sale, lease or listing for sale or lease of residential property on the grounds of loss in value, increase in crime, or decline of the quality of schools due to the present or prospective entry into the neighborhood of persons of a different race, color, religion, ancestry or national origin. This does not apply with respect to familial status as it applies to housing for older persons, and housing for senior citizens as provided in California law.

m. Violated the Franchise Investment Law or the regulations of the Commissioner of Corporations pertaining thereto.

n. Violated the Corporate Securities Law of 1968 or the regulations of the Commissioner of Corporations pertaining thereto.

o. Failure of the licensee to disclose to the buyer, where the licensee is an agent for the buyer, the nature and extent of the licensee's direct or indirect ownership interest in the property, the direct or indirect ownership interest by a person related to the licensee by blood or marriage, by entity in which the licensee has an ownership interest, or by any other person with whom the licensee has a special relationship.

p. Violation by a real estate broker that is a corporation of Article 6, Section 10237.

Section 490; The Commissioner may suspend or revoke a license for the following:

The licensee has been convicted of a crime which is substantially related to the qualifications, functions, or duties of the business or profession for which the license is issued.

B. PROBLEMS ACQUIRING A LICENSE

Generally, a real estate broker license or a real estate salesperson license is acquired by written application to the Real Estate Commissioner, meeting certain educational requirements, passing an examination, payment of the appropriate fee, and being fingerprinted. As a result of information that may surface during the application process for a license, the Commissioner may require the applicant to submit other evidence concerning his or her honesty and truthfulness. When the applicant is a corporation, the Commissioner will be concerned with determining whether the officers, directors, or persons owning more than ten percent of the stock have been truthful and honest in supplying information on the application. The Commissioner is authorized to hold a hearing to gather this extra evidence.

1. Statement of Issues

An administrative hearing to determine whether a license should be granted, issued, or renewed is started by filing a document called a statement of issues. The hearing process is initiated by the Commissioner filing a statement of issues. The *STATEMENT OF ISSUES identifies the issues being raised by the Commissioner and specifies the statutes and rules that are being violated.* The respondent must be served with the statement of issues and, if he or she desires, may request a hearing where evidence may be presented to counter the Commissioner's allegations. The hearing process is the same as the hearing process for suspending or revoking an existing license, which is discussed later, except that a document called an accusation is used when the Commissioner believes that an existing license should be suspended or revoked.

Case Example: In 2002, Bernard Berg applied for a real estate salesperson's license. The Department of Real Estate filed a statement of issues, citing Berg's disbarment as grounds for denying the license under Section 10177(f). After a hearing, the administrative law judge found that Berg was disbarred for acts that "constitute fraud or dishonest dealing" and would be grounds for revocation of a real estate license. The ALJ concluded it would be contrary to the public interest to issue a license, even on a restricted basis, to Berg. Berg was disbarred for violation of the Business and Professions Code by repeated bulk billing, which are dishonest acts involving moral turpitude and violation of the Rules of Professional Conduct by withdrawing funds disputed by a client from his trust account. The disbarment proceeding was preceded by a civil action filed against Berg by a client for fraud and deceitful billing in which the jury returned a verdict in favor of the client for $282,024.86. Among other things, Berg had one of his employees count the number of pages of pleadings and documents received and multiply that number by three minutes per page for billing purposes and sometimes billed for more than 24 hours a day, up to 100 plus. Regarding both the billing and the trust account, Berg was found to have had a reprehensible lack of insight into the wrongfulness of his actions and disbarred.

Berg petitioned for a writ of mandate to set aside the order denying him a real estate license. The trial court found substantial evidence supported the decision to deny the license. Berg appealed. The Court of Appeal affirmed the trial court judgment. *Berg v Davi*, 130 Cal. App. 4th 223, 29 Cal. Rptr. 3d 803 (2005).

---

2. License Obtained By Fraud

If the real estate license was obtained by fraud, misrepresentation, deceit, or by making any material misstatement of fact in the application for the license, the Commissioner may, without a hearing, suspend that person's license. The Commissioner has ninety days after the date of the license's issuance to order this suspension. The suspension remains in effect only until the effective date of the decision of the Commissioner after a hearing is conducted. A statement of issues is filed and served on the respondent with the order of suspension. The respondent has thirty days after service in which to file a written request for a hearing on the statement of issues. The Commissioner must hold a hearing within thirty days after receipt of the request for a hearing from the respondent. If the hearing is not commenced within thirty days after receipt of request for the hearing, or if the decision of the Commissioner is not rendered within thirty days after the completion of the hearing, the order of suspension is set aside.

C. RESTRICTED LICENSE

Under certain situations the Commissioner may believe it is necessary to issue only a restricted license to the applicant. The Commissioner can restrict licenses by limiting the term (for example, to one month), requiring that a salesperson be employed by a particular broke, limiting licensed activities to a certain geographic area or type of activity, requiring detailed reports of each transaction, requiring the licensee to post a surety bond, or requiring other conditions or combinations of conditions A restricted license may be issued when the Commissioner does not want to completely revoke or deny a license, yet does not want to grant the unrestricted retention or acquisition of a license.

A person acquires no property rights by the issuance of a restricted license. The holder has no right to renew the license and the Commissioner may, without a hearing, issue an order suspending the restricted licensee's right to any privileges granted under a restricted license pending a final determination to be made at a formal hearing.

 www2.dre.ca.gov/PublicASP/pplinfo.asp
DRE - Real Estate License Lookup

D. LICENSE REVOCATION OR SUSPENSION

When a person receives an unrestricted real estate license, he or she possesses a property right in that license that requires due process if it is to be taken away. This does not mean it is impossible to revoke or suspend the license, it simply means a hearing must take place for the revocation or suspension to be legal. Where a licensee commits fraud or participates in other forms of dishonest dealings, such as those mentioned in Sections 10176 and 10177, the license may be revoked or suspended by proving these acts at a hearing.

1. Suspension, Revocation, and Other Potential Discipline

A license suspension bars a licensee from engaging in activities that require a license for a specified period of time. Instead of suspending a license, the Commissioner may impose a fine of up to $250 per day of suspension, up to a maximum fine of $10,000. A license revocation bars a licensee from engaging in activities that require a license for an indefinite period of time and is, in theory, a permanent loss. If a license is suspended or revoked, the licensee may apply for reinstatement. The reinstatement process is discussed later in this Chapter. The Commissioner also has authority to issue desist and refrain orders and to obtain injunctions to prevent violations of the Real Estate Law.

2. Investigation

The Commissioner may, upon his or her own motion, and shall upon a verified written complaint, investigate the actions of any licensee and may permanently revoke or temporarily suspend the license if warranted. The department's investigator will interview the parties, accumulate and review documentation, and, when necessary, have subpoenas issued to get information. If the evidence accumulated by the department's investigation does not warrant the issuance of an accusation, no further action will be taken. If the evidence is substantially in support of the complaint, the matter is turned over to the legal section for the filing of the accusation.

The department may refer the matter to another agency, for example, for criminal prosecution. A licensee who has willfully violated, or knowingly participated in a violation of a Business and Professions Code section, is guilty of a misdemeanor punishable by a fine not exceeding ten thousand dollars or by imprisonment in a county jail not exceeding six months, or by both fine and imprisonment.

3. After Civil Action

The Commissioner, after conducting a hearing, also has the power to suspend or revoke a real estate license when a final judgment is obtained in a civil action against a licensee on the grounds of fraud, misrepresentation, or deceit with reference to any transaction for which the license is required.

The *RECOVERY FUND (funded by licensee's fees) is administered by the DRE to satisfy judgments for fraud or misrepresentation against licensed real estate agents, which would otherwise go unpaid.* In *Yergan v. Department of Real Estate*, 77 Cal. 4th 959, 968-970, 92 Cal.Rptr2d 189, 196-197 (App. 2 Dist. 2000), vendors who brought suit against a broker were not permitted to recover from the Recovery Fund because their settlement agreement provided for entry of judgment on only the alleged negligence and breach of duty claims, but not the alleged fraud claims.

E. ACCUSATION

When the Commissioner seeks to suspend or revoke a person's real estate license, a hearing must be held to satisfy the due process requirements. The hearing is initiated by filing an accusation and the complainant is the Real Estate Commissioner. The *ACCUSATION is a written statement in ordinary, concise language that sets forth the acts or omissions with which the respondent is charged, and it specifies any statutes and rules that the respondent is alleged to have violated.* A hearing is held before an **administrative law judge (ALJ)** and is conducted in the same manner as those where a statement of issues has been filed, except that with an accusation, the license is considered a property right and the Department of Real Estate has the burden of proof.

The "due process" hearing is held before an administrative law judge (ALJ) and the burden of proof rests with the DRE.

STATEMENT OF ISSUES: writing identifying Commissioner's concerns and specifying statutes and rules being violated; used to initiate license denial hearings.

ACCUSATION: a clear and concise writing setting forth acts or omissions that violate specified statutes or rules; used to initiate proceeding to suspend or revoke license.

When the accusation is filed, the licensee is served with a copy of the accusation, a statement of the respondent's legal rights, a notice of defense form, and copies of Government Code sections which deal with discovery procedures. The respondent is advised that unless a written request for a hearing is made within fifteen days after service of the accusation, the respondent will have waived the right to a hearing and the department may take disciplinary action without further notice. All the respondent has to do to request a hearing is sign the enclosed "notice and defense" and mail it to the Department of Real Estate. The respondent may, but need not be, represented by an attorney at respondent's expense during the hearing proceedings. The respondent is not entitled to the appointment of a free attorney. If the notice of defense is filed by the respondent, the Department of Real Estate will schedule a hearing and send a notice of hearing at least 10 days before the scheduled date.

The parties may reach a settlement before the hearing and propose that it be adopted by the Commissioner in order to eliminate the need for a hearing.

Names and addresses of witnesses who may testify at the hearing and relevant documents and investigative reports may be obtained through discovery. Subpoenas for the attendance of witnesses or production of documents can be issued and served.

A hearing is presided over by an administrative law judge in a manner resembling a civil trial: oral evidence taken under oath, witnesses examined, and documents introduced into evidence as exhibits. The respondent may be called as a witness and cross-examined even if the respondent does not want to be called as a witness.

F. THE DECISION

The administrative law judge prepares, within thirty days after the case is concluded, a proposed decision and delivers it to the Department of Real Estate. The decision must be in writing and contain findings of fact, a determination of the issues presented and the penalty, if any. The department may act on the proposed decision by adopting it in its entirety, or reducing the proposed penalty and adopting the balance of it, or rejecting it. If the proposed decision is not adopted by the department, the department itself may decide the case upon the hearing record, including the transcript, with or without taking additional evidence or may refer the case to the administrative law judge to take additional evidence. If additional evidence is taken by the administrative law judge, a proposed decision shall again be filed. Normally, the decision is effective thirty days after it is sent to the respondent.

If the Real Estate Commissioner determines that the public interest and the public welfare will be adequately served by permitting a real estate licensee to pay a monetary penalty to the department in lieu of an actual license suspension, the Commissioner may stay the execution of the suspension of the license, upon the condition that the licensee pay a monetary penalty and incur no other cause for disciplinary action within a stated period of time, provided by the Commissioner. The amount of the monetary penalty shall not exceed $250 for each day of suspension stayed, nor a total of $10,000 per decision, regardless the number of days of suspension stayed under the decision.

www.secure.dre.ca.gov/publicasp/unlicenseddnr.asp
Desist and Refrain Orders for Unlicensed Activities

G. RECONSIDERATION

Reconsideration of a decision can be ordered by the Department of Real Estate on its own motion or on petition of the respondent, and must be made prior to the effective day of the decision. The case may be reconsidered by the department itself, considering all pertinent parts of the record and such additional evidence and arguments as may be permitted, or it may be assigned to the administrative law judge. The proposed decision of the administrative law judge after reconsideration is subject to the same procedure as a proposed decision following a hearing on an accusation. The respondent may seek judicial review of the Commissioner's decision by filing a petition for a writ of mandate in the superior court. This appeal usually must be filed no later than 30 days after the Commissioner's decision was issued. Only if the respondent is successful in obtaining a discretionary stay order from the court will the respondent's license remain in effect while the matter is under appeal. Should the superior court grant the writ of mandate, the proceeding is remanded back to the department with directions concerning any further action. If the superior court denies the petition for a writ of mandate, the petitioner may appeal to the appellate court. The courts are unlikely to reverse a decision of the department, especially on a question involving facts.

H. REINSTATEMENT

When a license has been suspended or revoked, reinstatement is handled on an individual, case-by-case basis. A license suspension is temporary, and the period of suspension is specified (90 days, for example). But the license is not automatically reinstated after the suspension period ends. The respondent must apply for reinstatement. (If the license was suspended for more than one year, the respondent may apply for reinstatement after one year has passed, rather than waiting until the suspension period ends.)

Although, in theory, revocation is permanent (no period is specified), reinstatement is granted in some cases. The respondent may apply for reinstatement one year after the license was revoked.

The department gives notice to the attorney general of the filing of the petition and the petitioner is afforded an opportunity to present either an oral or a written argument before the department. The department decides the petition and the decision includes reasons therefore and the terms and conditions that the department deems appropriate to impose as a condition of reinstatement, if granted. If the department's investigation shows that the petitioner has not been rehabilitated, then the petition will be denied.

The Commissioner may require an applicant for reinstatement to retake the license examination. If an applicant whose license was revoked is not ordered to retake the exam, the applicant must show that he or she has complied with the Real Estate Law's continuing education requirements.

In some cases, the Commissioner will issue the reinstated licensee a *RESTRICTED LICENSE. The term of the license may be limited, and it may specify that the agent is only allowed to work for a particular broker*. The Commissioner may also place other restrictions on the license, and require the agent to file surety bonds. An agent with a restricted license doesn't have an automatic right to renewal—that's up to the Commissioner. And a restricted license may be suspended without a hearing.

Most real estate brokers and agents are honest and hard working, and very few intentionally commit fraud. But only the very lucky get through a long career without some problems arising. Careless mistakes or misunderstandings can have drastic consequences.

The best way to avoid problems is to know the law, keep up to date on changes in the law, communicate with your clients and customers, and be careful. Competent, diligent, ethical work is the surest road to success.

I. PREVENTING VIOLATIONS

If the Commissioner has evidence that a person is about to violate the Real Estate Law or is engaged in an ongoing violation, a desist and refrain order may be issued. The respondent is required to stop the activities in question immediately. He or she may request a hearing. If the respondent claims that the Commissioner's order substantially interferes with his or her real estate business, the order will be rescinded unless the commissioner obtains an injunction.

To obtain an injunction, the Commissioner must file a lawsuit in superior court. If the Commissioner proves that the respondent's activities violate the Real Estate Law, the court will enjoin the respondent from continuing those activities.

J. STATUTE OF LIMITATIONS

The Department of Real Estate must file an accusation within three years from the occurrence of the alleged grounds for taking disciplinary action. If the alleged grounds involved fraud, misrepresentation or a false promise the accusation must be filed within one year after the date of discovery by the aggrieved party or within three years after the occurrence of the act, whichever is later. However, no accusation can be filed later than 10 years from the occurrence of the alleged grounds for disciplinary action.

VI. CHAPTER SUMMARY

1. Negotiation. The use of alternative dispute resolution (ADR) is increasing. Negotiation, mediation, and arbitration offer alternatives to litigation as a means to resolve disputes.

2. Negotiation is still the primary method to resolve disputes. Needs and interests should be negotiated, not positions. Integrative negotiation (win-win) is preferable to distributive negotiation (win-lose).

3. Preparation is vital to good negotiating and makes the other two stages, the actual negotiations and conclusion of the negotiations, more efficient.

4. It's a good idea to determine your best alternative to a negotiated agreement (BATNA) and use it at the appropriate time.

5. Mediation. Mediation is voluntary negotiation involving a neutral third party to facilitate the parties in reaching an agreement. The mediator does not impose an agreement, but helps the parties reach their own agreement.

6. Mediation involves six steps: 1) the pre-session where parties agree to utilize mediation and select a mediator; 2) the mediation session where the mediator meets with the parties to explain processes to them and establish guidelines; 3) issues and needs are identified by the parties with the mediator's help; 4) alternatives and options are developed and analyzed; 5) agreement is either reached by the parties or the inability to reach an agreement is recognized and mediation stops, and 6) final agreement is reduced to a signed writing.

7. Arbitration. An arbitration is where a neutral third party resolves a dispute between parties by making a final decision. They are normally less formal, take less time, and are less costly than litigation. They are also private proceedings as opposed to the public nature of litigation.

8. Private arbitrations require the parties to agree to arbitrate the dispute. This agreement may occur either prior to or after the dispute has arisen.

9. Arbitration clauses in real estate contracts must comply with the state mandated language. Submission agreements are used to submit an existing dispute to arbitration.

10. Associations may require their members to arbitrate disputes as a condition of membership.

11. But for limited exceptions, binding arbitrations are not reviewable by the courts, but nonbinding arbitrations are reviewable by the courts.

12. Arbitrations start with a written notice being sent to the other party stating the nature of the dispute, the amount of money involved, and the remedy being sought. A response may be sent answering the demand.

13. Resolving Disputes Concerning a Real Estate License. A real estate license may be denied, suspended, or revoked.

14. A real estate license is obtained by a written application and all information must be truthful. The Commissioner may have concerns with the application and need further information from the applicant. A hearing may be used to obtain the information.

15. A statement of issues initiates the hearing involving denial of an application for a license (or to take away, within 90 days of issuance, a license obtained by fraud).

16. A restricted license may be issued by the Commissioner if questions exist as to the appropriateness of the applicant receiving an unrestricted license.

17. If the Commissioner seeks to suspend or revoke the license, an accusation must be filed and a hearing held.

18. Hearings are held by administrative law judges (ALJs) and their decisions are recommendations to the Commissioner.

19. After the Commissioner has taken action on a license, the matter may be reconsidered. If more than one year has lapsed from the date of the decision, the person may seek reinstatement. In the alternative, a person unhappy with the Commissioner's action may sue in court to set the action aside and reinstate or issue the license.

20. An arbitrator must comply with the "ethics standards" adopted by the California Judicial Council. They are not negotiable and cannot be waived.

VII. CASE PROBLEM
Frei v. Davey, 124 Cal. App. 4th 1506, 22 Cal. Rptr. 3d 429 (2004)

This case deals with Section **17. DISPUTE RESOLUTION; A. MEDIATION** and Section **22. ATTORNEYS' FEES** of the real estate purchase contract form in Chapter 8. Please reread both paragraphs before continuing.

The plaintiffs entered into a written contract to purchase the defendant's house on September 12, 2000. On October 11, the defendants canceled the purchase agreement. The plaintiffs sued the defendants for specific performance so a notice of pendency could be recorded. The trial court entered judgment for the plaintiffs. It was appealed, with the appellate court ordering a judgment in favor of the defendants. The trial court then granted the defendant's motion for $37,950 attorneys' fees incurred on the appeal and $119,935 in attorneys' fees for the trial. Plaintiffs appealed the attorneys' fee award on the ground that the defendants had failed to mediate the dispute as required in the purchase contract.

The defendants acknowledge receiving a letter from the plaintiffs dated November 30, 2000 demanding to mediate pursuant to paragraph 17 (at this point the parties were within $18,540 of reaching a settlement). The defendants did not respond so the plaintiffs filed a lawsuit on December 13. On January 5, plaintiffs' attorney wrote a letter to the defendants stating that he had not received a response with regard to mediation. On January 22 the defendant's attorney said the defendants were not interested in mediating the dispute. On February 27 the attorney called again stating that even though he had recommended mediation the defendants were not interested in doing so. Additionally, on January 5 the defendants declared that mediation would be fruitless. How will the appellate court rule on the attorney's fees and why?

CHAPTER 9

VIII. KEY TERMS

accusation	mediation clause
adjudicative	mediator
administrative law judge (ALJ)	negotiation
Alternative Dispute	nonadjudicative
Resolution (ADR)	petition to confirm
arbitration	private arbitrations
arbitrator	reconsideration
award	recovery fund
BATNA	reinstatement
binding/nonbinding	self-executing
arbitration	statement of issues
caucus	strike list
court-ordered arbitrations	submission agreement
distributive/integrative	subpoena duces tecum
negotiations	subpoena

IX. CHAPTER QUIZ

1. Which of the following is an advantage of alternative dispute resolution?
   - a. It is normally faster than that litigation
   - b. It is less formal than a court proceeding
   - c. It may be less expensive than litigation
   - d. All of the above

2. In which of the following proceedings is the result generally final and nonappealable?
   - a. Arbitration
   - b. Mediation
   - c. Negotiation
   - d. All of the above

3. Which of the following is an advantage to arbitration?
   - a. The parties may be able to select an arbitrator that has expertise in the subject matter of the dispute.
   - b. California law prohibits the parties from using an attorney during arbitration.
   - c. California law does not allow arbitration for disputes involving more than $10,000.
   - d. All of the above.

4. If a dispute is resolved by adjudicative procedures:
   - a   the dispute will be settled by mediation.
   - b. the dispute involves more than $10,000.
   - c. the dispute will be settled by negotiation.
   - d. the dispute could be settled by arbitration.

5. A respondent may seek judicial review of the Commissioner's decision regarding a license by filing in the superior court a petition for writ of:

    a. review.
    b. mandate.
    c. habeas corpus.
    d. reconsideration.

6. A petition for a writ of mandate must be filed in the superior court no later than:

    a. 15 days after the Commissioner's decision is issued.
    b. 25 days after the Commissioner's decision is issued.
    c. 30 days after the Commissioner's decision is issued.
    d. 60 days after the Commissioner's decision is issued.

7. After the license hearing is concluded, the administrative law judge must prepare a proposed decision and deliver it to the DRE within:

    a. 10 days.
    b. 15 days.
    c. 20 days.
    d. 30 days

8. Regarding a license hearing, when DRE receives a proposed decision by the administrative law judge, it may:

    a. adopt the entire decision.
    b. reject the proposed penalty and adopt the balance of it.
    c. reject a proposed decision entirely.
    d. do any of the above actions.

9. Assume a license is suspended for 60 days. What happens when the 60-day period ends?

    a. The license is automatically reinstated
    b. The license automatically becomes a restricted license for another 60 days
    c. The license is automatically revoked
    d. The person whose license has been suspended must apply for reinstatement

10. When the winning party in an arbitration asks a court to confirm the award, this means:

    a. they want a court trial to determine the validity of the award.
    b. they want a review of the award to see that the arbitrator's decision is correct.
    c. they want to determine the amount of attorneys fees to be added to the award.
    d. they want to turn the award into a court judgment.

ANSWERS: 1. d; 2. a; 3. a; 4. c; 5. b; 6. c; 7. d; 8. d; 9. d; 10. d

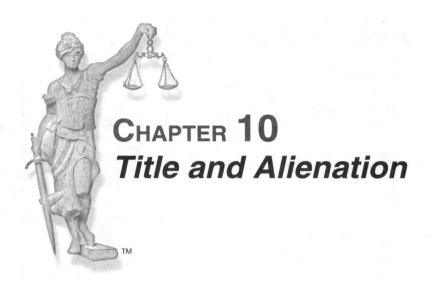

CHAPTER **10**
Title and Alienation

CHAPTER OVERVIEW

Ownership of real property is transferred from one person to another in a variety of ways. Sometimes a property owner voluntarily transfers title by deed or in a will. In other cases, property is transferred involuntarily, against the owner's wishes, as in a foreclosure sale or condemnation action. Alienation is the legal term that encompasses all the different methods of transfer, voluntary and involuntary. This chapter describes the requirements for the various types of transfers and their effects. It also discusses the recording system and title insurance, which play an essential role in the transfer of real property.

I. Voluntary Alienation

There are two primary ways to voluntarily transfer property: by deed and by will. A deed can only transfer title while the owner is alive, and a will only transfers title when the owner dies.

A. DEEDS

A *DEED is a document used by an owner of real property (the **GRANTOR**) to transfer all or part of his or her interest in the property to another party (the **GRANTEE**). The process of alienating real property by deed is sometimes called a **CONVEYANCE**.*

A deed transfers all or part of an interest in real property.

To be valid, a deed has to contain certain elements and meet specific requirements. An invalid deed doesn't transfer title; the intended grantor still owns the property. In California, a deed is valid if it:

1. is in writing,
2. includes words of conveyance,
3. is signed by a competent grantor,

CHAPTER OUTLINE

4. names an identifiable and living grantee,

5. contains an adequate description of the property, and

6. has been delivered and accepted.

1. Requirements for a Valid Deed

a. Written

A deed must always be in writing. A transfer of real property cannot be accomplished orally.

b. Words of Conveyance

A deed has to have a granting clause; words that convey the property to the new owner. This requirement is easily satisfied: any words that express the intention to transfer an interest or ownership will do the trick.

Usually a single word—"grant" or something similar—is sufficient. However, since some lawyers like to use five or six words when one will do, some granting clauses look like this:

"The grantors do hereby give, grant, bargain, sell, and convey unto the said grantees forever ..."

Not only are the extra technical words unnecessary, they can create confusion. It's better to keep it simple.

c. Competent Grantor

A grantor must be competent—of legal age and sound mind. Minors and incompetents can own real property, but they can't convey it without their legal guardian's approval. A deed is void if the grantor is a minor or has been declared incompetent by a court. A deed is voidable when the grantor hasn't been declared incompetent, but was not of sound mind when the deed was executed.

1. Grantor's Name

The grantor's name is the name under which title was originally taken by the grantor.

If the grantor took title under a different name than the one he or she is using now, the deed must state the former name as well as the current one.

Example: Eileen bought a house when she was single. The name on her deed is "Eileen R. Flannigan," her maiden name. A few years after buying the house, she married and took her husband's last name, Minuscoli.

Several years later, Eileen sells the house. On the deed to the buyer, she is identified as "Eileen R. Minuscoli, who acquired title as Eileen R. Flannigan."

If the deed had listed the grantor only under her current name, it would not be invalid. It would be effective to transfer title to the buyer, however, it would not give constructive notice of the transfer to later buyers or lienholders. That may also be true if the grantor's name is spelled differently on the two deeds, or if a nickname is used on one deed and not the other. These problems will be discussed later in the chapter in the section on recording.

Although it isn't a legal requirement, a deed should also indicate the grantor's marital status. Marital status can affect the grantor's right to convey the property since California is a community property state. As such, it's a good idea to state clearly in the deed whether the grantor is married or single.

2. Grantor's Signature

To be valid, a deed must be signed by the grantor (owner). (The grantee's signature isn't required.) The grantor should sign his or her current legal name—in the example above, Eileen Minuscoli should sign her married name, not her maiden name.

If the grantor is unable to write his or her own name (because of illiteracy or a physical disability), the deed may be signed by a mark. If the grantor signs by a mark, the name should be written or typed in near the mark. Two witnesses should also sign to attest that the mark is the grantor's signature.

Sometimes a deed is executed by the grantor's agent instead of the grantor. The agent must be the grantor's attorney in fact, authorized to sign by a recorded power of attorney (see Chapter 5). The attorney in fact must sign the grantor's name and then his or her own name beneath it.

Example: _____
        Eileen R. Flannigan, Grantor
    By _____, her Attorney in Fact

A grantee taking title by a deed signed by an attorney in fact should make sure that the power of attorney has not expired or been revoked, and that the grantor is alive and competent.

d. Identifiable Grantee

For a deed to transfer title, it must name an existing, living, and identifiable grantee. Note that the grantee does not have to be competent—property can be transferred to a minor or an insane person.

Example: A deed to "Zelda Higgins and her husband" is adequate to transfer ownership to Zelda and her husband. The identity of Zelda's husband can be determined, even though his name was not stated in the deed.

A deed to "Zelda Higgins's brother" would be effective as long as Zelda has only one brother. But if Zelda has two brothers, the grantee is not identifiable.

Example: J executes a deed to transfer his property to M, not realizing that M was killed in an accident the day before. M's heirs try to claim the property, but in fact they don't have any legal right to it. A deed can't transfer property to a dead grantee. The deed is void, and the property still belongs to J. If he wants M's heirs to have it, he must deed it to them.

If the grantee is an organization (such as a corporation or partnership) rather than a human being, it must legally exist when the deed is executed. In other words, it has to meet the requirements for incorporation, or have the proper certificates recorded, so that it's a legally recognized entity (see Chapter 4).

e. Adequate Property Description

A deed must contain an adequate description of the property being conveyed. A full legal description isn't required, but the property should be described well enough to identify it with reasonable certainty (see Chapter 2).

f. Delivery and Acceptance

1. Delivery

A deed has no legal effect until the grantor has delivered the deed with the intention of immediately transferring title and the grantee has accepted the deed.

Delivery of a deed is a legal concept that means more than physically handing the deed to the grantee. Legal delivery of a deed can happen in situations when the grantor does not physically give the deed to the grantee. And while legal delivery of a deed may be presumed if the grantor physically hands a deed to the grantee, physical delivery may not be held to be legal delivery. *Legal delivery means that the grantor must intend to immediately surrender control of, and transfer title of the property to the grantee. This is called* **DONATIVE INTENT**.

Case Example: Mr. Kimbro was seriously ill with pneumonia, and his doctor thought he might die. Mr. Kimbro owned several lots in Los Angeles. During his illness, Mrs. Kimbro asked her husband to deed two of his lots to her, and he agreed. Their lawyer drew up a deed. Mr. Kimbro signed it, but did not acknowledge it, before giving it to his wife.

After Mr. Kimbro recovered, he asked his wife to give him back the deed. He implied that she had taken advantage of his illness and bullied him into signing it. Outraged, Mrs. Kimbro gave him back the deed, and he destroyed it.

Several years later, the Kimbros decided to go their separate ways. In the divorce proceedings, Mrs. Kimbro claimed that she owned the two lots Mr. Kimbro had deeded to her, as her separate property.

But Mr. Kimbro testified that he believed the deed was invalid because it wasn't acknowledged. He claimed to have told his wife at the time, "Well, I will sign the deed, but it won't benefit you any for it is not acknowledged."

Of course, in California a deed does not have to be acknowledged to be valid. But the court ruled that Mr. Kimbro had not delivered the deed with donative intent, so it did not transfer title. As a result, the lots were never Mrs. Kimbro's separate property. *Kimbro v. Kimbro*, 199 Cal. 344, 249 P.180 (1926).

A deed must be delivered while the grantor is alive, or it has no legal effect. Sometimes, a person signs a deed intending that title only transfer after the grantor's death. Such a deed would never be valid, as the shown in the following case.

Case Example: Meta Rasmussen was old and didn't expect to live much longer. She wanted to leave some of her property to her sister, Maria Beck, and some to her friend, Robert Jansen.

But Rasmussen was concerned that if she willed her property to them, probate costs would eat up a large share of the estate, so she executed a deed for her house, granting a life estate to Beck, with the remainder interest in the property going to Jansen.

Asking another friend to act as a witness, Rasmussen sealed the deed in an envelope. On the outside of the envelope she wrote, "Signed, Sealed, and Delivered in the presence of Beatrice Myers Winslow," and "This envelope and contents is the property of Maria Beck of Ferndale and Robert N. Jansen of Manteca, California. [Signed] Meta Rasmussen. Witness B. M. Winslow." Instead of giving the deed to Beck or Jansen, Rasmussen placed the envelope in her safe deposit box.

Rasmussen died a little less than a year later, and the deed was found after her death. Jansen tried to claim an interest in Rasmussen's house, but the deed was held to be ineffective. It had not been delivered to Beck and Jansen while Rasmussen was alive. *Miller v. Jansen*, 21 Cal. 2d 473, 132 P.2d 801 (1943).

In some cases, a deed is considered to be constructively delivered when the grantor turns it over to a third person to give to the grantee. The deed would be valid as long as the grantor intended to immediately transfer title to the grantee.

Example: X has decided to deed property to his granddaughter Z. Z is out of town when X signs the deed, so he can't physically deliver the deed to Z. X hands the deed to his son S and say: "The property is now Z's property. Please give this deed to Z when she returns from her trip."

A court would likely consider the deed to constructively delivered, and thus valid, because X intended to immediately transfer title to the property to Z when he signed the deed.

2. Acceptance

$65

grantor needs to be alive

Not only is it necessary for the grantor to intend to transfer ownership, it is necessary for the grantee to accept the transfer in the deed. And the acceptance must take place while the grantee is alive.

Problems concerning acceptance are rare, because most grantees are happy to acquire title to and take control of property. Acceptance can be shown by acts, words, or conduct of the grantee. For example, if a grantee records a deed, it would be presumed that the grantee accepted the transfer. There are some exceptions. A grant of property to a public agency such as a city or county must formally accepted by the agency. And, as the Kelly case below shows, there may be other rare times when acceptance becomes an issue.

> **Case Example:** In 1943, Arthur Kelly was about to have a serious operation and there was a good chance he wouldn't survive it. He deeded his ranch to his son Everett and gave Everett the deed.
>
> Arthur came through the operation and recuperated. He and his wife Winnie (Everett's stepmother) continued to live on the ranch. They paid the taxes and other expenses, and took out loans using the ranch as collateral. On their income tax statements, Arthur and Winnie listed the ranch as their property, reported all the income from it, and deducted its operating expenses. Everett, on the other hand, did not live or work on the ranch, pay any of the taxes or expenses, collect any of the income, or list the ranch as his property on loan applications or income tax statements.
>
> Five years later, Arthur was dying of cancer. He asked Everett to return the deed to him, and Everett did so. Arthur made out a will, leaving all his property, including the ranch, to both Winnie and Everett. After his father's death, Everett tried to establish that he was the sole owner of the ranch. He claimed to have owned the property since 1943, when his father executed the deed. As a result, Everett contended his father didn't have the right to leave part of the property to Winnie in his will.
>
> The court held that Everett never owned the ranch before his father's death. The court questioned whether Arthur had delivered the deed with donative intent. Even if Arthur had, Everett hadn't accepted it (in the eyes of the law) because he didn't take on any of the rights or duties of ownership. *Kelly v. Bank of America*, 112 Cal. App. 2d 388, 246 P.2d 92 (1952).

2. Other Elements

Many deeds contain other elements that seem to be standard, but aren't required by California law for the deed to be valid (effective to transfer title)—a certificate of acknowledgment, a date, and a recital of consideration are examples. Also, it is not necessary that that the grantee sign a deed to make the deed valid, and it is not necessary

CHAPTER 10

that the deed be recorded to make it valid. However, recording a deed is important to give notice of the transfer and to protect the grantee's title against claims from persons who may later acquire and interest in the property (recording is discussed in detail later in this Chapter.

An *ACKNOWLEDGMENT is a formal declaration, made before an officer designated by statute (typically a notary public) that a person executed (signed) a document.*

The person signing a grant deed, quitclaim deed, or trust deed is required to place a right thumb print on the notary's sequential journal. This is because of a high rate of fraud by the use of false deeds. Additionally, a notary must immediately notify the secretary of state if the notary's sequential journal is stolen, lost, misplaced, destroyed, damaged, or otherwise rendered unusable.

A person signing a legal document will often make an acknowledgment of his or her signature in front of a notary public or other person authorized to take proof of acknowledgments. Acknowledgment of a deed is not required to make a deed valid, but a grantee should always insist on acknowledgment. A deed cannot be recorded in California unless it has been acknowledged by the grantor, and an acknowledgment may be used to prove the validity of the grantor's signature.

Because most acknowledgments are proved before notaries, taking a proof of acknowledgment is often referred to as "notarizing" the document. The notary taking the proof of acknowledgment usually completes or attaches a certificate of acknowledgment, which states that the document signer personally appeared before the notary on the date indicated and in the county indicated, that the signer provided sufficient evidence of his or her identity, and that the signer acknowledged executing (signing) the document. To have the document acknowledged, you must give the notary proof of your identity.

Almost all deeds are dated, but a date is not required to make the deed valid. However, a date is a good idea because a deed is presumed to be delivered on its date and a date may be important in establishing the priority of the grantor's interest in the property as compared to other interests.

A deed may contain the grantee's signature, but the grantee does not need to sign a deed. Only the grantor's signature is required to make a deed valid.

Many deeds contain a recital of consideration given in exchange for the transferred property, but consideration is not required to make a deed valid. A person can deed property to a grantee as a gift. When a recital of consideration is included, it typically does not state the actual purchase price, but contains language such as "For $1.00 and other valuable consideration." A recital may be important to show that the transfer was a sale rather than a gift, which may be important if the grantor's creditors claim that they can still reach the property because no value was paid.

A Valid Deed

I grant	words of conveyance
Razorback Farm	description of property
to Jacob Howard	identifiable grantee
[signed] Sylvia Peron	signature of competent grantor

1. In writing, delivered with donative intent, and accepted
2. Can't be recorded without grantor's acknowledgment

---

3. Types of Deeds

Only two types of deeds are frequently used in California: the grant deed and the quitclaim deed. Warranty deeds were common here at one time and are still popular in many states, but they're almost never used in California today.

www.homebuying.about.com/od/titleinsurance/qt/REdeeds.htm
Property Deeds in California

a. Grant Deeds and Warranty Deeds

Nearly every California real estate sale involves a grant deed. *The law treats any deed that uses "grant" in its words of conveyance as a GRANT DEED.* When that word is included, the deed carries two implied warranties (unless the deed expressly states it does not carry them). The grantor warrants to the grantee in a grant deed that:

1. the grantor has not previously conveyed title to anyone else, and
2. the grantor has not caused any encumbrances to attach to the property, other than those disclosed on the deed.

A grant deed contains two implied warranties.

Warranty deeds carry additional warranties, beyond the two implied in grant deeds. A general warranty deed gives the grantee the broadest protection.

With a *GENERAL WARRANTY DEED, the grantor warrants the title even against defects arising before he or she owned the property. A SPECIAL WARRANTY DEED isn't quite so sweeping; its warranties only extend to problems that may have arisen during the grantor's period of ownership.*

The grantee has the right to sue the grantor if any of the deed warranties are breached. For example, suppose the seller gives you a grant deed and it turns out that there's a surprise tax lien against the property. If you pay off the tax lien, you can sue the seller for breach of warranty and recover the amount of the lien.

Today, nearly every real estate transaction is covered by title insurance. As a result, deed warranties are no longer important. The insurance takes care of the kinds of problems that warranties were intended to address. That's why Californians use the simpler grant deed instead of bothering with general and special warranty deeds.

Both grant deeds and warranty deeds convey after-acquired title, which is discussed later in this section.

CHAPTER 10

b. Quitclaim Deeds

A quitclaim deed transfers, without warranty, only whatever interest or title a grantor may have at the time the conveyance is made.

A quitclaim deed merely conveys whatever interest the grantor has. It carries no warranties of any sort. If the grantor owns no interest in the property when the quitclaim deed is executed, the deed conveys nothing to the grantee.

→ signed

Example: A and B are neighbors and good friends. They're uncertain about the exact location of the boundary line between their lots. There's a fence between the properties 30 yards from B's house, but B thinks the true property line is really 32 yards from the house. A and B both want to sell their properties, but don't want to hire a surveyor. B gives A a quitclaim deed for the two yards of property on the other side of the fence.

When the properties are surveyed several years later, the survey shows that the fence is right on the true boundary line. Therefore, B's quitclaim deed didn't transfer any interest to A since B didn't actually own the two yards on the other side of the fence.

A common reason for using a quitclaim deed is to clear up a *CLOUD ON THE TITLE, which is a claim, encumbrance, or apparent defect that makes the title to real property unmarketable, such as a technical flaw, like the misspelling of grantee's name on an earlier deed, or a property description error.* The cloud might also be an expired option to purchase. If the optionee executes a quitclaim deed in favor of the optionor, it's absolutely clear that the optionee has no further claim against the property.

A quitclaim deed is also used when the grantor is not sure of the validity of his or her title and wants to avoid giving any warranties.

Example: J's uncle left J some property in his will, but the will is being challenged in court by J's cousin. If J wants to transfer the property before the lawsuit is resolved, she should use a quitclaim deed.

c. After-Acquired Title

An important difference between a grant deed and a quitclaim deed is that the grant deed conveys after-acquired title and the quitclaim deed doesn't. A quitclaim deed conveys only the interest that the grantor has when the deed is executed. The after-acquired title doctrine, found in Civil Code section 1106, provides that when a person purports grant greater title than he or she actually holds at the time of the transfer, and the grantor later acquires the title that he or she purported to convey after making that grant, the "after-acquired title" passes automatically to the grantee by operation of law.

> **Case Example:** Ms. Schwenn owned some property in Long Beach. She leased the oil and gas rights to the Atlantic-Richfield Company (ARCO). ARCO paid Schwenn royalties for the oil and gas her property produced.
>
> In 1969, Schwenn conveyed the oil and gas rights to her daughter as a gift. ARCO began paying the royalties to Schwenn's daughter. ▼

Five years later, Schwenn sold the property to the Kayes. The preliminary title report showed that the property was subject to ARCO's lease, but failed to show that Schwenn had conveyed the oil and gas rights to her daughter. Before closing, Schwenn agreed that the oil and gas lease would be assigned to the Kayes "if assignable." She didn't explain that she didn't have the right to assign the lease because it belonged to her daughter.

After closing, ARCO was notified of the sale and began sending the royalties to the Kayes instead of Schwenn's daughter. Schwenn protested, claiming that the royalties should still be sent to her daughter. ARCO said it would not disburse any more royalties without a court order resolving the dispute.

At this point, Schwenn asked her daughter to reconvey the oil and gas rights to her. She explained that there was going to be a lawsuit, and she didn't want her daughter to get mixed up in litigation over a gift. So the daughter deeded the rights back to Schwenn.

The court ruled that the Kayes now owned the oil and gas rights and were entitled to the royalties. Schwenn had given them a grant deed that purported to convey fee simple title to the property. She didn't own the oil and gas rights at that time, and so could not sell the rights to the Kayes. However, when Schwenn's daughter conveyed the rights back to Schwenn, they automatically belonged to the Kayes under the doctrine of after-acquired title. *Schwenn v. Kaye*, 155 Cal. App. 3d 949, 202 Cal. Rptr. 374 (1984).

The case wouldn't have worked out this way if Schwenn had transferred her property to the Kayes with a quitclaim deed instead of a grant deed. Since a quitclaim deed doesn't convey after-acquired title, the Kayes would not have automatically gained title to the oil and gas rights when Schwenn's daughter transferred the rights back to Schwenn.

B. WILLS

The second method of voluntary alienation is by will. A will only transfers property when the owner dies. An expectation under a will (knowing that Aunt Harriet is leaving you her house) is not an interest in property. You have no legal interest in the property and no rights in regard to it until Aunt Harriet is dead.

www.calbar.ca.gov/Public/Pamphlets/EstatePlanning.aspx
Do I Need Estate Planning - The State Bar of California

A person who makes out a will is called the **TESTATOR** *(male) or* **TESTATRIX** *(female)*. Under modern statutes, the term testator may be used to refer to either a male or female, and instead of testator or testatrix, the person who makes out a will is sometimes called a "maker." *A testator* **bequeaths** *personal property to* **LEGATEES** *and devises real property to* **DEVISEES**. (Legatees and devisees are lumped together as the **beneficiaries** of the will.) *The* **EXECUTOR** *or* **EXECUTRIX** *is the person appointed in the will to carry out the testator or testatrix's directions under the supervision of the probate court.* **PROBATE** *is the legal process in which a will is proved valid and the property is distributed according to its terms.* In California, probate matters are handled by the superior courts.

In the early 1980s, the California Legislature substantially revised the statutes governing wills. Although many rules remained the same, many changes went into effect in 1985. As a

CHAPTER 10

Will Terms

Testator/Testatrix – One who makes a will
Bequeath – To transfer personal property by will
Devise – Disposition of real or personal property by will
Codicil – An amendment to a will
Executor/Executrix – Someone appointed in the will to carry out the testator's or testatrix's directions
Probate – Legal procedure for proving a will's validity

result, a will written long ago might be treated differently depending on whether the testator or testatrix died before or after January 1, 1985. The rules outlined here, of course, are the current ones.

Any person of sound mind who is 18 years of age or older may make a will. Just like a grantor, a testator or testatrix must be competent. If he or she is found to have been incompetent at the time the will was executed, it is invalid. Then the property will pass just as if the testator or testatrix had died *INTESTATE—without making a will.* (The rules of intestate succession are discussed in the next section of this chapter.)

In California, a will must be in writing. Oral wills bequeathing personal property used to be recognized in very specific situations, but the legislature repealed that law. It was never possible to devise real property by an oral will.

A will must be signed by the testator or testatrix. However, as with deeds, a will may be signed with a mark or by someone else on behalf of the testator or testatrix. If the will is signed by someone else, it has to be signed in the presence of the testator or testatrix. The person signing must also sign his or her own name.

1. Formal, Witnessed Wills

Ordinarily, at least two witnesses must sign their names to a will. To be legitimate witnesses, they must be present either when the testator or testatrix signs the will, or when he or she acknowledges it. They must specifically understand that the document being signed is a will.

Generally, a beneficiary should not be a witness to a will.

Any competent adult may witness a will. However, someone who is a beneficiary under the will should not act as a witness unless there's no alternative. That wouldn't invalidate the will, but it might cause trouble for the witness/beneficiary.

Unless there were at least two other disinterested witnesses, it would be presumed that the witness/beneficiary used fraud, duress, menace, or undue influence to make the testator or testatrix execute the will in his or her favor. If the beneficiary could prove that presumption was false, he or she would get the full bequest or devise. If the beneficiary was unable to overcome the presumption, the beneficiary would get no more than what he or she would have inherited if the testator or testatrix had died intestate.

Example: Mrs. Cox drew up a will leaving her Palm Springs condominium to her hairdresser and all the rest of her property (including her house in San Francisco) to her

---

Wills

- In writing
- Signed by testator

FORMAL

Two witnesses
Competent adults
Disinterested if possible

Statutory will may be used

HOLOGRAPHIC

In testor's handwriting
No witnesses

---

cook. She expressly disinherited her daughter. Mrs. Cox's signature was witnessed by the cook and the gardener.

Since the cook was a beneficiary as well as a witness, there was only one disinterested witness (the gardener). In the probate proceedings after Mrs. Cox's death, the cook has to prove that he didn't use fraud or other underhanded methods to persuade Mrs. Cox to leave the bulk of her property to him. If he is able to convince the court that he did not, then he is entitled to the property.

If the cook can't convince the court, he will only be awarded what he would have received if Mrs. Cox had never made a will. Since he is not related to Mrs. Cox, that would be nothing at all. (If he were Mrs. Cox's son instead of her cook, he would receive a share of the estate according to the rules of intestate succession, outlined later in the chapter.)

If there had been a third witness to Mrs. Cox's will—also disinterested, like the gardener—then the cook would not have to defend himself against the presumption of fraud or underhandedness.

a. Statutory Will

The law governing wills and estates is complicated, and many wills need to be drawn up by a lawyer. However, people with simple estates can use California's *STATUTORY WILL, which is a basic will form set out in the Probate Code.* The legislature adopted the statutory will to help people with modest incomes avoid high legal fees. It's a good idea to have a statutory will reviewed by a lawyer, but that should cost considerably less than having a will drafted from scratch.

A statutory will, like any other formal will, must be witnessed by at least two people.

2. Holographic Wills

In California, the only exception to the witnessing requirement is the holographic will. A *HOLOGRAPHIC WILL is one that the testator or testatrix has written out by hand.* As long as the signature and the main provisions are in the testator or testatrix's handwriting, the will is valid even without witnesses. It used to be that the entire will, including the date, had to be handwritten, but that rule has been relaxed. A statement of testamentary intent (such as the heading "Last Will and Testament") in a holographic will may be part of a commercially printed form. Other provisions that are typewritten or preprinted will be disregarded when a court interprets a holographic will.

A person making a will should have it witnessed whenever possible. A holographic will is much more easily challenged in court than a witnessed will.

3. Foreign Wills

When someone executes a will in another state or another country in compliance with the laws of that place, California probate courts consider the will valid, even if it doesn't meet all of California's legal requirements.

> **Example:** R is vacationing in Islandia, a faraway country. While he's there, R becomes very ill and decides to execute a will in case he doesn't live. The only witness to the will is his nurse. This will is valid in Islandia because that country's laws require only one witness for a will.
>
> R recovers and comes home to California. He never bothers to make a new will. When R dies, his Islandian will is probated in a California court. Although one witness ordinarily would not be enough in California, the court holds that the will is valid here because it was valid in the place where it was executed.

The same rule applies if a citizen of another state or country executes a will while staying in California. If the will would be valid under the laws of the state or country of citizenship, California courts will accept it.

4. Family Rights Under a Will

In California, when a spouse dies, half of any community property automatically belongs to the surviving spouse, regardless of the terms of the will (see Chapter 4). The other half of the community property and any separate property owned by the deceased spouse may be disposed of by will. Aside from the surviving spouse's community property rights, he or she may be disinherited. A child may be completely disinherited.

Sometimes a will makes no provision for a surviving spouse because the testator or testatrix got married after executing the will and never wrote a new one. In that case, the omitted spouse will be awarded the community property and the share of the separate property he or she would have received if the testator or testatrix had died intestate. However, the court can't award an omitted spouse more than half the separate property.

There's a similar rule for children who aren't mentioned in a will because they were born or adopted after it was executed. These children generally receive the share of the estate they would have taken if the parent had died intestate.

Occasionally, the family home is willed to someone other than the family. The surviving spouse and minor children have the right to continue living in the home for at least 60 days after the inventory of the estate property is filed with the probate court. The court may extend that grace period if necessary.

The court may also decide to treat the home as a ***PROBATE HOMESTEAD****, setting it aside for the use of the spouse and children and giving it homestead protection (see Chapter 3) from some claims against the estate.* A probate homestead is held for a limited period, under conditions specified by the court. The devisee the home was willed to takes title subject to the probate homestead right.

5. Revocation

A will is revoked if the testator or testatrix executes another will later on. The earlier will is revoked to the extent it is inconsistent with the later one, or if the later one expressly states that the earlier one is completely revoked. A will is also revoked if it is burned, torn, canceled, obliterated, or destroyed with the intent to revoke it. This destruction must either be done by the testator or testatrix, or by another person in the testator or testatrix's presence and at his or her direction.

If a will is lost or destroyed inadvertently or as a result of fraud, the court may still establish the existence of the will on the testimony of at least two witnesses. If the will was last seen in the possession of the testator or testatrix and he or she was competent until the time of death, the court will presume that the will was destroyed with the intention of revoking it. The survivors have to present evidence to overcome that presumption.

When a testator or testatrix gets divorced, the will provisions involving the ex-spouse are automatically revoked. If the ex-spouse was to receive property under the will, that property will go to whoever would have taken it if the ex-spouse had died before the testator or testatrix. If the ex-spouse was to act as executor or executrix, the probate court will appoint an administrator to take his or her place.

Revocation of a Will

- **Execution of a later will**
- **Divorce**
- **Intentional destruction by the testator**

---

a. Codicil

In addition to revoking your current will and writing a new one, you can change your will by creating a codicil. A *CODICIL is a formal supplement to your will and must conform to the same requirements for executing a will (must be written and signed by you and your witness).*

II. Involuntary Alienation

INVOLUNTARY ALIENATION is any transfer of property that occurs against the owner's wishes or without any action by the owner. Property is involuntarily alienated when a person dies without leaving a will, or without any heirs. Title may also be involuntarily transferred by adverse possession, a court decision, or government action. Ownership also sometimes changes hands as a result of natural forces that cause geological changes in the land itself.

A. INTESTATE SUCCESSION

Someone who dies without leaving a will is said to die INTESTATE. The rules of intestate succession determine who is entitled to a share of the property of a person who dies intestate, or whose will is ruled invalid. (Like the statutes on wills, those governing intestate succession were changed in 1985.) *HEIRS are persons related to the deceased person by blood or marriage,* and the Probate Code establishes which heirs are entitled to receive property. The probate court will appoint an *ADMINISTRATOR to administer the estate of the deceased person and carry out the statutory distribution of the deceased person's property.*

CHAPTER 10

www.wwlaw.com/estate.htm
Estate Planning Tool

A person's *ISSUE are his or her lineal descendants, that is, his or her children, grandchildren, great-grandchildren, and so forth.* The issue of a person's parents are that person's brothers and sisters, nieces and nephews, great-nieces, and so on. The California Probate Code provides that an intestate person's property is distributed in the following manner:

1. The **surviving spouse** is entitled to all of the community property, plus:

   a. **One-half** of the separate property if the intestate person is survived by:
      1. only one child or issue of a deceased child, or
      2. one or both parents, or the issue of either parent.

   b. **One-third** of the separate property if the intestate person is survived by:
      1. more than one child,
      2. one child and the issue of one or more deceased children, or
      3. the issue of two or more deceased children.

   c. **All of the separate property** if there is no surviving issue, or parent, or brother or sister, or issue of a deceased brother or sister.

2. The portion of the separate property not going to the spouse (or the entire estate if there is no surviving spouse) is distributed to the issue of the intestate person—the children, grandchildren, and so on of the person who died.

   If the issue are all of the same degree of kinship, they take equally. In other words, if the intestate person had three children and they are all still living, each of the three would get an equal share. If all three children were already dead, but there were five grandchildren still living, each of those five would get an equal share.

   If the issue are not of the same degree of kinship, then those of a more remote degree divide up their deceased parent's (or grandparent's) share.

   Example: Arnold and Brenda had two children, Celia and David. Celia has been dead for some time. She had two children, Eliza and Francine, who are still living. David also has a living child, Greg.

   Arnold dies intestate. Brenda is entitled to all of the community property, plus one-third of Arnold's separate property. The other two-thirds of the separate property is divided among Arnold's issue (his children and grandchildren).

   The total value of the separate property is $60,000. Brenda gets $20,000. The remaining $40,000 is divided among the issue. David, Arnold's only living child, takes $20,000 (one-half of the $40,000). Celia would have been entitled to the other $20,000 if she were still alive. But since she is dead, her children divide her share instead. Thus, Eliza and Francine each receive $10,000. David's child, Greg, does not share in his grandfather's estate because his father is still living.

   Suppose that instead of $60,000 cash, Arnold's separate property was real estate worth approximately $60,000. The shares would still be the same, but instead of money, the heirs would each take an interest in the property as tenants in common. Brenda would have a one-third interest, David would have a one-third interest, and Eliza and Francine would each have a one-sixth interest in the property.

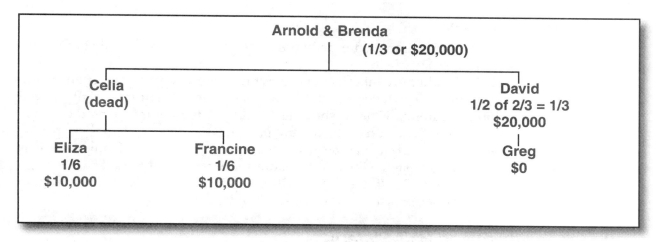

Rather than holding a small portion of the real property as tenants in common, the heirs may want to sell the property and receive its cash value instead. In order to sell the property, all of the heirs must sign the deed to give the new owner a clear title.

3. If the intestate person has no living issue (children, grandchildren, etc.), the share of separate property not taken by the surviving spouse is distributed in this order:

   a. to the intestate person's parents;

   b. then to the intestate person's brothers and sisters and the issue of any deceased brothers and sisters;

   c. then to the intestate person's grandparents, or to their issue if they're no longer living;

   d. then to issue of a predeceased spouse (someone who was married to the intestate person but died before he or she did);

   e. then to the next of kin, however remote (second cousins once removed and so forth);

   f. then to the parents of a predeceased spouse.

www.probateca.com
www.ca-trusts.com
Probate in California

Keep in mind that the members of category b only get a share if there are no living persons in category a, and the members of category c only get a share if there are no living persons in either category a or b, and so on down the list.

Example: Anna, a childless widow, died intestate. She was survived by her parents (category a), her nephew (category b), her paternal grandmother (category c), her dead husband's son (category d), and six second cousins (category e).

Anna's entire estate will be divided between her parents. None of her other relatives will receive a share. However, if her parents were dead, the entire estate would go to her nephew. If her parents and her nephew were dead, the entire estate would go to her grandmother, and so on. The six second cousins would only receive shares if everyone else had already died before Anna died.

CHAPTER 10

1. Adopted Children

Legally adopted children are treated exactly the same as a person's natural children for the purposes of intestate succession.

An adopted child ordinarily inherits only from his or her adoptive parents, not from his or her natural parents. However, the child may inherit from a natural parent (as well as from the adoptive parents) if he or she ever lived with the natural parent, or if the adoption took place after the death of the natural parent.

In some cases where a child has been treated as a member of a family and it is established that the foster parent intended to adopt the person but could not because of a legal barrier, the *DOCTRINE OF EQUITABLE ADOPTION is applied. Then the child inherits from an intestate parent just as if he or she had been legally adopted.*

2. Half-Brothers and Half-Sisters

As far as the rules of intestate succession are concerned, half-brothers and half-sisters are the same as other brothers and sisters.

3. Illegitimacy and Divorce

Generally, inheritance by (or from) a child doesn't depend on whether the parents are still married, or whether they were ever married. An illegitimate child is entitled to share in an intestate parent's estate just like a legitimate child.

> **Example:** Adrian was married to Becky, and they had two children (Edgar and Fred). He and Becky then divorced. Edgar and Fred live with their mother and Adrian has not seen them for 13 years.
>
> Adrian later married Corinne. Adrian and Corinne had one child (George). During his second marriage, Adrian had an affair with Dorothy and they had an illegitimate daughter (Helen).
>
> Adrian dies intestate. His current wife (Corinne) receives all of the community property and one-third of the separate property. The remaining two-thirds of the separate property is divided equally between all of Adrian's children. Edgar, Fred, George, and Helen each receive one-sixth of their father's estate.

4. Stepchildren

Stepchildren are the only group of children that are affected by divorce. Suppose that when Adrian married Corinne, she already had a son, Ira, from an earlier marriage. As long as Corinne and Adrian are married, Ira is Adrian's stepson. If Corinne and Adrian were married when Adrian died intestate, Ira might be entitled to a share of Adrian's separate property. Corinne and Ira would have to prove to the probate court that Adrian would have adopted Ira, except that there was a legal barrier to the adoption.

If Corinne and Adrian were divorced, however, Ira wouldn't be Adrian's stepson anymore. Then if Adrian died intestate, Edgar, Fred, George, and Helen would still share in Adrian's estate, but Ira would not.

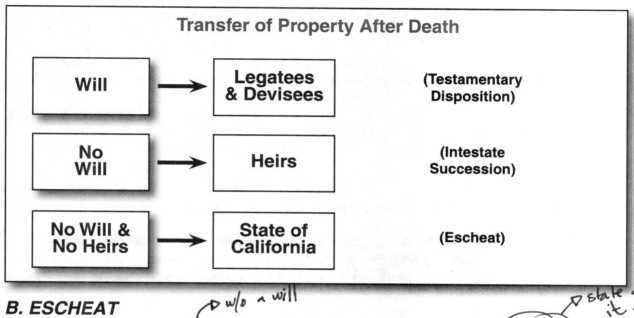

Transfer of Property After Death

Will	→	Legatees & Devisees	(Testamentary Disposition)
No Will	→	Heirs	(Intestate Succession)
No Will & No Heirs	→	State of California	(Escheat)

B. ESCHEAT

→ w/o a will

→ state gets it.

When a person dies intestate and no heirs can be located, the property *ESCHEATS, meaning ownership reverts to the state.* Since the state is the ultimate source of title to property, it is also the ultimate heir when there are no other claimants.

If no heirs have come forward two years after an intestate person's death, the attorney general may bring a court action to establish the state's title to the estate property. The court will enter a judgment ordering the property to be turned over to the state treasurer. It will then be sold at public auction.

Sometimes there are very remote heirs who can't easily be located, and who aren't aware that they are entitled to inherit. In California, any heir to escheated funds or real property has five years after the attorney general obtains a judgment in which to file a claim.

The heirs must establish their claim to the satisfaction of the court. The court then orders payment to the heirs of any escheated funds and delivery of any escheated property. When escheated property has already been sold, the heirs receive the proceeds of the sale.

If no valid claims are filed within the five-year period, the property permanently escheats. After that, the state's title to it can no longer be challenged by long-lost heirs.

Under certain circumstances, property that was left to someone in a valid will can escheat. If the beneficiary can't be located, the property goes to the state, rather than to the testator or testatrix's heirs.

C. COURT DECISIONS

Property can also be involuntarily alienated by court order. Aside from marital dissolutions (see Chapter 4), the most common forms of court action affecting title to property are foreclosure, partition, and quiet title actions.

1. Foreclosure

Foreclosure is a legal proceeding to enforce a lien by the sale of property in order to satisfy a debt.

Creditors holding liens against a piece of real property may bring a **foreclosure action** if the debt secured by the property is not paid. The court will order the property sold at a public auction (sheriff's sale, tax sale, or execution sale). After a waiting period, the buyer at a foreclosure sale receives a deed to the property—usually a **sheriff's deed**, **trustee's deed**, or a **tax deed**, depending on the type of sale. These deeds do not carry any warranties of title.

Foreclosure is available for any type of lien that attaches to real property, including deeds of trust, mortgages, mechanics' liens, tax liens, and judgment liens. Foreclosure of trust deeds and mortgages is discussed in more detail in Chapter 12.

2. Partition

A partition divides up the existing interests of the owners.

In a suit for *PARTITION, the court divides property owned by more than one person when the co-owners can't agree among themselves how to divide it*. In some cases, the court actually orders a physical division of the land, but more often the property is sold and the proceeds are divided among the co-owners.

Any co-owner can bring a partition action against the others, so the lawsuit may result in involuntary alienation. For example, if there's a good offer for the property but one co-owner doesn't want to sell, the others can sue for partition. The court-ordered sale accomplishes what persuasion could not, and the reluctant co-owner is forced to accept the money instead of keeping the property. Partition suits are discussed in more detail in Chapter 4.

3. Quiet Title

When there's a cloud on an owner's title, it makes the property unmarketable. As you've seen, in many cases the cloud can be cleared away with a quitclaim deed, but sometimes the owner can't get a quitclaim deed from the person who created the cloud. The person may be unknown, unavailable, uncooperative, or may believe that he or she has a legitimate claim against the title. Then the title holder may file a **quiet title action** to get a judicial ruling on ownership of the property.

Example: X has found a potential buyer for his property. But the title insurance company's search of the public record shows a gap in the chain of title: the recorded documents don't indicate who owned the property for a four-year period about 15 years before X bought the property.

X brings a quiet title action. The defendants in the action are all the parties who have a potential interest in the land. This includes the mystery person who held title during the gap, even though this person's name is unknown.

X asks the court to declare his title valid, thereby quieting title to the property. If no defendants appear to challenge X's title, the court will grant X's request. Then the buyer can go ahead with the purchase in reliance on the court's declaration.

It isn't just the record title holder who can file a quiet title action, however. The plaintiff can be anyone claiming title or an interest in the property. *For example, to make title acquired by adverse possession marketable, the adverse possessor has to bring a quiet title action against the record owner. This is called* **PERFECTING THE TITLE**. Adverse possession is discussed in the next section.

D. ADVERSE POSSESSION

ADVERSE POSSESSION *is the process by which possession and use of property can mature into title to the property*. The main purpose of the adverse possession laws is to encourage the fullest and most productive use of property. The idea is that it's better to give title to someone who makes good use of the property, rather than leaving title with someone who ignores the property for a long period of time.

Owners of vacant property or land held for future sale, use, or development should make periodic inspections of their property to check for any signs of adverse possession. Merely posting "no trespassing" signs isn't enough to prevent a claim of adverse possession.

1. Public Lands

Any property can be adversely possessed except public lands. Land owned by the United States, the state of California, a county, or a city is generally secure. For example, I can't acquire title to a corner of Yosemite through adverse possession, no matter how long I camp there.

California law also provides that property held by a public utility cannot be taken through adverse possession.

2. Requirements

In California, title can be acquired by adverse possession if the possession is:

1. actual, open, and notorious;
2. hostile to the owner's interest; Tresspassing
3. under claim of right or color of title; Telling others you own it
4. exclusive, continuous, and uninterrupted for five years, and
5. the property taxes are paid during the five year period of possession.

a. Actual, Open, and Notorious Possession

This means that the adverse possessor must use the property openly, in a way that will put the owner on notice that his or her title is threatened. In other words, you can't sneak around on someone's property for five years and then claim adverse possession. Your use must be open enough to make the owner aware of your presence if he or she is paying reasonable attention to the property.

> **Case Example:** The Benders owned two adjoining lots. In 1993, the Benders deeded one lot to their daughter Gayl as a gift. Gayl built a cabin on the lot and then moved to Ireland. In 1998, the Benders deeded the remaining lot, which included a house, to the Nielsons by grant deed. The Benders also gave a quit claim deed for the lot owned by Gayl to the Nielsons. The Nielsons moved into the house and immediately began to occupy, improve, and maintain both lots. ▼

They physically blocked the separate access to Gayl's lot and put a fence around both lots. They paid the annual property taxes for both properties each year beginning in 1997. Gayl died in 2003. The Nielsons brought a quiet title in 2006 claiming title to Gayl's lot by adverse possession. Gayl's executor claimed that the Nielsons did not satisfy the "open and notorious" element of adverse possession so as to give Gayl reasonable notice of the Nielson's possession of the property because she was in Ireland and did not have the means for acquiring knowledge of the possession.

But the court ruled that when the record owner fails to look after her interests and remains in ignorance of the possession and potential claim, was her own fault. The fact that the record owner resided out of state and apparently failed to visit the property was irrelevant. *Nielsen v. Gibson*, 178 Cal.App.4th 318 (2009).

b. Hostility, Claim of Right, and Color of Title

Possession of the property must also be hostile. This doesn't mean the adverse possessor has to hate the owner, or even be embroiled in a dispute over the title. It simply means that the nature of the possession must conflict with the owner's interest. If the owner has given someone else permission to use the property, that use is not hostile and can never develop into adverse possession.

The requirement that the possession be under a claim of right is virtually identical to the hostility requirement. The adverse possessor must be claiming the right to the property. In many cases, the adverse possessor's claim is simply a mistake, rather than a deliberate plan to take over someone else's property. *When the adverse possessor's claim to the property is based on a defective deed or some other invalid written document, he or she is said to have* **COLOR OF TITLE**.

California Code of Civil Procedure Section 323 states when a person has possession under color of title:

For the purpose of constituting an adverse possession by any person claiming a title founded upon a written instrument, or a judgment or decree, land is deemed to have been possessed and occupied in the following cases:

1. Where it has been usually cultivated or improved;
2. Where it has been protected by a substantial enclosure;
3. Where, although not enclosed, it has been used for the supply of fuel, or of fencing-timber for the purposes of husbandry, or for pasturage, or for the ordinary use of the occupant;
4. Where a known farm or single lot has been partly improved, the portion of such farm or lot that may have been left not cleared, or not included according to the usual course and custom of the adjoining country, shall be deemed to have been occupied for the same length of time as the part improved and cultivated.

However, when a person is claiming title, but not under a written document, California Code of Civil Procedure Section 325 applies:

For the purpose of constituting an adverse possession by a person claiming title, not founded upon a written instrument, judgment, or decree, land is deemed to have been possessed and occupied in the following cases only:

1. Where it has been protected by a substantial enclosure.
2. Where it has been usually cultivated or improved.

Case Example: Mr. Lowe owned a house as his separate property. He married Wyonna in August 1973 and she moved into the house and was repeatedly reminded that it belonged only to him. In 1978, unknown to Mrs. Lowe, Mr. Lowe deeded the house to himself and three sons from his first marriage as joint tenants. When Mr. Lowe died in August 1981, the sons demanded and continued to demand that Wyonna move from the property. Wyonna refused, stayed on the property believing she owned it under community property laws and made all mortgage and tax payments.

In December 1981, Wyonna sued to set aside Mr. Lowe's gift of community property to the sons and they sued to quiet title and for ejectment. In May 1988, the lawsuit was dismissed for failure to prosecute. In December 1988, the actions were refiled. Wyonna claimed title by adverse possession.

The court of appeal held that Wyonna did not have a community property interest in the house, however all of the elements of adverse possession had been established: 1) She made the tax payments; 2) had actual possession; 3) possession was open and notorious; 4) continuous and uninterrupted for five years; 5) hostile and adverse to the three owners' title; and 6) either under claim of right or color of title. The five-year time period was not tolled (interrupted) by Wyonna's lawsuit to set aside Mr. Lowe's deed to the sons when it was dismissed for failure to prosecute. *First Boston Credit Corp. v. Lowe*, 37 Cal. App. 4th 1798, 44 Cal. Rptr. 2d 784 (1995).

c. Exclusive, Continuous, and Uninterrupted

An adverse possessor must be the exclusive user of the property; he or she can't share possession with the owner. You can't adversely possess a summer cabin by using it every other weekend if the owner is there on the weekends in between.

The adverse possession must be continuous and uninterrupted for five years. Of course, that doesn't mean the adverse possessor can't ever leave the property during that period. The possession is considered continuous if the property is used as constantly as an owner would ordinarily use that type of property, but the use must be uninterrupted; there can't be a significant break in the period of exclusive possession.

Example: P is adversely possessing a cabin beside a mountain lake. She spends every summer there for five years in a row, but never goes there in the winter. This would probably be considered continuous possession, since the cabin is really only intended for summer use.

On the other hand, suppose P spent three summers at the cabin, didn't come up at all during the fourth summer, but returned the next summer and the summer after that. Over a period of six years she has used the property for a total of five summers. But her adverse possession claim would fail because her use was interrupted during the fourth summer; she wasn't in possession for five summers in a row. She would have to start counting her five years over again beginning the summer she came back.

P's possession would also be considered interrupted if the cabin's record owner turned up one summer. P would have to start counting her five years over again after the owner left.

371

CHAPTER 10

However, it doesn't necessarily have to be the same person adversely possessing the property during all five years. *In some cases, a court will tack together the periods of possession from a series of adverse possessors, so that they add up to five years. This is called TACKING.*

Case Example: In 1901, when Mr. Costa purchased unimproved property in a Benicia subdivision, he was given a deed describing the west half of Lot 7. When he took possession, he accidentally moved onto the east half of Lot 8 instead of the west half of Lot 7.

No one realized Costa's mistake, and it set up a chain reaction. Mr. Nelson held the deed to the east half of Lot 7, but he moved onto the west half of Lot 7. The person who received a deed for the west half of Lot 6 took possession of the east half of Lot 7, and so on down the street.

The property owned by Nelson changed hands several times over the years. Each time the new owners were given a deed describing the east half of Lot 7, and each time they moved onto the west half of Lot 7.

Meanwhile, Costa (whose deed described the west half of Lot 7) continued to live next door on the east half of Lot 8. In 1940 he bought property described as the east half of Lot 8 at a tax sale. He had a survey done, and discovered that the tax sale deed described the property he'd been living on for almost 40 years. This meant his neighbors had actually been living on his property all that time.

A dispute arose between Costa and Sorensen, the neighbor living on the west half of Lot 7, over the ownership of that parcel. Sorensen sued to quiet his title to the west half of Lot 7, claiming adverse possession. Sorensen had only purchased his lot and moved in a few months before.

In considering his adverse possession claim, the court treated all the owners who had held the deed to the east half of Lot 7 and lived on the west half of Lot 7 as a series of adverse possessors. Tacked together, their periods of possession added up to more than 40 years. The court confirmed Sorensen's ownership of the west half of Lot 7. (His neighbor to the east had, in turn, adversely possessed the property described in Sorensen's deed.) *Sorensen v. Costa,* 32 Cal. 2d 453, 196 P.2d 900 (1948).

LOT 8		LOT 7	
W 1/2	E 1/2	W 1/2	E 1/2
	Costa's House	Costa's Deed	Sorensen's Deed
		Sorensen's House	Unimproved Property

d. Payment of Taxes

The adverse possessor not only has to occupy the property for five years in a row, he or she has to pay the property taxes during those years. Recent legislation requires that the person claiming title to adverse possession must pay the taxes "timely." This probably means that the taxes must be paid before the delinquency date and would prevent someone from paying back taxes to support a claim of adverse possession. In the Sorensen case, the court found that Sorensen and his predecessors in interest had paid taxes on the west half of Lot 7 rather than the east half because the tax assessment rolls made the same mistake that everyone living on the street had made. This was easily shown because the east half of Lot 7 was unimproved and the west half of Lot 7 had a house on it. The tax rolls had always treated the unimproved property (the east half of Lot 7) as the west half of Lot 6, and the improved property (the west half of Lot 7) as the east half of Lot 7.

Often the adverse possessor can't prove that he or she has paid the taxes, and many claims fail because of this requirement.

Case Example: Because a survey stake was incorrectly placed, everyone thought the Hallams' property extended 15 feet further than it actually did. The Hallams planted poplar trees and grass on that 15-foot strip and put in a sprinkler system and a sidewalk. More than five years later, the neighbors (the Gilardis) had their property surveyed and discovered that the trees, lawn, and sidewalk were on their lot, not the Hallams'. They sued to quiet title.

The Hallams were able to establish all the necessary elements of an adverse possession claim, except that they couldn't prove that they had paid property taxes for the 15-foot strip of land. The tax assessments were done by lot number; the Hallams had paid for their lot number and the Gilardis had paid for theirs. There was nothing to indicate that the assessor had treated the 15-foot strip with its improvements as part of the Hallams' lot. The court quieted the Gilardis' title to the strip. *Gilardi v. Hallam*, 30 Cal. 3d 317, 636 P.2d 588 (1981).

The court noted that the Hallams might be able to claim a prescriptive easement over the 15-foot strip, even though they hadn't acquired title to it. The requirements for a *PRESCRIPTIVE EASEMENT are the same as those for adverse possession, except that the easement claimant's use doesn't have to be exclusive (the owner may be using the property at the same time), and it's not necessary to pay the taxes.*

E. CONDEMNATION

Condemnation of private property by the government is another form of involuntary alienation. *Under the U.S. Constitution, the government has the power to take private property for public use with just compensation. This power is called **EMINENT DOMAIN**.* The California state constitution also provides for eminent domain. Both constitutions require the government to pay just compensation to the owner.

www.eminentdomainlaw.net/propertyguide.html
Property Owners' Guide to Eminent Domain

Eminent domain can be exercised by the state, cities, counties, school districts, and other government entities, and limited use of the power has been delegated to some private entities by statute. For example, privately owned utility companies are authorized to condemn property for public utility uses. Nonprofit cemetery authorities can also use condemnation to expand existing cemeteries. Whether the entity is public or private, its intended use of the property must benefit the public.

In California, the government (or other authorized entity) must first offer to purchase the property it needs. If the owner rejects the offer, then the government files a condemnation lawsuit. The court will consider evidence concerning the fair market value of the property taken, and direct the government to compensate the owner. Then the court will order the property condemned.

When only part of a parcel of property is taken, the owner must also be compensated for any injury to the remainder of the parcel. *If the value of the remainder drops because of the condemnation, the government has to repay the owner for that loss of value. This payment is called* **SEVERANCE DAMAGES**.

Case Example: Mr. Daley owned a large tract of land known as the Rancho Jamul, which he was planning to subdivide. The San Diego Gas & Electric Company filed suit to condemn a 200-foot wide power line easement across part of the ranch.

The fair market value of the 200-foot strip was determined to be $190,000, but in addition to that amount, the jury awarded Daley $1,035,000 to compensate him for damage to the remainder of the property. The power line project was going to make the rest of the ranch much less desirable as a housing subdivision.

The jury considered not only the ugly steel transmission towers and the noise of the power lines, but also public fear of the electromagnetic fields generated by the lines. The utility argued that there was no conclusive scientific evidence that electromagnetic fields were hazardous to human beings. However, prospective buyers might be afraid (however unreasonably), and the jury was allowed to take that into account in deciding on the amount of compensation. *San Diego Gas & Electric Co. v. Daley*, 253 Cal. Rptr. 144 (Cal. App. 4 Dist. 1988).

---

1. Inverse Condemnation

Inverse condemnation is a court remedy for a private landowner whose interest or ownership in land has been interfered with or taken away outright by a governmental body.

> *INVERSE CONDEMNATION involves a situation where a private landowner's property is damaged by government conduct but the government takes no condemnation action.* This requires the landowner to sue the government for damages for inverse condemnation.

Case Example: In 1987, the City of San Luis Obispo had a severe drought problem. The city decided to draw down its surface water supply instead of using strict water conservation measures. In 1989, looking for more water, the city decided to drill new wells rather than take available agricultural water. The city's water policy caused subsidence and structural damage to LOVA'S shopping mall when the wells pulled water from the ground under the mall. LOVA sued for damages for inverse condemnation.

The court of appeal held that removal of the underground support for the mall caused by the city's water policy constituted a physical taking of property and damages were appropriate. *Los Osos Valley Associates v. City of San Luis Obispo*, 30 Cal. App 4th, 1670, 36 Cal. Rptr. 2d 758 (1994).

Inverse condemnation is difficult to establish. The property owner must prove that there was a physical seizure or occupation (as in the *Los Osos* case), that a government land use regulation is so strict that the property owner has no economically viable use of the property, or that there is no rational connection (called a nexus) between the public purpose for the land use regulation and the use condition being imposed. See the discussion of the police power in Chapter 13.

F. DEDICATION

DEDICATION *is a gift of privately owned land to the public.* Dedication can either create an easement or actually transfer title from the private owner to the local government. In some cases, dedication is voluntary, as when a wealthy philanthropist dedicates a portion of his estate to the city for use as a public park.

Usually, however, dedication is more or less involuntary. Cities often require developers to dedicate portions of their property to public use in exchange for permission to subdivide. For example, a developer almost always has to dedicate land within a subdivision for use as public streets and sidewalks. Dedication of recreational areas or open space in the subdivision may also be required.

Another kind of dedication can be completely involuntary: *IMPLIED DEDICATION. If the public makes use of private property for at least five years and the owner neither openly objects nor grants permission, the local government can declare that the owner has dedicated the property to the public by implication.*

Implied dedication may result in an public easement, or in a transfer of the property to public ownership. Either way, the government isn't required to pay the owner compensation. When an easement is created by implied dedication, it's very similar to a prescriptive easement, but the right created belongs to the public, not to particular individuals.

Unfortunately, the possibility of implied dedication discourages private owners from allowing public use of their property, so the legislature passed a statute that protects owners from implied dedication. Since 1971, a government body can claim implied dedication only if:

1. the property is coastal property (within 1,000 yards of the ocean), or
2. the government has been improving or maintaining the property to such an extent that the owner should be aware of the public use.

Even in these situations, the owner can prevent implied dedication by recording a notice, posting signs, or publishing a notice in the newspaper. The notice or signs must state that the right to use the property is by permission of the owner. As long as the owner has granted permission, implied dedication can't occur. If the owner doesn't want to permit public use, he or she must take steps to keep the public off the property, or else risk losing control of it through implied dedication.

G. ACCESSION

When something is added to a parcel of real property, the property owner acquires title to the addition by accession. Accession can occur in two ways: by annexation, or by the action of natural forces.

CHAPTER 10

1. Annexation by People

When someone builds a house or installs a swimming pool or plants a tree, personal property is annexed to real property. *As a general rule, ANNEXATION transforms personal property into a natural attachment or a fixture, part of the real property* (see Chapter 2). As such, the owner of the real property also owns the annexed property.

> **Example:** The neighbor kids think the big oak tree on the west edge of X's property would be perfect for a tree house. X isn't a very friendly man, so the kids build the tree house without asking his permission.
> Although X isn't even aware of the tree house, he owns it—it's part of his real property. If he finds out about it, he can require the neighbors to remove it, or chase the kids away and use it himself.

However, a different rule applies when property is annexed by a good faith improver. *A GOOD FAITH IMPROVER is someone who annexes personal property to real property in the mistaken belief that he or she owns the real property.*

> **Example:** Q thinks the row of sumac trees marks her property boundary, but her lot actually ends seven yards east of the trees. Q builds a gazebo beside the trees, on her neighbor's land. Her mistake isn't discovered for several months—not until the neighbor sells his property and the new owner has a survey done.

A good faith improver has the right to remove the annexed property: Q could have the gazebo moved over onto her own land. But if she chooses to do that, she will have to pay the neighboring landowner for any damages resulting from the annexation or the removal. A good faith improver also may have to pay damages to subsequent lienholders who believed their liens against the real property also covered the annexed property. This might be a lender who believed the improvement was on the property and, in good faith, made a secured loan relying on the improvement being part of the property. Or, it might be a mechanic's lien of someone who helped construct the improvement.

In special circumstances, a court may order a different remedy. For example, if the landowner would like to keep the improvement, and removal would destroy it, the court could order the landowner to pay the good faith improver the value of the improvement. Or, if it isn't possible to remove the improvement and the landowner doesn't want it, the court could order the improver to pay the landowner the value of the land. Then, title to the land and the improvement would be quieted in favor of the improver.

2. Forces of Nature

The land itself can move or change shape, which sometimes results in an involuntary transfer of title. *Land beside the ocean or a lake or river is increased by ACCRETION when waterborne silt is deposited on the shore. These deposits of sand or soil are called ALLUVION or ALLUVIUM.* A key feature of accretion is that the buildup of soil is very gradual, almost imperceptible. When land is added to by accretion, the landowner acquires title to the newly deposited soil.

Accretion is a buildup of land by natural forces, such as water.

When a body of water recedes, the adjoining landowner acquires title to the newly exposed land. This is called **RELICTION** *or* **DERELICTION**. Like accretion, reliction must be very gradual. The waterline must retreat little by little.

AVULSION is not a gradual process: land is violently torn away by flowing water or waves. Avulsion does not transfer title immediately; the land torn away still legally belongs to the original owner. If it's possible to identify the severed land, the original owner can reclaim it within one year. After one year, however, the severed land becomes part of the property where it ended up.

Avulsion can also refer to a sudden change in a watercourse. Suppose a river has always marked the boundary line between two properties. Then flood waters tear away the land, and when the flood subsides, the river flows in a different channel. The boundary between the two properties does not move, even though the river has moved.

Case Example: Mr. Butts owned land to the west of the Russian River in Sonoma County. When the property was first surveyed in 1856, it bordered on the river, but by the 1950s the river had moved 1,500 feet to the east.

Butts claimed that the river had moved very gradually. He sued to quiet title to the 1,500 feet of land between the river and the property line described in his deed. However, testimony in the case revealed that the river's position had changed suddenly, not gradually, as a result of flooding. This was avulsion, not accretion or reliction. Consequently, Butts had not acquired title to the 1,500-foot strip. It still belonged to the person who owned the parcel east of the river, even though the strip was now west of the river. *Butts v. Cummings*, 117 Cal. App. 2d 432, 256 P.2d 52 (1953).

When you consider all the different ways that title to real property can change hands, it's surprising that anyone can keep track of who owns what. That's what makes the recording system and title insurance invaluable for buyers and lenders. They don't take care of all the problems, but they're a big help.

III. Recording

Just because someone offers to sell real property doesn't necessarily mean he or she actually owns it. The seller may be lying, or (much more commonly) there may be some problem with the title that the seller isn't aware of. To limit these risks, every state has recording laws. By making it possible to determine who holds an interest in a piece of property, the recording system protects real estate buyers and lenders against secret conveyances and encumbrances.

www.cdph.ca.gov/CERTLIC/BIRTHDEATHMAR/Pages/CountyRecorderOffice.aspx
California County Recorders' Directory

After accepting a listing, a real estate agent isn't required to verify a seller's title. This takes place later, when a prospective buyer has been found and a preliminary report from a title company is requested. It's always helpful, however, to know as much as possible about the property you're trying to sell. Through the recording system, an agent can find out some useful information about the property, such as:

1. who is listed as the present owner,
2. the legal description, and
3. whether there are liens, easements, or restrictions.

RECORDING is the act of entering a record of documents affecting or conveying interest in real estate in a county recorder's office. Until such a document is recorded, a deed or mortgage generally is not effective against subsequent purchasers or mortgages or other third parties unless they actually know about the document.

Any legal document that transfers or encumbers title to real property can be recorded, and most should be: deeds, easements, restrictive covenants, court orders, long-term leases, trust deeds and reconveyances, land contracts, agreements relating to community or separate property, and so on. Most documents must be acknowledged before they can be recorded.

Certain documents have no legal effect unless they're recorded. These include mechanics' liens, declarations of homestead, attachment liens, execution liens, judgment liens, lis pendens, and powers of attorney for the conveyance of real estate. For other documents, recording is optional—the parties to the document are bound by it even if it's unrecorded. The purpose of recording documents is to provide notice to others. (The importance of notice is discussed below.)

A. THE RECORDER'S OFFICE

To have a document recorded, you file it at the county recorder's office in the county where the property is located and pay the recording fee. (If it's a deed, you'll also have to pay the documentary transfer tax.) The document is said to be **filed for record**. The recorder then places the document in the public record. Long ago, this meant that a clerk actually transcribed the document into a record book. Nowadays, the document is photographed onto microfilm or computerized.

The documents are processed in the order that they were filed for record—not just according to date, but also according to time of day. This is extremely important, since deed priority or lien priority often depends on when the competing documents were filed. Each document is stamped with a **recording number** so that it can be located in the public record.

After recording, the original document is returned to the person who submitted it. But once a document has been recorded, it generally doesn't matter if the original is lost or destroyed. The public record provides evidence of the document's existence and contents. If a recorded document has a defect in the execution of the instrument or the certificate of acknowledgment or it lacks a certificate, the document does not give constructive notice until one year after it is recorded.

1. Indexes

The recorder must keep an index of all the recorded documents. The index is usually divided into two parts: the grantor/grantee index (or direct index) and the grantee/grantor index (or inverted index). In the **GRANTOR/GRANTEE INDEX**, *documents are listed in alphabetical order under the last name of the grantor*. In the **GRANTEE/GRANTOR INDEX**, *they're listed in alphabetical order under the last name of the grantee*.

For the purpose of these indexes, a "grantor" is not just the grantor of a deed, but anyone transferring an interest in property, such as a lessor, or the trustor on a trust deed. And "grantee" refers to anyone receiving an interest in real property: a lessee, a trust deed beneficiary, and so on.

For each document, the index states the names of the grantor and grantee, the type of document, the recording date, and (usually) a brief property description. The index also tells you the recording number of the document so that you can locate it and request a copy.

These indexes are often divided according to time of recording. For instance, one set of indexes might include all instruments recorded from January 3, 2004, through June 30, 2004. As such, it's helpful to have some idea of when the property was transferred when searching the record for a deed.

2. Plat Maps

The recorder also keeps **PLAT BOOKS**, *containing all the subdivision plat maps for the county*. There's an alphabetical index listing each plat by name. (See Chapter 2 for more information about plats.)

B. NOTICE

When two people have conflicting claims, their rights and liabilities sometimes depend on whether one had notice of the other's claim. You have **ACTUAL NOTICE** *of something if you actually know about it because you saw it, read it, or were told about it*. You have constructive notice of something you ought to know about, even though you don't actually know about it. **CONSTRUCTIVE NOTICE** *is the notice of something that the law will treat you as knowing, whether or not you actually know about that thing*. All persons are charged with knowledge of recorded documents and their contents, whether or not they have actually examined them. Constructive notice can come from recordation of documents or being placed on a duty to inquire.

The law holds that everyone has constructive notice of recorded documents. Even if you didn't know about a particular recorded document, you could have found out about it by searching the public record. The law expects a buyer or lender to take that step for his or her own protection. The law won't look after a buyer or lender who doesn't bother.

Example: Summerville grants an easement across his property to Jones and Jones records the easement document. Summerville then sells his property to Kruger. Kruger claims that she doesn't have to honor the easement because she couldn't tell that it existed simply by looking at the property, and Summerville never told her about it.

The easement is still valid because Kruger is deemed to have constructive notice of it. Even though she didn't have actual notice, she could have found out about it by checking the public record.

However, recorded documents only give a buyer or lender constructive notice if they are within the chain of title for the property. The *CHAIN OF TITLE is the series of recorded deeds transferring title from one owner to the next.* The chain can be traced backwards using the grantee/grantor index: the current owner took title from so-and-so, and so-and-so took title from such-and-such, and so forth.

A recorded document is considered to be within the chain of title if the person who executed the document was the **record owner** of the property at the time the document was recorded. In other words, a search of the public record would show that person was the owner during the period when the document was recorded. *If the person who executed the document wasn't the record owner, the document is* **WILD** *(a "wild deed," "wild trust deed," or something similarly worded).* A wild document does not give a buyer or lender constructive notice.

Example: Richardson buys a house and records her deed. Later she sells the property to Singer, but Singer doesn't record his deed. Although Singer is now the actual owner, Richardson is still the record owner of the property. Someone searching through the grantor/grantee indexes would find that Richardson was the grantee on the most recently recorded deed and wouldn't find any sign of Singer's interest.

Singer sells the property to Tanabe, and Tanabe records his deed promptly. Now there's a break in the chain: the record shows only Richardson's deed and Tanabe's deed, and the link between them, Singer's deed, is missing. That makes Tanabe's deed a wild deed.

Richardson is aware that Singer never recorded his deed, and she decides to sell the same property a second time. This time she sells it to Sharif.

Sharif doesn't know about Singer or Tanabe, so he has no reason to look up those names in the grantee/grantor index. He looks up Richardson's name, and as far as he can tell from the record, she is still the owner of the property. Therefore, Sharif goes ahead with the purchase.

Sharif doesn't have constructive notice of Singer's deed because it wasn't recorded. And Sharif doesn't have constructive notice of Tanabe's deed—even though it was recorded—because it was outside the chain of title.

A person is held to also have constructive notice when there's some indication of a claim or a problem that would lead a reasonable person to inquire further into the condition of the title. This type of constructive notice is called **INQUIRY NOTICE**. If you don't find out about the claim because you fail to investigate any further, you may still be held to have had notice of the claim.

Example: Jarrell is thinking of buying Valencia's house. He visits the property a few times before closing. There's a well-worn path across the front yard that leads to the neighbor's property.

After buying the house, Jarrell learns that the neighbors claim Valencia granted them an easement across the front yard, although it was never recorded. Jarrell sues to prevent the neighbors from using the path. He says he took the property without notice of the easement. But the court holds that Jarrell was on inquiry notice. The path was so apparent that a reasonable person would have inquired about it.

1. The Race/Notice Rule

What happens when an owner sells property to one person, and then sells the same property to another person? California follows the *RACE/NOTICE RULE. The first part of this rule, race, means, figuratively speaking, the two grantees "race" each other to the recorder's office, and whoever records a deed first wins the race and has title to the property. However, the second part of the rule, notice, means that the race winner must not have actual or constructive notice of an earlier claim in order to take title free of that earlier claim.*

Example: Newkirk sells his property to Chang and gives him a deed on June 10. Chang fails to record his deed and does not move onto the property. Newkirk sells the same property to Murphy on August 15. Murphy has no knowledge of the sale to Chang. Murphy records her deed on August 15.

Murphy has valid title to the property even though Chang purchased it first. Murphy won the race by recording first, and she had no notice of the earlier sale. She didn't have actual notice, and couldn't be deemed to have constructive notice because Chang's deed wasn't recorded and Chang was not occupying the property when she received her deed.

Murphy is a *BONA FIDE PURCHASER for value and without notice—someone who in good faith pays for an interest in land that has already been conveyed to another, without any notice (actual or constructive) of the earlier conveyance.* Chang can sue Newkirk for damages, but he has no claim against Murphy or the property.

Under race/notice statutes, a subsequent bona fide purchaser is only protected if he/she records before the other person claiming an interest in the property and without notice of that interest.

In the same way, a trust deed lender can be a *GOOD FAITH ENCUMBRANCER without notice. Once the lender's trust deed is recorded, that lien isn't affected by earlier conveyances or encumbrances, as long as the lender did not have notice of them.* The good faith encumbrancer's lien attaches to the property and has priority over the earlier liens.

A subsequent purchaser who has notice of a previous conveyance never has valid title, even if he or she records first. A subsequent encumbrancer who has notice of a previous trust deed loan doesn't have first lien position, even if he or she records first.

Example: Newkirk sells his property to Chang and gives him a deed, but Chang fails to record the deed. A few weeks later, Newkirk negotiates a sale of the same property to Murphy.

Before Newkirk and Murphy actually close their transaction, Murphy drives by the property to take another look. She sees a man next door out mowing his lawn, so she goes over says, "Hi, I'm going to be your new neighbor." The man looks surprised and asks Murphy what happened to Mr. Chang. Murphy asks him who Mr. Chang is, and the man explains that he thought someone named Chang had bought the property from Newkirk a little while ago. In fact, she sees a sign on the house that says "Chang residence."

Murphy decides to put this conversation out of her mind and go ahead with the purchase. Newkirk gives her a deed and she records it immediately.

The conversation with the neighbor gave Murphy constructive notice of the earlier sale to Chang. She should have investigated further, and her failure to do so was not in good faith. She isn't a good faith purchaser. Even though her deed was recorded before Chang's, she does not have title to the property. However, how will Chang be able to prove what Murphy knew prior to purchase? If Murphy purchased the property "sight unseen," she is still bound by what she should have seen had she inquired.

The recording statutes are primarily intended to protect purchasers and lenders. Someone who inherits property or receives it as a gift is not protected in the way that a good faith purchaser is.

Example: Phillips gives the bank a trust deed on his property, but the bank fails to record it. Phillips later deeds the property to his son as a gift. The son records his deed. The son is not protected against the unrecorded trust deed because he is not a purchaser. The bank can still enforce the trust deed.

However, if the son sells the property to Monroe and Monroe records the deed, Monroe will take title free of the unrecorded trust deed. She is a good faith purchaser without notice.

2. Recording Problems

A county recorder may be liable for losses resulting from his or her negligence (or an employee's negligence) in recording a document. For instance, the recorder may be liable for failing to record an instrument in the order in which it was filed for record, recording an unacknowledged deed, indexing a document incorrectly, or altering records. Such a failure can seriously affect the parties.

Case Example: In 1983, Stuart and Romero Hochstein were divorced with Stuart receiving the house and an obligation for payments to Romero. Stuart married Portia in October 1986 and deeded the property to himself and Portia as joint tenants. In November 1986, Stuart died owing Romero $19,425. Subsequently, Romero recorded an abstract of judgment for that amount.

However, the abstract of judgment showed Stuart as the debtor and on the reverse side named Portia as an additional debtor. Portia was never named in the lawsuit, served or had any knowledge of it. In March 1988, the Evans purchased the house from Portia. In August, the recorder indexed the abstract under Portia's name. In November, Romero sought to sell the house by reason of her lien.

The court of appeal held that the Evans purchased the house without constructive notice of the abstract of judgment because it had not been indexed properly—the abstract under Portia's name was not recorded until several months after Evans purchased the property. *Hochstein v. Romero*, 219 Cal. App. 3d 447, 268 Cal. Rptr. 202 (1990).

The recorder is not liable for mistakes made by a person who submits a document for recording. For instance, if a name on the original document is incorrect or misspelled, the county recorder is not liable. The following case shows how important it can be to make sure the names on a document are absolutely correct before recording it.

Case Example: Mr. Orr won a lawsuit and was granted a $50,000 judgment against Mr. Elliott. However, on the abstract of judgment that Orr filed for record, Elliott's name was spelled "Elliot" and "Eliot." As a result, the Orange County recorder listed the judgment in the grantor/grantee index only under those two spellings. Elliott later acquired some property in Orange County, and Orr's judgment automatically became a lien against it. Then Elliott sold the property to Mr. Byers, but the title search failed to turn up Orr's judgment because of the misspelled name. As a result, Byers was unaware of the judgment lien and didn't require Elliott to satisfy it out of the sale proceeds.

Orr sued for a declaration of his rights against the Elliott/Byers property. The court held that the judgment lien no longer attached to the property since Byers acquired title without notice of the lien. *Orr v. Byers*, 198 Cal. App. 3d 666, 244 Cal. Rptr. 13 (1988).

IV. CHAPTER SUMMARY

1. A deed must be in writing and signed by a competent grantor, include words of conveyance and an adequate property description, and name an identifiable, living grantee. Consideration generally isn't necessary for a valid deed. A deed isn't effective until the grantor delivers it to the grantee with donative intent, and the grantee accepts it.

2. The only types of deeds commonly used in California now are grant deeds and quitclaim deeds. A grant deed carries limited implied warranties and conveys after-acquired title. A quitclaim deed carries no warranties and conveys only the interest that the grantor holds when the deed is executed.

3. A will must be in writing and signed by the testator or testatrix. Ordinarily, at least two witnesses must also sign the will, but a holographic will is valid even without witnesses. A new will revokes an earlier will to the extent that they're inconsistent. A will is also revoked if the testator or testatrix destroys the document with the intent to revoke it.

4. When a person dies without a valid will, the estate passes to the heirs according to the rules of intestate succession. If there are no heirs, the intestate person's property escheats to the state.

5. Property can be involuntarily transferred by court order, as in a foreclosure action, a partition suit, or a quiet title action.

6. An adverse possessor acquires title to another's property through possession and use. The possession must be actual, open, notorious, hostile, and under a claim of right or color of title. It must be exclusive, continuous, and uninterrupted for at least five years. The adverse possessor also has to pay the property taxes for at least five years.

7. Private property is transferred to the government for public use by condemnation or dedication. The government is constitutionally required to pay the property owner just compensation for condemned property. The owner isn't compensated for implied dedication, however.

8. A real property owner acquires title by accession when something is added to the property. Personal property annexed to real property belongs to the real property owner, unless it was annexed by a good faith improver. Title is transferred when natural forces gradually add to a parcel of land (accretion and reliction). Sudden natural changes generally don't transfer title (avulsion).

9. Most documents that affect title to property should be recorded. Each document filed for record is given a recording number, processed, and listed in the grantor/grantee and grantee/grantor indexes.

10. A buyer or lender has constructive notice of all recorded documents in the chain of title. Possession or use of the property by someone other than the record owner puts a prospective buyer on inquiry notice.

11. California follows the race/notice rule. A subsequent good faith purchaser who records a deed holds title free of earlier unrecorded claims or encumbrances, unless he or she had actual or constructive notice of them.

V. CASE PROBLEM

Far West Savings & Loan v. McLaughlin, 201 Cal. App. 3d 67, 246 Cal. Rptr. 872 (1988)

Mr. Geiger bought some property in Sylmar. His deed was recorded on June 1, 1982. On July 8, Geiger deeded the property to GTB Properties, but GTB didn't record its deed at that time. On August 3, GTB executed a $51,888 trust deed in favor of Ms. McLaughlin. McLaughlin recorded her trust deed on August 10.

Almost a year later, GTB sold the property to the Stapletons. The Stapletons borrowed $105,300 from Far West Savings, and executed a trust deed in favor of Far West. On July 1, 1983, the deed from GTB to the Stapletons and the Far West trust deed were recorded. On the same date, the old deed from Geiger to GTB was recorded for the first time.

The next year, the Stapletons stopped making loan payments to Far West, and Far West foreclosed. At the foreclosure sale, Far West ended up acquiring title to the property.

Shortly afterwards, McLaughlin (who had loaned money to GTB two years before) notified Far West that she was going to foreclose. GTB had never paid her, and she claimed her trust deed was still a lien against the property.

Far West sued, asking the court for a declaratory judgment to prevent McLaughlin from foreclosing. Far West argued that McLaughlin's trust deed lien could not be enforced because Far West had acquired its trust deed lien without actual or constructive notice of McLaughlin's lien. This gave Far West's lien priority over McLaughlin's, so her lien was extinguished in Far West's foreclosure.

On the other hand, McLaughlin contended that Far West had constructive notice of her lien since her trust deed was recorded long before Far West acquired its lien against the property.

Did Far West have constructive notice? Or was Far West a subsequent good faith encumbrancer without notice? Was McLaughlin allowed to foreclose?

VI. KEY TERMS

abstract of title	dedication	holographic will
acceptance	deed	intestate succession
accession	devise	inverse condemnation
accretion	devisee	involuntary alienation
acknowledgment	donative intent	issue
adverse possession	escheat	legatee
after-acquired title	executor/executrix	probate
alluvion	good faith purchaser for	probate homestead
annexation	value	quiet title action
avulsion	good faith improver	quitclaim deed
bequeath	grant deed	race/notice rule
cloud on the title	grantee	recording
codicil	grantee/grantor index	reliction (dereliction)
color of title	granting clause	tacking
condemnation	grantor	testator/testatrix
constructive notice	grantor/grantee index	voluntary alienation
conveyance	heir	

CHAPTER 10

VII. CHAPTER QUIZ

1. J conveys her property to M. J is 23 and M is 17. M signs the deed but J does not. The deed doesn't state how much M paid for the property, and M never has the deed recorded. This deed is invalid because:

    a. M is only 17.
    b. J didn't sign it.
    c. it doesn't contain a recital of the consideration.
    d. it wasn't promptly recorded.

2. A homebuyer in California is most likely to take title with a:

    a. grant deed.
    b. special warranty deed.
    c. express warranty deed.
    d. quitclaim deed.

3. A quitclaim deed:

    a. conveys after-acquired title.
    b. carries an implied warranty of marketability.
    c. conveys whatever interest the grantor holds when the deed is executed.
    d. all of the above.

4. R's friend just died, leaving a will giving R her house. R is:

    a. an heir.
    b. a legatee.
    c. a codicil.
    d. a devisee.

5. W died intestate. She is survived by her husband and his daughter, whom W legally adopted several years earlier. What share of W's estate is the daughter entitled to?

    a. Half of the separate property
    b. Half of the entire estate
    c. One-third of the entire estate
    d. None of it, since the daughter wasn't actually related to W

6. When property escheats, the title:

    a. passes to the next of kin.
    b. passes to the heirs.
    c. reverts to the state.
    d. reverts to the remainderman.

7. What's the difference between easement by prescription and title by adverse possession?

    a. An adverse possessor acquires title to the property, not just an easement.
    b. An adverse possessor must pay the property taxes.
    c. Adverse possession must be exclusive.
    d. All of the above.

8. When the government acquires an easement or title to property through public use, it's called:

    a. eminent domain.
    b. implied dedication.
    c. condemnation.
    d. annexation.

9. A trust deed has been recorded, and it's within the chain of title, but the prospective buyer hasn't checked the record. The prospective buyer has:

    a. constructive notice of the trust deed.
    b. actual notice of the trust deed.
    c. inquiry notice of the trust deed.
    d. none of the above.

10. Which type of title insurance policy insures the policyholder against adverse possession claims?

    a. Standard coverage policy
    b. Extended coverage policy
    c. Both a and b
    d. Neither a nor b

ANSWERS: 1. b; 2. a; 3. c; 4. d; 5. a; 6. c; 7. d; 8. b; 9. a; 10. b

CONSTRUCTION SITE
SAFETY RULES

1. HARD HATS REQUIRED.
2. PROPER WORK SHOES REQUIRED.
3. NO SHORTS.
4. NO RADIOS.
5. NO GLASS BOTTLES.
6. NO ALCOHOL OR DRUGS ALLOWED.

CHAPTER 11
Escrow and Closing

CHAPTER OVERVIEW

A seller listed property with a broker. The broker found an interested buyer, and the buyer and seller signed a purchase agreement, but there's still a lot to be done before title is actually transferred to the new owner. This stage of the transaction is known as the closing process. An escrow is opened to facilitate the closing.

This chapter describes the closing process. It discusses the role of the escrow agent, the requirements for a valid escrow, and the preparation of settlement statements.

I. Preparing for Closing

CLOSING is the consummation of a real estate transaction, when the seller delivers the deed to the buyer and the buyer pays the seller the purchase price. Before closing can take place, all preliminary matters must by taken care of, including: 1) obtaining title search; 2) clearing all liens; 3) performing all inspections; 4) completing required repairs; 5) paying off loans/obtaining new loans, and 6) securing title insurance.

When the purchase agreement is signed, the seller and buyer will have established a closing date as part of their contract. The *CLOSING DATE is when the documents transferring title from the seller to the buyer will be recorded.* The real estate agents representing the seller and buyer usually provide advice on the projected closing date based upon the likely amount of time needed to complete all of the tasks required to close the transaction. The real estate agents representing the seller and buyer usually provide advice on the projected closing date based upon the likely amount of time needed to complete all of the tasks required to close the transaction.

The most significant factor in estimating a closing date is the state of the finance market. A broker needs to be aware of the current market in order to make an accurate estimate. If many people are seeking financing at the same time, lenders and appraisers may be too busy to act immediately. Then the closing period will be fairly long, perhaps three or four months. If the finance market is not particularly busy, 45 days is a common period estimated for closing. The closing date may be set to take place as soon as reasonably possible, or the buyer and seller may agree to delay it.

CHAPTER 11

A real estate buyer seldom just hands the seller the cash when the seller transfers the title. Usually an escrow is opened to handle the details of the closing process. An escrow is not required by law in California, but it is more convenient and safer for both parties.

II. Escrow

*An **ESCROW** is any transaction in which a person delivers any written instrument, money, or evidence of title for the purpose of effecting the sale, transfer, encumbrance, or lease of real property to a third person to be held until the happening of an event or performance of a condition at which time it is delivered to the appropriate person.*

Escrow is an arrangement in which a third (disinterested) party (the escrow agent) holds money and documents on behalf of the principals in a transaction.

In the case of a real estate sale, the escrow agent holds the purchase money and the deed for the buyer and seller. The escrow agent distributes the money and delivers the deed according to instructions from the parties.

www.ceaescrow.org
California Escrow Association

In northern California, escrow services are most often provided by **title companies**. In the southern part of the state, **"independent" escrow corporations** are more common. An independent escrow corporation must be licensed as an escrow agent by the California Department of Corporations and is subject to strict regulation by the Department of Corporations. A number of organizations are allowed to act as escrow agents without a Department of Corporations escrow agent license: banks, trust companies, savings banks, insurance companies, title insurance companies, and California real estate brokers. Attorneys can also perform escrow services for their clients.

A real estate broker may act as an escrow agent, but only in a transaction where he or she is the buyer or seller, or is the listing or selling broker. A broker can't participate in a transaction only as an escrow agent. A broker also isn't permitted to delegate escrow duties (except for minor clerical tasks) to a salesperson or another broker. A broker's business name may not contain the term "escrow" unless the business name also includes the term, "a non-independent broker escrow," following the name.

If a broker's business name includes the term "escrow," the term "a non-independent broker escrow" must be included in any advertising, signs, or electronic promotional material

An escrow agent cannot pay, prior to the close of escrow, any compensation to a real estate agent or anyone else when it is contingent upon performance of the escrow. Nor can escrow agents pay a fee or commission to anyone for referring or soliciting escrow customers to them. A real estate developer selling single-family homes cannot require the use of a specific escrow company as a condition for the sale if the developer has more than a five percent ownership interest in

---

Facts About Escrow Organizations

Northern California uses mostly **title insurance companies**.
Southern California more commonly uses **independent escrow (agents) corporations**.

Organizations allowed to act as escrow agents without a special license include: **banks, trust companies, savings banks, insurance companies, and title insurance companies**.

Attorneys can also perform escrow services for their clients.

A **California real estate broker** may act as an escrow agent, but only in a transaction where he or she is the buyer or seller, or is the listing or selling broker. A broker can't participate in a transaction only as an escrow agent.

---

the escrow company. If the developer does so, the developer is liable for three times the amount charged for escrow services, but not less than $250 plus reasonable attorney's fees and costs.

A. GROUNDS FOR DISCIPLINARY ACTION

If a real estate broker is acting as an escrow agent, the following acts by the broker are grounds for disciplinary action under Section 2950 of the Commissioner's regulations:

(a) Soliciting or accepting an escrow instruction (or amended or supplemental escrow instruction) containing any blank to be filled in after signing or initialing of such escrow instruction (or amended or supplemental escrow instructions).

(b) Permitting any person to make any addition to, deletion from, or alteration of an escrow instruction (or amended or supplemental escrow instruction) received by such licensee, unless such addition, deletion, or alteration is signed or initialed by all persons who had signed or initialed such escrow instruction (or amended or supplemental escrow instruction) prior to such addition, deletion, or alteration.

(c) Failing to deliver at the time of execution of any escrow instruction (or amended or supplemental escrow instruction) a copy thereof to all persons executing the same.

(d) Failing to maintain books, records, and accounts in accordance with accepted principles of accounting and good business practice.

(e) Failing to maintain the office, place of books, records, accounts, safes, files, and papers relating to such escrows freely accessible and available for audit, inspection, and examination by the commissioner.

(f) Failing to deposit all money received as an escrow agent and as part of an escrow transaction in a bank trust account, or escrow account on or before the close of the next full working day after receipt thereof.

(g) Withdrawing or paying out any money deposited in such trustee account or escrow account without the written instruction of the party or parties paying the money into escrow.

(h) Failing to advise all parties in writing if he has knowledge that any licensee acting as such in the transaction has any interest as a stockholder, officer, partner, or owner of the agency holding the escrow.

(i) Failing upon closing of an escrow transaction to render to each principal in the transaction a written statement of all receipts and disbursements together with the name of the person to whom any such disbursement is made.

(j) Delivery or recording any instrument which purportedly transfers a party's title or interest in or to real property without first obtaining the written consent of that party to the delivery or recording.

B. PURPOSE OF ESCROW

An escrow comprises the intermediary steps in which to close a real estate transaction.

The purpose of escrow is to ensure that the concerns of the buyer, the seller, and the lender will all be met. A buyer is reluctant to make more than an earnest money deposit until it is certain that the seller can convey title as agreed. A seller is reluctant to deliver the deed before receiving the agreed payment from the buyer. The escrow arrangement helps ensure that the seller receives the purchase price, the buyer receives clear title, and the lender's security interest in the property is properly perfected.

Escrow protects each party from the other's change of mind. For example, once the deed is in escrow, the seller can't refuse to deliver it to the buyer just because he or she has had second thoughts about the sale. By turning the deed over to the escrow agent, the seller relinquishes control over it. When the buyer meets all the conditions specified in the escrow instructions, the escrow agent must deliver the deed.

Escrow makes it unnecessary for the buyer and seller to meet during the closing process. This allows them to avoid face-to-face confrontations over any conflicts that crop up. It's also a great convenience when the parties live in different states (or even different countries), travel extensively, or are occupied with other business. Escrow allows closing to go forward even when both parties aren't available.

C. OPENING ESCROW

Escrow may be opened by anyone involved in the sale transaction.

In many cases, it's opened by the broker or salesperson, who delivers a copy of the purchase agreement to the escrow agent. In other cases, escrow is opened when the lender delivers a copy of the purchase agreement or loan commitment to its escrow department or escrow subsidiary.

The escrow agent reviews the purchase agreement or loan commitment to determine whether it can serve as the basis for a valid sale escrow. Then he or she helps prepare the escrow instructions and explains them to the parties. The escrow agent orders a preliminary title report, while the real estate agent orders the structural pest control inspection and any other necessary tests. If the seller has an outstanding loan, the escrow agent will request a payoff figure from the seller's lender. If the preliminary title report shows encumbrances the buyer won't accept, the escrow agent arranges with the seller to have them cleared. The escrow agent collects and disburses funds required for closing, arranges for all necessary documents to be executed, recorded, and delivered, and finally prepares the settlement statements. In most transactions, the real estate agent works together with the escrow agent to get the sale closed.

CHAPTER 11

D. REQUIREMENTS FOR A VALID ESCROW

A legally binding contract must create an escrow designating an escrow holder and giving him/her escrow instructions.

> ### Requirements for a Valid Escrow:
>
> - An enforceable contract
> - Relinquishment of control of documents and funds
> - A valid deed
> - An escrow agent
> - Escrow instructions with conditions

1. Enforceable Contract

There should be an enforceable contract between the parties before escrow can be opened. In most cases, this requirement is fulfilled by a purchase agreement. If no purchase agreement is prepared, some other mutual agreement is necessary, such as escrow instructions signed by both parties.

2. Relinquishment of Control

In a valid escrow (mutually executed escrow instructions), each party's deposit of funds or documents must be irrevocable. The depositor must give up all right to retrieve or control the deposit for as long as the escrow is in effect.

> **Case Example:** Mr. Wade agreed to sell his walnut grove to Mr. Mosier. They opened an escrow, and Mosier gave the escrow agent a check for $15,000 as earnest money for the purchase. However, Mosier told the escrow agent to hold onto the check until Mosier instructed him to put it into the escrow account. The agent attached a note to the check ("Hold, do not deposit—Mosier will notify us") and kept it in the file.
>
> Mosier retained control over the check since it was to be processed only under his direction. Because he did not relinquish control, the check was not validly delivered into escrow. (Mosier went bankrupt shortly afterwards, so the check never could be cashed.) *Wade v. Lake County Title Co.*, 6 Cal. App. 3d 824, 86 Cal. Rptr. 182 (1970).

In the event the other party does not execute (sign) the mutually binding escrow instructions, the depositor can withdraw the deposit at any time. However, once the depositor has given up control (signed the escrow instructions), he or she cannot regain control unless the escrow is terminated or the other party agrees to allow the deposit to be withdrawn.

3. Valid Deed

A deed can't be the subject of escrow unless it's valid. If the deed is invalid, it can be recalled by the seller. If an item can be recalled, it isn't adequately delivered into escrow.

Example: Q signs a deed and delivers it to the escrow agent, but the deed doesn't contain a description of the property conveyed, so it's invalid and Q can recall it. Since Q retains the power to recall the deed, the escrow isn't valid. If Q requested the escrow agent to insert the correct legal description it would be valid.

E. ESCROW AGENT

The buyer and seller should agree on the selection of the escrow agent as part of their purchase contract. The buyer and seller often defer to their real estate agents for a recommendation on which escrow agent to select. If the sale transaction is subject to the Real Estate Settlement Procedures Act (RESPA), discussed later in this Chapter, the agents are prohibited from receiving any type of referral fee or kickback, and any referral to an affiliated business must be properly disclosed to the parties.

Avoid escrow holders who are affiliated with the broker.

An escrow agent is a special agent; his or her authority is limited by the escrow instructions. An escrow agent is also a dual agent with fiduciary duties toward both parties in the closing process.

For this reason, it's a good idea for the escrow agent to be a disinterested third party, independent of the seller and the buyer, although an escrow agent is not legally required to be a completely neutral third party. One party's lawyer or real estate broker can act as the escrow agent, as long as the other party approves and no fiduciary duties are violated. A lawyer or real estate broker can even act as the escrow agent when he or she is the buyer or seller, if the other party agrees.

www.ceaescrow.org/_consumer.asp
Escrow Consumer Information

Case Example: A divorce property settlement provided that the ex-wife could buy the ex-husband's community property interest in their Newport Beach home for $70,000. Instead of paying cash, she was to give him a security interest in the property. The ex-husband delivered a quitclaim deed to his ex-wife's lawyer, instructing the lawyer to record it as soon as the ex-wife executed the promissory note and trust deed.

The quitclaim deed was recorded even though the ex-wife never signed the note and trust deed. The ex-husband sued the lawyer for negligence. The lawyer argued that his only duty was to his client, the ex-wife. The court disagreed. In accepting the quitclaim deed he acted as an escrow agent, and as an escrow agent he owed fiduciary duties to both parties to the transaction. *Wasmann v. Seidenberg*, 202 Cal. App. 3d 752 (1988).

---

1. Escrow Instructions

The *ESCROW INSTRUCTIONS (also called the escrow agreement) are the escrow agent's written authorization to deliver the deposited funds and documents.* They tell the agent exactly what conditions each party must fulfill in order to be entitled to delivery. For example, the buyer's instructions might state that the purchase money can't be turned over to the seller until all encumbrances, except the utility easement, have been cleared from the title.

Escrow instructions can differ greatly from one transaction to another. Escrow agents and lenders usually provide preprinted forms, but the parties should review the forms

Escrow Progress Chart

	Sch. Date	Actual Date	Escrow Operations
1.			Notice of sale to multiple listing service
2.			Buyer's deposit increased to $
3.			Escrow opened with
4.			Preliminary title searched
5.			Clouds on title eliminated
6.			Credit report ordered from
7.			Credit report received
8.			Report of residential record ordered
9.			Report of residential record received
10.			Pest control inspection ordered
11.			Pest control report received; work—
12.			Pest control report accepted by seller
13.			Pest control work ordered
14.			Pest control work completed
15.			Other inspections ordered
16.			Report received; work—
17.			Report accepted by
18.			Special contingencies eliminated
19.			Payoff or beneficiary statement ordered
20.			Payoff or beneficiary statement received
21.			Payoff or beneficiary statement ordered
22.			Payoff or beneficiary statement received
23.			1st loan commitment ordered from
24.			Received: @ % Fee Pts.
25.			2nd loan commitment ordered from
26.			Received: @ % Fee Pts.
27.			Loan application submitted to
28.			Loan application approved
29.			Loan/assumption papers received by escrow
30.			Hazard insurance placed with
31.			Escrow closing instructions requested
32.			Client called for closing appointment
33.			Closing papers signed
34.			Closing papers to escrow holder
35.			Funds ordered
36.			Deed recorded

Received	Delivered	AFTER CLOSE OF ESCROW	Received	Delivered	AFTER CLOSE OF ESCROW
		Final adjusted closing statement			Seller's loss payee ins. policy
		Check of seller's proceeds			Record deed
		Check of buyer's refund			Title insurance policy
		Commission check			

carefully. Sometimes a form includes a provision that isn't suitable for a particular transaction. All escrow instructions must contain the license, name and the department issuing the license or the authority under which the person is operating.

Written escrow instructions can serve as the parties' contract of sale if they have no other enforceable contract.

Example: J agreed to sell K his house for $175,000, but they never signed a purchase agreement or put their agreement in writing. When they opened an escrow, however, they both signed written escrow instructions.

J later tries to get out of the sale, and K sues. Without the escrow instructions, K would lose his lawsuit because the statute of frauds makes an unwritten agreement to sell real property unenforceable. However, the escrow instructions are considered a written memorandum of the parties' agreement, and they satisfy the statute of frauds.

As long as the parties have some other written contract, the escrow instructions don't have to be in writing to be binding. If the buyer and seller signed a purchase agreement and then gave an escrow agent oral instructions, the escrow agent would be required to carry out those instructions. Of course, it's always safer to put everything in writing.

The buyer and seller may prepare separate escrow instructions, or use joint escrow instructions.

Separate instructions are used frequently in northern California, whereas joint instructions are standard in southern California. In some instances, primarily in northern California, escrow instructions are prepared but not signed until the escrow is ready to close.

Separate instructions allow each party to keep certain information confidential from the other party. (The seller might not want the buyer to know what the broker's commission is, for example.) On the other hand, joint instructions eliminate the risk of conflicting statements or inconsistencies. If separate instructions are prepared and the seller's don't match up with the buyer's in some important respect, the instructions can't be treated as a contract of sale between the parties. (Remember that there can't be a contract without mutual consent to all material terms.)

Once the parties have signed joint instructions or matching separate instructions, they are legally bound to go through with the transaction. If a buyer or seller tries to back out, he or she can be sued for breach of contract, even if no purchase agreement was signed.

On the other hand, what if the buyer and seller did sign a purchase agreement, and that earlier agreement doesn't match the escrow instructions? As a general rule, when two consecutive contracts involve the same subject matter, the two are interpreted together to determine the whole agreement. If the two contracts have material terms that are inconsistent and can't be reconciled, the later contract supersedes the earlier one. So when the escrow instructions conflict with the purchase agreement, the terms of the escrow instructions control.

Example: The purchase agreement states that the seller will pay for the pest inspection. But the escrow instructions provide that the buyer will pay it.

Since the two contracts are inconsistent, the later contract controls. The buyer will be required to pay for the pest inspection, as agreed in the escrow instructions.

When the buyer is taking out a loan, the escrow instructions must match the lender's loan commitment. If there's a discrepancy between those two documents (such as different loan amounts or interest rates), the lender will require the parties to sign amended escrow instructions. Obviously, it's important to prepare and review the escrow instructions very carefully.

a. Provisions

The escrow instructions usually state which party is responsible for paying the various transaction costs: inspection fees, escrow fees, the broker's commission, recording charges, appraisal fees, title insurance costs and premiums, and so forth. Later in this chapter, we'll run through a settlement statement to show how these charges are ordinarily allocated.

The instructions generally include a list of the deposits each party must make (and when they must make them). For the seller, these might be the deed, a bill of sale for any personal property, receipts showing paid taxes, a hazard insurance policy, leases, service contracts, a pest inspection report, and other inspection reports. Depending on how the purchase is financed, the buyer may be required to deposit the full price in cash, or a down payment and a trust deed in favor of the lender or the seller.

Case Example: The Amens opened an escrow for the purchase of a tavern (bulk sale—personal property) by signing escrow instructions on forms provided by the escrow company (Merced County Title Company). The instructions provided how much the Amens were paying, which included the assumption of $10,000 of certain debts. The instructions also stated that the escrow company would pay any debts over the $10,000 out of the proceeds of the sale. The State Board of Equalization mailed to the Amens, in care of the escrow company, a notice that they should obtain a tax clearance certificate to avoid liability for state sales taxes owed by the seller.

A second warning by telephone was given to the person handling Amen's escrow for the company. The Amens were never advised of this, no certificate was requested and the escrow closed. Several months later the Amens received a notice of unpaid sales taxes of the seller of $4,749.48 and of their liability as seller's successor. The Amens sued the escrow company. The California Supreme Court held that an escrow holder must strictly follow the escrow instructions and a failure to do so makes the escrow holder liable for the loss occasioned thereby. *Amen v. Merced County Title Company*, 58 Cal. 2d 528, 25 Cal. Rptr. 65 (1962).

b. Escrow Agent's Duty

An escrow agent is limited to exercising ordinary care in strictly carrying out the escrow instructions.

An escrow agent must follow the instructions to the letter. An agent who acts contrary to the instructions is liable for any resulting damages.

The instructions also set the limit of the escrow agent's obligations. Furthermore, there is a statutory obligation to give notice to the buyer of the advantages of title insurance if no policy of title insurance is to be issued in the transaction.

> **Case Example:** A title company provided escrow services for a complicated transaction. The seller was an elderly widow who didn't understand the risk involved in carrying back the trust deed that gave her fourth lien position. Her trust deed became worthless after a senior lienholder foreclosed.
>
> The seller sued most of those involved in the transaction. She sued the title company for negligence and breach of fiduciary duty because its escrow agent didn't advise her that she was taking a very weak security interest in the property. The court ruled that the company had not acted negligently, since it had followed the seller's escrow instructions exactly. In so doing, the company fulfilled its fiduciary duty to the seller. *Axley v. Transamerica Title Insurance Co.*, 88 Cal. App. 3d 1, 151 Cal. Rptr. 570 (1978).

III. Termination of Escrow

When the parties have performed all the conditions and the escrow agent has delivered the deed and the purchase money, the escrow ends automatically.

An escrow is set up for a particular transaction. When that transaction is consummated, the escrow terminates.

What happens if the escrow conditions are not fulfilled? Then the escrow may be cancelled by mutual agreement, or expire, or be terminated as a result of one party's default.

A. MUTUAL AGREEMENT

The parties may terminate escrow at any time by mutual agreement. This happens when unforeseen events make both buyer and seller decide they don't want to go through with the transaction.

> **Example:** The sellers plan to retire, sell the house, and spend the next year traveling around Europe, but after escrow is opened, the husband dies. The wife decides she would rather keep the house instead of going on the voyage by herself.
>
> Meanwhile, the buyers have decided to get a divorce, and neither wants to go ahead with the purchase of the new house. After discussing their situations, the seller and buyers agree to cancel the escrow.

When the parties agree to cancel, they notify the escrow agent. The escrow agent will usually send a letter or cancellation agreement to all of the parties to clarify the situation and resolve any questions. The cancellation agreement should explain which party is responsible for paying any costs (such as title insurance and inspection fees) that have already been incurred. The escrow agent may also charge a cancellation fee. After the parties have signed the cancellation agreement, the escrow agent will return any deposits.

Cancelling escrow doesn't terminate the buyer and seller's underlying agreement.

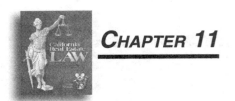

CHAPTER 11

Note, however, that a mutual agreement to cancel the escrow does not automatically cancel the purchase contract between the parties, as demonstrated in the following case.

Case Example: The Shearers agreed to sell their home to the Cohens, and escrow was opened. However, a few months later the escrow agent received a cancellation notice signed by both the buyers and the sellers: "All previous instructions given by Buyer and Seller in the above escrow are hereby cancelled, and this escrow is not to be consummated." The earnest money deposit was returned to the Cohens.

Shortly afterwards, the Cohens filed a specific performance action, asking the court to order the Shearers to go through with the sale. The trial judge dismissed their case. The judge interpreted the escrow cancellation notice as a mutually agreed rescission of the property sale contract.

The appellate court reversed that decision. The notice cancelled only the escrow, not the parties' contract. The Cohens might be entitled to specific performance. *Cohen v. Shearer*, 108 Cal. App. 3d 939, 167 Cal. Rptr. 10 (1980).

B. EXPIRATION

Escrow instructions usually state that the conditions must be performed within a certain time limit. As a general rule, when that time expires and the conditions have not been performed, the escrow continues until one of the parties makes a written demand to stop. Once escrow instructions are executed by the seller and buyer, the escrow holder generally will not automatically release funds or return funds until mutually executed cancellation instructions have been provided to the escrow holder.

Case Example: Mr. Pothast agreed to sell some property to Mr. Cly. On April 26, they executed escrow instructions that allowed Cly 90 days to deposit $2,000 into the escrow.

Pothast changed his mind about the sale. On July 16, he sent the escrow agent a letter canceling the escrow and demanding the return of his deed. This was ineffective, because he had relinquished control of the deed, and one party can't cancel escrow unilaterally. Cly still wanted to go through with the purchase and on August 3, he gave the escrow agent $2,000.

Pothast brought a quiet title action, and the court ruled in his favor. Although Pothast's attempt to cancel the escrow didn't work, Cly failed to make the 90-day deadline stated in the escrow instructions. The escrow expired on July 25, more than a week before Cly deposited the $2,000. After that date, the escrow agent wasn't authorized to deliver Pothast's deed to Cly. *Pothast v. Kind*, 218 Cal. 192, 24 P.2d 771 (1933).

As with most contracts, however, courts don't always strictly enforce time limits in escrow instructions. If the instructions didn't state that time was of the essence, or one party didn't insist that the deadline be met, a court might hold that the time limit was waived. And if one party causes a delay, he or she can't hold the other party to a time limit.

Example: The closing date was set for July 25, but neither party performed on that date. The seller hadn't cleared her title yet, so the buyer didn't deposit the purchase money.

On August 20, the escrow agent finally received the paperwork necessary for clearing title. On October 9, the escrow agent asked the buyer to deposit the purchase money, and he promptly complied.

But the seller had changed her mind, and she refused to complete the transaction by delivering the deed. She believed she was not required to since the July 25 closing date was long past.

In the ensuing lawsuit, the court awarded the buyer specific performance. The buyer had been ready to go on July 25, and it was the seller's fault that the transaction didn't close then. The buyer was not required to perform until the title had been cleared. The seller couldn't use the missed deadline as an excuse for backing out of the sale. (Based on *Langston v. Huffacker*, 36 Wash. App. 779, 678 P.2d 1265 [1984].)

Case Example: Mr. and Mrs. Wong (plaintiffs) sold property to Mr. and Mrs. Vaughan (defendants). The defendants placed the money in escrow with Title Insurance and Trust Company (escrow). The escrow instructions provided that "time is of the essence" and out in the event escrow was not in "condition to close by May 29, 1946, any party who then shall have fully complied with his instructions may, in writing, demand the return of his money and/or property." Escrow was not in a condition to be closed on May 29, but on June 18 escrow notified the defendants not on receipt of the unpaid balance of $30,000 and was ready to issue its policy of title insurance and close escrow. On July 1, the defendants paid an additional $5,000 into escrow. On July 15, the defendants signed and delivered to escrow, with the plaintiffs' approval, amended escrow instructions regarding payment of interest on a note which was in lieu of the previous instructions. No more money was paid into escrow by the defendants. On August 27, plaintiffs filed a lawsuit to declare a forfeiture of the escrow money. Ultimately, judgment was for the defendants and plaintiffs appealed.

Where time is made of the essence in a contract for the payment of money and this covenant has been waived by the acceptance of money after it is due, with knowledge of the facts, such conduct will be regarded as creating a temporary suspension of the right of forfeiture as could only be restored by giving a definite and specific notice of intention to enforce it. The evidence shows that the transaction was still pending on July 15, with the plaintiff's approval. Therefore, the "time is of the essence" is deemed to have been waived. Any right of forfeiture which may have existed was thus suspended until definite notice to perform the contract by a specific date was given. Although there was conflicting evidence, the trial court determined that no such notice had been given. In the absence of such notice plaintiff cannot enforce any right of forfeiture and the defendants were entitled to restitution of the escrow payments they had made. *Chan v. Title Insurance and Trust Company*, 39 Cal. 2d 253, 246 P. 2d 632 (1952).

C. DEFAULT

The escrow instructions may provide for cancellation of escrow in the event of default. In that case, it's not necessary to wait for the escrow to expire if one party clearly fails to fulfill a condition. For example, the instructions might provide that if the seller refuses to correct a termite problem as agreed, the buyer may cancel escrow before the scheduled closing date without the seller's consent. Even with such an instruction, an escrow agent will probably require mutual instructions to cancel.

Most purchase agreements provide that if the buyer defaults, the seller keeps the earnest money deposit. If the seller defaults, the buyer gets it back, but the escrow agent shouldn't let either one have the deposit without the other's consent.

Whenever there's a dispute over which party is entitled to funds in escrow, it's not up to the escrow agent to resolve the issue. The escrow agent can either hold onto the funds until the parties work it out, or start an interpleader action. In an **INTERPLEADER**, *the escrow agent turns the funds over to the court. The parties then argue the case to the judge, who decides what to do with the funds.*

Case Example: A broker was acting as both real estate broker and escrow agent in a transaction. The parties disagreed about the terms of the sale, and the buyer told the broker the escrow was cancelled. The broker released the earnest money deposit to the buyer without asking the seller about it.

The seller protested that he hadn't authorized cancellation of escrow or the return of the deposit. The broker believed he was allowed to release the deposit because the sale was dead. The Department of Real Estate disciplined the broker for acting without authorization from both parties. The broker appealed, but the appellate court affirmed the DRE's action. *Mullen v. Dept. of Real Estate*, 251 Cal. Rptr. 12 (1988).

A special statutory rule applies to a sale of residential property with one-to-four units (one of which is to be occupied by the buyer) when the transaction isn't completed by the scheduled closing date. If one party submits a written request for the return of funds in escrow, within 30 days, the other party must sign a release allowing the escrow agent to return the funds. Otherwise, the party making the request can sue. The court will order the other party to release the funds, and in addition, to pay the plaintiff treble damages and attorney fees. (Treble damages would be three times the amount of the deposited funds. The treble damages award can't be more than $1,000 or less than $100, however.) This rule only applies when the plaintiff is clearly entitled to the funds and the defendant is not holding them in good faith to resolve a dispute.

IV. When Title Passes

When does title to funds or property that one party places in escrow pass to the other party? Unless otherwise agreed, title passes only when all the conditions for delivery have been performed. So the buyer still holds title to the deposited funds, and the seller still holds title to the property. The seller ordinarily stays in possession of the property, collects any rents, and pays the taxes. But when all the conditions have been performed, legal title to the funds or property passes to the other party. In some cases, California courts have held that title passes even before the escrow agent actually delivers the funds or the deed.

The risk of loss as to property or funds in escrow follows legal title or possession of the property. As long as the seller has both title and possession of the property, it's the seller's loss if the property is destroyed. However, once legal title or possession has been transferred to the buyer, the risk of loss is the buyer's.

Example: The deed is in escrow, but the seller is still living on the property. The house is destroyed by fire. The buyer doesn't have to go through with the purchase. The seller had both legal title and possession, so the risk of loss was his or hers.

If the buyer has already taken possession of the property when the fire occurs, it's his/her loss, even though the deed is still in escrow and the seller holds legal title. The buyer is not relieved of the obligation to pay the seller.

A similar rule applies to funds in escrow. If the escrow agent steals the deposited funds, the party who holds legal title to the funds suffers the loss.

> **Case Example:** Mr. Beck listed his Los Angeles property with the H.B. Eshelman Realty Company. Mr. Hildebrand offered to buy Beck's property for $1,800, and Beck agreed. The broker, Mr. Eshelman, acted as escrow agent for the sale.
>
> Beck deposited a deed in escrow, and Hildebrand deposited $1,800. The escrow instructions authorized Eshelman to deliver the purchase money to Beck as soon as a title insurance policy was issued.
>
> However, a few days after receiving Hildebrand's deposit, Eshelman embezzled all the money he held as an escrow agent for several transactions (totaling more than $40,000). As you might imagine, he left Los Angeles immediately.
>
> Two weeks later, the title company issued a policy for the Beck-Hildebrand transaction. Hildebrand brought a quiet title action to establish that he now owned Beck's property. Hildebrand argued that he had deposited the purchase money as agreed, and all conditions of the sale had been met, so the property was his. But Beck, who never saw a penny of Hildebrand's money, disagreed.
>
> The court ruled in favor of Beck. Hildebrand still held title to the deposited funds when Eshelman ran off with them. Since Beck never took title to the funds, he could not be compelled to complete the sale. *Hildebrand v. Beck*, 196 Cal. 141, 236 P. 301 (1925).

A. UNAUTHORIZED DELIVERY

If the escrow agent delivers a deposit before one of the conditions has been performed, title does not pass unless the depositor ratifies the escrow agent's action. *The unauthorized transfer or use of another person's money or property is a tort called* **CONVERSION**. The injured party may recover damages from the escrow agent or from the other party who accepted the wrongful delivery.

B. DOCTRINE OF RELATION BACK

In special circumstances, there's an exception to the rule that title doesn't pass until all the escrow conditions have been performed. To avoid injustice and carry out the parties' intentions, a court may rule that title passed on the date the deed or funds were deposited in escrow, instead of the date all conditions were performed. This is known as the *DOCTRINE OF RELATION BACK: the transfer relates back to the date of deposit in escrow.* (This doctrine is also used in connection with option contracts. See Chapter 8.)

The doctrine of relation back is often applied when a seller deposits a deed in escrow, but dies before the deed is delivered to the buyer. Under the ordinary rules governing transfer, the buyer would be out of luck. A deed must be delivered to the grantee while the grantor is alive. However, if the delivery is held to relate back to the date the deed was deposited (when the seller was still alive), the transfer is effective.

> **Case Example:** Mrs. Brunoni was dying of cancer. She asked her lawyer to draw up a will dividing her property equally between her children, but she wanted the will to provide that her son Antonio could buy her ranch for $6,500 (considerably less than its market value). ▼

The lawyer explained that it would be simpler if Mrs. Brunoni sold the ranch to Antonio while she was still living, rather than having him purchase it from her estate. Mrs. Brunoni agreed.

The lawyer wrote up a will leaving Mrs. Brunoni's property to all her children, and also prepared escrow instructions. The instructions required the lawyer to deliver the deed to the ranch to Antonio if he paid $6,500 and agreed to support his mother for the remainder of her life. On June 18, Mrs. Brunoni signed the will and the escrow instructions, and gave the lawyer a deed transferring the ranch to Antonio.

Two days later (June 20), Antonio signed a document in which he agreed to purchase the ranch for $6,500 and fulfill the other conditions in his mother's escrow instructions.

On June 23, Mrs. Brunoni died. Antonio didn't deposit the $6,500 in escrow until July 1. The lawyer delivered the deed to him.

Some of the decedent's children sued to establish (1) that the deed to Antonio was invalid and (2) the decedent lacked mental capacity to convey the property. With regard to her mental capacity, none of the witnesses were more specific in their testimony than to state that the decedent was forgetful. None of them testified that she was mentally incompetent. Old age does not render a person incompetent to execute and deed. Nor will sickness, duress, or the debility of the body affect mental capacity if sufficient intelligence remains. With regard to the deed, while it is elementary that a deed must be delivered "inter vivos," the rule is also well established that when a valid escrow agreement is created, the death of the grantor prior to delivery by the escrow agent to the grantee relates back to the delivery by the grantor to the escrow agent and thus constitutes an "inter vivos" delivery, as she was alive at that time. Also, a valid underlying purchase contract constitutes a complete and binding escrow when deposited with the escrow holder. This contract arose when Antonio accepted that his mother's offer to sell by agreeing to all the terms set forth by her. Judgment for Antonio. *Brunoni v. Brunoni*, 93 Cal. App. 2d 215, 208 P.2d 1028 (1949).

The outcome in this case would have been different if Mrs. Brunoni had died on June 19, the day after she deposited the deed in escrow. Antonio didn't sign a purchase agreement until June 20. It wasn't until he signed the agreement that a valid escrow was created. Remember that there can't be a valid escrow unless there's a binding agreement between the parties.

Without a valid escrow, the doctrine of relation back would not apply.

V. Real Estate Settlement Procedures Act (RESPA)

The *REAL ESTATE SETTLEMENT PROCEDURES ACT (RESPA) is a federal law passed by Congress in 1974. It requires lenders to disclose information about closing costs to loan applicants*. RESPA applies to most federally related loans. A loan is federally related if it meets all of the following criteria:

1. used to purchase or refinance residential property with up to 4 units;

2. secured by a first or subordinate lien, and

3. made by any lender who has federally-insured deposit account, is federally regulated, makes loans insured, guaranteed, or assisted by any federal agency, makes loans intended

to be sold to or guaranteed by Fannie Mae, Freddie Mac, or Ginnie Mae, or makes or invests in residential real estate loans totaling more than $1,000,000 per year.

In short, the act applies to almost all institutional lenders and to most residential loans. RESPA has four basic requirements:

1. The lender must give a copy of the booklet *Settlement Procedures and You* (prepared by HUD) to each loan applicant within three days of receiving a written loan application.

2. The lender must give the applicant a good-faith estimate (GFE) of settlement costs within three days after receiving the loan application. Closing costs that may increase by a maximum of 10% over GFE include title insurance premiums, recording fees, escrow fees, and any closing costs from providers selected by the lender. Closing costs that may not increase are loan origination fees and transfer taxes. In 2011, authority for enforcing RESPA was transferred from the U. S. Department of Housing and Urban Development (HUD) to the **Consumer Financial Protection Bureau (CFPB)**. The CFPB has issued proposed regulations that would combine the GFE disclosures with disclosures required to be given to a borrower at time of application under the Truth-in-Lending Act (TILA). The TILA is discussed in more detail in the next section. As proposed by the CFPB, the combined disclosures would be contained in a document called a "Loan Estimate."

3. The lender must itemize all loan settlement charges on a Uniform Settlement Statement (see Figure 11-1).

4. The lender may not pay kickbacks or referral fees to anyone for referring customers for any settlement service business involving a federally related loan.

Violations of RESPA's anti-kickback, referral fees and unearned fees provisions are subject to criminal and civil penalties. In a criminal case, a person may be fined up to $10,000 and imprisoned up to one year. In a private lawsuit may be liable to the person who paid for the settlement service for an amount equal to three times the amount of the charge paid for the service.

www.hud.gov/offices/hsg/sfh/res/respa_hm.cfm
RESPA

VI. Settlement Statement

A **SETTLEMENT STATEMENT** (*also called a* **closing statement**) *sets out the financial details of a real estate transaction.* It itemizes the sums to be paid by each party, and to be paid to each party. It also shows the net amount of cash the buyer will have to pay at closing and the net cash that the seller will receive.

If the transaction is subject to RESPA, a **Uniform Settlement Statement** form (**Figure 11-1**) must be used. If RESPA doesn't apply, any one of several different forms may be used. There may be separate statements for buyer and seller, or the statements may be combined. The regulations proposed by the CFPB would also combine the RESPA closing statement disclosures with disclosures required at time of closing under the TILA. As proposed by the CFPB, the combined disclosures would be contained in a document called a **Closing Disclosure Form**.

Figure 11-1

 A. **Settlement Statement (HUD-1)**

B. Type of Loan

1. ☐ FHA	2. ☐ RHS	3. ☐ Conv. Unins.	6. File Number:	7. Loan Number:	8. Mortgage Insurance Case Number:
4. ☐ VA	5. ☐ Conv. Ins.				

C. Note: This form is furnished to give you a statement of actual settlement costs. Amounts paid to and by the settlement agent are shown. Items marked "(p.o.c.)" were paid outside the closing; they are shown here for informational purposes and are not included in the totals.

D. Name & Address of Borrower:	E. Name & Address of Seller:	F. Name & Address of Lender:
G. Property Location:	H. Settlement Agent:	I. Settlement Date:
	Place of Settlement:	

J. Summary of Borrower's Transaction		K. Summary of Seller's Transaction	
100. Gross Amount Due from Borrower		**400. Gross Amount Due to Seller**	
101. Contract sales price		401. Contract sales price	
102. Personal property		402. Personal property	
103. Settlement charges to borrower (line 1400)		403.	
104.		404.	
105.		405.	
Adjustment for items paid by seller in advance		**Adjustment for items paid by seller in advance**	
106. City/town taxes to		406. City/town taxes to	
107. County taxes to		407. County taxes to	
108. Assessments to		408. Assessments to	
109.		409.	
110.		410.	
111.		411.	
112.		412.	
120. Gross Amount Due from Borrower		**420. Gross Amount Due to Seller**	
200. Amount Paid by or in Behalf of Borrower		**500. Reductions In Amount Due to seller**	
201. Deposit or earnest money		501. Excess deposit (see instructions)	
202. Principal amount of new loan(s)		502. Settlement charges to seller (line 1400)	
203. Existing loan(s) taken subject to		503. Existing loan(s) taken subject to	
204.		504. Payoff of first mortgage loan	
205.		505. Payoff of second mortgage loan	
206.		506.	
207.		507.	
208.		508.	
209.		509.	
Adjustments for items unpaid by seller		**Adjustments for items unpaid by seller**	
210. City/town taxes to		510. City/town taxes to	
211. County taxes to		511. County taxes to	
212. Assessments to		512. Assessments to	
213.		513.	
214.		514.	
215.		515.	
216.		516.	
217.		517.	
218.		518.	
219.		519.	
220. Total Paid by/for Borrower		**520. Total Reduction Amount Due Seller**	
300. Cash at Settlement from/to Borrower		**600. Cash at Settlement to/from Seller**	
301. Gross amount due from borrower (line 120)		601. Gross amount due to seller (line 420)	
302. Less amounts paid by/for borrower (line 220)	( )	602. Less reductions in amounts due seller (line 520)	( )
303. Cash ☐ From ☐ To Borrower		603. Cash ☐ To ☐ From Seller	

The Public Reporting Burden for this collection of information is estimated at 35 minutes per response for collecting, reviewing, and reporting the data. This agency may not collect this information, and you are not required to complete this form, unless it displays a currently valid OMB control number. No confidentiality is assured; this disclosure is mandatory. This is designed to provide the parties to a RESPA covered transaction with information during the settlement process.

Previous edition are obsolete   Page 1 of 3   HUD-1

L. Settlement Charges

700. Total Real Estate Broker Fees

	Paid From Borrower's Funds at Settlement	Paid From Seller's Funds at Settlement
Division of commission (line 700) as follows :		
701. $ to		
702. $ to		
703. Commission paid at settlement		
704.		

800. Items Payable in Connection with Loan

801. Our origination charge $ (from GFE #1)		
802. Your credit or charge (points) for the specific interest rate chosen $ (from GFE #2)		
803. Your adjusted origination charges (from GFE #A)		
804. Appraisal fee to (from GFE #3)		
805. Credit report to (from GFE #3)		
806. Tax service to (from GFE #3)		
807. Flood certification to (from GFE #3)		
808.		
809.		
810.		
811.		

900. Items Required by Lender to be Paid in Advance

901. Daily interest charges from to @ $ /day (from GFE #10)		
902. Mortgage insurance premium for months to (from GFE #3)		
903. Homeowner's insurance for years to (from GFE #11)		
904.		

1000. Reserves Deposited with Lender

1001. Initial deposit for your escrow account (from GFE #9)		
1002. Homeowner's insurance months @ $ per month $		
1003. Mortgage insurance months @ $ per month $		
1004. Property Taxes months @ $ per month $		
1005. months @ $ per month $		
1006. months @ $ per month $		
1007. Aggregate Adjustment -$		

1100. Title Charges

1101. Title services and lender's title insurance (from GFE #4)		
1102. Settlement or closing fee $		
1103. Owner's title insurance (from GFE #5)		
1104. Lender's title insurance $		
1105. Lender's title policy limit $		
1106. Owner's title policy limit $		
1107. Agent's portion of the total title insurance premium to $		
1108. Underwriter's portion of the total title insurance premium to $		
1109.		
1110.		
1111.		

1200. Government Recording and Transfer Charges

1201. Government recording charges (from GFE #7)		
1202. Deed $ Mortgage $ Release $		
1203. Transfer taxes (from GFE #8)		
1204. City/County tax/stamps Deed $ Mortgage $		
1205. State tax/stamps Deed $ Mortgage $		
1206.		

1300. Additional Settlement Charges

1301. Required services that you can shop for (from GFE #6)		
1302. $		
1303. $		
1304.		
1305.		

1400. Total Settlement Charges (enter on lines 103, Section J and 502, Section K)

407

Comparison of Good Faith Estimate (GFE) and HUD-1 Charrges		Good Faith Estimate	HUD-1
Charges That Cannot Increase	HUD-1 Line Number		
Our origination charge	# 801		
Your credit or charge (points) for the specific interest rate chosen	# 802		
Your adjusted origination charges	# 803		
Transfer taxes	# 1203		

Charges That In Total Cannot Increase More Than 10%		Good Faith Estimate	HUD-1
Government recording charges	# 1201		
	#		
	#		
	#		
	#		
	#		
	#		
	#		
Total			
Increase between GFE and HUD-1 Charges		$ or	%

Charges That Can Change		Good Faith Estimate	HUD-1
Initial deposit for your escrow account	# 1001		
Daily interest charges $ /day	# 901		
Homeowner's insurance	# 903		
	#		
	#		
	#		

Loan Terms

Your initial loan amount is	$
Your loan term is	years
Your initial interest rate is	%
Your initial monthly amount owed for principal, interest, and any mortgage insurance is	$ includes ☐ Principal ☐ Interest ☐ Mortgage Insurance
Can your interest rate rise?	☐ No ☐ Yes, it can rise to a maximum of %. The first change will be on and can change again every after . Every change date, your interest rate can increase or decrease by %. Over the life of the loan, your interest rate is guaranteed to never be lower than % or higher than %.
Even if you make payments on time, can your loan balance rise?	☐ No ☐ Yes, it can rise to a maximum of $
Even if you make payments on time, can your monthly amount owed for principal, interest, and mortgage insurance rise?	☐ No ☐ Yes, the first increase can be on and the monthly amount owed can rise to $. The maximum it can ever rise to is $
Does your loan have a prepayment penalty?	☐ No ☐ Yes, your maximum prepayment penalty is $
Does your loan have a balloon payment?	☐ No ☐ Yes, you have a balloon payment of $ due in years on
Total monthly amount owed including escrow account payments	☐ You do not have a monthly escrow payment for items, such as property taxes and homeowner's insurance. You must pay these items directly yourself. ☐ You have an additional monthly escrow payment of $ that results in a total initial monthly amount owed of $. This includes principal, interest, any mortgage insurance and any items checked below: ☐ Property taxes ☐ Homeowner's insurance ☐ Flood insurance ☐ ☐

Note: If you have any questions about the Settlement Charges and Loan Terms listed on this form, please contact your lender.

A. ALLOCATING EXPENSES

Preparing a settlement statement involves little more than determining the amounts of the charges and credits that apply to the transaction and allocating them to the right parties. The division of expenses is usually determined by the terms of the purchase agreement or local custom that doesn't conflict with written agreements between the buyer and seller.

> **Example:** It's customary for the buyer to pay for the appraisal. However, in the purchase agreement, the seller agreed to pay the appraisal fee. As a result, the custom will be disregarded, and the seller will be charged for the appraisal.

Neither local custom nor the parties' agreement may be contrary to local, state, or federal law. Veterans Administration regulations, which have the effect of law, prohibit buyers seeking VA guaranteed financing from paying any portion of the loan discount (points).

B. TRANSACTION SETTLEMENT GUIDE

A *TRANSACTION SETTLEMENT GUIDE (Figure 11-2) shows how the various debits and credits are usually allocated. A DEBIT is an amount owed or a charge that must be paid. A CREDIT is the opposite of a debit: it is an amount to be received.* A transaction settlement guide will help the real estate agent determine what costs will be paid by each party.

Although it generally isn't possible to calculate the exact closing costs in advance, a reasonably accurate estimate can be prepared. Real estate agents are often called upon to make an estimate since the parties should have a good idea of the closing costs before they sign the purchase agreement. There are standard forms that agents may use in estimating the costs and proceeds, such as the California Association of REALTORS® forms shown in **Figure 11-3** and **11-4**.

C. BUYER'S COST (Debits)

Obviously, the main cost for the buyer will be the **purchase price**. It appears on the settlement statement as a debit to the buyer and a credit to the seller. In most transactions the purchase price will be offset by some form of **financing**, such as an institutional loan or seller financing. New loans or assumption of existing loans are listed as credits for the buyer. The difference between the price and the financing is the down payment.

After the purchase price, the buyer's second largest debit at closing is typically the *LOAN ORIGINATION FEE (also called the loan fee or loan service fee), a fee charged by the lender to cover the administrative costs of making the loan; it's stated as a percentage of the loan amount.* The VA limits loan fees to 1% of the loan amount. Conventional lenders usually charge more (between 1% and 3%). To calculate the loan fee, simply multiply the loan amount (not the purchase price) by the fee percentage.

A lender may charge an **assumption fee** when the buyer assumes an existing loan. FHA and VA fees are minimal, but some conventional lenders' assumption fees are quite substantial—as large as a loan origination fee.

In addition to the origination fee or assumption fee, some lenders charge a **loan processing fee**. This is likely to be between $200 and $300.

For some loans, the lender charges discount points. *DISCOUNT POINTS are a percentage of the loan amount paid up front to increase the lender's yield on the loan.* One point is 1% of the loan amount. The VA prohibits borrowers from paying any points (they can only be paid by

Figure 11-2

Transaction Settlement Guide

	BUYER'S STATEMENT		SELLER'S STATEMENT	
	DEBIT	CREDIT	DEBIT	CREDIT
Purchase Price	X			X
Deposit		X	X	
Documentary Transfer Tax			X	
Sales Commission			X	
Pay-Off Existing Loan			X	
Assume Existing Loan		X	X	
New Loan		X		
Seller Financing		X	X	
Owner's Title Insurance	VARIES ACCORDING TO LOCAL CUSTOM			
Lender's Title Insurance	VARIES ACCORDING TO LOCAL CUSTOM			
Loan Discount (Points)	BY AGREEMENT, EXCEPT VA			
Loan Fee	X			
Property Taxes				
Arrears		X	X	
Current/Not Due		X	X	
Prepaid	X			X
Hazard Insurance				
Assume Policy	X			X
New Policy	X			
Interest				
Pay-off Existing Loan			X	
Assume Existing Loan		X	X	
New Loan (Prepaid Interest)	X			
Impound Accounts				
Pay-off Existing Loan				X
Assumption	X			X
Credit Report	X			
Survey	X			
Pest Inspection	BY AGREEMENT			
Appraisal	X			
Escrow Fee	BY AGREEMENT, EXCEPT VA			
Sale of Chattels (Personal Property)	X			X
Recording Fees	X		X	
Balance Due From Buyer		X		
Balance Due Seller			X	
TOTALS	**X**	**X**	**X**	**X**

Figure 11-3

CALIFORNIA ASSOCIATION OF REALTORS®

ESTIMATED SELLER PROCEEDS
(C.A.R. Form ESP, Revised 4/06)

SELLER: _____ DATE: _____

PROPERTY ADDRESS: _____

This estimate is based on costs associated with _____ type of financing.

PROJECTED CLOSING DATE: _____ PROPOSED SALE PRICE: $ _____

Current Annual Property Taxes: $ _____ Rate: _____ % Monthly Homeowners Dues, if any: $ _____

CHARGES BY EXISTING LIEN HOLDERS

Interest to payoff date (first loan)	# Days _____	$ _____
Interest (secondary financing)	# Days _____	$ _____
Interest on lines of credit or other financing		$ _____
Prepayment penalty		$ _____
Demand and Reconveyance fees		$ _____
Other lender fees (wire transfers, courier, etc.)		$ _____

ESCROW AND TITLE CHARGES

Escrow Fee ☐ including any Exchange Fees $ _____
Title Insurance Policy $ _____
Drawing, Notary and Recording Fees $ _____

OTHER EXPENSES & PRORATIONS

Brokerage -Listing ☐Amount $_____ or☐ _____ % $ _____
Fee -Selling ☐Amount $_____ or☐ _____ % $ _____
Transfer Tax-County Rate per $1,000 $ _____ $ _____
-City Rate per $1,000 $ _____ $ _____
Property Taxes # Days _____ $ _____
Homeowners Dues # Days _____ $ _____
Buyer's Closing Costs $ _____
Natural Hazard Disclosure and/or other Reports $ _____
Wood Destroying Pest and/or other Inspection Fees $ _____
Corrective Work and/or other Repairs $ _____
Home Warranty Program $ _____
Rents and Security Deposits $ _____
VA/FHA Discount Points and Fees $ _____
HOA Transfer and/or Move-Out Fees $ _____
Other _____ $ _____
_____ $ _____

TOTAL ESTIMATED EXPENSES $ _____

ENCUMBRANCES (EXISTING LIENS)

First Loan	Rate: _____ %	$ _____
Secondary Financing	Rate: _____ %	$ _____
Secured Lines of Credit		$ _____
Bonds, Liens, etc.		$ _____
Other _____		$ _____
TOTAL ENCUMBRANCES		$ _____

GROSS EQUITY $ _____
(Expected sale price less encumbrances)

ESTIMATED CREDITS

Prorated Property Taxes # Days _____ $ _____
Prorated Homeowners Dues # Days _____ $ _____
Other _____ $ _____
Other _____ $ _____

TOTAL ESTIMATED CREDITS $ _____

PROCEEDS RECAP

Expected Sale Price $ _____
LESS Total Encumbrances - _____
LESS Total Estimated Expenses - _____
PLUS Total Estimated Credits + _____

ESTIMATED TOTAL SELLER PROCEEDS $ _____

LESS any Note Carried by Seller - _____
LESS any Federal/State Withholding - _____

ESTIMATED SELLER CASH PROCEEDS $ _____

This estimate, based upon the above sale price, type of financing and projected closing date, has been prepared to assist Seller in estimating costs and proceeds. Amounts will vary depending upon differences between actual and estimated repairs that may occur in the transaction, unpaid loan balances, assessments, liens, impound accounts, charges by lenders, escrow companies, title insurers and other service providers and other items. Not all liens may yet have been identified. Neither Broker nor Agent guarantee these figures represent the actual, or only, amounts and charges. By signing below Seller acknowledges that Seller has read, understands and received a copy of this Estimated Seller Proceeds.

Seller _____ Date _____
Seller _____ Date _____
Real Estate Broker (Firm) _____ DRE Lic. # _____
By (Agent) _____ DRE Lic. # _____ Date _____
Address _____ City _____ State _____ Zip _____
Telephone _____ Fax _____ E-mail _____

SURE TRAC
The System for Success™

Published and Distributed by:
REAL ESTATE BUSINESS SERVICES, INC.
a subsidiary of the California Association of REALTORS®
525 South Virgil Avenue, Los Angeles, California 90020

Reviewed by _____ Date _____

EQUAL HOUSING OPPORTUNITY

ESP REVISED 4/06 (PAGE 1 OF 1) **ESTIMATED SELLER PROCEEDS (ESP PAGE 1 OF 1)**

Agent: Walt Huber	Phone:	Fax:	Prepared using WINForms® software
Broker: WALT HUBER, REALTOR	123 Winsail	, MARINA DEL REY CA 90292	

Figure 11-4

CALIFORNIA ASSOCIATION OF REALTORS®

ESTIMATED BUYER COSTS
(C.A.R. Form EBC, Revised 4/06)

BUYER: _____ DATE: _____

PROPERTY ADDRESS: _____

PROJECTED CLOSING DATE: _____ PROJECTED PURCHASE PRICE: $ _____

New First Loan: $_____ Rate: _____% ☐ Fixed or ☐ Adjustable ☐ Interest Only Term: _____ years

New Second Loan: $_____ Rate: _____% ☐ Fixed or ☐ Adjustable ☐ Interest Only Term: _____ years

Current Annual Property Taxes: $_____ Rate: _____% If Rented, Current Monthly Rent $ _____

FINANCING CHARGES

New First Loan Origination Fee/Points _____%	$ _____
Secondary Financing Orig. Fee/Points _____%	$ _____
Prepaid Interest (First Loan) # Days _____	$ _____
Prepaid Interest (Secondary Financing) # Days _____	$ _____
Impounds: - Property Taxes # Months _____	$ _____
- Insurance # Months _____	$ _____
Processing/Underwriting Fees	$ _____
Document Preparation Fees	$ _____
Appraisal Fees	$ _____
Funding Fees	$ _____
Other Lender Fees (Tax Service, Flood Certificates, etc.)	$ _____

ESCROW AND TITLE CHARGES

Escrow Fee ☐ including any Sub-Escrow Fee	$ _____
Owner's Title Insurance Policy	$ _____
Lender's Title Insurance Policy	$ _____
Document Preparation, Recording, Notary & other Fees	$ _____

OTHER EXPENSES & PRORATIONS

Prorated Property Taxes # Days _____	$ _____
Homeowners Dues # Days _____	$ _____
Transfer Tax (if charged to Buyer) Rate per $1,000 $_____	$ _____
Buyer Brokerage Fee	$ _____
Annual Insurance Premium (excluding flood & earthquake) $	$ _____
Home Warranty Program	$ _____
Wood-Destroying Pest Inspection	$ _____
Other Physical Inspection Fees _____	$ _____
HOA Transfer and/or Move-In Fees	$ _____
Other	$ _____
_____	$ _____

TOTAL ESTIMATED EXPENSES $ _____

ESTIMATED CREDITS

Prorated Property Taxes # Days _____	$ _____
Prorated Rents # Days _____	$ _____
Tenant Security Deposits	$ _____
Credit from Seller	$ _____
Other _____	$ _____
Total Estimated Credits	$ _____

ESTIMATED CASH NEEDED TO CLOSE

Purchase Price	$ _____
LESS Total Loans	- _____
Down Payment	= _____
PLUS Total Estimated Expenses	+ _____
LESS Total Estimated Credits	- _____
LESS Initial Deposits	- _____
Est. Cash Needed to Close Escrow	$ _____

ESTIMATED MONTHLY PAYMENTS

New First Loan*	$ _____
Secondary Financing*	$ _____
New Property Taxes	$ _____
Insurance (ex. flood & earthquake)	$ _____
Mortgage Insurance	$ _____
Homeowners Dues	$ _____
Mello Roos	$ _____
Other _____	$ _____
Total Estimated Payment	$ _____

* Buyer is aware that with regard to adjustable rate loans, the monthly payments may increase at various times over the life of the loan. Buyer should confirm directly with lenders all terms and conditions of said loans.

This estimate, based upon the above proposed purchase price, type of financing and projected closing date, has been prepared to assist Buyer in computing costs. Amounts will vary depending upon differences between actual and estimated repairs that may occur in the transaction, assessments, liens, impound accounts, charges by lenders, escrow companies, title insurers and other service providers and other items. Not all liens may yet have been identified. Neither Broker nor Agent guarantee these figures represent the actual, or only, amounts and charges.
By signing below Buyer acknowledges that Buyer has read, understands and received a copy of this Estimated Buyer's Costs.

Buyer _____ Date _____

Buyer _____ Date _____

Real Estate Broker (Firm) _____ DRE Lic. # _____

By (Agent) _____ DRE Lic. # _____ Date _____

Address _____ City _____ State _____ Zip _____

Telephone _____ Fax _____ E-mail _____

Published and Distributed by:
REAL ESTATE BUSINESS SERVICES, INC.
a subsidiary of the California Association of REALTORS®
525 South Virgil Avenue, Los Angeles, California 90020

SURE TRAC — The System for Success™

Reviewed by _____ Date _____

EQUAL HOUSING OPPORTUNITY

EBC REVISED 4/06 (PAGE 1 OF 1)   **ESTIMATED BUYER COSTS (EBC PAGE 1 OF 1)**

Agent: Walt Huber	Phone:	Fax:	Prepared using WINForms® software
Broker: WALT HUBER, REALTOR	123 Winsail	, MARINA DEL REY CA 90292	

the seller), but in other transactions the buyer may be responsible for the points. If buyer pays points, they are shown as a debit on the buyer's statement.

Several other loan costs are customarily charged to the buyer in a real estate sale. These include the appraisal fee, the credit report fee, reserve amounts for taxes and insurance, and prepaid interest.

The **appraisal fee** and **credit report fee** are usually set at a flat rate, which varies depending on the location of the property and the person or firm preparing the report. Residential appraisals usually cost a few hundred dollars and credit reports are generally less than $100.

An *IMPOUND ACCOUNT* (or *reserve account*) *is a trust account maintained by the lender for paying property taxes and mortgage insurance premiums.* The borrower pays a portion of these expenses as a part of each monthly loan payment, and the lender deposits those contributions in the impound account. When the taxes or insurance premiums become due, the lender pays them out of the impound account.

In some cases a lender requires the borrower to make an initial deposit into an impound account at closing. It might be enough to cover six months' or one year's taxes and insurance. In California, a lender can't require an impound account for a conventional loan on an owner-occupied, single-family home unless the loan amount is more than 80% of the appraised value of the property.

PREPAID INTEREST (*also called* **interim interest**) *is the amount of interest due on the loan during the first (partial) month of the loan term.* Interest on real estate loans is generally paid in arrears. In other words, the interest for a given month is paid at the end of that month; the loan payment due on October 1 includes the interest accrued during September. However, when a new loan is made, the interest is paid in advance (at closing) for the month in which closing takes place.

> **Example:** Closing occurs on June 15. Interest for the period from June 15 through June 30 is paid at closing. The first regular payment on the loan is then due on August 1, and it covers the interest due for the month of July.

To calculate the interim interest due, you need to find out the approximate amount of interest owed per day. First multiply the loan amount by the annual interest rate to get an annual interest amount. Divide that amount by 365 to get the amount of interest owed per day. Multiply the daily amount times the number of days between the closing date and the end of the month (in the example above, it's 16 days). This gives you the amount of interim interest that will have to be paid at closing.

> **Example:** Suppose that the buyer's loan in the previous example was for $200,000 with a 12% annual interest rate.
>
> $200,000 x .12 = $24,000 (annual interest)
> $24,000 ÷ 365 = $65.75 (daily interest)
> $65.75 x 16 days = $1,052 (interim interest)

The buyer will also be required to take out a **hazard insurance policy** (or assume the seller's policy). A premium for at least one year's coverage is usually paid at closing.

Other items typically charged to the buyer include a share of the **escrow fee** and some of the **notary fees** and **recording fees**. The buyer will also be charged an **attorney's fee** if he or she retained a lawyer. The cost of the **structural pest control inspection** (required by most lenders) may be the buyer's responsibility, depending on the parties' agreement.

CHAPTER 11

The buyer will probably also be charged for **title insurance**. Although the allocation of this expense varies according to local custom, it's common to have the buyer pay for the lender's policy while the seller pays for the owner's policy. Of course, the parties may agree to any other allocation of the costs, as long as they include that agreement in the purchase agreement or escrow instructions.

Depending on the status of the **property taxes**, the buyer may get a credit or may owe an amount to the seller. If the seller has paid the property taxes for a period after the closing date, the buyer will have to reimburse the seller. If the taxes are in arrears, the seller will owe the buyer. Delinquent taxes (past due) are always owed by seller.

> **Example:** The closing date is June 15, and the taxes have been paid through the end of June. The buyer owes the seller an amount equal to the tax for the last half of June.
>
> If the closing date was not until July 15, the seller would owe the buyer the amount of tax due from the end of June until July 15.

To calculate the amount of tax payable, you need to know the daily rate of the tax and the number of days for which each party is responsible. The expense can then be prorated (allocated) between the parties. Proration is also used to allocate interest on assumed loans, premiums on assumed insurance policies, and rents from income property. (See the proration discussion at the end of this section.)

All California property buyers are required to fill out a transfer statement for the county assessor. A fee is charged to buyers who file a late or incorrect filing. Escrow agents are now suggesting that the buyer file this form as part of closing.

D. BUYER'S CREDITS

To determine how much the buyer will actually be required to pay at closing, certain credits must be deducted from the buyer's closing costs. The proceeds of a new or assumed loan are a credit for the buyer. If the buyer has already given the lender a deposit to cover initial loan costs such as the appraisal and credit report, this will also be listed as a credit on the settlement statement. As mentioned above, the buyer may be entitled to credits for some prorations such as taxes, insurance, or rents.

E. SELLER'S COST (Debits)

The seller's major cost at closing is usually the **payoff of any existing loans**. The seller may also be charged a **prepayment penalty** in connection with the payoff (see Chapter 12), and will be responsible for a prorated portion of the **interest** due for the month of closing. All of these appear as debits on the seller's settlement statement. If the buyer is assuming or taking subject to the seller's loan, or if the seller is carrying back a trust deed from the buyer, those would also be debits for the seller.

The seller is usually also debited for the **broker's commission,** part of the **escrow fee**, and some **notary fees** and **recording fees**. If the seller was represented by a lawyer, he or she will also have to pay an **attorney's fee**.

Depending on local custom or the parties' agreement, the seller may be responsible for all or part of the **title insurance premium**, the **pest control inspection** (and any necessary repairs), and **discount points** on the buyer's loan. If the property taxes are in arrears, the seller will also owe the tax due up to the date of closing.

414

The documentary transfer tax is ordinarily paid by the seller. The **DOCUMENTARY TRANSFER TAX** *is a tax applied to every transfer of real estate in most California cities and counties. The rate is $ .55 for each $500 of the sales price or $1.10 for each $1,000.*

Example: The house is being sold for $100,000.

$100,000 ÷ 500 = 200
200 x $.55 = $110
The seller is required to pay $110 for the documentary transfer tax.

Note that the documentary transfer tax doesn't apply to the amount of any loans the buyer is assuming or taking subject to. If the buyer in the example above had assumed the seller's existing $70,000 trust deed, the tax would only be due on the $30,000 difference between the sales price and the assumed loan. The tax would then be only $33.

For income property, the seller may get a credit for prorated **rents** paid in advance.

F. SELLER'S CREDITS

The seller's major credit is, of course, the **purchase price**. In addition to this, the seller may be credited for **prorated taxes** and **insurance premiums**. If there was an impound account for an existing loan, any remaining balance in the account will be credited to the seller.

G. PRORATIONS

The term **PRORATE** *means to divide or distribute proportionately.* In a real estate sale, there are often expenses that must be prorated so that each party takes care of amounts owed during his or her ownership of the property.

Some of the items that may need to be prorated are property taxes, hazard insurance premiums, rents, and interest on loans.

Although prorating may seem complicated, it's really just a process of dividing an expense as of a specific date. The date most commonly used for computing prorations is the date of close of escrow, since that's usually the date when the actual change of ownership occurs. The buyer's responsibility begins on the closing date—that is, the buyer pays the costs for that day.

Example: The seller paid for a one-year hazard insurance policy in advance. The policy runs from January 1 through December 31. The premium was $675. Escrow closes on April 1. The insurance payment must be prorated; the buyer must reimburse the seller for the amount paid for the period from April 1 through December 31.

The first step in prorating this expense is to figure out how much the insurance costs per day. Divide the total cost by the number of days in the year: $675 ÷ 365 days = $1.85 per day.

Since the buyer becomes responsible for the insurance costs as of April 1, the seller is required to pay for the period from January 1 through March 31 (90 days). Multiply the number of days by the cost per day: 90 days x $1.85 = $166.50. That's the seller's portion of the cost.

Subtract the seller's portion from the total amount paid: $675 - $166.50 = $508.50. The buyer must pay the seller $508.50 as the prorated portion of the hazard insurance premium.

Of course, the buyer should get an assignment from the hazard insurance company. The assignment will name the new owner as the insured party on the policy.

When figuring prorations, a 360-day year and 30-day months are sometimes used to simplify the calculations. (Thus, although February has 28 days and March has 31, in the proration process both would be treated as having 30 days.) However, now that calculators are available in almost every office, there is a trend toward using a 365-day year (or 366 days for a leap year) and the actual number of days in each month. The method used in a particular transaction depends on the preference of the escrow agent or lender. If the lender is using a 360-day year on a conventional loan, it may tell the escrow agent to use a 360-day year. A 365-day year is used for most new VA and FHA loans.

Some title companies still use preprinted forms that calculate prorations based on a 360-day year and **30-day months**. However, if the client requests it, they will change the form and calculate using the actual number of days. The real estate agent should ask which method is being used; the parties may request one method or the other.

H. CLOSING

Once the buyer's loan is approved, the lender forwards the loan documents to the escrow agent. Then the buyer is in a position to fulfill his or her obligations by signing the loan documents, which the escrow agent returns to the lender. If all other conditions in the escrow instructions have been met, the transaction is ready to close.

At this point, the buyer may not have seen the property for weeks or even months. It's a good idea for the buyer to inspect the property again personally just before closing. He or she should make sure that the property and the fixtures are in the same condition that they were in when the purchase agreement was signed.

In most transactions, the buyer's lender disburses the loan funds to the title company insuring the transaction. The escrow agent also sends the seller's deed to the title company, with instructions to record it on receipt of the loan funds. A final title search is run to make sure that no new liens have attached to the property. Then the title company has the deed, loan documents, and any other documents recorded. The title company turns the loan funds over to the escrow agent.

The actual closing may take place at the escrow agent's office, or it may be carried out by mail. The deed is delivered to the buyer and the purchase money is delivered to the seller. Each party receives a final settlement statement. The buyer will also receive copies of the loan documents, insurance policies, and inspection reports. An escrow agent is required by law to issue a settlement statement.

Sometimes there is money left over in an escrow account after closing. This can happen when the actual cost of a particular item (such as the pest inspection) turns out to be less than the amount deposited for that purpose. Often the parties (and the agents) are so concerned with the details of closing that they forget to tie up loose ends. Check to see that there aren't any leftovers in the escrow account.

VII. Title Insurance

A title insurance policy is a contract in which the insurance company agrees to **INDEMNIFY** the policyholder against losses caused by defects in title. In other words, if there turns out to be something

416

wrong with the title, and the policyholder loses money (or even the property) as a result, the company will compensate or reimburse the policyholder. Different types of title policies cover different types of title problems, and no policy covers every possible risk.

 www.clta.org/for-consumers/consumer-general.html
Title Insurance FAQs

A. OBTAINING TITLE INSURANCE

Almost all title insurance policies are taken out when property is about to be transferred or encumbered. The policyholder is usually a buyer or lender.

There are generally two steps in taking out a title insurance policy. The first step is ordering a **title search**.

Most title insurance companies have their own *TITLE PLANT—a microfilmed copy of the public record—which is constantly updated.* This way the title searchers don't have to spend all their time in the county recorder's office.

Title companies also have tract indexes of recorded documents. In a *TRACT INDEX, the recorded documents pertaining to a particular piece of property are listed together.* So you can look up Lot 3, Block 9 of the Hindenberg Addition and find a list of all the recorded deeds, trust deeds, easements (and so forth) with that legal description. A tract index is much easier to use than a grantor/grantee index.

The title searcher finds the most recent deeds for the property in question, tracking the chain of title backwards in time. The searcher also looks for other recorded documents that affect the chain of title or create encumbrances. In addition, probate, domestic, and bankruptcy court files may have to be checked, since court orders based on wills, intestate succession, dissolution of marriage, and bankruptcy are often not recorded.

After the title search is completed, a title examiner prepares a *PRELIMINARY REPORT on the condition of the title, which lists all the defects and encumbrances of record.* These will be listed as exceptions in the insurance policy and excluded from coverage. (At this stage, the property owner may eliminate some of the exceptions by paying off liens.)

The second step in the process is the issuance of the title insurance policy itself. The title company charges a single premium, which covers the entire life of the policy. The policy lasts as long as the policyholder has a legal interest in the property. The amount of the premium depends on the amount of the coverage. A policy with $100,000 worth of coverage would indemnify the policyholder for any losses up to $100,000.

1. How Title Insurance Works

Sometimes there are *LATENT* (hidden) title defects that can't be discovered by a search of the public record. These include forgery or fraud by a grantee, a deed or release of lien executed by a minor or incompetent person, a deed or trust deed that indicates the wrong marital status, and deeds that weren't properly delivered. This kind of hidden defect is usually covered by a title insurance policy; the title company takes on the risk that these defects may exist. Other problems that don't show up on the public record, such as adverse possession, are often not covered.

The title company also insures against its own errors. If there's a recorded lien or an easement that the title searcher fails to discover, that encumbrance won't be listed as an

417

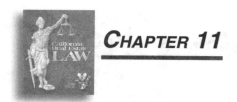

exception to the policy. As a result, any losses that result from that encumbrance will be covered. This is also true if the policy lists an encumbrance incorrectly.

> **Case Example:** The J.H. Trisdale Company was buying some property, so it applied for title insurance. The title search revealed that Pacific Gas & Electric had a recorded easement across the property.
>
> The title company's preliminary report and the policy itself listed this easement as an exception from coverage. Unfortunately, the report and policy erroneously stated that the easement holder was Pacific Telephone & Telegraph, not Pacific Gas & Electric. As a result, the report and policy gave the impression that there was an easement for telephone poles and lines, not one for electrical transmission lines.
>
> The Trisdale Company went ahead and bought the property. When the company later discovered the true nature of the easement, it sued the title insurer. Power lines have a much greater impact on the value of property than telephone lines, so the Trisdale Company claimed it would not have paid the same price for the property (or might not have bought it at all) if it had been aware of the power line easement. Since the policy had failed to accurately list the easement as an exception from coverage, the title company was liable for any loss resulting from the easement. *J.H. Trisdale, Inc. v. Shasta County Title Co.*, 146 Cal. App. 2d 831, 304 P.2d 832 (1956).

B. TYPES OF COVERAGE

A title insurance policy can generally be classified either as a standard coverage policy or an extended coverage policy. Either type of policy can be an owner's policy (insuring the buyer), a lender's policy (insuring the lender), or a joint protection policy (insuring both the buyer and the lender). Lenders require title insurance to make sure that their trust deed has first lien position (see Chapter 12), and they generally insist on extended coverage. Extended coverage is also becoming a more common choice for owners.

[handwritten: NO SURVEY OR INSPECTION] The **STANDARD COVERAGE POLICY** *insures against any recorded encumbrances that aren't listed as exceptions in the policy. It also insures against hidden title defects such as forgery, fraud, incompetency, and improperly delivered deeds.* The standard policy doesn't insure against claims and problems that might be disclosed by an inspection or survey of the property, such as unrecorded easements, encroachments, boundary disputes, and adverse possession.

[handwritten: INCLUDES: • survey • inspection] The **EXTENDED COVERAGE POLICY** *insures against all matters covered by the standard policy, plus problems that should be discovered through inspection of the property.* In fact, before issuing an extended policy, a title company sends an inspector out to take a look around. The inspector is trained as a surveyor, and in some cases will actually survey the property. If the inspection turns up encroachments, adverse possessors, boundary problems, and so on, these will be listed as exceptions to the coverage. However, if any of these problems aren't specifically listed as exceptions, the extended policy covers them. It also insures against unrecorded easements, restrictions, and liens, including mechanics' liens for work begun before the closing date.

A policyholder can obtain coverage for a specific type of problem the policies don't ordinarily cover by paying extra for a **SPECIAL ENDORSEMENT** *to cover that problem.* However, title insurance companies generally refuse to insure against losses due to government action such as condemnation or changes in zoning. And they won't cover defects and encumbrances created by the policyholder, or unrecorded defects and encumbrances that the policyholder is aware of but doesn't disclose to the title company.

Title Insurance Coverage

Standard Coverage

Latent title defects:
- Forged deeds
- Incompetent grantors

Recorded encumbrances not listed as exceptions

Marketable title

Access to public street

Extended Coverage

All of the above, plus:

Defects that should be apparent from inspection or survey
- Adverse possessors
- Encroachments
- Boundary problems

Unrecorded encumbrances

C. DUTY TO DEFEND

A title insurance policy obligates the title company to handle the legal defense of the title if someone makes a claim against it.

Case Example: The Jarchows and the Canaviers wanted to buy a three-acre parcel. They took out a title policy with $72,000 worth of coverage. The title search turned up a recorded deed that gave an easement to a neighbor, Mr. Perez, but by an oversight, the Perez easement wasn't disclosed in the preliminary report or the policy.

Shortly after closing, Perez told the Jarchows and Canaviers about his easement. They, in turn, contacted the title company about Perez's claim. The title company refused to take any action, leaving it up to the Jarchows and the Canaviers to clear their title.

After a successful quiet title suit against Perez (the conveyance of the easement was held to be void), the Jarchows and the Canaviers sued the title company. In the policy, the title company agreed to defend the policyholders' title; by failing to do so the company breached the insurance contract. A judgment was entered against the title company for $7,100 to cover the policyholders' attorney's fees, plus $200,000 for bad faith and negligent infliction of emotional distress. *Jarchow v. Transamerica Title*, 48 Cal. App. 3d 917,122 Cal. Rptr. 470 (1975).

The title insurance company is not required to initiate a lawsuit for the policyholder.

Case Example: In September 1986, the Mannecks purchased a home for $200,000, and had a policy of title insurance from Lawyers Title Insurance Corporation (Lawyers). In 1988 they had the property surveyed to replace a fence. The survey showed that "virtually everything beyond their back door, including their swimming pool, surrounding deck and appurtenant equipment, was constructed on adjoining property not owned by the plaintiffs." ▼

The Mannecks notified Lawyers and demanded an immediate lawsuit for a prescriptive easement. Lawyers stated that they were covered under their policy only in the event they were "forced to remove your existing structure other than a boundary wall or fence" and since there was no impeding removal, there was no coverage for their claim.

The Mannecks sued Lawyers for breach of contract for failing to litigate on their behalf and to indemnify them for their losses. Subsequently, Mannecks sold the home. The problem was later settled by Lawyers for the benefit of the new owners by getting title to the land under the improvement.

The court of appeal held that the language of the policy was clear and Lawyers was not obligated to bring a lawsuit on behalf of Mannecks. Since the Mannecks were not forced to remove their improvements, they were not covered under the title insurance policy. *Manneck v. Lawyers Title Ins. Corp.*, 28 Cal. App. 4th 1294, 33 Cal. Rptr. 2d 771 (1994).

1. Abstract and Opinion

Before title insurance was developed, a buyer would obtain an *ABSTRACT OF TITLE, which is a condensed history of the title based on the public record*. The buyer would then have the abstract examined by a lawyer, who would give a professional opinion on the condition of the title. However, this process did not protect the buyer against latent or undiscovered defects in the title. If the lawyer was negligent, the buyer could sue for malpractice, but that was the only recourse.

It's still possible to get an abstract instead of title insurance, but todays virtually all real estate purchase and loan transactions in California are insured.

VIII. CHAPTER SUMMARY

1. Escrow is an arrangement in which money and documents are held by a third party on behalf of the buyer and seller. The purpose of escrow is to ensure that the concerns of the buyer, the seller, and the lender are all met before the transaction is final.

2. An escrow agent may be a bank or other financial institution, a title insurance company, an independent escrow firm, a lawyer, or a real estate broker.

3. The requirements for a valid escrow are an enforceable contract between the parties, relinquishment of control, a valid deed, an escrow agent, and escrow instructions with conditions.

4. Escrow instructions are the escrow agent's written authorization to deliver the funds and the deed. They set out the conditions that the buyer and seller must meet before they will be entitled to delivery.

5. Escrow may be terminated when all of the conditions have been met and the transaction concludes; or when the parties agree to cancel the escrow; or when the escrow instructions expire; or when there is a default.

6. Title does not pass to the new owner until all of the conditions specified in the instructions have been performed. However, the relation back doctrine provides that in special circumstances, the date of delivery of the deed to the new owner relates back to the date it was deposited in escrow.

7. The Real Estate Settlement Procedures Act (RESPA) requires lenders to disclose information regarding closing costs to loan applicants. RESPA applies to almost all institutional loans for residential purchases. When RESPA applies, the lender must itemize all loan settlement charges on a Uniform Settlement Statement.

8. A settlement statement sets out the costs each party is to pay and the amounts each is to receive at closing. A transaction settlement guide shows how the various charges and credits are usually allocated, but the buyer and seller may agree to a different allocation.

9. Certain expenses, such as rents, taxes, or hazard insurance premiums, may need to be prorated between the parties. Proration is simply the division of an expense or revenue based on a 30-day month so that each party is responsible for the amount owed during his or her ownership of the property.

10. A title insurance policy indemnifies a buyer or lender for losses resulting from undiscovered title defects. The title company prepares a preliminary report listing the known defects and encumbrances. Then the company issues a standard or extended coverage policy. A standard policy insures against latent defects and recorded encumbrances that aren't listed as exceptions. An extended coverage policy also insures against unrecorded encumbrances, and against problems that should be discovered by an inspection or survey of the property.

IX. KEY TERMS

closing	documentary transfer tax	prorations
conversion	escrow	relation back doctrine
credits	good faith estimate (GFE)	RESPA
debits	impound account	settlement statement
delivery	interpleader	title insurance
deposit	loan origination fee	transaction settlement
discount points	prepaid (interim) interest	guide

CHAPTER 11

X. CHAPTER QUIZ

1. In northern California, escrows are usually handled through which of the following?

    a. Independent escrow companies
    b. Attorneys
    c. Real estate brokers
    d. Title insurance companies

2. In southern California, escrows are usually handled through which of the following?

    a. Real estate brokers
    b. Real estate attorneys
    c. Independent escrow companies
    d. Lending institutions

3. Regarding escrow agents, which of the following is correct?

    a. They cannot pay a fee to someone for referring customers to them
    b. They can pay a fee for a customer referral provided it does not exceed $50
    c. They can pay a fee for a customer referral provided it does not exceed $100
    d. They can pay a fee for a customer referral provided it does not exceed 15% of the escrow fee paid by the seller

4. When Walker deposited a deed in a valid escrow:

    a. if he gives the escrow holder written notice, the deed must be returned to him.
    b. the deed cannot be removed by Walker unless the escrow terminates.
    c. Walker must give an escrow holder either a written or verbal five-day notice after which the deed will be returned to him.
    d. the law requires Walker to post a $1,000 bond in order to have the deed returned to him.

5. Which of the following is not a requirement for a valid sale escrow?

    a. Escrow instructions with conditions
    b. A valid deed
    c. An enforceable contract
    d. The use of an attorney

6. The parties verbally agreed on the purchase and sale of the property and subsequently each signed escrow instructions. With regard to the escrow:

    a. the escrow is invalid without an underlying signed written purchase agreement.
    b. the escrow is valid only if the parties signed a written purchase agreement.
    c. the written escrow instructions can serve as the parties' contract.
    d. only the court can determine if the escrow is valid.

7. When the time for an escrow expires and the conditions have not been performed:

    a. the escrow is automatically terminated.
    b. escrow generally continues until the parties give mutual instructions to cancel.
    c. the escrow can be terminated only upon a court order.
    d. the escrow is automatically extended for 60 days.

8. If the escrow is cancelled due to default:
   a. that also cancels the underlying purchase contract.
   b. the underlying purchase contract is still valid.
   c. only the seller decides whether the underlying purchase contract is canceled or valid.
   d. none of the above are correct answers.

9. The Doctrine of Relation Back:
   a. means the transfer of title relates back to the date the deed was deposited in escrow.
   b. applies when the property owner dies and title to property relates back to the closest heir.
   c. is a test for incompetency if the person cannot remember relationships that occurred back in their past.
   d. applies if the legal description on the current deed is inaccurate and the legal description relates back to the most recent recorded deed with the correct legal description.

10. A debit is which of the following?
   a. An amount to be received
   b. An amount owed or charge that must be paid
   c. A machine that dispenses cash
   d. All of the above

ANSWERS: 1. d.; 2. c.; 3. a.; 4. b.; 5. d.; 6. c.; 7. b.; 8. b.; 9. a.; 10. b.

CHAPTER 12
Real Estate Financing

CHAPTER OVERVIEW

It takes a lot more than pocket change to buy real estate. As a result, most real estate purchases involve a loan, and some involve more than one. Buyers, sellers, and real estate agents need to understand the rights and obligations of borrowers and lenders: buyers, since they'll be borrowers; sellers, since they may be lenders; and agents, since they'll have to help the parties obtain financing.

This chapter explains promissory notes and security agreements, the basic financing documents. It describes the foreclosure process—what happens when a borrower defaults. It also takes a brief look at the land contract, a security device no longer widely used in California. The chapter closes with an overview of some state and federal consumer protection laws that regulate real estate lending.

I. Promissory Notes

A **PROMISSORY NOTE** *makes a promise to repay a debt*. One person loans another money, and the other signs a promissory note, promising to repay the loan (plus interest, in most cases). *The borrower who signs the note is called the **MAKER**, and the lender is called the **PAYEE**.* Today, almost all promissory notes are negotiable instruments. One reason this is true is because of secondary marketing. Unless the promissory note given for a real estate loan is negotiable, it will be very difficult for the lender to sell the loan on the secondary market. The big agencies such as Fannie Mae and Freddie Mac, also known as the Federal National Mortgage Association (FNMA) and Federal Home Loan Mortgage Corporation (FHLMC), won't even consider it.

A. RELATIONSHIP BETWEEN PROMISSORY NOTE AND SECURITY AGREEMENT

A person borrowing money to buy real estate signs a promissory note in favor of the lender. In addition, the borrower signs a security agreement, such as a deed of trust or mortgage. The **SECURITY AGREEMENT** *is a contract that makes the real property collateral for the loan*. It creates a lien on the property. If the borrower doesn't repay as agreed in the promissory note,

CHAPTER 12

the security agreement gives the lender the right to foreclose. Basically, in foreclosure the property is sold and the proceeds are used to pay off the loan balance.

A promissory note can be enforced whether or not it is accompanied by a security agreement. The payee/lender can file a lawsuit and obtain a judgment if the maker/borrower breaches by failing to repay. Without a security agreement, however, the judgment may turn out to be uncollectible. For example, the borrower may already have resold the property, so there's nothing left for a judgment lien to attach to.

By creating a lien on the property at the time of the loan, a security agreement ensures that the lender will be able to get at least some of its money back. Because real estate loans are substantial sums, they are virtually always secured. Security agreements will be discussed in detail in the next section of the chapter. For now, let's look more closely at promissory notes.

B. BASIC NOTE PROVISIONS

In a real estate loan transaction, the promissory note should state that it is secured. The note should identify the security agreement by date or recording number. The note and the security agreement are signed on the same date, and are linked together. If the lender negotiates the note, the security interest in the property is automatically transferred along with it. The security agreement can't be assigned unless the right to payment under the note is also transferred.

The note generally states the *loan amount (the **PRINCIPAL**)*, the amount of the payments, and when and how the payments are to be made. It includes the **MATURITY DATE**, *when the loan is to be fully paid*. The note also lists the interest rate, which may be either fixed or adjustable.

CHAPTER 12

> 1. **PROMISSORY NOTE** – A promise to repay a loan. States the terms of repayment and gives the lender the right to sue.
>
> 2. **SECURITY AGREEMENT** – Creates a lien against the property and gives the lender the right to foreclose after default (deed of trust or mortgage).

When a noninstitutional lender (a private individual or business, as opposed to a bank, savings bank, or similar regulated lending institution) makes an adjustable-rate loan secured by residential property with four units or less, California law requires the promissory note to include this warning in large, boldface type: **NOTICE TO BORROWER: THIS DOCUMENT CONTAINS PROVISIONS FOR AN ADJUSTABLE INTEREST RATE**. The law also places a number of restrictions on noninstitutional, residential, adjustable-rate loans; for example, the rate can't change more than once every six months.

Promissory notes are classified according to the way the principal and interest are to be paid. With a *STRAIGHT NOTE, the periodic payments are interest only, and the full amount of the principal is due in a lump sum when the loan term ends* (see **Figure 12-1**). With an *INSTALLMENT NOTE, the periodic payments include part of the principal as well as interest*. If the installment note is fully amortized, the amount of the payments is enough to pay off the entire loan, both principal and interest, by the end of the term. If it is only partially amortized, the payments don't cover the full amount of principal and interest, and a balloon payment will be due at the end of the term.

A *BALLOON PAYMENT LOAN is one that provides for a final payment that is more than twice the amount of the immediately preceding six regularly scheduled payments or contains a call provision*. Borrowers often find it more difficult than they anticipated to come up with the extra money at the end of the loan. As a result, California law doesn't allow balloon payments on certain loans secured by residential property. (This rule is explained in connection with the Mortgage Loan Broker Law, at the end of this chapter.) When a residential loan with a term longer than one year calls for a balloon payment, the lender is usually required to send the borrower by certified mail a reminder notice at least 90 days (but not more than 150 days) before the balloon payment is due.

A promissory note usually contains provisions that explain the consequences of failure to pay as agreed. Real estate lenders often protect themselves with late charges, acceleration clauses, and similar provisions. All of these are recited in the promissory note. We'll discuss these and other optional loan terms later in the chapter, after an overview of security agreements.

II. Security Agreements

A security agreement is made between a lender and a borrower and creates a security interest in property pledged or hypothecated.

As you've seen, a loan can be secured or unsecured. An unsecured lender has a legal right to be repaid, but there's no assurance that a judgment against the borrower will be collectible. Therefore, lenders prefer to obtain a security interest in the borrower's property. Then if the borrower defaults, the lender can recover the money by having the property sold.

The oldest and simplest security arrangement is the pawnbroker's. To borrow money from a pawnbroker, you have to bring in some property as security for the loan—your great-grandfather's gold watch, for example. If you repay the loan within a specified period, you get the watch back. *If that period expires and you haven't paid the pawnbroker, he or she will sell the watch and keep the proceeds. The legal term for this system is PLEDGING*; your great-grandfather's watch is the pledge.

Figure 12-1

Escrow No.

STRAIGHT NOTE

$ California   20

after date, for value received,

I/We promise to pay in lawful money of the United States of America, to

or order, at place designated by payee, the principal sum of

DOLLARS,

with interest in like lawful money from   , until paid at the

rate of   per cent per annum, payable

Principal and interest payable in lawful money of the United States of America. Should default be made in payment of interest when due the whole sum of principal and interest shall become immediately due at the option of the holder of this note. If action be instituted on this note I promise to pay such sum as the Court may fix as Attorney's fees. This note is secured by a Deed of Trust.

FTG-3014

CHAPTER 12

In pledging, you're required to turn over possession of the security property to the lender, but the security arrangement for a real estate loan is more sophisticated. *You don't have to give up possession of your house to get the loan. You only have to grant the lender the right to sell the house in case you default. This is called HYPOTHECATION.*

According to the original theory behind real estate security agreements, the borrower transferred title to the property to the lender (or a neutral third party) during the loan period. When the loan was paid off, title was transferred back to the borrower. The language in some security agreements still reflects this theory, stating that the borrower "conveys" the property; after the loan is paid off, a "reconveyance" is recorded. This is essentially a legal fiction. For all practical purposes, the security agreement merely creates a voluntary lien against the property (see Chapter 3), and no real transfer of title is involved. The lien enables the lender to foreclose if the borrower defaults.

There are two main types of real property security agreements: **deeds of trust** (also called **trust deeds**) and **mortgages**. Either type must be in writing and must meet the formal requirements for a deed (see Chapter 10). Either creates a lien on everything that would be transferred by a deed—so it includes the fixtures and the appurtenances such as water rights, as well as the land and the improvements (see Chapter 2).

The key difference between the two types is their foreclosure procedures. Mortgages historically did not have a power of sale clause, requiring foreclosure judicially—that is, by filing a lawsuit. A deed of trust may also be foreclosed judicially, but because a deed of trust does contain a power of sale clause, the lender may foreclose without going to court (called a trustee's sale or nonjudicial foreclosure). That saves the lender a lot of time, money and effort.

In California, nearly all lenders use deeds of trust instead of mortgages.

A survey of California title insurers indicated that deeds of trust are used in about 98% of all recorded real estate transactions. For this reason, our discussion will focus on deeds of trust.

A. DEEDS OF TRUST

There are three parties to a deed of trust: the *TRUSTOR (the borrower)*, the *BENEFICIARY (the lender)*, and the *TRUSTEE (a neutral third party)*. The trustor/borrower makes payments to the beneficiary/lender; the trustee only has two possible duties: to reconvey the deed of trust if the loan is repaid in full or to conduct foreclosure proceedings if the borrower defaults.

Institutional lenders (that is, banks and savings banks) almost always use standard forms for their trust deeds. This is necessary if the loan is going to be sold to the FNMA or FHLMC. These secondary marketing agencies require the use of standard forms because they don't have time to review all the terms of a complicated security agreement for each transaction, and because they insist on certain protective provisions. (A copy of a different type of deed of trust is shown in **Figure 12-2**.)

1. Basic Provisions

A trust deed identifies the parties and should include a full legal description of the security property. A lender doesn't want there to be any doubt about what its lien covers in case foreclosure is necessary.

The trust deed refers to the underlying debt and the promissory note that it secures.

Figure 12-2

RECORDING REQUESTED BY

ORDER #
APN

WHEN RECORDED MAIL TO

Name
Street
Address
City &
State

SPACE ABOVE THIS LINE FOR RECORDER'S USE

SHORT FORM DEED OF TRUST AND ASSIGNMENT OF RENTS

This Deed of Trust, made this ___ day of ___, between ___, herein called TRUSTOR,

whose address is ___

(number and street)　(city)　(state)　(zip)

OLD REPUBLIC TITLE COMPANY, a California corporation, herein called TRUSTEE, and

___, herein called BENEFICIARY,

Witnesseth: That Trustor IRREVOCABLY GRANTS, TRANSFERS AND ASSIGNS TO TRUSTEE IN TRUST, WITH POWER OF SALE, that property in ___ County, California, described on *"Exhibit A" attached hereto*

In the event the herein described property or any part thereof, or any interest therein is sold, agreed to be sold, conveyed or alienated by the Trustor, or by the operation of law or otherwise, all obligations secured by this instrument, irrespective of the maturity dates expressed therein, at the option of the holder hereof and without demand or notice shall immediately become due and payable.

TOGETHER WITH the rents, issues and profits thereof, SUBJECT, HOWEVER, to the right, power and authority given to and conferred upon Beneficiary by paragraph (10) of the provisions incorporated herein by reference to collect and apply such rents, issues and profits.

For the Purpose of Securing: 1. Performance of each agreement of Trustor incorporated by reference or contained herein. 2. Payment of the indebtedness evidenced by one promissory note of even date herewith, and any extension or renewal thereof, in the principal sum of $ ___ executed by Trustor in favor of Beneficiary or order. 3. Payment of such further sums as the then record owner of said property hereafter may borrow from Beneficiary, when evidenced by another note (or notes) reciting it is so secured.

To Protect the Security of This Deed of Trust, Trustor Agrees: By the execution and delivery of this Deed of Trust and the note secured hereby, that provisions (1) to (14), inclusive, of the fictitious deed of trust recorded in Santa Barbara County and Sonoma County October 18, 1961, and in all other counties October 23, 1961, in the book and at the page of Official Records in the office of the county recorder of the county where said property is located, noted below opposite the name of such county, viz.:

COUNTY	BOOK	PG	COUNTY	BOOK	PG	COUNTY	BOOK	PG	COUNTY	BOOK	PG	COUNTY	BOOK	PG
Alameda	435	684	Imperial	1091	501	Modoc	184	851	San Diego Series 2 Book 1961 Page 183887			Sonoma	1851	689
Alpine	1	250	Inyo	147	598	Mono	52	429	San Francisco	A332	905	Stanislaus	1715	456
Amador	104	348	Kern	3427	60	Monterey	2194	538	San Joaquin	2470	311	Sutter	572	297
Butte	1145	1	Kings	792	833	Napa	639	86	San Luis Obispo	1151	12	Tehama	401	289
Calaveras	145	152	Lake	362	39	Nevada	305	320	San Mateo	4078	420	Trinity	93	366
Colusa	296	617	Lassen	171	471	Orange	5889	611	Santa Barbara	1878	860	Tulare	2294	275
Contra Costa	3978	47	Los Angeles	T2055	899	Placer	895	301	Santa Clara	5336	341	Tuolumne	135	47
Del Norte	78	414	Madera	810	170	Plumas	151	5	Santa Cruz	1431	494	Ventura	2062	386
El Dorado	568	456	Marin	1508	339	Riverside	3005	523	Shasta	684	528	Yolo	653	245
Fresno	4626	572	Mariposa	77	292	Sacramento	4331	62	Sierra	29	335	Yuba	334	486
Glenn	422	184	Mendocino	579	530	San Benito	271	383	Siskiyou	468	181			
Humboldt	657	527	Merced	1547	538	San Bernardino	5567	61	Solano	1105	182			

(which provisions, identical in all counties, are printed on the reverse hereof) hereby are adopted and incorporated herein and made a part hereof as fully as though set forth herein at length; that he will observe and perform said provisions; and that the references to property, obligations, and parties in said provisions shall be construed to refer to the property, obligations, and parties set forth in this Deed of Trust.

The undersigned Trustor requests that a copy of any Notice of Default and of any Notice of Sale hereunder be mailed to him at his address hereinbefore set forth.

STATE OF CALIFORNIA
COUNTY OF ___ } SS.

On ___ before me, the undersigned, a Notary Public in and for said State, personally appeared ___

personally known to me (or proved to me on the basis of satisfactory evidence) to be the person(s) whose name(s) is/are subscribed to the within instrument and acknowledged to me that he/she/they executed the same in his /her /their authorized capacity(ies), and that by his/her/their signature(s) on the instrument the person(s), or the entity upon behalf of which the person(s) acted, executed the instrument.
WITNESS my hand and official seal.

Signature ___

Notary Public in and for said County and State　(Type or Print)　(Seal)

ORT 215 [1/94]　**Note: Legal Description Must Be Attached As "Exhibit A" Prior To Recordation**

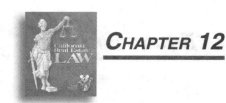

CHAPTER 12

It states the total amount of the debt and the maturity date, but usually doesn't go into more detail. The interest rate and the amount of the payments, late charges, and other charges are generally found only in the note. However, when a noninstitutional loan secured by residential property (one-to-four units) is subject to an adjustable interest rate, a provision explaining the rate must be included in the trust deed as well as the note.

Deeds of trust do go into considerable detail about the borrower's obligations regarding care of the property and the title. The borrower agrees to insure the property against fire and other hazards. (California law prevents the lender from requiring insurance for more than the replacement value of the improvements, however.) The borrower must not commit WASTE (*something that substantially decreases the value of the property*) or allow the property to deteriorate. The trust deed grants the lender the right to inspect the property, to make sure the borrower is maintaining it.

The borrower agrees to keep property taxes, special assessments, and insurance up to date. If the borrower allows any of these bills to become delinquent, the lender has the right (but not the obligation) to pay them. This is important to the lender, since delinquent taxes reduce the value of the security property. If the delinquencies become severe, the taxing authority can foreclose—and the tax liens have higher priority than the trust deed (see Chapter 3). Any amounts the lender pays to prevent the taxes from becoming delinquent or the insurance from lapsing will be added to the borrower's debt and may cause the lender to declare a default and foreclose.

The key provision in a deed of trust—the one that makes it different from a mortgage—is the **POWER OF SALE CLAUSE**, *where the borrower grants the trustee the power to sell the property in case of default.* This is what enables the lender to foreclose nonjudicially rather than having to file a judicial foreclosure suit. (Modern mortgages generally do have power of sale clauses, like deeds of trust, but are still infrequently used in California.)

A trust deed usually briefly outlines the procedures to be followed if the trustee exercises the power of sale and forecloses. For the most part, however, these procedures are prescribed by law. The foreclosure process is described later in this chapter.

2. Recording
A lender always records its trust deed since its lien priority is determined by the recording date.

In California, a county recorder cannot accept a trust deed unless the grantor's (borrower's) signature on the document is acknowledged and notarized. The document must also include the grantor's address, along with a request that any notice of default or notice of sale be sent to that address.

Title insurance companies often serve as trustees for deeds of trust, and one company may record hundreds of documents each month. To cut down on recording costs, a title company may record a **FICTITIOUS TRUST DEED**, *which is a standard trust deed form that hasn't been filled out.* Once the company's blank form has been recorded, it's only necessary to record the first page and signature page of any actual trust deed that is executed on that form. The standard provisions on the middle pages are incorporated into the actual trust deed by reference to the recording number of the fictitious trust deed. Therefore, if you look up a trust deed in the public record or request a certified copy from the recorder, don't be surprised if the document is incomplete.

3. Reconveyance

If the borrower is going to pay off the existing loan, the lender must give the borrower a beneficiary statement if requested by the borrower. The *BENEFICIARY STATEMENT shows the borrower the exact amount due on the loan.* Once a trust deed borrower has paid off the entire amount of the debt, he or she is entitled to a *FULL RECONVEYANCE of the trust deed, a document stating that the debt secured by the deed of trust has been discharged.*

On receiving the final payment, the lender/beneficiary must send the trustee the original promissory note and trust deed, along with a request for reconveyance. The trustee is then required to execute and record the reconveyance document within 21 days. This makes it a matter of public record that the debt has been paid off and the trust deed is no longer a lien on the property. The borrower may ask the trustee for the original note and trust deed. (The trustee and beneficiary are allowed to charge the borrower a reasonable fee for these reconveyance services.)

The Civil Code outlines steps the borrower can take to clear title, such as the substitution of the trustee, if the beneficiary and trustee don't execute a reconveyance within the timelines provided by law. A willful (intentional) failure to reconvey is a misdemeanor with a fine of not less than $50, nor more than $400, or imprisonment in the county jail for a period not to exceed six months, or both. Additionally, the trustor is entitled to recover all damages caused by the failure to reconvey plus a mandatory statutory penalty of $500. Damages may include those for emotional distress and attorneys' fees.

When several parcels of property are the security under a single trust deed, the borrower may be given a partial reconveyance after a certain portion of the debt has been repaid. The *PARTIAL RECONVEYANCE removes the trust deed lien from specified parcels; the lien still attaches to the other parcels.*

III. Common Optional Loan Terms

A promissory note is a borrower's promise to repay a loan, and a security agreement gives the lender the power to have the borrower's property sold in case of default.

These are the basic terms for every real estate loan. Most real estate loan agreements also include additional provisions governing prepayment, default, and transfer or encumbrance of the security property. Some of these provisions appear in the note, some in the trust deed, and some in both.

These common additional terms generally provide extra protection for the lender. This is not surprising; when the parties work out the details of their agreement, the lender is ordinarily in a better bargaining position than the borrower. If you apply for a loan at a bank and start haggling about the prepayment clause, the loan officer may wish you good afternoon and turn her attention to the next customer. However, as you'll see, California and federal law places some limits on the protective provisions a lender can impose, especially on a loan secured by residential property.

A. PREPAYMENT PROVISIONS

When a contract states a specific time for performance, the law requires it to be performed at the stated time—not after that time, and also not before that time. Suppose our loan agreement obligates me to pay you $789 on the 15th of each month. I don't necessarily have the right to pay more or pay sooner.

CHAPTER 12

However, a loan agreement may expressly give the borrower the right to *PREPAY, that is, make a larger payment than required, or pay off the entire loan before its maturity date.* In fact, prepayment is permitted by the terms of most promissory notes. The note may simply state that the monthly payment is $789 "or more," or that the payments are due "on or before" the 15th of each month. The note may include a provision expressly stating that the borrower has the right to prepay. There may be a *PREPAYMENT PENALTY, which is an added expense to the borrower, if the loan is paid before the due date.*

When a loan agreement doesn't give the borrower the option to prepay, the loan is said to be *LOCKED IN.* It is extremely unusual for a real estate loan to be completely locked in, but some loan agreements include a lock-in clause that prevents prepayment during a certain period.

Case Example: To develop an office building complex in West Los Angeles, the Trident Center partnership borrowed $56,500,000 from the Connecticut General Life Insurance Company in 1983. The interest rate was 12.25%, and the loan was to be paid off in 15 years. The promissory note stated that the partnership "shall not have the right to prepay the principal amount hereof in whole or in part" during the first 12 years of the loan.

Everything went smoothly for a few years, but interest rates were dropping during that period. By 1987, the 12.25% rate on the Trident Center loan was good for the lender, but bad for the borrower. The partnership wanted to refinance to take advantage of the lower rates that were available. However, refinancing would involve paying off the original loan long before its due date. Connecticut General refused to accept the prepayment, and the partnership sued. The court held that Connecticut General's lock-in clause was enforceable; the partnership could not prepay without the lender's consent during the first 12 years of the loan period. *Trident Center v. Connecticut General Life Ins.*, 847 F.2d 564 (9th Cir. 1988).

1. Residential Property

The California legislature enacted a statute that prohibits lock-in clauses for loans on residential property with one-to-four units. With these loans, the borrower has the right to make a partial prepayment or to pay off the entire loan balance at any time. The lender is allowed to impose a **prepayment charge** only if agreed to in writing.

Even prepayment charges are limited if the property is owner-occupied. For owner-occupied property, during the first five years of the loan, the borrower must be allowed to prepay up to 20% of the original loan amount in any 12-month period without penalty. But if the borrower prepays more than 20%, the lender can assess a prepayment charge. The charge cannot be more than the equivalent of six months' interest on the amount of prepayment over 20%.

During the first five years of a loan for owner-occupied property, the borrower must be allowed to prepay up to 20% of the loan amount in any 12-month period without penalty.

434

Prepayment

Nonresidential Property

- No right to prepay unless agreed
- Lock-in clauses allowed
- Prepayment penalties allowed (if reasonable)

Residential Property (1-4 units)

- Right to prepay at any time (seller financing exception)
- Lock-in clauses not allowed
- Borrower must initial prepayment provisions
- Owner-occupied: limited penalties for first 5 years (unless Mortgage Loan Broker Law applies)

The maximum prepayment penalty on a high priced mortgage loan shall not exceed 2% during the first 12 months of the loan or 1% during the second 12 months. If a mortgage broker arranges only higher-priced mortgage loans, it must be disclosed orally and in writing at the time services are engaged. A higher-priced mortgage loan is: (a) a first-lien loan with an annual percentage rate that is 1.5 percentage points or more above the "average prime offer rate," based on Freddie Mac Primary Mortgage Market Survey, or (b) a subordinate-lien loan (junior loan) with an APR that is 3.5 percentage points or more above the average prime offer rate.

Example: Suppose a bank has loaned you $100,000 at 10% interest so that you can buy a condominium unit. If you prepay $20,000 (20%) in one year, the lender can't require you to pay a prepayment charge.

However, if you prepay more than that in one year—for example, $25,000 (25%)—the lender may add on a prepayment charge. The charge cannot exceed the equivalent of six months' interest on 5% of the original loan amount (25% - 20% = 5%). One year's interest on $5,000 at a 10% annual rate would be $500, so six months' interest would be $250. The prepayment charge could not be more than $250.

After a loan on owner-occupied property has been in place for five years, the borrower can't be required to pay any further prepayment charges. A different rule applies to loans secured by single-family, owner-occupied homes that are covered by the Mortgage Loan Broker Law, which is discussed at the end of this chapter.

The federal Truth-in-Lending Act, discussed in more detail later in this chapter, contains additional restrictions on prepayment penalties. For loans covered by this Act and secured by the borrower's dwelling, the loan may have a prepayment penalty only if the loan is a fixed-rate, qualified mortgage (meeting certain underwriting criteria) and not a higher-priced loan. Adjustable rate loans and higher-priced loans may not have a prepayment penalty. If the loan is permitted to provide for a prepayment penalty, the prepayment penalty may not exceed two percent of the amount prepaid, and no prepayment penalty may be charged after three years.

2. Seller Financing

The statute that establishes the residential borrower's right to prepay makes an exception for seller financing. Under this exception, a home seller who carries back a deed of trust for the purchase price can prevent any prepayment during the year of the sale.

435

CHAPTER 12

This addresses a seller's concern about income tax liability. When a buyer prepays all or part of a carryback loan in a large lump, the seller may end up in a higher rate tax bracket, owing much higher taxes on that money than if the payments had been spread out over a few years.

Note, however, that this exception doesn't apply to a seller who carries back four or more residential deeds of trust in one year. In that situation, the seller is required to allow prepayment during that year, just like an institutional lender.

These rules on lock-in clauses and prepayment charges apply only to loans on residential property where the owner lives in one of the one-to-four units. There are no statutory restrictions on lock-in clauses and prepayment charges for other real estate loans.

3. Natural Disaster

No prepayment charge is allowed if the residence cannot be occupied, for example, if damage occurs from a natural disaster for which a state of emergency is declared by the governor.

B. DEFAULT PROVISIONS

1. Late Charges and Default Rates

Many promissory notes provide for a late payment penalty. The penalty may take the form of a flat fee; for example, $5 per month is added to the debt until the overdue payment is received. Or there may be a **default interest rate**. For example, the interest rate on the loan balance is ordinarily 8%, but 10% is charged on any delinquent amounts.

Late payment charge provisions such as these generally must comply with the rules for liquidated damages (see Chapter 7). This means the amount of the late charge must have been reasonable at the time the loan agreement was made. Thus, if a promissory note provided that a $200 late fee would be added to the $500 monthly payment whenever the payment was overdue, a court would undoubtedly refuse to enforce that provision.

The borrower must be given notice that a late fee or default rate will be charged. The notice must state the amount of the fee and the date it will be charged, and explain how the penalty is calculated.

A default interest rate can be assessed on the delinquent amount until it is paid, but not on the entire loan balance.

Example: The interest rate on my loan is 8.5%, but the note provides for a default rate of 10%. My payments are $500 a month, and the loan balance is currently $59,432. For one reason or another, I miss my October payment. The lender can charge 10% interest on the delinquent $500 until I pay it. However, the lender can't charge 10% on $59,432; the interest rate on the nondelinquent balance must remain at 8.5%.

a. Residential Property

The California Civil Code has placed special restrictions on late charges for loans on single-family, owner-occupied residences. A late charge can't be imposed until a payment is more than ten days overdue. There is a ten-day advance notice requirement before assessing the first late charge. The late charge on a single delinquent payment cannot exceed $5 or 6% of the payment amount, whichever is greater. Only one charge can be assessed against each delinquent payment. Whatever the borrower does pay must be applied first to the most recent payment due.

2. Acceleration on Default

An acceleration clause allows the lender to demand payment of the outstanding loan balance for various reasons, including if the buyer defaults on a loan payment.

Virtually every real estate loan agreement provides for acceleration of the loan in case of default. *If the borrower defaults, the lender has the right to declare the entire balance due immediately, no matter how many years away the original maturity date might be. This is sometimes referred to as "calling the note"; the provision in the loan agreement is an ACCELERATION CLAUSE or call provision.*

A lender does not have the right to accelerate unless expressly included in the loan agreement. An acceleration clause in the promissory note allows the lender to accelerate if the borrower fails to make payments on time. An acceleration clause in the trust deed gives the lender the right to accelerate if the borrower breaches any part of the security agreement, for example, by failing to pay the property taxes or keep the property insured.

Acceleration is a lender's option, not an automatic event. The lender decides whether or not to accelerate and when—after the borrower has missed two payments, or five or six. But the right to accelerate ends as soon as the borrower cures the default by tendering payment of the delinquent amounts, renewing the insurance, or taking whatever other action is necessary. The borrower can cure the default even after the lender has accelerated the loan. If the default isn't cured, the lender will foreclose.

a. Prepayment Charges and Acceleration

When a lender accelerates a loan because of default and has the property sold, the proceeds from the foreclosure sale are used to pay off the debt. This usually occurs long before the loan's original maturity date, so, in effect, acceleration and foreclosure lead to prepayment of the loan. A lender may not impose a prepayment penalty on a loan secured by residential property with up to 4 units if the lender accelerates the loan pursuant to a due-on-sale (alienation) clause.

C. TRANSFER PROVISIONS

When real property is sold (or otherwise transferred), the new owner takes title *SUBJECT TO any existing liens, meaning the lienholders still have the power to foreclose on the property in spite of the transfer.* If the new owner fails to pay, the original debtor is still liable for payment. However, the new owner does not necessarily take on personal responsibility for the liens.

Personal responsibility becomes important if the lienholder forecloses and the foreclosure sale proceeds aren't enough to pay off the full amount of the lien. *In some cases, the lienholder can sue for the remainder. That's called a DEFICIENCY JUDGMENT*—it makes up for the deficiency in the sale proceeds. When a new owner takes property subject to existing liens, he or she may lose the property to foreclosure, but isn't personally liable for a deficiency judgment. The lienholder has to collect the deficiency judgment from the former owner.

CHAPTER 12

It's different if the new owner assumes an existing lien instead of merely taking title subject to it. In an *ASSUMPTION*, *the new owner agrees to take on personal responsibility for the lien.* Then if the lender obtains a deficiency judgment, the new owner will be liable. However, the original borrower (the former owner) remains secondarily liable for a deficiency judgment. If the new owner doesn't pay, the lender can collect from the former owner. The former owner can then go after the new owner for payment, but may be out of luck. Deficiency judgments and anti-deficiency judgment rules are discussed later in the chapter.

Even though the original borrower is still liable, an assumption may increase the lender's risk. The lender wants to be paid as agreed—foreclosure is a last resort. The new owner could be a much worse credit risk than the former owner, or might be more likely to allow the security property to deteriorate.

Because of these concerns, most conventional real property loan agreements contain a due-on-sale clause.

1. Due-on-Sale Clauses

A lender can't include a provision in the loan agreement that prevents the borrower from selling or transferring the security property. In the eyes of the law, that would be an **unreasonable restraint on alienation**. Transfer of property from one person to another is generally good for commerce, so the law protects an owner's right to freely transfer property.

However, lenders can use due-on-sale clauses to protect their interests. A *DUE-ON-SALE CLAUSE provides that if the borrower sells or transfers any interest in the property without the lender's consent, the lender has the right to accelerate the loan and demand immediate payment in full.*

These provisions are also called alienation clauses. *ALIENATION CLAUSES are always acceleration clauses—but don't confuse them with the provisions for acceleration on default that were discussed earlier. Here there's no default; the monthly payments, taxes, and so forth have been paid reliably. The borrower has simply exercised his or her right to sell or transfer the property.* If a lender chooses to use the due-on-sale clause to accelerate the loan, the full balance must be paid. If it isn't, the lender can foreclose.

A due-on-sale clause (also called an alienation clause) is a type of acceleration clause that demands payment of the entire balance of the loan upon sale or transfer of title.

Sometimes (if the new owner is a good credit risk) instead of exercising its due-on-sale rights, the lender is willing to agree to an assumption of the loan. In that case, the new owner is usually required to pay an assumption fee, or a higher interest rate on the assumed loan, or both. The lender and the new owner sign a written assumption agreement, and the former owner has no further liability for the debt.

a. Residential Property

The California Legislature has adopted some rules for due-on-sale clauses in loans on residential property with one-to-four units.

For loans made since July 1, 1972, if the loan agreement includes a due-on-sale provision, it must appear in full in both the promissory note and the trust deed.

For loans made since January 1, 1976, a due-on-sale clause can't be triggered by certain types of transfers. The lender can't accelerate the loan when:

1. the borrower's spouse becomes a co-owner of the security property.
2. the borrowers are a married couple, and one of them dies, making the other sole owner of the property.
3. married borrowers separate or divorce and one of them becomes the sole owner.
4. the borrower transfers the property to a trust in which he or she is a beneficiary.
5. the borrower uses the property as security for junior-priority loan.

b. Prepayment Charges and Due-On-Sale Clauses

For most residential loans, if a loan agreement contains both a prepayment provision and a due-on-sale clause, the lender cannot collect prepayment charges after accelerating the loan because the property has been sold.

For some loans, a lender can collect a prepayment penalty if the loan is accelerated following default as long as the deed of trust contains a clause specifically allowing the prepayment penalty and that clause is separately initialed or signed by the borrower. However, federal law prohibits prepayment charges on most loans secured by an owner-occupied home, and state law prohibits prepayment charges on a loan on residential property with one-to-four units if the due-on-sale clause is exercised.

Due-on-Sale Clauses

For residential property:

- Clause must be in both note and security agreement
- Certain transfers are exempt
- Prepayment penalties can't be charged after acceleration pursuant to a due-on-sale clause

---

2. Due-on-Encumbrance Provisions

Some due-on-sale clauses allow the lender to accelerate the loan not only if ownership is transferred, but even if the borrower encumbers the property with another lien. The borrower can't take out an additional loan using the property as security, even though the first lender's trust deed would have higher priority than the second trust deed. These due-on-encumbrance provisions are generally enforceable. However, federal law prohibits them in loans secured by owner-occupied homes, and California law prohibits them in loans on residential property with one-to-four units.

D. SUBORDINATION PROVISIONS

Lien priority is extremely important to every lender. The higher the lender's priority, the more likely that lender is to recover all (or most) of the debt if any lienholder forecloses.

As you know, the priority of a trust deed depends on the date it was recorded. A trust deed has lower priority than any voluntary liens on the same property that were recorded earlier, and higher priority than any that were recorded later.

A lender can agree to accept a lower priority position than the one established by the recording date. The lender may **subordinate** its trust deed to another trust deed that was (or will be) recorded later. *The earlier trust deed that takes on a lower priority is called a SUBORDINATED TRUST DEED. The later trust deed that is given a higher priority is called the SUBORDINATING TRUST DEED.*

Subordination is most common when a seller carries back a trust deed for part of the purchase price. The borrower/buyer intends to improve the security property, but to do so, he or she will have to obtain a construction loan. Construction lenders generally insist on having *FIRST LIEN POSITION (the highest priority).* As a result, the buyer won't be able to get the construction loan unless the seller is willing to subordinate the purchase loan.

A subordination clause can be included in the earlier trust deed, or a separate subordination agreement may be drawn up. The provision may subordinate the trust deed to a loan that has already been arranged, or to one that the borrower intends to apply for.

Because subordination can have a drastic effect on the strength of a lender's security, any subordination provision must be drafted or carefully reviewed by a competent lawyer. When the other loan hasn't been arranged yet, the provision should establish strict standards for the quality and purpose of the other loan. Otherwise, the borrower can subordinate the earlier trust deed to any kind of loan and do anything he or she wants with the money. This can make the subordinated lender's security worthless.

Case Example: Mr. Handy contracted to buy the 320-acre Gordon Ranch for $1,200,000. The contract provided that Handy would sign a ten-year deed of trust in favor of the Gordons to cover the purchase price. Handy intended to obtain other loans for construction and permanent financing, and the Gordons agreed to subordinate their trust deed to these other loans.

A few months later, however, the Gordons had changed their minds about selling the property to Handy. Handy sued for specific performance of the contract.

The court stated that a subordination clause "must contain terms that will define and minimize the risk that the subordinating liens will impair or destroy the seller's security." Nothing in the Gordons' subordination provision ensured that Handy would use all of the proceeds from the other loans to improve the security property.

As a result, the amount of those loans might be much greater than the amount Handy's improvements added to the value of the property. If he defaulted and the subordinating lenders foreclosed, their claims would probably absorb all the foreclosure sale proceeds. Thus, the contract leaves defendants with nothing but plantiff's good faith and business judgment to insure them that they will ever receive anything for conveying their land. The court ruled that this was not just and reasonable for the Gordons, and refused to make them go through with the contract. *Handy v. Gordon*, 65 Cal. 2d 578, 55 Cal. Rptr. 769 (1967).

In California, to lessen the chances that an unsophisticated lender will subordinate a trust deed without realizing it, certain trust deeds with subordination provisions must have the words **SUBORDINATED TRUST DEED** printed in large, bold type at the top of the document. The document also has to include certain warnings about the risks involved in subordination. However, these rules don't apply when either the subordinated loan or the subordinating loan (the later loan) will be for more than $25,000.

IV. Foreclosure

The purpose of every real estate security agreement is to give the lender the right to foreclose: to have the property sold and the debt paid out of the sale proceeds. The **power of sale clause** in a deed of trust enables the lender to foreclose nonjudicially without filing a lawsuit. The foreclosure must take place within 10 years of maturity date of the note, or 60 years after recording the deed of trust.

> *The power of sale clause permits nonjudicial foreclosure in accordance with specific terms.*

A power of sale clause can also be included in a mortgage, making the mortgage just like a trust deed. A standard mortgage does not contain a power of sale clause, and can only be foreclosed through judicial process.

For a trust deed lender, on the other hand, judicial foreclosure is an option. There is rarely any advantage to it; nonjudicial foreclosure is always faster and cheaper. (Nonjudicial foreclosure can be accomplished in less than four months and usually costs less than $500; judicial foreclosure can take years and cost thousands of dollars.) Since most foreclosures in California are nonjudicial, we'll look at the nonjudicial procedure in detail. Later in the chapter, we'll compare the judicial foreclosure process.

A. NONJUDICIAL FORECLOSURE OF A TRUST DEED

There are three main steps in the nonjudicial foreclosure process:

1. Notice of default
2. Notice of sale
3. Trustee's sale

1. Notice of Default

When a trust deed beneficiary (the lender) asks the trustee to start the foreclosure process, the first step is to record a *NOTICE OF DEFAULT, which identifies the trust deed, states that the borrower has breached the terms of the trust deed, and describes the nature of the breach.* A Notice of Default cannot be recorded until 30 days after the lender contacts the borrower. Remember, default doesn't have to be failure to make monthly payments on time.

The notice of default is recorded in the county where the property is located. Within ten business days after it is recorded, the trustee must mail a copy to the borrower by certified or registered mail. In addition, a second copy must be sent to the borrower by first class mail, and the sender has to execute an affidavit of mailing.

In that same ten business-day period, the trustee must also send a copy of the notice of default, by certified or registered mail, to everyone who requested notice. *Anyone who wants to receive notice of default on a particular trust deed can record a REQUEST FOR NOTICE OF DEFAULT.* (Sometimes a request for notice of default is included in the trust deed itself.) The request must include an address so that the trustee knows where to send the notice. A commercial tenant wants to know if the landlord is in default.

In addition, the trustee has to send a copy of the notice of default to:

1. the borrower's successors in interest (that's everyone who has acquired an ownership interest in the property—heirs, for example),

2. the junior trust deed beneficiaries (the lenders with lower lien priority than the foreclosing lender),

3. the vendee in a land contract with lower priority than the trust deed, and

4. the lessee in a lease with lower priority than the trust deed.

Like the others, these copies must be sent by certified or registered mail, but they don't have to be sent within ten business days. The trustee has one month after the notice of default is recorded to send copies to these parties. (If any of them want to be notified sooner, they have to record a request for notice.)

2. Notice of Sale

The trustee's next step is to issue a notice of sale. This can't be done until at least three months after the notice of default was recorded, but it must be done at least 20 days before the date set for the trustee's sale.

The **NOTICE OF SALE** *states the time and place that the trustee's sale will be held*. It gives the name, address, and phone number of the trustee conducting the sale; it identifies the borrower and the property to be sold. The notice states the amount of the unpaid loan balance and an estimate of the costs and expenses, including a warning to the borrower:

"UNLESS YOU TAKE ACTION TO PROTECT YOUR PROPERTY, IT MAY BE SOLD AT A PUBLIC SALE. IF YOU NEED AN EXPLANATION OF THE NATURE OF THE PROCEEDING AGAINST YOU, YOU SHOULD CONTACT A LAWYER."

To issue a notice of sale, the trustee must do **all of the following at least 20 days before the sale date**:

1. Post a copy of the notice in a public place (such as the courthouse) in the city or judicial district where the property is located.

2. Begin publishing the notice once a week in a newspaper of general circulation in the city or judicial district where the property is located.

3. Post a copy in a conspicuous place on the property to be sold.

4. Send borrower one copy by registered or certified mail, and one by first class mail.

5. Send a copy to each of the other parties that were sent a notice of default.

For loans secured by residential real property where the billing address for the loan is different than the property address, the trustee is required to post and mail a notice, when the Notice of Sale is given, addressed to the "Resident of property subject to foreclosure sale" that foreclosure may result in termination of a lease and eviction. The notice must be given in six different languages: English, Spanish, Chinese, Tagalog, Vietnamese, and Korean.

In addition, at least 14 days before the sale, the trustee must record a copy of the notice of sale in the county where the property is located.

3. Preventing a Trustee's Sale

Once the foreclosure process has begun, there are three ways the borrower can prevent a trustee's sale:

1. Cure the default to reinstate the loan.
2. Redeem the property.
3. Give the lender a deed in lieu of foreclosure.

a. Cure and Reinstatement

When the borrower has defaulted by failing to make payments, or failing to pay taxes, assessments, or insurance, the default can be cured. (Note that a cure isn't always permitted: not if the borrower has committed waste, or if the loan has been accelerated pursuant to a due-on-sale clause, for example.)

A default can be cured by paying the delinquent taxes or assessments, reinsuring the property, or paying the overdue amounts (including late charges). In addition, the costs incurred because of the default must be paid (the cost of recording and mailing notices, for example). The trustee's fees and any attorney's fees must also be paid, and these are limited by statute.

Before the notice of sale is mailed. Until the notice of sale is deposited in the mail, if the borrower wishes to reinstate, the trustee's or attorney's fees that may be recovered may not exceed $300 for an unpaid principal of $150,000 or less, or $250 if the unpaid principal exceeds $150,000, plus 1/2 of 1 percent of the amount from $50,001 to $150,000, plus 1/4 of 1 percent of the unpaid amount from $150,001 through $500,000 plus 1/8 of 1 percent of any portion of the unpaid principal sum exceeding $500,000.

After the notice of sale is mailed. If the borrower wishes to redeem after the notice of sale has been deposited in the mail, the trustee's or attorney's fees are set at an amount that does not exceed $425 on the first $150,000 or unpaid principal, or $360 if the unpaid principal exceeds $150,000, plus 1 percent of the unpaid principal exceeding $50,000 through $150,000 plus 1/2 of 1 percent from $150,000 through $500,000, 1/4 of 1 percent of the unpaid principal sum exceeding $500,000.

Trustee's or attorney's fees. Any charge for trustee's or attorney's fees are presumed to be lawful when they do not exceed these authorized amounts.

It's not just the borrower and the borrower's successors in interest who can cure the default. A junior lienholder might pay off the delinquencies, costs, and fees in order to protect its lien.

The default can be cured any time after the notice of default has been recorded, until five business days before the date of the trustee's sale. This is known as the **REINSTATEMENT PERIOD**. If the sale is postponed, the right to cure the default revives until five business days before the new sale date. ~~5 days extended~~

When the default is curable, the notice of default must contain an explanation of the right to reinstate the loan. It must also inform the borrower that the lender may be willing to allow additional time or arrange a payment schedule. The amount necessary for curing the default as of the notice date must be listed, along with a phone number to call for an update of the necessary amount.

Once a default has been cured, the loan is reinstated.

Regular payment resumes—the lender can't demand higher payments or a higher interest rate because of the earlier default. The borrower may ask the lender to record a notice of rescission. The **NOTICE OF RESCISSION** *gives public notice that the notice of default and notice of sale have been rescinded.* The lender must record a notice of rescission within 30 days after receiving a written request from the borrower.

b. Redemption

Five days before the sale date, the borrower (and all interested parties, such as a junior lienholder) loses the right to cure the default. In that five-day period, there's still a chance to prevent the sale and retain control of the property, but now it becomes necessary to pay the lender the entire loan balance—not merely the delinquencies—plus costs and fees. If the borrower can come up with that much, he or she will own the property free and clear of the lender's interest. This doesn't happen often.

Once the trustee's sale is over, the right to redeem the property is lost.

c. Deed in Lieu of Foreclosure

The only other way for the borrower to prevent a trustee's sale is by giving the lender a **DEED IN LIEU OF FORECLOSURE,** *where the borrower simply deeds the property to the lender, surrendering ownership.* Why would a borrower do that? Often the borrower is going to lose the property anyway, since he or she can't afford to cure the default, much less pay off the entire loan. By giving the lender a deed in lieu, the borrower can avoid liability for costs and fees, and may be able to protect his or her credit rating.

A lender isn't required to accept a deed in lieu of foreclosure. The lender can decide whether accepting it will be more advantageous than foreclosing. That may not be the case, for example, if the property is encumbered with other liens. (As explained later in this chapter, foreclosure eliminates all liens junior to foreclosing trust deed.) A lender may also choose not to accept a deed in lieu for bankruptcy or income tax reasons.

Special Foreclosure Laws for Owner-Occupied Residential Properties

California law has established some special rules that apply to the foreclosure processes (nonjudicial and judicial) to first-priority loans secured by residential property with up to 4 units occupied as the owner's primary residence. Included in these special rules:

A lender may not record a Notice of Default until 30 days after the lender contacts (or makes a diligent effort to contact) the borrower to assess the borrower's financial condition and options to avoid foreclosure and to notify the borrower of the right to request a meeting with the lender.

A lender is prohibited from "dual-tracking"—starting or continuing a foreclosure process (recording a Notice of Default, Notice of Sale, conducting a trustee's sale) while the lender is reviewing a loan modification request or has approved a short sale that is still in process.

A lender is prohibited from recording a Notice of Default until the lender has notified the borrower of the borrower's right to obtain copies of the promissory note, deed of trust, any assignment of the deed of trust, and payment history.

The lender must, upon the request of a borrower, create a "single point of contact" (an individual or a team) to communicate with the borrower and coordinate any requested loan modification or other foreclosure alternative (Applies only to lenders who had 175 or more foreclosures in the previous calendar year).

---

4. Trustee's Sale

A trustee's sale is a public auction; the foreclosure property is sold to the highest bidder.

The sale must be held during ordinary business hours, in the county where the property is located. The trustee's role is to conduct the sale in a fair and open manner, to protect all interested parties (the borrower, the foreclosing lender, and the other lienholders) and obtain a reasonable price for the property. Upon the sale of the property, the trustee may deduct from the proceeds of the sale those reasonable costs and expenses which are actually incurred in enforcing the terms of the obligation or which are authorized by law to be in an amount which does not exceed $425 or 1% of the unpaid principal sum secured, whichever is greater. The unpaid sum secured is determined as of the date the notice of default was recorded. If the charge does not exceed this dollar amount provided, it is conclusively presumed to be valid.

The trustee can postpone the sale, if necessary, to protect the interests of the beneficiary or borrower. Remember that when a trustee's sale is postponed, the right to cure the default is revived until five business days before the new sale date.

The foreclosing lender is allowed to credit bid at the sale. With *CREDIT BIDDING*, *the amount owed to the lender is offset against the amount of the bid*. No other lienholders are allowed to credit bid.

Example: The amount due to the foreclosing lender is $100,000. (This includes the unpaid balance on the trust deed, plus costs and fees.) The lender bids $100,000, which is the highest bid. The lender gets the property without actually paying anything for it. If the lender bid had been $120,000, the lender would only pay $20,000.

Suppose there's a junior trust deed on the property with a $15,000 unpaid balance. If the lender on that junior trust deed bid $100,000, he or she would have to pay the full $100,000 (not $85,000).

Nonjudicial Foreclosure

Default and Acceleration
Notice of Default
Notice of Trustee's Sale .... 3 months after notice of default
Cure and Reinstatement .... until 5 business days before sale
Redemption .... until the sale
Trustee's Sale .... 20 days after notice of sale
    Trustee's Deed .... issued immediately after sale
    Junior Liens Extinguished
    No Deficiency Judgments

---

a. Sale Proceeds

After the property has been sold at the trustee's sale, the proceeds are applied in the following order:

1. First, the costs of the foreclosure are paid (including costs of publishing, recording, and mailing notices, a title search, and trustee's and attorney's fees).

445

CHAPTER 12

2. Next, the note underlying the trust deed that was foreclosed is paid.

3. Then, any junior liens are paid off in order of priority.

4. Finally, anything left over is paid to the borrower.

If there's nothing left after the foreclosed trust deed is paid off, the junior lienholders get nothing. If there is something left, junior lienholders are sent a notice to file a written claim, and the trustee determines priority. If there's only enough left to pay the first junior lienholder, the second and third get nothing (and so on). If the trustee cannot determine priority, the matter is transferred for determination to the superior court. The foreclosure extinguishes the junior liens: the junior lienholders have lost their security interest in the property—they can't foreclose later on. Not only that, because of the antideficiency rules (discussed below), a junior lienholder may have no other recourse—they may not be able to sue the borrower for payment.

However, the foreclosure does not extinguish any liens that had higher priority than the foreclosed trust deed (a property tax lien, for example). The purchaser at the trustee's sale takes the property subject to those senior liens.

b. Trustee's Deed

The purchaser at a trustee's sale receives title to the property immediately. The borrower has no further right to redeem the property. If the borrower is still in possession of the property, he or she can be evicted.

The purchaser at a trustee's sale is given a *TRUSTEE'S DEED (not the same thing as a trust deed!). Like a quitclaim deed, it conveys whatever ownership rights the borrower had, but carries no warranties of title.*

5. Protection for Junior Lienholders

The beneficiary of a junior trust deed (or any other junior lienholder) has the same right to foreclose as the beneficiary of the senior trust deed. However, as you've seen, if the senior lender forecloses first, the junior lender's security interest will be wiped out altogether. The junior lender may receive full payment, partial payment, or nothing at all.

The only protection for a junior lender (besides choosing the borrower carefully) is to submit a **request for notice of delinquency** to the senior lender(s).

If a junior lender knows that the borrower is having trouble with a senior loan, the junior lender can cure the default and reinstate the senior loan.

The amount it costs to cure the default is added to what the borrower already owes the junior lender. With the senior loan reinstated, the junior lender can decide whether to foreclose on its own lien.

A junior lender can only use a request for notice of delinquency if the security property is residential property with one-to-four units, or if the junior lien is for $300,000 or less. And the junior lender must first obtain written permission from the borrower. Delinquencies of four months or more are reported. The notice fee is $40 and is good for five years; it can be renewed.

Any junior lender can (and should) record a **request for notice of default**. The borrower's consent is not necessary. The request for notice of default was described earlier in this chapter. When a junior lender has filed a request for notice of default, the trustee has to send a notice of default to the junior lender within ten business days (rather than a month) after recording it. The notice of default doesn't warn the junior lender as early as a notice of delinquency, but it's better than nothing.

B. JUDICIAL FORECLOSURE OF A MORTGAGE

There are only two parties to a mortgage. The *borrower is the MORTGAGOR, the lender is the MORTGAGEE,* and there's no trustee. Up until the point of foreclosure, the mortgagor and mortgagee have the same rights and obligations as a trust deed trustor and beneficiary. A promissory note secured by a mortgage is the same as one secured by a trust deed, usually containing an acceleration clause and providing for late charges. Like a trust deed, a mortgage requires the borrower to maintain the property and keep it insured, and there's usually a due-on-sale clause.

Unlike a trust deed, a mortgage doesn't ordinarily have a power of sale clause. As a result, nonjudicial foreclosure is not permitted.

To foreclose, the mortgagee has to file a complaint in the superior court of the county where the property is located within four years of payment being due. The defendants in a foreclosure lawsuit are the borrower and junior lienholders. If the mortgagee doesn't include one of the junior lienholders as a defendant, that junior lien isn't affected by the foreclosure. As with nonjudicial foreclosure, however, all the other junior liens are extinguished.

After filing a foreclosure suit, the mortgagee records a notice called a lis pendens. The **LIS PENDENS** *states that a legal action is pending that may affect title to the property.* It provides constructive notice of the foreclosure, so anyone who acquires an interest in the property takes it subject to the outcome of the foreclosure suit.

The mortgagor and junior lienholders have the right to cure the default and reinstate the loan while the lawsuit is pending, but once the court issues a decree of foreclosure, the right to reinstate the loan ends.

The decree of foreclosure establishes the amount that the mortgagor owes the mortgagee. It also states whether or not the mortgagee is entitled to a deficiency judgment if the foreclosure sale proceeds are less than the debt. (This depends on the anti-deficiency rules, discussed below.)

The sale after a judicial foreclosure is called a SHERIFF'S SALE or an execution sale (as opposed to a trustee's sale). The court appoints a receiver to conduct the sale. The receiver records a **notice of levy**.

The rest of the process depends on whether the lender is seeking a deficiency judgment. If not, the receiver must wait at least 120 days after recording the notice of levy before posting, publishing, and mailing out the notice of sale. The foreclosure sale purchaser receives a **sheriff's deed** immediately after the sale. (Like a trustee's deed, it carries no warranties.)

On the other hand, if the mortgagor will be liable for any deficiency, the receiver may issue the notice of sale immediately, but the property will be sold subject to the mortgagor's right of redemption. *The foreclosure sale purchaser is given a CERTIFICATE OF SALE instead of a deed.*

The mortgagor can redeem the property by paying the amount that the foreclosure sale purchaser paid for it (plus interest), and whatever the purchaser has spent on taxes, insurance, and maintenance. If the purchaser was a junior lienholder, the mortgagor must also pay off that junior lien, plus interest. If the purchaser has used the property during the redemption period, the reasonable value of that use can be offset against the redemption price.

If it turns out that no deficiency judgment is necessary, then the redemption period only lasts for three months after the sale. If the mortgagor hasn't redeemed the property by then, the purchaser receives a sheriff's deed.

When the sale proceeds don't cover the debt, costs, and fees, and a deficiency judgment is entered against the mortgagor, the redemption period lasts one year. That's a long period of uncertainty for the purchaser. As a general rule, the borrower is entitled to remain in possession of the property during the redemption period, paying rent to the purchaser.

California law used to allow junior lienholders to redeem the property after a judicial foreclosure sale. However, now the defaulting mortgagor and the mortgagor's successors in interest are the only ones with the right of redemption within 12 months of the sale.

If they do redeem the property, a **certificate of redemption** is issued and recorded. If a deficiency judgment was entered and they haven't paid it, a judgment lien attaches to the redeemed property. Junior liens that were extinguished by the foreclosure sale aren't revived by the redemption. They're gone for good.

Judicial Foreclosure

Default and Acceleration
Lawsuit Filed and Lis Pendens Recorded
Cure and Reinstatement (Until Decree of Foreclosure)
Decree of Foreclosure
Notice of Levy
Notice of Sale
Sheriff's Sale
    – Junior Liens Extinguished
    – Certificate of Sale (Issued Immediately)
Redemption: – 3 months after sale if no deficiency judgment
               – 1 year after sale if deficiency judgment
Sheriff's Deed (Issued After Redemption Period Ends)

The same procedures are followed when a trust deed beneficiary chooses to foreclose judicially instead of using the power of sale. There are real disadvantages to the judicial foreclosure process in terms of both time and money. So why would a trust deed beneficiary choose judicial foreclosure? The most common reason is that it's the only way to obtain a deficiency judgment. Let's take a look at the rules that govern when deficiency judgments are available.

C. DEFICIENCY JUDGMENTS

During the Great Depression in the 1930s, thousands of families lost their homes to foreclosure. Legislatures in many states, including California, passed laws to grant some relief to borrowers. For example, legislation was enacted that delayed foreclosure sales, extended redemption periods, and limited lenders' ability to obtain deficiency judgments. Most of these laws were temporary, emergency measures that later lapsed or were repealed, but restrictions on deficiency judgments are still in effect.

When a foreclosing lender is entitled to a deficiency judgment, the lender must apply to the court for the judgment within three months after the property is sold at the foreclosure sale.

The court will order an appraisal of the property's fair market value as of the time of the sale. The deficiency judgment will be the difference between the amount owed to the lender (including costs and fees) and either:

1. the fair market value at the time of the sale, or
2. the actual sale proceeds.

The deficiency judgment will always be the smaller of these two amounts. If the fair market value is less than or equal to the sale proceeds, the lender's total recovery (sale proceeds plus deficiency judgment) will equal the full amount owed. This won't be true if the fair market value is more than the sale proceeds.

Example: The borrower owes the foreclosing lender $100,000, including foreclosure costs and attorney's fees. At the foreclosure sale, the property was purchased for $75,000. The lender applies to the court for a deficiency judgment.

The court orders an appraisal. The appraiser estimates the property's fair market value at the time of the sale was $85,000. Then the deficiency judgment would be for only $15,000, the difference between the appraised value and the debt. The lender's total recovery would be less than the $100,000 owed: $75,000 (sale proceeds) + $15,000 (deficiency judgment) = $90,000.

This rule may seem hard on the lender, but it prevents an abuse that was once widespread. Foreclosing lenders used to purchase the property at the foreclosure sale for much less than its fair market value, and then obtain a deficiency judgment for the difference between the sale proceeds and the debt. As a result, the lender came away from the foreclosure with far more than the borrower had owed.

Beyond this limitation on the amount of a deficiency judgment, there are rules that prohibit some deficiency judgments altogether. A lender cannot obtain a deficiency judgment:

1. after a nonjudicial foreclosure; or
2. after foreclosing on certain purchase money loans.

When a trust deed lender believes that a foreclosure sale is likely to result in a substantial deficiency, it may be worth the extra trouble to start a foreclosure lawsuit and get a deficiency judgment instead of exercising the power of sale. Even after a judicial foreclosure, a deficiency judgment is often prohibited if the loan was a purchase money loan—that is, the loan funds were used to purchase the security property.

No deficiency judgment is allowed for a purchase money trust deed or mortgage carried back by the seller.

Suppose you sell me your land, and I give you a $40,000 trust deed as part of the purchase price. If I default and you foreclose, the sale proceeds are all you can get, no matter how severe the deficiency. There's an important exception, however. If the seller has subordinated the

449

purchase money loan to a nonpurchase money loan (such as a construction loan), the anti-deficiency rule doesn't apply. The subordinated seller can obtain a deficiency judgment.

No deficiency judgment is allowed after a third-party lender forecloses on a purchase money loan if the security was residential property with one-to-four units, and one of the units was occupied by the borrower/purchaser. Most residential real estate loans fall into that category. This rule has been interpreted to include loans for the construction of a residence on vacant land. If a purchase money loan is refinanced after January 1, 2013, the lender on the refinanced loan is also prevented from obtaining a deficiency judgment except to the extent that the new refinance loan exceeded the balance of the original purchase money loan.

Case Example: The Pruntys used their savings to buy an unimproved lot in Oakland, intending to build a home there. They borrowed $40,000 from Bank of America, giving the bank a trust deed on their lot.

Without improvements, the land was worth $7,500. After the house was built, the property value rose to $96,000. A landslide then destroyed the house, and the hazard insurance didn't cover landslides.

Foreclosure was inevitable, so the borrowers sued for a declaratory judgment. They contended that the $40,000 loan was a purchase money loan, and asked the court to rule that the bank could not obtain a deficiency judgment. The bank argued that it was a construction loan, not a purchase money loan.

The court agreed with the borrowers. Using the funds to build a home was essentially the same as using them to buy one. The bank wouldn't be allowed to apply for a deficiency judgment. *Prunty v. Bank of America*, 37 Cal. App. 3d 430, 112 Cal. Rptr. 370 (1974).

The Anti-Deficiency Judgment Rules

A lender cannot obtain a deficiency judgment after:

1. Foreclosing nonjudicially;
2. Foreclosing judicially on a seller-financed purchase money loan (unless it was subordinated to a nonpurchase money loan), or
3. Foreclosing on a residential purchase money loan (one-to-four units and borrower occupied).
4. Foreclosing on a loan used to refinance a purchase money loan secured by owner-occupied residential property with 1-4 units (except to the extent new principal is advanced).

V. Reverse Mortgages

A *REVERSE MORTGAGE*, also known as a reverse annuity mortgage (RAM), enables older homeowners (62+) to convert their home equity into tax-free income without having to sell their home, give up title, or take on a mortgage.

Prior to accepting an application for a reverse mortgage or charging any fees, the lender must refer the borrower to a reverse mortgage counseling agency approved by HUD. The lender must provide the borrower with a list of ten counseling agencies, including two that can do counseling by telephone. Then the lender must receive a certification from the applicant that the applicant has received counseling from an approved agency. The certification must be signed by the applicant and the agency counselor. To emphasize this, the applicant must receive the following notice from the lender in conspicuous **16-point type** or larger (not shown here in 16 Pt.):

IMPORTANT NOTICE

To Reverse Mortgage Applicant

A reverse mortgage is a complex financial transaction that provides a means of using the equity you have built up in your home, or the value of your home, as a source of additional income. If you decide to obtain a reverse mortgage loan, you will sign binding legal documents that will have important legal and financial implications for you and your estate. It is therefore important to understand the terms of the reverse mortgage and its effect. Before entering into this transaction, you are required to consult with an independent loan counselor. A list of approved counselors will be provided to you by the lender. You may also want to discuss your decision with family members or others in whom you rely for financial advice.

The most basic reverse mortgage is the *TERM LOAN*, *which provides monthly advances for a fixed period of time (generally three to 12 years). At the end of the period, all principal advances, plus interest, are due.* With a *TENURE LOAN*, *the lender makes monthly payments as long as the borrower occupies the home as a primary residence—the loan comes due when the borrower moves, sells the home, or dies. The LINE OF CREDIT LOAN is slightly different from the other reverse mortgages in that payments are not made on a regular basis.*

The following are some of the major provisions required in a reverse mortgage:

1. Must allow prepayment in whole or in part without penalty at any time during the loan.
2. May provide for a fixed or adjustable interest rate, which may be contingent upon the value of the property or changes in the value between closing and maturity.
3. Periodic advances to the borrower cannot be reduced in amount or number based on any adjustment in the interest rate.
4. A lender who fails to make loan advances as required must forfeit to the borrower treble the amount wrongfully withheld plus interest at the legal rate.
5. The reverse mortgage may become due if:
   a. The home is sold, or
   b. The borrower ceases occupying the home as a residence, or
   c. A specified event in the loan occurs that jeopardizes the lender's security, or
   d. The maturity date has occurred.
6. Borrower cannot be required to purchase an annuity. The lender or mortgage broker cannot offer an annuity or refer the borrower to an annuity provider before the loan closes.
7. Lender, mortgage broker, counseling agency, and others involved in the loan are prohibited from receiving any compensation from any insurance company or other company who provides annuities.

8. Lender or mortgage broker must provide a written checklist on matters to cover with the counseling agency.

Obviously, unlike a normal loan where presumably the lender's risk regarding the value of the collateral decreases with each payment, in a reverse mortgage the value of the property is critical since the debt increases with each advance. Consequently, the legislation addresses some particular concerns when the borrower is absent from the property. The temporary absence from the home not exceeding 60 consecutive days cannot cause the mortgage to become due. Extended absences from the home exceeding 60 consecutive days, but less than one year, cannot cause the mortgage to become due if the borrower has taken prior action that secures and protects the home in a manner satisfactory to the lender, as specified in the loan documents.

The reverse mortgage is a lien on the home to the extent of all advances and interest. This lien has priority over any lien recorded after the reverse mortgage. Unless federal law provides otherwise, loan payments to the borrower are treated as proceeds of a loan and not as income for the purposes of determining eligibility and benefits under means-tested programs of aid to individuals. Additionally, undisbursed reverse mortgage funds are treated as equity in the home and not as proceeds from a loan, resources or assets for determining eligibility and benefits.

VI. Real Property Sales Contracts

There's another type of security agreement besides trust deeds and mortgages. We'll call them land contracts, although they go by various similar names: land sales contracts, installment land contracts, installment sales contracts, or real property sales contracts.

Land contracts were once a popular form of seller financing. They used to have some advantages over a trust deed, from the seller's point of view. However, court decisions have trimmed back the seller's rights, and added to the seller's obligations. As a result, land contracts are rarely used in California anymore. (One important exception: the CalVet program uses land contracts to finance purchases by veterans.)

In a **LAND CONTRACT** *purchase, the buyer pays the seller in installments over a long period of time. Although the buyer usually takes possession of the property immediately, the seller retains title to the property as security for payment of the contract price.* The seller doesn't deliver the deed to the buyer until the full price has been paid off, which is often many years later.

Under a valid land sales contract, the buyer (vendee) holds an equitable title and is entitled to full use and enjoyment of the property. The seller (vendor) keeps legal title until the last payment is made.

> **Vendor –** The seller under a land contract.
>
> **Vendee –** The buyer under a land contract.

The parties to a land contract are called the *VENDOR (the seller)* and the *VENDEE (the buyer)*. The vendor has **legal title**; the vendee has **equitable title**. The vendor's interest in the property decreases as the contract is paid off, and the vendee's interest increases. Any payments received by the vendor for insurance and taxes must be held in trust for this purpose. The vendee of residential housing can prepay all or any part of the balanced owed. However, the vendor may in writing prevent prepayment for up to 12 months after the purchase.

A land contract should be recorded to give constructive notice of the vendee's interest in the property.

It's illegal for a vendor to transfer the property without assigning the contract to the new owner. If the vendor violates that rule, anyone who buys the property with actual or constructive notice of the contract takes title subject to the vendee's interest. When the vendee tenders full payment, the buyer will have to deliver title to the vendee, just as the vendor would have had to.

If the contract isn't recorded and someone buys the property without notice of the vendee's interest, the buyer can cut off the vendee's rights. The vendor will be liable to the vendee for breach of contract, but the vendee will lose the property. However, that can only happen if the vendee isn't in possession of the property, since possession gives constructive notice of an interest (see Chapter 10).

A. THE VENDOR'S REMEDIES

If the vendee defaults, the vendor can **terminate** the contract by sending the vendee a **notice of election to terminate**. However, to regain possession and cut off the vendee's right to redeem the property, the vendor will need to foreclose judicially (if possible) or get a court judgment quieting the vendor's title against the vendees' right of redemption.

The vendor may have to reimburse the vendee for the amount paid on the contract. However, the vendee's recovery may be reduced by any damages that the vendor incurred, or the vendee may be charged the rental value of the property during the period he or she was in possession.

VII. Lending Disclosure Laws

A number of federal and state laws require real estate lenders to fully inform borrowers about the terms of their loans. Here's an overview of the main consumer protection laws affecting California lenders.

A. TRUTH IN LENDING ACT (TILA)

The *TRUTH IN LENDING ACT (TILA) is a federal law that requires lenders to disclose the complete cost of credit to consumer loan applicants*. The act also regulates advertising of consumer loans. Congress outlined these goals in the act, and delegated the responsibility for carrying them out to the Federal Reserve Board. The Federal Reserve Board's Regulation Z implements the Truth in Lending Act. *REGULATION Z sets out the detailed rules that lenders must comply with.*

1. Coverage of the Act

A consumer loan is used for personal, family, or household purposes.

A consumer loan is covered by the Truth in Lending Act if it is to be repaid in more than four installments, or is subject to finance charges, and is either:

1. for $25,000 or less; or
2. secured by real property.

Thus, any loan secured by a trust deed is covered by the Truth in Lending Act, as long as the proceeds are used for personal, family, or household purposes (such as buying a home or college tuition). If the loan is used for business, commercial, or agricultural purposes, or made to other than a natural person, i.e., a partnership, however, the act doesn't apply. A loan for more than $25,000 isn't covered by the act if it isn't secured by real property.

2. Disclosure Requirements

The Truth in Lending Act's disclosure requirements apply not only to lenders but also to **CREDIT ARRANGERS** *(go-betweens who help would-be borrowers find willing lenders)*. The primary disclosures that a lender or credit arranger must make to a loan applicant are the total finance charge and the annual percentage rate. The *TOTAL FINANCE CHARGE is the sum of all fees the lender charges a borrower in exchange for granting the loan.* This includes the interest on the loan, plus charges like the origination fee, points, finder's fees, and service fees. Title insurance costs, credit report charges, the appraisal fee, and points paid by the seller are not included.

The **ANNUAL PERCENTAGE RATE (APR)** *states the relationship of the total finance charge to the amount of the loan expressed as an annual percentage.* The APR is a percentage rate reflected as an annual rate and includes all interest, points, and fees. A loan's APR is higher than its annual interest rate, since it reflects all the other finance charges in addition to the interest. A loan with an 11% annual interest rate might have an 11.25% APR.

The lender or credit arranger must give the loan applicant a clear, easily understandable disclosure statement within three days of application and before any fees or charges are collected, other than reasonable credit report fees. In addition to the total finance charge and the APR, the statement must disclose the total amount financed, the payment schedule, the total number of payments, the total amount of payments, and information regarding any balloon payments, due-on- sale clauses, late fees, or prepayment charges. A real estate loan must also state whether the loan may be assumed by someone who buys the security property from the borrower.

Additional disclosures are required for adjustable-rate loans. The lender must give the applicant an informational brochure on ARM loans, the Consumer Handbook on Adjustable Rate Mortgages, published jointly by the Federal Reserve and the Federal Housing Finance Board. The lender must also provide specific information regarding the particular ARM loan program being applied for, such as the index, the initial rate, and any rate or payment caps.

The Truth in Lending Act has some special rules for only home equity loans. A **HOME EQUITY LOAN** *is a loan secured by the borrower's existing residence, as opposed to a loan financing the purchase or construction of a residence.* When the security property is the borrower's principal residence, the act gives a home equity borrower a right of rescission up until midnight on the third business day (Sunday and federal holidays excluded) after signing the agreement, receiving the disclosure statement, or receiving notice of the right of rescission, whichever comes latest. If the borrower never receives the statement or notice, the right of rescission does not expire for three years. The Truth in Lending Act also requires certain disclosures for home equity plans that involve repeated extensions of credit, versus a single loan.

3. Advertising

The Truth in Lending Act strictly controls advertising of credit terms. Its advertising rules apply to anyone who advertises consumer credit.

For example, a real estate broker advertising financing terms for a listed home has to comply with Regulation Z.

The cash price for a property and a loan's annual percentage rate can always be advertised. If any other particular loan terms (the down payment or the interest rate, for example) are stated in an ad, then all the terms must also be included. For example, if an ad says, "Assume 11% VA loan," it will violate the Truth in Lending Act unless it goes on to reveal the APR and all the terms of repayment. However, general statements such as "low down" or "easy terms" don't trigger the full disclosure requirement.

The Truth-in-Lending Act also bans the following advertising practices:

1. Advertisements that state "fixed" rates or payments for loans whose rates or payments can vary without adequately disclosing that the interest rate or payment amounts are "fixed" only for a limited period of time, rather than for the full term of the loan;

2. Advertisements that compare an actual or hypothetical rate or payment obligation to the rates or payments that would apply if the consumer obtains the advertised product unless the advertisement states the rates or payments that will apply over the full term of the loan;

3. Advertisements that characterize the products offered as "government loan programs," "government-supported loans," or otherwise endorsed or sponsored by a federal or state government entity even though the advertised products are not government supported or -sponsored loans;

4. Advertisements, such as solicitation letters, that display the name of the consumer's current mortgage lender, unless the advertisement also prominently discloses that the advertisement is from a mortgage lender not affiliated with the consumer's current lender;

5. Advertisements that make claims of debt elimination if the product advertised would merely replace one debt obligation with another;

6. Advertisements that create a false impression that the mortgage broker or lender is a "counselor" for the consumer; and

7. Foreign-language advertisements in which certain information, such as a low introductory "teaser" rate, is provided in a foreign language, while required disclosures are provided only in English.

B. SELLER FINANCING DISCLOSURE LAW

When a seller carries back a purchase money loan on residential property, California law requires that certain disclosures be made to both buyer and seller if an "arranger of credit" is involved. For the purposes of the statute, an arranger of credit is anyone (other than the buyer or the seller) who:

1. is involved in negotiating the terms of the loan agreement;

2. participates in preparing the financing documents, or
3. is directly or indirectly compensated for arranging the financing or the sale.

There's an exception for escrow agents and for lawyers representing either party—these aren't considered arrangers of credit. If the buyer or seller is a lawyer or real estate agent, he or she is considered an arranger of credit if neither party is represented by a real estate agent.

1. Coverage of the Law

It applies if a seller gives the buyer credit for some of the purchase price, if:

1. the property is residential with one-to-four units,
2. the credit arrangements involve a finance charge or provide for four or more payments of principal and interest or interest only (not including the down payment), and
3. an arranger of credit is involved.

However, a transaction is exempt if it's already covered by other disclosure laws, such as the Truth in Lending Act, the Real Estate Settlement Procedures Act, or the Mortgage Loan Broker Law.

2. Disclosure Requirements

When the seller financing disclosure law applies to a transaction, the required disclosures must be made before the buyer signs the note or security agreement. The seller must make disclosures to the buyer, and the buyer must make disclosures to the seller. The arranger of credit is responsible for ensuring that each party discloses all required information to the other and each party sign and receive a copy of the disclosure statement.

The statute contains a long list of required disclosures, including but not limited to:

1. The terms of the note and security agreements.
2. The terms and conditions of senior encumbrances (such as a first trust deed that the buyer will be assuming or taking subject to).
3. Whether the financing may result in negative amortization.
4. Whether the financing will result in a balloon payment (if so, the buyer must be warned it may be difficult to obtain refinancing to cover the payment).
5. Employment, income, and credit information about the buyer, or a statement that the arranger of credit has made no representation regarding the buyer's creditworthiness.
6. A statement suggesting filing of a "request for notice of delinquency" and a "request for notice of default."
7. A warning of possible limitations on seller's ability, with a foreclosure, to recover proceeds of the sale financed.

C. MORTGAGE LOAN BROKER LAW

Real estate agents often help buyers obtain financing. This assistance may go beyond simply helping the buyer apply to one institutional lender. In some cases, it's necessary to get loans from two or more lenders to raise enough cash to close the transaction.

California's **MORTGAGE LOAN BROKER LAW** (also known as the **Necessitous Borrowers Act** or the **Real Property Loan Law**) regulates real estate agents who act as loan brokers. The law requires a loan broker to give the borrower a disclosure statement, and for loans secured by residential property, the law places restrictions on the fees and commissions paid by the borrower or received by the loan broker, and regulates other aspects of the loan terms. We'll give only an overview of some of the law's key provisions here.

1. Disclosure Statement

The disclosure statement required by the Mortgage Loan Broker Law must be on a form approved by the California Real Estate Commissioner. It discloses all the costs, including fees received by the broker involved in obtaining the loan, and the actual amount the borrower will receive after all costs and fees are deducted. The borrower must receive the statement within three business days of receipt of the loan application or before the borrower becomes obligated to complete the loan, whichever is earlier.

A disclosure statement is required whenever a real estate agent negotiates a loan or performs services for borrowers or lenders in connection with a loan.

It's required for loans secured by commercial property as well as for residential loans. However, there's an important exception. The disclosure statement is not required if:

1. the lender is an institutional lender, and
2. the commission paid by the borrower is 2% of the loan amount or less.

2. Commissions and Costs

The Mortgage Loan Broker Law limits the commissions and costs that a real estate agent may charge the borrower for arranging a loan secured by residential property with one-to-four units. These restrictions only apply when the security agreement is as stated in the chart at the top of the next page.

For these loans, the costs of making the loan (such as appraisal and escrow fees) cannot exceed 5% of the loan amount, or $390, whichever is greater. However, the costs charged to the borrower must never exceed $700, or exceed the actual costs.

The Maximum Commissions That An Agent Can Charge Are:

First Trust Deeds for less than $30,000:

- 5% of the principal if the loan term is less than three years, and
- 10% of the principal if the term is three years or more.

Junior Trust Deeds for less than $20,000:

- 5% of the principal if the term is less than two years,
- 10% of the principal if the term is at least two years, but less than three years, and
- 15% of the principal if the term is three years or more.

---

3. Balloon Payments

The Mortgage Loan Broker Law prohibits balloon payments in certain residential loans secured by first trust deeds for less than $30,000 or junior trust deeds for less than $20,000.

Balloon payments are prohibited in these loans if the loan is to be paid off in less than three years. If the security property is an owner-occupied home, balloon payments are prohibited when the loan term is less than six years. These rules don't apply to seller financing, however. For the purposes of this law, a balloon payment is one that is more than twice as large as the smallest payment required by the loan agreement.

4. Language Translation

When a loan is negotiated in Spanish, Chinese, Tagalog, Vietnamese, or Korean and not English, the broker must give the borrower a written translation of the loan documents in that negotiated language before the borrower signs them. This rule only applies to loans used for personal, family, or household purposes (such as the purchase of a home).

5. Prepayment Charges

The borrower can prepay up to 20% of the unpaid balance at the time of payment in any 12-month period during the first seven years of the loan without a prepayment penalty. If more than the 20% is paid, the excess is subject to a maximum of six months' interest. After seven years there is no prepayment charge.

6. Late Charges

The late charge provisions are the same as for residential property, except the rate is 10% of the installment or $500, whichever is greater.

D. HOME EQUITY PURCHASERS OF FORECLOSURE PROPERTY

The California Legislature found that homeowners whose residences are in foreclosure have been subjected to fraud and unfair dealings by home equity purchasers. During a foreclosure period, the poor, elderly, and financially unsophisticated are vulnerable to the harassment of equity purchasers who induce homeowners to sell their homes for a small fraction of their fair market value through the use of schemes, which often involve misrepresentations, deceit, intimidation and other unfair dealing practices. Consequently, the legislature adopted some rules for home equity purchasers of owner-occupied property with one-to-four units after the recording of a notice of default.

The contents of the equity purchase contract and the cancellation notice are set by the legislature. The seller may not waive any rights under this law and can cancel the contract until midnight of the fifth business day after the equity sales contract was signed, or until 8:00a.m on the foreclosure sale date, whichever occurs first. Taking unconscionable advantage of the equity seller is unlawful and the seller has two years from recording the equity sale to rescind the contract. However, there can be no rescission in the event of a subsequent bona fide purchaser or encumbrancer. The equity seller has four years to bring a civil action against the equity buyer and may recover damages or equitable relief, attorney's fees and possible exemplary damages (not less than three times the equity seller's actual damages) or a civil penalty of up to $2,500. If the equity purchaser fails to comply with the statutory law, the purchaser may be fined not more than $10,000, sentenced to jail for not more than one year, or both. An equity purchaser is one who acquires title to a residence in foreclosure, except one who acquired title:

1. for use as a residence;
2. by a deed in lieu of foreclosure;
3. by trustee's deed;
4. by a statutory sale;
5. pursuant to a court order; or
6. from a spouse, blood relative, or blood relative of a spouse.

The homeowner in distress is typically approached by a "representative" of an "interested financial party" offering to help the homeowner in foreclosure. The homeowner needs to know that the representative must provide the following: (1) a valid current California Real Estate Sales License, (2) written proof that the representative is bonded by an admitted surety insurer in an amount equal to twice the fair market value of the property, and (3) a statement in writing, signed under penalty of perjury, that the representative is both (1) and (2) above.

E. MORTGAGE FORECLOSURE CONSULTANT'S LAW

The California Legislature placed numerous restrictions on foreclosure consultants who were found to use fraud and harassment to obtain a fee from the property owner, representing that the consultant could provide beneficial services to save the home from foreclosure. These consultants often charged high fees, secured their fee by a deed of trust on the residence to be saved, or performed worthless services in order to collect a fee. A foreclosure consultant is any person who, for compensation, will:

1. stop or postpone the foreclosure;
2. obtain any forbearance from the beneficiary or mortgagee;
3. assist with reinstatement of the loan;
4. obtain an extension of time to reinstate the loan;
5. obtain a waiver of the acceleration clause in the note;
6. assist the owner with obtaining any loan or other funds;
7. protect the owner's credit; or
8. save the residence from foreclosure.

There are a number of persons who are not considered foreclosure consultants: for example, attorneys providing legal services, licensed accountants, the person holding the lien being foreclosed, and institutional lenders. The law covers owner-occupied residences of one-to-four units and starts after the recording of the notice of default. The contents of the foreclosure consultant contract are established by the law. No waiver of rights or limitations of liability are allowed in the contract. The property owner can cancel the contract within three business days following its signing. Foreclosure consultants may not:

1. receive any compensation until full performance of all terms of the contract;
2. receive a fee of more than 10 percent per year of the loan amount;
3. take any security interest for the consulting fee;
4. receive a fee from a third party without a full disclosure to the property owner;
5. acquire any interest in the property being foreclosed;
6. receive a power of attorney from the property owner except to inspect the documents, or
7. induce the property owner to enter into a contract that does not comply with the law.

The property owner has four years from a violation of the law to sue for recovery of actual damages, attorney's fees and court costs, plus, it is possible to recover exemplary damages.

Any violation of law subjects the financial consultant or representative to a fine of not more than $10,000, a jail term not exceeding one year, or both for each violation. The financial consultant is liable for all actions of any representative. The representative must provide the owner with written proof of a valid sales license and bonding (for twice the fair market value of the residence). This must be done prior to any interest being transferred by the owner.

VIII. SAFE Act

The **SAFE ACT** requires all states and 5 territories to implement a licensing system for residential mortgage loan originators. A **MORTGAGE LOAN ORIGINATOR** is someone who takes applications for or negotiates the terms of loans secured by one-to-four unit residential property. California passed legislation allowing the Department of Real Estate (DRE) and the Department of Corporations (DOC) to implement the requirements of the SAFE Act.

Real estate licensees must file a report with the DRE within 30 days of making, arranging, or servicing loans secured by 1-4 unit residential property. Real estate brokers or salespersons who make or arrange these loans must have a Mortgage Loan Originator endorsement to their license. Current information on the MLO endorsement requirements is available on the DRE website: **www.dre.ca.gov**. Mortgage loan originators who work for lenders supervised by the DOC must have a Mortgage Loan Originator license issued by the DOC. Current information on the MLO license required for DOC supervised lenders is available on the DOC website: **www.corp.ca.gov**.

Each Mortgage Loan Originator must have a unique identification number assigned by the Nationwide Mortgage Licensing System and Registry (NMLS), the national governing organization. Information on the NMLS registration is available on the NMLS website: **http://mortgage.nationwidelicensingsystem.org/SLR/COMMON/RENEWALS/Pages/default.aspx**.

IX. Agricultural Security Interests

Suppose a borrower wants to give the lender a security interest in standing timber to be cut, as extracted minerals, or crops growing in a field (agricultural lien) with the idea that the lender or more removed the collateral if there is a default. How is this accomplished? The secured party with a security interest in standing timber or as extracted minerals will record (in the county where the real property is located) a financing statement (Form UCC-1) that describes the collateral and includes a description of the real property on which the collateral is located. Once recorded, it becomes constructive notice of the security interest to subsequent purchasers or lenders. The secured party with a security interest in growing crops will use the same financing statement, but has a choice of recording it in the county where the collateral is located or filing it with the Secretary of State's office in Sacramento or both (probably the best choice).

Borrower's Right to Receive Copy of Appraisal Report

A borrower has the right to a copy of the appraisal report to be obtained in connection with the loan for which he or she is applying, providing he or she is willing to pay for it.

Credit Scoring

What is Credit Scoring?

Credit scores are assigned numbers used by lenders to determine whether a consumer will get a loan and at what interest rate. Individual lenders often contract with a credit reporting agency, such as Trans Union, Experian, or Equifax, who compile consumer credit information. These companies then contract with a credit scoring company, more often than not, Fair Issac Corporation (www.fico.com), who own the mathematical model used to create the score. They provide the lender with a list of "reason codes" that the lender can choose from when receiving scores for consumers applying for mortgages. The "reason codes" can include things like, "too few bank card accounts," "too many subprime accounts," etc. The credit scoring company uses information from a consumer's credit report, together with these "reason codes" and the mathematical formula to create an individual's credit score.

The law now:

1. requires lenders to provide consumers with their specific credit score, what credit information went into making up the score, and an explanation of how credit scores work in the loan approval process,

2. compels credit reporting agencies to correct inaccurate information in a timely manner, and

3. provides consumers with additional legal recourse if an agency continues to report inaccurate information once they become aware that a mistake has been made.

 www.TransUnion: transunion.com
www.Experian: experian.com
www.Equifax: equifax.com

X. CHAPTER SUMMARY

1. A promissory note is the maker's promise to repay a debt. The payee may transfer the note to another person. Almost all promissory notes are negotiable.

2. A promissory note can be a straight note (with interest-only payments) or an installment note (with payments of principal and interest). An installment note may be fully amortized, or partially amortized with a balloon payment required at the end of the loan term.

3. A security agreement makes real property collateral for a loan, creating a lien and giving the lender the right to foreclose if the debt isn't paid. A deed of trust includes a power of sale clause, which enables the lender to foreclose nonjudicially. Mortgages historically did not have power of sale clauses, and therefore had to be foreclosed judicially. Nonjudicial foreclosure is faster and cheaper than a foreclosure lawsuit.

4. Most loan agreements permit the borrower to prepay, but nonresidential loans can be locked in. A residential borrower must be allowed to prepay. If residential property is owner occupied, only a limited prepayment penalty may be charged, and only during the first five years of the loan term.

5. A lender may impose late fees and charge a default interest rate on delinquent amounts. An acceleration clause gives the lender the right to declare the entire loan balance due if the borrower defaults. The loan agreement may provide that the lender can impose a prepayment penalty after accelerating the loan.

6. A due-on-sale clause gives the lender the right to accelerate the loan if the borrower transfers the security property to a new owner. The lender may be willing to let the new owner assume the loan at a higher rate of interest, or upon payment of an assumption fee.

7. When a trust deed contains a subordination clause, the lender agrees to subordinate its lien to another trust deed that would otherwise have lower lien priority. The clause should establish strict standards for the subordinating trust deed to minimize the subordinated lender's risk.

8. To foreclose nonjudicially, the trustee records a notice of default and mails copies to the borrower, all junior lienholders, and other interested parties. At least three months after recording the notice of default and at least 20 days before the sale, the trustee must record, post, publish, and mail out a notice of sale.

9. A trustee's sale can be prevented by curing the default and reinstating the loan, by paying off the entire loan (plus costs) to redeem the property, or by giving the lender a deed in lieu of foreclosure.

10. Trustee's sale proceeds are first applied to the foreclosure costs, then to the foreclosed trust deed, then to junior liens in order of priority. Anything left over belongs to the borrower. All junior liens are extinguished by the sale. The purchaser is given a trustee's deed.

11. For judicial foreclosure, the lender files a lawsuit against the borrower and junior lienholders. The court issues a decree of foreclosure, and the property is sold at a sheriff's sale. If the lender obtains a deficiency judgment, the sale purchaser is only given a certificate of sale, and the borrower has one year to redeem the property. If the borrower doesn't redeem it, the purchaser is finally given a sheriff's deed.

12. If the foreclosure sale proceeds don't cover the debt and the lender's costs, in a few cases the lender is entitled to a deficiency judgment. A deficiency judgment is never available after a nonjudicial foreclosure, or if the loan was a residential purchase money loan. A deficiency judgment also isn't available after foreclosure of a seller-financed purchase money loan (on any type of property), unless it was subordinated to a nonpurchase money loan.

13. In a land contract purchase, the vendee (buyer) takes possession of the property immediately, but the vendor (seller) retains legal title as security for payment. The vendee has equitable title. The vendor doesn't deliver the deed to the vendee until the contract price has been paid off.

14. The federal Truth in Lending Act (TILA) and California's seller financing disclosure law and Mortgage Loan Broker Law require lenders and credit arrangers to fully inform residential loan applicants about the cost of financing. The Truth in Lending Act also regulates consumer finance advertising.

15. Because of problems with equity purchasers of foreclosure property and those selling foreclosure consulting services, both practices are regulated in California.

16. The SAFE Act requires all states and five territories to implement a licensing system for residential mortgage loan originators. Within 30 days of commencing loan activity, all licensees must report to the DRE if they make, arrange, or service loans secured by real property. When all requirements are met, the DRE will issue a mortgage loan originator (MLO) license endorsement.

17. Recording a financing statement gives constructive notice of a security interest in timber to be cut or as extracted minerals. Recording or filing with the secretary of state works for agricultural liens.

XI. CASE PROBLEM
Williams v. Fassler, 110 Cal. App. 3d 7, 167 Cal. Rptr. 545 (1980)

Mr. Fassler owned a 20-acre ranch with a house on it in Stanislaus County. He agreed to sell it to Mr. Williams for $114,000. For income tax reasons, Fassler didn't want to collect the full price at the time of the sale, so Williams executed an $80,940 promissory note and a trust deed in favor of Fassler. Williams was to pay $8,709 (principal and 8.75% annual interest) each year for 20 years. The note provided that if Williams paid anything extra during the first five years of the loan, Fassler would charge a 50% penalty on the extra amounts.

Seven months after buying the property, Williams decided to build a new house there. He couldn't obtain financing for the project unless he paid off Fassler's trust deed. But if Williams did that, Fassler would charge the 50% prepayment penalty on more than $70,000—so the penalty alone would come to more than $35,000.

Williams sued for a declaratory judgment, asking the court to rule that the prepayment penalty was invalid. Could Fassler enforce the penalty provision? Does it make any difference whether the court treated the ranch as residential property? Could Fassler have included a lock-in clause in the loan agreement?

XII. KEY TERMS

acceleration	certificate of sale	fictitious trust deed
amortized	credit bid	foreclosure
annual percentage rate	cure	hypothecation
assumption	deed in lieu of foreclosure	judicial/nonjudicial
balloon payment	deed of trust	foreclosure
beneficiary statement	deficiency judgment	junior lienholders
beneficiary	due-on-sale (alienation)	land contract
call provision	clause	legal/equitable title

lending disclosure laws	pledging	senior/junior lienholder
line of credit loan	power of sale	sheriff's deed
lis pendens	prepayment penalty	split-term loan
lock-in clause	principal	subject to
maker	promissory note	subordination
maturity date	real property sales contract	tenure loan
mortgage	reconveyance	term loan
mortgagee/mortgagor	redemption	trustee
mortgage loan broker law	Regulation Z	trustee's deed
natural disaster	reinstatement period	trustee's sale
negotiable instrument	reverse mortgage	trustor
notice of default	SAFE Act (2010)	Truth in Lending Act (TILA)
notice of sale	security agreement	vendee/vendor
payee	seller financing	

XIII. CHAPTER QUIZ

1. The lender loaned borrower $10,000 evidenced by a signed written promissory note. Borrower verbally agreed that the note would be secured by a vacant residential lot owned by the borrower. Borrower's payments are in default. The lender can:

    a. foreclose on the residential lot in payment of the note.

    b. sue on the unpaid balance of the note.

    c. only foreclose on the residential lot in payment of the note.

    d. sue on the unpaid balance of the note and include judicial foreclosure on the residential lot as part of the lawsuit.

2. The monthly payments on the debt are interest only. The full amount of the principal is due in a lump sum at the end of the loan term. This is an example of a(n):

    a. fully amortized note.

    b. acceleration note.

    c. straight note.

    d. due on sale balloon note.

3. ARM stands for:

    a. Acceleration Recovery Mortgage.

    b. Alternative Reinstatement Mortgage.

    c. American Rates Manual.

    d. Adjustable Rate Mortgage.

4. A balloon payment is generally defined as:

    a. a payment more than twice the amount of the immediately preceding six regularly scheduled payments.

    b. a payment more than three times the amount of any preceding payment.

    c. a payment which is $100 more than any preceding payment.

    d. any payment over $5,000.

5. To cut down on recording costs, a title company may record a standard trust deed form that has not been filled out called a(n):

    a. blank trust deed.
    b. open trust deed.
    c. empty trust deed.
    d. fictitious trust deed.

6. If no deed of reconveyance is recorded within the required time, the trustor could bring a lawsuit to recover, among other things, a mandatory statutory penalty of:

    a. $100.
    b. $500.
    c. $2,500.
    d. $5,000.

7. In a promissory note, it states that the monthly payment is "$1,370 or more." This can be interpreted as:

    a. a prepayment provision.
    b. a balloon payment.
    c. illegal interest.
    d. none of the above.

8. For loans secured by owner-occupied residential loan with four or fewer unit, during the first five years of the loans, the borrower must be allowed to prepay up to what percent of the original loan amount in any 12-month period, without penalty?

    a. 2%
    b. 10%
    c. 20%
    d. 25%

9. California law on residential property with one-to-four units prohibits prepayment charges on a loan when which of the following is exercised?

    a. The foreclosure clause
    b. The due-on-sale clause
    c. The subordination clause
    d. The disclosure clause.

10. During a foreclosure, issuing a notice of sale cannot be done until at least how many months after the notice of default was recorded?

    a. One month
    b. Three months
    c. Six months
    d. Nine months

ANSWERS: 1. b; 2. c; 3. d; 4. a; 5. d; 6. b; 7. a; 8. c; 9. b; 10. b

CHAPTER 13
Land Use Controls

CHAPTER OVERVIEW

A prospective buyer considers property with particular plans in mind—remodeling the house, opening a gas station, or planting a lemon grove. To decide whether the property is suitable, the buyer needs to find out what restrictions there are on the use of the property. Real estate agents and the seller are required to disclose known restrictions to the buyer.

This chapter discusses public restrictions on land use, which are laws imposed by federal, state, and local governments on private owners. It also explains private restrictions, imposed by a previous owner or the developer.

I. Public Restrictions

Public restrictions on the use of privately owned land have proliferated in the past few decades in the form of zoning ordinances, building codes, subdivision laws, and environmental legislation.

A. ZONING

In colonial times, a landowner could do just about anything he wanted with his property. He could build a house or raise pigs or run a blacksmith shop, or even do all three on the same piece of property. But as the country's population grew and cities became crowded, people began to see a pig farm right next to a shopping district as a problem.

To prevent that kind of conflict and to gain some control over the problems of overcrowding, U.S. cities began to enact zoning laws. (New York City adopted the first major zoning ordinance in 1916, and the California Legislature enacted a statewide zoning law in 1917.) A zoning law divides a city or county into zones, and segregates different types of land use in different zones. The typical ordinance creates residential zones, commercial zones, industrial zones, and agricultural zones. Zoning laws also regulate the size of lots, the size and height of buildings, and the placement of buildings on each lot.

CHAPTER OUTLINE

B. POWER TO REGULATE LAND USE

At first it was argued that zoning laws were an unconstitutional interference with a landowner's property rights. But in 1926, in the landmark case *Village of Euclid v. Ambler Realty Co.* (272 U.S. 365), the U.S. Supreme Court ruled that zoning was a constitutional exercise of police power. **POLICE POWER** *is a state government's power to adopt and enforce laws for the protection of the public health, safety, morals, and general welfare* (Article XI, Section 7 of the California Constitution). A state may delegate this power to local governments (county or city). Because zoning ordinances prevent overcrowding and the problems with sanitation, fire protection, and law enforcement that overcrowding creates, they protect the public health, safety, and welfare. As a general rule, they are a legitimate use of the police power and are constitutional.

But the constitutionality of a particular zoning law can still be challenged. For example, a plaintiff may argue that an ordinance isn't necessary for the protection of the public. That argument rarely wins a lawsuit, however; courts allow local governments a lot of discretion in deciding what the public good requires.

Case Example: The area in San Diego known as Old Town is the site of the city's original settlement; many of the buildings there were built before 1871. The San Diego City Council adopted an ordinance requiring property owners in Old Town to apply to an architectural review board before constructing new buildings, altering old buildings, or putting up signs. The goal was to make all the buildings look like those built before 1871.

Mr. Bohannan, who owned a store in Old Town, filed a lawsuit challenging the constitutionality of the law. He argued that because the ordinance regulated only the appearance of buildings, its purpose was merely esthetic. It didn't protect the public health, safety, morals, or welfare.

Ruling that the ordinance was constitutional, the court stated, "Police power extends to measures designed to promote the public convenience and the general prosperity." Preservation of the historical character had educational value for the public. It also encouraged tourism, which helped the local economy. *Bohannan v. City of San Diego*, 30 Cal. App. 3d 416 (1973).

A landowner whose property has been severely restricted by a zoning law can challenge the law as unconstitutionally excessive. But to win the lawsuit, the owner has to prove that the zoning law has deprived the owner of "all economically beneficial use" of the property.

It isn't enough to show that the value of the property was lowered—even if it was lowered substantially.

Case Example: HFH, a limited partnership, bought a tract of unimproved land in Cerritos for $388,000. At the time of the purchase, the property was zoned for commercial use, but the city adopted a new zoning law a few years later. Now HFH's property was in a low-density residential zone, where very few commercial uses were permitted.

HFH decided to sell its property, and Diversified Associates contracted to buy it for $400,000. The contract was conditional, however: Diversified wouldn't go through with the purchase unless the tract was rezoned for commercial use. HFH applied to the city to have it rezoned, but the request was turned down.

HFH sued the city, claiming the zoning change had lowered the value of its land from $400,000 to approximately $75,000. The court dismissed the case. Even though the property's value was sharply reduced as a result of the zoning law, it could be developed for residential use. The law was constitutional, and the city was not required to compensate HFH for its loss. *HFH, Ltd. v. Superior County of Los Angeles County*, 15 Cal. 3d 508, 125 Cal. Rptr. 365 (1975).

Zoning laws can be challenged on a number of other constitutional grounds. Generally, a citizen has 90 days after the zoning ordinance is adopted to challenge it. An ordinance can't be discriminatory—that is, it must be applied in the same manner to all similarly situated property owners. It also can't be exclusionary, excluding certain classes of people from a community. (For example, requiring all residences in a town to be large single-family homes would effectively prevent low-income families from living there.) And ordinances regulating signs can't violate the right to freedom of speech.

Also, some zoning laws have been struck down because they invade the property owner's right to privacy. For instance, a Santa Barbara ordinance prohibited more than five unrelated people from sharing a single-family home. It didn't limit the number of people who could share a home as long as they were related by blood, marriage, or adoption. The California Supreme Court ruled that the ordinance's arbitrary distinction between families and groups of unrelated people violated privacy rights. The court stated "In general, zoning ordinances are much less suspect when they focus on the use than when they command inquiry into who are the users." (*City of Santa Barbara v. Adamson*, 27 Cal. 3d 123, 164 Cal. Rptr. 539 (1980).)

1. Land Use Planning

California has many examples of the problems that haphazard, unplanned growth causes. To promote more rational development, the state now requires each city and county to have a planning agency. Most counties and cities have an independent **planning commission**. In smaller communities the city council often acts as the planning agency.

The **PLANNING COMMISSION** is responsible for preparing a comprehensive, long-term general plan for all development within the city or county. The **GENERAL PLAN** outlines the community's development policies and establishes an overall design for the various land uses in the area. The general plan must address a collection of seven subject categories called "elements"—land use, circulation (transportation), housing, conservation, open space, noise, and safety. A city or county may include other elements covering issues of local interest. While developing the plan, the commission must hold public hearings to gather ideas and opinions from citizens, public agencies, and developers. The general plan is the basis for all local land use decisions. Zoning (except for some charter cities), subdivisions, and other land use approvals may only be approved when they are consistent with the general plan.

Several state and regional agencies help coordinate the general plans of neighboring communities. *When a city expands (by annexing new land) or two communities merge, the* **LOCAL AGENCY FORMATION COMMISSION (LAFCO)** *supervises the change to make sure it accords with the general plans of the communities involved.* The **METROPOLITAN TRANSPORTATION COMMISSION (MTC)** *oversees transportation planning on a regional basis.* The **ASSOCIATION OF BAY AREA GOVERNMENTS (ABAG)** *works to coordinate the general plans of all cities and counties in the San Francisco Bay area.*

2. Implementing the General Plan

A general plan sets out the community's land use policies in general terms.

To carry out those policies, detailed zoning ordinances must be drafted that conform to the plan. In most cases, these are enacted by the county board of supervisors or city council (usually with the planning commission's advice). Since zoning can have far-reaching effects, the council or board is required to hold a public hearing before adopting a new ordinance or changing a current ordinance.

3. Typical Zoning Provisions

Early zoning laws usually established only four land use categories: residential, commercial, industrial, and agricultural/rural. Modern zoning regulations tend to be much more complicated, including numerous subcatagories.

A Zoning Map

Example: In Nowhere City, there are several types of residential zones. In zones designated R1, only detached single-family houses are allowed; in R2 zones, row houses and duplexes (as well as detached single-family houses) are permitted; R3 zones also have apartments and condominiums; and any kind of housing (including manufactured housing) is allowed in an R4 zone.

An industrial zone might be divided into a section for light industry and a section for heavy industry. Sometimes a mixture of uses is allowed in a single zone: commercial and light industrial in the same zone, or multi-family residential and retail in the same zone.

Each zone generally has its own minimum lot size and building height limits. There are usually **setback** and **side yard** rules requiring buildings to be at least a specified distance from the property lines. There may be a limit on how much of a lot can be covered by a building.

Example: Nowhere City's ordinance provides that office buildings in a C2 commercial zone may not be higher than ten stories and must be set back at least 20 feet from property lines. In that zone, no more than 80% of a lot can be taken up by a building.

Instead of strictly prescribing height and coverage limits and setback requirements, some ordinances allow developers to use the *FLOOR AREA RATIO (FAR) METHOD, which controls the ratio between the area of the building's floor space and the area of the lot.* For example, a floor area ratio of two might permit 100% of the lot to be covered by a two-story building, or 50% of the lot to be covered by a four-story building. The FAR method gives architects and developers more flexibility in deciding the shape and height of buildings.

Zoning ordinances regulate many other aspects of development in addition to type of use and building size and placement. For instance, an ordinance is likely to include requirements for off-street parking, landscaping, and outdoor lighting.

Even if a proposal satisfies the requirements of the general plan and zoning ordinances, there is no guarantee that a permit will be issued.

4. Exceptions to Zoning Regulations

Zoning can have a big impact on the use and value of property. To be constitutional, a zoning law must be applied in the same manner to all similarly situated property owners. But if zoning regulations are rigidly applied, it can lead to unnecessarily harsh results for a few owners. Zoning laws usually have special provisions for existing uses that conflict with the new rules. They also establish procedures for creating limited exceptions to the regulations.

a. Nonconforming Uses

When a new zoning designation is imposed on a neighborhood, some owners find that the way they've been using their property is no longer permitted, even though it was fine under the old law.

Example: B opens a small bakery in an area zoned for mixed residential and commercial use. A few years later, the city council rezones that neighborhood to allow only single-family homes.

B's bakery is now a nonconforming use and it doesn't conform to the new law. If an owner were ordered to discontinue a nonconforming use immediately, this might be considered a taking of the property, and the government would have to pay compensation (see the discussion of eminent domain in Chapter 10). This practice could also create a lot of uncertainty: if I open a business here, will I be ordered to shut it down six months from now?

Zoning laws usually provide that existing nonconforming uses may continue.

However, a nonconforming use is subject to a number of restrictions. These restrictions are intended to gradually phase out the nonconforming use. For instance, as a general rule, a nonconforming use may not be enlarged or expanded.

Case Example: Mr. and Mrs. Rehfeld owned a grocery store on the corner of Filbert and Baker Streets in San Francisco. The neighborhood was not zoned when the store first opened, but many years later it was zoned for residential use. The Rehfelds were allowed to continue operating their grocery store as a nonconforming use.

After the zoning ordinance went into effect, the Rehfelds applied to the planning commission for a permit to expand the store. The Rehfelds wanted to extend the store 22 feet onto a vacant lot behind the store. The permit was denied; the ordinance didn't allow nonconforming uses to be enlarged. *Rehfeld v. San Francisco*, 218 Cal. 83, 21 P.2d 419 (1933).

When the buildings involved in a nonconforming use become obsolete, the owners are usually not allowed to renovate them. Even maintenance and repairs may be restricted: minor repairs are okay, but major repairs that would extend the lifespan of the building aren't permitted. Ordinances also generally provide that if a nonconforming building is destroyed by a hazard such as a fire or an earthquake, it may not be rebuilt. Any new structure must comply with the current zoning regulations. If the Rehfelds' store burned down, they could build a house on their property, but would not be allowed to rebuild the store.

Instead of relying on obsolescence or destruction to phase out nonconforming uses, some ordinances simply establish time limits. For example, the zoning authority might have ruled that the Rehfelds could only go on running their store for ten years after the zoning ordinance went into effect. As long as the time limit is reasonable, it will generally be upheld by the courts. One factor in determining whether a time limit is reasonable is the life expectancy of the buildings involved. If at the time the ordinance was passed the life expectancy of the Rehfelds' building was ten years, that would probably be considered a reasonable time limit for the nonconforming use.

Under most ordinances, if a nonconforming use is discontinued, it can't be resumed later on. If the Rehfelds closed their store for a year or more, they might not be allowed to reopen it. However, a court may require proof of intent to abandon the use. A nonconforming use would usually be allowed to resume after a temporary closure due to events the owner has no control over (a war, for example).

Permission to continue a nonconforming use ordinarily isn't tied to a particular owner. If the Rehfelds sold their property, the new owner could continue to operate the store as a nonconforming use, but the same restrictions would apply. A prospective buyer should find out whether there's a time limit on the existing use of the property, or restrictions on expansion, renovation, or rebuilding.

b. Variances

Sometimes a zoning ordinance creates special problems for a particular owner because his or her property is unusual in some way. To deal with this, zoning ordinances provide for variances. *A VARIANCE is a permit that lets an owner build a structure or use property in a way that isn't otherwise allowed.*

> **Case Example:** The Pasadena zoning ordinance required swimming pools in R1 residential zones to be set back at least 25 feet from the property lines.
>
> Ms. Brown's home was in an R1 zone. She wanted to have a pool installed in her backyard. Her yard was smaller than the other yards in the neighborhood, and there wasn't enough room to place a pool 25 feet from the rear property line.
>
> Ms. Brown was granted a variance permitting her to install a pool only 20 feet from the property line. *Ames v. City of Pasadena*, 167 Cal. App. 2d 510, 334 P.2d 653 (1959).

Variances are a zoning law's safety valve; they provide flexibility when the injury to the property owner would be greater than the public benefit from strict enforcement. The property owner must apply for a variance with the proper agency (for example, zoning board or planning commission).

In most cases, a variance authorizes only a minor deviation from the regulations.

California law provides that variances from the terms of the zoning ordinances can be granted only if the property owner can prove three elements: (1) that there are exceptional circumstances that apply to the property (size, shape, topography, location or surroundings) compared other property in the vicinity with the identical zoning classification, (2), that because of these unusual circumstances, the strict application of the zoning ordinance would deprive the property owner of privileges enjoyed by owners of nearby lands in the same zone, and (3) that the exception to the zoning ordinance would not be detrimental to the public or change the essential character of the neighborhood. If a property owner needs the rules loosened too much, a variance is inappropriate.

California law also prohibits local authorities from granting *USE VARIANCES. A variance cannot be used to authorize a use or activity which is not otherwise expressly authorized by the zoning regulations that apply to a parcel of property (for example, a commercial use may not be approved in a residential zone by variance).*

The zoning authority's decision can be appealed to the **board of zoning appeals** (or to the county board of supervisors or city council if there is no board of appeals). The appeals board's decision may in turn be appealed to a Superior Court. However, courts usually won't overrule a local authority's zoning decision unless there has clearly been an abuse of discretion.

Case Example: An investment company owned 28 acres in Topanga Canyon. The Los Angeles County zoning ordinance permitted only light agricultural and single-family residential use in that area, and set the minimum lot size at one acre. The investment company was granted a variance to establish a 93-space mobile home park on its land. The Topanga Association for a Scenic Community appealed the variance decision.

The investment company defended the variance by pointing out that its property was unusually difficult to develop; it was hilly, and extremely steep in places. Using the property for one-acre homes would generate much lower profits than the proposed mobile home park.

The California Supreme Court ruled that the variance should be denied. The investment company's property was difficult to develop because of its terrain, but the same was true of the surrounding properties affected by the zoning law. The variance would have put the investment company in a better position than its neighbors. *Topanga Association for a Scenic Community v. Los Angeles*, 11 Cal. 3d 506, 113 Cal. Rptr. 836 (1974).

It should be noted that these state variance rules (no use variances, and the unusual circumstances requirement) don't apply to municipalities that were organized as **chartered cities**. San Diego and San Francisco are examples of chartered cities. The zoning ordinances for a chartered city may or may not follow the state zoning laws.

c. Conditional Use Permits

*Most zoning ordinances allow the local zoning authority to issue special permits (after public notice and hearing—unless permitted otherwise by law) for certain uses that are inconsistent with a neighborhood's zoning designation, but are necessary or beneficial to the community. These are called **CONDITIONAL USE PERMITS** or special exception permits.* Those issued these permits include schools, hospitals, churches, cemeteries, and public utility structures. A conditional use permit will impose special development requirements to insure that the use will not be detrimental to the surrounding neighborhood (for example, additional landscaping, soundproofing, limited hours of operation, additional parking, or road improvements).

A city or county's zoning ordinance will list any conditional uses that may be allowed in a zone and the public hearing procedure that applies to a request for a conditional use permit. Notice of the public hearing must be mailed or delivered to the owners of surrounding properties. The zoning authority will usually want to control the number and placement of conditional use permits. One church or hospital in a residential neighborhood may not be a problem, but if there were two or three, the neighborhood would lose its residential character.

> **Exceptions to Zoning Regulations**
> ● Nonconforming Uses
> ● Variances
> ● Conditional Uses

5. Rezoning

In many situations, neither a variance nor a conditional use permit is available. There's one other possibility for a property owner who doesn't want to accept the zoning law's restrictions: requesting a rezone. A *REZONE is actually an amendment to the zoning law,*

CHAPTER 13

not just an authorized exception to the law. For example, a property owner in an R1 zone (detached single-family homes only) might ask to have part of that zone redesignated R3 (multi-family housing allowed).

A rezone must be consistent with the community's general plan, so drastic changes are usually not allowed (for instance, a rezone from residential to heavy industrial use is very unlikely). But a property owner may be able to show that circumstances have changed since the original ordinance was passed, and a new zoning designation would be more appropriate. The planning commission holds a public hearing on a proposed zoning amendment (or new ordinance) after giving a judge notice.

a. Spot Zoning (Illegal)

The rezoning process can be abused. *If a zoning authority grants an isolated zoning change that favors a particular property owner without real justification, it's called* **SPOT ZONING**. This is illegal.

> **Case Example:** Mr. Kerr bought a large tract of property in South Lake Tahoe. The maximum building height limit in that area of the city was 50 feet. Kerr wanted to build a high-rise, so he applied to the city planning commission for a variance. There weren't legal grounds for a variance; Kerr's property didn't have unusual characteristics that made it more difficult to develop than the surrounding lots. The variance was denied.
>
> However, the city council then passed an ordinance removing the height limit from Kerr's property. Neighboring landowners sued, and the court ruled that the rezoning was invalid. The change violated the community's general plan without justification and gave Kerr special treatment. *Silvera v. City of South Lake Tahoe*, 3 Cal. App. 3d 554, 83 Cal. Rptr. 698 (1970).

Sometimes a legitimate zoning change can look like spot zoning. As long as there are sound reasons and the rezone doesn't conflict with the general plan, it isn't illegal.

Example: Homeowners in a residential area complain that they have to travel too far for groceries, gas, and other basic services. The city council rezones the four corner lots at an intersection in the neighborhood for commercial use. This would probably be considered a legitimate change.

In deciding whether or not a particular rezone is illegal spot zoning, the courts consider all the circumstances: How large an area was rezoned? Does the new use meet community needs, or does it benefit a few owners without serving the community?

b. Interim Zoning

The appropriate local legislative body may adopt an **INTERIM** (*temporary—45 days unless extended*) **ZONING** ordinance as an emergency measure. This is done to protect public health, welfare, and safety without compliance with notice and hearing requirements.

6. Enforcement of Zoning Ordinances

A zoning ordinance usually provides that fines and other penalties can be imposed on a property owner who violates its rules. The owner may be required to tear down an illegal structure or stop an illegal use. However, most counties and cities don't have enough personnel to make routine checks on all the land uses in their jurisdiction. Unless a complaint is filed, a property owner may get away with a minor zoning violation.

C. BUILDING CODES

Building codes establish minimum standards for construction, requiring builders to use particular methods and materials. There are usually several specialized building codes: a fire code, a plumbing code, an electrical code, and so on. Like zoning laws, they are an exercise of the police power, protecting public health and safety. To establish some uniformity, California has adopted the **State Building Standards Code** and the **State Housing Law**. These set minimum standards; some local governments require more.

Building codes are mainly enforced through the permit system. A property owner intending to build or remodel a structure must submit plans to the local building department for approval. A building permit will be issued only if the plans comply with the codes. Once construction begins, an inspector may visit the site at different stages. If there are problems, the inspector can stop work on the project until they're resolved. The completed building is inspected, and a **certificate of occupancy** will be issued only if every aspect of the building is in compliance with the codes.

It isn't just new or remodeled structures that have to comply with building codes. In some cases (see following case example), when the government imposes a new, stricter standard, a property owner may be required to bring an old building "up to code."

Case Example: The Hotel Padre in Bakersfield was built in 1929. It was constructed in accordance with the laws that applied at that time.

In 1951, Bakersfield adopted a new building code. Many aspects of the Hotel Padre violated the fire safety provisions of the new code: unenclosed stairways and inadequately enclosed elevator shafts, a dangerous boiler room, and unsafe fire escapes, among other things.

The city tried to work with the hotel's owner to correct the violations, but he was extremely uncooperative. The owner claimed he couldn't afford the changes, and couldn't be required to comply with the new law. The city sued, and the court ruled against the hotel owner—he had to bring the hotel up to the new standards. The city wasn't trying to penalize the owner for the construction methods used in 1929; it was trying to eliminate a present danger to public safety. *City of Bakersfield v. Miller*, 64 Cal. 2d 93, 48 Cal. Rptr. 889 (1966).

It's a good idea for a prospective buyer (or the buyer's real estate agent) to check with the building department to verify that all structures on the property have been inspected and approved for occupancy. All sorts of information can be obtained from the building department about the property improvements.

Sometimes the construction permit involves nonoccupancy structures and a different standard for approval.

Case Example: Sprint PCS has a wireless telecommunications company and it applied for five Public Right-of-Way Above Ground Communication permits seeking to install wireless towers in the city La Canada Flintridge. Two permits were granted. The city denied the two applications finding that they would obstruct the right-of-way and would have a deleterious aesthetic impact (antennas are "unsightly") on the neighborhood. Sprint sued the city alleging

▼

---

violations of the federal Telecommunications Act of 1996. The District Court agreed. Sprint appealed.

California law provides that the only restriction on telephone companies is they may not incommode (obstruct) the public use of roads. State law preempts local ordinances if they duplicate, contradict or enter an area fully occupied by the general laws of the state. State law gives the city the "right to exercise reasonable control as to the time, place, and manner in which roads, highways, and waterways are accessed." Therefore, local regulators retain no authority to deny permits based on aesthetics. Because the city overstepped its regulatory authority under state law, it's wireless ordinance is invalid. Judgment reversed. *Sprint PCS Assets L.L.C. v. City of La Canada Flintridge*, 435 F.3d 993 (2005).

1. Second Units

The legislature of California has recognized that second units are a valuable and useful form of housing.

If a local ordinance regulates second unit permits, there is no guarantee that one will be issued. The Desmonds discovered this (see Case Example below) when their application was denied because of a finding under the Contra Costa County Ordinance Codes that "there was ample evidence of community concern with the impact of a residential second rental unit on the general aesthetic character of the neighborhood, as well as on traffic, safety, and protection of property values." *Desmond v. County of Contra Costa*, 21 Cal. App. 4th 308, at 339, 25 Cal. Rptr. 2d 842, at 848 (1993).

This legislation was adopted to encourage local governments to enact their own ordinances allowing and regulating so-called "granny flat" residential second units in single-family and multifamily zones where they would otherwise be prohibited. This legislation sets up a three option approach under which a local government may: (1) choose to ban all residential second units by making findings that the ordinance may limit housing opportunities of the region and additional findings that specific adverse impacts on the public health, safety, and welfare would result from allowing second units within single-family and multifamily zone areas; or (2) adopt its own ordinance providing for the creation of a second units and establish a various criteria for approving them, or (3) do neither and follow the state prescribed procedure for approving or disapproving applications for the creation of second units.

The following case involves a local ordinance adopted according to (2) above.

Case Example: The Desmonds (plaintiffs) submitted an application for a permit to build a residential second unit. The County zoning administrator approved it. A group of neighbors appealed the issuance of the permit to the County Planning Commission. Following a public hearing, the commission voted unanimously to uphold the neighbors' appeal and deny the application of the grounds that a second unit was not architecturally compatible with the overall character of the neighborhood, and the second unit will present a threat to public health, safety and welfare. The decision was appealed to the County Board which upheld the denial. Plaintiff sued.

The County ordinance provides that the planning agency "shall make" findings before granting a permit that: (1) the second unit has architecturally compatible with the overhaul neighborhood character; (2) the second unit does not result in excessive neighborhood noise,

▼

traffic, or parking problems, and (3) the second unit does not present a threat to public health, safety or welfare. Failure to make any one of these findings must result in a denial of the application. The County Board heard ample evidence of community concern with the general aesthetic character of the neighborhood, traffic issues, and protection of property values. The board concluded these opinions constituted substantial evidence that the second unit was intrusive to the character of the surrounding neighborhood. Judgment affirmed. *Desmond v. County of Contra Costa*, 21 Cal. App. 4th the 330; 25 Cal. Rptr. 2d 842; (1993).

2. Manufactured Homes

Manufactured homes must be allowed on lots zoned for single-family dwellings provided they are certified under the **National Manufactured Housing Construction and Safety Standards Act of 1974** and are installed on a foundation system. The manufactured home is subject to the same standards as conventional housing except for architectural requirements. Architectural requirements are limited to roof overhang, roofing materials and siding materials and cannot exceed those required of conventional housing. If there are no existing requirements for overhangs on both conventional housing and manufactured housing, 16 inches is the maximum. However, an ordinance may be adopted that prevents installation of a manufactured home if it is more than 10 years old.

D. SUBDIVISION LAWS

Local authorities also control land use by regulating the development of new subdivisions. Subdivision regulations may control the size of the lots and the location of streets, sidewalks, and sewer and water lines. They may also require the developer to provide open spaces and recreational areas within the subdivision.

California has two laws that govern the subdivision of land in the state: the Subdivision Map Act and the Subdivided Lands Law.

www.dot.ca.gov/hq/row/landsurveys/Study_material/Laws_Surveyors/Subdivision_Map_Act_and_Division_3.pdf
The Subdivision Map Act

1. Subdivision Map Act

The *SUBDIVISION MAP ACT gives cities and counties the power to regulate subdivisions and sets out rules for the exercise of that power. The purpose of the Map Act is to ensure that new subdivisions comply with the local general plan for development.* It also ensures that adequate utilities (water, sewer, electricity, and so on) are provided for each new subdivision. The act applies to any subdivision of land into two or more parcels, but its most important provisions only affect subdivisions with five or more parcels.

> **Subdivision Map Act** – required for two or more lots or parcels; administered by local officials; no public report required.
>
> **Subdivided Lands Law** – required for five or more lots or parcels; administered by the California Real Estate Commissioner; public report required.

When land is subdivided into five or more parcels, the subdivider must file a tentative subdivision map with the local planning agency. The *TENTATIVE SUBDIVISION MAP shows the proposed lot boundaries, the width and location of utility easements and access roads, and provisions for the control of flooding, among other things.* The planning agency can approve or reject the tentative map, or approve it on condition that the subdivider takes certain actions. For example, the agency may require the subdivider to dedicate some of the property for public streets.

After the planning agency approves the tentative map, the subdivider has 24 months to file a *FINAL MAP, showing the subdivision in its final form.* No sale, lease, or contract for sale or lease of a subdivision lot is valid until the final map has been filed.

Instead of tentative and final maps, a PARCEL MAP can be filed for subdivisions with two-to-four lots, and for condominiums and cooperatives. A parcel map doesn't have to be as detailed as tentative and final maps. Parcel maps can also be used for subdivisions with lots that are 40 acres or larger, certain subdivisions with access to existing streets, and some subdivisions zoned for commercial or industrial use.

2. Subdivided Lands Law

Lots in a subdivision covered by the *SUBDIVIDED LANDS ACT cannot be sold, leased, or financed until the Real Estate Commissioner investigates the subdivision and issues a final subdivision public report.* The *FINAL SUBDIVISION PUBLIC REPORT provides information about title to the property, liens that affect the entire subdivision, utilities and improvements, and terms and warranties that will apply to a transaction.*

As a general rule, the developer must give a copy of the final report to a prospective buyer, renter, or lender before he or she enters a transaction. In some cases the Commissioner issues a **preliminary report**. If the developer gives a prospective buyer a copy of the preliminary report, the buyer can reserve a lot in the subdivision. However, until the buyer receives the final report, he or she has the right to back out and have any deposit refunded in full.

The Subdivided Lands Act also applies to manufactured home parks and planned unit developments with five or more lots, to condominiums and cooperatives with five or more units, to some residential timeshare projects, and to rural land projects with fifty vacant lots or more. Leases of apartments, offices, and retail space within a building are generally exempt from the law. Standard subdivisions that are entirely within the limits of an incorporated city may also be exempt if the developer complies with certain rules.

www.leginfo.ca.gov/.html/bpc_table_of_contents.html
Subdivided Lands Act - Business & Professions Code 11000-11200

Another consumer protection law concerning subdivision sales is the *INTERSTATE LAND SALES FULL DISCLOSURE ACT (ILSFDA), which is a federal law that applies when subdivision property in one state is offered for sale in another state.* For example, when a subdivision in California is advertised in a magazine that is distributed in other states, the subdivider may have to comply with ILSFDA.

3. Common Interest Developments (CIDs)

The *DAVIS STIRLING COMMON INTEREST DEVELOPMENT ACT (Civil Code Section 1350-1376) contains the statutory provisions with respect to the creation and essential attributes of common interest developments*. The act covers:

1. condominium projects,*
2. community apartment projects,*
3. planned developments, and
4. stock cooperatives.*
(* See Chapter 4 for details of these common interest developments)

It is very comprehensive and, among other things, requires necessary documentation, provides for management by an association, sets up a procedure enforcing assessments, liens, covenants and restrictions; and establishes a procedure to amend existing documentation. In essence, a common interest development consists of separately owned spaces and additional space owned in common.

E. ENVIRONMENTAL REGULATIONS

When land use controls first developed, not much thought was given to protection of the environment. In recent years, however, this has become an area of great concern. Use of land, air, and water need to be controlled not just for the public health and welfare, but also for the preservation of natural resources. To this end, several federal and state environmental laws have been enacted. Here's a list of the more important ones.

1. National Environmental Policy Act (NEPA)

The National Environmental Policy Act (NEPA) of 1969 was enacted by Congress, and in addition to defining our nation's environmental policy, it establishes the **Environmental Protection Agency (EPA)**, the **Council on Environmental Quality (CEQ)**, and the **Environmental Impact Statements (EIS)**. The CEQ, which consist of three members appointed by the President, assists and advises the President on national environmental quality. The EPA is responsible for carrying out environmental policy. An EIS is required on all federal actions that may significantly affect the quality of the human environment.

NEPA applies to all kinds of federal development projects, such as dam and highway construction and waste control plans. NEPA also applies to private action when the use or development requires a license or permit from a federal agency, or even a federal loan. In these cases, the federal agencies may require submission of an EIS before granting approval.

An EIS should examine the impact of the development on energy consumption, sewage systems, school population, drainage, water facilities, and other environmental, economic, and social factors, as well as alternatives including a "no action" alternative.

2. Clean Air Act

The federal *CLEAN AIR ACT requires the Environmental Protection Agency (EPA) to regulate emission of air pollutants that are harmful to the public's health*. National standards have been issued for certain pollutants. Each state is required to prepare a **State Implementation Plan (SIP)** for meeting the national standards.

Developers of projects that will involve direct emission of pollutants into the air must obtain permits from state or regional air pollution control authorities. States are given authority to prevent development that would interfere with attainment or maintenance of clean air objectives.

The **California Health and Safety Code** contains most of California's law governing air quality. The legislation establishes air basins in an attempt to coordinate local, regional and state pollution control. The State Air Resources Board and numerous Regional Air Pollution Control Districts have been established and use control officers to enforce air pollution control standards. Each district has to adopt plans and regulations to maintain air quality standards.

The **State Air Resources Board** coordinates these pollution control activities and enforces compliance with the standards for air quality adopted by the Legislature by reviewing the districts' enforcement practices, rules and regulations, programs and goals.

3. Clean Water Act

The federal *CLEAN WATER ACT sets water quality standards.* A permit is required for discharging pollutants into a lake, stream, or other navigable waterway. Any land use that would discharge an unacceptable level of water pollutants is prohibited. Developers are often required to take measures, such as building retention basins or installing silt fences, to protect from runoff of contaminants.

The Clean Water Act also regulates wastewater treatment systems. It encourages local governments to investigate new technology and alternatives to traditional sewage treatment plants. The wastewater facilities available may have a significant effect on the type and amount of new construction permitted.

4. Resource Conservation and Recovery Act

The *RESOURCE CONSERVATION AND RECOVERY ACT allows regulation of hazardous waste facilities through the EPA.* The Office of Solid Waste issues permits for storage, treatment and disposal of hazardous wastes. Hazardous substances are identified, site inventories are conducted and information is stored as part of the ongoing effort to keep track of hazardous materials.

5. The Comprehensive Environmental Response, Compensation, and Liability Act (CERCLA)

The **COMPREHENSIVE ENVIRONMENTAL RESPONSE, COMPENSATION, AND LIABILITY ACT (CERCLA)**, *a federal law, concerns liability for environmental cleanup costs. Under the act, the current owner of contaminated property may be required to pay for cleanup, even if the owner did not cause the contamination, and even if someone else owned the property when the contamination occurred.*

6. Endangered Species Act

Enacted in 1973, this very important federal conservation law became one of the most highly publicized and controversial laws. The general purpose is to provide a means whereby the ecosystems upon which endangered species and threatened species depend may be conserved, and to provide a program for the conservation of such endangered species and threatened species. Private property owners may be required to take measures designed to minimize and mitigate the effects that any development of their property may have on endangered or threatened species or their habitat.

7. California Environmental Quality Act (CEQA)

This state law is similar to the National Environmental Policy Act. The *CALIFORNIA ENVIRONMENTAL QUALITY ACT (CEQA) requires state or local agencies to prepare an environmental impact report (EIR) for any project (public or private) that may have a significant impact on the environment.* Private projects are subject to CEQA review if any state agency or local government must approve the project or provides funding for the project (examples would be rezoning or subdivision approvals). A development can only be excepted from this requirement if the public agency overseeing the project rules that it will not have significant adverse effects on the environment.

A public hearing is held for each EIR. Alternatives to the proposed action must be considered, and a developer may be required to make changes to reduce its impact. For judicial review, no lawsuit can be brought unless the alleged noncompliance with the act was presented to the public agency verbally before the close of the public hearing before the notice of determination is issued.

Case Example: Martin owns a house located on Broadway in San Francisco. The Atkinson House was originally erected in 1853. It is one of the oldest houses in San Francisco. The noted 19th-century architect Willis Polk designed the remodeling of its interior in 1893. The neighborhood is listed on the National Register of Historic Places and the California Register of Historic Resources. Martin submitted plans to the city for alterations to the interior and exterior of his house that contemplated destruction of the Polk-designed redwood interior. The city determined that the application involved space considered to be part of historic resorts and consequently under the CEQA. Martin submitted an Environmental Evaluation application. The city's position was that the proposed interior alterations would cause a substantial adverse change in the significance of a historic resource. Martin sued for a declaration that the CEQA does not apply to his proposed interior modifications and that the city has no discretion to deny a permit for renovation. Judgment for the city. Martin appealed.

The CEQA exempts interior alterations to an existing private structure that entail negligible or no expansion of existing use. The CEQA deals with tangible physical manifestations that are perceptible by the senses. No one not actually inside Martin's house will have any awareness that the interior modifications have been made. A purely intellectual understanding that work by Willis Polk may no longer be within an unobservable part of another person's private living quarters will not suffice to establish a significant effect on the environment. We can scarcely believe the Legislature envisioned turning local agencies into censors of homeowners' plans for interior decoration. Mr. Martin's project is exempt from the environmental report. However, since the city has yet to deny Martin a permit, we cannot grant his request ordering the issuance of a permit. *Martin v. City and County of San Francisco*, 135 Cal. App. 4th 392, Cal. Rptr. 3d 470 (2005).

8. California Coastal Act

The *CALIFORNIA COASTAL ACT established the California Coastal Zone Conservation Commission.* The commission researches ways to protect the California coastline and controls development along the coast. It has several regional divisions, and no development is permitted in the coastal zone without a permit from the appropriate regional board. A coastal zone is normally from the highest coastal mountain peak to the outer sea limits, but this distance has been reduced in large urban areas.

9. Alquist-Priolo Special Studies Zone Act

Under the *ALQUIST-PRIOLO SPECIAL STUDIES ZONE ACT, any application for new residential development or construction in certain areas of the state must include a geologic report.* The report considers the earthquake risks for the property. Additionally, a seller must disclose to a potential buyer if the property is in a special studies zone, where there is a recently active or potentially active earthquake fault.

10. Safe Drinking Water and Toxic Enforcement Act

Proposition 65 generated the *SAFE DRINKING WATER AND TOXIC ENFORCEMENT ACT of 1986, which is enforced by the Department of Health Services. The purpose of the Act is to warn the public of health hazards and protect drinking water from toxic contamination through discharge into the water or onto the land.* Actions for enforcement are brought by public prosecutors or can be brought by any person in the public interest.

11. Environment Responsibility Acceptance Act

An owner of property who is actually aware of a release of a hazardous material must send notice of potential liability to those identified as potentially responsible parties for the release and to the appropriate government agency. Those receiving the notice of potential responsibility are given an opportunity to assess the magnitude of the release and seek agreement for proportional division of the cleanup task and cost.

12. Integrated Waste Management Act of 1989

This legislation mandated local jurisdictions to meet solid waste diversion goals of 25 percent by 1995 and 50 percent by 2000. This diversion would be determined by looking at the base-year solid waste generation (waste normally disposed of into landfills) to determine the amount of solid waste diverted.

13. California Coastal Sanctuary Act of 1994

To encourage conservation, maintenance, and utilization of the living resources of the ocean and other waters under the jurisdiction of the State of California, this legislation creates a sanctuary consisting of all state waters subject to tidal influence. There is an exception for those waters subject to oil and gas leases.

14. Williamson Act

The Legislature enacted the Williamson Act in an attempt to preserve agricultural land by allowing farmers and ranchers to enter into commitments of no less than 10 years that restrict the property to only agricultural uses. The benefit to the landowner or gain to the restriction is a special property tax assessment rate.

15. Telecommunications Act of 1996

Congress directed, in Section 207 of the Telecommunications Act of 1969, that the Federal Communications Commission adopt an Over-the-Air Reception Devices Rule. This rule would cover governmental and nongovernmental restrictions on a viewer's ability to receive video programming signals from direct broadcast satellites, wireless cable providers, and television broadcast stations. Essentially, the rule prohibits restrictions that impair the installation, maintenance, or use of antennas used to receive video programming by viewers. The rule covers video antennas, including direct-to-home satellite dishes that are less then 1 meter in diameter, TV antennas, and wireless cable antennas.

16. Solar Shade Control Act

No person owning or in control of a property shall allow a tree or shrub to be planted, or, if placed, to grow on such property subsequent to the installation of a solar collector on the property of another so as to cast a shadow on greater than 10% of the collector absorption area at any one time between the hours of 10 A.M. and 2 P.M. This does not apply to specific trees and shrubs that at the time of installation of a solar collector cast a shadow upon the collector.

II. Private Restrictions

In some cases, private restrictions on the use of property are simply a contract between a seller and a buyer, or between an owner and the neighboring owner.

Example: A and B are neighbors. A is concerned that B might put an addition on her house that would block his view of the mountains. He discusses this with B. B says that if A pays her $500, she will never obstruct his view. A puts this agreement in writing, they both sign it, and A gives B the $500.

This is an enforceable contract between A and B. If B breaks her promise, A can sue her. This kind of agreement is called a **restrictive covenant**.

But what if B sells her property to X? X is interested in astronomy; she builds an observation tower that blocks A's view of the mountains. A would not have the right to sue X because X was not a party to the contract between A and B.

However, by following certain statutory rules, A and B could have made their restrictive covenant run with the land in the same way that an easement can (see Chapter 3). Then the restriction against blocking the view would apply to X (or anyone else who bought B's property). If A sold his property to someone else, the new owner would have the right to enforce the restrictive covenant and protect the view, just as A did.

A. RESTRICTIVE COVENANTS RUNNING WITH THE LAND

To make a restrictive covenant run with the land, the original parties must record a document that states the terms of the restriction. This document is often a deed.

Example: Q owns a large lot; he sells part of it to P. Q can include a restrictive covenant in the deed that will prevent P from building within 40 feet of their common property line. By accepting the deed, P agrees to the restriction.

1. Requirements for a Covenant to Run with the Land

A *COVENANT RUNS WITH THE LAND if it binds not only the person who originally made the promise but also binds subsequent owners of the land, even though they did not personally make the promise.* For a promise to run with the land:

1. the covenant must be in a recorded document,
2. the document must describe the property that benefits from the restriction and the property that is burdened by the restriction,
3. the covenant must expressly state that future owners of the burdened property are bound by the covenant for the benefit of the other property, and
4. the covenant must relate to the use, repair, maintenance or improvement of, or payment of taxes and assessments on, the burdened property.

If the document does not fulfill all four of these requirements, the restrictions will not run with the land. The original promisor will have to comply with the restriction, but a subsequent owner would not.

A restrictive covenant will not run with the land unless it relates to the use, repair, maintenance, or improvement of the property, payment of taxes on the property, or otherwise directly benefits the property.

2. Subdivision Restrictions

Today, most private restrictions are imposed by subdivision developers. A developer often places restrictions on all the lots in a new subdivision by recording a declaration of covenants, conditions, and restrictions (better known as CC&Rs). As the Anthony case suggests, a developer's CC&Rs are generally intended to keep the subdivision attractive and protect the market value of the homes.

Case Example: The Anthonys bought a home in the Glenbrook Hills subdivision in Brea, a community in Orange County. The recorded CC&Rs for the subdivision required all homeowners to belong to the Brea Glenbrook Club. The private club owned and operated a recreational area in the subdivision, with a swimming pool and a clubhouse. Every homeowner had to pay membership dues, which were used to maintain the club's facilities.

The Anthonys didn't want to be members of the club or use its facilities. They sued for a declaration that the membership requirement in the CC&Rs was not a covenant running with the land.

The court disagreed. The covenant related to the use, repair, and maintenance of the club's property. It also directly benefited the other properties in the subdivision since the recreational facilities increased the market value of the homes. *Anthony v. Brea Glenbrook Club*, 58 Cal. App. 3d 506, 130 Cal. Rptr. 32 (1976).

By following certain rules, a developer can establish a common plan of restrictions for the whole subdivision. When there's a **COMMON PLAN**, *any homeowner in the subdivision can enforce the CC&Rs against any other homeowner*. The lots are mutually burdened and benefited by the restrictions.

Example: In the Maytag Meadows subdivision, Lot 47 is half a mile away from Lots 18, 19, and 20. The family that lives on Lot 19 hangs its laundry out to dry in the back yard, which violates one of the rules in the CC&Rs. The owners of Lot 18 and Lot 20 don't mind. The owner of Lot 47 is outraged. Because the developer established a common plan of restrictions for the entire subdivision, the owner of Lot 47 can enforce the restriction against Lot 19, even though she doesn't live next door.

To establish a common plan, the developer must clearly state in the CC&Rs that the restrictions are mutually binding on all the homeowners in the subdivision, and the developer must make sure that the CC&Rs are recorded before any parcels are sold. Once the CC&Rs have been recorded, the restrictions are binding on subsequent buyers of the lots, even if the deeds don't mention the CC&Rs. Private restrictions work basically the same way easements do: once they're in the recorded chain of title for the burdened property, subsequent purchasers have constructive notice and take title subject to the restrictions.

Example: J was the first person to buy Lot 10, and his deed from the developer states that the property is subject to the recorded CC&Rs. J records his deed. When J sells Lot 10 to K, he doesn't tell K about the restrictions, and they aren't mentioned in the new deed.

K violates the restrictions by putting a large fountain in his front yard. One of his neighbors sues. K claims he isn't bound by the CC&Rs because they weren't mentioned in his deed. The court rules against K. The CC&Rs bind all successive owners of Lot 10, since J put them in the chain of title by recording his deed. It doesn't matter that they weren't expressly incorporated into K's deed.

B. ENFORCING PRIVATE RESTRICTIONS

When a court finds that a property owner has violated a restrictive covenant, the owner may be required to pay damages to the person who is asking to have the restriction enforced. In addition (or instead), the court may issue an injunction ordering the owner to comply with the restriction: take down the basketball hoop, stop mowing the lawn at midnight, or get rid of the chickens. If the owner doesn't do what the court orders, he or she can be fined or even put in jail for contempt of court.

Example: L purchased a home overlooking a lake. All lots in this subdivision were bound by a restrictive covenant stating that no structure should be more than one story high, except that the Architectural Control Committee could grant a special variance if it wouldn't restrict the view from other lots.

L builds a one-story house. Several years later (without a variance), he begins adding a second story that would block the view of the lake for his neighbor N. N brings a lawsuit to enforce the covenant and stop construction.

L argues that N is only entitled to damages, but a view is a special asset, and it would be extremely difficult to place a monetary value on it. N testifies that the view was one of the main reasons he bought that particular house. The court orders L to remove the partially constructed addition to restore N's view.

1. Covenants vs. Conditions

Breach of Covenant – results in an order to comply with restriction or pay damages.

Breach of Condition – may result in reversion of title to grantor (previous owner).

So far we've discussed only restrictive covenants. But a restriction in a deed can be either a covenant or a condition, and there's a significant difference between them. A *COVENANT, as you've seen, is a promise to do or not do something.* It may just be a contract between two parties, or it may run with the land. In either case, someone who breaches a covenant will be ordered to comply with the restriction and/or pay damages.

A 90

Breach of a condition is a much more serious matter than breach of a covenant. A *CONDITION in a deed makes the owner's title subject to forfeiture.* Someone who breaches a condition may forfeit title to the property, so that it reverts to the previous owner (who placed the condition in the deed). In other words, if there's a condition in the deed, the grantee has a fee simple defeasible estate instead of a fee simple absolute (see Chapter 3).

Because forfeiture of title (or "power of termination") is an extremely harsh result, a court will always try to interpret a deed restriction as a covenant rather than a condition. If the wording is absolutely clear and leaves no room for interpretation, the restriction will be enforced as a condition. The power of termination expires 30 years after it is recorded or after a notice of intent to preserve the power is recorded under the marketable record title legislation. The power can also expire if it becomes obsolete for reasons like changed conditions over time. Additionally, there is a five-year statute of limitations from the date of the breach.

Case Example: General Petroleum sold some property to Kelley and Clark. The deed included a restriction prohibiting the grantees from opening a service station on the property for 20 years. The deed stated: "Should the property be used for service station purposes ... the title should be revested and revert to General Petroleum Corporation."

A few years later, Kelley and Clark sold the property to Mr. Boughton. Boughton sued for a declaration that General Petroleum's restriction was unenforceable. The court held that Boughton would forfeit his title if he violated the condition. *Boughton v. Socony Mobil Oil Co.*, 231 Cal. App. 2d 188, 41 Cal. Rptr. 714 (1964).

Nearly all private restrictions are covenants rather than conditions. Even though "CC&Rs" stands for covenants, conditions, and restrictions, they virtually never make a grantee's title subject to forfeiture.

C. TERMINATING RESTRICTIVE COVENANTS

Many restrictive covenants have no time limit, but others state that they will expire after a certain date. In that case, the covenant becomes unenforceable when time runs out.

Some states impose statutory time limits on restrictive covenants. In New York, for example, private restrictions terminate automatically after 30 years, unless they're formally renewed. There is no statutory time limit in California; if a restrictive covenant doesn't limit itself, it can be enforced indefinitely—unless something happens to terminate it.

One of the ways a restrictive covenant can be terminated is by agreement. The owner of the benefited property agrees to release the burdened property from the restriction. In that case, the parties should be sure to record a release.

A restrictive covenant can also be terminated by **merger**, just like an easement. If the owner of the burdened property also acquires title to the benefited property, the restriction disappears. It won't revive if the two properties are sold separately again later on.

If a restrictive covenant isn't enforced, it may become unenforceable. This is called TERMINATION BY ABANDONMENT.

Case Example: The subdivision restrictions required all buildings to be set back at least 20 feet, with side yards at least four-feet wide. The Whitneys built their home only three feet, eight inches from one of the side boundaries of their lot, and a neighbor sued.

The Whitneys offered evidence that there were many similar violations in the subdivision. For instance, on Lots 21 and 23 the side yards were less than four-feet wide, and on Lot 5 the side yards were only one-foot wide. There was a house built right on top of the side boundary between Lots 17 and 18.

The court ruled that because there hadn't been uniform enforcement of the restrictions, they should be treated as abandoned. Enforcing the side yard requirements against the Whitneys wouldn't restore the area to its intended design, and failing to enforce them didn't diminish the value of the surrounding properties. *Bryant v. Whitney*, 178 Cal. 640, 174 P. 32 (1918).

Similarly, *a restrictive covenant may no longer be enforceable if the character of the restricted neighborhood has changed. This is called* **TERMINATION DUE TO CHANGED CIRCUMSTANCES** (see the following Case Example).

In other cases, other courts have reached different conclusions. As long as the original purpose of the restrictive covenants can still be realized, they are supposed to be enforceable.

Case Example: A 24-lot subdivision in Orange County was restricted to single-family residential use. Commercial uses were forbidden. These restrictions were placed in 1940.

In 1955, Mr. McCabe bought Lot 1, which fronted on Highway 101. Part of that lot was zoned for commercial use, and part of it was zoned for multifamily residential use. Although McCabe was aware of the subdivision restrictions, he started constructing a commercial building on his lot. Some of the neighbors sued.

McCabe argued that conditions around Lot 1 had changed since the subdivision restrictions were imposed, and it was no longer suitable for single-family residential use. Traffic on that stretch of Highway 101 had increased, and the authorities were considering expanding it to four lanes. The court agreed with McCabe that Lot 1 wasn't suitable for single-family homes, and decided that commercial use of the property wouldn't have adverse effects on the other lots in the subdivision. As a result, the court refused to enforce the restriction. *Key v. McCabe*, 54 Cal. 2d 736, 8 Cal. Rptr. 425 (1960).

CHAPTER 13

Termination of Restrictive Covenants

Expiration   Release   Merger   Abandonment   Changed Circumstances

D. PUBLIC POLICY LIMITS ON PRIVATE RESTRICTIONS

Just several decades ago, it was commonplace for CC&Rs to prohibit conveyance of property within a subdivision to blacks, Jews, or other minorities. Now private restrictions forbidding transfer based on race, religion, ancestry, national origin, sex, or physical disability are illegal. You may still run across discriminatory provisions in CC&Rs recorded half a century ago, but those provisions are unenforceable and can be removed.

In some subdivisions, the CC&Rs prevented homeowners from putting up "For Sale" signs on their properties. In passing California Civil Code Sections 712 and 713, the legislature decided such restrictions were an unreasonable restraint on alienation if the signs are reasonably located, in plain view of the public, of reasonable size and dimension, and do not adversely affect public (including traffic) safety.

Additionally, any covenant, restriction, or condition that effectively prohibits or restricts the installation or use of a solar energy system is void and unenforceable.

It is a state policy in California to encourage the use of solar energy systems and remove obstacles to their use, however, reasonable restrictions are allowed.

It's also illegal for private restrictions to forbid an owner from having a manufactured home installed. The manufactured home can be required to comply with the restrictions that apply to all homes in the subdivision—size, building materials, and so on. But it can't be ruled out just because it was constructed in a factory instead of on the property.

California laws limit restrictions against flying flags on an owner's property and restrictions related to posting noncommercial signs on an owner's property. Both California law and federal regulations prohibit restrictions on installing a TV antennae or satellite dishes that would unreasonably increase the cost of installation or impair reception of an acceptable quality signal.

Finally, CC&Rs prohibiting a residence from being used as any business or for non-residential purposes does not prohibit a residence being used as a family daycare home under Health & Safety Section 1597.40(c) or a group home for the disabled elderly under Government Code Section 12955.

E. CALGREEN (California Green Building Standards Code)

Effective January 1, 2011, California, through the *CALIFORNIA GREEN BUILDING STANDARDS CODE, or CALGreen, became the first state to adopt a green building code that imposes energy efficiency and other green standards on new construction in an effort to achieve reductions in natural resource consumption and greenhouse gas emissions.* Despite its first-in-the-nation status, CALGreen represents only a modest change from prior California green building requirements.

CALGreen establishes minimum uniform standards for green building that apply to many types of new construction, including commercial, low-rise residential, state owned and educational buildings.

CALGreen encompasses residential and non-residential mandatory measures. The non-residential mandatory measures are classified into the following categories: Planning and Design; Energy Efficiency; Water Efficiency and Conservation; Material Conservation and Resource Efficiency; and Environmental Quality.

Among the mandatory measures, developers must divert 50 percent of construction waste from landfills through recycling or re-use of materials. They must provide designated, and in some cases preferred, parking for bicycles, carpool, and clean-air vehicles. They must use low pollutant-emitting construction and finishing materials. They must install separate water meters for indoor and outdoor uses for buildings over 50,000 square feet. They must also install moisture-sensing or "smart" irrigation systems for larger landscape projects. Additionally, developers must reduce potable water consumption by 20 percent through performance or prescriptive standards, and wastewater by 20 percent through installation of water-conserving fixtures or the use of graywater, rainwater or recycled water. Light pollution from the site must be reduced, and building commissioning is required for buildings 10,000 square feet and larger.

III. CHAPTER SUMMARY

1. The government's power to regulate land use is based on the police power: the power to pass laws for the protection of the public health, safety, morals, and general welfare. Land use regulations are unconstitutional if they are discriminatory or exclusionary, or if they are excessive, preventing the owner from making any use of the property.

2. State law requires every city and county in California to have a planning agency. The agency is responsible for creating a long-range general plan for development. Local authorities adopt detailed zoning ordinances to carry out the general plan.

3. Zoning ordinances segregate different types of land use into different areas. They usually also regulate the size of lots, height of buildings, building setbacks, lighting, signs, and off-street parking. Zoning ordinances provide for certain exceptions to their rules: nonconforming uses, variances, and conditional uses.

4. A nonconforming use is an established use that violates a new zoning ordinance, but is permitted to continue. A nonconforming use generally can't be expanded, renovated, rebuilt after destruction, or resumed after abandonment.

5. A variance allows an owner to build a structure or use property in a way that violates the zoning ordinance. Variances usually only authorize a minor deviation from the rules. Under California law, a variance can only be granted when the zoning regulations have a greater impact on the property (because of its unusual size, shape, or topography) than on neighboring properties. California law also prohibits use variances.

6. A rezone is a revision of the zoning ordinance. Spot zoning—rezoning to benefit or restrict a particular property owner without justification—is illegal.

7. Building codes establish minimum standards for construction methods and materials. Building inspectors issue a certificate of occupancy for new construction that complies with the codes. Existing buildings may also be required to comply with new building codes.

8. The Subdivision Map Act requires a subdivider (land or condos) to file a map with the local planning agency (city or county) for approval. Under the Subdivided Lands Law, lots in a subdivision can't be sold, leased, or financed until the Real Estate Commissioner issues a public report on the development.

9. The National Environmental Policy Act and the California Environmental Quality Act require government agencies to prepare environmental impact statements before approving major development projects. The developers may be required to modify their plans to reduce the adverse effects on the environment. The federal Clean Air Act and Clean Water Act set standards for air and water quality and regulate pollution.

10. Private restrictions relating to the use, maintenance, or improvement of property, or benefiting property, can run with the land. A recorded document must state that future owners of the burdened property will be bound by the restrictions.

11. If the developer establishes a common plan of restrictions for a subdivision, any lot owner can enforce the restrictions against any other lot owner. To establish a common plan, CC&Rs must be recorded and also incorporated into the first deed for each lot.

12. Restrictive covenants can be terminated by agreement, merger, abandonment, or a change in the character of the neighborhood.

13. CALGreen (California Green Building Standards Code) imposes energy efficiency and other green standards on new construction in an effort to achieve reductions in natural resource consumption and greenhouse gas emissions.

IV. CASE PROBLEM
City of National City v. Wiener, 3 Cal. 4th 832, 12 Cal. Rptr. 2d 701, (1992)

The City of National City, (The City) has 17.9 percent of its land zoned for commercial use, 40.6 percent zoned for residential use, 16.9 percent for industrial use and 24.6 percent zoned for institutional and military use. The City has an ordinance prohibiting an adult entertainment business within 1,500 feet of another adult business, school or public park, or within 1,000 feet of a residential zone, unless it is located in an enclosed mall or a mall where the business front is isolated from public off-site view. The ordinance does not limit the number of adult businesses or the hours of operation. Wiener and his sister opened Chuck's Bookstore, an adult bookstore and arcade on National City Boulevard. The City sought an injunction against the bookstore for violating the ordinance by being too close to another adult business and a residential area. Weiner claimed the ordinance was unconstitutional as a violation of his First Amendment rights of free speech, especially since there was only one other adult business in The City, a theater. Additionally, The City is mostly strip zoned and the distance requirements make all locations almost impossible except for a mall.

The City claimed the ordinance was a reasonable regulation designed to serve a substantial government interest and that it provided a reasonable alternative avenue of communication since there are other shopping malls that could accommodate an adult business and plenty of commercial property that could do likewise. Weiner responded that even though there were vacancies in the three shopping malls, no mall would rent space to an adult business. He would, therefore, have to build his own mall. Is the ordinance unconstitutional?

V. KEY TERMS

Board of Adjustment	floor area ratio	restrictive covenant
building code	general plan	rezone
CC&Rs	LAFCO	setback
certificate of occupancy	NEPA	side yard
conditional use	nonconforming use	special exception
Environmental Impact	parcel map	spot zoning
Statement (EIS)	planned unit development	tentative subdivision map
EQA	planning commission	use variance
exclusionary zoning	police power	variance

VI. CHAPTER QUIZ

1. California law prevents local governments from allowing commercial use in a residential zone by granting:

    a. use variances.
    b. zoning waivers.
    c. spot waivers.
    d. selective zoning.

2. How many days does a citizen generally have to challenge a zoning ordinance after it has been adopted?

    a. 30 days
    b. 60 days
    c. 90 days
    d. 180 days

3. What document outlines the community's development policies and establishes an overall design for the various land uses in the area?

    a. Zoning plan
    b. General plan
    c. Community plan
    d. Zoning authorization plan

4. If the citizens are not happy with the land-use controls adopted by their local government, they can:

    a. do nothing about it.
    b. adopt local land-use controls by the initiative process.
    c. ignore them because land-use controls are unconstitutional.
    d. none of the above.

5. The floor area ratio:

    a. computes the square footage of a building.
    b. is the ratio between the square footage of the floor and the cubic footage of the attic.
    c. is the ratio between the square footage in the residence and the garage.
    d. is the ratio between the area of the building's floor space and the area of the lot.

6. If a nonconforming building is destroyed, most ordinances provide that:

    a. a new building can replace the destroyed building and continue the nonconforming use.
    b. no building is allowed on the property.
    c. a new building can be constructed, but it cannot continue the nonconforming use.
    d. none of the above.

7. With regard to building a second unit ("granny flat"), the California Legislature:
    a. has declared construction of second units illegal.
    b. has declared second units are important in California and do not require a building permit.
    c. has established rules regarding local ordinances adopted for regulating second unit permits.
    d. none of the above.

8. With regard to lots zoned for single-family dwellings, manufactured homes:
    a. must be allowed on those lots if they are certified under the National Manufactured Housing Construction and Safety Standards Act.
    b. must be allowed on most lots if they are installed on a foundation.
    c. both a and b are correct.
    d. none of the above.

9. The purpose of the Subdivision Map Act is to:
    a. ensure that new subdivisions comply with the local general plan for development.
    b. set zoning for the property.
    c. establish the value of the subdivision for tax purposes.
    d. protect the buyers from dishonest salespersons.

10. A restrictive covenant can be terminated by which of the following?
    a. Abandonment
    b. The owner of the benefited property releases the burdened property
    c. A change in circumstances
    d. All of the above

ANSWERS: 1. a; 2. c; 3. b; 4. b; 5. d; 6. c; 7. c; 8. c; 9. a; 10. d

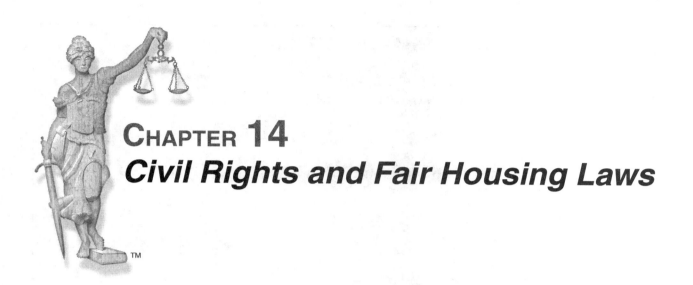

CHAPTER 14
Civil Rights and Fair Housing Laws

CHAPTER OVERVIEW

Numerous federal and state civil rights and fair housing laws prohibit discrimination against persons in certain groups based upon their characteristics or backgrounds (*the groups of persons protected from discrimination are called* **PROTECTED CLASSES**).

A real estate agent needs to be able to recognize conduct that violates anti-discrimination laws in order to avoid liability. A violation could lead to the suspension or revocation of the agent's license, and could result in a civil lawsuit or even criminal prosecution.

An agent can combat discrimination by explaining the fair housing laws to clients. Sellers and landlords want to avoid liability, and buyers and tenants want to know their rights.

This chapter discusses the most important federal and California state anti-discrimination laws. It explores how these laws affect the day-to-day relationships between real estate agents and their clients.

I. Historical Background

In the United States, the first civil rights laws were passed more than 120 years ago. The Thirteenth, Fourteenth, and Fifteenth Amendments to the Constitution were adopted right after the Civil War. They abolished slavery, guaranteed equal protection of the laws, and established that citizens of all races had the right to vote. The Civil Rights Act of 1866 was enacted during the same period.

Early civil rights laws were originally interpreted only to prohibit discrimination that involved **state action**—that is, action by a federal, state, or local governmental body (see the discussion of the Constitution in Chapter 1). As such, it was illegal for a city government to enact discriminatory ordinances, or for the police to enforce the laws in a discriminatory way, favoring one group over another. It wasn't illegal for private citizens to discriminate, however.

The landmark case concerning real estate discrimination was decided by the U.S. Supreme Court in 1948. At that time, it wasn't unlawful for a deed to include a covenant restricting property ownership to members of a particular race or religion. But in *Shelley v. Kraemer*, 334 U.S.1, the Court held that it was unconstitutional for a government to enforce discriminatory restrictions. A court order enforcing the restrictions would be discriminatory state action.

CHAPTER 14

Therefore, even though the restrictive covenants (private action) were legal, a court order enforcing them (state action) was illegal. Without enforcement, a restrictive covenant isn't very effective, so *Shelley v. Kraemer* was an early step toward eliminating housing discrimination by private citizens. The *Shelley* rule still depended on state action, however.

In the last few decades, court decisions and legislation have extended laws against discrimination to purely private activities involving no state action. Federal and state laws now make it illegal to include discriminatory covenants in deeds or other documents, or to honor such provisions already in existing documents. It is also now unlawful for county recorders to record documents containing discriminatory covenants.

II. Federal Legislation

http://portal.hud.gov/hudportal/HUD?src=/program_offices/fair_housing_equal_opp
Fair Housing and Equal Opportunity

The federal government uses legislation and regulations to carry out a policy of eliminating discrimination in housing and other real estate related areas, such as lending and employment.

As you read the following discussion of federal discrimination laws, it's important to remember that California state law in this area is often stricter than federal law. California law prohibits more types of discrimination in more types of transactions, and with far fewer exceptions.

The stricter law is the one that must be followed. With that in mind, you can treat the material covering exemptions from the Federal Fair Housing Act as general background information, recognizing that for the most part, those exemptions do not exist under California law.

A. CIVIL RIGHTS ACT OF 1866

The *CIVIL RIGHTS ACT OF 1866 prohibits discrimination based on race or ancestry in any property transaction in the United States.* The act states, "…all citizens of the United States shall have the same right, in every state and territory as is enjoyed by white citizens thereof to inherit, purchase, lease, sell, hold and convey real and personal property."

Unlike the 1968 Fair Housing Act (discussed below), which applies only to housing and certain other particular types of property, the 1866 Civil Rights Act contains no exceptions and applies to all property, whether real or personal, residential or commercial, improved, or unimproved.

Civil Rights Act of 1866

- Only prohibits discrimination based on race or ancestry
- Applies to any real estate or personal property transaction
- No exceptions

#92

---

1. Enforcement

A lawsuit based on the 1866 Act can only be filed in federal district court. The federal law doesn't specify a time limit for filing an action; the lawsuit must be filed within the time limit specified by state law for similar claims. In California, that's three years.

Since the statute itself doesn't specifically mention remedies, the court fashions the remedies it finds necessary. The case law shows that the remedies available to a claimant who proves unlawful discrimination under the 1866 Act include:

1. injunctions,
2. compensatory damages, and
3. punitive damages.

An *INJUNCTION is a court order requiring the defendant to do or refrain from doing a particular act* (see Chapter 1). In a discrimination case, a court might order the defendant to sell his or her house to the plaintiff, for example.

CHAPTER 14

An award of **COMPENSATORY DAMAGES** *in a discrimination suit could include out-of-pocket expenses (such as rent or transportation payments) and compensation for emotional distress.* In many discrimination cases, awards for compensatory damages total thousands of dollars; in exceptional cases, hundreds of thousands of dollars have been awarded.

PUNITIVE DAMAGES *are intended to punish the wrongdoer and discourage others from engaging in similar behavior (see Chapter 6). There is no limit on the amount of punitive damages that may be awarded for claims under the 1866 Act.* Punitive damage awards have exceeded $100,000 in some cases.

2. Constitutionality

The constitutionality of the 1866 Act was challenged in a landmark case decided by the U.S. Supreme Court just a few weeks after Congress passed the 1968 Civil Rights Act.

www.withylaw.com/history.htm
A Short History of American Civil Rights Laws

> **Case Example:** Mr. and Mrs. Jones, a black couple, attempted to buy a home in a subdivision being developed near St. Louis by the Mayer Company. When their offer was refused, they brought suit against the Mayer Company based on the 1866 Civil Rights Act. They claimed they were turned down because of their race. The court ruled in favor of the Joneses and held that the 1866 Act was constitutional. *Jones v. Alfred H. Mayer Co.*, 392 U.S. 409 (1968).

The ruling in favor of the Joneses established three important points:

1. The 1866 Act prohibits all racial discrimination in the sale and rental of property—the actions of private parties as well as state action—because the right to buy or lease property can be impaired as effectively by those who place property on the market as by government actions.

2. The 1866 Act is constitutional under the Thirteenth Amendment to the Constitution, which abolished slavery and also gave Congress the power to enforce the amendment through appropriate legislation. The Court held that the 1866 Act was an example of "appropriate legislation." The Thirteenth Amendment was intended to eliminate not only slavery but also the various conditions associated with slavery, often referred to as "badges of slavery." One of these badges was the inability to own or exchange property. Thus, Congress eliminated this incident of slavery through legislation.

3. The provisions of the 1866 Act are independent of and not superseded by the 1968 Civil Rights Act. The Court noted that the 1866 Act is not a comprehensive fair housing law. It doesn't address discrimination on grounds other than race or ancestry; it doesn't deal with discrimination in the provision of services or facilities connected with housing, financing, advertising, or brokerage; and it doesn't provide for any federal agency to assist aggrieved parties, or for intervention by the U.S. Attorney General. The 1866 Act is a general statute enforceable only by private parties bringing private lawsuits. By contrast, the Fair Housing Act is a detailed housing law covering a great variety of discriminatory practices and enforceable by federal authorities.

www.en.wikipedia.org/wiki/Civil_Rights_Act_of_1964
Civil Rights Act of 1964

B. FEDERAL FAIR HOUSING ACT (1968)

Title VIII of the Civil Rights Act of 1968 is commonly called the Federal Fair Housing Act. The first section of Title VIII states, "It is the policy of the United States to provide, within constitutional limitations, for fair housing throughout the United States." To that end, the act prohibits discrimination based on **race, color, national origin, religion, sex, familial status,** or **handicap (disability)** in the sale or lease of residential property. It also prohibits discrimination in advertising, lending, brokerage, and other services in residential transactions.

1. Application

The law applies to most sales, rentals, and exchanges of residential property. It covers transactions involving:

1. any building or structure, or portion of a building or structure, that is occupied as (or designed or intended to be occupied as) a residence for one or more persons; and,

2. vacant land offered for sale or lease for the construction of any buildings to be used (entirely or in part) for residential purposes.

2. Exemptions

Although the act covers the majority of residential transactions in the U.S., there are several specific exemptions. The following transactions are completely exempted from the act:

1. The law doesn't apply to a single-family home sold or rented by a private individual owner, provided that:

   a. the owner owns no more than three such homes,
   b. no discriminatory advertising is used, and
   c. no real estate broker (or anyone in the business of selling or renting homes) is employed.

   If the owner isn't the occupant or most recent occupant, he or she may use this exemption only once every 24 months.

2. The law doesn't apply to the rental of a room or unit in a dwelling with up to four units, provided that:

   a. the owner occupies one unit as his or her residence,
   b. no discriminatory advertising is used, and
   c. no real estate broker is employed.

   This is often referred to as "the Mrs. Murphy exemption."

3. In dealing with their own property in noncommercial transactions, religious organizations or societies or affiliated nonprofit organizations may limit occupancy to or give preference to their own members, provided that membership isn't restricted on the basis of race, color, or national origin.

4. Private clubs with lodgings that aren't open to the public and that aren't operated for a commercial purpose may limit occupancy to or give preference to their own members.

5. The Fair Housing Act prohibits discrimination on the basis of familial status: it's illegal to discriminate against a person because he or she has custody of a child under 18 years of age. However, that rule does not apply to "housing for older persons." The act defines housing for older persons as any housing that is:

   a. provided under a state or federal program designed to assist the elderly; or
   b. intended for and solely occupied by persons 62 or older; or
   c. designed to meet the physical or social needs of older persons, if the management publishes and follows policies and procedures demonstrating an intent to provide housing for persons 55 or older, and at least 80% of the units are occupied by at least one person 55 or older.

3. Disability

A disability under the law is a long-term physical or mental impairment or condition that substantially limits a person's major life activities.

For example, blindness, wheelchair users, those who cannot hear, mental illness, those recovering from drug or alcohol addictions (not covered are those who are illegally using or addicted to illegal drugs). In the landlord-tenant area, property owners may receive a request from a tenant to change existing policies or rules so that a person with the disability can enjoy the premises in the same way as everyone else. This is called a **reasonable accommodation request**. For example, a landlord must allow a person with a visual impairment to have a guide dog even though occupants are not allowed to have pets or providing a person with a wheelchair a preferred or handicapped parking space. Landlords may also be requested to make a reasonable modification that amounts to an alteration of the premises so that the person with a disability can enjoy the premises in the same way as everyone else. For example, the installation of grab bars in the bathroom or an access ramp to the entrance. These modifications are paid for by the tenant and must be allowed by the landlord as long as the requested modifications are reasonable. Additionally, the tenant may be required to use a licensed contractor to do the modifications and the landlord may, under certain circumstances, require that the tenant restore the premises to its original condition upon vacating the premises.

The *AMERICANS WITH DISABILITIES ACT (ADA) is a federal civil rights law that applies to people with disabilities and protects them from discrimination.*

ADA prohibits state and local governments from discriminating against disabled persons in their programs and sets forth the applicable structural accessibility requirements for the public and private individuals. The law also covers public accommodations and services (e.g., hotels, restaurants, and transit systems) from denying goods, services, and programs to people based on their disabilities.

4. Prohibited Acts

The following acts are unlawful under the Federal Fair Housing Act if they are based on race, color, national origin, religion, sex, familial status, or handicap (disability):

Federal Fair Housing Act

In residential transactions, prohibits discrimination based on:

Race   **Color**   **National Origin**   **Religion**

Sex   **Familial Status**   **Handicap (Disability)**

---

1. refusing to rent or sell residential property after receiving a bona fide offer;
2. refusing to negotiate for the sale or rental of residential property;
3. any action that would otherwise make residential property unavailable or deny it to any person (this general clause covers **steering**, **redlining**, and many other discriminatory practices);
4. discriminating in the terms or conditions of any sale or rental of residential property, or in providing any services or facilities in connection with such property;
5. discriminatory advertising or any other notice that indicates a limitation or preference or intent to make any limitation, preference, or discrimination;
6. making any representation that property is not available for inspection, sale, or rent when it is in fact available;
7. inducing or attempting to induce, for profit, any person to sell or rent property based on representations regarding entry into the neighborhood of persons of a particular race, color, national origin, religion, or sex (**blockbusting**);
8. discrimination by a commercial lender in making a loan for buying, building, repairing, improving, or maintaining a dwelling, or in the terms of such financing;
9. denying access to a multiple listing service or any similar real estate brokers' organization, or discriminating in the terms or conditions for access to the organization, or
10. coercing, intimidating, threatening, or interfering with anyone on account of his or her enjoyment, attempt to enjoy, or encouragement or assistance to others in enjoying the rights granted by the Fair Housing Act.

In 1972, the Fair Housing Act was amended to require **display of fair housing posters** (see **Figure 14-1**) and use of the fair housing logo in advertising. If a real estate broker or other person or business required to display the poster is investigated, failure to display the poster and logo may be considered evidence of discrimination.

As you can see, most discriminatory behavior in connection with residential transactions would violate federal law. Three terms mentioned above frequently come up in discussions of fair housing and fair lending laws:

1. steering,
2. blockbusting, and
3. redlining

STEERING refers to directing prospective buyers or tenants to, or away from, specific neighborhoods based upon their race (or religion, national origin, or other protected class), or

Figure 14-1

Equal Housing Lender

**We Do Business In Accordance With The
Federal Fair Housing Law**

**(Title VIII of the Civil Rights Act of 1968,
as Amended by the Housing and Community
Development Act of 1974)**

**IT IS ILLEGAL TO DISCRIMINATE AGAINST ANY PERSON
BECAUSE OF RACE, COLOR, NATIONAL ORIGIN, RELIGION,
SEX, FAMILIAL STATUS (including children under the age of 18
living with parents or legal custodians, pregnant women, and
people securing custody of children under the age of 18),
and HANDICAP, TO:**

- Deny a loan for the purpose of purchasing, constructing, improving, repairing or maintaining a dwelling or

- Discriminate in fixing of the amount, interest rate, duration, application procedures or other terms or conditions of such a loan.

**IF YOU BELIEVE YOU HAVE BEEN DISCRIMINATED
AGAINST, YOU MAY SEND A COMPLAINT TO:**

**U.S. DEPARTMENT OF HOUSING AND URBAN DEVELOPMENT
Assistant Secretary for Fair Housing and Equal Opportunity
Washington, D.C. 20410**

or call your local HUD Area or Insuring Office.

based upon the composition (racial, religious, etc.) of any occupants of the area in which the real property is located.. For example, white customers might only be shown homes in white neighborhoods, and black customers only shown homes in black neighborhoods.

> **Case Example:** In the Detroit area it was a widespread practice to code listing agreements with an "X" or some other mark to indicate that the home could be shown to black prospects. One real estate brokerage used a separate phone number in ads for properties located in black neighborhoods. The telephone setup in the office allowed the person answering the phone to see if the call was coming in on the special line. If so, he or she would direct the caller to one of the black sales associates working in the office. *U.S. v. Real Estate One*, 433 F. Supp. 1140 (E.D. Mich. 1977).

Certainly, it is a violation for a real estate agent, by words or actions, to direct or advise a buyer to buyer or not buy based upon the composition (racial or other protected class) of the neighborhood.

Example: "You probably wouldn't be interested in looking at that house, it is in a (black or white, as appropriate) neighborhood."

A real estate agent's good-faith answer to a question from a prospective buyer about the composition of a neighborhood (racial, ethnic, religious, etc.) may not be a violation. However, a Fair Housing Act the Act prohibits housing practices that have a discriminatory effect, regardless of any motive or intent to discriminate. It is best for the agent to decline to answer questions about neighborhood composition.

*BLOCKBUSTING (or **panic selling**) refers to the practice of predicting the entry of minorities into a neighborhood, and stating or implying that this will result in lower property values, higher crime rates, or some other undesirable consequence.* The purpose is to induce property owners to list their property for sale or sell their property at a reduced price, so the individual making the predictions (often a real estate agent) can profit. A wide variety of blockbusting "techniques"—many of them shocking—appear in the case law. For example:

1. passing out pamphlets stating that a member of a minority group has purchased a home nearby;
2. "wrong number" phone calls where the callers indicate that they thought they were calling "the black family that just moved in," or
3. purchasing a home in the area and selling it on contract to a minority buyer, then suggesting to white owners that it's time to move.

REDLINING is refusal, for discriminatory reasons, to make loans on property located in a particular neighborhood. In the past, many lenders assumed that an integrated or predominantly black neighborhood was automatically a neighborhood where property values were declining. Based on that assumption, they refused to make loans in those neighborhoods. In many cases, this worked as a self-fulfilling prophecy. Since it was almost impossible to obtain purchase or renovation loans, it was extremely difficult to market, maintain, or improve homes in those neighborhoods, causing values to decline.

Lenders may still deny loans in neighborhoods where property values are declining. However, that action must be based on objective economic criteria concerning the condition and value of the particular property or the surrounding neighborhood, without regard to the racial or ethnic composition of the neighborhood. A lender may not simply equate an integrated or minority neighborhood with declining values.

5. Enforcement

An individual who feels he or she has been discriminated against in violation of the Federal Fair Housing Act may file a complaint with the **OFFICE OF FAIR HOUSING AND EQUAL OPPORTUNITY (FHEO)** of the Department of Housing and Urban Development (HUD). In addition (or instead), he or she may file a lawsuit in federal or state court. HUD may also file a complaint on its own initiative. A complaint must be filed with HUD within one year; a lawsuit must be brought within two years.

When a complaint is filed with HUD, the agency will attempt to obtain voluntary compliance through negotiation and conciliation. If that's unsuccessful, the parties may have the dispute decided by HUD. The agency can award compensatory damages to the plaintiff, issue injunctions against the defendants, and impose civil penalties (fines ranging from a maximum of $11,000 for a first offense, up to $55,000 for a third offense).

Where there are state or local fair housing laws substantially equivalent to the federal law, HUD may refer complaints to the state or local agency that has similar responsibilities (for example, the California Department of Fair Employment and Housing).

A complainant may file suit in federal district court or in the state trial court having general jurisdiction (in California, a superior court). The court may grant the relief it deems appropriate, including:

1. a temporary or permanent injunction,
2. compensatory damages,
3. punitive damages, and
4. attorney's fees if the court believes the plaintiff is not able to pay the fees.

The defendant may also be ordered to take certain steps to insure that no discrimination occurs in the future.

The U.S. Attorney General may also bring a civil suit in federal district court if he or she has reason to believe that anyone is engaged in a pattern of discriminatory activities, or if there is a group of people who have been denied their rights in such a manner that it raises an issue of general public importance. The attorney general may request temporary or permanent injunctions or other orders to insure that all persons are able to exercise the rights granted under the Fair Housing Act. The court may also impose civil penalties of up to $110,000.

C. FAIR LENDING LAWS

There are several federal laws and regulations designed to eliminate discrimination in lending. They include:

1. the Fair Housing Act (discussed above),
2. the Equal Credit Opportunity Act, and
3. the Home Mortgage Disclosure Act.

The **FAIR HOUSING ACT** *prohibits discrimination in home loans and other aspects of residential financing*. It does not apply to any credit transactions other than residential financing.

The *EQUAL CREDIT OPPORTUNITY ACT (ECOA)* *applies to all consumer credit, including residential real estate loans. CONSUMER CREDIT is credit extended to an individual (not a corporation or business) for personal, family, or household purposes.* The ECOA prohibits any institution or lender regularly engaged in financing from discriminating on the basis of **race, color, national origin, religion, sex,** or **marital status**. It also prohibits discrimination based on age, as long as the applicant is of legal age to contract. And it prohibits discrimination against an applicant because his or her income is derived (partly or entirely) from public assistance.

The *HOME MORTGAGE DISCLOSURE ACT is a tool for gathering information on whether lenders are fulfilling their obligation to serve the housing needs of their communities.* The act facilitates enforcement of laws against redlining. Large institutional lenders are required to make annual reports on the residential mortgage loans (both purchase money and improvement loans) that were originated or purchased during the fiscal year. Each loan is categorized according to its dollar amount, type (FHA, VA, FMHA, other), and geographic location by census tract (or by county, for small counties with no established census tracts). If analysis of the reports discloses areas where few or no home loans have been made, this alerts investigators to the possibility that these areas are being redlined.

III. California Legislation

In California, the Unruh Civil Rights Act, the Fair Employment and Housing Act, the Housing Financial Discrimination Act, and the Real Estate Law all include provisions designed to promote fair housing within the state.

The California courts have taken a somewhat different approach to interpreting civil rights legislation than the courts in other states. The result has been that California laws against discrimination often have a far greater impact than is immediately apparent from the language of the statutes themselves.

Under federal law and in most states, discrimination is unlawful only if the discrimination is based upon one of the protected classes expressly listed in a particular law. For example, if you don't like lawyers, you could refuse to rent or sell to a lawyer unless a state law specifically prohibited discrimination based on profession or occupation.

A. UNRUH CIVIL RIGHTS ACT

It doesn't work that way in California, primarily for historical reasons. The precursor to the current Unruh Act (which prohibits discrimination by business establishments) was a rather broad statute that required full and equal treatment for all citizens, rather than specifying certain classes (such as sex, race, national origin, and religion) that were to be protected from discrimination. Additionally, individuals with disabilities are entitled to full and equal access to public facilities, as are other members of the general public.

As a result, California courts have taken the approach that if a state civil rights law includes a list of protected classes, the list is only illustrative, not a complete list of all groups that may not be discriminated against. Thus, the courts could find and did find that arbitrary discrimination against anyone was prohibited, even when it was not directed against a class listed in a statute. For example, California courts have held that it is unlawful to discriminate against the following groups, although it was not expressly prohibited by any statute: homosexuals, students, welfare recipients, persons of a particular occupation or profession, children, persons who associate with blacks, and unmarried persons.

This doesn't mean that all discrimination is prohibited in California, just arbitrary discrimination. Discrimination is considered arbitrary if it is based solely on the fact that the person belongs to a particular class or group. If there is an objective reason for the discrimination, or if it is based on particular conduct, it is not unlawful.

The **UNRUH CIVIL RIGHTS ACT** *states that all persons are entitled to the full use of any services provided by a business establishment.* "All persons within the jurisdiction of this state are free and equal, and no matter what their sex, race, color, religion, ancestry, national origin, disability, medical condition, marital status, genetic information, or sexual orientation are entitled to the full accommodations, advantages, facilities, privileges, or services in all business establishments of every kind whatsoever."

The California courts have determined that the Unruh Act covers common interest developments and real estate brokers. Real estate brokers are required to offer their facilities and services to everyone who wants to make use of them, without arbitrary discrimination. If a broker refuses a listing or turns away a customer, it must not be for discriminatory reasons. The Act specifically provides that "No business establishment of any kind whatsoever shall discriminate against, boycott or blacklist, refused to buy from, or sell to, or trade with any person in the state because of the race, creed, religion, color, national origin, or sex of any such person …"

However, where accommodations are designed to meet the physical and social needs of senior citizens, there may be established and preserved housing for senior citizens as provided under a state law, unless that law has been preempted by the Fair Housing Amendments Act.

Rental properties, condominiums, and other real estate developments are considered business establishments for the purposes of the Unruh Act. The general terms of the act make it illegal for an apartment complex or condo to have a "no kids" rule. The act was amended to allow developments designed for senior citizens to require that at least one member of each household be 62 or older, and to exclude people younger than 45. Large developments that comply with certain other rules can have a slightly lower age limit, requiring at least one member of each household to be 55 or over.

The California Legislature adopted this amendment to the Unruh Act before Congress amended the Federal Fair Housing Act to prohibit discrimination based on familial status. The state law must be interpreted in conjunction with the federal law's rules concerning "housing for older persons" (see above). The state law may be applied to give more protection against age discrimination than the federal law, but it may not be applied to give less protection.

1. Enforcement

Someone who has been discriminated against in violation of the Unruh Act may sue for an injunction, compensatory damages, attorney's fees, and punitive damages. (The punitive damages award can't be more than three times the amount of the compensatory damages.) In addition, the victim of discrimination may file a complaint with the California Department of Fair Employment and Housing. The state attorney general also has the right to sue for violations of the Unruh Act.

B. CALIFORNIA FAIR EMPLOYMENT AND HOUSING ACT (FEHA)

1. Illegal Discrimination Defined

The legislature in California has declared that "the practice of discrimination because of race, color, religion, sex, marital status, national origin, ancestry, familial status, source of income, disability, genetic information, or sexual orientation in housing accommodations is declared to be against public policy." The purpose of California's legislation is "to provide effective remedies that will eliminate these discriminatory practices." Illegal discrimination is defined to include the following when based on any of the above characteristics:

- Refusal to sell, rent, or lease housing accommodations;
- Refusal to negotiate for the sale, rental or lease of housing accommodations;
- Representation that a housing accommodation is not available for inspection, sale, or rental when that housing accommodation is in fact so available;
- Any other denial or withholding of housing accommodations;
- Includes provisions of inferior terms, conditions, privileges, facilities, or services in connection or with those housing accommodations;
- Includes harassment in connection with those housing accommodations;
- Includes the cancellation or termination of a sale or rental agreement;
- Includes the provision of segregated or separated housing accommodations;
- Includes the refusal to permit, at the expense of the disabled person, reasonable modifications of existing premises occupied or to be occupied by the disabled person, if the modifications may be necessary to afford the disabled person full enjoyment of the premises, except that, in the case of a rental, the landlord may, where it is reasonable to do so condition permission for a modification on the renter's agreeing to restore the interior of the premises to the condition that existed before the modification (other than for reasonable wear and tear), and
- Includes refusal to make reasonable accommodations in rules, policies, practices or services when these accommodations may be necessary to afford a disabled person an equal opportunity to use and enjoy a dwelling.

However, discrimination does NOT include any of the following:

- Refusal to rent or lease a portion of an owner-occupied single-family house to a person as a roomer or border living within the household, provided that no more than one roomer or border is to live within the household and the owner complies with the subdivision (c) of Section 12955, which prohibits discriminatory notices, statements and advertisements.
- Where the sharing of living areas in a single dwelling unit is involved, the use of words stating or tending to imply that the housing being advertised is available only to persons of one sex.
- Conduct by a religious organization, association or society, or any non profit institution or organization operated, supervised, or controlled by that organization from limiting the sale, rental, or occupancy of dwellings that it owns or operates for other than commercial purposes to persons of the same religion or from giving preference to those persons, unless membership in that religion is rejected on account of race, color, or national origin.

2. Illegal Discriminatory Activities

The above is a lengthy definition of types of illegal discrimination. The list below contains unlawful conduct in housing accommodations when the issue is race, color, religion, sex, sexual orientation, marital status, national origin, ancestry, familial status, source of income, or disability of a person:

- For the owner of any housing accommodation to discriminate against or harass any person because of the above characteristics.

- For the owner of any housing accommodation to make or cause to be made any written or oral inquiry concerning the above characteristics.

- For any person to make, print, or publish, or cause to be made, printed, or published any notice, statement, or advertisement with respect to the sale or rental of a housing accommodation that indicates any preference, limitation, or discrimination based on the above characteristics. Or an intention to make any such preference, limitation or discrimination.

- For any owner of a housing accommodation to harass, evict, or otherwise discriminate against any person in the sale or rental of housing accommodations when the owner's dominate purpose is retaliation against a person who has opposed practices unlawful under the law.

- For any person to aid, abet, insight, compel, or coerce the doing of any of the acts or practices declared above to be unlawful.

- For any person, for profit, to induce any person to sell or rent any dwelling by representations regarding the entry or perspective entry into the neighborhood of a person or persons who have the above characteristics.

- To otherwise make unavailable or deny a dwelling based on discrimination because of the above characteristics.

- Includes a perception that a person has any of those characteristics or that the person is associated with a person who has, or is perceived to have, any of those characteristics.

- For any person or other organization whose business involves real estate transactions to discriminate against any person in making available a transaction, or in the terms and conditions of a transaction, because of the above characteristics.

- To deny a person access to, or membership or participation in, a multiple listing service, real estate brokerage organization, or other service because of the above characteristics.

- To use a financial or income standard in the rental of housing that fails to account for the aggregate income of persons residing together or proposing to reside together on the same basis as the aggregate income of married persons residing together or proposing to reside together.

- In instances where there is a government rent subsidy, to use a financial or income standard in accessing eligibility for the rental of housing that is not based on the portion of the rent to be paid by the tenant.

- For purposes of this section, "source of income" means lawful, verifiable income paid directly to a tenant or paid to a representative of the tenant. It shall not constitute discrimination based on source of income to make a written or oral inquiry concerning the level or source of income.

- For any person, bank, mortgage company, or other financial institution to discriminate against any person or group of persons because of the above characteristics.

With regard to the characteristics listed above, "familial status" means one or more individuals under 18 years of age who resides with a parent, another person with care and legal custody of that individual, a person who has care and custody of the individual given by a state or local government agency who is responsible for the welfare of children, or the designee of that parent or other person with legal custody of the individual by written consent of the parent or designated custodian. Familial status protection is also applicable to any individual who is pregnant, who is in the process of securing legal custody of any individual under 18 years of age, or who is in the process of being given care and custody of any individual under 18 years of age by a government agency.

Under California law, no declaration or governing document can include a restrictive covenant in violation of the above provisions.

3. Enforcement

A person who has been discriminated against in violation of the Fair Employment and Housing Act may file a complaint with the Department of Fair Employment and Housing within one year of the date of the alleged discrimination. The attorney general may also file a complaint for any practices that appear to violate the act. After receiving a complaint, the department may bring an action in superior court to obtain an injunction preventing the alleged violator from renting or selling the property until after the department has completed its investigation.

If the investigation appears to confirm the charges, the department will hold a formal hearing. If the department finds that there has been a violation, the violator will be ordered to stop the discriminatory practices. He or she may also be ordered to sell or rent the property (if it is still available), or similar property, to the complainant, or to provide financial assistance or other services that had been denied. The violator may also be liable for compensatory damages and for punitive damages of up to $1,000.

In addition to the department's actions, the victim of discrimination may bring a civil action in superior court.

C. HOUSING FINANCIAL DISCRIMINATION ACT

The *HOUSING FINANCIAL DISCRIMINATION ACT states that it is against public policy to deny mortgage loans or give stricter terms for loans because of neighborhood characteristics unrelated to the creditworthiness of the borrower or the value of the real property.* Under this Act, financial institutions in California are prohibited from:

1. discriminating in the provision of financial assistance to purchase, construct, rehabilitate, improve, or refinance housing on the basis of the characteristics of the neighborhood surrounding the property, unless the lender can demonstrate that such consideration is necessary to avoid an unsound business practice;

2. discriminating in the provision of financial assistance for housing, based on race, color, national origin, religion, sex, marital status, or ancestry; and

3. considering the racial, ethnic, religious, or national origin composition of the neighborhood surrounding the property when providing financial assistance.

CHAPTER 14

The Housing Financial Discrimination Act doesn't prohibit a financial institution from taking the fair market value of the property into consideration when deciding whether or not to grant a loan.

D. REAL ESTATE COMMISSIONER'S REGULATIONS

www.dre.ca.gov/pdf_docs/regs2010.pdf
Regulations of the Real Estate Commissioner

The Business and Professions Code (Section 125.6) prohibits discrimination by anyone holding a state business license—including real estate brokers and salespersons. This provision of the law is implemented by Commissioner's Regulations 2780, 2781, and 2725, which specifically address the duties of real estate agents with respect to unlawful discrimination based on race, color, sex, religion, ancestry, physical disability, marital status, or national origin.

Regulation 2780 is essentially an explanatory regulation. It gives licensees some guidance as to the types of discriminatory conduct that are prohibited, and also describes some conduct that is permitted even though it may involve discriminatory treatment.

The regulation takes the form of several pages of examples of prohibited conduct. The examples are merely illustrative—they don't cover all prohibited actions. Other conduct by licensees, even though not specifically listed in the regulation, may constitute unlawful discrimination and be the basis for license suspension or revocation.

Here are some of Regulation 2780's examples of conduct that is prohibited when it is based on the prospect's race, color, sex, religion, ancestry, physical disability, marital status, or national origin:

1. refusing or failing to provide information regarding real property;
2. using codes or other means of identifying the applications of minority prospects with a discriminatory intent or effect;
3. processing an application more slowly or otherwise acting to delay or hinder a sale, rental, or financing of real property;
4. soliciting sales, rentals, or listings from one person but not another in the same area;
5. informing some persons but not others of the existence of waiting lists or other procedures concerning the future availability of property; or
6. providing different information to different persons concerning the desirability of a particular property or neighborhood.

It is also a violation of Regulation 2780 to assist anyone in the sale, rental, or financing of real property when there is reason to believe that person intends to discriminate.

In addition to the numerous examples of prohibited conduct, Regulation 2780 recites several examples of permissible discriminatory conduct. For example, it is not unlawful discrimination to fail to show, rent, sell, or finance property to a prospect with a physical disability if the property is dangerous or inaccessible to the physically disabled. Advertising directed at the physically disabled (such as an ad that mentions the presence or absence of particular features that are useful to the disabled) is also permissible.

Regulation 2781 concerns panic selling or blockbusting. The regulation states that a licensee may not solicit listings by making any written or oral statement, warning, or threat, or taking any other action, to induce owners to sell or lease property because persons of another race, color, national origin, religion, sex, marital status, or ancestry have moved into the neighborhood, or may be about to move in.

Regulation 2725 addresses the supervisory duties of real estate brokers in connection with civil rights laws. The regulation requires brokers to take reasonable steps to familiarize themselves with state and federal laws relating to discrimination in the sale, rental, and financing of real property. They must also take reasonable steps to familiarize their salespersons with the requirements of those laws.

IV. Case Examples of Discrimination

The overall effect of federal and state legislation and regulations is to outlaw discrimination based on race or ancestry in all property transactions, with no exceptions. Discrimination based on other classes (religion, national origin, sex, familial status, disability, medical condition, marital status, or sexual orientation) is also generally prohibited, but there are a few exceptions.

Therefore, in most cases discrimination by an owner or real estate agent violates one or more laws. This section of the chapter briefly discusses real estate case examples in which the courts have applied anti-discrimination legislation. These examples cover the sale and rental of real estate, MLS membership, brokers' employment and business practices, advertising, lending, and zoning and other regulatory actions.

A. RENTING AND SELLING

It's unlawful to refuse to sell or rent after receiving a good-faith offer if it can be shown that the offeror's race, religion, sex, national origin, or disability was a factor, even if it wasn't the only reason for the refusal. In one case, the landlord claimed that a sub-tenant was unacceptable for several reasons, including a poor credit history. Even though there were some legitimate reasons for rejecting the subtenant, a federal court held that the landlord had violated the law if race was one of the reasons for the refusal.

Sometimes discrimination is straightforward. A seller or landlord might tell a potential buyer or renter to get lost. More often, the landlord or seller avoids minority applicants, or pretends that all applicants are being treated equally.

Case Example: Philip J. Frantz (plaintiff) filed a complaint against Jack R. Blackwell and others (defendant) alleging discrimination in violation of the Unruh Civil Rights Act seeking to enjoin the alleged discrimination. Defendant develops and sells single-family homes to the public. Plaintiff and defendant closed escrow on Lot 159 in the Pierce Ranch subdivision developed by defendants. Plaintiff contracted to purchase Lot 282 and signed an agreement that he was purchasing the lot as an owner-occupant. Regarding Lot 282, defendant concluded plaintiff was purchasing as an investor-speculator rather than an owner-occupant. After a disagreement, defendant rescinded the contract. Plaintiff sued for specific performance. The suit was settled with a dismissal by the plaintiff and defendant paying plaintiff $35,000.

Plaintiff tried to purchase Lot 484, but defendant refused to deal with plaintiff. Plaintiff sued claiming discrimination solely because of the fact plaintiff was successful in the prior lawsuit and that the plaintiff represents a class with whom the defendant did not want to conduct business, that is, persons who have filed lawsuits against defendant. ▼

The defendant claims plaintiff purchases units in new developments, delays escrow closing, and attempts to resell the units before his escrow closes, using the time delay and defendant's promotional efforts on the balance of the subdivision units to create a profit. The defendant claims that if the plaintiff cannot resell, the plaintiff can merely default on the purchase contract. The issue is whether the defendant's refusal to do business with the plaintiff is arbitrary discrimination. The trial court dismissed the lawsuit. Plaintiff appealed.

The Unruh Civil Rights Act is intended to prohibit all arbitrary discrimination by business establishments. There are previous cases in which a person's conduct, as opposed to his/her status, produced the discrimination alleged to be arbitrary. The Act does not seek to remedy discrimination based on purely personal grounds. The plaintiff is merely taking parasitical advantage of the developer's skills. We cannot say such a refusal to sell a home to a perceived investor-speculator is unreasonable. Judgment affirmed. *Frantz v. Blackwell*, 189 Cal. App. 3d 91, 234 Cal. Rptr. 178, (1987).

B. ADVERTISING

Both federal law and California law prohibit any advertising that indicates a restriction, preference, or intent to discriminate based on race or other protected classes. Discriminatory advertising or solicitations may be very subtle. Apparently innocent statements may be intended or interpreted as discriminatory.

Example: In some areas of the country, an advertisement that describes a home as "near schools and churches" may be taken to mean that it is a gentile neighborhood and that Jews (who attend temple or synagogue, not church) are not welcome.

Case Example: The plaintiffs represent a number of individuals, including a former manager, who are African-American, African-Jamaican, Latino, or Caucasian who reside at or formerly were residents of, the apartment building at 691 S. Irolo St., in Los Angeles. Defendants include Donald T. Sterling who has been in the Los Angeles real estate business for 40 years, and either personally or through various affiliated entities, has purchased 99 apartment buildings in Southern California, including the Irolo St. apartment building. This is a housing discrimination case and the plaintiffs allege violations of the Fair Housing Act and made a motion for a preliminary injunction. The following is a brief summary of the numerous discriminatory statements and housing practices alleged by the plaintiffs. Defendants vehemently deny most of the allegations and fault the plaintiffs for being unreliable tenants and for being driven by hidden agendas.

Discriminatory Statements, Advertisements, or Inquiries.

1. Shortly after Sterling purchased the property, he conducted a meeting of the building's staff, during which he told the manager, among others, he did not like Hispanic or African-American tenants, that he preferred Korean-American tenants, and that he wanted the staff to rent only to Korean-Americans.

▼

2. A former property supervisor for Sterling declared she heard Donald and Rochelle Sterling make disparaging comments about African-American and Hispanic tenants. Another plaintiff stated she once spoke to a real estate agent for Sterling about a potential tenant and was told she could sign a lease with the applicant provided the applicant was Korean.

3. The defendants have used the words "Korean" or "Asian" in the names of many of their rental properties. The subject property was changed from "Mark Wilshire Towers" to "Korean World Towers" (which was subsequently renamed "Ambassador Towers"); along with name changes of apartments to "Wilshire Korean Towers," "The Sterling Korean Plaza," "Windsor Square Korean Towers," "Fremont Place Korean Plaza," and "Hancock Park Asian Towers."

4. The defendants have featured the South Korean flag touching the American flag in advertising that the American Korean Land Company purchased several real estate properties.

The Court finds evidence sufficient to establish that defendants used the word "Asian" in referring to a Sterling building in a published announcement, and used the South Korean flag in a second announcement, and currently use the word "Korean" in the names of at least two apartment buildings. Plaintiffs must prove that defendants' statements would discourage an ordinary reader of a particular protected group from applying for an apartment or would suggest to an ordinary reader that people of a particular race or national origin are preferred or dis-preferred for the housing in question. The Court will not enjoin the use of the word "Asian," since it has not been used in notices or advertisements with respect to the rental of a dwelling. The Court will not enjoin the use of the South Korean flag since an ordinary reader would likely view the flag as a symbolic representation of the "American Korean Land Company" corporate name, not as a discriminatory message—particularly because the American flag also appears in the announcement. The very word used by defendants—"Korean"—is necessarily and commonly understood to signify a particular national origin. Given this ordinary understanding, the use of the word "Korean" in the names of residential apartment buildings would indicate to the ordinary reader that the buildings' owner is not only receptive to but actually prefers tenants of Korean national origin. This will discourage potential applicants. Defendants are preliminarily enjoined from using the term "Korean" in a building name or printed material with respect to the rental of a unit in such building.

Questions about National Origin.

The Court finds that in February 2003 defendants sent tenants of the building a notice that the garage would be closed and tenants who wanted a garage remote control would be required to complete an application. The application asked tenants to identify the place where they and their spouses were born, as well as state their citizenship and date of naturalization. The notice emphasized a "complete" response was necessary and that "incomplete information" would delay processing of the application. Defendants are preliminarily enjoined from asking or requiring tenants to state their national origin or place of birth on any application or questionnaire used in connection with building facilities and from conditioning the provision of such facilities on national origin. *Housing Rights Center v. Donald Sterling Corp.*, 274 F. Supp. 2d 1129 (2003).

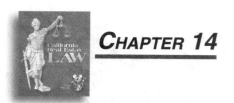

CHAPTER 14

C. DISABILITY

The following case involves a question of what is a reasonable accommodation for a disabled person under the California Fair Employment and Housing Act.

Case Example: Jayne and Abdelfatah "Ed" Elebiari sought permission from their condominium association to keep a small dog. They suffer from severe depression and found that taking care of a dog alleviated their symptoms and enable them to function more productively. The association refused the request because association rules do not allow dogs. They filed a complaint with the Department of Fair Employment and Housing. Ed was involved in a serious car accident and suffered brain damage, which required three surgeries. He is hydrocephalic, has a seizure disorder, has severe headaches, and suffers from depression. Jayne suffers from major depression, which is recurrent. She has sleeping problems, lacks concentration, engages in acts of self-mutilation, and avoids social interaction. The previous diagnoses was prepared by their psychiatrist. Despite the ban on dogs, they brought home a small terrier. With the dog, Jayne's agitation lessened, her concentration improved, her interpersonal relationships improved, she slept better and the acts of self-mutilation became less severe. The dog also alleviated depression for both Jane and Ed and enabled them to enjoy each other's company more. The psychiatrist believed that the improvement in moods occurred after getting the dog. Therefore, the psychiatrist recommended a reasonable accommodation in the rules be made to allow Jayne to continue to have her companion animal.

The association's rules allow cats, so the association recommended they get a cat and the request for special accommodation was not acceptable. "The Association does have reasonable accommodations for people who want companion pets, and the pets include cats, rabbits, hamsters, guinea pigs, birds, et cetera. Ms. Elebiari could have a pet, but the fact that she prefers a dog is what is keeping her from having a companion at accommodation."

The case was heard by an administrative law judge who concluded that Jayne and Ed were disabled and the defendants had notice of their disabilities; the association never requested documentation of their medical conditions, which they would have been entitled to had they requested it; that a companion dog would have been a reasonable accommodation; and the repeated denials constituted unlawful discrimination. The judge awarded Ed $5,000 and Jayne $7,500 in emotional distress damages. The association went to court. The trial court agreed with the association, finding there was no medical evidence to support a request for accommodation and no evidence that a companion dog was a necessary reasonable accommodation. It also found that emotional damages were based on an inappropriate standard. Ed and Jayne appealed.

In reviewing a decision of the Fair Employment and Housing Commission, the Commission's interpretation is entitled to great respect. There was abundant evidence introduced at the hearing that their disabilities interfered with the use and enjoyment of their home, and that having a dog improved the situation. Each inquiry regarding a reasonable accommodation with companion pets requires a case-by-case determination. Under the right circumstances, allowing a pet despite a no pets policy might constitute a reasonable accommodation. The Commission's decision that a companion dog constituted a reasonable accommodation was supported by substantial evidence and the court erred in reaching a contrary conclusion. Decision reversed. *Auburn Woods I Homeowners Association v. Fair Employment and Housing Commission*, 121 Cal. App. 4th 1578, 18 Cal. Rptr. 3d 669 (2004).

D. AGE

The following case deals with the frequent problem of adults living in an environment where children are present and the rules used to try and govern the conduct of the two groups.

Case Example: This case involves a motion for summary judgment by plaintiffs seeking a declaration that the park rules of several mobile home parks in California restrict or deny access to facilities or areas on the basis of age in violation of the Fair Housing Act. The preambles to the park's rules state that the park was "designed and built as an adult facility," or that it was "designed as an ADULT facility." The essence of the lawsuit is discrimination on "familial status," which is defined as one or more individuals who have not attained the age of 18 years being domiciled with a parent or other person having legal custody of such individual(s).

The age restrictive rules fall into three categories:

1. Absolute Prohibitions. These rules impose various age restrictions prohibiting children from engaging in certain activities or access to common areas. Any concern the defendants may have for health and safety is not necessarily linked to age, and problem behavior can be addressed with rules. Requiring adult supervision rather than imposing an absolute ban is clearly a less restrictive means.
2. Adult Supervision Requirements. These rules require adult supervision for the use of numerous facilities, including swimming pools, saunas, tennis courts, etc. by children of various ages ranging from 18 to 10 years of age. Adult supervision is required for children under the age of 14 to ride bicycles and for children of any age to walk around the park. Certainly, prohibiting all children from walking around the park without adult supervision is overly broad regardless of the concern. There is nothing magical about the age of 14 or 18 if defendants' concerns are for the protection of health and safety. Such concerns should be addressed through the use of rules. Moreover, rather than being connected to such ages, bicycle and pool safety would be better served with a proficiency requirement.
3. Hours of Access Restrictions. These rules include a prohibition on the use of swimming pool and sundeck to children under 18 except during certain hours (i.e., between 10 a.m. and 12 noon). Defendants attempt to justify the swimming pool hour restrictions "equitably accounting for the interest of tenants." Clearly, this is not a compelling interest. Nor can the interest or desire of the adult tenants to discriminate against children ever justify such discrimination.

It is clear from these restrictive rules that they treat children, and thus, families with children, differently and less favorably than adults-only households. The preambles that describe certain parks as "adult" parks are clear examples of illegal steering. The defendants must now articulate a legitimate justification for their rules. They must establish that their rules constitute a compelling business necessity and that they have used the least restrictive means to achieve that end. Based on the foregoing, the plaintiffs are entitled to summary judgment for declaratory and injunctive relief against defendants on the grounds that the rules have restricted or denied access to facilities and/or areas on the basis of age in violation of the Fair Housing Act. *United States of America v. Plaza Mobile Estates*, 273 F. Supp. 2d 1084 (US District Court for the Central District of California, Western Division 2003).

V. Extent of Liability for Discrimination

Compensatory Damages – an award intended to reimburse a plaintiff for actual out-of-pocket expenses and provide compensation for mental and emotional distress caused by discrimination.

Punitive Damages – an award intended to punish the wrongdoer and discourage other from discriminating.

As discussed earlier in this chapter, a plaintiff in a discrimination lawsuit may be awarded compensatory and punitive damages. Awards for both compensatory and punitive damages have been growing much larger in recent years. The court opinions suggest one possible reason for larger judgments is that the more time that passes since the enactment of fair housing and other civil rights laws, the more inexcusable any discrimination becomes. Whatever the reasons, the awards can be substantial.

Discrimination cases may involve the use of *TESTERS, who are essentially undercover agents posing as potential buyers or renters sent out to investigate discrimination complaints.* If preferential treatment is given to members of one racial, ethnic, religious, or other group over another, it may validate the accusation of discrimination. Someone who believes he or she is being lied to about the unavailability of housing complains to a government agency or a community organization. Then the agency or organization sends out testers who pretend they're interested in renting or buying the property. Often a "sandwich test" is used. A white tester is shown available space; then a minority tester is told there are no vacancies; then another white tester is shown available space. This kind of test is very convincing evidence of discrimination.

Of course the original rental applicant (who complained to the fair housing organization) can sue for damages. However, the testers and the fair housing organization may also be able to sue.

Case Example: Sheryl McCoy (McCoy), an African-American police officer, inquired about renting a unit in a duplex that Nancy Konig, who is Caucasian, owned. As McCoy read a rental notice posted on Konig's door, Konig came to the door and stated to her: " Shame on you. What are you doing on my porch? Get off my porch. You're trying to break into my house." McCoy inquired about the unit, after which Konig responded: "You know you don't want to rent this place. You're here to break in. Shame on you. I'm not going to rent to you. I'm not going to rent to a person like you." Koenig then slammed the door in McCoy's face. To see if the response was racially motivated, McCoy asked another police officer, Terrence Smith, also African-American, to inquire about the rental. When he approached Konig, she ran into her residence, slammed the door, and did not respond to knocks on the door. He left his name, address and telephone number on a piece of paper, which he slipped into the mail slot as directed by the notice on the door. Konig never made contact.

When the unit was again advertised for rent approximately 1 year later, the Fair Housing Council of Long Beach sent two female "testers" to the residence to inquire about the unit. Konig discouraged the African-American tester from renting the premises because it was too large. She asked whether the tester had given notice at her residence. The tester said she had not, but that her landlord had waived such a notice. Konig, however, insisted that the tester was not free to leave her present residence because she had not given proper notice. When the tester asked for an application, Konig refused to give her one. In contrast, Konig treated the Caucasian tester with deference, did not ask whether she had given notice at her present residence, and told her to telephone her if she wished to rent the unit.

▼

McCoy became distraught and was humiliated by Konig's insults and rebuff. The event caused McCoy to relive an emotionally painful episode in her life when she and her family were victims of racial discrimination. Both McCoy's mother and Smith noticed the adverse effect the incident had on McCoy.

McCoy filed a complaint with the Department of Fair Employment and Housing. After a hearing before the Commission, the Commission found that Konig had discriminated against McCoy because of her race. The Commission ordered Konig to cease and desist the discriminatory conduct and to pay McCoy a civil penalty of $10,000 and $10,000 as actual damages for McCoy's emotional distress and a lost housing opportunity. Of the $10,000 actual damages, nominal damages of one dollar were for lost housing opportunity. McCoy suffered no out-of-pocket loss. Konig appealed.

Actual damages are compensatory damages that include nonquantifiable general damages for emotional distress and pecuniarly measurable special damages for out-of-pocket losses. Due to recent amendments to the Fair Employment and Housing Act by the Legislature which make it clear that the Legislature was attempting to insure the availability of emotional distress damage awards in administrative proceedings rather than requiring a court action for such an award, the judgment is affirmed. *Konig v. Fair Employment and Housing Commission*, 28 Cal. 4th 743, 50 P.3d 718, 123 Cal. Rptr. 2d 1 (2002).

So just about everyone affected by an act or practice of unlawful discrimination can sue. Just about everyone connected with the violation can be held liable, either because of their own actions, or on the basis of agency responsibility: property managers, real estate brokers, real estate salespersons, and property owners. Remember, too, that if a seller refuses to go through with a transaction because of the prospective buyer's race, religion, ethnic background, or sex, the broker may sue the seller for the commission.

Who Can Sue for Violations of Anti-Discrimination Laws?

1. Prospective Buyer/Tenant
2. Tester
3. Fair Housing Organization
4. California Department of Fair Employment and Housing
5. State Attorney General
6. U.S. Attorney General

Who Can Be Held Liable for Unlawful Discrimination?

Seller/Landlord	Property Manager
Homeowner's Association	Resident Manager
Real Estate Broker	Rental Agent
Real Estate Salesperson	Lender
Multiple Listing Service (MLS)	Loan Officer

Refusing to deal with someone who has sued you for discrimination may be considered unlawful retaliation.

VI. CHAPTER SUMMARY

1. The Civil Rights Act of 1866 prohibits discrimination based on race or ancestry in any real estate transaction in the United States. The Supreme Court held that the law applies to private action as well as state action.

2. The Federal Fair Housing Act prohibits discrimination based on race, color, national origin, religion, sex, familial status, or handicap (disability) in the sale or lease of residential property. It also prohibits discrimination in advertising, lending and real estate brokerage in residential transactions. Steering, blockbusting, and redlining are among the practices outlawed by the act. The act's limited exceptions never apply to racial discrimination (because of the Civil Rights Act of 1866), and don't matter in California (because of stricter state laws).

3. The Americans with Disabilities Act (ADA) is a federal civil rights law that applies to people with disabilities and protects them from discrimination.

4. The Equal Credit Opportunity Act prohibits discrimination in residential lending on the basis of race, color, religion, national origin, sex, marital status, age, or receipt of public assistance. To detect redlining, the Home Mortgage Disclosure Act requires lenders to make annual reports on residential loans.

5. California civil rights laws are interpreted to prohibit all arbitrary discrimination, not just discrimination against the groups expressly listed in the statutes.

6. The Unruh Civil Rights Act prohibits any discrimination by a business establishment in California. An exception to the act allows housing developments designed for senior citizens to impose age limits.

7. The Fair Employment and Housing Act (FEHA) prohibits all housing discrimination in California. The act specifically makes it illegal for a seller or lessor to ask questions about a prospective buyer or tenant's race, religion, sex, marital status, national origin, or ancestry. It prohibits advertising that indicates an intent to discriminate. There are few exceptions to the act. It doesn't apply to rental of part of a single-family, owner-occupied home, to roommates limiting occupancy of a single dwelling unit to persons of one gender, or to accommodations operated by nonprofit religious, fraternal, or charitable organizations.

8. California's Holden Act prohibits discrimination in residential lending.

9. Commissioner's Regulations 2780, 2781, and 2785 explain the duties of real estate agents in regard to unlawful discrimination.

10. Nearly everyone connected with a discriminatory act can be held liable for it: the owner, homeowners' association, property manager, broker, or salesperson. They may be ordered to pay compensatory and punitive damages, attorney's fees, court costs, and civil penalties. Testers and fair housing organizations may be entitled to damages, as well as the victim. A court can also issue an injunction requiring the defendant to sell or lease property to the plaintiff, or to stop a discriminatory business practice.

VII. KEY TERMS

Americans With Disabilities Act (ADA)
blockbusting
Civil Rights Act of 1866
compensatory damages
Department of Housing and Urban Development (HUD)
Department of Fair Employment and Housing
disparate impact
Equal Credit Opportunity Act (ECOA)
exclusionary zoning
Fair Employment and Housing Act (FEHA)
Fair Lending Laws
Federal Fair Housing Act (1968)
Home Mortgage Disclosure Act
Housing Financial Discrimination Act
injunction
mortgage loan originator (MLO)
Mrs. Murphy Exemption
Office of Equal Opportunity (OEO)
panic selling
punitive damages
Real Estate Commissioner's Regulations
redlining
steering
testers
Title VIII
Unruh Civil Rights Act

CHAPTER 14

VIII. CHAPTER QUIZ

1. Congress enacted the first Civil Rights Act in what year?
    a. 1850
    b. 1860
    c. 1866
    d. 1896

2. Regarding deeds containing discriminatory covenants:
    a. it is unlawful for county recorders to record them.
    b. they are legally enforceable in California.
    c. they are legally enforceable in California until 2010.
    d. they are legally enforceable in California as long as the discriminatory covenant does not involve race.

3. If California law is more restrictive than federal law, the result is:
    a. federal law prevails.
    b. California law prevails.
    c. the judge may choose whichever law to enforce.
    d. the parties to the litigation are allowed to choose which law to use.

4. The law in California that states that all persons are entitled to the full use of any services provided by a business establishment is which of the following?
    a. The Fair Employment and Housing Act
    b. The Fair Housing Act
    c. The Civil Rights Act of 1866
    d. The Unruh Civil Rights Act

5. The Unruh Civil Rights Act lists all of the following protected classes except:
    a. sexual orientation.
    b. disability.
    c. physical appearance.
    d. marital status.

6. The "Mrs. Murphy exemption" primarily deals with which of the following?
    a. Occupational preference in employment
    b. Racial preferences by large apartment complex landlords
    c. Equal opportunity for real estate loans to women
    d. Renting of a unit in a dwelling with up to four units with one unit occupied by the owner

7. In order to fully enjoy the premises in a manner similar to or like other occupants, a renter with a disability can ask for:

    a. special preferences.
    b. reasonable accommodation.
    c. a rent reduction.
    d. a kitchen window with a view.

8. In California, the Real Estate Commissioner has:

    a. implemented regulations regarding discrimination, but limited only to race, color and ancestry.
    b. unfortunately not implemented any regulations regarding discrimination.
    c. implemented regulations concerning panic selling or blockbusting.
    d. none of the above.

9. The term "disability" refers to:

    a. physical disability only.
    b. mental impairment only.
    c. those in a wheelchair only.
    d. physical disability or mental impairment.

10. The manager of the Mesa apartment complex was looking for an independent contractor to provide landscaping services. He refused to negotiate with two sisters who offered their services because he didn't believe that women could provide the required services. In this case, which of the following is true?

    a. Under California law, this conduct is permissible since it doesn't involve discrimination against prospective tenants.
    b. The manager's conduct violates the Unruh Act.
    c. The manager's conduct is a specific exception listed in Unruh Act.
    d. None of the above.

***ANSWERS:** 1. c; 2. a; 3. b; 4. d; 5. c; 6. d; 7. b; 8. c; 9. d; 10. b*

CHAPTER 15
Landlord/Tenant Law

CHAPTER OVERVIEW

One of the most common of all real estate transactions is renting a place to live or work. This chapter describes the different types of leases and explains the rights, duties, and liabilities of the landlord and tenant. Real estate agents need a basic knowledge of landlord/tenant law since they may be asked to act as rental agents. When property is for sale, but no buyer can be immediately found, some sellers rent it with an option to buy (at the right price and terms acceptable to the owner). Because many licensees specialize in property management, an understanding of landlord/tenant law is essential.

I. Leases

A lease is both a conveyance and a contract.

As a conveyance, it temporarily transfers an interest in the right of possession, occupancy, quiet enjoyment, and use of property from the owner (the **landlord** or **lessor**) to another (the **tenant** or **lessee**). Although the landlord still retains the ownership of the estate, the tenant has a leasehold estate (see Chapter 3).

As a contract, the lease states the terms of the parties' relationship: what has each agreed to do? Leases are often called **rental agreements**.

A landlord and tenant are free to negotiate the terms of their lease, just as with any contract, but landlords are often in a much better bargaining position than tenants (especially residential tenants). As a result, in the past, many leases were slanted in the landlord's favor. To protect tenants against overreaching, the law now prohibits landlords from including certain unfair provisions in a lease. The law also imposes a number of duties on landlords that apply regardless of what terms are expressed in the lease. Thus, there are several limits on the freedom of contract between landlord and tenant.

CHAPTER 15

Lease

Conveyance: Transfer leasehold estate to tenant

Leasehold-to-Tenant

Contract (Rental or Lease): Capacity, Offer, Acceptance, and Consideration

– In writing, if term ends more than one year from signing –

A. REQUIREMENTS FOR VALIDITY

Since a lease or rental agreement is a contract, the basic requirements for a valid contract are necessary for a valid lease. The lessor and lessee must have the legal capacity to contract—they can't be incompetent or under age, and a lease has to be supported by consideration. In most cases, the consideration is a sum of money paid as rent.

Under the statute of frauds, a lease must be in writing if it is for more than one year, or if it won't be fully performed within one year from the date it is signed.

Example: M is a college student. In June, she signs a lease for the next school year. The lease runs from September 10 through August 30. It has to be in writing even though the lease term is less than one year, since it won't end until more than a year from June, when it was made (signed).

If the lease has to be in writing under the statute of frauds, and it is signed by an agent on behalf of a principal, then the agent's authority from the principal must also be in writing.

A written lease must be signed by the landlord or owner's authorized agent. All landlords must sign if the property is owned jointly. A tenant usually also signs the lease, but the tenant's signature isn't required. A tenant who takes possession and pays rent is considered to have accepted the terms of the lease. However, the tenant must sign the lease in order for the landlord to enforce certain contract provisions in the lease against the tenant (for example, a covenant to repair). It is the best practice to have both parties sign the lease.

California law limits the duration of some leases. A lease of land for agricultural purposes can't last more than 51 years; a lease of a town or city lot or the lease of land for oil, gas or mineral production can't last more than 99 years.

B. BASIC PROVISIONS

Every written lease should include certain basic information: the parties' names, an adequate description of the property (the address may be enough for residential or business property), the amount of the rent, when rent it is due, how payable, and the duration of the lease.

If the lease doesn't specify its duration, the law presumes it is a month-to-month tenancy, but there are two important exceptions to this rule. An agricultural lease is presumed to be for one year unless otherwise stated. A residential lease is presumed to last as long as the rental period: if rent is due every week, it's presumed to be a week-to-week tenancy; if rent is due every month, it's presumed to be a month-to-month tenancy.

Most leases also contain clauses concerning acceptable uses of the property, the right to assign or sublet, required security deposits, and the responsibility for repairs and maintenance. Other issues that are often addressed in a lease: the landlord's access to the property during the lease term, alterations or damage by the tenant, the consequences of default, extensions or renewals, and each party's duties if the property is destroyed.

C. TYPES OF LEASES   All #99

1. Fixed Lease

A fixed lease may also be called a **flat**, **gross**, or **straight lease**. Most residential leases are fixed. Under a *FIXED LEASE, the rent is set at a fixed amount, and that's all the tenant has to pay the landlord.* Operating expenses such as maintenance and repair costs, taxes, special assessments, and insurance are all the landlord's responsibility. However, the tenant under a fixed lease often has to pay for utilities (electricity, heat, and so on) in addition to the rent.

2. Graduated Lease

A *GRADUATED LEASE may also be called a "cost of living adjustment" or "step-up" lease and is similar to a fixed lease, except that it provides for periodic increases, called BUMPS, in the rent.* These increases are usually set for specific future events, such as a date, an occupancy rate for the building (or by other tenants), or by attainment of a certain sales volume. The amount of each increase may be based on a fixed amount or an index, such as the Consumer Price Index (CPI). This is also called a **stepped lease**.

3. Net Lease

When a tenant pays rent plus some or all of the operating expenses (such as utilities, taxes, insurance, and repairs), it's called a NET LEASE, or sometimes a "triple-net" lease. The rent is pure "net" to the landlord. Many commercial leases are net leases.

4. Percentage Lease

Some commercial leases provide for a percentage rent. With a *PERCENTAGE LEASE, the rental amount is based on a percentage of the tenant's monthly or annual gross sales.* Percentage leases are common for retail stores, especially in large shopping centers.

There are many types of percentage leases. For instance, under a *PURE PERCENTAGE LEASE, the entire rental amount is a percentage of gross sales.* Under the most common type of percentage lease, a fixed minimum rent is required.

> **Example:** ARCO closed its gas station three years before the 20-year lease expired. ARCO contended that it only had to pay the $1,000 monthly minimum rent for the remaining three years of the lease term. The court held that ARCO might be required to pay more than the minimum, even though it was no longer selling gas on the property. A percentage lease tenant is generally expected to continue operating its business for the entire lease term.

Case Example: Circle K Corporation leased property for 20 years from Frank Collins, agreeing to pay rent calculated at 2% of "gross sales." Subsequently, state law legalized lotteries and Circle K began selling lottery tickets.

The issue became whether Circle K paid 2% on the commission it received on lottery ticket sales or 2% of the total sale price of lottery tickets. The court held that "Circle K acts more nearly as a tax collector for the state than as a retailer." Circle K is paid for its services by a commission and that commission is considered a "gross receipt" for services performed on the premises.

The 2% is calculated on the commission, not the total lottery ticket sales. *In Re Circle K Corp.*, 98 F. 3d 484 (9th Cir. 1996).

---

5. Ground Lease

In a *GROUND LEASE, the owner leases vacant land to a tenant who agrees to erect a building on it.* The property involved in the ARCO case was vacant until ARCO built its gas station.

To make construction of a building worth the tenant's while, ground leases tend to be long term. They are popular in large metropolitan areas where land is particularly valuable. For example, a tenant might lease a block from the landowner, demolish the existing structures, put up a 40-story office building, and lease office space to various businesses. This also creates a *SANDWICH LEASE, where the tenant who constructed the building is both a tenant (as to the land), and landlord (as to the building).*

D. TRANSFERRING LEASED PROPERTY

A lessor is free to sell the leased property at any time. Occasionally, a lease provides that it will terminate if the property is sold. In most cases, however, the new owner takes the property subject to the existing lease and must honor the terms. However, what if the lessor sells the leased property, but fails to tell the purchaser that it is leased? The purchaser would be on constructive notice if the tenant was in possession or the lease was recorded. How important is recording the lease? The answer is found in California Civil Code Section 1214:

CHAPTER 15

If the lease term is for more than one year the tenant cannot force the lease on the new owner who purchased the property in good faith unless the lease is recorded. Where the owner fails to notify the buyer or a new lender of the tenancy, the tenant's only recourse is to sue the previous owner.

1. Sale

Once the property has been transferred, all of the former owner's rights and duties under the lease are transferred to the new owner. If the tenant gave the former owner a security deposit or paid any rent in advance, the former owner must either turn that money over to the new owner or refund it to the tenant (Civil Code Section 1950.5[f]).

> **Case Example:** In 1971, Ms. Trypucko leased some commercial property in Pasadena from Mr. Clark. The lease term was five years, with an option to renew for an additional five years. Trypucko gave Clark a $2,500 security deposit.
>
> Two years later, Clark sold the property to Security Pictures. He told Trypucko to start sending her rent payments to Security, but didn't tell her he'd sold the property. He also didn't transfer Trypucko's deposit to Security.
>
> In 1976, Trypucko exercised her option and renewed the lease for five more years. When the renewal expired in 1981, Trypucko moved out and demanded her security deposit back from Clark. Clark refused to return the money. Trypucko sued.
>
> Clark claimed that Trypucko had violated the terms of the lease in 1980, so she wasn't entitled to the return of her deposit. The court ruled that Clark's rights under the lease ended when he sold the property. Trypucko's conduct after that point had nothing to do with Clark, and certainly didn't excuse his failure to refund the deposit. Judgment for Trypucko. *Trypucko v. Clark*, 142 Cal. App. 3d Supp. 1, 191 Cal. Rptr. 165 (1983).

2. Assignment

A tenant has the right to assign the lease to someone else unless the lease expressly states that it can't be assigned without the landlord's consent. (Many leases do require consent.) *ASSIGNMENT transfers the right of occupancy to a new tenant (assignee on the original; tenant/ assignor for the entire remainder of the lease term).* The statute of frauds requires a lease assignment for more than one year to be in writing. Tenant transfers all

After assignment, the assignee is responsible for paying the rent to the landlord, but the original tenant also remains liable to the landlord. If the assignee doesn't pay, the landlord can demand the rent from the original tenant (assignor).

If the landlord wants the assignee to be bound by every contractual obligation in the current lease, it's very important to get a written assumption of the lease signed by the assignee.

3. Sublease

A sublease may also involve the lease by the tenant to a subtenant of a portion of the leased premises or for the remaining lease term.

Case Example: The trustees of the Meredith estate leased some commercial property in Los Angeles to Mr. Dardarian. The lease was for five years, from July 1, 1971, to June 30, 1976. It could not be assigned without consent.

In November 1971, Dardarian asked the trustees for permission to assign the lease to DA&W Commercial Corporation. The trustees gave their consent. DA&W took over the lease from November 1971 through June 30, 1976.

All went well for a few years, but DA&W stopped paying rent in April 1975. In May 1976, the trustees finally filed a lawsuit to evict DA&W and collect the rent. They also made Dardarian a defendant in the lawsuit. A judgment for the unpaid rent was entered against Dardarian, the original tenant, as well as against DA&W, the assignee. *Meredith v. Dardarian*, 83 Cal. App. 3d 248, 147 Cal. Rptr. 761 (1978).

Tenant transfers LESS than all

A *SUBLEASE* is different than an assignment. In a sublease, the original tenant retains the right under the lease to occupy the leased premises for the entire remaining term of the lease, but enters into a separate agreement with a subtenant giving the subtenant the right to occupy some portion of the leased premises for the remaining term or the right to occupy the entire leased premises for part of the remaining term. Thus, a sublease involves two different landlord/tenant relationships—one between the original landlord and tenant under the lease, and a second between the tenant and subtenant in which the original tenant acts as a landlord. In a sublease, the subtenant owes duties including the duty to pay rent to the original tenant, not to the landlord. The original tenant is still primarily obligated to pay rent to the landlord and to perform all of the other lease covenants. As with assignments, a tenant has the right to sublease a property unless the lease prohibits subleasing. If the lease prohibits assignments but does not mention subleasing, the tenant has the right to sublease.

> **Example:** T leases an apartment. His tenancy will last from October through the following September. In March, T's company gives him a four-month assignment in Taiwan. He subleases his apartment to S for the four months he will be gone. S agrees to pay rent to T from April 1 through July 31. T continues to pay rent to the landlord.
>
> When T returns from Taiwan, S moves out and T moves back in for the final two months of the lease term.

A sublease doesn't alter the legal relationship between the landlord and the original tenant. If not paid, ordinarily the landlord can sue only the original tenant.

a. Withholding Consent

Many commercial leases prohibit both assignment and subleasing without the landlord's consent. For commercial leases executed on or after January 1, 1990, the lease may include a restriction on transfer of the tenant's interest in the lease. A transfer by a tenant may be absolutely prohibited in the lease, or a restriction on transfer may provide that it is subject to any express standard or condition, including a provision that the landlord is entitled to some or all of any consideration the tenant receives from the transfer in excess of the rent under the lease.

If the transfer restriction in the lease requires the landlord's consent for the transfer but no standard for giving or withholding consent, it is implied that the consent may not be unreasonably withheld. Whether it is unreasonably withheld is a question of fact on which the tenant has the burden of proof. The burden of proof may be satisfied by showing that, in response to the tenant's written request for a statement of reasons for withholding consent, the landlord failed within a reasonable time to state a reasonable objection in writing to the tenant. Also, a landlord's acceptance of rent, or a failure to object in a timely manner after the tenant's breach of a transfer restriction, may constitute a waiver of the breach and therefore the landlord's consent.

Case Example: Mr. Schweiso leased some commercial property. The lease stated that it could not be assigned without the lessors' written consent. Sometime later, Schweiso wanted to sell his business to the Grofs, so he asked the lessors for permission to assign the lease to the Grofs.

    The lessors would not consent unless they were paid $6,000. They said the lease gave them the right to be unreasonable and arbitrary; the consent provision was their "license to steal." After the lessors withheld consent, the Grofs cancelled their conditional contract to buy Schweiso's business.

    Schweiso sued the lessors. The court ruled that the lessors did not have the right to arbitrarily withhold consent. They couldn't turn down the tenant's request just on the basis of personal taste or whim, or in order to demand more money. *Schweiso v. Williams*, 150 Cal. App. 3d 883, 198 Cal. Rptr. 238 (1984).

If there is no restriction on transfer in the lease, the tenant's transfer rights are unrestricted. Remember this legislation does not apply to residential leases.

4. Novation

Neither an assignment nor a sublease takes the original tenant off the hook. He or she is still liable to the landlord for the rent. To avoid any further liability under the lease, the original tenant has to arrange a novation rather than an assignment or sublease.

A *NOVATION replaces the lease between the landlord and the original tenant with a new lease between the landlord and the substitute tenant.* The original tenant is released. Of course, a novation always requires the landlord's consent.

II. Rights and Duties of the Landlord and Tenant

In the lease, landlord and tenant each agree to take on certain duties in exchange for certain rights. The law also imposes duties on each party, creating corresponding rights for the other. These duties imposed by law apply even when they aren't expressly stated in the lease, and they override any inconsistent lease provisions. They're sometimes called **implied covenants** or **implied warranties**; the law makes them part of the lease.

There are often different legal rules for residential tenancies and nonresidential tenancies.

Commercial tenants are presumed to be more sophisticated than residential tenants, and better able to protect their interests during lease negotiations. As a result, the law imposes duties on residential landlords that don't apply to commercial and other nonresidential landlords.

California also has a special landlord/tenant law for mobilehome parks, which will be discussed later. For now, we'll look at the general rules.

A. DELIVERY OF POSSESSION

There's an implied covenant in every lease that the landlord will deliver possession of the property to the tenant on the date the lease term begins. If the tenant is prevented from taking possession, it is a breach of this implied covenant.

> **Example:** The apartment rental agreement says the tenancy will begin on August 1. When the new tenant shows up on that day ready to move in, she discovers that the previous tenant hasn't moved out yet. It was up to the landlord to make sure the old tenant was out before August 1, and his failure to do so is a breach of the new lease.

When the covenant to deliver possession is breached, the tenant has the option of rescinding the lease: asking the landlord to return any money already paid, and looking for another place to live or set up shop. If the tenant decides not to rescind and just waits for the landlord to deliver possession, the tenant may only request compensatory damages.

As stated earlier, compensatory damages are an award of money intended to compensate someone for the consequences or results of a wrongful act. Suppose the apartment in the previous example wasn't ready for the new tenant until August 6. If the new tenant chooses to wait instead of rescinding the lease, she must still pay rent, but may demand that the landlord pay her compensatory damages. These may include a six-day hotel bill, cost of storing her furniture for six days, and only additional moving expenses.

B. RENT

Not surprisingly, the tenant's primary duty is to pay the rent as agreed. Most leases state a specific date when rent is due, usually at the beginning of the rental period. But if the lease doesn't specify when rent is to be paid, it isn't due until the end of the rental period (unless the period is longer than one year).

Many landlords require tenants to pay a late charge if the rent isn't paid within a certain time after the due date. There is a presumption that a late charge would have to be a "reasonable" amount because no specific amount has been set by legislation or court decision. What would be reasonable? A late charge of 6% of the delinquent amount is permitted by legislation on a note secured by a deed of trust. In any event, the landlord would have the burden of proving the late charge is reasonable. A landlord has the right to terminate a lease or evict a tenant for nonpayment of rent. Some cities have rent control ordinances (discussed later) limiting the amount of and ability to increase rent amounts.

A landlord may not require cash as the exclusive form of payment of rent or deposit of security. The landlord may require cash if the tenant has previously attempted to pay with a check drawn on insufficient funds or has stopped payment on the check. However, the landlord must have given the tenant a written notice stating the rent check was dishonored, attaching a copy of the dishonored check, and informing the tenant that future rent must be paid in cash for the time stated therein which cannot exceed three months.

C. EVICTION

Eviction can be either actual or constructive. There's *ACTUAL EVICTION if the landlord orders the tenant to leave the leased property, or physically forces the tenant out (by changing the locks, for example). But sometimes the tenant is forced to leave because the property has become uninhabitable*

CHAPTER 15

or can no longer be used as intended. When that's the landlord's fault, it's called CONSTRUCTIVE EVICTION.

Constructive Eviction

- Substantial interference with use of property
- Problem must be landlord's responsibility
- Tenant must actually move out
- Duty to pay rent ends

Case Example: Ms. Buckner rented an apartment in Mr. Azulai's building. Sometime later, the building became infested with vermin. Buckner did her best to exterminate them in her own apartment, but it was hopeless, since the whole building was infested, the bugs kept coming back. The landlord didn't take action, so Buckner moved out. In the ensuing lawsuit, the court held that she had been constructively evicted. The judgment for her last month's rent is afirmed. *Buckner v. Azulai*, 251 Cal. App. 2d Supp. 1013, 59 Cal. Rptr. 806 (1967).

D. COVENANT OF QUIET ENJOYMENT

The implied *COVENANT OF QUIET ENJOYMENT provides that the tenant has a right to undisturbed possession of the property during the lease term.* The tenant is protected from intrusion by the landlord or by anyone else claiming a right to the property. This covenant is breached if the tenant is wrongfully evicted.

A breach of the covenant of quiet enjoyment (either actual or constructive eviction) relieves the tenant of the duty to pay rent. However, to claim constructive eviction, the tenant must actually move off the property within a reasonable period of time. Buckner couldn't have stopped paying rent because of the bugs if she were still living in that apartment. Not every problem or disturbance can be the basis for a claim of constructive eviction. The problem must substantially interfere with the tenant's use of the property, and it must be the landlord's responsibility. (Of course, the tenant may stay and sue for damages.)

Case Example: Mr. Brown leased an apartment. The lease stated that the landlord was not liable to the tenant for any damage resulting from the acts of other tenants in the building.

It turned out that the family in the apartment below Brown liked to sing and quarrel loudly at all hours. Brown couldn't get a good night's sleep. He complained to the family and to the landlord, but without effect, so he moved out and stopped paying rent. The landlord sued Brown for the money.

The court ruled in the landlord's favor. Since the lease expressly stated that the landlord wasn't responsible for the acts of other tenants, the neighbors' noise wasn't constructive eviction. Brown was required to pay his rent. *Conterno v. Brown*, 263 Cal. App. 2d 135, 69 Cal. Rptr. 393 (1968).

E. PRIVACY

Unless otherwise agreed, a landlord doesn't have the right to enter the leased property without the tenant's consent.

If the landlord is supposed to maintain the property, it's understood that he or she may enter to make necessary repairs. Most leases contain a clause stating that the landlord may show the premises to a prospective tenant or purchaser after receiving the notice of intent to vacate. California has special rules to protect the privacy of residential tenants. A residential landlord may not enter the property without the tenant's consent to merely "inspect the premises." An exception is for an emergency that threatens to injure someone or damage property—then notice must be given immediately afterwards.

> **Example:** A water pipe bursts and begins flooding a tenant's apartment. The tenant isn't home. This is an emergency—the landlord may enter the apartment without the tenant's consent to stop the flood, then leave notice.

When there's no emergency, however, a residential landlord must obtain the tenant's permission or give reasonable notice before entering and can enter for only the following reasons: to make necessary or agreed repairs, or show the property to a prospective new tenant, prospective buyer, lender or workmen. Twenty-four hours' notice is considered reasonable under state law; some local ordinances may require more notice. Except in emergencies or unusual circumstances, the landlord may only enter during ordinary business hours, unless the tenant agrees. Otherwise, in some instances, it may be necessary for the landlord to get a court order to enter.

These rules don't apply when the landlord believes the tenant has abandoned the property. Abandonment is discussed later in this chapter.

F. MAINTENANCE, REPAIRS, AND HABITABILITY

1. Tenant's Duties

Unless otherwise agreed, the tenant has a duty to keep the leased property clean and in good condition, dispose of garbage in a clean and sanitary manner, properly use all fixtures and keep them clean, and to use each portion of the premises as they are intended. Of course, if the tenant is just renting part of a building, that duty applies only to the tenant's own apartment or office space, not to the hallways and other common areas.

The tenant must not intentionally or negligently damage any part of the property, or permit guests to damage it. The tenant is expected to repair damage caused by unauthorized alterations, failure to exercise ordinary care, or use of the property in a way it wasn't intended to be used. If the tenant doesn't make these repairs, he or she is liable to the landlord for their cost, but a tenant isn't liable for the ordinary wear and tear that results from normal use of the property or for defective conditions that preexisted the tenancy.

www.dca.ca.gov/publications/landlordbook/index.shtml
California Department of Consumer Affairs - Landlord/Tenant Publication

a. Security Deposits

Unfortunately, it's not uncommon for a tenant to move out without paying all the rent that's due, leaving the property in a mess or even badly damaged. To protect themselves, most landlords require a tenant to pay a security deposit before the tenancy begins.

If the tenant pays the rent and keeps the apartment in good condition, the security deposit is refunded when the lease ends. The landlord can retain as much of the deposit as is reasonably necessary to cover unpaid rent, damage caused by the tenant, or cleaning costs. A security deposit cannot be used for ordinary wear and tear, however.

Example: T rents an apartment from L and pays her a $1,000 security deposit. When T moves in, the living room carpet isn't new, but it's in fairly good shape. T moves out two years later. Now the carpet looks worn and shabby, so L decides to replace it before renting the apartment again. L is not allowed to use T's security deposit for new carpet, as the deterioration of the old carpet was ordinary wear and tear.

On the other hand, suppose the carpet was new when T moved into the apartment. When she moves out a year later, there are cigarette burns and coffee stains in several places. L wouldn't usually have replaced the carpet this soon, but was forced to because of the burns and stains. In this case, L could legitimately apply T's security deposit to the cost of new carpet.

California law limits the amount a residential landlord can demand as a security deposit.

For unfurnished apartments or houses, the deposit can't be more than the equivalent of two months' rent. (If the rent is $1,500 a month, the deposit can't be more than $3,000.) For furnished property, the deposit can't be more than three months' rent. The deposit is usually collected in addition to the first month's rent prior to giving possession.

Commercial landlords may charge nonrefundable deposits, but residential landlords are not allowed to. To get around these rules, some residential landlords began making new arrangements and giving new names to special charges. However, the law now treats any advance payment as a security deposit, no matter what it is called (e.g., key deposits, pet deposit, water bed deposit).

Case Example: The Parkmerced Company owned a huge apartment complex. All tenants had one-year leases, paid rent by the month, and were required to give Parkmerced a refundable security deposit. But the first month's rent was $65 higher than the rent for the remaining 11 months of the year. For example, if the annual rent was $3,665, the tenant would have to pay $365 the first month and $300 each month thereafter.

On behalf of the tenants, the state of California sued Parkmerced for this practice. The court held that the additional $65 was actually an illegal nonrefundable fee, not part of the rent. Even in Parkmerced's internal accounting records, the $65 was noted separately from the rent payments. The court ordered Parkmerced to refund the $65 charges to all the tenants (even former tenants), and also pay $221,700 in punitive damages and $40,000 in attorney fees. *People v. Parkmerced Company*, 198 Cal. App. 3d 683, 244 Cal. Rptr. 22 (1988).

In most California rental agreements, no interest is due to the tenant on the security deposit; where exceptions occur, the requirements are specific.

Upon notification of termination of tenancy, or before the end of the lease term, the landlord must notify the tenant in writing of the option to request an initial inspection and to be present at the inspection. The initial inspection should be made within a reasonable time, but not earlier than two weeks before the termination of the tenancy. The purpose is to allow the tenant an opportunity to correct identified deficiencies pursuant to the rental agreement in order to avoid deductions from the security deposit. If the inspection is requested, the parties should agree to a mutually acceptable date and time. The landlord must give a 48-hour prior written notice of the mutually agreed time or, if a mutually agreed time cannot be scheduled but the tenant still wishes the inspection, both the landlord and the tenant can waive the 48-hour notice. The landlord proceeds with the inspection whether or not the tenant is present, unless the tenant previously withdrew the request. Based on the inspection, the landlord gives the tenant an itemized statement specifying the repairs and cleaning required by the tenant that can be deducted from the security deposit.

Within 21 days after a residential tenant moves out, the landlord must give the tenant an itemized statement with any refund and explanation of why all or part of the deposit has been retained.

Any residential landlord who keeps a security deposit in bad faith can be ordered to pay up to twice the amount of the security in statutory damages in addition to actual damages. In commercial tenancies, if the landlord's only claim against the deposit is for unpaid rent, the remainder of the deposit (if any) and an itemized statement must be sent to the tenant within 21 days. If deductions are made for cleaning or damage, then he or she has 30 days to send the remainder and the statement. Any commercial landlord who keeps a security deposit in bad faith can be ordered to pay $200 in punitive damages, in addition to having to pay actual damages.

Security Deposits

- Unpaid rent, damage, and cleaning—not ordinary wear and tear
- Not treated as liquidated damages; landlord may sue
- Full refund and itemized explanation required (residential: 21 days, commercial: 21 days)
- Residential property—no more than two months' rent (three months' rent if furnished)—no nonrefundable deposits.

If a tenant caused severe damage and the repair costs are greater than the security deposit, the landlord may bring a lawsuit against the former tenant to collect the additional amount. The security deposit doesn't limit the tenant's liability; it isn't treated as liquidated damages. A lease may include a liquidated damages provision.

Example: In the earlier example involving a burned and stained carpet, the tenant gave the landlord a $1,000 damage deposit. Suppose it cost the landlord $2,500 to replace the carpet. The landlord could sue the tenant for $1,500, the amount the deposit didn't cover. The court would consider whether or not it was reasonably necessary to replace the carpet. If so, the landlord would be entitled to the full amount of damages.

On the other hand, if the tenant could prove that it wasn't necessary to replace the carpet, then the landlord wouldn't collect a judgment. Perhaps the carpet could have

CHAPTER 15

been restored for only $400. If so, the restoration costs would have been less than the security deposit. The landlord would be ordered to refund the tenant the extra $600.

2. Landlord's Duties to Repair and Maintain

a. Commercial Property

Under common law, the landlord had no duty to maintain the premises; it was the tenant's obligation to maintain and repair the leased property. For leases of commercial real property, the common law still applies. Unless the landlord agrees in the lease to repair or maintain the premises, the landlord has no duty to repair or maintain the premises, and it is the tenant's responsibility to repair maintain the premises that are exclusively controlled by the tenant. The landlord will have a duty to maintain and repair property over which the landlord retains control, such as common areas. A landlord can promise in a lease to repair and maintain the premises, and if so, the landlord can be liable for failure to repair or maintain as promised.

In commercial leases, if the landlord has a duty to repair or maintain, that duty is independent of the tenant's duty to pay rent. The tenant must pay rent even if the landlord has breached the duty to repair or maintain. There is no right to make the repairs and deduct the cost of the repairs from rent. The tenant's remedy is to sue for damages. The breach of duty to repair or maintain the premises cannot be raised as a defense in an unlawful detainer action.

b. Residential Property

In California, there is an obligation on the part of the landlord to make the residential premises fit for occupancy and to maintain the premises.

Tenant's Right to Repair and Deduct

When a problem develops that makes the property untenantable, the tenant must notify the landlord. If the landlord doesn't fix the problem within a reasonable time, the tenant has the right to hire someone to do the repairs, and then deduct the cost from the rent. The cost can't be more than one month's rent, and the tenant can use this remedy no more than twice in any twelve-month period.

The California Civil Code requires that property rented as a dwelling must meet a basic standard of *TENANTABILITY, meaning that the landlord, to make the dwelling tenantable, must provide effective waterproofing and weather protection; plumbing, heating, and electrical wiring that's up to code: hot and cold running water; adequate garbage receptacles, and safe floors, stairs, and railings.* At the beginning of a residential lease, the landlord must have made sure that the tenant's unit (or house) is free from trash, garbage, rodents, and insects. In the case of a residential building with more than one tenant, the landlord is always responsible for keeping the common areas uninfested and reasonably clean. The landlord must meet the standards of tenantability before renting the property and throughout the term of the lease.

538

How long does the tenant have to wait for the landlord? Thirty days is presumed to be a reasonable time, but in many cases the tenant would be justified in taking action sooner. An example would be a broken hot water heater.

Instead of having the property repaired and deducting the cost, the tenant has the option of terminating the lease if the landlord doesn't make repairs as required by law (or as agreed in the lease). This is constructive eviction, discussed earlier in the chapter. If the tenant moves out, he or she will not owe the landlord any further rent.

If the dwelling is untenantable and the landlord has not, without good cause, corrected the problem within 30 days, the tenant can repair and deduct. A landlord cannot demand or collect rent when the premises are not habitable, a housing official has given the landlord notice of the habitability violation, and the landlord failed to correct the violations within 35 days. A landlord who does so is liable to the tenant for actual damages and special damages of not less than $100 or more than $5,000, plus reasonable attorneys' fees, and the court can order the landlord to correct the problem.

Although the landlord has the duty to maintain the leased property in accordance with habitability standards, tenants have these duties:

1. keeping the premises clean and sanitary and disposing of garbage and waste;
2. properly using fixtures and appliances; and
3. not willfully damage the premises.

Other statutory obligations for residential landlords relating to property condition include:

1. provide the tenant with and maintain wiring for one telephone jack;
2. disclose to the tenant the lack of separate utility meters, and reach an agreement regarding payment;
3. allow the tenant to install a water bed provided certain requirements are met;
4. disclose any occupants' deaths (except AIDS) on the premises within the last 3 years;
5. disclose any former state or federal ordnance (military explosives) location within one mile, if the landlord has knowledge of it;
6. provide the tenant with a notice about the existence of a database maintained by law enforcement that gives the locations of registered sex offenders;
7. install and maintain locks on doors and windows. The bolt on dead bolt locks on each main (swinging) entry door must protrude 13/16 inches into the doorjamb at a minimum; and
8. notify the tenant in writing of the release of all illegal controlled substances on the property if the landlord knows of it.

The only exception is when the tenant agrees to perform repairs or improvements in exchange for lower rent. The landlord should also provide adequate locks and lighting to help prevent crime. In the *Hinson* case that follows, an implied "**warranty of habitability**" was created by the court for residential property. This is separate and distinct from the Civil Code requirements of tenantability.

Case Example: Ms. Hinson rented an apartment in Richmond for $90 a month and moved in with her children. The apartment was in adequate condition at that time, but over the next few months, several problems developed. Dry rot caused a large hole in the bathroom floor, the toilet leaked badly, and a glass panel in the front door let in a cold draft that made it difficult to keep the main room warm.

Hinson repeatedly asked the landlord to take care of all these problems, but she got no response. An official inspection showed the defects violated city codes. There was so little low-income housing in the area that Hinson couldn't find another place to live. Finally, Hinson told the landlord's manager that she wouldn't pay her rent until the apartment was repaired. When the unpaid rent amounted to $200, the landlord sent an eviction notice, stating that Hinson had to pay up within three days or get out.

Hinson sued to prevent the landlord from evicting her. The court held that she wasn't required to pay the full $90 a month as long as the landlord was breaching the implied warranty of habitability. Until the apartment was made habitable, Hinson was only required to pay the reasonable rental value of the property. *Hinson v. Delis*, 26 Cal. App. 3d 62, 102 Cal. Rptr. 661 (1972).

If the landlord breaches the implied warranty of habitability, the tenant doesn't have to pay the full amount of rent charged while the landlord's breach continues.

Instead, the tenant is required to pay only the reasonable rental value of the property in its substandard condition.

In the *Hinson* case, the appellate court didn't decide what was the reasonable rental value of the nonrepaired apartment. (The appellate court remanded the case back to the trial court to determine the reasonable rental value.) Presumably, the reasonable rental value was very low. Note that Hinson could have avoided any further liability for rent if she'd moved out of the apartment and claimed constructive eviction, but she and her family had nowhere else to go.

In addition to using the implied warranty of habitability as a defense against eviction, a residential tenant can also bring a tort suit against the landlord for failing to maintain the property.

Case Example: Ms. Stoiber's apartment had sewage leaking from the bathroom plumbing, dangerous electrical wiring, structurally unsound walls and floors, a leaking roof, broken windows, cockroaches, and a few other problems. Stoiber notified her landlords about all of these conditions. On one occasion, they sent out a plumber to fix the toilet, but that was it. Eventually the Kern County Health Department ordered the property vacated and demolished.

Stoiber sued the landlords for breach of the warranty of habitability, asking them to repay the difference between the rent she'd paid and the fair rental value of the property. She also sued them for damage to her personal property (some of it had been destroyed by water leaking into the apartment), and for discomfort, annoyance, and emotional distress. The Court of Appeal allowed her lawsuit to continue. *Stoiber v. Honeychuck*, 101 Cal. App. 3d 903, 162 Cal. Rptr. 194 (1980).

3. Tenant's Smoking Ban

California landlords, who have long had the right to restrict pets, noise, and even water beds in their units, can now prohibit smoking under a new law, California Senate Bill 332. As of January 1, 2012, all new leases must state the smoking policy and specify where tenants cannot smoke. For leases entered into prior to January 1, 2012, a prohibition against smoking on any portion of the property in which smoking was previously permitted constitutes a change of terms of tenancy requiring adequate notice, as specified. This bill states that a landlord who exercises the above authority shall be subject to state and local notice requirements governing changes to the terms of rental agreements that are in existence at the time the policy is adopted (SB 332, Cal Civ. Code 1947.5).

4. Protecting Pets from Being Declawed or Devocalized

A landlord or other person or corporation that occupies, owns, manages, or provides services in connection with any real property that allows an animal as defined on the premises, is prohibited from requiring that the animal be declawed or devocalized (SB 1229, Cal. Civ. Code 1942.7).

G. LIABILITY FOR PERSONAL INJURIES

When someone—a tenant, a tenant's guest, or a meter reader—is injured on leased property, is the landlord liable? Regarding common areas under the landlord's control, the answer is nearly always "yes."

> **Example:** A steep stairway leads up to the main entrance of the apartment building. The steps are covered with moss, and they become quite slick after a rain. A tenant slips on the top step and breaks his arm. He sues the landlord. The landlord is held liable for negligence because the landlord failed to use ordinary care in maintaining the property's common areas. When it happens inside a unit, the answer isn't as simple.

The rule used to be that the landlord usually wasn't liable in these cases. Once the lease term started, the landlord was no longer in control of the single-family home or the office space; the tenant had control. The landlord was only held liable if he or she knew that there was a hidden hazard on the property before the tenant moved in. Then the landlord had a duty to warn the tenant. The landlord was virtually never liable for injuries resulting from a problem that developed after the lease began.

For a short period, California courts expanded the landlords' liability well beyond those limits. For example, a landlord who was engaged in the business of leasing dwellings was held strictly liable for injuries resulting from a latent defect on the premises when the tenant rented the premises. Under the strict liability standard, the landlord was liable for injuries caused by defects that the landlord had not created, that would not have been disclosed by a reasonable inspection, and of which the landlord had no knowledge, even if the landlord had exercised extraordinary care. In *Peterson v. Superior Court*, 10 Cal. 4th 1185, 43 Cal. Rptr. 2d 836 (Cal. 1995) (explained later), the California Supreme Count reconsidered whether a landlord should be held strictly liable for injuries to tenants caused by defects in the premises, and determined that the reasons for imposing strict liability on a retailer or manufacturer of a defective product do not apply to landlords. A landlord still may be held liable for negligence if he/she breaches the applicable standard of care.

> **Case Example:** A real estate broker owned several single-family rental homes in one neighborhood in Modesto. He rented one of these homes to a family with a large German shepherd. He specifically granted them permission to keep the dog on the leased property.
>
> The dog was vicious. Although it was usually kept chained, it attacked neighbors on two separate occasions. One day it attacked Juliana, a girl who had come over to play with the tenants' children. Juliana was badly injured.
>
> After this, many of the neighbors signed a petition demanding that the tenants get rid of the dog, but the tenants didn't give up the dog until several months later, after it attacked their own daughter.
>
> Juliana's parents sued the dog owners and their landlord, requesting compensation for Juliana's injuries. The trial judge dismissed the case against the landlord, but the appellate court reversed. The tenants had a month-to-month lease, which the landlord could have terminated at any time. Thus, the landlord retained considerable control over the leased property. If the landlord was aware of the dog's vicious character, he was negligent in failing to make the tenants remove the dog from his property. The landlord, as well as the tenants, could be held liable for Juliana's injuries.
>
> However, "a landlord is under no duty to inspect the premises for the purpose of discovering the existence of a tenant's dangerous animal; only when the landlord has actual knowledge of the animal, coupled with a right to have it removed from the premises, does a duty of care arise." *Uccello v. Laudenslayer*, 44 Cal. App. 3d 504, 118 Cal. Rptr. 741 (1975).

However, commercial landlords, not small residential landlords, must conduct reasonable inspections to maintain the safety of any premises open to the public. A landlord is not liable for injuries when a reasonable inspection was conducted but the presence of the dangerous condition was not discovered.

> **Case Example:** While delivering beer to a liquor store, Portillo was severely injured by the store owner's guard dog. Portillo sued the store owner and Aiassa who was the landlord. Aiassa had not inspected the premises prior to the tenant's renewal of the lease, but stated he visited the premises several times a year and the dog did not appear vicious. Store customers testified the dog was always there, was dangerous, and had bitten people. The tenant posted a sign that read "Beware of Dog... WE HAVE A GUARD DOG! DO NOT PET OR TEASE!" A newspaper article was also posted concerning the dog's recent attack on a robber in which the dog was described as "a furry juggernaut, replete with iron trap jaws, razor sharp fangs and a rotten disposition."
>
> The jury found for Portillo and awarded damages of $300,000. The court of appeal agreed and held that "a landlord has a duty to exercise reasonable care in the inspection of his commercial property and to remove a dangerous condition. A dog should be removed from the premises if he knew, or in the exercise of reasonable care would have known, the dog was dangerous and usually on the premises. The risk of harm to the general public clearly outweighs the presence of a particular tenant on the premises." *Portillo v. Aiassa*, 27 Cal. App. 4th 1128, 32 Cal. Rptr. 2d 755 (1994).

Case Example: Olga Kiymaz (tenant) rented a condominium from Jerome Brown (landlord) and owned a Jack Russell terrier which was allowed under the condominium CC&Rs (condo rules). The dog ran out of the tenant's unit and jumped upon the 71-year-old plaintiff who rented the property next door causing her to fall and sustain numerous injuries. The plaintiff sued the landlord, Homeowners Association, the property managers, and the tenant.

The plaintiff failed to present any evidence that the landlord or the Association had knowledge of the dog's dangerous propensities. The only evidence presented was that the dog was seen off-leash, and engaged in the normal animal functions of urinating and defecating (not cleaned up) which resulted in a $50 fine and a warning. The fact that the landlord was aware that the dog was a Jack Russell terrier and that its name was "Thunder" does not support an inference of the knowledge of dangerous propensities. The expert witness for the plaintiff declared that Jack Russell terriers, as a breed, are not recommended for apartments or condominiums because the dogs will try to escape confinement, jump and leap, and be dangerously playful. The property managers duty of care was no different than that of the landlord since they had no actual knowledge regarding the dog. Summary judgment for the defendants affirmed (the tenant filed bankruptcy and was dismissed from the lawsuit). *Chee v. Amanda Goldt Property Management*, 143 Cal. App. 4th 1360, 50 Cal. Rptr. 3d 40 (2006).

The landlord's liabilities in the *Uccello* case and the *Portillo* case were based on negligence, a failure to use ordinary care. Most cases in which a landlord is held liable for injuries involve negligence: negligently failing to repair the property, or making repairs in a negligent manner.

Case Example: Nadine Peterson claimed that while she was a guest at the Palm Springs Marquis Hotel, she slipped and fell in the bathtub while taking a shower, sustaining serious head injuries. She alleged that the bottom surface of the bathtub was extremely slick and slippery and the bathtub had no safety measures like anti-skid surfaces, grab rails or rubber mats. In addition to a cause of action for negligence, she brought a cause of action for strict liability asserting the bathtub was a defective product, relying on Becker. The court held that landlords and hotel owners should not be held strictly liable in tort for injuries to tenants and guests caused by defects in the premises. Landlords may still be held liable for injuries resulting from defects on the premises if they were negligent in handling the property. The case was sent back for trial on her negligence claim. *Peterson v. Superior Court (Paribas)*, 10 Cal. 4th 1185, 43 Cal. Rptr. 2d 836 (1995).

In summary, for residential property, a landlord may be negligent if the landlord has failed to disclose a dangerous condition on the premises and it is foreseeable that the defect is likely to cause personal injury to the tenant or guest of the tenant. This means every property owner owes a duty to a tenant to exercise ordinary care in the management of the property to prevent injury to other persons. This is especially true in the common areas. Therefore, if the landlord has knowledge of defects in the property that are unknown to the tenant and not apparent to the tenant, and the landlord fails to disclose these defects to the tenant, the landlord will be liable for injuries. A landlord is not liable for injuries to a tenant caused by a condition of the property that occurs after the tenant has taken occupancy and of which the landlord has no knowledge or is a condition created by the tenant. If the landlord has knowledge of a dangerous condition or defect, the landlord's obligation is to repair it and make the property safe or warn the tenant.

CHAPTER 15

1. Criminal Acts

In the past, landlords weren't held to have a duty to protect tenants against crimes committed by third parties on the leased property. However, in recent years California courts have found landlords liable for failing to protect tenants against foreseeable crimes, especially if the building was advertised as a security building, or if it's in a neighborhood where criminal activity is likely or has previously occured. In other words, the same negligence standard applies—did the landlord have notice of prior similar incidents of crime on the landowner's premises and fail to take reasonable precautions to prevent future incidents. If the act could not have been anticipated or prevented, there is no landlord liability.

Case Example: Ms. O'Hara rented an apartment in a San Jose complex owned by Western Seven Trees Corporation. She was told that professional guards patrolled the property at night, and the complex was safe. She wasn't told that several of the tenants had been raped in their apartments and the rapist had not yet been arrested.

Three months after moving in, O'Hara was raped in her apartment by the same man who committed the earlier crimes. She sued her landlords for failing to provide adequate security, and for deceit. The trial judge dismissed the case, but the appellate court ruled that the landlords could be held liable. *O'Hara v. Western Seven Trees Corp.*, 75 Cal. App. 3d 798, 142 Cal. Rptr. 487 (1978).

At least one court has held that the landlord's duty to protect tenants from crime only creates liability for personal injuries, not for a loss of property. That case, *Royal Neckware Company, Inc. v. Century City, Inc.*, 252 Cal. Rptr. 810 (1988), involved a burglary at a clothing and jewelry store in a shopping mall. The court said it's up to the tenant to insure personal property against theft.

III. Termination of a Lease

A lease for a set term (an **estate for years** – see Chapter 3) expires on a specified date. Sometimes when a lease is about to expire, the parties decide to renew it. They may renegotiate the terms of the lease at this point; the rent may be raised or lowered.

A. EXPIRATION, RENEWAL, AND NOTICE

A lease can be renewed even if the landlord and tenant don't expressly arrange for renewal. If the tenant remains in possession after the lease term expires, and the landlord continues to accept rent, it's presumed that they've renewed the lease on the same terms. With this type of implied renewal, if the rent is paid monthly, the new lease will be from month-to-month.

Example: T rented L's house for a one-year term, paying $575 a month in rent. At the end of the year, the lease expired, but T doesn't move out. He continues to pay L $575 a month. This is an implied renewal, and T and L have the same duties as they had under the original lease. Now, instead of an estate for years, T has a month-to-month periodic tenancy.

Nothing seems to have changed (T is paying L $575 each month, just as he always has), but the lease term is now only one month long, not one year. Either T or L can terminate the periodic tenancy by giving notice to the other party.

In California, notice of termination must be in writing.

For a month-to-month tenancy (or any periodic tenancy with a rental period longer than one month), tenants or landord must give written notice at least 30 days before the end of the period, unless otherwise agreed. However, for leases of residential property, the landlord must give a 60-day notice if the tenant has lived on the property for more than one year. If the rental period is less than a month, the notice period must be at least as long as the rental period, unless otherwise agreed. The parties can agree to a longer or shorter notice period in the lease, but it can't be less than seven days. If neither party gives notice, the tenancy is automatically renewed for another rental period.

Although a periodic lease can be terminated at any time just by giving notice, a lease for a set term doesn't work that way. In that case, both the landlord and tenant are bound by the lease until the term expires. However, a lease for a set term can end before the expiration date in one of six ways:

1. Surrender
2. Foreclosure
3. Destruction of the premises
4. Illegal use of the premises
5. Tenant default
6. Abandonment

B. SURRENDER

Sometimes both landlord and tenant would like to terminate their lease before its term expires. When they agree to terminate the lease, it's called surrender. Surrender is often preferred by the tenant and landlord when a novation is used to begin a new lease with a new tenant.

C. FORECLOSURE (90 Days' Notice)

The title conveyed to a purchaser at a trustee's sale relates back to the date when the trust deed was recorded. A lease is subordinate to the trust deed if it was executed after the trust deed was recorded. Therefore, the lease is terminated by the foreclosure sale. However, both California and federal law require that residential tenants must be given 90 days' notice to vacate if the foreclosure purchaser chooses to terminate the lease. And for residential leases, except where the foreclosure purchaser will occupy the property as a primary residence, the purchaser cannot terminate any bona fide fixed-term lease before its expiration date.

D. DESTRUCTION OF THE PREMISES

If a lease is for a part of a building (such as an office or apartment), the entire purpose of the lease is frustrated if the building is destroyed by fire, flood or an earthquake. The tenant is released from the duty to pay rent.

Of course, the landlord and tenant can (and should) include a provision in the lease concerning destruction of the premises. Most leases specify who will maintain insurance on the property, and who is liable for rebuilding if a structure is destroyed. If there is no express stipulation and the building is destroyed without fault, it's generally the landlord's loss. Most commercial landlords require the landlord to be named as a co-insured on the hazard insurance policies.

E. ILLEGAL USE OF THE PREMISES

California law provides that if the tenant's uses the property for "maintaining, committing, or permitting the maintenance or commission of a nuisance upon the demised premises or using the premises for an unlawful purpose," the lease is terminated upon service of a three-day notice to quit. This includes using the property illegally for the sale of a controlled substance.

F. TENANT DEFAULT - UNLAWFUL DETAIN AND EVICTION

Almost every lease provides that, if the tenant doesn't pay the rent, or is otherwise in default under the lease, the landlord may terminate the lease and evict the tenant from the property. However, that doesn't mean the lease terminates automatically if the tenant fails to pay.

1. Notice to Quit

First the landlord must serve on the tenant a written *NOTICE TO REMEDY OR QUIT*. *The notice states the amount due and warns that if it isn't paid within three days, the tenant must move out.* If the tenant doesn't move out, the landlord may begin legal proceedings to recover the unpaid rent and evict the tenant. If the tenant moves out within three days, the lease terminates.

The landlord also has the right to end the tenancy if the tenant violates other terms of the lease or uses the property in an unauthorized manner. Again, before taking legal action, the landlord must give the tenant a written notice to remedy or quit ("If the boa constrictors are not removed from the apartment within three days ..."). Sometimes just a notice to quit is enough as the problem cannot be remedied.

A landlord who makes a tenant move out without legal justification can be held liable for **wrongful eviction**. The landlord would be required to compensate the tenant for any damages suffered as a result of the eviction.

2. Unlawful Detainer

The landlord served a notice to quit, but the tenant still hasn't paid the rent or gotten rid of the snakes. At this point, if the tenant stays in possession of the property, he or she is "unlawfully detaining" it. The landlord's next step is to file an *UNLAWFUL DETAINER ACTION, which is a lawsuit to recover possession of leased property from a defaulting tenant.* It can also be used against a holdover tenant—one who stays on without the landlord's permission after the lease expires or when the landlord gives notice of termination.

An unlawful detainer action is filed in superior court. Because possession of the property is at issue (not just money), unlawful detainer suits are supposed to be resolved as quickly as possible. They take priority on a court's trial schedule, and the procedures are expedited. For example, the tenant has only five days from service to respond to the summons and complaint, compared to 30 days for defendants in other civil suits.

At the trial, the tenant might argue that the landlord breached the implied warranty of habitability, or a lease provision, or the property was untenantable. If the tenant proves that charge, he or she will not be evicted or held liable for the full amount of unpaid rent.

Usually, possession of the premises is given to the landlord along with a judgment for a lesser amount against the tenant.

If the court finds that the tenant has, in fact, defaulted and the landlord is entitled to possession of the property, a judgment for possession and rent will issue. After that, a writ of possession will be issued. The writ of possession orders the sheriff to remove the tenant from the rental unit. The sheriff posts the property with a lock-out order (eviction notice). The lock-out order will allow the sheriff to lock the tenant out if the tenant does not leave the premises with his or her belongings within 5 days of the posting. If the tenant does not leave by the end of the fifth day, the writ of possession authorizes the sheriff to physically remove and lock the tenant out, and seize (take) the tenant's belongings that have been left in the rental unit. The landlord is not entitled to possession of the rental unit until after the sheriff has removed the tenant.

3. Self-Help Eviction

Despite expedited procedures, the process of legal eviction often seems slow from the landlord's point of view. However, a landlord should never try to force the tenant off the property by other means. It's illegal for a landlord to remove or exclude a tenant from the leased property without a court order.

Sometimes a landlord tries to force a tenant to leave by cutting off utility services to the property. It's hard to stay in an apartment with no electricity or water, or no heat in the middle of January. And some landlords use a variety of ways to get rid of unwanted tenants: changing the apartment's locks when the tenant isn't home (lockout tenants); removing windows or doors, or removing the tenants' personal property from the dwelling. These practices are illegal. The landlord can be ordered to pay $100 in punitive damages for each day of violation, with a minimum of $250. The landlord can also be required to pay any actual damages the tenant suffers, plus the tenant's reasonable attorney's fees.

4. Retaliatory Eviction

When a landlord raises the rent sharply, decreases services, or terminates a lease because the tenant exercises a legal right, such as making a complaint about the condition of the property, requesting repairs, organizing or participating in a tenant's organization, it's called RETALIATORY EVICTION. The landlord is retaliating against the tenant for asserting a lawful right. Retaliatory eviction is illegal.

Case Example: For four years, Mr. Schweiger had been a month-to-month tenant in an apartment building owned by Mr. Bonds. The rent for Schweiger's apartment was $75 a month, like most of the other apartments in the building. Schweiger sent Bonds a letter on June 16, asking Bonds to repair some long-standing problems in Schweiger's apartment. There were two broken windows, and the back door wouldn't lock.

On July 1, Bonds notified Schweiger that his rent would be raised to $125 a month as of August 1. Bonds didn't raise the rent for any of the other apartments in the building. Sometime in July, Bonds had Schweiger's windows fixed, but not the back door.

On August 1, Schweiger paid Bonds only $60. This represented his ordinary rent payment, less $15, the estimated cost of repairing the back door. (When Schweiger actually carried out the repairs, it cost him $35.)

▼

CHAPTER 15

Schweiger refused to pay the higher rent, claiming Bonds had raised it in retaliation against his complaint.

Bonds brought an unlawful detainer action to evict Schweiger. The California Supreme Court ruled that if the rent hike and the lawsuit were retaliatory, Bonds was not entitled to evict Schweiger. *Schweiger v. Superior Court of Alameda County*, 3 Cal. 3d 507, 90 Cal. Rptr. 729 (1970).

However, in order for a tenant to use the defense of retaliatory eviction, the tenant cannot: (1) be in default in the payment of rent, (2) use the retaliatory eviction defense more than once in any 12 month period, and (3) use the defense after the passage of 180 days. Additionally, a landlord cannot retaliate against the tenant for organizing or participating in a tenant's rights organization and there is no 180 day limit on the tenant.

An unlawful detainer action is retaliatory when it occurs within 180 days after the tenant complains to the landlord about the condition of the property, files a complaint with a housing authority, sues the landlord for breach of the implied warranty of habitability, or is awarded a judgment against the landlord in such a lawsuit. If the landlord raises the rent or evicts the tenant during that 180-day period, the landlord will have to prove that a valid reason (not retaliation) was the cause for the action. The tenant has the overall burden of proving his landlord's retaliatory motive by a preponderance of the evidence.

If retaliatory action is taken within the 180-day period, the landlord will have to compensate the tenant for any damages suffered, and also pay the tenant's attorney's fees. Punitive damages of not less than $100 nor more than $2,000 for each retaliatory act are included if the court finds that the landlord was also guilty of fraud, oppression, or malice.

Case Example: For four years, Alice Barela rented an apartment from Leonard Valdez on a month-to-month tenancy at $200 per month. She called the police to complain that Valdez had sexually molested her nine-year-old daughter. Valdez then served her with a 30-day notice terminating her tenancy. She did not move and was sued for unlawful detainer. Barela alleged an affirmative defense that she was being evicted in retaliation for her exercise of constitutionally protected rights.

The California Supreme Court noted that Civil Code Section 1942.5 provides that it is unlawful for a landlord to sue to recover the property "for the purpose of retaliating against the lessee because he or she has ... lawfully and peaceably exercised any rights under the law." Reporting a crime is such a right. Public policy is served by reporting crimes. Barela's defense of retaliatory eviction is valid. *Barela v. Superior Court of Orange County*, 30 Cal. 3d 244, 178 Cal. Rptr. 618 (1981).

G. ABANDONMENT

Sometimes a tenant moves out (or simply disappears) before the lease expires. *When a tenant relinquishes possession of the property, it's called ABANDONMENT.* In this situation, the landlord usually wants to retake possession of the property and rent it out again as soon as possible, rather than waiting until the lease term runs out.

When the landlord reasonably believes that the property has been abandoned and the rent is at least 14 days overdue, he or she can terminate the lease and sue the tenant for damages.

To terminate the lease, the landlord must send a **NOTICE OF BELIEF OF ABANDONMENT** *to the tenant's last known address. The notice states that the lease will be terminated unless the tenant responds before a specified date.* The termination date (of the notice period) must be at least 18 days after the notice was mailed to the tenant (or, if the notice was served on the tenant in person, at least 15 days after the date of service).

To prevent termination, the tenant must inform the landlord in writing that he or she does not intend to abandon the property. The tenant must also give the landlord an address where he or she can be served if the landlord files an unlawful detainer action.

If the tenant doesn't respond by the specified date, the lease is terminated. Then the landlord can rent the property to a new tenant, and sue the former tenant for damages (see below). However, when a tenant abandons the rental unit, they often leave behind personal property. The law is specific on the storage of tenant's property. The landlord must give a notice of intent to dispose of it, and the tenant must pay reasonable cost of storage to reclaim the property.

Under some leases, the landlord has another option after abandonment. Instead of terminating the lease and suing for damages, the landlord may choose to let the lease continue. The tenant will still have the right of possession of the property (although he or she is not taking advantage of it), and will still owe the landlord the rent as it becomes due. This remedy is only available to the landlord if the lease expressly provides for it, and if the lease allows the tenant to assign or sublease, subject only to reasonable limitations.

H. LANDLORD'S DAMAGES

When a lease is terminated after abandonment or by an unlawful detainer action, the landlord is usually entitled to a judgment against the tenant for unpaid rent. In some cases, the award for landlord's damages is only the unpaid rent up to the termination date. In other cases, however, the tenant will also be charged for rent that would have been owed if the lease had not been terminated.

> **Example:** In January 2005, T signed a two-year lease for L's house, agreeing to pay $1,000 a month. But in June, T lost her job. She couldn't pay the rent due on July 1, and a few days later she moved out and went to stay with her brother.
>
> Near the end of July, L sent T a notice of belief of abandonment stating that the lease would be terminated on August 15. T didn't respond, so the lease was terminated.
>
> L cleaned up the house and began advertising it for rent again. However, L didn't find a new tenant until November 1.

If L sues T for damages, she can be required to pay him not just the rent due from July 1 through August 15, but the rent due up until November 1—a total of $4,000, plus interest (and any costs L incurred in trying to find a new tenant). In some cases, there will be additional damages.

> **Example:** Suppose rental rates have fallen, and L can only charge the new tenant $900 a month instead of the $1,000 that T was paying. Then T would owe L the difference for the rest of her original lease term, from November 1, 2005, all the way to December 31, 2006: $100 x 14 months = $1,400.

Depending on when the lawsuit is filed, the landlord may be asking the court to award damages for future losses—losses the landlord has not incurred yet. The court can award damages for future losses only if the lease expressly provides for that, or if the landlord acts reasonably and in good faith to re-rent the property. An award for future losses will be discounted to represent the present value of the money.

1. Mitigation

Keep in mind that the landlord has a duty to mitigate the damages by trying to rent the property to a new tenant as soon as possible. If the former tenant can prove that the landlord could have rented the property again sooner, or for more money, the damages award will be reduced.

> **Example:** Continuing with the previous example, suppose T's friend Joe offers to rent the house from L for $1,000 a month starting on October 1, 2005. Joe has a good credit rating and rental history. L's niece tells him that she wants to rent the house, so L turns Joe down. L's niece moves in on November 1 and pays only $900 a month.
>
> T would not be required to pay L for the month of October or the $100 difference in the rent. These were damages that L could have avoided by accepting Joe's offer.

I. TENANT'S PERSONAL PROPERTY

If a tenant leaves personal property behind after vacating the leased property (either by abandonment or at the end of the term), the landlord must either leave it where it is or place it in storage. Within 18 days after moving out, the tenant must request in writing that the landlord surrender the property. The tenant must pay the landlord's itemized reasonable removal and storage expenses. The landlord and tenant mutually agree when the property will be picked up, but not later than 72 hours after payment of the landlord's expenses. A landlord's failure to comply with the tenant's request subjects the landlord to liability for actual damages, not to exceed the value of the personal property, plus up to $250, if the landlord's failure to comply was in bad faith, and reasonable attorney's fees.

If the tenant doesn't contact the landlord about the property, the landlord must send the tenant a *NOTICE OF RIGHT TO RECLAIM ABANDONED PROPERTY*. *The notice tells the former tenant where the property can be claimed, and usually sets a deadline for claiming it.* The deadline must be at least 15 days after the notice is served on the tenant in person, or at least 18 days after it's mailed. Again, the tenant must pay the landlord's expenses when claiming the property.

If the tenant doesn't claim the property by the deadline, it will be sold at public auction. If the landlord reasonably believes that the resale value of the property is less than $300, the landlord can keep it for his or her own use, or dispose of it in any way, such as putting it in the trash. After deducting the costs of storage, advertising, and sale, any unclaimed proceeds of the public auction are paid into the county treasury not later than 30 days after the sale. The tenant has one year to claim the sale proceeds from the county.

IV. Mobilehome Residency Law

In a mobilehome park, the tenants usually own their mobilehomes and rent a space from the park owner. It's much more difficult for a mobilehome owner to move than for an ordinary tenant. In many communities, there are few mobilehome parks and very few vacancies in those parks. Also, it can be expensive to move a mobilehome, especially a large one. The landlord has the right to require a picture of the unit as part of the application process and to inspect the unit prior to approving the mobilehome for the park.

To address these problems, the California legislature adopted the **Mobilehome Residency Law** (Civil Code Section 798-798.88). It governs the relationship between mobilehome owners and park management. The statute applies to manufactured homes, but not to recreational vehicles.

A. RENTAL AGREEMENTS

There are two sections in the law relating to rental agreements. One section sets out the requirements for all agreements. The other describes optional provisions. If these are included in the agreement, it will be exempted from local rent control ordinances.

1. Requirements

All mobilehome park rental agreements must be in writing. They must include:

1. the length of the lease term, where the park offers a one-year minimum,
2. the rent to be charged and how payable,
3. a description of the physical improvements to be provided to the homeowner,
4. a description of the services to be provided and any fees that will be charged for the services with separate billing for those fees, and
5. the park's rules and regulations with the owner's name, address, and phone number.

The agreement must state that it is the management's responsibility to maintain the common facilities. It also has to explain that the management may charge a fee for maintaining the property on which a home is located if the homeowner fails to do so after being given 14 days' notice. A copy of the Mobilehome Residency Law must be attached and incorporated into the agreement by reference. Management must also post a sign showing the name, address and phone number of the state mobilehome ombudsman.

The mobilehome owner must be offered at least a one-year lease. A shorter lease term can be arranged only if that's what the homeowner wants. Neither party can have the sole option of automatically extending or renewing the lease for a term longer than 12 months.

Of concern for the owners and management of a mobilehome park is the risk of paying an amount not to exceed $2,000 to homeowners who are successful in enforcing their legal rights against the park management for a willful violation of the statute. The amount is discretionary with the court and is in addition to any other damages awarded.

2. Rent Control Exemption

A mobilehome park rental agreement is exempt from local rent control laws if:

1. The agreement is for longer than one year.
2. The agreement is for personal residence by the owner of the mobilehome.
3. A written notification and receipt that the owner is given at least 30 days from the time the agreement is first offered to decide whether to accept it or reject it.
4. A written notification and receipt that the owner may rescind the agreement within 72 hours after signing it.

CHAPTER 15

Although the management must offer a lease for one year, the mobilehome owner must have the option of taking a shorter lease. However long or short the lease, the rent and other provisions of the agreement must be the same as those offered for a 12-month lease, at least during the first 12 months of the term. (For example, the management can't charge a higher or lower rent on a six-month lease than it would on a 12-month lease.)

The first sentence of the first paragraph of an exempt rental agreement must be printed in 12-point bold type to notify the tenant that the rent control ordinance won't apply. When the rental agreement is first offered to the homeowner, the management must give a written notice of a 30-day right to inspect the agreement and a 72-hour right to void the agreement.

Any newly constructed spaces in a mobilehome park that were initially held out for rent after January 1, 1990, are exempt from rent control, whether or not their rental agreements comply with these rules. Park rules can be amended with homeowner's consent (or without upon 6 months' notice), but they must be reasonable to be enforced.

A security deposit is limited to a maximum of two months' rent and is refunded after 12 consecutive months of prompt rental payment (no interest required) or resale of the mobilehome if requested by the homeowner in writing.

B. GROUNDS FOR TERMINATION

Because of the high cost of moving mobilehomes, the statute severely limits the landlord's right to terminate or refuse to renew a lease. Park management may terminate a lease or refuse to renew it only for one of these reasons:

1. The homeowner has failed to comply with park rules and regulations, or with local or state laws regulating mobilehomes within a reasonable time after notice;

2. The homeowner has engaged in conduct that is a substantial annoyance to other park residents;

3. The homeowner (or someone residing in the home) is convicted of prostitution, battery, assault, lewd or lascivious acts, arson, or a felony controlled substance offense, if the crime was committed in the mobilehome park (including the mobilehome);

4. The homeowner hasn't paid rent, utilities, or reasonable service charges after receiving proper notice of nonpayment;

5. The park has been condemned;

6. There is going to be a change in the use of the park; or

7. Failure of the homeowner to comply with the rules and regulations of the park contained in the rental agreement.

Management generally must give a mobilehome owner 60 days' notice before terminating the tenancy and 90 days before raising the rent. When the management is changing the use of the park and has received governmental approval for the change, it must give the tenants at least six months' notice. If governmental approval isn't necessary, tenants must be given at least one year's notice.

1. Removal Upon Sale

When a mobilehome is sold, the management ordinarily can't require that it be removed. They may require notice of the sale, and the right to approve the buyer as a tenant, but approval can't be withheld unless the buyer isn't financially able to pay the rent, or the buyer's rental history indicates he or she probably won't comply with park rules.

The management can require removal of a home upon sale in order to upgrade the park. Even in that case, they can only require removal if the home is old and doesn't meet construction and safety standards, or if it's dilapidated or in disrepair. When these conditions are met, the management can order the buyer to remove the home even if the seller's lease hasn't expired yet. Management can also sell an abandoned mobilehome.

2. Floating Home Residency Law

California has enacted regulations involving the landlord-tenant relationship in a floating home marina. The comprehensive regulations can be found starting with California Civil Code Section 800.

V. Rent Control

www.cato.org/pubs/pas/pa-274.html
Analysis - How Rent Control Drivers Out Affordable Housing

RENT CONTROL *laws are local ordinances that set maximum limits on the amount of rent a landlord may charge.* The intent of these laws is to make rental property available at reasonable rates when there is a housing shortage. Unfortunately, rent control discourages new construction and forces out other lower income people. State law prohibits local governments from imposing rent controls on commercial property, single-family units, and new construction of residential units. However, some communities in California have adopted residential rent control ordinances.

Some rent control ordinances have exemptions for new construction and other property being offered for rent for the first time. Some ordinances have a **VACANCY DECONTROL PROVISION**: *when an apartment becomes vacant, the rent can be raised to the current market rate.* In effect, these ordinances only limit rent increases once the tenancy has begun. When an ordinance doesn't have a vacancy decontrol provision, the rent control limits apply for new tenants. Ordinances with vacancy decontrol provisions usually restrict the landlord's right to terminate a tenancy. Many ordinances prohibit eviction for grounds other than those stated in the ordinance and some require landlords to register their units and pay registration fees.

State law now prohibits a landlord from evicting a tenant from a rent-controlled unit to make it available to a relative, or for the landlord's own use, unless the relative or the landlord lives there for at least six months. A landlord who fraudulently evicts a tenant or intentionally charges an illegal rent may be ordered to pay treble damages. On the other hand, state law limits the penalties a city may impose on a landlord who has made a good-faith effort to comply with the rent control ordinance.

State law also prohibits local governments from compelling property owners to continue offering their property for rent. If an owner doesn't want to rent the property for the amount allowed by the rent control ordinance, he or she may withdraw it from the market. The landlord may have to pay compensatory damages and in some cases punitive damages (not to exceed six months' rent) to tenants who are displaced when the property is withdrawn.

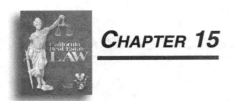

> **Case Example:** Ms. Castillo had been renting a two-bedroom apartment from Mr. Friedman on a month-to-month basis for more than eight years. There had never been any problems between Castillo and Friedman.
>
> The apartment was subject to the Los Angeles Rent Stabilization Ordinance. The ordinance limited the amount of rent Friedman could charge and the grounds on which he could terminate a tenancy. Under the ordinance, Castillo paid $346 per month. The ordinance's vacancy decontrol provision would allow Friedman to raise the rent if Castillo moved out.
>
> In July 1982, Friedman sent Castillo a notice of termination stating that her tenancy would end on August 31. To comply with the city ordinance, Friedman attached a rent stabilization declaration form to the notice. On the form, he explained that he wanted Castillo's apartment so that his mother could move into it. The ordinance permitted termination of a tenancy if the apartment was going to be occupied by the landlord or the landlord's spouse, children, or parents.
>
> So Castillo and her daughter moved out. Castillo tried to find another two-bedroom apartment in the same neighborhood, but they were being rented for $450 to $500, and Castillo couldn't afford that much. She finally signed a one-year lease on a one-bedroom apartment several miles away. The rent was $350 a month. Because her new apartment was so much smaller, she had to store some of her furniture. The storage cost her $25 a month.
>
> In October Castillo drove by her old building and saw a "For Rent" sign advertising a two-bedroom apartment. Suspicious, she asked her friend Mr. Silva to inquire about the apartment. Friedman showed Silva Castillo's old apartment and told him the rent was $565 a month.
>
> Since Castillo had signed a lease on her new apartment, she wasn't in a position to demand her old apartment back from Friedman, but she sued him for fraud and wrongful eviction. Friedman was ordered to pay Castillo the difference between what it would have cost her to stay in her rent-controlled apartment for another two years (at $346 a month) and what a comparable apartment would cost her at current market rates. He also had to pay her storage expenses. *Castillo v. Friedman*, 197 Cal. App. 3d Supp. 6, 243 Cal. Rptr. 206 (1987).

There are specific requirements that must be met if the property comes back on the market for rent, depending on how long it has been since the withdrawal.

If the withdrawn property is offered for rent again within one year, it may be subject to the controls in effect at the time of withdrawal. If it's put back on the market more than a year after withdrawal, the controls currently in effect may be applied. When property returns to the market any time within ten years after withdrawal, a local ordinance may require the landlord to first offer the units to the displaced tenants.

VI. Unlawful Detainer Assistants

The California Legislature has determined that there are numerous unscrupulous individuals and associations who purport to offer protection to tenants from eviction. In fact, these individuals defraud tenants of both their funds and their rights under the law while filing thousands of frivolous or fraudulent legal pleadings in both state and federal courts. Not only have there been thousands of defrauded tenants, but also severe economic losses to landlords as well as the clogging of both state and federal courts, severely taxing the judicial system. Consequently, the legislature passed a law (Business and Professions Code Sections 6400 et. seq.) regulating unlawful detainer assistants. An *UNLAWFUL DETAINER ASSISTANT is an individual who, for compensation, assists or advises in the prosecution or defense of an unlawful detainer action.*

These assistants must register with the county clerk where they reside and work and must post a bond of $25,000, or the same amount in cash. The registration is effective for two years and can be renewed. Once registered, the assistant is given a photo identification card with an assigned number. The registration number and county registration has to appear on any advertisement or work product of the assistant. A written contract containing certain requirements is mandatory along with a 24-hour right of recession. The county clerk retains power to revoke the registration under certain conditions. Additionally, a person who practices as an assistant, but has failed to comply with the registration requirements, is guilty of a misdemeanor with a fine of not less than a $1,000, no more than $2,000 for each violation, or imprisonment for a maximum of one year or both. Exempt from the registration requirements are government employees, attorneys and their employees, employees of nonprofit tax exempt corporations who assist clients free of charge, and licensed real estate brokers or salespersons who are parties to the unlawful detainer action or perform certain acts, such as the collection of rent.

VII. Property Management

Residential buildings containing 16 or more units require an onsite resident manager (no real estate license is required).

Many real estate licensees perform **offsite management services** on behalf of the landlord for a fee. The **management contract** (employment contract) must comply with the requirements of a valid contact, and must be in writing if performed by a licensee.

VIII. Electric Vehicle (EV) Charging Station

Effective January 1, 2012, any restriction that prohibited or restricted the installation or use of an electric vehicle ("EV") charging station in a common interest development became void and unenforceable (Civil Code §1353.9(a)). If a homeowner wants to install an EV charging station in a common area or an exclusive use common area (his parking space), he must meet applicable health and safety standards and requirements imposed by state and local authorities as well as all other applicable zoning, land use or other ordinances, or land use permits. In addition, he/she must obtain HOA approval and agree in writing to the following:

1. Comply with the association's architectural standards.
2. Use a licensed contractor to install the station.
3. Within 14 days of approval, provide a certificate of insurance that names the common interest development as an additional insured under the homeowner's insurance policy.
4. Pay for electricity usage associated with the station.

IX. CHAPTER SUMMARY

1. A lease is both a conveyance and a contract, and must meet all the requirements for a valid contract. It must be in writing and signed by the lessor if it will end more than one year after it was made.

2. There are fixed leases, graduated leases, net leases, percentage leases, and ground leases. The differences generally concern who pays which expenses and how rent is calculated.

3. Unless the lease expressly forbids assignment and subleasing, the tenant has the right to transfer possession of the property to a third person. Neither assignment nor subleasing relieves the original tenant of liability as does novation. Many leases require the tenant to obtain the landlord's consent before assigning the lease or subleasing.

4. A landlord is required to deliver possession of the property to the tenant on the date the lease begins. If the property isn't ready for possession, the tenant may rescind the lease or demand consequential damages.

5. The implied covenant of quiet enjoyment gives the tenant the right to undisturbed possession of the property. The covenant is breached by actual or constructive eviction. An evicted tenant is no longer required to pay rent. To claim constructive eviction, the tenant must move out.

6. A landlord may not enter the property without the tenant's permission, unless otherwise agreed. Except in an emergency, a residential landlord must obtain the tenant's consent and give reasonable notice (usually 24 hours' notice) before entering.

7. Unless otherwise agreed, the tenant is required to keep the leased property clean and in good repair. The landlord is responsible for the common areas. The landlord can keep the tenant's security deposit to cover unpaid rent, damage, or cleaning costs, but not for ordinary wear and tear. California law limits the amount a residential landlord can charge as a security deposit, and prevents residential landlords from charging nonrefundable fees.

8. A landlord must make a dwelling fit for human occupancy before leasing it. The landlord must also keep it up to that standard during the lease term. A nonresidential tenant may waive these requirements, however.

9. There's an implied warranty of habitability in every residential lease. The landlord must keep the property habitable. This requirement can't be waived by the tenant. If the landlord breaches the implied warranty, the tenant is only required to pay the reasonable rental value of the nonrepaired property.

10. If the landlord fails to make repairs (as agreed or as required by law) within a reasonable time, the tenant may arrange for the repairs and deduct the cost from the rent. If the problems interfere with use of the property, the tenant may move out and claim constructive eviction.

11. A landlord may be held liable for injuries that occur on leased property if the landlord is held to have retained some control over the property. A landlord generally won't be liable unless the injuries resulted from his or her negligence.

12. A periodic lease is renewed automatically unless one of the parties gives notice of termination. A lease for a set term expires on the specified date unless the parties agree to renew it. It can be terminated before it expires by surrender, foreclosure, eviction, abandonment, or destruction of the leased property.

13. To evict a tenant, the landlord must send a notice to remedy or quit if that is possible. If the tenant doesn't comply with the notice, the landlord has to file an unlawful detainer action. Self-help eviction is illegal. It's also illegal to evict a tenant in retaliation for making a complaint against the landlord or participating in a tenants' rights group.

14. When a lease is terminated by abandonment or an unlawful detainer action, the landlord may be entitled to a judgment for the unpaid rent and other damages.

15. The Mobilehome Residency Law requires mobilehome parks to offer tenants at least one-year leases. It also limits the grounds for termination of leases.

16. Many cities in California have adopted residential rent control ordinances. State law prohibits rent controls on most commercial property. Local governments are also prohibited from compelling a landlord to continue offering a property for rent.

17. Because of problems involving those who offer assistance involving unlawful detainer actions, these activities are regulated in California.

18. Effective January 1, 2012, any restriction that prohibited or restricted the installation or use of an electric vehicle ("EV") charging station in a common interest development became void and unenforceable.

X. CASE PROBLEM
Evans v. Thomason, 72 Cal. App. 3d 978, 140 Cal. Rptr. 525 (1977)

The Evans family rented an unfurnished one-bedroom apartment in Healdsburg on a month-to-month basis. They plugged their refrigerator and their freezer into a double electrical outlet in the kitchen. In December, the lower outlet stopped working. There wasn't another outlet nearby, so the tenants bought a extension cord, plugged it in to the top outlet, and plugged both the refrigerator and freezer into that.

The landlords were renovating the apartment next door at that time. One of the Evanses went over and told the landlords about the problem with the electrical outlet. The landlords said they'd fix it, but they never did. Two of them were experienced electricians, and it would have taken them less than ten minutes to do the repairs. On at least two occasions, one of the landlords was in the Evans's kitchen and saw their extension cord arrangement.

In May, the overloaded extension cord started a fire. Mr. and Mrs. Evans and their children were severely injured and lost most of their possessions. They sued the landlords for damages.

Could the landlords be held liable when it was the tenants themselves who had created the dangerous extension cord arrangement? Did the landlords have a duty to repair the electrical outlet? If so, was it based on their agreement with the tenants, or imposed by law?

What if the lease had stated that the landlords had no duty to repair any problems that arose after the lease began? What if the lease had provided that the landlords could not be held liable for injuries occurring on the property during the tenancy? Would the answers to these questions be different if this had been a commercial lease?

If this had been a one-year lease instead of a month-to-month lease, would the tenants have had a right to move out and stop paying rent because of the landlords' failure to make the repairs? What could the tenants have done aside from moving out?

XI. KEY TERMS

abandonment	lockout	retaliatory eviction
actual eviction	mitigation	security deposit
assignment	Mobilehome Residency Law	self-help eviction
consequential damages	net lease (triple net)	strict liability
constructive eviction	notice of belief of	sublease
electric vehicle (ev) charging	abandonment	surrender
station	notice of right to reclaim	unlawful detainer
fixed (gross, straight) lease	abandoned property	unlawful detainer assistants
graduated lease (step-up)	notice to remedy or quit	untenantable/tenantability
ground lease	novation	vacancy decontrol provision
implied warranty of	percentage lease	writ of possession
habitability	quiet enjoyment	wrongful eviction
lessor/lessee	rent control	

XII. CHAPTER QUIZ

1. If a tenant is forced to leave the residential property because it has become uninhabitable because of mice, this is known as:
    a. actual eviction.
    b. constructive eviction.
    c. retaliatory eviction.
    d. unlawful detainer.

2. Regarding entry into the dwelling and by the landlord:
    a. a landlord can never enter the dwelling without the tenant's permission.
    b. a landlord can enter the dwelling without the tenant's permission in an emergency.
    c. the landlord must give a 48-hour notice before entering.
    d. the landlord may enter the dwelling at any time to "inspect the premises."

3. With regard to ordinary wear and tear in the dwelling unit:
    a. a tenant is liable for ordinary wear and tear up to a maximum of $1000.
    b. a tenant is liable for ordinary wear and tear up to a maximum of one month's rent.
    c. a tenant is not liable for ordinary wear and tear.
    d. a tenant is liable for ordinary wear and tear and that there is no maximum amount.

4. With regard to a security deposit and a tenant with a water bed:
    a. a landlord may not charge an additional security deposit because of the water bed.
    b. a landlord may charge an additional security deposit amounting to one months rent.
    c. A landlord may charge an additional security deposit amounting to one half of one months rent.
    d. a landlord may charge an additional security deposit not to exceed $300.

5. For the residential property to be tenantable, the landlord has all of the following obligations except which one?
    a. Provide the tenant with and maintain wiring for one telephone jack
    b. Disclose any ordnance located within 1 mile that the landlord is aware of
    c. Disclose to the tenant the lack of separate utility meters and reach an agreement regarding payment
    d. Disclose any occupants death on the premises within the last seven years

6. The tenant has the following obligations with regard to renting residential property, except which one?
    a. Keep the premises clean and sanitary
    b. Properly dispose of garbage and waste
    c. Properly use the included fixtures and appliances
    d. Install and maintain a fire alarm

CHAPTER 15

7. With regard to the "warranty of habitability":

    a. it was created in the case of *Hinson v. Delis*.

    b. it was established by legislation.

    c. it was created by the courts.

    d. answers a and c above are correct answers.

8. A landlord is legally allowed to require a cash payment for the rent:

    a. at any time.

    b. if previous rent payments by check have been dishonored due to insufficient funds.

    c. if the tenant loses his/her job.

    d. a landlord has never legally allowed to require a cash payment for the rent.

9. The management of a mobilehome park may terminate a lease or refuse to renew it if:

    a. the park has been condemned.

    b. the homeowner has failed to pay rent.

    c. the homeowner has engaged in conduct that is a substantial annoyance to other park residents.

    d. all of the above are correct answers.

10. Unlawful detainer of assistance must:

    a. register with the county clerk where they reside.

    b. register with the county clerk where they work.

    c. post a bond of at least $25,000.

    d. all of the above are correct answers.

***ANSWERS:** 1. b; 2. b; 3. c; 4. c; 5. d; 6. d; 7. d; 8. b; 9. d; 10. d*

A

Abandonment – Failure to occupy and use property; may result in a loss of rights.

Abstract of Judgment – A summary of the provisions of a court judgment; when recorded, it creates a lien on all the real property of the debtor in the county where recorded.

Abstract of Title – A brief, chronological summary of the recorded documents affecting the title to a particular parcel of real property. COMPARE: Title Report.

Acceleration Clause – 1. A provision in a loan agreement allowing the lender to declare the entire debt due immediately if the borrower defaults. Also known as a call provision. 2. A due-on-sale clause.

Acceptance – 1. Agreeing to the terms of an offer to enter into a contract, thereby creating a binding contract. 2. Taking delivery of a deed.

Accession – The acquisition of title to additional property by its annexation to real estate already owned. This can be the result of human actions or natural processes. SEE: Annexation; Accretion; Reliction.

Accord and Satisfaction – An agreement to accept something different than (and usually less than) what the original contract called for.

Accretion – A gradual addition to dry land by the forces of nature, as when the tide deposits waterborne sediment on shoreline property. SEE: Accession: Alluvion.

Accusation – A written statement of rules violated, used in a property right hearing.

Acknowledgment – When a person who has signed a document formally declares to an authorized official (usually a notary public) that he or she signed voluntarily. The official attests that the signature is voluntary and genuine.

Act – A statute.

Actual Notice – SEE: Notice, Actual.

Adjustable-Rate Mortgage (ARM) – A mortgage or deed of trust with a variable interest rate (an interest rate that changes periodically).

Adjudicative Methods – The resolution of a dispute by mirroring the judicial process in that a third party decides the controversy much as a judge does in court. SEE: Alternative Dispute Resolution (ADR)

Administrative Agency – A government agency (federal, state, or local) that administers a complex area of law, adopting and enforcing detailed regulations that have the force of law.

Administrative Law Judge – A law judge that conducts hearings enforcing the detailed regulations that have the force of law, by a government agency (federal, state, local and DRE.) It is a complex area of law.

Administrator – A person appointed by the probate court to manage and distribute the estate of a deceased person when no executor is named in the will or there is no will.

Ad Valorem – A Latin phrase meaning "according to value"; used to refer to taxes assessed on the value of property.

Adverse Possession – Acquiring title to someone else's real property by possession of it. The possession must be actual, open, notorious, hostile, exclusive, continuous, and uninterrupted for five years. COMPARE: Prescription.

Affidavit – A sworn statement that has been written down and acknowledged; may be submitted as evidence in a trial.

Affirm – In an appeal, to rule that the lower court's decision was correct, rejecting the appellant's arguments.

After-Acquired Title – SEE:Title, After-Acquired.

Agency – A relationship of trust created when one person (the principal) gives another (the agent) the right to represent the principal in dealings with third parties.

Agency, Dual – When an agent represents both parties in a transaction, as when a broker represents both buyer and seller.

Agency, Ostensible – 1. When someone who has not been authorized to represent another acts as if he or she is that person's agent. 2. When an agent acts beyond the scope of his or her authority, giving a third party the impression that the acts are authorized. Also called apparent agency.

Agency Coupled With an Interest – When the agent has an personal interest in the subject of the agency; as when one co-owner has been authorized by the others to sell their property.

Agency Disclosure Form – An agency disclosure of relationships form that acknowledges that an agent works for a seller or buyer or both. Required for residential property transactions of one to four units.

GLOSSARY

Agent – A person authorized to represent another (the principal) in dealings with third parties.

  Agent, Dual – SEE: Agency, Dual.

  Agent, General – An agent authorized to handle all of the principal's affairs in one area or in specified areas.

  Agent, Special – An agent with limited authority to do a specific thing or conduct a specific transaction.

  Agent, Universal – An agent authorized to do everything that can be lawfully delegated to a representative.

Air Rights – The right to undisturbed use and control of the airspace over a parcel of land; may be transferred separately from the land.

Alienation – The transfer of ownership or an interest in property from one person to another, by any means.

  Alienation, Involuntary – Transfer of an interest in property against the will of the owner, or without action by the owner, occurring through operation of law, natural processes, or adverse possession.

  Alienation, Voluntary – When an owner voluntarily transfers an interest to someone else.

  Alienation Clause – SEE: Due-on-sale Clause.

Alternative Dispute Resolution (ADR) – The resolution of disputes by negotiation, mediation, and arbitration.

Alluvion – The solid material deposited along a shore by accretion. Also called alluvium.

Amortized – SEE: Note, Installment.

Annexation – Attaching personal property to land so that the law views it as part of the real property (a fixture). Annexation can be actual or constructive.

  Annexation, Actual – A physical attachment of personal property to land. SEE: Fixture.

  Annexation, Constructive – When personal property is associated with real property in such a way that the law treats it as a fixture, even though it is not physically attached to the real property.

Annual Percentage Rate (APR) – the charges a borrower pays a lender for a loan (interest, discount points, loan fees, etc.), expressed as an annual percentage.

Answer – The document a defendant must file with the court in response to the plaintiff's complaint.

Anticipatory Repudiation – When one party to a contract informs the other before the time set for performance that he or she does not intend to perform as agreed. SEE: Tender.

Anti-Deficiency Rules – Laws that prevent a secured lender from suing the borrower for a deficiency judgment after foreclosure, in certain circumstances.

Appeal – The process in which a higher court reviews the decision of a lower court or an administrative tribunal.

Appellee – In an appeal, the party who did not file the appeal. Also known as the respondent.

Appraisal – An estimate or opinion of the value of a piece of property as of a certain date. Also called valuation.

Appraiser – One who appraises property, especially an expert qualified to do so by education and experience.

Appurtenance – A right that goes along with ownership of a piece of real property; usually transferred with the property, but may be sold separately.

APR – Annual percentage rate.

Arbitration – A neutral third party who listens to each party's position and makes a final binding decision.

  Arbitrator – A neutral third party who receives evidence and resolves the dispute. SEE: Alternative Dispute Resolution

ARM – Adjustable rate mortgage.

Artificial Person – A person created by law, as distinguished from a natural person, a human being; usually refers to a corporation.

"As Is" Clause – A provision in a purchase agreement stating that the buyer accepts the property in its present condition.

Assessment – 1. A government's valuation of property for tax purposes. 2. A special assessment.

Assessor – An official who determines the value of property for taxation.

Assign – To transfer a right or an interest in property to another.

  Assignee – One to whom a right or interest has been assigned.

  Assignor – One who assigns a right or interest to another.

Assumption – When a buyer takes on personal responsibility for paying off a mortgage or deed of trust that was originally taken out by the seller.

Assumption Fee – A sum paid to the lender, usually by the buyer, when a mortgage or deed of trust is assumed.

Attachment – Court ordered seizure of property belonging to a defendant in a lawsuit, so that it will be available to satisfy a judgment. In the case of real property, attachment creates a lien.

Attachments, Man-Made – SEE: Fixture.

Attachments, Natural – Things growing on a piece of land, such as trees, shrubs, or crops. SEE: Emblements; Fructus Industriales; Fructus Naturales. COMPARE: Fixture.

Attorney in Fact – Any person authorized to act for another by a power of attorney; not necessarily a lawyer (an attorney at law). Authority, Actual-Authority actually given to an agent by the principal, either expressly or by implication.

Authority, Implied – An agent's authority to do everything reasonably necessary to carry out the principal's express orders.

Avulsion – 1. When land is suddenly (not gradually) torn away by the action of water, potentially causing a transfer of title. 2. A sudden shift in a watercourse, which doesn't cause a transfer of title.

Award – The decision of the arbitrator.

B

Balloon Payment – A final payment on a loan that is significantly larger than the earlier installment payments. SEE: Note. Installment.

Base Line – In the government survey system, a main east-west line from which township lines are established. Each principal meridian has one base line associated with it.

Basis – A figure used in calculating gain on the sale of real estate for income tax purposes. Initially, the basis is the amount the owner originally paid for the property, but the figure is adjusted to reflect improvements, cost recovery deductions, and other factors.

BATNA – Best Alternative To A Negotiated Agreement.

Bench Mark – A metal disk set in a stable position at a known elevation, used as a reference point in calculating the elevation of land and other objects in a surveyed area.

Beneficiary – 1. One for whom a trust is created and on whose behalf the trustee administers the trust. 2. The lender in a deed of trust transaction. 3. One entitled to receive real or personal property under a will; a legatee or devisee.

Beneficiary Statement – A statement of the amount necessary to pay off a loan.

Bequeath – To transfer personal property to another by a will.

Bequest – Personal property transferred by a will. Also called a legacy.

Best Alternative To A Negotiated Agreement (BATNA) – SEE: Alternative Dispute Resolution.

Bill – A proposed law, formally submitted to a legislature for consideration.

Bill of Sale – A document used to transfer title to personal property from one person to another.

Binding Arbitration – The decision of the arbitrator is final and not reviewable by the courts.

Blanket Trust Deed (Mortgage) – SEE: Deed of Trust, Blanket.

Block – In reference to platted property, a group of lots surrounded by streets or unimproved land.

Blockbusting – The illegal practice of inducing owners to sell their homes (often at a deflated price) by suggesting that the ethnic or racial composition of the neighborhood is changing, with the implication that property values will decline as a result. Also called panic selling.

Bona Fide – In good faith; genuine.

Boot – In an exchange, any property that isn't treated as like-kind for income tax purposes; for example, if a building is traded for vacant land and a yacht, the yacht is boot.

Boundary – The perimeter or border of a parcel of land; the dividing line between one piece of property and another.

Breach – Violation of an obligation, duty, or law.

Breach, Material – A breach of contract important enough so that it excuses the nonbreaching party from performing his or her contractual obligations.

Breach of Contract – An unexcused failure to perform according to the terms of a contract.

Broker – One who is licensed to represent one or more of the parties in a real estate transaction, for compensation.

Broker, Associate – One who is licensed as a real estate broker but works for another broker.

Brokerage – A broker's business.

Building Code – A set of rules establishing minimum standards for construction methods and materials.

Burden of Proof – SEE: Proof, Burden of.

Business Compulsion – SEE: Duress, Economic.

C

Call Provision – SEE: Acceleration Clause.

Cancellation – Termination of a contract without undoing acts that have already been performed under the contract. COMPARE: Rescission.

Capacity – Legal ability to perform some act, such as enter into a contract or execute a deed or will. SEE: Competence; Minor.

Capital Expenditure – Money expended on improvements and repair or prolong its life; not deductible. COMPARE: Deduction, Repair.

CAR – California Association of Realtors.

Case Law – Rules of law developed in court decisions, as opposed to constitutional law, statutory law, or administrative regulations. Also called decisional law.

Case or Controversy Requirement – A provision in the U.S. Constitution that limits judicial power to deciding actual, active conflict (as opposed to hypothetical questions). Declaratory relief is an exception to this rule.

Caucus – Occurs when the mediator meets with each party individually.

Caveat Emptor – A Latin phrase meaning "let the buyer beware." It expresses the common law rule that a buyer is expected to examine the property carefully, instead of relying on the seller to disclose problems. The rule has lost most of its strength, particularly in residential transactions.

CC&Rs – A declaration of covenants, conditions, and restrictions; usually recorded by a developer to create a common plan of private restrictions for a subdivision.

Certificate of Occupancy – A statement issued by a local government verifying that a newly constructed building is in compliance with all codes and may be occupied.

Certificate of Sale – The document given to the purchaser at a mortgage foreclosure sale, instead of a deed; replaced with a sheriff's deed only after the redemption period expires.

Chain of Title – SEE: Title, Chain of.

Chattel – A piece of personal property.
    Chattel Real – Personal property that is closely associated with real property, such as a lease.

Civil Law – The body of law concerned with the rights and liabilities of one individual in relation to another; includes contract, tort, and property law. COMPARE: Criminal Law.

Civil Rights – Fundamental rights guaranteed to all persons by the law. The term is primarily used in reference to constitutional and statutory protections against discrimination based on race, religion, sex, or national origin.

Civil Wrong – SEE: Tort.

Client – One who employs a broker, lawyer, or other professional. A real estate broker's client can be the seller, the buyer, or both, but usually is the seller.

Closing – The final stage in a real estate transaction, when the seller receives the purchase money and the buyer receives the deed.

Closing Costs – Expenses incurred in the transfer of real estate in addition to the purchase price; for example, the appraisal fee, title insurance premiums. broker's commission, transfer tax.

Closing Statement – SEE: Settlement Statement.

Cloud on the Title – A claim, encumbrance, or apparent defect that makes the title to real property unmarketable. SEE: Title, Marketable.

Codicil – An addition to or revision of a will. It must be executed with the same formalities as a will.

Codification – Collection and organization of piecemeal laws into a comprehensive code.

Collateral – Anything of value used as security for a debt or obligation.

Collusion – An agreement between two or more persons to defraud someone.

Color of Title – Title that appears to be good title, but which in fact is not.

Commercial Property – Property zoned and used for business purposes, such as a store, restaurant or office building; as distinguished from residential, industrial, or agricultural property.

Commingling – Illegally mixing personal funds with money held in trust on behalf of a client. SEE: Conversion.

Commission – The compensation paid a broker for services in a real estate transaction; usually a percentage of the sales price, rather than a flat fee.

Common Areas – The land and improvements in a condominium, planned development, or cooperative that are owned and used collectively by all the residents, such as the parking lot, hallways, and recreational facilities; does not include the individual apartment units or homes.

Common Law – 1. Early English law. 2. Long-established rules based on English law, followed in many states. 3. Case law.
   Common Law Remedy – Money awarded to the plaintiff in a civil lawsuit; damages. COMPARE: Equitable Remedy.

Community Property – Property owned jointly by a married couple in California; any property acquired through the labor or skill of either spouse during marriage. COMPARE: Separate Property.

Competent – 1. Of sound mind, for the purposes of entering a contract or executing a will; not suffering from mental illness, retardation, or senility. 2. Of sound mind and having reached the age of majority.

Complaint – The document a plaintiff files with the court to start a lawsuit.

Condemnation – 1. Taking private property for public use, through the government's power of eminent domain. 2. A declaration that a structure is unfit for occupancy and must be closed or demolished.

Condition – A provision in an agreement or deed that makes the parties' rights and obligations depend on the occurrence (or nonoccurrence) of a particular event. Also called a contingency clause.

Conditional Use Permit – A permit issued by a zoning authority that allows property to be used in a manner not ordinarily allowed in the zone where it's located; primarily for uses that benefit the public, such as hospitals, schools, and cemeteries. Also called a special exception permit.

Condominium – Property developed for concurrent ownership, where each co-owner has a separate interest in an individual unit, combined with an undivided interest in the common areas of the property. COMPARE: Cooperative.
   Condominium Association – The organization that manages the operation of a condominium, imposing assessments and arranging for the maintenance of the common areas. The association's members are the unit owners, and they usually elect a board of directors.
   Condominium Declaration – The document that must be filed for record when property is developed as or converted to a condominium.

Consideration – Anything of value given to induce another to enter into a contract, such as money, services, goods, or a promise. Sometimes called valuable consideration.
   Consideration, Adequate – Consideration that is comparable in value to the consideration the other party to the contract is giving. A contract is enforceable even if the consideration is inadequate, but a court can't order specific performance in that case.

Constitution – A fundamental document that establishes a government's structure and sets limits on its power.

Constitutional – 1. Pertaining to or based on a constitution. 2. Not in violation of the U.S. Constitution or a state constitution.

Constructive Eviction – SEE: Eviction, Constructive.
   Constructive Notice – SEE: Notice, Constructive.

Consummate – To complete.

Contingency Clause – SEE: Condition.

Contract – An agreement between two or more persons to do or not do a certain thing. The requirements for an enforceable contract are capacity, mutual consent, a lawful purpose, and consideration. In addition, many contract must be in writing to be enforceable.
   Contract, Bilateral – A contract in which each party promises to do something. COMPARE: Contract, Unilateral.
   Contract, Executed – A contract in which both parties have completely performed their contractual obligations.
   Contract, Executory – A contract in which one or both parties have not yet completed performance of their obligations.

GLOSSARY

Contract, Express – A contract that has been put into words, either spoken or written.

Contract, Implied – An agreement that has not been put into words, but is implied by the actions of the parties.

Contract, Installment Land – SEE: Contract, Land.

Contract, Land – A contract for the sale of property in which the buyer pays in installments, taking possession of the property immediately, but not taking title until the purchase price has been paid in full. Also called an installment land contract, installment sales contract, land sales contract, real estate contract, and other names.

Contract, Oral – A spoken agreement, as opposed to a written one.

Contract, Unenforceable – An agreement that a court would refuse to enforce; for example, it may be unenforceable because its contents can't be proven, or because it isn't in writing, or because the statute of limitations has run out.

Contract, Unilateral – When one party promises to do something if the other party performs a certain an, but the other party does not promise to perform it; the contract is formed only if the other party does perform the requested act. COMPARE: Contract, Bilateral.

Contract, Valid – A binding, legally enforceable contract.

Contract, Void – An agreement that isn't an enforceable contract because it lacks a required element or is defensive in some other respect.

Contract, Voidable – A contract that one of the parties can disaffirm without liability, because of lack of capacity or a negative factor such as fraud or duress.

Conversion – 1. Misappropriating property or funds belonging to another. 2. Changing an existing rental apartment building into a condominium.

Conveyance – The transfer of title to real property from one person to another by means of a written document, such as a deed.

Cooperative – A building owned by a corporation, where the residents are shareholders in the corporation; each shareholder receives a proprietary lease on an individual unit and the right to use the common areas. COMPARE: Condominium.

Corporation – An association organized according to strict regulations, in which individuals purchase ownership shares; regarded by the law as an artificial person, separate from the individual shareholders. COMPARE: Partnership.

    Corporation, Domestic – A corporation doing business in the state where it was created (incorporated).

    Corporation, Foreign – A corporation doing business in one state, but created (incorporated) in another state.

Correction Lines – Adjustment lines used in the government survey system to compensate for the curvature of the earth. They occur at 24-mile intervals (every fourth township line), where the distance between range lines is corrected to 6 miles.

Co-Tenant – Anyone who shares ownership of a piece of property with another; may be a joint tenant, a tenant in common, a tenant in partnership, or a spouse owning community property.

Counter Offer – A response to an offer to enter into a contract, changing some of the terms of the original offer. A counter offer is a rejection of the offer (not a form of acceptance), and does not create a binding contract unless accepted by the original offeror.

Course – A direction, stated in terms of a compass bearing, in a metes and bounds description of property.

Court-Annexed – A court mandated arbitration.

Covenant – 1. A contract. 2. A promise. 3. A guarantee (express or implied) in a document such as a deed or lease. 4. A restrictive covenant.

    Covenant, Restrictive – SEE: Restrictive Covenant.

    Covenant of Quiet Enjoyment – A promise that a buyer or tenant's possession will not be disturbed by the previous owner, the lessor, or anyone else claiming an interest in the property.

    Covenants, Conditions, and Restrictions – SEE: CC&Rs.

Credit – A payment receivable (owed to you), as opposed to a debit, which is a payment due (owed by you).

Credit Bid – When a lienholder purchasing the security property at a foreclosure sale is allowed to apply the amount the borrower owes him or her to the purchase, rather than having to pay the full amount of the bid in cash.

Creditor – One who is owed a debt.

    Creditor, Secured – A creditor with a lien on specific property, which enables him or her to foreclose and collect the debt from the sale proceeds if it isn't otherwise paid.

Criminal Law – The body of law concerned with crimes, an individual's actions against society. COMPARE: Civil Law.

Cure – To remedy a default, by paying money that's overdue or fulfilling other obligations.

Customer – A prospective property buyer.

D

Damages – An amount of money a defendant is ordered to pay to a plaintiff.

Damages, Actual – Compensatory damages.

Damages, Compensatory – Damages intended to compensate the plaintiff for harm caused by the defendant's an or failure to an, including personal injuries (physical and mental), property damage, and financial losses.

Damages, Consequential – Damages compensating for losses that were not the direct result of the defendant's wrongful act, but which were a foreseeable consequence of it.

Damages, Exemplary – Punitive damages.

Damages, Liquidated – A sum that the parties to a contract agree in advance (at the time of entering into the contract) will serve as compensation in the event of a breach.

Damages, Punitive – An award added to compensatory damages, to punish the defendant for malicious or outrageous conduct and discourage others from similar acts.

Datum – An artificial horizontal plane of elevation, established in reference to sea level, used by surveyors as a reference point in determining elevation.

Dealer – One who regularly buys and sells real estate in the ordinary course of business.

Dealer Property – Property held for sale to customers rather than as a long-term investment; a developer's inventory of subdivision lots, for example.

Debit – A charge or a debt owed to another.

Debtor – One who owes money to another.

Decedent – A person who has died.

Declaration of Abandonment – A document recorded by an owner that voluntarily releases a property from homestead protection.

Declaration of Homestead – The recorded document that establishes homestead protection.

Declaratory Relief – When a court issues a binding judgment that explains the plaintiff's and defendant's rights and duties in advance, rather than waiting until a breach of contract or other violation has occurred. SEE: Case or Controversy Requirement.

Dedication – An appropriation or gift of private property for public use; may transfer ownership or simply create a public easement.

Dedication, Implied – Involuntary dedication, resulting from an owner's acquiescence to public use of his or her property for at least five years. Also called common law dedication. COMPARE: Prescription.

Dedication, Statutory – A dedication required by law; for example, dedication of property for streets and sidewalks as a prerequisite to subdivision approval.

Deduction – An amount a taxpayer is allowed to subtract from his or her income before calculating the tax on the income.

Deduction, Cost Recovery – An income tax deduction that allows the taxpayer to recover the cost of depreciable property used for the production of income or used in a trade or business. Formerly called a depreciation deduction.

Deduction, Depreciation – SEE: Deduction, Cost Recovery.

Deduction, Repair – An income tax deduction allowed for expenditure made to keep property in ordinary, efficient operating condition; not allowed for a principal residence or personal use property. COMPARE: Capital Expenditure.

Deed – An instrument that conveys ownership of real property from the grantor to the grantee.

Deed, Correction – A deed used to correct minor mistakes in an earlier deed, such as misspelled names or errors in the legal description.

Deed, General Warranty – A deed in which the grantor warrants the title against defects that might have arisen before or during his or her period of ownership. COMPARE: Deed, Special Warranty.

Deed, Gift – A deed that isn't supported by valuable consideration; often lists "love and affection" as the consideration.

Deed, Grant – Any deed that uses the word "grant" in its words of conveyance; carries two implied warranties and conveys after-acquired title. The most commonly used deed in California. COMPARE: Deed, Quitclaim.

GLOSSARY

Deed, Quitclaim – A deed that conveys any interest in a piece of real property the grantor has at the time the deed is executed. Often used to clear up a cloud on the title. It contains no warranties of any kind, and does not convey after-acquired title. COMPARE Deed, Grant.

Deed, Sheriff's – A deed delivered by the sheriff, on court order, to the holder of the certificate of sale when the redemption period after a mortgage foreclosure has expired.

Deed, Special Warranty – A deed in which the grantor warrants title only against defects arising during the time he or she owned the property, and not against defects arising before that time; often used by executors and administrators of estates. COMPARE: Deed, General Warranty.

Deed, Tax – A deed given to a purchaser of property at a tax foreclosure sale.

Deed, Trustee's – A deed given to a purchaser of property at a trustee's sale.

Deed, Warranty – A deed carrying warranties (guarantees) of clear title and the grantor's right to convey. SEE: Deed, General Warranty; Deed, Special Warranty.

Deed in Lieu of Foreclosure – A deed given by a borrower to the lender to satisfy the debt and avoid foreclosure.

Deed of Trust – An instrument that creates a voluntary lien on real property to secure the repayment of a debt. The parties to a deed of trust are the grantor or trustor (borrower), beneficiary (lender), and trustee (neutral third party). Unlike a mortgage, a deed of trust includes a power of sale, allowing the trustee to foreclose nonjudicially. Also called a trust deed.

Deed of Trust, Blanket – 1. A trust deed that covers more than one parcel of real estate. 2. A trust deed that covers an entire building or development, rather than an individual unit or lot.

Deed of Trust, First – The deed of trust that has higher priority than any other on a property. This is usually the one that was recorded first, unless there's a subordination agreement.

Deed of Trust, Junior – A second (or third, etc.) deed of trust, with lower lien priority than the first trust deed.

Deed of Trust, Senior – A deed of trust with higher priority than another deed of trust on a property.

Deed Restriction – A restrictive covenant in a deed.

Default – Failure to fulfill an obligation, duty, or promise, as when a borrower fails to make payments, or a tenant fails to pay rent.

Defeasible Fee – SEE: Fee Simple Defeasible.

Defendant – 1. The person being sued in a civil lawsuit. 2. The accused person in a criminal lawsuit.

Deficiency Judgment – A personal judgment entered against a debtor if the proceeds from a foreclosure sale of security property are not enough to pay off the debt.

Delivery – The legal transfer of a deed (or other instrument). A valid deed doesn't convey title until it has been delivered (actually or constructively) to the grantee. SEE: Donative Intent.

Deposit – 1. Money offered as an indication of good faith regarding the future performance of a contract to purchase. Also called earnest money. 2. A security deposit.

Deposition – The formal, out-of-court testimony of a witness in a lawsuit, taken before the trial; used as part of the discovery process, to determine the facts of the case, or if the witness won't be able to attend the trial. A transcript of a deposition can be introduced as evidence in the trial.

Depreciable Property – Property that's eligible for depreciation (cost recovery) deduction, because it will wear out and have to be replaced. SEE: Deduction, Cost Recovery.

Depreciate – To decline in value.

Devise – 1. (noun) Real property transferred in a will. 2. (verb) To transfer real property by will. COMPARE: Bequest; Bequeath; Legacy.

Devisee – A recipient of real property under a will. COMPARE: Beneficiary; Legatee.

Disaffirm – To ask a court to terminate a voidable contract.

Disclosures – Agents, buyers, and sellers must inform all principles and third parties of any known material fact that may affect the value of a property.

Discount Point – One percent of the principal amount of a loan, paid to the lender at the time the loan is made, to give the lender an additional yield above the interest rate. Because of the points paid at the outset, the lender is willing to make the loan at a lower interest rate.

Discovery, Pretrial – When each of the opposing parties in a lawsuit is required to disclose requested information and evidence to the other party, and each is allowed to examine witnesses who will testify for the other side at trial. Depositions and interrogatories are used during discovery.

Discrimination – Arbitrarily treating people unequally because of their race, religion, sex, national origin, age, or some other characteristic.

Distributive Negotiation – Goals of the parties are interdependent but not compatible, win-lose.

Domicile – The state where a person has his or her permanent home.

DRE – California Department of Real Estate.

Dual Agent – SEE: Agency, Dual.

Due-on-Sale Clause – A clause in a loan agreement giving the lender the right to declare the entire amount of the loan due immediately if the security property is sold. Also called an alienation clause.

Due Process – A fair hearing before an impartial judge. Under the U.S. Constitution, no one may be deprived of life, liberty, or property without due process of law.

Duress – Unlawfully confining someone to force him or her to sign a document; or confining the signer's spouse, child, or other close relative. COMPARE: Menace.

  Duress, Economic – Threatening to take some action that will be financially harmful to a person, to force him or her to sign a document; for example, threatening to breach a contract. Also called business compulsion.

E

Earnest Money – SEE: Deposit.

Easement - A right to use some part of another person's real property for a particular purpose; unlike a license, an easement is irrevocable and creates an interest in the property.

  Easement, Appurtenant – An easement that benefits a particular piece of property, the dominant tenement. COMPARE: Easement in Gross.

  Easement by Express Grant – An easement granted to another in a deed or other document.

  Easement by Implication – An easement created by law (not by express grant) when a parcel of land is divided, if there is a long-standing, apparent use that is reasonably necessary for the enjoyment of the dominant tenement. Also called an implied easement.

  Easement by Necessity – A special type of implied easement; when the dominant tenement would be completely useless without an easement, an easement exists even if it isn't a long-standing, apparent use.

  Easement, Implied – SEE: Easement by Implication.

  Easement in Gross – An easement that benefits a person instead of a piece of land; there's a dominant tenant, but no dominant tenement. COMPARE: Easement, Appurtenant.

  Easement, Prescriptive – An easement acquired by prescription.

Emblements, Doctrine of – The rule that an agricultural tenant has the right to enter the land to harvest crops after the lease ends.

Eminent Domain – The government's constitutional power to take (condemn) private property for public use, as long as the owner is paid just compensation.

Employee – Someone who works under the direction and control of another. COMPARE: Independent Contractor.

Encroachment – A physical intrusion onto neighboring property, usually due to a mistake regarding the boundary.

Encumbrance – A nonpossessory interest in property; a lien, easement, or restrictive covenant burdening the property owner's title.

Endorsement – When the payee on a negotiable instrument (such as a check or promissory note) assigns the right to payment to another, by signing the back of the instrument.

Enjoin – To prohibit an act, or command performance of an act, by court order; to issue an injunction.

EQA – The California Environmental Quality Act.

Equal Protection Requirement – Under the U.S. Constitution, all citizens are entitled to equal protection of the laws; no law may arbitrarily discriminate between different groups, or be applied to different groups in a discriminatory manner.

Equitable Remedy – A judgment granted to a plaintiff that is something other than an award of money (damages); an injunction, quiet title, rescission, and specific performance are examples. COMPARE: Common Law Remedy.

GLOSSARY

Equity – 1. An owner's unencumbered interest in his or her property; the difference between the value of the property and the liens against it. 2. A judge's power to soften or set aside strict legal rules, to bring about a fair and just result in a particular case.

Erosion – A gradual loss of soil due to the action of water or wind.

Error, Harmless – A mistake by a trial judge that did not affect the final judgment in the case.
   Error, Prejudicial – A mistake by a trial judge that may have affected the final judgment in the case. Also called reversible error (because it's grounds for reversing the trial court's decision).

Escheat – When property reverts to the state after a person dies and the heirs (or the beneficiaries of the will) cannot be located.

Escrow – The system in which things of value (such as money or documents) are held on behalf of the parties to a transition by a disinterested third party (an escrow agent), until specified conditions have been complied with.
   Escrow Instructions – The document that authorizes an escrow agent to deliver items deposited in escrow once the parties have complied with specified conditions.

Estate – 1. A possessory interest in real property; either a freehold or a leasehold. 2. The property left by someone who has died.
   Estate for Life – SEE: Life Estate.
   Estate for Years – A leasehold estate set to last for a definite period (one week, three years, etc.), after which it terminates automatically. Also called a term tenancy.
   Estate of Inheritance – An estate that can be willed or descend to heirs, such as a fee simple estate.

Estoppel – A legal doctrine that prevents a person from asserting rights or facts that are inconsistent with his or her earlier actions or statements.

Ethics – A system of accepted principles or standards of moral conduct.

Eviction – Dispossessing or expelling someone from real property. SEE: Unlawful Detainer.
   Eviction, Actual – Physically forcing someone off of property (or preventing them from re-entering), or using the legal process to make someone leave. COMPARE: Eviction, Constructive.
   Eviction, Retaliatory – When a landlord evicts a tenant in retaliation for requesting repairs, filing a complaint against the landlord, or organizing or participating in a tenants' rights group.
   Eviction, Wrongful – When a landlord evicts a tenant in violation of the tenant's rights.

Evidence – Testimony, documents, and objects used in a lawsuit as proof of a fact.

Execute – 1. To sign. 2. To perform or complete. SEE: Contract, Executed.

Execution – The legal process in which a court orders an official (such as a sheriff) to seize and sell the property of a judgment debtor to satisfy a judgment lien.

Executive – The head of a government, such as president, governor, or mayor.

Executor/Executrix – A person named in a will to carry out its provisions. If it's a man, he's an executor; if it's a woman, she's an executrix. COMPARE: Administrator.

Exemption – A provision holding that a law or rule doesn't apply to a particular person or group. For example, a person entitled to a property tax exemption is not required to pay property taxes. An exemption can be full or partial.

Exhibit – 1. Documentary or physical evidence submitted in a trial. 2. An attachment to a document.

Express – Stated in words, spoken or written. COMPARE: Implied.

Extender Clause – A clause in a listing agreement providing that for a specified period after the listing expires, the broker will still be entitled to a commission if the property is sold to someone the broker dealt with during the listing term. Also called a carryover clause or safety clause.

F

Failure of Purpose – When the intended purpose of an agreement or arrangement can no longer be achieved; in most cases, this releases the parties from their obligations.

Fair Market Value – SEE: Value, Fair Market. Fannie Mae-The FNMA.

Federal Question – A legal issue involving the U.S. Constitution, a treaty, or a federal statute. Federal courts have jurisdiction to hear federal question cases, but they may also be decided in state court.

Fee – An estate of inheritance; title to real property that can be willed or descend to heirs.

Fee, Conditional – Title that may be terminated by a former owner if conditions stated in the deed are not met. The only type of defeasible fee that's recognized in California now. Also called fee simple subject to a condition subsequent. SEE: Power of Termination.

Fee Simple Absolute – The greatest estate one can have in real property; freely transferable and inheritable, and of indefinite duration, with no conditions on the title. Often called fee simple or fee title.

Fee Simple Defeasible – A fee estate in real property that may be defeated or undone if certain events occur or certain conditions are not met. SEE: Fee, Conditional; Fee Simple Determinable.

FHA – Federal Housing Administration.

FHLMC – Federal Home Loan Mortgage Corporation; also known as "Freddie Mac." SEE: Secondary Marketing.

Fiduciary Relationship – A relationship of trust and confidence, where one party owes the other (or both parties owe each other) loyalty and a higher standard of good faith than they owe to third parties. For example, an agent is a fiduciary in relation to the principal; husband and wife are fiduciaries in relation to each other.

Finance Charge – Any charge a borrower is assessed, directly or indirectly, in connection with the loan.

Financing Statement – A brief document that, when recorded, gives constructive notice of a creditor's security interest in an item of personal property.

Finder's Fee – A referral fee paid to someone for directing a buyer or seller to a real estate agent.

First Lien Position – The spot held by the deed of trust with highest lien priority, when there's more than one deed of trust on the property. SEE: Deed of Trust, First.

Fixed Term – A period of time with a definite ending date.

Fixture – An item of personal property that has been attached to or closely associated with real property in such a way that it has legally become part of the real property. SEE: Annexation, Actual; Annexation, Constructive.

Floor Area Ratio Method – A flexible method of limiting the size of a building in relation to the size of a lot; used in some zoning ordinances as an alternative to strict size and coverage limits.

FNMA – Federal National Mortgage Association; also known as "Fannie Mae." SEE: Secondary Marketing.

Foreclosure – When a lienholder causes property to be sold, so that the unpaid lien can be satisfied from the sale proceeds.

Foreclosure, Judicial – A lawsuit filed by a mortgagee or deed of trust beneficiary to foreclose on the security property when the borrower has defaulted.

Foreclosure, Nonjudicial – Foreclosure by a trustee under the power of sale clause in a deed of trust.

Forfeiture – Loss of a right or something else of value as a result of failure to perform an obligation or condition.

Fraud – An intentional or negligent misrepresentation or concealment of a material fact.

Fraud, Actionable – Fraud that meets certain criteria, so that the victim can successfully sue. The victim/plaintiff usually must prove that the defendant concealed a material fact or made a false statement (intentionally or negligently) with the intent to induce the victim to enter a transaction, and that the victim was harmed because he or she relied on the misrepresentation.

Fraud, Actual – Intentional misrepresentation or concealment, or negligent misrepresentation, which is making a false statement without reasonable grounds for believing it is true.

Fraud, Constructive – A breach of duty that misleads the person the duty was owed to, without an intention to deceive.

Freddie Mac – The FHLMC.

Freehold – An ownership estate in real property; either a fee simple or a life estate. The holder of a freehold estate has title, whereas the holder of a less-than-freehold estate (leasehold estate) is merely a tenant, having a temporary right to possession, but no title.

Frontage – The distance a piece of property extends along a street or a body of water.

Fructus Industriales – Plants planted and cultivated by people, such as crops ("fruits of industry").

Fructus Naturales – Naturally occurring plants ("fruits of nature").

G

Gain – The portion of the proceeds from the sale of an asset that the IRS recognizes as taxable profit.

GLOSSARY

Gain, Capital – A gain realized on the sale of a capital asset. Real estate is considered a capital asset if it is income property, investment property, or property used in a trade or business.

Garnishment – A legal process by which a creditor gains access to the funds or personal property of a debtor that are in the hands of a third party. For example, if the debtor's wages are garnished, the employer is required to turn over part of each paycheck to the creditor.

General Lien – SEE: Lien, General.

General Plan – A long-term, comprehensive plan for the development of a city or county, used as a guide in preparing zoning ordinances.

Ginnie Mae – The GNMA.

GNMA – Government National Mortgage Association. SEE: Secondary Marketing.

Government Lot – A parcel of land that can't be divided into a regular section in the government survey, because of the convergence of range lines, or because of a body of water or some other obstacle or irregularity.

Government Survey – A system of land description that divides the land into squares called townships (each approximately six miles square, containing 36 square miles), which are divided into 36 sections (each approximately one mile square and containing approximately 640 acres). Also called the rectangular survey or the section, township, and range system.

Grant – To transfer or convey an interest in real property by means of a written instrument.
   Grantee – One who receives a grant of real property.
   Granting Clause – Words in a deed that indicate the grantor's intent to transfer an interest in property.
   Grantor – One who grants an interest in real property to another.
   Grantor/Grantee Indexes – Indexes of recorded documents, with each document listed in alphabetical order according to the last name of the grantor (in the grantor/grantee index) and grantee (in the grantee/grantor index). The recording number of each document is given, so that they can be located in the public record. COMPARE: Tract Index.

Guardian – A person appointed by a court to administer the affairs of a minor or an incompetent person.

H-I

Heir – Someone entitled to inherit another's property under the laws of intestate succession.

Holder in Due Course – A person who obtains a negotiable instrument for value, in good faith, without notice that it is overdue or notice of any defenses against it.

Holdover Tenant – A tenant who fails to surrender possession of the premises at the end of a tenancy.

Homeowner's Association (HOA) – A nonprofit association made up of homeowners in a subdivision, responsible for enforcing the subdivision's CC&Rs and managing other community affairs.

Homestead Protection – Limited protection against the claims of judgment creditors, for property used as the debtor's residence. SEE: Declaration of Homestead; Declaration of Abandonment.

HUD – The Department of Housing and Urban Development.

Hypothecate – To make property security for a loan without giving up possession of it. COMPARE: Pledge.

Implied – Not expressed in words, but understood from actions or circumstances. COMPARE: Express.

Implied by Law – Required by law to be part of an agreement; read into an agreement even if it contradicts the express terms the parties agreed to.

Implied Warranty of Habitability – A warranty implied by law in every residential lease, that the property is safe and fit for habitation.

Impound Account – A bank account maintained by a lender for paying property taxes and insurance premiums on the security property; the lender requires the borrower to make regular deposits, and pays the expenses out of the account. Also called a reserve account.

Improvements – Man-made additions to real property.

Income Property – Property that generates rent (or other income) for the owner, such as an apartment building.

Incompetent – Not legally competent; not of sound mind; mentally ill, senile, or feebleminded.

Independent Contractor – A person who contracts to do a job for another but maintains control over how he or she will carry out the task, rather than following detailed instructions. COMPARE: Employee.

Ingress and Egress – Entering and exiting; usually refers to a road or other means of access to a piece of property. An easement for ingress and egress is one that gives the dominant tenant access to the dominant tenement.

Inherit – In strict legal usage, to acquire property by intestate succession, but commonly used to mean acquiring property either by intestate succession or by will.

Injunction – A court order prohibiting anact or compelling anact to be done. SEE: Enjoin; Equitable Remedy.

Installment Sale – A sale in which less than 100% of the sales price is received in the year the sale occurs.

Instrument – A document that transfers title, creates a lien, or gives a right to payment, such as a deed, deed of trust, or contract. SEE: Negotiable Instrument.

Insurance – The act of insuring, or assuring, against loss or damage by a contingent event; a contract whereby, for a stipulated consideration, called premium, one party undertakes to indemnify or guarantee another against loss by certain specified risks.

Insurance Hazard – Insurance against damage to real property caused by fire, flood, or other disasters.
Insurance, Homeowner's – Insurance against damage to the real property and the homeowner's personal property.
Insurance, Mortgage – Insurance that protects a lender against losses resulting from the borrower's default.
Insurance, Title – Insurance that protects against losses resulting from undiscovered title defects.
Insurance, Title, Extended Coverage – Title insurance that covers problems that should be discovered by an inspection of the property (such as encroachments and adverse possession) in addition to the problems covered by standard coverage policies.
Insurance, Title, Standard Coverage – Title insurance that protects against latent title defects (such as forged deeds) and undiscovered recorded encumbrances, but does not protect against problems that would only be discovered by an inspection of the property.

Integration Clause – A provision in a contract document stating that the document contains the entire agreement between the parties.

Integrative Negotiation – Goals of the parties are mutual gain, win-win.

Intent, Objective – A person's manifested intention; what he or she appears to intend, whether or not that is what he or she actually intends.

Intent, Subjective – What a person actually intends, whether or not that is apparent to others.

Interest – 1. A right or share in something (such as a piece of real estate). 2. A charge a borrower pays to a lender for the use of the lender's money. COMPARE: Principal.

Interest, Future – An interest in property that will or may become possessory at some point in the future. SEE: Remainder; Reversion.
Interest, Prepaid – Interest on a new loan that must be paid at the time of closing; covers the interest due for the first month of the loan term. Also called interim interest.
Interest, Undivided – A co-tenant's interest, giving him or her the right to possession of the whole property, rather than to a particular section of it. SEE: Unity of Possession.

Interpleader – A court action filed by someone who is holding funds that two or more people are claiming. The holder turns the funds over to the court to resolve the dispute and deliver the money to the party to whom it is entitled.

Interrogatories – Written questions submitted to the opposing party in a lawsuit during discovery, which he or she is required to answer in writing and under oath.

Intestate – Dying without leaving a will.
Intestate Succession – Distribution of the property of a person who died intestate to his or her heirs.

Invalid – Not legally binding or legally effective; not valid.

Inverse Condemnation Action – A court action by a private landowner against the government, seeking compensation for damage to property that resulted from government action.

Inverted Pyramid – A way of visualizing ownership of real property; theoretically, a property owner owns all the earth, water, and air enclosed by a pyramid that has its tip at the center of the earth and extends up through the property boundaries out into the sky.

Investment Property – Unimproved property held as an investment because it is appreciating in value.

IRS – Internal Revenue Service.

Issue – A person's direct descendants: children, grandchildren, great-grandchildren, and so on.

GLOSSARY

J

Joinder Requirements – The rules requiring both husband and wife to consent to and sign agreements and conveyances concerning community property.

Joint Tenancy – SEE: Tenancy, Joint.

Joint Venture – Two or more individuals or companies joining together for one projects or a related series of projects, but not as an ongoing business. COMPARE: Partnership.

Judgment – 1. A court's binding determination of the rights and duties of the parties in a lawsuit. 2. A court order requiring one party to pay the other damages.
  Judgment Creditor – A person who is owed money as a result of a judgment in a lawsuit.
  Judgment Debtor – A person who owes money as a result of a judgment in a lawsuit.
  Judgment Lien – SEE: Lien, Judgment.

Judicial Review – When a court considers whether or not a statute or regulation is constitutional.

Jurisdiction – The extent of a particular court's authority; a court can't hear a case that's outside its jurisdiction.
  Jurisdiction, Appellate – The authority to hear an appeal (as opposed to conducting a trial).
  Jurisdiction, Diversity – The federal courts' power to hear cases in which a citizen of one state sues a citizen of another state (or country).
  Jurisdiction, General – When a court's jurisdiction is not limited to specific types of cases.
  Jurisdiction, Original – The authority to conduct a trial (as opposed to hearing an appeal).
  Jurisdiction, Personal – A court's authority over a particular individual; usually obtained by service of process.
  Jurisdiction, Subject Matter – The types of cases a particular court has authority to hear.

L

LAFCO – Local Agency Formation Commission.

Land Contract – SEE: Contract, Land.

Landlocked Property – A parcel of land without access to a road or highway.

Landlord – A landowner who has leased his or her property to another. Also called a lessor.

Land Patent – Evidence of title issued by a government of a conveyance of a portion of the public domain.

Latent Defects – Defects that are not visible or apparent; hidden defects.

Lateral Support – SEE: Support, Lateral.

Lawful Object – A legal purpose.

Lease – A conveyance of a leasehold estate from the fee owner to a tenant; a contract in which one party pays the other rent in exchange for the possession of real estate.
  Lease, Fixed – A lease in which the rent is set at a fixed amount, and the landlord pays most or all of the operating expenses (such as taxes, insurance, and repair costs). Also called a flat lease, gross lease, or straight lease.
  Lease, Graduated – A lease in which it is agreed that the rental payments will increase at intervals by an agreed amount or according to an agreed formula.
  Lease, Ground – A lease of the land only, usually for a long term, to a tenant who intends to construct a building on the property.
  Lease, Net – A lease requiring the tenant to pay all the costs of maintaining the property (such as taxes, insurance, and repairs), in addition to the rent paid to the landlord.
  Lease, Percentage – A lease in which the rent is based on a percentage of the tenant's monthly or annual gross sales.

Leasehold Estate – An estate that gives the holder (the tenant) only a temporary right to possession, without title. Also called a less-than-freehold estate.

Legacy – A gift of personal property by will. Also called a bequest. SEE: Legatee.

Legal Description – A precise description of a piece of property; may be a lot and block description, a metes and bounds description, or a government surrey description.

Legatee – Someone who receives personal property (a legacy) under a will.

Legislature – The arm of a government that has primary responsibility for making new laws.

Lender, Institutional – A bank, savings and loan, or similar regulated lending institution; as opposed to an individual or private business that loans money.

Lessee – One who leases property from another; a tenant.
  Lessor – One who leases property to another; a landlord.

Less-Than-Freehold Estate – A leasehold estate.

Levy – To impose a tax.

Liable – Legally responsible.

License – 1. Official permission to do a particular thing that the law doesn't allow everyone to do. 2. Revocable, nonassignable permission to enter another person's land for a particular purpose. COMPARE: Easement.

License, Restricted – A real estate broker's or salesperson's license that includes limitations on the licensee's right to do business; usually issued after a suspended or revoked license has been reinstated.

Lien – A nonpossessory interest in property, giving the lienholder the right to foreclose if the owner doesn't pay a debt owed to the lienholder; a financial encumbrance on the owner's title.
  Lien, Attachment – A lien intended to prevent transfer of the property pending the outcome of litigation.
  Lien, General – A lien against all the property of a debtor, rather than a particular piece of his or her property.
  Lien, Involuntary – A lien that arises by operation of law, without the consent of the property owner. Also called a statutory lien.
  Lien, Judgment – A general lien against a judgment debtor's property, which the judgment creditor creates by recording an abstract of judgment in the county where the property is located.
  Lien, Materialman's – Similar to a mechanic's lien, but based on a debt owed to someone who supplied materials (as opposed to labor) for a project.
  Lien, Mechanic's – A specific lien claimed by someone who performed work on the property (construction, repairs, or improvements) and has not been paid. This term is often used in a general sense, referring to materialmen's liens as well as actual mechanics' liens.
  Lien, Property Tax – A specific lien on property to secure payment of the property taxes.
  Lien, Specific – A lien that attaches only to a particular piece of property (as opposed to a general lien, which attaches to all of the debtor's property).
  Lien, Tax – A lien on property to secure the payment of taxes.
  Lien, Voluntary – A lien placed against property with the consent of the owner; a deed of trust or a mortgage.
  Lienholder, Junior – A secured creditor whose lien is lower in priority than another's lien.
  Lien Priority – The order in which liens are paid off out of the proceeds of a foreclosure sale.

Life Estate – A freehold estate that lasts only as long as a specified person lives. That person is referred to as the measuring life.
  Life-Estate Pur Autre Vie – A life estate "for the life of another," where the measuring life is someone other than the life tenant.
  Life Tenant – Someone who owns a life estate; the person entitled to possession of the property during the measuring life.

Limited Liability Company – A business entity where each owner has the limited liability of a corporate shareholder and the tax advantages of a partner.

Liquidated Damages – SEE: Damages, Liquidated.

Lis Pendens – A recorded notice stating that there is a lawsuit pending that may affect title to the defendant's real estate.

Listing – A written agency contract between a seller and a real estate broker, stipulating that the broker will be paid a commission for finding (or attempting to find) a buyer for the seller's property.
  Listing, Exclusive Agency – A listing agreement that entitles the broker to a commission if anyone other than the seller finds a buyer for the property during the listing term.
  Listing, Exclusive Right to Sell – A listing agreement that entitles the broker to a commission if anyone—including the seller—finds a buyer for the property during the listing term.
  Listing, Net – A listing agreement in which the seller sets a net amount he or she is willing to accept for the property; if the actual selling price exceeds that amount, the broker is entitled to keep the excess as his or her commission.
  Listing, Open – A non-exclusive listing, given by a seller to as many brokers as he or she chooses. If the property is sold, a broker is only entitled to a commission if he or she is the procuring cause of the sale.

Litigant – A party to a lawsuit; a plaintiff or defendant.

Litigation – A lawsuit (or lawsuits).

GLOSSARY

Loan, Carryback – When a seller extends credit to a buyer to finance the purchase of the property, accepting a deed of trust or mortgage instead of cash. Sometimes called a purchase money loan. SEE: Seller Financing.

Loan, Construction – A loan made to cover the cost of construction of a building, usually arranged so that the money is advanced in installments as the work progresses.

Loan, Conventional – Loan with only the property as security, without the government insuring (FHA) or guaranteeing (VA) the loan.

Loan, Guaranteed – A loan in which someone (the VA, for example) guarantees repayment; so that if the borrower defaults, the guarantor reimburses the lender for some or all of the loss.

Loan, Purchase Money – 1. A loan the borrower uses to buy the security property (as opposed to a loan secured by property the borrower already owns). 2. A carryback loan.

Loan Assumption Fee – A fee a lender charges a buyer in return for granting the buyer permission to assume an existing loan.

Loan Fee – A loan origination fee.
  Loan Origination Fee – A fee a lender charges a borrower in exchange for issuing a loan; also called a loan fee.

Lock-in Clause – A clause in a promissory note or land contract that prohibits prepayment before a specified date, or prohibits it altogether.

Loss, Capital – A loss taken on the sale of a capital asset. Real estate is considered a capital asset if it's income property, investment property, or property used in a trade or business.

Loss, Passive – A loss taken in connection with income property. SEE: Passive Income.

Lot – A parcel of land; especially, a parcel in subdivision.
  Lot and Block Description – The type of legal description used for platted property. The description states only the property's lot number and block number in a particular subdivision. To find out the exact location of the property's boundaries you consult the plat map for that subdivision at the county recorder's office.

M

Mailbox Rule – An acceptance of a contract offer is effective as of the moment it is mailed, even though the other party hasn't received it yet.

Majority, Age of – The age at which a person gains legal capacity; in California, 18 years old. COMPARE: Minor.

Maker – A person who signs a promissory note; the borrower who promises to repay the debt.

Marketable Title – SEE: Title, Marketable Market Price-The price actually paid for property. Not the same as market value.

Market Value – SEE: Value, Fair Market.

Material Breach – SEE: Breach, Material.

Material Fact – An important fan; one that is likely to influence a decision.

Materialman – Someone who supplies materials for a construction project. SEE: Lien, Materialman's. COMPARE: Mechanic.

Maturity Date – The date by which a loan is supposed to be paid off in full.

Mechanic – Someone who performs work (construction, improvement, or repairs) on real property. SEE: Lien, Mechanic's. COMPARE: Materialman.

Mediation Clause – A clause in a contract requiring mediation in the event of a dispute. SEE: Alternative Dispute Resolution.

Mediator – A person who helps the parties reach a voluntary agreement.

Meeting of Minds – SEE: Mutual Consent.

Megan's Law – California law that provides the public with certain information on the whereabouts of sex offenders so that members of local communities may protect themselves and their children.

Menace – Threatening physical harm to a person, or threatening harm to a person's reputation, to force someone to sign a document. COMPARE: Duress; Duress, Economic.

Merger – Uniting two or more separate properties by transferring ownership of all of them to one person.

Meridian, Principal – In the government survey system, the main north-south line in a particular grid, used as the starting point in numbering the ranges. California has the Humboldt Meridian, the Mt. Diablo Meridian, and the San Bernardino Meridian.

Meridians, Guide – In the government survey system, lines running north-south (parallel to the principal meridian) at 24-mile intervals.

Metes – Measurements.

Metes and Bounds Description – A legal description that starts at an easily identifiable point of beginning, then describes the property's boundaries in terms of courses compass directions) and distances, ultimately returning to the point of beginning.

Mineral Rights – Rights to the minerals located beneath the surface of a piece of property.

Minor – A person who has not yet reached the age of majority; in California, a person under 18.

Minor, Emancipated – A minor who is or has been married, is on active duty in the armed forces, or has a declaration of emancipation from a court. An emancipated minor has legal capacity to contract.

Misrepresentation – A false or misleading statement. SEE: Fraud.

Mistake, Mutual – When both parties to a contract were mistaken about a fact or a law.

Mistake, Unilateral – When only one of the parties to a contract was mistaken about a fact or a law.

Mitigation – When the nonbreaching party takes action to minimize the losses resulting from a breach of contract.

MLS – Multiple Listing Service.

Monument – A visible marker (natural or artificial) used in a survey or a metes and bounds description to establish the boundaries of a piece of property.

Mortgage – An instrument that creates a voluntary lien on real property to secure repayment of a debt. The parties to a mortgage are the mortgagor (borrower) and mortgagee (lender). Unlike a deed of trust, a mortgage does not include a power of sale, so it can only be foreclosed judicially.

Mortgage, Satisfaction of – The document a mortgagee gives the mortgagor when the mortgage debt has been paid in full, acknowledging that the debt has been paid and the mortgage is no longer a lien against the property. COMPARE: Reconveyance.

Mortgagee – A lender who accepts a mortgage as security for repayment of the loan.

Mortgagor – A person who borrows money and gives a mortgage to the lender as security.

Multiple Listing Service (MLS) – An organization of brokers who share their exclusive listings.

Mutual Consent – When all parties freely agree to the terms of a contract, without fraud, undue influence, duress, menace, or mistake. Mutual consent is achieved through offer and acceptance; it is a "meeting of the minds."

N

NAR – National Association of REALTORS®.

Natural Person – A human being, an individual (as opposed to an artificial person, such as a corporation).

Negligence – Conduct that falls below the standard of care that a reasonable person would exercise under the circumstances; carelessness or recklessness. Negligence that causes harm is a tort. COMPARE: Strict Liability.

Negotiable Instrument – An instrument containing an unconditional promise to pay a certain sum of money, to order or to bearer, on demand or at a particular time. It can be a check, promissory note, bond, draft, or stock. SEE: Note, Promissory.

Negotiation – A voluntary process where parties attempt to settle agreements and conflicts in a peaceful manner.

Negotiation, Distributive – (Win-Lose)

Negotiation, Integrative – (Win-Win)

NEPA – National Environmental Policy Act.

Nonbinding Arbitration – The decision of the arbitrator is reviewable by the court.

Nonconforming Use – A property use that doesn't conform to current zoning requirements, but is allowed because the property was being used in that way before the present zoning ordinance was enacted.

Nonpossessory Interest – An interest in property that does not include the right to possess and occupy the property; an encumbrance, such as a lien or an easement.

GLOSSARY

Nonrecognition Provision – A provision in the income tax law that allows a taxpayer to defer recognition and taxation of a gain until a later time or later transaction.

Notary Public – An official whose primary function is to witness and certify the acknowledgment made by someone signing a legal document.

Note – SEE: Note, Promissory.

Note, Demand – A promissory note that is due when-ever the holder of the note demands payment.

Note, Installment – A promissory note that calls for regular payments of principal and interest until the debt is fully paid. The note is fully amortized if the regular payments are enough to pay it off in full by the maturity date. The note is partially amortized if the payments won't pay it off, so that a balloon payment is due at the end of the term.

Note, Promissory – A written promise to repay a debt; may or may not be negotiable.

Note, Straight – A promissory note that calls for regular payments of interest only, so that the entire principal amount is due in one lump sum at the end of the loan term.

Notice, Actual – Actual knowledge of a fact, as opposed to knowledge imputed by law.

Notice, Constructive – Knowledge of a fact imputed to a person by law. A person is held to have constructive notice of something when he or she should have known it, even if he or she didn't know it. Everyone has constructive notice of the contents of recorded documents, since everyone is expected to protect his or her interests by searching the public record.

Notice, Inquiry – When there were circumstances that should have alerted someone to a possible problem and caused him or her to investigate further, he or she may be held to have had notice of the problem.

Notice of Cessation – A notice recorded by a property owner when construction on the property has ceased, although the project hasn't been completed; it limits the period in which laborers and suppliers can file mechanics' liens.

Notice of Completion – A recorded notice that announces the completion of a construction project and limits the period in which mechanics' liens can be filed.

Notice of Default – A notice issued by a trustee, stating that the deed of trust borrower has breached the loan agreement.

Notice of Levy – A notice recorded by the receiver after a court has issued a decree of foreclosure.

Notice of Sale – A notice issued by a trustee (or by the receiver after a decree of foreclosure) setting the date for the foreclosure sale.

Notice to Quit – A notice to a tenant, demanding that he or she vacate the leased property.

Novation – 1. When one party to a contract withdraws and a new party is substituted, relieving the withdrawing party of liability. 2. The substitution of a new obligation for an old one.

O

Offer – When one person proposes a contract to another; if the other person accepts the offer, a binding contract is formed. SEE: Acceptance.

Offeree – One to whom an offer is made.

Offeror – One who makes an offer.

Opinion, Judicial – A judge's written statement of a decision in a court case, outlining the facts of the case and explaining the legal basis for the decision.

Option – A contract giving one party the right to do something, without obligating him or her to do it.

Optionee – The person to whom an option is given.

Optionor – The person who gives an option.

Option to Purchase – An option giving the optionee the right to buy property owned by the optionor at an agreed price during a specified period.

Ordinance – A law passed by a local legislative body, such as a county board of supervisors or city council.

Ouster – One co-tenant refuses to allow occupancy by the other co-tenant.

Ownership – Title to property, dominion over property; the rights of possession and control.

Ownership in Severalty – Ownership by a single individual. COMPARE: Concurrent Ownership.

P

Panic Selling – SEE: Blockbusting.

Parcel – A lot or piece of real estate, particularly a specified part of a larger tract.

Parol Evidence – Evidence concerning negotiations or oral agreements that were not included in a written contract, often altering or contradicting the terms of the written contract.

Partition, Judicial – A court action to divide up a property among its co-owners, so that each owns part of it m severalty, or (if it's not practical to divide the property physically) each gets a share of the sale proceeds.
   Partition, Voluntary – When co-owners agree to terminate their co-ownership, dividing up the property so that each owns a piece of it in severalty.

Partner, General – A partner who has the authority to manage and contract for a general or limited partnership, and who is personally liable for the partnership's debts.
   Partner, Limited – A partner in a limited partnership who is primarily an investor and does not participate in the management of the business, and who is not personally liable for the partnership's debts.

Partnership – An association of two or more persons to carry on a business for profit. The law regards a partner ship as as a group of individuals, not as an entity separate from its owners. COMPARE: Corporation.
   Partnership, General – A partnership in which each member has an equal right to manage the business and share in the profits, as well as an equal responsibility for the partnership's debts. All of the partners are general partners.
   Partnership, Limited – A partnership made up of one or more general partners and one or more limited partners.
   Partnership Property – All property that partners bring into their business at the outset or later acquire for their business; property owned as tenants in partnership. SEE: Tenancy in Partnership.

Passive Income – Income (rents) received from income property, as opposed to wages, salaries, interest, dividends, or royalties. An IRS term.

Patent – The instrument used to convey government land to a private individual.

Payee – The person entitled to payment under a promissory note.

Personal Property – Any property that is not real property; movable property not affixed to land. Also called chattels or personalty.

Personal Use Property – Property that a taxpayer owns for his or her own use (or family use), as opposed to income property, investment property, dealer property, or property used in a trade or business.

Petition to Confirm – Filed with the court when a party refuses to comply with the arbitration award.

Petitioner – 1. An appellant. 2. A plaintiff (in some actions, such as a dissolution of marriage).

Plaintiff – The party who starts a civil lawsuit; the one who sues.

Planned Unit Development (PUD) – A development (usually residential) with small, clustered lots designed to leave more open space than traditional subdivisions have.

Planning Commission – A local government agency responsible for preparing the community's general plan for development. SEE: General Plan.

Plat – A detailed survey map of a subdivision, recorded in the county where the land is located. Subdivided property is often called platted property.
   Plat Book – A large book containing subdivision plats, kept at the county recorder's office.

Pledge – When a debtor transfers possession of property to the creditor as security for repayment of the debt. COMPARE: Hypothecate.

Point of Beginning (POB) – The starting point in a metes and bounds description; described by reference to a monument.

Points – SEE: Discount Points.

Police Power – The constitutional power of state and local governments to enact and enforce laws that protect the public's health, safety, morals, and general welfare.

Possession – 1. The holding and enjoyment of property. 2. Actual physical occupation of real property.

Possessory Interest – An interest in property that includes the right to possess and occupy the-property; not necessarily ownership.

Power of Attorney – An instrument authorizing one person (the attorney in fact) to an as another's agent, to the extent stated in the instrument.

Power of Sale Clause – A clause in a deed of trust giving the trustee the right to foreclose nonjudicially (sell the debtor's property without a court action) if the borrower defaults.

Power of Termination – The right to terminate a conditional fee estate if the state holder fails to meet the required conditions. Also called a right of reentry. SEE: Fee, Conditional.

Precedent – A published judicial opinion that serves as authority for determining a similar issue in a later case. SEE: Stare Decisis.

    Precedent, Binding – A precedent that a particular court is required to follow.

Prepayment – Paying off part or all of a loan before payment is due.

    Prepayment Penalty – A penalty charged to a borrower who prepays.

    Prepayment Privilege – A provision in a promissory note allowing the borrower to prepay. COMPARE: Lock-in Clause.

Prescription – Acquiring an interest in real property (an easement) by using it openly and without the owner's permission for at least five years. In contrast to adverse possession, a prescriptive use does not have to be exclusive (the owner may be using the property, too), and the user does not acquire title to the property.

Principal – 1. One who grants another person (an agent) authority to represent him or her in dealings with third parties. 2. One of the parties to a transaction (such as a buyer or seller), as opposed to those who are involved as agents or employees (such as a broker or escrow agent). 3. The loan amount originally borrowed, as opposed to the interest.

Principal Residence Property – Real property that is the owner's home, his or her main dwelling. A person can only have one principal residence at a time. The term is most often used in connection with the income tax laws.

Prior Appropriation – A system of allocating water rights. Under this system, a person who wants to use water from a particular lake or river is required to apply for an appropriation permit. It is not necessary to own property beside the body of water in order to acquire an appropriative right. COMPARE: Riparian Rights.

Probate – A judicial proceeding in which the validity of a will is established and the executor is authorized to distribute the estate property; or, when there is no valid will, an administrator is appointed to distribute the estate to the heirs.

    Probate Court – A court that oversees the distribution of property under a will or by intestate succession.

Procedural Law – A law that establishes a legal procedure for enforcing a right. COMPARE: Substantive Law.

Procuring Cause – The real estate agent who is primarily responsible for bringing about a sale; for example, by introducing the buyer to the property, or by negotiating the agreement between the buyer and seller.

Promisee – Someone who has been promised something; someone who is supposed to receive the benefit of a contractual promise.

Promisor – Someone who has made a contractual promise to another.

Proof, Burden of – The responsibility for proving or disproving a particular issue in a lawsuit. In most cases, the plaintiff has the burden of proof.

    Proof, Standard of – The extent to which the plaintiff or prosecutor must have convinced the jury or judge in order to win the case. In most civil suits, a preponderance of the evidence must support the plaintiff's case. In a criminal action, the prosecutor's case must be proven beyond a reasonable doubt.

Property – 1. The rights of ownership in a thing, such as the right to use, possess, transfer, or encumber the thing. 2. Something that is owned.

    Property Manager – A person hired by a property owner to administer, market, and maintain rental property.

    Property Tax – SEE: Tax, Property.

    Property Used in a Trade or Business – Property such as business sites and factories used in one's trade or business.

Proposition 13 – The initiative measure passed in 1978 that led to major revisions in California's property tax laws.

Proration – The process of dividing something (especially a sum of money or an expense) proportionately.

Public Record – The official collection of legal documents that individuals have filed with the county recorder in order to make the information contained in them public. SEE: Constructive Notice; Recording.

Puffing – Superlative statements about a property that shouldn't be considered assertions of fact. "The best buy in town," or "It's a fabulous location" are examples of puffing.

Punitive Damages – SEE: Damages, Punitive.

Pur Autre Vie – "For the life of another." SEE: Life Estate.

Purchase Agreement – The document used for a prospective real estate buyer's offer to a seller, which also serves as the buyer's receipt for the deposit. If the seller accepts the buyer's offer, the purchase agreement becomes their contract; also called an earnest money agreement or purchase and sale agreement.

Q

Question of Fact – In a lawsuit, a question about what actually occurred, as opposed to a question about the legal consequences of what occurred (a question of law).

  Question of Law – In a lawsuit, what the legal rights and duties of the parties were.

Quiet Enjoyment – Use and possession of real property without interference from the previous owner, the lessor, or anyone else claiming title. SEE: Covenant of Quiet Enjoyment.

Quiet Title Action – A lawsuit to establish who has title to a piece of property, or to remove a cloud on the title.

Quitclaim Deed – SEE: Deed, Quitclaim.

R

Race/Notice Rule – When the same property has been sold to two different buyers, if the second buyer records his or her deed before the first buyer (wins the "race" to the recorder's office), the second buyer has good title to the property—as long as he or she did not have notice of the first buyer's interest.

Range – In the government survey system, a strip of land six miles wide, running north and south.

  Range Lines – In the government survey system, the north-south lines located six miles apart.

Ratification – The later confirmation or approval of an act that was not authorized when it was performed.

Ready, Willing, and Able – Making an offer to purchase on terms acceptable to the seller, and having the financial ability to complete the purchase.

Real Estate Contract – 1. A purchase and sale agreement. 2. A land contract. 3. Any contract having to do with real property.

Real Estate Investment Trust (REIT) – A real estate investment business with at least 100 investors, organized as a trust.

Realization – The point at which a gain or profit is actually obtained; for example, the value of a piece of property has been increasing steadily, but the owner's profit won't be realized until she sells the property.

Real Property – Land and everything attached to or appurtenant to it. COMPARE: Personal Property.

REALTOR® – A broker or salesperson who is an active member of a state or local real estate board that is affiliated with the National Association of REALTORS®.

Realty – Real property.

Receiver – A person appointed by a court to manage and look after property or funds involved in litigation.

Recognition – The point at which a gain is taxed (which is ordinarily in the year it was realized, but may be later if a nonrecognition provision applies).

Reconsideration – A request by The Department of Real Estate or the respondent made before the effective day of the hearing decision.

Reconveyance – An instrument that releases the security property from the lien created by a deed of trust; a trustee is required to record one when the borrower has paid off the debt.

  Reconveyance, Partial – A reconveyance that releases some parcels from the lien of a blanket deed of trust, usually recorded when the borrower has paid off a certain amount of the debt.

Recording – Filing a document at the county recorder's office, so that it will be placed in the public record.

  Recording Number – The numbers stamped on documents when they're recorded, used to identify and locate the documents in the public record (each page is stamped with a consecutive number).

Redemption – 1. When a defaulting borrower prevents foreclosure by paying the full amount of the debt, plus costs. 2. When a mortgagor regains the property after foreclosure by paying whatever the foreclosure sale purchaser paid for it, plus interest and expenses. COMPARE: Reinstatement.

  Redemption, Equitable Right of – The right of a borrower to redeem property prior to the foreclosure sale.

  Redemption, Statutory Right of – The right of a mortgagor to redeem property after a foreclosure sale.

Redlining – When a lender refuses to make loans secured by property in a certain neighborhood because of the racial or ethnic composition of the neighborhood.

Reformation – A legal action to correct a mistake, such as a typographical error, in a deed or other document. The court will order the execution of a correction deed.

Regulation – 1. A rule adopted by an administrative agency. 2. Any governmental order having the force of law.

Regulation Z – The Federal Reserve Board's regulation that implements the Truth in Lending Act.

GLOSSARY

Reinstatement – Preventing foreclosure by curing the default. COMPARE: Redemption.

Relation Back – A legal doctrine that allows a court to rule that a party acquired title at some point before he or she actually received the deed. Applied in cases involving escrow or the exercise of an option to purchase.

Release – 1. To give up a legal right. 2. A document in which a legal right is given up.

Relation – When a body of water gradually recedes, exposing land that was previously under water.

Remainder – A future interest that becomes possessory when a life estate terminates, and that is held by someone other than the grantor of the life estate; as opposed to a reversion, which is a future interest held by the grantor.

Remainderman – The person who has an estate in remainder.

Remand – When an appellate court orders further trial proceedings in a case, sending the case back to the court that originally tried it, or to a different trial court.

Rent – Compensation paid by a tenant to the landlord in exchange for the possession and use of the property.
   Rent Control – Government restrictions on how much rent a landlord can charge.

Renunciation – When someone who has been granted something or has accepted something later gives it up or rejects it; as when an agent withdraws from the agency relationship. COMPARE: Revocation.

Rescission – When a contract is terminated and each party gives anything acquired under the contract back to the other party. The verb form is rescind.) COMPARE: Cancellation.

Reservation – A right retained by a grantor when conveying property; for example, mineral rights, an easement, or a life estate can be reserved in the deed.

Reserve Account – SEE: Impound Account.

Res Judicata – The legal doctrine holding that once a lawsuit between two parties has been tried and a final judgment has been issued, neither one can sue the other over the same dispute again.

RESPA – Real Estate Settlement Procedures Act.

Respondent – 1. An appellee. 2. In a DRE disciplinary hearing, the licensee accused of misconduct. 3. In a dissolution of marriage, the party who did not file the action.

Restitution – Restoring something to a person that he or she was unjustly deprived of.

Restriction – A limitation on the use of real property.
   Restriction, Deed – A restrictive covenant in a deed.
   Restriction, Private – A restriction imposed on property by a previous owner, or the subdivision developer; a restriction covenant or a condition in a deed.
   Restriction, Public – A law or regulation limiting or regulating the use of real property.
   Restrictive Covenant – A promise to do or not do an act relating to real property; usually an owner's promise to not use property in a particular way. May or may not run with the land.

Restricted License – A license with restrictions attached.

Revenue Stamps – SEE: Tax, Documentary Transfer.

Reverse – To overturn a lower court's decision on appeal, ruling in favor of the appellant. COMPARE: Affirm.

Reversion – A future interest that becomes possessory when a temporary estate (such as a life estate) terminates, and that is held by the grantor (or his or her successors in interest). COMPARE: Remainder.

Revocation – When someone who granted or offered something withdraws it; as when a principal withdraws the authority granted to the agent, an offeror withdraws the offer, or the Real Estate Commissioner cancels a real estate agent's license. COMPARE: Renunciation.

Rezone – An amendment to a zoning ordinance, usually changing the uses allowed in a particular zone. Requires the approval of the local legislative body. Also called a zoning amendment. COMPARE: Zoning, Spot.

Right of First Refusal – A right of reemption.

Right of Preemption – A right to have the first chance to buy or lease property if the owner decides to put it up for sale or make it available. Also called a right of first refusal. COMPARE: Option.

Right of Survivorship – A characteristic of joint tenancy; surviving joint tenants automatically acquire a deceased joint tenant's interest in the property.

Right of Way – An easement that gives the holder the right to cross another person's land.

Riparian Rights – The water rights of a landowner whose property is adjacent to or crossed by a body of water. COMPARE: Prior Appropriation.

Rollover – When a taxpayer sells his or her principal residence and reinvests the sale proceeds in another home, deferring recognition of the gain on the sale.

Rule of Capture – A legal principle that grants a landowner the right to all oil and gas produced from wells on his or her land, even if it migrated from underneath land belonging to someone else.

Running with the Land – Binding or benefiting the successive owners of a piece of property, rather than terminating when a particular owner transfers his or her interest. Usually said in reference to an easement or a restrictive covenant.

S

Safety Clause – SEE: Extender Clause.

Secondary Marketing – Buying and selling existing mortgage and trust deed loans. The primary market is the one in which lenders loan money to borrowers; the secondary market is the one in which the lenders sell their loans to the large secondary marketing agencies (FNMA, FHLMC, and GNMA) or to other investors.

Secret Profit – A financial benefit that an agent takes from a transaction without informing the principal; usually the result of self-dealing.

Section – In the government survey system, a section is one mile square and contains 640 acres. There are 36 sections in a township.

Security Agreement – An instrument that creates a voluntary lien on property to secure repayment of a loan. For debts secured by real property, a security agreement is either a deed of trust or a mortgage.

Security Deposit – Money a tenant gives a landlord at the beginning of the tenancy to ensure that the tenant will comply with the terms of the lease. The landlord may retain all or part of the deposit to cover unpaid rent or repair costs at the end of the tenancy.

Security Interest – The interest a creditor may acquire in the debtor's property to ensure that the debt will be paid.

Seisin – The possession of a freehold estate; ownership. Also spelled seizen or seizin.

Self-Dealing – When a real estate agent buys the principal's property him or herself (or sells it to a relative, friend, or associate, or to a business he or she has an interest in), without disclosing that fact to the principal, and in violation of his or her fiduciary duties to the principal.

Self-Executing Arbitration Clause – The parties do not need to use the court to compel arbitration.

Seller Financing – When a seller extends credit to a buyer to finance the purchase of the property; as opposed to having the buyer obtain a loan from a third party, such as an institutional lender. SEE: Loan, Carryback.

Separate Property – Property owned by a married person that is not community property; includes property acquired before marriage, or by gift or inheritance after marriage.

Service of Process – Delivery of a legal document (especially a summons) to a person in accordance with the rules prescribed by statute, so that he or she is held to have received it (whether or not he or she actually did).

Setback Requirements – Provisions in a zoning ordinance that do not allow structures to be built within a certain distance of the property line.

Settlement – 1. An agreement between the parties to a civil lawsuit, in which the plaintiff agrees to drop the suit in exchange for money or the defendant's promise to do or refrain from doing something. 2. Closing.

    Settlement Statement – A document that presents a final, detailed accounting for a real estate transaction, listing each party's debits and credits and the amount each will receive or be required to pay at closing (closing statement).

Severable – When one provision in a law or a contract can be held unenforceable, without making the entire law or contract unenforceable.

Severalty – SEE: Ownership in Severalty.

Severance – Termination of a joint tenancy, turning it into a tenancy in common.

Sheriff's Sale – A foreclosure sale held after a judicial foreclosure. Sometimes called an execution sale.

Short Platting – Subdividing a parcel of land into two, three, or four lots.

Side Yard – The area between a building and one of the side boundaries of the lot on which it's located.

GLOSSARY

Special Assessment – A tax levied only against the properties that have benefited from a public improvement (such as a sewer or a street light), to cover the cost of the improvement; creates a special assessment lien.

Specific Performance – A legal remedy for breach of contract in which a court orders the breaching party to actually perform the contract as agreed, rather than simply paying money damages.

Stare Decisis – The legal doctrine holding that in resolving a lawsuit, a court should try to follow precedents decided in the same jurisdiction, to make the law evenhanded and predictable.

State Action – In constitutional law, action by a government (federal, state, or local) rather than by a private party.

Statement of Issues – A written allegation by the commissioner identifying the issues and listing the rules violated, used in a non-property right hearing.

Statute – A law enacted by a state legislature or the U.S. Congress. SEE: Statutory Law. COMPARE: Ordinance.

Statute of Frauds – A law that requires certain types of contracts to be in writing and signed in order to be enforceable.

Statute of Limitations – A law requiring a particular type of lawsuit to be filed within a specified time after the event giving rise to the suit occurred.

Statutory Construction – When a judge interprets and applies a statute in the course of resolving a lawsuit.

Statutory Law – Laws adopted by a legislative body (Congress, a state legislature, or a county or city council), as opposed to constitutional law, case law, or administrative regulations.

Steering – Channeling prospective buyers or tenants to particular neighborhoods based on their race, religion, national origin, or ancestry.

Strict Liability – When someone is held legally responsible for an injury to another, even though he or she did not act negligently. COMPARE: Negligence.

Strike List – An arbitration service sends a list of arbitrators to each party and the parties strike the names that are unacceptable.

Subagent – A person that an agent has delegated authority to, so that the subagent can assist in carrying out the principal's orders.

Subdivision – 1. A piece of land divided into two or more parcels. 2. A residential development.

   Subdivision Regulations – State and local laws that must be complied with before land can be subdivided.

Subject to – When a purchaser takes property subject to a trust deed or mortgage, he or she is not personally liable for paying off the loan; in case of default, however, the property can still be foreclosed on. COMPARE: Assumption.

Sublease – When a tenant grants someone else the right to possession of the leased property for part of the remainder of the lease term; as opposed to an assignment, where the tenant gives up possession for the entire remainder of the lease term.

Subordination Clause – A provision in a mortgage or deed of trust that permits a later mortgage or deed of trust to have higher lien priority than the one containing the clause.

Submission Agreement – An agreement by the parties to submit a dispute to arbitration.

Subpoena – A document ordering a person to appear at a deposition or court proceeding to testify or produce documentary or physical evidence. An order requiring a witness to attend.

   Subpoena Duces Tecum – An order to produce books, records or other documents.

Substantial Performance – When a promisor doesn't perform all of his or her contractual obligations, but does enough so that the promisee is required to fulfill his or her side of the bargain. COMPARE: Breach, Material.

Substantive Law – A law that establishes a right or a duty. COMPARE: Procedural Law.

Successor in Interest – A person who has acquired property previously held by someone else; for example, a buyer or an heir.

Summons – A document informing a defendant that a lawsuit has been filed against him or her, and ordering the defendant to file an answer to the plaintiff's complaint with the court.

Support, Lateral – The support that a piece of land receives from the land adjacent to it.

Support, Subjacent – The support that the surface of a piece of land receives from the land beneath it.

Surrender – Giving up an estate (such as a life estate or leasehold) before it has expired.

Survey – The process of precisely measuring the boundaries and determining the area of a parcel of land.

Suspension – When a real estate agent's license is temporarily withdrawn.
   Suspension, Summary – License suspension before a hearing has been held.

Syndicate – An association formed to operate an investment business. A syndicate is not a recognized legal entity; it can be organized as a corporation, partnership, or trust.

T

Tacking – When successive periods of use or possession by more than one person are added together to make up the five years required for prescription or adverse possession.

Taking – When the government acquires private property for public use by condemnation, it's called "a taking." The term is also used in inverse condemnation lawsuits, when a government action has made private property useless.

Tax, Documentary Transfer – A tax on the transfer of real property; revenue stamps, indicating the tax has been paid, usually must be attached to a deed before it can be recorded.
   Tax, General Real Estate – Property taxes.
   Tax, Property – An annual ad valorem tax levied on real and personal property.
   Tax Deed – SEE: Deed, Tax.
   Tax Sale – Sale of property after foreclosure of a tax lien.

Tenancy – Lawful possession of real property; an estate.
   Tenancy, Joint – A form of concurrent ownership in which the co-owners have equal undivided interests and the right of survivorship. The right of survivorship means that when one joint tenant dies, the surviving tenants automatically acquire his or her interest in the property. SEE: Unities, Four. COMPARE: Tenancy in Common.
   Tenancy, Periodic – A leasehold estate that continues for successive periods of equal length (such as from week-to-week or month-to-month), until terminated by proper notice from either party. COMPARE: Estate for Years.
   Tenancy at Will – When a tenant is in possession with the owner's permission, but there's no definite lease term; as when a landlord allows a holdover tenant to remain on the premises until another tenant is found.
   Tenancy by the Entirety – A form of co-ownership of property by husband and wife (in states that don't use a community property system).
   Tenancy in Common – A form of concurrent ownership in which two or more persons each have an undivided interest in the entire property (unity of possession), but no right of survivorship. COMPARE: Tenancy, Joint.
   Tenancy in Partnership – The form of concurrent ownership in which general partners own partnership property, whether or not title to the property is in the partnership's name. Each partner has an equal undivided interest, but no right to transfer the interest to someone outside the partnership.

Tenant – Someone in lawful possession of real property; especially, someone who has leased property from the owner.
   Tenant at Sufferance – A tenant who holds over beyond the expiration of the tenancy without lanlord's permission.
   Tenant, Dominant – A person who has easement rights on another's property; either the owner of a dominant tenement, or someone who has an easement in gross.
   Tenant, Holdover – A lessee who remains in possession of the property after the lease term has expired.
   Tenant, Life – Someone who holds a life estate.
   Tenant, Servient – The owner of a servient tenement—that is, someone whose property is burdened by an easement.

Tender – An unconditional offer by one of parties to a contract to perform his or her part of the agreement; made when the offeror believes the other party is breaching, it establishes the offeror's right to sue if the other party doesn't accept it. Also called a tender offer.

Tenement, Dominant – Property that receives the benefit of an appurtenant easement.
   Tenement, Servient – Property burdened by an easement. In other words, the owner of the servient tenement (the servient tenant) must allow someone who has an easement (the dominant tenant) to use the property.

Tenements – Everything of a permanent nature associated with a piece of land and ordinarily transferred with the land. Tenements are both tangible (buildings, for example) and intangible (air rights, for example).

Term – A prescribed period of time; especially, the length of time a borrower has in which to pay off a loan, or the duration of a lease.

Testate – Refers to someone who has died and left a will. COMPARE: Intestate.
   Testator – A man who makes a will.
   Testatrix – A woman who makes a will.

GLOSSARY

Tester – A person working with a fair housing organization, who pretends to be interested in buying or renting property from someone suspected of unlawful discrimination.

Time is of the Essence – A clause in a contract that means performance on the exact dates specified is an essential element of the contract; failure to perform on time is a material breach.

Timeshare Estate – An ownership interest that gives the owner a right to possession of the property only for a specific, limited period each year.

Timeshare Use – A license for the holder to possession of the property only for a specific, limited period each year.

Title – Lawful ownership of real property. Also, the deed or other document that is evidence of that ownership.
   Title, After-Acquired – Title acquired by a grantor after he or she attempted to convey property he or she didn't own.
   Title, Chain of – The chain of deeds (and other documents) transferring title to a piece of property from one owner to the next, as disclosed in the public record.
   Title, Clear – Title that is free of encumbrances or defects: marketable title.
   Title, Equitable – The vendee's interest in property under a land contract. Also called an equitable interest. COMPARE: Title, Legal.
   Title, Legal – The vendor's interest in property under a land contract. COMPARE: Title, Equitable.
   Title, Marketable – Title free and clear of objectionable liens, encumbrances, or defects, so that a reasonably prudent person with full knowledge of the facts would not hesitate to purchase the property.
   Title Company – A title insurance company.
   Title Insurance – SEE: Insurance, Title.
   Title Plant – A duplicate (usually microfilmed) of a county's public record, maintained by a title company at its offices for use in title searches.
   Title Report – A report issued by a title company, disclosing the condition of the title to a specific piece of property. A preliminary title report is one issued early on in a transaction, before the actual title insurance policy is issued.
   Title Search – An inspection of the public record to determine all rights and encumbrances affecting title to a property.

Tort – A breach of a duty imposed by law (as opposed to a duty voluntarily taken on in a contract) that causes harm to another person, giving the injured person the right to sue the one who breached the duty. Also called a civil wrong (in contrast to a criminal wrong, a crime). SEE: Negligence; Strict Liability.

Township – In the government survey system, a parcel of land 6 miles square, containing 36 sections; the intersection of a range and a township tier.
   Township Lines – Lines running east-west, spaced six miles apart, in the government survey system.
   Township Tier – In the government survey system, a strip of land running east-west, six miles wide and bounded on the north and south by township lines.

Tract – 1. A piece of land of undefined size. 2. In the government survey system, an area made up of 16 townships; 24 miles on each side.
   Tract Index – An index of the public record, grouping together all recorded documents that carry a particular legal description. COMPARE: Grantor/grantee Indexes.

Trade Fixtures – Articles of personal property annexed to real property by a tenant for use in his or her trade or business.

Transfer Disclosure Statement – Facts about a property are filled out on a form by the seller.

Transmutation Agreement – A contract in which co-owners agree to change their form of ownership; usually one in which husband and wife agree to change community property to separate property.

Trespass – An unlawful physical invasion of property owned by another.

Trial – The fundamental court proceeding in a lawsuit, in which a judge (and in some cases, a jury) hears evidence presented by both parties and issues a judgment. COMPARE: Appeal.

Trier of Fact – The one who decides questions of fact in a lawsuit. In a jury trial, it's the jury; in a nonjury trial, it's the judge. (Questions of law are always decided by the judge.)

Trust – A legal arrangement in which title to property (or funds) is vested in one or more trustees, who manage the property on behalf of the trust's beneficiaries, in accordance with instructions set forth in the establishing documents.
   Trust Account – A bank account, separate from a real estate broker's personal and business accounts, used to segregate trust funds from the broker's own funds.

Trust Deed – SEE: Deed of Trust.

Trustee – 1. A person appointed to manage a trust on behalf of the beneficiaries. 2. A neutral third party appointed in a deed of trust to handle the nonjudicial foreclosure process in case of default.

Trustee's Sale – A non-judicial foreclosure sale under a deed of trust.

Trust Funds – Money or things of value received by an agent, not belonging to the agent but being held for the benefit of others.

Trustor – The borrower on a deed of trust. Also called the grantor.

U

Unconstitutional – Violating a provision of the U.S. Constitution or a state constitution.

Undivided Interest – SEE: Interest, Undivided.

Undue Influence – Exerting excessive pressure on someone so as to overpower the person's free will and prevent him or her from making a rational or prudent decision; often involves abusing a relationship of trust.

Uniform Settlement Statement – A closing statement required for any transaction involving a loan that's subject to the Real Estate Settlement Procedures Act (RESPA).

Unilateral Contract – SEE: Contract, Unilateral.

Unilateral Mistake – SEE: Mistake, Unilateral.

Unincorporated Association – The legal designation for an organization that has recorded a statement listing the names of those who are authorized to execute conveyances on its behalf, which makes it possible for title to be held in the association's name.

Unities, Four – The unities of time, title, interest, and possession. These are required for a joint tenancy.
Unity of Interest – When each co-owner has an equal interest (equal share of ownership) in a piece of property.
Unity of Possession – When each co-owner is equally entitled to possession of the entire property, because the ownership interests are undivided.
Unity of Time – When each co-owner acquired title at the same time.
Unity of Title – When each co-owner acquired title through the same instrument (deed, will, or court order).

Unjust Enrichment – An undeserved benefit.

Unlawful Detainer – A summary legal action to regain possession of real property; especially, a suit filed by a landlord to evict a defaulting tenant.

Untenantable – Not fit for occupancy.

Usury – Charging an interest rate that exceeds legal limits.

V

VA – Department of Veterans Affairs.

Valid – The legal classification of a contract that is binding and enforceable in a court of law.

Valuation – SEE: Appraisal.

Value – The amount of goods or services offered in the marketplace in exchange for a given thing.
Value, Assessed – The value placed on property by the taxing authority (the county assessor, for example) for the purposes of taxation.
Value, Base – Under Proposition 13, the initial assessed value of a piece of property, used in calculating a particular owner's property taxes; this figure is later adjusted to reflect inflation and improvements.
Value, Fair Market – The amount of money that a piece of property would bring if placed on the open market for a reasonable period of time, with a buyer willing (but not forced) to buy, and a seller willing (but not forced) to sell, if both buyer and seller were fully informed as to the possible use of the property. Also called market value.
Value, Full Cash – Under Proposition 13, the assessed value of newly transferred property; it's the purchase price of the property, unless it can be shown that the property wouldn't have been sold at that price on the open market.

Variable Interest Rate – An interest rate on a mortgage or deed of trust that is adjusted periodically, usually to reflect changes in a particular economic index. A loan with a variable interest rate is often called an adjustable-rate mortgage or ARM.

Variance – A permit obtained from the local zoning authority allowing the holder to use property or build a structure in a way that violates the zoning ordinance. COMPARE: Nonconforming Use, Conditional Use Permit.

GLOSSARY

Variance, Use – A variance that permits an owner to use the property in a way that isn't ordinarily allowed in that zone; for example, a commercial use in a residential zone.

Vendee – A buyer or purchaser; particularly, someone buying property under a land contract.

Vendor – A seller; particularly, someone selling property by means of a land contract.

Vested – When a person has a present, fixed right or interest in property, even though he or she may not have the right to possession until sometime in the future. For example, a remainderman's interest in property vests when it is granted, not when the life estate ends.

Veto – When the president or governor formally rejects a bill that Congress or the legislature has passed. The bill won't become law unless the legislative body votes to override the veto.

Void – Having no legal force or effect.

Voidable – SEE: Contract, Voidable.

W

Waiver – The voluntary relinquishment or surrender of a right.

Warranty, Implied – In the sale of property, a guarantee created by operation of law, whether or not the seller intended to offer it.

Warranty of Habitability – SEE: Implied Warranty of Habitability.

Waste – Destruction, damage, or material alteration of property by someone in possession who holds less than a fee estate (such as a life tenant or lessee), or by a co-tenant.

Water Rights – SEE: Prior Appropriation; Riparian Rights.

Will – A person's stipulation (testament) regarding how his or her estate should be disposed of after he or she dies.

Will, Formal – A written, witnessed will.

Will, Holographic – A will written entirely in the testator or testatrix's handwriting, which may be valid even if it was not witnessed.

Writ of Execution – A court order directing a public officer (sheriff) to seize and sell property to satisfy a debt.

Writ of Possession – A court order issued after an unlawful detainer action, informing a tenant that he or she must vacate the landlord's property within a specified period or be forcibly removed by the sheriff.

Z

Zoning – Government regulation of the uses of property within specified areas. SEE: Conditional Use Permit; Nonconforming Use; Rezone; Variance.

Zoning, Exclusionary – A zoning law that has the effect of preventing certain groups (such as minorities or poor people) from living in a community.

Zoning, Spot – An illegal rezone that favors (or restricts) a particular property owner (or a small group of owners) without justification.

INDEX

INDEX

INDEX

INDEX

INDEX

INDEX

INDEX

INDEX

INDEX

Textbooks From
Educational Textbook Company

www.etctextbooks.com

Sometimes our textbooks are hard to find!

If your bookstore does not carry our textbooks, please send us a check or money order and we'll mail them to you with our 30-day money back guarantee.

Other Great Books from Educational Textbook Company:*

California Real Estate Principles, 13th ed., 2nd Printing, by Huber	$100.00	____
California Real Estate Practice, 7th ed., by Huber & Lyons	$100.00	____
How To Pass The Real Estate Exam, 7th ed. - e-book (850 Exam Questions), by Huber	$99.00	____
California Real Estate Law, 8th ed., by Huber & Tyler	$100.00	____
Real Estate Finance, 7th ed., third printing, by Huber & Messick	$100.00	____
Real Estate Finance: Appraiser's Edition, 6th ed., by Huber & Messick	$100.00	____
Real Estate Economics, 5th ed., by Huber, Messick, & Pivar	$100.00	____
Real Estate Appraisal – Principles and Procedures, 4th ed., by Huber, Messick, & Pivar	$100.00	____
Residential Real Estate Appraisal, by Huber & Messick	$100.00	____
Mortgage Loan Brokering, 4th ed., by Huber, Pivar, Zozula	$100.00	____
Property Management, 5th ed., by Huber, Lyons, & Pivar	$100.00	____
Escrow I: An Introduction, 3rd ed., by Huber & Newton	$100.00	____
Real Estate Computer Applications, by Grogan & Huber	$100.00	____
Homeowner's Association Management, by Huber & Tyler	$100.00	____
California Business Law, 3rd ed., by Huber, McGrath, & Tyler	$100.00	____
Hubie's Power Prep 700 CD – 700 Questions, by Huber	$100.00	____

---

* <u>PRICES EXPIRE 1/1/2014</u>

Allow 2-3 weeks for delivery

Subtotal _____
Add shipping and handling @ $10.00 per book _____
Add California sales tax @ 9.75% _____
TOTAL _____

Name: _____

Address: _____

City, State, Zip: _____

Phone: _____

Check or money order: Educational Textbook Company, P.O. Box 3597, Covina, CA 91722